BOOK SALE
Solano College Library

Democracy, Liberty, and Property

THE MACMILLAN COMPANY
NEW YORK · BOSTON · CHICAGO · DALLAS
ATLANTA · SAN FRANCISCO

MACMILLAN AND CO., Limited
LONDON · BOMBAY · CALCUTTA · MADRAS
MELBOURNE

THE MACMILLAN COMPANY
OF CANADA, Limited
TORONTO

DEMOCRACY, LIBERTY, AND PROPERTY

Readings in the American Political Tradition

Edited, with Introductions, by

FRANCIS W. COKER

Alfred Cowles Professor of Government,
Yale University

NEW YORK · The Macmillan Company · 1949

COPYRIGHT, 1942,
BY THE MACMILLAN COMPANY

All rights reserved—no part of this book may be reproduced in any form without permission in writing from the
publisher, except by a reviewer who wishes to quote brief
passages in connection with a review written for inclusion
in magazine or newspaper.

— PRINTED IN THE UNITED STATES OF AMERICA —
Published May, 1942

Reprinted March, 1947; May, 1947; April, 1948; April,
1949.

JK
11
D4
C
29344

PREFACE

FREE speculation upon the nature and purpose of government has been an element of the American tradition from the days of the first settlements. Our writers have stood predominantly for government by consent, freedom in regard to belief and expression, and free economic enterprise. This is not to say that we have all been of one mind in these matters. The principles themselves have been challenged from time to time; and we have engaged in continual debate upon their quantitative and qualitative implications. What should be the form and extent of popular participation in government? What rightful limits are to be set upon the power of government over personal liberties or property rights? How may we determine the pace of political change, or preserve that responsiveness to emerging public demands which is the essence of democracy? These and kindred questions have provided the dynamic which has made our political speculation the vital thing it has always been.

The purpose of this collection is to indicate the main lines of our political tradition by means of representative excerpts from a variety of sources—essays and addresses, public documents, revolutionary pronouncements, formal treatises; and the attempt has been made to indicate typical attitudes on both sides of the fundamental questions at issue.

The editor is greatly indebted for advice and criticism given by colleagues in Yale University: Professors C. H. Driver, A. W. Griswold, and H. C. Mansfield; Mrs. Margaret Lippiatt Van Houten, research assistant in government; Mr. Paul F. Boller, Foote-Sheldon Clark fellow in History, the Arts, and Letters; Mr. Maurice J. Klain, Cowles fellow in government; and Miss Frances Astrachan, graduate student in government.

F. W. C.

NEW HAVEN, CONN.
April, 1942

v

ACKNOWLEDGMENTS

THE author gratefully acknowledges the kindness of publishers in giving permission to reprint selections in this volume as follows:

D. APPLETON-CENTURY COMPANY for the selections from *The Complete Works of Abraham Lincoln* (c. 1894, 1905).

THE JOHN DAY COMPANY for the selection from Franklin D. Roosevelt, *Looking Forward* (1933).

DOUBLEDAY, DORAN AND COMPANY, INC. for the selection from Woodrow Wilson, *The New Freedom* (c. 1913, 1933).

HARPER & BROTHERS for the selections from Horace Greeley, *Hints Towards Reform* (1850); and from The Rt. Rev. Msgr. John A. Ryan, *A Better Economic Order* (1935).

THE PRESIDENT AND FELLOWS OF HARVARD COLLEGE for the selection from Thomas Nixon Carver, *Essays in Social Justice* (1915).

HENRY HOLT AND COMPANY, INC. for the selection from Frederick Jackson Turner, *The Frontier in American History* (1920).

HOUGHTON MIFFLIN COMPANY for the selections from Herbert Agar and Allen Tate, eds., *Who Owns America?* (1936); from *Emerson's Complete Works* (1883); and from *The Writings of Henry David Thoreau* (c. 1906).

MITCHELL KENNERLEY for the selection from Walt Whitman, *Complete Prose Works* (1914).

ALFRED A. KNOPF, INC. for the selections from Charles A. Beard, *The Economic Basis of Politics* (1922, 1934); from James Fenimore Cooper, *The American Democrat* (reprint, 1931); and from H. L. Mencken, *Notes on Democracy* (1926).

FOLA LA FOLLETTE for the selection from Robert M. La Follette, *La Follette's Autobiography* (1913).

THE LATE RT. REV. WILLIAM LAWRENCE for his article, "The Relation of Wealth to Morals" in *The World's Work*, Vol. I (1900–01).

J. B. LIPPINCOTT COMPANY for the selection from H. C. Carey, *Principles of Social Science* (ed. 1871).

LITTLE, BROWN & COMPANY for the selections from *The Works of John Adams* (1850–56); from *The Works of Fisher Ames* (1854); from

Theodore Parker, *Additional Speeches* (1855); and from *The Works of Daniel Webster* (1851).

MACMILLAN COMPANY for the selections from *The Writings of John Quincy Adams* (1913–17); from *The Writings of Benjamin Franklin* (1905–07); and from Norman Thomas, *After the New Deal, What?* (1936).

MASSACHUSETTS HISTORICAL SOCIETY for the selection from *The Winthrop Papers* (1931).

G. P. PUTNAM'S SONS for the selections from *The Writings of Samuel Adams* (1904–08); *The Works of Alexander Hamilton* (1904); *The Writings of Thomas Jefferson* (1892–99); and *The Writings of Thomas Paine* (1894–96).

REYNAL & HITCHCOCK, INC. for the selection from Henry A. Wallace, *New Frontiers* (1934).

ROOSEVELT MEMORIAL ASSOCIATION, INC. for the selection from *The Works of Theodore Roosevelt* (1923–26).

ROBERT SCHALKENBACH FOUNDATION for the selection from Henry George, *Progress and Poverty* (reprint, 1940).

CHARLES SCRIBNER'S SONS for the selections from E. G. Conklin, *The Direction of Human Evolution* (rev. ed., 1934); from Charles Horton Cooley, *Social Organization* (1909); from Edwin Lawrence Godkin, *Problems of Modern Democracy* (3rd. ed., 1907); from Herbert Hoover, *The Challenge to Liberty* (1934); and from Thorstein Veblen, *The Theory of Business Enterprise* (1904).

THE VIKING PRESS, INC. for the selection from Thorstein Veblen, *The Theory of the Leisure Class* (1899).

YALE UNIVERSITY PRESS for the selections from Carl L. Becker, *Modern Democracy* (1941); from *Records of the Federal Convention*, ed. by Max Farrand (rev. ed., 1937); and from *Essays of William Graham Sumner*, ed. by A. G. Keller and M. R. Davie (1934).

CONTENTS

CONTENTS

CONTENTS xi

IV. THE PROBLEM OF CHANGE

INTRODUCTION

ORIGINS OF THE AMERICAN POLITICAL TRADITION

I

FEW of the original European settlers of America were inspired
by any intention of experimenting with novel ideas of government, liberty, or property. What Governor Bradford said of the
founders of Plymouth was probably true as well of most of the other
seventeenth-century immigrants. They came, he declared, "not out
of any newfangledness, or other such like giddie humor, by which
men are oftentimes transported to their great hurt & danger, but for
sundrie weightie & solid reasons." Among those solid reasons, certain preoccupations with religion were conspicuous. Bradford's
history of Plymouth, other contemporary narratives, and the early
colonial charters all put the conversion of the Indians high among
the purposes of the colonizing endeavor. Yet most of those who
came over for religious reasons were more concerned with fortifying
their own beliefs and keeping their fellow-settlers on the narrow
path than with saving the souls of the natives. For the majority of
these early settlers came from the religious minorities of their home
countries, where they were denied the freedom to preach and practise their particular tenets. The move to America offered them the
opportunity to worship, preach, and teach according to their own
unorthodox convictions.

On the other hand, more worldly aims were predominant in the
minds of most of the promoters and financial sponsors of the settlements; and solid economic reasons moved many of the migrants
themselves. England had manifestly been lagging behind Portugal
and Spain in the century-old race to build a colonial empire. Now,
however, the circumstances seemed propitious for renewed efforts.
An enterprising temper was spreading; and concerted efforts, both
public and private, were being made to induce in Englishmen a
realization of the rich resources of the New World, in materials and

1

markets for England's manufacturers and traders, supplies for her navy, and new opportunities for finding employment and getting rich. Captain John Smith, hardy explorer and soldier of fortune, reveals the realism of this expanding mood in his *Description of New England*, written in 1616. After discanting on the sublime joy of "discovering things unknowne," "erecting Townes, peopling Countries," and converting "the poore Salvadges," he added that he was "not so simple to thinke, that ever any other motive than wealth will ever erect there a Commonweale, or draw companie from their ease and humours at home." No less significant is a Puritan minister's pamphlet of the same decade wherein we find that a chapter entitled "New England is a fit Country for the Seating of an English Colony for the Propagation of Religion" is devoted mainly to descriptions of the fish, fowl, venison, furs, wines, and (particularly) the "Planks, Masts, Oares, Pitch, Tarre and Iron, and hereafter (by the aptnesse of the Soyle for Hempe) if the Colonie increase, Sailes and Cordage."

Much of this publicity describing the resources of the New World was put forth to promote imperial aims or to serve the interests of investors who had no thought of migrating to such remote regions themselves. Yet America did offer prospects of a better livelihood for ordinary craftsmen, laborers and others who were willing to endure the hazards of actual settlement; and such men were numerous. Inflation, war, and changes in fiscal policy had seriously upset certain industries during the preceding generation. And although at the time of the first settlements England was apparently emerging from this depression, many farmers, traders, and professional men were still finding it difficult to maintain their accustomed standards of living, or believed they were not sharing sufficiently in the recovery. Unemployment was still widespread; towns and parishes were overwhelmed by the task of taking care of beggars and vagabonds; and the belief was growing that England was overpopulated. "We are a great people," said a pamphleteer in 1609, "and the lande is too narrow for us."

Few colonial leaders looked upon these diverse religious and economic motives as incompatible. Indeed they were inclined to regard them as interdependent. Even the strongest conviction and the most resolute courage needed a vigorous body and some assurance of a secure place in society. Thus, said Bradford of the Pilgrims, life was so hard in the country to which they had first gone, in their flight from religious trouble at home, that some of them preferred imprisonment in England "rather than this libertie in Holland with these afflictions"; and the leaders concluded that "an easier place of living . . . would draw many, and take away these discouragements." Their pastor, John Robinson, said that many now writing and preaching against the Pilgrim doctrine would adopt it "if they were in a place where they might have libertie and live comfortably." The Puritans were even more explicit in acknowledging the connection between spiritual strength and economic well-being. They frankly accepted what Rev. John Cotton called "a combination of virtues, strangely mixed." "We know that nothing sorts better with piety than competency," said Rev. John White, another Puritan divine.

The settlers came over during a period of unusually active discussion of civic affairs. Yet they were not utopians and the writers among them had drawn up no clear schemes for defining the location of public authority or the scope of private rights. Although the dissenting sects had arisen as adherents of a new, liberal, idea in religion—of spiritual regeneration through man's own inner experience—most of them clung to the belief that ordinary mortals needed instruction, guidance, perhaps even coercion, by their enlightened and duly designated leaders. The Puritans, who were the most intellectual and articulate of the seventeenth-century settlers, had no exalted opinion of human nature. For the most part they believed in the moral right and practical necessity of authority and rank, in both church and state. Men, according to the Puritan creed, were not by nature either reasonable or good and they were certainly not born equal. As for the financial promoters of the settlements, they were men of wealth, accustomed to the enjoyment of social and political privileges. It was therefore in accord with their convictions and generally in their interest to have familiar social distinctions recognized in the colonies. Among the actual settlers, it is true, there were very few men of aristocratic origins. Yet the resources of the new continent created new occasions for inequality as well as for equality. When the colonists set up their own governments, they merely followed tradition in requiring property and religious qualifications for voting and the holding of office; and the conflicts between privileged and unprivileged groups formed the substance of political controversy throughout the colonial period.

There were difficulties in the way of a government of laws rather than of men in the colonies. Lawyers were rare among the early settlers. Early charters and codes repeated the traditional prescriptions to govern according to the law or to proceed only according to the "due course of law" in punishing criminals and adjudicating civil disputes; and colonial magistrates generally followed the traditional procedure of English courts. Both magistrates and lawmakers, however, had confused and vacillating ideas as to what (if any) system of laws limited their discretion. Sometimes they proclaimed the Bible to be the supreme law, binding on civil authority as well as the church. Sometimes they acted on the assumption that the substantive rules of common law must prevail in America as in England. Sometimes they appealed to rules of "natural law" —universally binding principles of reason and justice, understood by all normally reasonable men—as the final arbiter. Occasionally, legislators in enacting statutes and magistrates in deciding questions at issue in criminal and civil litigation claimed a right to act according to their own ideas of civic justice and expediency.

Very few of the colonial leaders desired to make America a home for religious freedom. Most of the colonies gave a privileged position to a particular religion and officially concerned themselves with the religious and moral behavior of their inhabitants. Thus the Puritans, although they opposed certain doctrines and rituals of the Church of England, were yet not opposed to the principle of religious uniformity, a uniformity sustained if need be by the force of the civil authority itself. They came to America in order to worship and teach as they pleased, but not to provide such freedom for others. The Fundamental Orders of Connecticut authorized the civil authorities to see that "the peace, ordinances, and rules of Christ be observed in every Church according to His Word," and the "blue" laws of that colony are famous. Civil authorities in Massachusetts dealt harshly with persons who advocated unorthodox beliefs, in however orderly a manner. This religious authoritarianism was not confined to the Puritan colonies. Most of the colonies maintained churches supported by public taxation; and many of them compelled church attendance and narrowly restricted Sabbath-day activities. The first Virginia charter, for example, prescribed that the word of God must be preached and applied "according to the rites and ordinances of the Church of England"; the second charter provided that all who wanted to settle in the colony must first take the oath of supremacy, thereby excluding non-conformists; early statutes fixed the minister's salary and his fees for christening, marrying, and burying, and followed the Elizabethan practice of levying a fine (in this case of five pounds of tobacco) on any person who absented himself from Church on Sunday; and later laws were enacted during the first colonial century to protect the colony against "infection" by Roman Catholics, Presbyterians, Baptists, and "that unreasonable and turbulent sort of people, comonly called Quakers." Even the famous "Toleration Act" of Maryland (1646) granted tolerance only to professed believers in Jesus Christ and provided the death penalty for a denial of the Trinity; a law of 1664 repealed that act and withdrew all civil protection from Roman Catholics.

The colonists brought with them no unusual doctrines as to how wealth should be distributed and regulated. Nowhere in the seventeenth century was there any idea that public authority should pursue a hands-off policy in dealing with private property. The original migrants settled generally in groups rather than as individuals; and in many respects the settlements were operated as community enterprises for a considerable time. Thus in Massachusetts Bay the original title to lands was vested in the joint-stock company of that name. The company later transferred titles to the towns. When the towns made allotments to individuals they not only restricted the owners' rights of alienation but also retained considerable areas for common use; and they knew no law, theory or tradition that would deny them the right to regulate private property in the public interest as they conceived it. Occasions for regulation appeared at the very beginning. A scarcity of workers resulted in high wages and this in turn led to high prices for the necessities of life; whereupon the Massachusetts general court (according to Governor Winthrop's account) taking note of these "evils," made an order "that carpenters, masons, etc., should take but two shillings the day, and the laborers but eighteen pence, and that no commodity should be sold at above four pence in the shilling more than it cost for ready money in England." As in Elizabethan England both town and central authorities intervened frequently in the economic life of the community, fixing wages and prices, regulating the quality of goods and the choice of occupations, and carrying on various community enterprises. Thus in 1639 a fine of £100 was imposed on Boston's richest merchant when he persisted in taking more than fifty percent profit on his goods despite repeated admonitions from the civil authorities. Some of the early colonial regulations were soon abandoned, others were long retained. At no time, in New England or the other regions, was there any prevailing idea that private property and public regulation were antagonistic conceptions.[1]

II

Only a romantic distortion of history, therefore, would represent the original settlers and their immediate successors as the bearers and conscious importers of those ideas which we are now accustomed to regard as fundamental in the American political tradition —the freedoms of religion, expression and assembly; economic laisser-faire; and the basic right of the ordinary citizen to a voice in government. Nevertheless, it is to the background of the seventeenth century immigrants, to the spiritual and intellectual climate in which they lived, and to the constitutional development of the Empire of which they were citizens that we must look if we are to understand the later emergence of those attitudes which are the specific American heritage.

The settlers came from a land which, despite all the limitations of public policy against which they were protesting, still enjoyed a greater degree of freedom than any other European country. Parliament was already a venerable institution with a history of some four hundred years behind it; the Common Law courts of England were older still; and the franchises of borough and corporate town, of manor and shire, had roots that went far back into English his-

[1] The quotations in the foregoing paragraphs are taken from the following: William Bradford, *Of Plimoth Plantation* (written 1630–1650, first published in 1856), bk. i, ch. 4; John Smith, *A Description of New England* (1616); John White, *The Planter's Plea* (1630), ch. 4; *A Good Speed to Virginia*, an anonymous London pamphlet, 1609; John Cotton, *Christ the Fountaine of Life* (1651), pp. 119–120; the Virginia charters of 1606 and 1609; Hening's *Statutes of Virginia*, Vol. I, pp. 122, 124; John Winthrop, *Journal* (1630–49), entry for November, 1633.

For general accounts of colonial origins: Edward P. Cheney, "Some English Conditions Surrounding the Settlement of Virginia," *American Historical Review*, Vol. XII (1907), pp. 507–528; N. M. Crouse, "Causes of the Great Migration," *New England Quarterly*, Vol. V (1932); Sanford H. Cobb, *Rise of Religious Liberty in America* (1902); Perry Miller, *The New England Mind* (1940); Charles M. Andrews, *The Colonial Period of American History*, 4 vols. (1934–38).

tory.   Local government and local loyalties were vital forces and
Parliament provided them with a forum for expression.   The emigrants to America took these things for granted.   Moreover, they
came over at a time of rapidly expanding social consciousness.   The
growth of trade, the extension of industry, the opening of new
markets, the increase in social mobility, the migration to the towns,
the consequences of war, and the multifarious results of the Reformation—all these and various other factors conspired to generate a
new spirit of mutual criticism and a fresh sense of the relevance of
political questions.   Another consideration related to this is that
most of the early settlers came from the middle and lower-middle
classes which were most likely to be affected by the impact of the
new forces—artisans, small farmers, business and professional men.
Neither the lower classes nor the aristocracy figured extensively in
the migration, as historians have often pointed out.

Equally important is the intellectual environment in which the
settlers had lived in England.   They were coming over to America
during an epoch of unusually active speculation and experimentation in political affairs.   New ideas were being elaborated and new
organizations proposed and tried to a degree never before witnessed
in British history.   First there were the repercussions from the Reformation.   Matters of church organization and government; the relation of Church to State; the nature of man's relation to God and
the qualifications of political obligation which that entailed—these
and similar matters of intensely personal significance hitherto left
to the learned and to those in high places now became subjects of
discussion among more ordinary persons.   Secondly, there were the
complex issues arising out of the classic constitutional struggle under the Stuarts.   On the one hand there was the contest between
Common Law and Prerogative jurisdiction, and on the other that
between Parliament and the King's servants.   Out of the two there
emerged talk of judicial supremacy and fundamental law, claims as
to the omnicompetence of a sovereign legislature, drafts for a re-
fashioning of the constitutional structure, and new proposals as to
the parliamentary franchise and the ownership of property.   Out of
all this came the Civil War, the Cromwellian Experiments, the Restoration of Monarchy and the final Revolution of 1689; and the
whole was accompanied by an astonishing amount of political speculation.   Books, broadsides and pamphlets, drawing their doctrine

and idiom from diverse sources—the Bible, English case law and history, and philosophical discussions of the nature of man and the laws of Nature—set forth new ideas of popular political rights, religious toleration, and the supremacy of law over government. Many of these discussions were soon forgotten; but in sum they changed the political atmosphere of England and they constituted the milieu in which were written the great political classics (by Milton, Harrington, Sidney, Locke, and others) which did survive. Many of the ideas they embodied found later acceptance in the New World.

III

From almost the beginning of the colonial settlements there were minority groups who were determined to create a relatively free and tolerant society in America, and the new ideas were not without effect on the more conservative groups. Thus doubts of the complete validity of the Puritan authoritarianism appeared at times to influence the decisions of the most orthodox leaders in Massachusetts and Connecticut. The size of the country, the opportunities for wealth, and the opportunities too for mobility militated in favor of experimentation with libertarian ideas.

As population expanded and moved inland, the influence of the more restrictive traditions derived from the social stratification of England tended to disappear. It is true that substantial numbers of the settlers had been property-owners in England and had come to America with the hope of acquiring property and finding greater security in its enjoyment. But circumstances favored an increasing competence for all alike and opinion endorsed economic aspirations. Energy and thrift in amassing wealth ranked high among the Puritan virtues. Few would have been found to disagree with Cotton that "diligence in worldly business gives Christians more liberty for the service of God in their callings." So although it is true that the property qualifications for voting and holding office were retained until well after the close of the colonial period, it must be equally remembered that the opportunities for acquiring such property were far greater than in England. Indeed, at times in some of the Northern and Middle colonies, the owners of small farms and small concerns were so numerous that the qualified voters constituted substantial majorities of the adult male freemen; and in most of the colonies the small owners who were predominant in the frontier sections were able from time to time to wrest concessions from the coastal aristocracies so as to secure a fairer apportionment of representation.

The mere fact of space was a circumstance favorable to the testing of minority views. When the rulers of Massachusetts Bay banished Roger Williams because they feared that the whole colony was "like to be set on fire" by his ideas, he moved some fifty miles away, bought lands of the Indians in order to set up a community based on separation of church and state and a more liberal system of representation. Charles II gave his blessing to what he called "the lively experiment" and a royal charter for Providence Plantations (in 1663) provided that "No person within the said colony, at any time hereafter, shall be any wise molested, punished, disqualified, or called in question for any difference of opinion in matters of religion: every person may at all times freely and fully enjoy his own judgment and Conscience in matters of religious concernments." William Penn also set up what he called a "holy experiment," to be based on the principle that "We must give the liberty we ask." Penn's "Frame of Government" (1682) declared that all who acknowledge belief in "the one Almighty and Eternal God" and who "hold themselves obliged in conscience to live peaceably and justly in civil society, shall in no ways be molested or prejudiced for their religious profession or practice in matters of faith and worship; nor shall they be compelled, at any time, to frequent or maintain any religious worship, place, or ministry whatever." Although Jews and other non-Christians were excluded from voting or holding office, there were no prosecutions on religious grounds. Neither Rhode Island nor Pennsylvania made any effort to establish a state-supported church. Other colonies—the Carolinas, New York, New Jersey, and Maryland—were generally more tolerant than Massachusetts, Connecticut, and Virginia, although less so than Rhode Island and Pennsylvania. There was considerable vacillation in most of the colonies. Repressive acts, often the occasions for menacing protests, were repealed, amended, and sometimes reenacted; or they were applied with varying degrees of rigor.

IV

The colonies evolved during the seventeenth century from trade and plantation corporations into provinces. During the eighteenth century they developed from provinces into self-conscious common-wealths. Within the same periods drastic changes had come over the British constitution itself. The Revolution of 1689 may be taken as the great turning point. Prior to that event colonists and Englishmen alike had the same relation to the Crown. After it the formal status of the colonists depreciated. The ultimate result of the Revolution of 1689 was to establish an omnicompetent Parliament at Westminster. In Britain Parliament now controlled the Executive, and, moreover, claimed to control the colonies too. In the colonies, however, there was no thought of making the legislatures omnicompetent. There the executives remained essentially irresponsible in their relations to colonial legislatures and in most instances exercised only an authority delegated by Parliament. Parliament, moreover, had fallen heir to the mercantilist policy of Charles II.

Some sort of challenge to this whole conception of parliamentary power and delegated authority was almost inevitable. The culminating effects of the measures of Parliament in execution of her mercantilist policy led to the familiar Revolutionary protests of the latter eighteenth century. In making the challenge the colonists revived, refurbished, and considerably enlarged seventeenth-century arguments and doctrines which had been formulated in very different circumstances and for different purposes. Contentions used against the claims of monarchy now became useful against the pretension of Parliament. Doctrines which had been formulated as principles to determine the internal ordering of a community were now put forth to justify self-determination and a right of revolution. Yet again, the Revolutionary "liberals" (such as Samuel Adams, Tom Paine, and Thomas Jefferson) intended that principles put forward to justify resistance to an oppressive regime in England should be applied also to justify attacks on the authority of colonial aristocracies.

V

The major steps in setting up the means for a liberal democracy did not get well under way until after the close of the colonial period. Bills of rights were adopted during the Revolutionary period, churches were disestablished and primogeniture and entail abolished soon afterwards, and religious and property qualifications for voting were eliminated in the course of the first half of the nineteenth century. The main trend has been towards a more general acceptance of the ideal values of democratic government, freedom of opinion, equality before the courts, and free economic enterprise. Yet there have been wide divergencies of opinion concerning means for realizing these ideals. There have indeed been notable repudiations of the ideals themselves: warnings of the practical incompetence and of the intellectual and spiritual tyranny and barrenness of democracy; disparagements of free speech, assembly, and association where these liberties appear to endanger the preservation of other traditional values; and denials that private property promotes free enterprise.

Few political writers in America have constructed formal systems of ideas, comparable in scope to the works of European political philosophers (such as Hobbes, Locke and Rousseau). John Adams and Thomas Jefferson are the notable exceptions: the former wrote with considerable historical perspective and achieved a comprehensive view; and Jefferson's varied writings and activities make, in sum, a coherent and impressive system. Ordinarily our most significant political discussions have been in the nature of arguments supporting one side or the other of some fundamental question in dispute. Obviously such questions are not basically severable, and most of the writers have not assumed that they are. Many of the discussions take clear account of such matters as the relations of forms of government to the distribution of wealth, the effects of economic regulation on the preservation of civil liberties, and the dependence of democracy upon the maintenance of those liberties.

The selections in this book are chosen to represent the classic American discussions concerning (1) the problem of locating political control, (2) the lines to be drawn between governmental authority and individual liberty, (3) the nature and limits of property rights, and (4) the problem of political change. They cover a span of over three hundred years (1630 to 1941) and are taken from a wide variety of sources: essays and sermons, revolutionary proclamations, legal documents, the deliberations of constitutional and legislative assemblies, presidential messages, court opinions, the personal correspondence of statesmen, and a few systematic treatises. The arrangement of these discussions according to the fundamental questions at issue supplies, it is believed, a clear and faithful picture of the main lines of development of American political thought.

1. DEMOCRACY VERSUS ARISTOCRACY

1. JOHN WINTHROP (1588–1649)

JOHN WINTHROP, first governor of Massachusetts Bay and one of the few non-clerics among the original leaders of that colony, was born of a family of the lesser gentry, in the village of Groton, Suffolk County, England. His people were Church-of-England Puritans, who urged "purification" of the forms, ceremonies, and practices of the church, yet remained within the church, conforming generally to its rules until they could be changed. He entered Trinity College (educational stronghold of Puritanism), Cambridge, at the age of fifteen, withdrawing two years later to marry. He became a lawyer and a member of the Inner Temple and soon established a successful practice in London. He was also justice of the peace at Groton and acted as steward of his father's estate until the lordship of the manor was relinquished to him in his early thirties. Deeply religious, public spirited, and ambitious, he was increasingly disturbed by the political, religious, and social confusion of his day, and he was convinced that God was about to bring heavy afflictions on England. He was also troubled over his domestic circumstances; there was an economic depression in his region, and he was finding it increasingly difficult to maintain his growing family in the scale of living demanded by his social position. Things were getting so, he said, that "no man is able to continue in that place and employment where he now iss." He thought for a while of moving to Ireland. In the summer of 1629 he became interested in the recently chartered Massachusetts Bay Company and took part in a meeting that resulted in the radical decision to transfer the charter and government of the company to America. He prepared a paper for the company, setting forth "Reasons to be considered for iustifieinge the undertakers of the intended Plantation in New England. . . ." His statement epitomizes very well the varied motives that impelled so many competent and stable Englishmen to pull up roots and move to a remote and uncivilized country: the move would enable them "to carry the Gospell into those parts of the world," to follow the Gospel in their own way, and to get away from the religious and civil turmoil of the old country; and it might afford them the opportunity to make a better economic living. "Why then," asked Winthrop, "should we stand striving here for places of habitation, etc., (many men spending as much labour & coste to recover or

keepe sometimes an acre or twoe of Land, as would procure them many &
as good or better in another Countrie) & in the meane time suffer a whole
Continent as fruitfull & convenient for the use of man to lie waste without any improvement?"   In October the "General Court" (directing
board) of the company, "having received extraordinary great commenda-
tions of MR. JOHN WYNTHROP, both for his integrity and sufficiency,"
chose him as governor.

He sailed in April, 1630.   Soon after embarking he began his *Journal*,
which he continued intermittently until his death; it is concerned
mainly with public affairs and is a principal source of our knowledge of
the early history of New England.   He also prepared a lay sermon aboard
ship, to remind the voyagers of the objects of the "Solemn Venture" and
to advise them as to the sort of community they must set up in order
to achieve those objects.   He called his sermon "A Modell of Christian
Charity"; it was of supreme importance, he said, that they should set
up the right sort of community; for they were to be "as a Citty upon a
hill" with "the eies of all people" upon them.

Winthrop was governor of the colony for nine of his remaining years
and either deputy-governor or "assistant" for the other ten years.   He
was thus a central and influential figure in the early political and religious conflicts of the community.   He appears to have been a humane
and able administrator, generally aligned (reluctantly at times) with
the more conservative and intolerant ecclesiastical leaders of the colony.

[See: Perry Miller and Thomas H. Johnson, *The Puritans* (1938), pp.
1–63: "The Puritan Way of Life"; Herbert L. Osgood, "The Political Ideas
of the Puritans," *Political Science Quarterly*, Vol. VI (1891), pp. 1–28.

Robert C. Winthrop, *Life and Letters of John Winthrop* (2 vols.,
1864–67), esp. pp. 309–317, 348; Cotton Mather, *Magnalia Christi
Americana* (1702), Vol. I, bk. ii, ch. 4, pp. 118–131; Samuel E. Morison,
Builders of the Bay Colony (1930), ch. 3; Stanley Gray, "The Political
Thought of John Winthrop," *New England Quarterly*, Vol. III (1930), pp.
681–705; E. A. J. Johnson, "The Economic Ideas of John Winthrop," *ibid.*,
pp. 234–250.]

From A MODELL OF CHRISTIAN CHARITY (1630) [1]

Written

On Boarde the Arrabella,
On the Attlantick Ocean.

By the Honorable JOHN WINTHROP Esquire.

In His passage, (with the great Company of Religious people, of which Christian Tribes he was the Brave Leader and famous Governor;) from the Island of Great Brittaine, to New-England in the North America.
Anno 1630.

CHRISTIAN CHARITIE.

A MODELL HEREOF.

God Almightie in his most holy and wise providence hath soe disposed of the Condicion of mankinde, as in all times some must be rich some poore, some highe and eminent in power and dignitie; others meane and in subieccion.

THE REASON HEREOF.

1. Reas: *First*, to hold conformity with the rest of his workes, being delighted to shewe forthe the glory of his wisdome in the variety and differance of the Creatures and the glory of his power, in ordering all these differences for the preservacion and good of the whole, and the glory of his greatnes that as it is the glory of princes to haue many officers, soe this great King will haue many Stewards counting himselfe more honoured in dispenceing his guifts to man by man, then if hee did it by his owne immediate hand.

2. Reas: *Secondly*, That he might haue the more occasion to manifest the worke of his Spirit: first, vpon the wicked in moderateing and restraineing them: soe that the riche and mighty should not eate vpp the poore, nor the poore, and dispised rise vpp against theire superiours, and shake off theire yoake; 2ly in the regenerate in exerciseing his graces in them, as in the greate ones, theire loue mercy, gentlenes, temperance etc., in the poore and inferiour sorte, theire faithe patience, obedience etc:

[1] In *The Winthrop Papers*, 2 vols. (Massachusetts Historical Society, Boston, 1931), Vol. II, pp. 282–295, at 282–284, 292–295.

3. Reas: Thirdly, That every man might haue need of other, and from hence they might be all knitt more nearly together in the Bond of brotherly affeccion: from hence it appeares plainely that noe man is made more honourable then another or more wealthy etc., out of any perticuler and singuler respect to himselfe but for the glory of his Creator and the Common good of the Creature, Man. . . . All men being thus (by divine providence) rancked into two sortes, riche and poore; vnder the first, are comprehended all such as are able to liue comfortably by theire owne meanes duely improued; and all others are poore according to the former distribution. . . .

It rests now to make some applicacion of this discourse by the present designe which gaue the occasion of writeing of it. Herein are 4 things to be propounded: first the persons, 2ly, the worke, 3ly, the end, 4ly the meanes.

1. For the persons, wee are a Company professing our selues fellow members of Christ, In which respect onely though wee were absent from eache other many miles, and had our imploymentes as farre distant, yet wee ought to account our selues knitt together by this bond of loue . . .

2ly. for the worke wee haue in hand, it is by a mutuall consent through a speciall overruleing providence, and a more then an ordinary approbation of the Churches of Christ to seeke out a place of Cohabitation and Consorteshipp vnder a due forme of Government both ciuill and ecclesiasticall. In such cases as this the care of the publique must oversway all private respects, by which not onely conscience, but meare Ciuill pollicy doth binde vs; for it is a true rule that perticuler estates cannott subsist in the ruine of the publique.

3ly. The end is to improue our liues to doe more seruice to the Lord the comforte and encrease of the body of christe whereof wee are members that our selues and posterity may be the better preserued from the Common corrupcions of this euill world to serue the Lord and worke out our Salvacion vnder the power and purity of his holy Ordinances.

4ly for the meanes whereby this must bee effected, they are 2fold, a Conformity with the worke and end wee aime at, these wee see are extraordinary, therefore wee must not content our selues with vsuall ordinary meanes whatsoever wee did or ought to haue

2. JOHN COTTON (1584–1652)

JOHN COTTON, scholarly ecclesiastical leader of Massachusetts Bay and a power also in the political life of the colony, was born in a market town in Derbyshire, England, son of a devout and prosperous lawyer. He entered Trinity College, Cambridge, at the age of thirteen, and obtained his A.B. and M.A. degrees there. Later he held a fellowship at Emmanuel College (most Puritan of the colleges), where he became head lecturer and dean and received the degree of Bachelor of Divinity. For twenty years he was vicar of the wealthy church of St. Botolf's in the seaport town of Boston, Lincolnshire. He appears to have been a highly popular minister, and somewhat unorthodox; he declared his adherence to some of the Puritan doctrines and made changes in the legally prescribed church ritual. Lincolnshire friends of Cotton (including Thomas Dudley, first deputy-governor of Massachusetts) were active in the organization of the Massachusetts Bay Company and when the boat carrying Winthrop was about to sail from Southampton, Cotton delivered the farewell sermon ("God's Promise to His Plantation"). Two years later he was summoned before the Court of High Commission to answer charges of nonconformity. Prominent friends aided him in flight and concealment until, in July, 1633, he set sail for New England.

A few weeks after landing Cotton was elected teacher of the Boston Church; and he soon became the dominating personality among the New England clergy. He wrote a series of treatises that were promptly accepted as the most authoritative statements of the doctrines and discipline of New England Congregationalism. He was chief among the clerical advisers and prodders of Winthrop, and exercised a political influence second only to that of Winthrop himself.

In 1636, in response to demands for a civil constitution for the colony, Cotton prepared a body of laws (named, by Winthrop, "Model of Moses His Judicials"); the General Court rejected it in favor of a somewhat more practical and slightly less scriptural code prepared by a lawyer, Nathaniel Ward.[1] Cotton's code, however, was of considerable influence on later colonial compacts, particularly the "Fundamental Agreement" of New Haven. He discussed civic questions in his Sunday and Thursday sermons and participated actively in several political and reli-

[1] See pp. 295ff., below.

21

gious debates that disturbed the colony. In the celebrated "antinomian" controversy, arising out of the popular preachings of Mrs. Anne Hutchinson and her brother-in-law, Rev. John Wheelwright, dealing with the relative weights to be given to "Grace" and "Works" in effecting salvation, Cotton at first defended the Hutchinson group (Mrs. Hutchinson had been one of Cotton's admiring parishioners in Lincolnshire). He appeared to agree, partially and vaguely, with the doctrine that a dispensation of grace (a "personal indwelling of the Holy Spirit") relieved a person from the necessity of sanctification through any sort of works. But as he became disturbed by what seemed to him to be exaggerated statements of that doctrine, and by fears that the controversy would lead to dangerous civic disunity, he yielded to the pleas of other clerical and civic leaders and aligned himself vehemently with the prosecution.

Cotton engaged in a long controversy with Roger Williams concerning two of the issues that had led to Williams' banishment from the colony. On the question of the relations of New England Congregationalists to the Church of England, Cotton took the more liberal side: Williams contended that only persons who had explicitly renounced the Church of England should be heard or admitted to membership in the new Congregations, while Cotton maintained that "those ought to be received into the Church who are Godly, though they doe not see, nor expressly bewaile all the polutions in Church-fellowship, Ministry, Worship, Government." Another issue, concerning the power of civil authorities in religious matters, was the occasion for a famous battle of pamphlets between the two, Cotton defending the orthodox position of the New England Puritan theocracy and Williams taking his stand for a complete separation of religious and secular affairs.[1]

Cotton's style is ponderous, often obscure. The clearest statement of his political doctrine appears in a letter he wrote to a Puritan noble, Lord Say and Seal, who, desiring to move to the colony, was disturbed by reports that only church members approved by the local theocracy could be admitted to citizenship. Cotton's letter reveals his basic ideas on the proper location of political authority and the relations between church and state.

[See: Cotton Mather, *Magnalia* (1702), Vol. I, bk. ii, ch. 1 (pp. 252–286); Williston Walker, *Ten New England Leaders* (1901), ch. 2; Vernon L. Parrington, *Main Currents of American Thought*, Vol. I (1927), pp. 27–37.

Cotton's most important expositions of New England congregationalism are *The Keyes of the Kingdom of Heaven* (1644), and *The Ways of the Churches of Christ in New England* (1645). For his controversy with

---

[1] See pp. 300ff., below.

Williams on the question of membership in the New England churches, see his "Reply to Mr. Williams," probably written in 1637, printed in 1643, reprinted in *Publications of the Narragansett Club*, Vol. I, pp. 295–311.]

From COPY OF A LETTER FROM MR. COTTON TO LORD SAY AND SEAL IN THE YEAR 1636.[1]

. . . It is very suitable to Gods all-sufficient wisdome, and to the fulnes and perfection of Holy Scriptures, not only to prescribe perfect rules for the right ordering of a private mans soule to everlasting blessednes with himselfe, but also for the right ordering of a mans family, yea, of the commonwealth too, so farre as both of them are subordinate to spiritual ends, and yet avoide both the churches usurpation upon civill jurisdictions, *in ordine ad spiritualia,*[2] and the commonwealths invasion upon ecclesiasticall administrations, *in ordine* to civill peace, and conformity to the civill state. Gods institutions (such as the government of church and of commonwealth be) may be close and compact, and co-ordinate one to another, and yet not confounded. God hath so framed the state of church government and ordinances, that they may be compatible to any commonwealth, though never so much disordered in his frame. But yet when a commonwealth hath liberty to mould his owne frame (*scripturae plenitudinem adoro*[3]) I conceyve the scripture hath given full direction for the right ordering of the same, and that, in such sort as may best mainteyne the *euexia*[4] of the church. Mr. Hooker doth often quote a saying out of Mr. Cartwright (though I have not read it in him) that noe man fashioneth his house to his hangings, but his hangings to his house. It is better that the commonwealth be fashioned to the setting forth of Gods house, which is his church, than to accommodate the church frame to the civill state. Democracy, I do not conceyve that ever God did ordeyne as a fitt government eyther for church or commonwealth. If the people be governors, who shall be governed? As for monarchy, and aristocracy, they are both of them clearly

---

[1] In Thomas Hutchinson, *The History of Massachusetts, from the First Settlement Thereof in 1628, until the year 1750*, 3rd ed., 2 vols. (Boston, 1795), Vol. I, pp 436–439.

[2] In reference to spiritual concerns.

[3] I respect the full authority of the Scriptures.

[4] Vigor.

approoved, and directed in scripture, yet so as referreth the sov-
eraigntie to himselfe, and setteth up Theocracy in both, as the best
forme of government in the commonwealth, as well as in the
church. . . .

When your Lordship doubteth, that this corse will draw all
things under the determination of the church, *in ordine ad spiritualia* (seeing the church is to determine who shall be members,
and none but a member may have to doe in the government of a
commonwealth) be pleased (I pray you) to conceyve, that magistrates are neyther chosen to office in the church, nor doe governe
by directions from the church, but by civill lawes, and those enacted in generall corts, and executed in corts of iustice, by the governors and assistants. In all which, the church (as the church)
hath nothing to doe: onely, it prepareth fitt instruments both to
rule, and to choose rulers, which is no ambition in the church, nor
dishonor to the commonwealth; the apostle, on the contrary,
thought it a great dishonor and reproach to the church of Christ,
if it were not able to yield able judges to heare and determine all
causes amongst their brethren, I Cor. vi. 1 to 5. which place alone
seemeth to me fully to decide this question; for it plainely holdeth
forth this argument: It is a shame to the church to want able
judges of civill matters (as v. 5.) and an audacious act in any church
member voluntarily to go for judgment, other where than before
the saints (as v. 1.) then it will be noe arrogance nor folly in church
members, nor prejudice to the commonwealth, if voluntarily they
never choose any civill judges, but from amongst the saints, such
as church members are called to be. But the former is cleare: and
how then can the latter be avoyded. If this therefore be (as your
Lordship rightly conceyveth) one of the maine objections if not
the onely one which hindereth this commonwealth from the enter-
tainment of the propositions of those worthy gentlemen, wee in-
treate them, in the name of the Lord Jesus, to consider, in meek-
nes of wisdome, it is not any conceite or will of ours, but the holy
counsell and will of the Lord Jesus (whom they seeke to serve as
well as wee) that overruleth us in this case: and we trust will overrule them also, that the Lord onely may be exalted amongst all his
servants. What pittie and griefe were it, that the observance of
the will of Christ should hinder good things from us! . . .

Nor neede wee feare, that this course will, in time, cast the commonwealth into distractions, and popular confusions. For (under correction) these three things doe not undermine, but doe mutually and strongly mainteyne one another (even those three which wee principally aime at) authority in magistrates, liberty in people, purity in the church. Purity, preserved in the church, will preserve well ordered liberty in the people, and both of them establish well-ballanced authority in the magistrates. God is the author of all these three, and neyther is himselfe the God of confusion, nor are his wayes the wayes of confusion, but of peace. . . .

3. THE "FUNDAMENTAL AGREEMENT" OF
NEW HAVEN (1639)

THE early settlers had to carry on government as well as write about it. In some cases they had to create their own governments. The settlements that were made under express grants of authority from England had the main lines of their governmental organization laid down in their charters (e.g., the Virginia charter of 1606 and the Massachusetts Bay charter of 1629). Other settlements (Providence Plantations, Connecticut, New Haven) were begun without any such authorization; and the settlers devised their own governmental arrangements. The formal agreements they adopted are important sources of our knowledge of the political ideas of the early settlers.

After squatters from Massachusetts Bay had, during 1635 and 1636, formed settlements (Windsor, Hartford, and Wethersfield) along the Connecticut River they conducted their civic affairs through provisional arrangements until, in 1637, they set up a "court," which was empowered to negotiate with the Indians, organize a militia, appoint constables, and levy taxes. On January 14, 1639, "voting" (in what form we do not know) "to associate and conjoyne . . . as one Publike State or Commonwealth" with "an orderly and decent Government established according to God," they adopted a document setting forth formally the fundamental rules for such a government. This document, subsequently known as "The Fundamental Orders of Connecticut," has been called "the first written constitution of America" and "the first written constitution of modern democracy." The document is a "constitution" in the sense that it is made up of rules defining a basic framework of government (the choice, terms, and duties of chief officials, qualifications of voters, structure of the courts) and that it was apparently adopted by a substantial fraction of the population that was to be subject to its rules. But it set up only a very limited form of democracy. Voters for deputies to the general court were only the "admitted inhabitants" of the several towns, and these were only such as were adjudged, by existing townsmen, to be of "honest Conversation" and qualified to take an oath (prescribed in the Orders) the terms of which implied a belief in the Trinity. Moreover, only "freemen" could vote for governor and magistrates or serve as deputies, and only the general court could make a man a freeman.

The "Fundamental Agreement" of New Haven reveals more clearly the ideas of the early Puritans as to how to set up civil government and as to who should hold the reins of political power. This settlement had been made in 1638 by a group of Londoners (led by John Davenport, a Puritan divine, and Theophilus Eaton, a merchant), who in the previous year had landed in the Massachusetts colony, apparently intending to found a separate commercial community within the limits of that colony. They were unable to find an unoccupied harbor in that region; and they were dissatisfied with the stand of the Massachusetts clergy in the Antinomian controversy. Accordingly they explored other regions and found a harbor on the north shore of Long Island Sound, at the mouth of the Quinnipiac River. A lease of land from the Quinnipiac Indians was their only foundation of authority; and they set about framing their own arrangements for the regulation of their common concerns. On June 4, 1639, some sixty free planters of the settlement assembled (in a barn belonging to a Mr. Francis Newman, according to tradition) to adopt basic rules of civil government and to prepare for the organization of a church. How they went about this, and what they considered to be the most important matters to be determined in setting up a civil order, is well revealed in the original account below, as recorded by Thomas Fugill, one of the signers of the document and first secretary of the settlement.

[Sixty-three names, headed by Eaton and Davenport, are affixed to the agreement. There then follow forty-eight "autograph signatures"—apparently names written in for the illiterate endorsers.
See: Charles M. Andrews, *The Colonial Period of American History* (1934–38), Vol. II, chs. 3–5; Henry White, "The New Haven Colony," in *Papers of the New Haven County Historical Society*, Vol. I (1865), pp. 1–10, and Leonard Bacon, "Civil Government in New Haven Colony," *ibid.*, pp. 11–28.]

THE "FUNDAMENTAL AGREEMENT" OF NEW HAVEN (JUNE 4, 1639) [1]

The 4th day of the 4th moneth called June 1639, all the free planters assembled together in a general meetinge to consult about settling civill Government according to God, and about the nomination of persons thatt might be founde by consent of all fittest in all respects for the foundacion worke of a church which was intend

[1] In *Records of the Colony and Plantation of New Haven, from 1638 to 1649*, ed. by Charles J. Hoadly (Hartford, 1857), pp. 11–17.

to be gathered in Quinipieck. After solemne invocation of the name of God in prayer for the presence and help of his speritt, and grace in those weighty businesses, they were reminded of the busines whereabout they mett (viz) for the establishment of such civill order as might be most pleasing unto God, and for the chuseing the fittest men for the foundacion worke of a church to be gathered. For the better inableing them to discerne the minde of God and to agree accordingly concerning the establishment of civill order, Mr. John Davenport propounded divers quaeres to them publiquely praying them to consider seriously in the presence and feare of God the weight of the busines they met about, and nott to be rash or sleight in giveing their votes to things they understoode nott, butt to digest fully and throughly whatt should be propounded to them, and without respect to men as they should be satisfied and perswaded in their owne mindes to give their answers in such sort as they would be willing they should stand upon recorde for posterity.

This being earnestly pressed by Mr. Davenport, Mr. Robt. Newman was intreated to write in carracters and to read distinctly and audibly in the hearing of all the people whatt was propounded and accorded on that itt might appeare thatt all consented to matters propounded according to words written by him.

QUAER. 1. Whether the Scripturs doe holde forth a perfect rule for the direction and government of all men in all dueties which they are to performe to God and men as well in the government of famylyes and commonwealths as in matters of the church.

This was assented unto by all, no man dissenting as was expressed by holding up of hands. Afterward itt was read over to them thatt they might see in whatt words their vote was expressed: They againe expressed their consent thereto by holdeing up their hands, no man dissenting.

QUAER. 2. Whereas there was a covenant solemnly made by the whole assembly of freeplanters of this plantation the first day of extraordenary humiliation which we had after wee came together, thatt as in matters thatt concerne the gathering and ordering of a church so likewise in all publique offices which concerne civill order, as choyce of magistrates and officers, makeing and repealing of lawes, devideing allottments of inheritance and all things of like nature we would all of us be ordered by those rules which the scripture holds forth to us. This covenant was called a plantation covenant to distinguish itt from a church covenant which could nott att thatt time be made, a church nott being then gathered, butt was deferred till a church might be gathered according to God: Itt was demaunded whether all the free planters doe holde themselves bound by thatt covenant in all businesses of thatt nature which are expressed in the covenant to submitt themselves to be ordered by the rules held forth in the scripture.

This also was assented unto by all, and no man gainesaid itt, and they did testefie the same by holdeing up their hands both when itt was first propounded, and confirmed the same by holdeing up their hands when itt was read unto them in publique, John Clarke being absent when the covenant was made, doth now manefest his consent to itt, allso Richard Beach, Andrew Low, Goodman Banister, Arthur Halbidge, John Potter, Robert Hill, John Brockett and John Johnson, these persons being nott admitted planters when the covenant was made doth now express their consent to itt.

QUAER. 3. Those who have desired to be received as free planters, and are settled in the plantation with a purpose, resolution and desire thatt they may be admitted into church fellowship according to Christ as soone as God shall fitt them thereunto: were desired to express itt by holdeing up of hands: Accordingly all did expresse this to be their desire and purpose by holdeing up their hands twice, (viz) both att the proposall of itt, and after when these written words were read unto them.

QUAER. 4. All the free planters were called upon to expresse whether they held themselves bound to establish such civill order as might best conduce to the secureing of the purity and peace of the ordinances to themselves and their posterity according to God. In answer hereunto they expressed by holding up their hands twice as before, thatt they held them selves bound to establish such civil order as might best conduce to the ends aforesaid.

Then Mr. Davenport declared unto them by the scripture whatt kinde of persons might best be trusted with matters of government, and by sundry arguments from scripture proved thatt such men as were discribed in Exod. 18. 2. Deut. 1. 13, with Deut. 17. 15, and 1. Cor. 6: 1 to 7, ought to be intrusted by them, seeing they were free to cast themselves into thatt mould and forme of comonn wealth which appeareth best for them in referrence to the secureing of the pure and peaceable injoyment of all Christ his ordinances in

the church according to God, whereunto they have bound themselves as hath beene acknowledged. Having thus said he satt
downe, praying the company freely to consider whether they would
have it voted att this time or nott: After some space of silence Mr.
Theophilus Eaton answered itt might be voted, and some others
allso spake to the same purpose, none att all opposeing itt. Then
itt was propounded to vote.

QUAER. 5. Whether Free Burgesses shalbe chosen out of church
members they thatt are in the foundation worke of the church being
actually free burgesses, and to chuse to themselves out of the like
estate of church fellowship and the power of chuseing magistrates
and officers from among themselves and the power off makeing
and repealing lawes according to the worde, and the devideing of
inheritances and decideing of differences thatt may arise, and all
the businesses of like nature are to be transacted by those free
burgesses.

This was putt to vote and agreed unto by the lifting up of hands
twice as in the former itt was done. Then one man stood up after
the vote was past, and expressing his dissenting from the rest in part
yett grantinge 1. That magistrates should be men fearing God.
2. Thatt the church is the company whence ordenaryly such men
may be expected. 3. Thatt they that chuse them ought to be men
fearing God: onely att this he stuck, That free planters ought nott
to give this power out of their hands: Another stood up and answered that in this case nothing was done but with their consent.
The former answered thatt all the free planters ought to resume
this power into their owne hands againe if things were nott orderly
carryed. Mr. Theophilus Eaton answered thatt in all places they
chuse committyes, in like manner the companyes of London chuse
the liveryes by whom the publique magistrates are chosen. In this
the rest are not wronged because they expect in time to be of ye
livery themselves, and to have the same power. Some others intreated the former to give his arguments and reasons whereupon he
dissented. He refused to doe itt and said they might nott rationally
demaund itt, seeing he lett the vote passe on freely and did nott
speake till after itt was past, because he would nott hinder whatt
they agreed upon. Then Mr. Davenport, after a short relation of
some former passages between them two about this question prayed
the company thatt nothing might be concluded by them in this

weighty question butt whatt themselves were perswaded to be agreeing with the minde of God and they had heard whatt had beene said since the voteing, intreated them againe to consider of itt, and putt itt againe to vote as before.—Againe all of them by holding up their hands did shew their consent as before, And some of them professed thatt whereas they did waver before they came to the assembly they were now fully convinced thatt itt is the minde of God. One of them said that in the morning, before he came, reading Deut. 17. 15. he was convinced att home, another said thatt he came doubting to the assembly butt he blessed God by whatt had beene said he was now fully satisfied thatt the choyce of burgesses out of church members, and to intrust those with the power before spoken off is according to the minde of God revealed in the scriptures. All haveing spoken their apprehensions, itt was agreed upon, and Mr. Robert Newman was desired to write itt as an order whereunto every one thatt hereafter should be admitted here as planters should submitt and testefie the same by subscribeing their names to the order, namely, that church members onely shall be free burgesses, and thatt they onely shall chuse magistrates & officers among themselues to have the power of transacting all the publique civill affayres of this Plantation, of makeing and repealing lawes, devideing of inheritances, decideing of differences thatt may arise and doeing all things or businesses of like nature.

This being thus settled as a foundamentall agreement concerning civill government Mr. Davenport proceeded to propound some things to consideracion aboute the gathering of a church. And to prevent the blemishing of the first beginnings of the church worke, Mr. Davenport advised thatt the names of such as were to be admitted might be publiquely propounded, to the end thatt they who were most approved might be chosen, for the towne being cast into severall private meetings wherein they thatt dwelt nearest together gave their accounts one to another of Gods gracious worke upon them, and prayed together and conferred to their mutuall edificacion, sundry of them had knowledg one of another, and in every meeting some one was more approved of all then any other, For this reason, and to prevent scandalls, the whole company was intreated to consider whom they found fittest to nominate for this worke.

QUAE. 6. Whether are you all willing and doe agree in this thatt twelve men be chosen thatt their fitnesse for the foundacion worke may be tried, however there may be more named yett itt may be in their power who are chosen to reduce them to twelve, and itt be in the power of those twelve to chuse out of themselves seaven that shall be most approved of the major part to begin the church.

This was agreed upon by consent of all as was expressed by holdeing up of hands, and thatt so many as should be thought fitt for the foundacion worke of the church shall be propounded by the plantation, and written downe and passe without exception unlesse they had given publique scandall or offence, yett so as in case of publique scandall or offence, every one should have liberty to propound their exception att thatt time publiquely against any man that should be nominated when all their names should be writt downe, butt if the offence were private, thatt mens names might be tendered, so many as were offended were intreated to deale with the offender privately, and if he gave nott satisfaction, to bring the matter to the twelve thatt they might consider of itt impartially and in the feare of God. The names of the persons nominated and agreed upon were Mr. Theoph. Eaton, Mr. John Davenport, Mr. Robt. Newman, Mr. Math. Gilbert, Mr. Richard Malbon, Mr. Nath: Turner, Eze: Chevers, Thomas Fugill, John Ponderson, William Andrewes, and Jer. Dixon. Noe exception was brought against any of those in publique, except one about takeing an excessive rate for meale which he sould to one of Pequanack in his need, which he confessed with griefe and declared thatt haveing beene smitten in heart and troubled in his conscience, he restored such a part of the price back againe with confession of his sin to the party as he thought himselfe bound to doe. And itt being feared thatt the report of the sin was heard farther than the report of his satisfaction, a course was concluded on to make the satisfaction known to as many as heard of the sinn. Itt was also agreed upon att the said meeting thatt if the persons above named did finde themselves straitened in the number of fitt men for the seaven, thatt itt should be free for them to take into tryal of fittnes such other as they should thinke meete, provided thatt itt should be signified to the towne upon the Lords day who they so take in, thatt every man may be satisfied of them according to the course formerly taken.

4. JOHN WISE (1652–1725)

JOHN WISE, an influential figure in civic and ecclesiastical affairs of the Boston region in the late seventeenth and early eighteenth centuries, has been called "the first great American democrat" and "the father of American democracy." Over half a century earlier, Roger Williams (banished from Massachusetts, because of his advocacy of religious toleration) had founded a colony ("Providence Plantations") in which he had made a serious attempt to set up a government based on principles of democracy and toleration; and in several writings, notably his *Bloudy Tenent of Persecution* (1644),[1] he had ably challenged the doctrine of the Massachusetts hierarchy that political authority rested on a divine delegation of power to an elect minority. But Williams wrote in a difficult idiom and some phases of his doctrine are not clear. In the early eighteenth century Wise set forth a lucid and cogent statement of the democratic theory.

We know relatively little of the life of Wise. He was born in the village of Roxbury, to which his father had come as an indentured servant. After his graduation from Harvard in 1673 he preached for brief terms in Branford, Connecticut, and in several Massachusetts towns; in 1680 he was called to Chebacco (now Essex), a newly established parish in the town of Ipswich, and he was a popular minister there for the remainder of his life. He was chaplain in the colonial expedition against Quebec in 1690; the attack ended disastrously, but the Massachusetts legislature, several years after Wise's death, voted three hundred acres to his heirs, in recognition of the piety, wisdom, heroism, and "Military Skill" he had displayed on the expedition.

Wise was a liberal and pugnacious minister and played aggressive and effective parts in several public controversies. When Governor Andros levied his tax of a penny on the pound, Wise led the discussion by the town meeting and drew up the protest. The colonists, he said, had "a good God, and a good King, and should do well to stand to our privileges," and he appealed to *Magna Charta* and other great English statutes. The outcome of the protest led him to say: "we too boldly endeavoured to persuade ourselves we were English Men," for in trials before Andros several of the leaders were convicted and Wise was fined,

[1] See below, pp. 301ff.

removed from his ministry, and jailed for three weeks. After Andros'
deposition in 1689, Wise was one of two Ipswich representatives in a
meeting held at Boston to draw up plans for reorganizing the old legislature. He was one of the few ministers to protest against the witchcraft
prosecutions of the sixteen-nineties; he prepared a remonstrance and
signed the petition of 1703 to the general court to clear the names of
all who had been convicted. The court did appoint a fast day in apology
for the tragic events and a few years later declared the convictions null
and void. Wise fought in other liberal causes—for inoculation against
smallpox (opposed by most of the ministers) and for a more flexible
currency system; he is the supposed author of a pamphlet on the latter
subject ("A Word of Comfort to a Melancholy Country . . .", issued
under the pseudonymn, *Amicus Patriae*).

Wise's two most important writings were occasioned by a controversy
over church organization. In 1705 an unsigned document ("Questions
and Proposals," supposedly prepared by Increase and Cotton Mather)
was issued in Boston, proposing to transfer control of the churches from
the members to the clergy and to put an end to the independence of the
several churches. Wise responded, first with a sarcastic and humorous,
but earnest and thoughtful, pamphlet, entitled "The Churches Quarrel
Espoused" (1710), and later with a more learned and systematic treatise
—*A Vindication of the Government of the New-England Churches*
(1717). In the latter he derived his ideas on church organization from
a general theory concerning the natural rights of man, the justification
of authority, and the different forms of civil polity. The *Vindication*
is an exceptionally comprehensive and thoughtful defense of democracy.
Both of Wise's works were in demand by the revolutionary leaders of
New England half a century later.

[See: Moses Coit Tyler, *A History of American Literature* (1878),
Vol. II, pp. 104–116; John L. Sibley, *Biographical Sketches of the Graduates
of Harvard University*, Vol. II (1881), pp. 428–441; Vernon L. Parrington,
Main Currents in American Thought, Vol. I (1927), pp. 118–125.]

From A VINDICATION OF THE GOVERNMENT OF NEW-ENGLAND CHURCHES (1717) [1]

I shall consider Man in a state of Natural Being, as a Free-Born
Subject under the Crown of Heaven, and owing Homage to none

[1] *A Vindication of the Government of New-England Churches. Drawn from Antiquity; the Light of Nature; Holy Scripture; its Noble Nature; and from the Dignity
Divine Providence has put upon it* (Boston, 1717), pp. 33–40, 41, 42–44, 47–50,
60–63.

but God himself. It is certain Civil Government in General, is a very Admirable Result of Providence, and an Incomparable Benefit to Man-kind, yet must needs be acknowledged to be the Effect of Humane Free-Compacts and not of Divine Institution; it is the Produce of Mans Reason, of Humane and Rational Combinations, and not from any direct Orders of Infinite Wisdom, in any positive Law wherein is drawn up this or that Scheme of Civil Government. Government (says the Lord *Warrington*) is necessary—in that no Society of Men can subsist without it; and that Particular Form of Government is necessary which best suits the Temper and Inclination of a People. Nothing can be Gods Ordinance, but what he has particularly Declared to be such; there is no particular Form of Civil Government described in Gods Word, neither does Nature prompt it. The Government of the *Jews* was changed five Times. Government is not formed by Nature, as other Births or Productions; If it were, it would be the same in all Countries; because Nature keeps the same Method, in the same thing, in all Climates. If a Common Wealth be changed into a Monarchy, is it Nature that forms, and brings forth the Monarch? Or if a Royal Family be wholly Extinct (as in *Noah*'s Case, being not Heir Apparent from Descent from *Adam*) is it Nature that must go to work (with the King Bees, who themselves alone preserve the Royal Race in that Empire) to Breed a Monarch before the People can have a King, or a Government sent over them? And thus we must leave Kings to Resolve which is their best Title to their Crowns, whether Natural Right, or the Constitution of Government settled by Humane Compacts, under the Direction and Conduct of Reason. . . .

1. The Prime Immunity in Mans State, is that he is most properly the Subject of the Law of Nature. He is the Favourite Animal on Earth; in that this Part of Gods Image, viz. Reason is Congenate with his Nature, wherein by a Law Immutable, Instampt upon his Frame, God has provided a Rule for Men in all their Actions, obliging each one to the performance of that which is Right, not only as to Justice, but likewise as to all other Moral Vertues, the which is nothing but the Dictate of Right Reason founded in the Soul of Man. . . . That which is to be drawn from Mans Reason, flowing from the true Current of that Faculty, when unperverted, may be said to be the Law of Nature; on which account, the Holy Scriptures declare it written on Mens hearts. For being indowed

with a Soul, you may know from your self, how, and what you ought to act, Rom. 2. 14. *These having not a Law, are a Law to themselves.* So that the meaning is, when we acknowledge the Law of Nature to be the dictate of Right Reason, we must mean that the Understanding of Man is Endowed with such a power, as to be able, from the Comtemplation of humane Condition to discover a necessity of Living agreeably with this Law: And likewise to find out some Principle, by which the Precepts of it, may be clearly and solidly Demonstrated. . . . A Man must be a very dull Scholar to Nature not to make Proficiency in the Knowledge of her Laws. But more Particularly in pursuing our Condition for the discovery of the Law of Nature, this is very obvious to view, *viz.*

1. A Principle of Self-Love, & Self-Preservation, is very predominant in every Mans Being.

2. A Sociable Disposition.

3. An Affection or Love to Man-kind in General. And to give such Sentiments the force of a Law, we must suppose a God who takes care of all Mankind, and has thus obliged each one, as a Subject of higher Principles of Being, then meer Instincts. For that all Law properly considered, supposes a capable Subject, and a Superiour Power; And the Law of God which is Binding, is published by the Dictates of Right Reason as other ways: Therefore says *Plutarch, To follow God and obey Reason is the same thing.* But moreover that God has Established the Law of Nature, as the General Rule of Government, is further Iilustrable from the many Sanctions in Providence, and from the Peace and Guilt of Conscience in them that either obey, or violate the Law of Nature. But moreover, the foundation of the Law of Nature with relation to Government, may be thus Discovered. *scil.* Man is a Creature extreamly desirous of his own Preservation; of himself he is plainly Exposed to many Wants, unable to secure his own safety, and Maintenance without the Assistance of his fellows; and he is also able of returning Kindness by the furtherance of mutual Good; But yet Man is often found to be Malicious, Insolent, and easily Provoked, and as powerful in Effecting mischief, as he is ready in designing it. Now that such a Creature may be Preserved, it is necessary that he be Sociable; that is, that he be capable and disposed to unite himself to those of his own species, and to Regulate himself towards them, that they may have no fair Reason to do him harm; but rather incline to

promote his Interests, and secure his Rights and Concerns. This then is a Fundamental Law of Nature, that every Man as far as in him lies, do maintain a Sociableness with others, agreeable with the main end and disposition of humane Nature in general. For this is very apparent, that Reason and Society render Man the most potent of all Creatures. And finally, from the Principles of Sociableness it follows as a fundamental Law of Nature, that Man is not so Wedded to his own Interest, but that he can make the Common good the mark of his Aim: And hence he becomes Capacitated to enter into a Civil State by the Law of Nature; for without this property in Nature, viz. Sociableness, which is for Cementing of parts, every Government would soon moulder and dissolve.

2. The Second Great Immunity of Man is an Original Liberty Instampt upon his Rational Nature. He that intrudes upon this Liberty, Violates the Law of Nature. In this Discourse I shall wave the Consideration of Mans Moral Turpitude, but shall view him Physically as a Creature which God has made and furnished essentially with many Enobling Immunities, which render him the most August Animal in the World, and still, whatever has happened since his Creation, he remains at the upper-end of Nature, and as such is a Creature of a very Noble Character. For as to his Dominion, the whole frame of the Lower Part of the Universe is devoted to his use, and at his Command; and his Liberty under the Conduct of Right Reason, is equal with his trust. Which Liberty may be briefly Considered, Internally as to his Mind, and Externally as to his Person.

1. The Internal Native Liberty of Mans Nature in general implies, a faculty of Doing or Omitting things according to the Direction of his Judgment. But in a more special meaning, this Liberty does not consist in a loose and ungovernable Freedom, or in an unbounded Licence of Acting. Such Licence is disagreeing with the condition and dignity of Man, and would make Man of a lower and meaner Constitution then Bruit Creatures; who in all their Liberties are kept under a better and more Rational Government, by their Instincts. Therefore as *Plutarch* says, *Those Persons only who live in Obedience to Reason, are worthy to be accounted free: They alone live as they Will, who have Learnt what they ought to Will.* So that the true Natural Liberty of Man, such as really and truely agrees to him, must be understood, as he is Guided and Restrained

by the Tyes of Reason, and Laws of Nature; all the rest is Brutal, if
not worse.

2. Mans External Personal, Natural Liberty, Antecedent to all
Humane parts, or Alliances must also be considered. And so every
Man must be conceived to be perfectly in his own Power and dis-
posal, and not to be controuled by the Authority of any other.
And thus every Man, must be acknowledged equal to every Man,
since all Subjection and all Command are equally banished on both
sides; and considering all Men thus at Liberty, every Man has a
Prerogative to Judge for himself, viz. What shall be most for his
Behoof, Happiness and Well-being.

3. The Third Capital Immunity belonging to Mans Nature, is
an equality amongst Men; Which is not to be denied by the Law
of Nature, till Man has Resigned himself with all his Rights for the
sake of a Civil State; and then his Personal Liberty and Equality is
to be cherished, and preserved to the highest degree, as will consist
with all just distinctions amongst Men of Honour, and shall be
agreeable with the publick Good. For Man has a high valuation
of himself, and the passion seems to lay its first foundation (not in
Pride, but) really in the high and admirable Frame and Constitution
of Humane Nature. The Word Man, says my Author, is thought
to carry somewhat of Dignity in its sound; and we commonly make
use of this as the most proper and prevailing Argument against a
rude Insulter, viz. *I am not a Beast or a Dog, but am a Man as well
as your self.* Since then Humane Nature agrees equally with all
persons; and since no one can live a Sociable Life with another that
does not own or Respect him as a Man; It follows as a Command
of the Law of Nature, that every Man Esteem and treat another
as one who is naturally his Equal, or who is a Man as well as he.
There be many popular, or plausible Reasons that greatly Illustrate
this Equality, viz. that we all Derive our Being from one stock, the
same Common Father of humane Race. . . .

And also that our Bodies are Composed of matter, frail, brittle,
and lyable to be destroyed by thousand Accidents; we all owe our
Existence to the same Method of propagation. The Noblest Mortal
in his Entrance on to the Stage of Life, is not distinguished by any
pomp or of passage from the lowest of Mankind; and our Life
hastens to the same General Mark: Death observes no Ceremony,
but Knocks as loud at the Barriers of the Court, as at the Door of

the Cottage. This Equality being admitted, bears a very great force in maintaining Peace and Friendship amongst Men. For that he who would use the Assistance of others, in promoting his own Advantage, ought as freely to be at their service, when they want his help on the like Occasions. . . . That it would be the greatest absurdity to believe, that Nature actually Invests the Wise with a Sovereignty over the weak; or with a Right of forcing them against their Wills; for that no Sovereignty can be Established, unless some Humane Deed, or Covenant Precede: Nor does Natural fitness for Government make a Man presently Governour over another; for that as *Ulpian* says, *by a Natural Right all Men are born free*; and Nature having set all Men upon a Level and made them Equals, no Servitude or Subjection can be conceived without Inequality; and this cannot be made without Usurpation or Force in others, or Voluntary Compliance in those who Resign their freedom, and give away their degree of Natural Being. . . .

1. Every Man considered in a Natural State, must be allowed to be Free, and at his own dispose; yet to suit Mans Inclinations to Society; And in a peculiar manner to gratify the necessity he is in of publick Rule and Order, he is Impelled to enter into a Civil Community; and Divests himself of his Natural Freedom, and puts himself under Government; which amongst other things Comprehends the Power of Life and Death over Him; together with Authority to Injoyn him some things to which has an utter Aversation, and to prohibit him other things, for which he may have as strong an Inclination; so that he may be often under this Authority, obliged to Sacrifice his Private, for the Publick Good. So that though Man is inclined to Society, yet he is driven to a Combination by great necessity. For that the true and leading Cause of forming Governments, and yielding up Natural Liberty, and throwing Mans Equality into a Common Pile to be new Cast by the Rules of fellowship; was really and truly to guard themselves against the Injuries Men were lyable to Interchangeably; for none so Good to Man, as Man, and yet none a greater Enemy. So that,

2. The first Humane Subject and Original of Civil Power is the People. For as they have a Power every Man over himself in a Natural State, so upon a Combination they can and do bequeath this Power unto others; and settle it according as their united discretion shall Determine. For that this is very plain, that when the

Subject of Sovereign Power is quite Extinct, that Power returns to the People again. And when they are free, they may set up what species of Government they please; or if they rather incline to it, they may subside into a State of Natural Being, if it be plainly for the best. . . .

1. The Forms of a Regular State are three only, which Forms arise from the proper and particular Subject, in which the Supream Power Resides. As,

1. A Democracy, which is when the Sovereign Power is Lodged in a Council consisting of all the Members, and where every Member has the Priviledge of a Vote. This Form of Government, appears in the greatest part of the World to have been the most Ancient. For that Reason seems to shew it to be most probable, that when Men [being Originally in a condition of Natural Freedom and Equality] had thoughts of joyning in a Civil Body, would without question be inclined to Administer their common Affairs, by their common Judgment, and so must necessarily to gratifie that Inclination establish a Democracy; neither can it be rationally imagined, that Fathers of Families being yet Free and Independent, should in a moment, or little time take off their long delight in governing their own Affairs, & Devolve all upon some single Sovereign Commander; for that it seems to have been thought more Equitable, that what belonged to all, should be managed by all, when all had entered by Compact into one Community. The Original of our Government, says *Plato*, (speaking of the *Athenian* Commonwealth) *was taken from the Equality of our Race. Other States there are composed of different Blood, and of unequal Lines, the Consequence of which are disproportionable Soveraignty, Tyrannical or Oligarchycal Sway; under which men live in such a manner, as to Esteem themselves partly Lords, and partly Slaves to each other. But we and our Country-men, being all Born Brethren of the same Mother, do not look upon our selves, to stand under so hard a Relation, as that of Lords and Slaves; but the Parity of our Descent incline us to keep up the like Parity by our Laws, and to yield the precedency to nothing but to Superiour Vertue and Wisdom.* And moreover it seems very manifest that most Civil Communities arose at first from the Union of Families, that were nearly allyed in Race and Blood. And though Ancient Story make frequent mention of Kings, yet it appears that most of them were such

that had an Influence rather in perswading, then in any Power of Commanding. So *Justin* discribes that Kind of Government, as the most Primitive, which *Aristotle* stiles an Heroical Kingdom. viz. Such as is no ways Inconsistent with a Democratical State. *De Princip. Reru.* I. L. I. C.

A democracy is then Erected, when a Number of Free Persons, do Assemble together, in Order to enter into a Covenant for Uniting themselves in a Body: And such a Preparative Assembly hath some appearance already of a Democracy; it is a Democracy in *Embrio* properly in this Respect, that every Man hath the Priviledge freely to deliver his Opinion concerning the Common Affairs. Yet he who dissents from the Vote of the Majority, is not in the least obliged by what they determine, till by a second Covenant, a Popular Form be actually Established; for not before then can we call it a Democratical Government, viz. Till the Right of Determining all matters relating to the publick Safety, is actually placed in a General Assembly of the whole People; or by their own Compact and Mutual Agreement, Determine themselves the proper Subject for the Exercise of Sovereign Power. And to compleat this State, and render it capable to Exert its Power to answer the End of a Civil State: These Conditions are necessary.

1. That a certain Time and Place be Assigned for Assembling.

2. That when the Assembly be Orderly met, as to Time and Place, that then the Vote of the Majority must pass for the Vote of the whole Body.

3. That Magistrates be appointed to Exercise the Authority of the whole for the better dispatch of Business, of every days Occurrence; who also may with more Mature diligence, search into more Important Affairs; and if in case any thing happens of greater Consequence, may report it to the Assembly; and be peculiarly Serviceable in putting all Publick Decrees into Execution. Because a large Body of People is almost useless in Respect of the last Service, and of many others, as to the more Particular Application and Exercise of Power. Therefore it is most agreeable with the Law of Nature, that they Institute their Officers to act in their Name, and Stead

2. The Second Species of Regular Government, is an Aristocracy; and this is said then to be Constituted when the People, or Assembly United by a first Covenant, and having thereby cast themselves into the first Rudiments of a State; do then by Common

Decree, Devolve the Sovereign Power, on a Council consisting of some Select Members; and these having accepted of the Designation, are then properly invested with Sovereign Command; and then an Aristocracy is formed.

3. The Third Species of a Regular Government, is a Monarchy which is settled when the Sovereign Power is confered on some one worthy Person. It differs from the former, because a Monarch who is but one Person in Natural, as well as in Moral account, & so is furnished with an Immediate Power of Exercising Sovereign Command in all Instances of Government; but the fore named must needs have Particular Time and Place assigned; but the Power and Authority is Equal in each. . . .

. . . an Aristocracy is a dangerous Constitution in the Church of Christ, as it possesses the Presbytery of all Church Power: What has been observed sufficiently Evinces it. And not only so but from the Nature of the Constitution, for it has no more Barrier to it, against the Ambition, Insults, and Arbitrary measures of Men, then an absolute Monarchy. But to abbreviate; it seems most agreeable with the Light of Nature, that if there be any of the Regular Government settled in the Church of God it must needs be.

3. A Democracy. This is a form of Government, which the Light of Nature does highly value, & often directs to as most agreeable to the Just and Natural Prerogatives of Humane Beings. This was of great account, in the early times of the World. And not only so, but upon the Experience of several Thousand years, after the World had been tumbled, and tost from one Species of Government to another, at a great Expence of Blood and Treasure, many of the wise Nations of the World have sheltered themselves under it again; or at least have blendished, and balanced their Governments with it.

It is certainly a great Truth, *scil.* That Mans Original Liberty after it is Resigned, (yet under due Restrictions) ought to be Cherished in all wise Governments; or otherwise a man in making himself a Subject, he alters himself from a Freeman, into a Slave, which to do is Repugnant to the Law of Nature. Also the Natural Equality of Men amongst Men must be duly favoured; in that Government was never Established by God or Nature, to give one Man a Prerogative to insult over another; therefore in a Civil, as well as in a Natural State of Being, a just Equality is to be indulged so far as that every Man is bound to Honour every Man, which is agreeable both with Nature and Religion, 1 Pet. 2. 17. *Honour all Men.*—The End of all good Government is to Cultivate Humanity, and Promote the happiness of all, and the good of every Man in all his Rights, his Life, Liberty, Estate, Honour, &c. without injury or abuse done to any. Then certainly it cannot easily be thought, that a company of Men, that shall enter into a voluntary Compact, to hold all Power in their own hands, thereby to use and improve their united force, wisdom, riches and strength for the Common and Particular good of every Member, as is the Nature of a Democracy; I say it cannot be that this sort of Constitution, will so readily furnish those in Government with an appetite, or disposition to prey upon each other, or imbezle the common Stock; as some Particular Persons may be apt to do when set off, and Intrusted with the same Power. And moreover this appears very Natural, that when the aforesaid Government or Power, settled in all, when they have Elected certain capable Persons to Minister in their affairs, and the said Ministers remain accountable to the Assembly; these Officers must needs be under the influence of many wise cautions from their own thoughts (as well as under confinement by their Commission) in their whole Administration: And from thence it must needs follow that they will be more apt, and inclined to steer Right for the main Point, *viz.* The peculiar good, and benefit of the whole, and every particular Member fairly and sincerely. And why may not these stand for very Rational Pleas in Church Order?

For certainly if Christ has settled any form of Power in his Church he has done it for his Churches safety, and for the Benefit of every Member: Then he must needs be presumed to have made choice of that Government as should least Expose his People to Hazard, either from the fraud, or Arbitrary measures of particular Men. And it is as plain as day light, there is no Species of Government like a Democracy to attain this End. There is but about two steps from an Aristocracy, to a Monarchy, and from thence but one to a Tyranny; an able standing force, and an Ill-Nature, *Ipso facto*, turns an absolute Monarch into a Tyrant; this is obvious among the Roman *Caesars*, and through the World. And all these direful Transmutations are easier in Church affairs (from the different

Qualities of things) then in Civil States. For what is it that cunning and learned Men can't make the World swallow as an Article of their Creed, if they are once invested with an Uncontroulable Power, and are to be the standing Oratours to Mankind in matters of Faith and Obedience? . . .

5. THOMAS PAINE (1737–1809)

TOM PAINE was born of a Quaker family in the village of Thetford in Norfolk County, England, where his father was a corset maker. After quitting school in his fourteenth year, he pursued several vocations (including that of his father), in none of them displaying much concern for earning more than a modest livelihood. He appears to have devoted considerable time to self-education and he had serious intellectual interests, attending public lectures and taking part in the debates (described by a contemporary as "warm and high") of a local Whig club. He met Benjamin Franklin in London and, carrying out a plan he had considered for some time, decided to go to America. He arrived in November, 1774, thirty-seven years old and without distinction in any line. But he brought letters of introduction from Franklin and almost immediately became a man of importance. He was appointed editor of the *Pennsylvania Magazine* and made a success of it; to this and a rival magazine he contributed poems, and numerous articles on scientific and political subjects. The dispute with England and the battles of Lexington and Concord aroused his intense interest. In the autumn of 1775 he wrote a forty-seven-page pamphlet advocating an immediate declaration of independence by the colonies. The pamphlet appeared on January 9, 1776, under the title "Common Sense"; it attempted to show the moral justification and practical advantages of independence, the importance of prompt action, and the superiority, on grounds of both justice and utility, of popular to hereditary government. It was more comprehensive in its argument and more graphic and forceful in its style than other appeals of the time; and it met with an immediate and impressive response. Over a hundred thousand copies were sold within a few months; George Washington wrote that "the sound doctrine and unanswerable reasoning" of the pamphlet was bringing about "a powerful change" in the minds of Virginians, and there were unmistakable evidences of its influence in other parts of the country. During the war Paine wrote other pamphlets (the famous *American Crisis* series) designed to revive and strengthen the spirit of resistance, despite military blunders and defeats, and to offer advice on problems of the war. He made no money out of his pamphlets, but in various ways the colonists gave official recognition of his services. He was

45

secretary of the Committee on Foreign Affairs in the Continental Congress (1777–79) and clerk of the Pennsylvania Assembly (1779–81); and after the war the state of New York presented him with a three-hundred-acre estate in New Rochelle, the Pennsylvania Assembly gave him five hundred pounds, and Congress voted him three thousand dollars.

In 1787 Paine returned to England, where he published *The Rights of Man* (in two parts, 1791, 1792), designed as a reply to Edmund Burke's *Reflections on the French Revolution* and as a general exposition and defense of the political ideals of the American and French Revolutions. An alleged "libel" in the book led to a trial in an English court, resulting in a conviction for treason. Meanwhile, however, he had gone to France and he was received there as a hero, made a citizen of France (along with Washington, Hamilton, and Madison), and elected to membership in the National Convention. But his opposition to the extreme policies of the Jacobins brought him into trouble again. While serving a term in prison he wrote parts of his *Age of Reason*, which contains a vigorous criticism of orthodox Christianity and a plea for a simple morality based on a "scientific" and "natural" religion. He also published a pamphlet (in French) on *Agrarian Justice* (1797), in which he held that land was originally and naturally "the common property of the human race," and proposed that land and other forms of inherited property be taxed in order to raise public funds for popular education, pensions for the aged, and aid for the unemployed.

Paine returned to America in 1802. He now lost most of his American popularity. He was too nationalistic for advocates of States' rights, too "republican" and too much of a friend of Jefferson for the Federalists. Moreover he was widely held to be an "infidel" because of his deistic beliefs; and he wrote a letter questioning Washington's record as military leader and as President. Six persons attended his burial.

[See: Moncure D. Conway, *The Life of Thomas Paine* (2 vols., 1892); Arthur W. Peach, "Introduction" to *Selections from the Works of Thomas Paine* (1928), pp. ix–xlviii; Harry H. Clark, "Towards a Reinterpretation of Thomas Paine," *American Literature*, Vol. V (1933–34), pp. 132–145; William E. Dodd, "Tom Paine," *American Mercury*, Vol. XXI (1930), pp. 477–483.]

From COMMON SENSE (JANUARY 10, 1776)[1]

On the Origin and Design of Government in General, With Concise Remarks on the English Constitution

Some writers have so confounded society with government, as to leave little or no distinction between them; whereas they are not only different, but have different origins. Society is produced by our wants, and government by our wickedness; the former promotes our happiness *possitively* by uniting our affections, the latter *negatively* by restraining our vices. The one encourages intercourse, the other creates distinctions. The first is a patron, the last a punisher.

Society in every state is a blessing, but Government, even in its best state, is but a necessary evil; in its worst state an intolerable one: for when we suffer, or are exposed to the same miseries *by a Government*, which we might expect in a country *without Government*, our calamity is heightened by reflecting that we furnish the means by which we suffer. Government, like dress, is the badge of lost innocence; the palaces of kings are built upon the ruins of the bowers of paradise. For were the impulses of conscience clear, uniform and irresistibly obeyed, man would need no other lawgiver; but that not being the case, he finds it neccessary to surrender up a part of his property to furnish means for the protection of the rest; and this he is induced to do by the same prudence which in every other case advises him, out of two evils to choose the least. Wherefore, security being the true design and end of government, it unanswerably follows that whatever form thereof appears most likely to ensure it to us, with the least expence and greatest benefit, is preferable to all others.

In order to gain a clear and just idea of the design and end of government, let us suppose a small number of persons settled in some sequestered part of the earth, unconnected with the rest; they will then represent the first peopling of any country, or of the world. In this state of natural liberty, society will be their first thought. A thousand motives will excite them thereto; the strength of one man

[1] In *The Writings of Thomas Paine*, ed. by Moncure Daniel Conway, 4 vols. (New York, 1894–96), in Vol. I, pp. 69–120, at 69–76, 79–84. By courtesy of G. P. Putnam's Sons.

is so unequal to his wants, and his mind so unfitted for perpetual solitude, that he is soon obliged to seek assistance and relief of another, who in his turn requires the same. Four or five united would be able to raise a tolerable dwelling in the midst of a wilderness, but one man might labour out the common period of life without accomplishing any thing; when he had felled his timber he could not remove it, nor erect it after it was removed; hunger in the mean time would urge him to quit his work, and every different want would call him a different way. Disease, nay even misfortune, would be death; for though neither might be mortal, yet either would disable him from living, and reduce him to a state in which he might rather be said to perish than to die.

Thus necessity, like a gravitating power, would soon form our newly arrived emigrants into society, the reciprocal blessings of which would supercede, and render the obligations of law and government unnecessary while they remained perfectly just to each other; but as nothing but Heaven is impregnable to vice, it will unavoidably happen that in proportion as they surmount the first difficulties of emigration, which bound them together in a common cause, they will begin to relax in their duty and attachment to each other: and this remissness will point out the necessity of establishing some form of government to supply the defect of moral virtue.

Some convenient tree will afford them a State House, under the branches of which the whole Colony may assemble to deliberate on public matters. It is more than probable that their first laws will have the title only of Regulations and be enforced by no other penalty than public disesteem. In this first parliament every man by natural right will have a seat.

But as the Colony encreases, the public concerns will encrease likewise, and the distance at which the members may be separated, will render it too inconvenient for all of them to meet on every occasion as at first, when their number was small, their habitations near, and the public concerns few and trifling. This will point out the convenience of their consenting to leave the legislative part to be managed by a select number chosen from the whole body, who are supposed to have the same concerns at stake which those have who appointed them, and who will act in the same manner as the whole body would act were they present. If the colony continue encreasing, it will become necessary to augment the number of representatives, and that the interest of every part of the colony may be attended to, it will be found best to divide the whole into convenient parts, each part sending its proper number: and that the *elected* might never form to themselves an interest separate from the *electors*, prudence will point out the propriety of having elections often: because as the *elected* might by that means return and mix again with the general body of the *electors* in a few months, their fidelity to the public will be secured by the prudent reflection of not making a rod for themselves. And as this frequent interchange will establish a common interest with every part of the community, they will mutually and naturally support each other, and on this, (not on the unmeaning name of king,) depends the *strength of government, and the happiness of the governed.*

Here then is the origin and rise of government; namely, a mode rendered necessary by the inability of moral virtue to govern the world; here too is the design and end of government, viz. Freedom and security. And however our eyes may be dazzled with show, or our ears deceived by sound; however prejudice may warp our wills, or interest darken our understanding, the simple voice of nature and reason will say, 'tis right.

I draw my idea of the form of government from a principle in nature which no art can overturn, viz. that the more simple any thing is, the less liable it is to be disordered, and the easier repaired when disordered; and with this maxim in view I offer a few remarks on the so much boasted constitution of England. That it was noble for the dark and slavish times in which it was erected, is granted. When the world was overrun with tyranny the least remove therefrom was a glorious rescue. But that it is imperfect, subject to convulsions, and incapable of producing what it seems to promise, is easily demonstrated.

Absolute governments, (tho' the disgrace of human nature) have this advantage with them, they are simple; if the people suffer, they know the head from which their suffering springs; know likewise the remedy; and are not bewildered by a variety of causes and cures. But the constitution of England is so exceedingly complex, that the nation may suffer for years together without being able to discover in which part the fault lies; some will say in one and some in another, and every political physician will advise a different medicine.

I know it is difficult to get over local or long standing prejudices, yet if we will suffer ourselves to examine the component parts of the English constitution, we shall find them to be the base remains of two ancient tyrannies, compounded with some new Republican materials.

First.—The remains of Monarchical tyranny in the person of the King.

Secondly.—The remains of Aristocratical tyranny in the persons of the Peers.

Thirdly.—The new Republican materials, in the persons of the Commons, on whose virtue depends the freedom of England.

The two first, by being hereditary, are independant of the People; wherefore in a *constitutional* sense they contribute nothing towards the freedom of the State.

To say that the constitution of England is an *union* of three powers, reciprocally *checking* each other, is farcical; either the words have no meaning, or they are flat contradictions.

To say that the Commons is a check upon the King, presupposes two things.

First.—That the King is not to be trusted without being looked after; or in other words, that a thirst for absolute power is the natural disease of monarchy.

Secondly.—That the Commons, by being appointed for that purpose, are either wiser or more worthy of confidence than the Crown.

But as the same constitution which gives the Commons a power to check the King by withholding the supplies, gives afterwards the King a power to check the Commons, by empowering him to reject their other bills; it again supposes that the King is wiser than those whom it has already supposed to be wiser than him. A mere absurdity!

There is something exceedingly ridiculous in the composition of Monarchy; it first excludes a man from the means of information, yet empowers him to act in cases where the highest judgment is required. The state of a king shuts him from the World, yet the business of a king requires him to know it thoroughly; wherefore the different parts, by unnaturally opposing and destroying each other, prove the whole character to be absurd and useless.

Some writers have explained the English constitution thus: the King, say they, is one, the people another; the Peers are a house in behalf of the King, the commons in behalf of the people; but this hath all the distinctions of a house divided against itself; and though the expressions be pleasantly arranged, yet when examined they appear idle and ambiguous; and it will always happen, that the nicest construction that words are capable of, when applied to the description of something which either cannot exist, or is too incomprehensible to be within the compass of description, will be words of sound only, and though they may amuse the ear, they cannot inform the mind: for this explanation includes a previous question, viz. *how came the king by a power which the people are afraid to trust, and always obliged to check?* Such a power could not be the gift of a wise people, neither can any power, *which needs checking*, be from God; yet the provision which the constitution makes supposes such a power to exist.

But the provision is unequal to the task; the means either cannot or will not accomplish the end, and the whole affair is a *Felo de se:* for as the greater weight will always carry up the less, and as all the wheels of a machine are put in motion by one, it only remains to know which power in the constitution has the most weight, for that will govern: and tho' the others, or a part of them, may clog, or, as the phrase is, check the rapidity of its motion, yet so long as they cannot stop it, their endeavours will be ineffectual: The first moving power will at last have its way, and what it wants in speed is supplied by time.

That the crown is this overbearing part in the English constitution needs not be mentioned, and that it derives its whole consequence merely from being the giver of places and pensions is self-evident; wherefore, though we have been wise enough to shut and lock a door against absolute Monarchy, we at the same time have been foolish enough to put the Crown in possession of the key.

The prejudice of Englishmen, in favour of their own government, by King, Lords and Commons, arises as much or more from national pride than reason. Individuals are undoubtedly safer in England than in some other countries: but the will of the king is as much the law of the land in Britain as in France, with this difference, that instead of proceeding directly from his mouth, it is handed to the people under the formidable shape of an act of parliament. For the fate of Charles the First hath only made kings more subtle—not more just.

Wherefore, laying aside all national pride and prejudice in favour of modes and forms, the plain truth is that *it is wholly owing to the constitution of the people, and not to the constitution of the government* that the crown is not as oppressive in England as in Turkey.

An inquiry into the *constitutional errors* in the English form of government, is at this time highly necessary; for as we are never in a proper condition of doing justice to others, while we continue under the influence of some leading partiality, so neither are we capable of doing it to ourselves while we remain fettered by any obstinate prejudice. And as a man who is attached to a prostitute is unfitted to choose or judge of a wife, so any prepossession in favour of a rotten constitution of government will disable us from discerning a good one.

OF MONARCHY AND HEREDITARY SUCCESSION

Mankind being originally equals in the order of creation, the equality could only be destroyed by some subsequent circumstance: the distinctions of rich and poor may in a great measure be accounted for, and that without having recourse to the harsh ill-sounding names of oppression and avarice. Oppression is often the *consequence*, but seldom or never the *means* of riches; and tho' avarice will preserve a man from being necessitously poor, it generally makes him too timorous to be wealthy.

But there is another and greater distinction for which no truly natural or religious reason can be assigned, and that is the distinction of men into KINGS and SUBJECTS. Male and female are the distinctions of nature, good and bad the distinctions of Heaven; but how a race of men came into the world so exalted above the rest, and distinguished like some new species, is worth inquiring into, and whether they are the means of happiness or of misery to mankind.

In the early ages of the world, according to the scripture chronology there were no kings; the consequence of which was, there were no wars; it is the pride of kings which throws mankind into confusion. Holland, without a king hath enjoyed more peace for this last century than any of the monarchical governments in Europe. Antiquity favours the same remark; for the quiet and rural lives of the first Patriarchs have a happy something in them, which vanishes when we come to the history of Jewish royalty.

Government by kings was first introduced into the world by the Heathens, from whom the children of Israel copied the custom. It was the most prosperous invention the Devil ever set on foot for the promotion of idolatry. The Heathens paid divine honours to their deceased kings, and the Christian World hath improved on the plan by doing the same to their living ones. How impious is the title of sacred Majesty applied to a worm, who in the midst of his splendor is crumbling into dust!

As the exalting one man so greatly above the rest cannot be justified on the equal rights of nature, so neither can it be defended on the authority of scripture; for the will of the Almighty as declared by Gideon, and the prophet Samuel, expressly disapproves of government by Kings. All anti-monarchical parts of scripture, have been very smoothly glossed over in monarchical governments, but they undoubtedly merit the attention of countries which have their governments yet to form. *Render unto Cesar the things which are Cesar's,* is the scripture doctrine of courts, yet it is no support of monarchical government, for the Jews at that time were without a king, and in a state of vassalage to the Romans.

Near three thousand years passed away, from the Mosaic account of the creation, till the Jews under a national delusion requested a king. Till then their form of government (except in extraordinary cases where the Almighty interposed) was a kind of Republic, administered by a judge and the elders of the tribes. Kings they had none, and it was held sinful to acknowledge any being under that title but the Lord of Hosts. And when a man seriously reflects on the idolatrous homage which is paid to the persons of kings, he need not wonder that the Almighty, ever jealous of his honour, should disapprove a form of government which so impiously invades the prerogative of Heaven.

Monarchy is ranked in scripture as one of the sins of the Jews, for which a curse in reserve is denounced against them. The history of that transaction is worth attending to. . . .

To the evil of monarchy we have added that of hereditary succession; and as the first is a degradation and lessening of ourselves, so the second, claimed as a matter of right, is an insult and imposition on posterity. For all men being originally equals, no one by birth could have a right to set up his own family in perpetual preference to all others for ever, and tho' himself might deserve some decent degree of honours of his cotemporaries, yet his descendants might be far too unworthy to inherit them. One of the strongest natural proofs of the folly of hereditary right in Kings, is that nature disapproves it, otherwise she would not so frequently turn it into ridicule, by giving mankind an *Ass for a Lion*.

Secondly, as no man at first could possess any other public honors than were bestowed upon him, so the givers of those honors could have no power to give away the right of posterity, and though they might say "We choose you for our head," they could not without manifest injustice to their children say "that your children and your children's children shall reign over ours forever." Because such an unwise, unjust, unnatural compact might (perhaps) in the next succession put them under the government of a rogue or a fool. Most wise men in their private sentiments have ever treated hereditary right with contempt; yet it is one of those evils which when once established is not easily removed; many submit from fear, others from superstition, and the more powerful part shares with the king the plunder of the rest.

This is supposing the present race of kings in the world to have had an honorable origin: whereas it is more than probable, that, could we take off the dark covering of antiquity and trace them to their first rise, we should find the first of them nothing better than the principal ruffian of some restless gang, whose savage manners or pre-eminence in subtilty obtained him the title of chief among plunderers: and who by increasing in power and extending his depredations, overawed the quiet and defenceless to purchase their safety by frequent contributions. Yet his electors could have no idea of giving hereditary right to his descendants, because such a perpetual exclusion of themselves was incompatible with the free and unrestrained principles they professed to live by. Wherefore, hereditary succession in the early ages of monarchy could not take place as a matter of claim, but as something casual or complemental; but as few or no records were extant in those days, and traditionary history stuff'd with fables, it was very easy, after the lapse of a few generations, to trump up some superstitious tale conveniently timed, Mahomet-like, to cram hereditary right down the throats of the vulgar. Perhaps the disorders which threatened, or seemed to threaten, on the decease of a leader and the choice of a new one (for elections among ruffians could not be very orderly) induced many at first to favour hereditary pretensions; by which means it happened, as it hath happened since, that what at first was submitted to as a convenience was afterwards claimed as a right.

England since the conquest hath known some few good monarchs, but groaned beneath a much larger number of bad ones: yet no man in his senses can say that their claim under William the Conqueror is a very honourable one. A French bastard landing with an armed Banditti and establishing himself king of England against the consent of the natives, is in plain terms a very paltry rascally original. It certainly hath no divinity in it. However it is needless to spend much time in exposing the folly of hereditary right; if there are any so weak as to believe it, let them promiscuously worship the Ass and the Lion, and welcome. I shall neither copy their humility, nor disturb their devotion.

Yet I should be glad to ask how they suppose kings came at first? The question admits but of three answers, viz. either by lot, by election, or by usurpation. If the first king was taken by lot, it establishes a precedent for the next, which excludes hereditary succession. Saul was by lot, yet the succession was not hereditary, neither docs it appear from that transaction that there was any intention it ever should. If the first king of any country was by election, that likewise establishes a precedent for the next; for to say, that the right of all future generations is taken away, by the act of the first electors, in their choice not only of a king but of a family of kings for ever, hath no parallel in or out of scripture but the doctrine of original sin, which supposes the free will of all men lost in Adam; and from such comparison, and it will admit of no other, hereditary succession can derive no glory. For as in Adam all sinned, and as in the first electors all men obeyed; as in the one all mankind were subjected to Satan, and in the other to sovereignty; as our innocence was lost in the first, and our authority in the last; and as both disable us from re-assuming some former state and privilege, it unanswerably follows that original sin and hereditary succession are parallels. Dishonourable rank! inglorious connection! yet the most subtle sophist cannot produce a juster simile.

As to usurpation, no man will be so hardy as to defend it; and that William the Conqueror was an usurper is a fact not to be contradicted. The plain truth is, that the antiquity of English monarchy will not bear looking into.

But it is not so much the absurdity as the evil of hereditary succession which concerns mankind. Did it ensure a race of good and wise men it would have the seal of divine authority, but as it opens a door to the *foolish*, the *wicked*, and the *improper*, it hath in it the nature of oppression. Men who look upon themselves born to reign, and others to obey, soon grow insolent. Selected from the rest of mankind, their minds are early poisoned by importance; and the world they act in differs so materially from the world at large, that they have but little opportunity of knowing its true interests, and when they succeed to the government are frequently the most ignorant and unfit of any throughout the dominions.

Another evil which attends hereditary succession is, that the throne is subject to be possessed by a minor at any age; all which time the regency acting under the cover of a king have every opportunity and inducement to betray their trust. The same national misfortune happens when a king worn out with age and infirmity enters the last stage of human weakness. In both these cases the public becomes a prey to every miscreant who can tamper successfully with the follies either of age or infancy.

The most plausible plea which hath ever been offered in favor of hereditary succession is, that it preserves a nation from civil wars; and were this true, it would be weighty; whereas it is the most barefaced falsity ever imposed upon mankind. The whole history of England disowns the fact. Thirty kings and two minors have reigned in that distracted kingdom since the conquest, in which time there has been (including the revolution) no less than eight civil wars and nineteen Rebellions. Wherefore instead of making for peace, it makes against it, and destroys the very foundation it seems to stand upon.

The contest for monarchy and succession, between the houses of York and Lancaster, laid England in a scene of blood for many years. Twelve pitched battles besides skirmishes and sieges were fought between Henry and Edward. Twice was Henry prisoner to Edward, who in his turn was prisoner to Henry. And so uncertain is the fate of war and the temper of a nation, when nothing but

personal matters are the ground of a quarrel, that Henry was taken
in triumph from a prison to a palace, and Edward obliged to fly
from a palace to a foreign land; yet, as sudden transitions of temper
are seldom lasting, Henry in his turn was driven from the throne,
and Edward re-called to succeed him.   The parliament always following the strongest side.

This contest began in the reign of Henry the Sixth, and was not
entirely extinguished till Henry the Seventh, in whom the families
were united.   Including a period of 67 years, viz. from 1422 to 1489.

In short, monarchy and succession have laid (not this or that
kingdom only) but the world in blood and ashes.   'Tis a form of
government which the word of God bears testimony against, and
blood will attend it.

If we enquire into the business of a King, we shall find that in
some countries they may have none; and after sauntering away
their lives without pleasure to themselves or advantage to the nation, withdraw from the scene, and leave their successors to tread
the same idle round.   In absolute monarchies the whole weight of
business civil and military lies on the King; the children of Israel
in their request for a king urged this plea, "that he may judge us,
and go out before us and fight our battles."   But in countries where
he is neither a Judge nor a General, as in England, a man would be
puzzled to know what *is* his business.

The nearer any government approaches to a Republic, the less
business there is for a King.   It is somewhat difficult to find a proper
name for the government of England.   Sir William Meredith calls
it a Republic; but in its present state it is unworthy of the name,
because the corrupt influence of the Crown, by having all the places
in its disposal, hath so effectually swallowed up the power, and
eaten out the virtue of the House of Commons (the Republican
part in the constitution) that the government of England is nearly
as monarchical as that of France or Spain.   Men fall out with names
without understanding them.   For 'tis the Republican and not
the Monarchical part of the constitution of England which Englishmen glory in, viz. the liberty of choosing an House of Commons
from out of their own body—and it is easy to see that when Republican virtue fails, slavery ensues.   Why is the constitution of England sickly, but because monarchy hath poisoned the Republic; the
Crown hath engrossed the Commons.

In England a King hath little more to do than to make war and
give away places; which, in plain terms, is to empoverish the nation
and set it together by the ears.　A pretty business indeed for a man
to be allowed eight hundred thousand sterling a year for, and worshipped into the bargain!　Of more worth is one honest man to
society, and in the sight of God, than all the crowned ruffians that
ever lived. . . .

6. THE DECLARATION OF INDEPENDENCE (1776)

IN THE Second Continental Congress, on June 7, 1776, Richard
Henry Lee, on behalf of the Virginia delegation, moved three resolutions: the first declared "that these United Colonies are, and of right
ought to be, free and independent States, that they are absolved from
all allegiance to the British Crown, and that all political connection between them and the State of Great Britain is, and ought to be, totally
dissolved"; the other resolutions proposed that steps be taken to form
foreign alliances and a confederation of the colonies. John Adams of
Massachusetts seconded the resolutions. On June 10, Congress adopted
a motion providing for a committee "to prepare a declaration to the
effect of the said first resolution," and on the following day appointed
to this committee Thomas Jefferson, John Adams, Benjamin Franklin,
Roger Sherman, and Robert Livingston. The committee entrusted the
framing of the declaration to Jefferson, who prepared a draft, inserted
a number of changes and additions suggested by Adams and Franklin,
and submitted the revised declaration to the full committee. On June
28, the committee reported this draft, without further change, to Congress. On July 2, Congress adopted Lee's first resolution; and this, it is
sometimes said, is the "real" declaration of independence. On the following day Congress debated, in committee of the whole, the declaration
previously reported by the committee of five. The discussion continued into the next day, the fourth, on which date the declaration was
adopted, with a few changes—notably, the elimination of a paragraph
condemning the King for having promoted the trade in slaves and for
having thwarted every effort to abolish or limit that "execrable commerce." On July 19, Congress resolved "That the Declaration passed
on the 4th, be fairly engrossed on parchment, with the title and stile of
'The unanimous declaration of the United States of America,' and that
the same, when engrossed, be signed by every member of Congress."
The names of most of the fifty-six signers were affixed on August 2.

The latter document (the historic "Declaration of Independence")
is chiefly Jefferson's work. Nearly half a century after its adoption,
John Adams said that Jefferson had been chosen to the committee and
given the highest votes (which made him chairman) because he had
come to Congress with "a reputation for literature, science, and a happy

talent of composition," but that no one had contributed very much to the substance of the declaration; there was "not an idea in it," said Adams, "but what had been hackneyed in Congress for two years before." A year later Jefferson replied to Adams' comments. Commending Adams' "zeal and ability" in advocating the declaration before Congress, he said that, although he (Jefferson) had "turned to neither book nor pamphlet while writing" the Declaration, he had not tried to find "new principles, or new arguments." Jefferson continued with this description of the Declaration: "Neither aiming at originality of principle or sentiment, nor yet copied from any particular and previous writing, it was intended to be an expression of the American mind, and to give to that expression the proper tone and spirit called for by the occasion. All its authority rests then on the harmonizing sentiments of the day, whether expressed in conversation, in letters, printed essays, or in the elementary books of public right, as Aristotle, Cicero, Locke, Sidney, &c."

[*Journals of the Continental Congress 1774–1789* (ed. by Worthington Chauncey Ford, Washington, 1904–37), Vol. V, pp. 425–431, 491–516, 590–591, 626; *Works of John Adams* (ed. by Charles Francis Adams) Vol. II, pp. 512–514 (letter to Timothy Pickering May 6, 1822); *Writings of Thomas Jefferson* (ed. by Paul Leicester Ford), Vol. X, pp. 266–269, 342–343 (letters to James Madison, August 30, 1823, and to Henry Lee, May 8, 1825); Carl Becker, *The Declaration of Independence: a Study in the History of Political Ideas* (1922); John H. Hazelton, *The Declaration of Independence: Its History* (1906); Herbert Friedenwald, *The Declaration of Independence* (1904).]

THE UNANIMOUS DECLARATION OF THE THIRTEEN UNITED STATES OF AMERICA

When, in the Course of human events, it becomes necessary for one people to dissolve the political bands which have connected them with another, and to assume, among the Powers of the earth, the separate and equal station to which the Laws of Nature and of Nature's God entitle them, a decent respect to the opinions of mankind requires that they should declare the causes which impel them to the separation.

We hold these truths to be self-evident, that all men are created equal, that they are endowed by their Creator with certain unalienable Rights, that among these, are Life, Liberty, and the pursuit of Happiness. That, to secure these rights, Governments are instituted among Men, deriving their just Powers from the consent of the governed. That, whenever any form of Government becomes destructive of these ends, it is the Right of the People to alter or to abolish it, and to institute new Government, laying its foundation on such Principles, and organizing its Powers in such form, as to them shall seem most likely to effect their Safety and Happiness. Prudence, indeed, will dictate that Governments long established should not be changed for light and transient causes; and, accordingly, all experience hath shewn, that mankind are more disposed to suffer, while evils are sufferable, than to right themselves by abolishing the forms to which they are accustomed. But, when a long train of abuses and usurpations, pursuing invariably the same Object, evinces a design to reduce them under absolute Despotism, it is their right, it is their duty, to throw off such Government, and to provide new Guards for their future Security. Such has been the patient sufferance of these Colonies; and such is now the necessity which constrains them to alter their former Systems of Government. The history of the present King of Great Britain is a history of repeated injuries and usurpations, all having in direct object the establishment of an absolute Tyranny over these States. To prove this, let Facts be submitted to a candid world.

He has refused his Assent to Laws the most wholesome and necessary for the public good.

He has forbidden his Governors to pass Laws of immediate and pressing importance, unless suspended in their operation till his Assent should be obtained; and when so suspended, he has utterly neglected to attend to them.

He has refused to pass other Laws for the accommodation of large districts of People, unless those People would relinquish the right of Representation in the legislature; a right inestimable to them and formidable to tyrants only.

He has called together legislative bodies at places unusual, uncomfortable, and distant from the depository of their Public Records, for the sole Purpose of fatiguing them into compliance with his measures.

He has dissolved Representative Houses repeatedly, for opposing, with manly firmness, his invasions on the rights of the People.

He has refused for a long time, after such dissolutions, to cause others to be elected; whereby the Legislative Powers, incapable of

Annihilation, have returned to the People at large for their exercise; the State remaining in the mean time exposed to all the dangers of invasion from without, and convulsions within.

He has endeavoured to prevent the Population of these States; for that purpose obstructing the Laws for Naturalization of Foreigners; refusing to pass others to encourage their migrations hither, and raising the conditions of new Appropriations of Lands.

He has obstructed the Administration of Justice, by refusing his Assent to Laws for establishing Judiciary Powers.

He has made Judges dependent on his Will alone, for the tenure of their offices, and the amount and payment of their salaries.

He has erected a multitude of New Offices, and sent hither swarms of Officers to harrass our People, and eat out their substance.

He has kept among us, in times of Peace, Standing Armies, without the Consent of our legislatures.

He has affected to render the Military independent of and superior to the Civil Power.

He has combined with others to subject us to a jurisdiction foreign to our constitution, and unacknowledged by our laws; giving his Assent to their Acts of pretended Legislation:

For quartering large bodies of armed troops among us:

For protecting them, by a mock Trial, from Punishment for any Murders which they should commit on the Inhabitants of these States:

For cutting off our Trade with all parts of the world:

For imposing Taxes on us without our Consent:

For depriving us, in many cases, of the benefits of Trial by Jury:

For transporting us beyond Seas to be tried for pretended offences:

For abolishing the free System of English Laws in a neighbouring province, establishing therein an Arbitrary government, and enlarging its Boundaries, so as to render it at once an example and fit instrument for introducing the same absolute rule into these Colonies:

For taking away our Charters, abolishing our most valuable Laws, and altering fundamentally the Forms of our Governments:

For suspending our own Legislatures, and declaring themselves invested with Power to legislate for us in all cases whatsoever.

He has abdicated Government here, by declaring us out of his protection, and waging War against us.

He has plundered our seas, ravaged our Coasts, burnt our towns, and destroyed the Lives of our People.

He is at this time transporting large Armies of foreign Mercenaries to compleat the works of death, desolation and tyranny, already begun with circumstances of Cruelty and perfidy scarcely paralleled in the most barbarous ages, and totally unworthy the Head of a civilized nation.

He has constrained our fellow Citizens, taken Captive on the high Seas, to bear Arms against their Country, to become the executioners of their friends and Brethren, or to fall themselves by their Hands.

He has excited domestic insurrections amongst us, and has endeavoured to bring on the inhabitants of our frontiers, the merciless Indian Savages, whose known rule of warfare, is an undistinguished destruction of all ages, sexes and conditions.

In every stage of these Oppressions, We have Petitioned for Redress, in the most humble terms: Our repeated Petitions, have been answered only by repeated injury. A Prince, whose character is thus marked by every act which may define a Tyrant, is unfit to be the ruler of a free People.

Nor have We been wanting in attentions to our Brittish brethren. We have warned them from time to time of attempts by their legislature to extend an unwarrantable jurisdiction over us. We have reminded them of the circumstances of our emigration and settlement here. We have appealed to their native justice and magnanimity, and we have conjured them by the ties of our common kindred, to disavow these usurpations, which, would inevitably interrupt our connexions and correspondence. They too have been deaf to the voice of justice and of consanguinity. We must, therefore, acquiesce in the necessity, which denounces our Separation, and hold them, as we hold the rest of mankind, Enemies in War, in Peace Friends.

We, therefore, the Representatives of the united States of America, in GENERAL CONGRESS assembled, appealing to the Supreme Judge of the World for the rectitude of our intentions, DO, in the Name, and by Authority of the good People of these Colonies, solemnly PUBLISH and DECLARE, That these United Colonies are, and of Right, ought to be *Free and Independent States;* that they are Absolved from all Allegiance to the British Crown, and that all political connexion between them and the State of Great Britain, is and ought to be totally dissolved; and that, as FREE and INDEPENDENT STATES, they have full Power to levy War, conclude Peace, contract Alliances, establish Commerce, and to do all other Acts and Things which INDEPENDENT STATES may of right do. AND for the support of this Declaration, with a firm reliance on the protection of divine Providence, we mutually pledge to each other our Lives, our Fortunes, and our sacred Honour.

7. THE CONVENTION OF 1787

ON FEBRUARY 21, 1787, the Congress of the Confederation adopted a resolution calling on the States to appoint delegates to a convention to be held in Philadelphia on the second Monday of the following May "for the sole and express purpose of revising the Articles of Confederation and reporting to Congress and the several legislatures such alterations and provisions therein as shall when agreed to in Congress and confirmed by the states render the federal constitution adequate to the exigencies of Government & the preservation of the Union." There appeared, on the designated date (May 14), only a small number of delegates from a few of the States. These delegates, with others as they arrived, adjourned from day to day until on May 25 they were able to organize, with twenty-nine delegates from seven States; and on that day George Washington was unanimously elected president of the Convention. Other delegates arrived during the next few days and deliberations on the proposed revision began on May 29. Rhode Island was not represented in the Convention at any time. From the other twelve original States, seventy-four delegates were elected; some of these declined membership, and others failed to attend; this left a total membership of fifty-five, of whom thirty-nine signed the completed document on the day of adjournment, September 17.

Early in its deliberations the Convention made the bold and (in a legal sense) revolutionary decision to draft a new constitution; a majority of the members concluded that if they followed the official instruction to confine their work to "revising the Articles of Confederation" they could not obey the other instruction to make the constitution "adequate to the exigencies of Government and the preservation of the Union." At the conclusion of its deliberations the Convention disregarded both the instructions by Congress and the provisions of the Articles of Confederation, by deciding to submit the constitution to State conventions (instead of legislatures) and by providing that the constitution would be in effect when ratified by nine (instead of all) of the States.

The Convention held its sessions in secret, for fear, apparently, that publicity would lead to dangerously exaggerated reports of any differences of opinion among the members. It provided for no record of its

65

debates; its official journal (first published in 1819) recorded only motions, resolutions, votes, committee reports, and other official actions. A few of the members kept diaries or other memoranda (usually continued for only brief periods) in which they recorded discussions on the floor of the Convention. James Madison made careful notes for every day, wrote these out in full between sessions, and later revised them from the official journal and from the notes of other members. His record is the chief source of our knowledge of the debates of the Convention.[1]

The Convention was made up of a large proportion of the ablest and most experienced men of the time. Most of the members had been members of Congress and most had had other public careers, as members of State legislatures, governors, or judges, or officers in the Revolutionary army. Seven had signed the Declaration of Independence. A few were widely read in history and politics. Most of them were prosperous property owners. But there were considerable differences of opinion among them, and there were, for the most part, no fixed alignments of opinion. The closed meetings facilitated a full and frank exchange of opinion. Many decisions on important issues were reached through compromises. The completed document turned out to be a unique and skillful blending of tradition and innovation.

[See: Max Farrand, *The Framing of the Constitution* (1913), and *The Fathers of the Constitution* (1921); Charles Warren, *The Making of the Constitution* (1928); Robert L. Schuyler, *The Constitution of the United States: an Historical Survey of Its Formation* (1923).]

DEBATES ON REPRESENTATION AND THE SUFFRAGE [2]

Wednesday June 6th. In Committee of the whole

Mr. Pinkney according to previous notice & rule obtained, moved "that the first branch of the national Legislature be elected by the

[1] The Madison notes were first published in 1845 (nine years after his death) as Volume V of *Elliot's Debates* (2d ed., 1836–45). Later publications have given the work the inappropriate title of *The Journal of the Federal Convention*.

[2] In *Records of the Federal Convention*, ed. by Max Farrand, rev. ed., 4 vols. (New Haven, 1937), Vol. I, pp. 132–134, 298–301, 421–425; Vol. II, pp. 201–205. The names (often misspelled) of the participants in the passages quoted are Charles Pinckney, Pierce Butler and John Rutledge of South Carolina, Elbridge Gerry and Nathaniel Gorham of Massachusetts, James Madison and George Mason of Virginia, Alexander Hamilton of New York, James Wilson, Gouverneur Morris, Thomas Fitzsimmons and Benjamin Franklin of Pennsylvania, Roger Sherman and Oliver Ellsworth of Connecticut, George Read and John Dickinson of Delaware, Hugh Williamson of North Carolina, and John Francis Mercer of Maryland. By courtesy of Yale University Press.

State Legislatures, and not by the people". contending that the people were less fit Judges in such a case, and that the Legislatures would be less likely to promote the adoption of the new Government, if they were to be excluded from all share in it.

Mr. Rutledge 2ded. the motion.

MR. GERRY. Much depends on the mode of election. In England, the people will probably lose their liberty from the smallness of the proportion having a right of suffrage. Our danger arises from the opposite extreme: hence in Massts. the worst men get into the Legislature. Several members of that Body had lately been convicted of infamous crimes. Men of indigence, ignorance & baseness, spare no pains however dirty to carry their point agst. men who are superior to the artifices practiced. He was not disposed to run into extremes. He was as much principled as ever agst. aristocracy and monarchy. It was necessary on the one hand that the people should appoint one branch of the Govt. in order to inspire them with the necessary confidence. But he wished the election on the other to be so modified as to secure more effectually a just preference of merit. His idea was that the people should nominate certain persons in certain districts, out of whom the State Legislatures shd. make the appointment.

MR. WILSON. He wished for vigor in the Govt. but he wished that vigorous authority to flow immediately from the legitimate source of all authority. The Govt. ought to possess not only 1st. the *force* but 2ndly. the *mind* or *sense* of the people at large. The Legislature ought to be the most exact transcript of the whole Society. Representation is made necessary only because it is impossible for the people to act collectively. The opposition was to be expected he said from the *Governments*, not from the *Citizens* of the States. The latter had parted as was observed (by Mr. King) with all the necessary powers; and it was immaterial to them, by whom they were exercised, if well exercised. The State officers were to be losers of power. The people he supposed would be rather more attached to the national Govt. than to the State Govts. as being more important in itself, and more flattering to their pride. There is no danger of improper elections if made by *large* districts. Bad elections proceed from the smallness of the districts which give an opportunity to bad men to intrigue themselves into office. . . .

COL. MASON.   Under the existing Confederacy, Congs. represent the *States* not the *people* of the States: their acts operate on
the *States* not on the individuals.   The case will be changed in the
new plan of Govt.   The people will be represented; they ought
therefore to choose the Representatives.   The requisites in actual
representation are that the Reps. should sympathize with their constituents; shd. think as they think, & feel as they feel; and that for
these purposes shd. even be residents among them.   Much he sd.
had been alledged agst. democratic elections.   He admitted that
much might be said; but it was to be considered that no Govt. was
free from imperfections & evils; and that improper elections in
many instances, were inseparable from Republican Govts.   But compare these with the advantage of this Form in favor of the rights
of the people, in favor of human nature.   He was persuaded there
was a better chance for proper elections by the people, if divided
into large districts, than by the State Legislatures.   Paper money
had been issued by the latter when the former were against it.
Was it to be supposed that the State Legislatures then wd. not
send to the Natl. legislature patrons of such projects. if the choice
depended on them. . . .

Monday, June 19,[1] 1787

MR. HAMILTON.[2]—. . . I see great difficulty of drawing forth a
good representation.   What, for example, will be the inducements
for gentlemen of fortune and abilities to leave their houses and
business to attend annually and long?   It cannot be the wages; for
these, I presume, must be small.   Will not the power, therefore,
be thrown into the hands of the demagogue or middling politician,
who, for the sake of a small stipend and the hopes of advancement,
will offer himself as a candidate, and the real men of weight and
influence, by remaining at home, add strength to the state governments?   I am at a loss to know what must be done—I despair that
a republican form of government can remove the difficulties.
Whatever may be my opinion, I would hold it however unwise to
change that form of government.   I believe the British government

[1] Mistake for June 18.
[2] Discussing the general proposals for the new constitution.

forms the best model the world ever produced, and such has been
its progress in the minds of the many, that this truth gradually
gains ground. This government has for its object *public strength*
and *individual security*. It is said with us to be unattainable. If
it was once formed it would maintain itself. All communities divide themselves into the few and the many. The first are the rich
and well born, the other the mass of the people. The voice of the
people has been said to be the voice of God; and however generally
this maxim has been quoted and believed, it is not true in fact.
The people are turbulent and changing; they seldom judge or determine right. Give therefore to the first class a distinct, permanent
share in the government. They will check the unsteadiness of the
second, and as they cannot receive any advantage by a change, they
therefore will ever maintain good government. Can a democratic
assembly, who annually revolve in the mass of the people, be supposed steadily to pursue the public good? Nothing but a permanent body can check the imprudence of democracy. Their turbulent and uncontrouling disposition requires checks. The senate of
New-York, although chosen for four years, we have found to be
inefficient. Will, on the Virginia plan, a continuance of seven
years do it? It is admitted that you cannot have a good executive
upon a democratic plan. See the excellency of the British executive—He is placed above temptation—He can have no distinct interests from the public welfare. Nothing short of such an executive
can be efficient. The weak side of a republican government is the
danger of foreign influence. This is unavoidable, unless it is so
constructed as to bring forward its first characters in its support.
I am therefore for a general government, yet would wish to go the
full length of republican principles.

Let one body of the legislature be constituted during good
behaviour or life.

Let one executive be appointed who dares execute his powers.

It may be asked is this a republican system? It is strictly so, as
long as they remain elective.

And let me observe, that an executive is less dangerous to the
liberties of the people when in office during life, than for seven
years.

It may be said this constitutes an elective monarchy? Pray what
is a monarchy? May not the governors of the respective states be

[Handwritten marginalia:]

Upper class will use their positions for personal and class gain and much of aim of revolution was to overthrow enormous over Lords. Their will be a class structure and equilibrium. The guy can be an idiot. He grows lazy and craves power.

A static, conservative, aristocratic tendency.

He can build up a machine and designate his successor.

It is a question of power not experience. Enough will be accomplished within framework of Republic. People recognize good men.

considered in that light? But by making the executive subject to impeachment, the term monarchy cannot apply. These elective monarchs have produced tumults in Rome, and are equally dangerous to peace in Poland; but this cannot apply to the mode in which I would propose the election. Let electors be appointed in each of the states to elect the executive [Yates's notes indicate that here Hamilton presented a paper, obviously recording his plan for the federal "legislature"] to consist of two branches—and I would give them the unlimited power of passing *all laws* without exception. The assembly to be elected for three years by the people in districts—the senate to be elected by electors to be chosen for that purpose by the people, and to remain in office during life. The executive to have the power of negativing all laws—to make war or peace, with the advice of the senate—to make treaties with their advice, but to have the sole direction of all military operations, and to send ambassadors and appoint all military officers, and to pardon all offenders, treason excepted, unless by advice of the senate. On his death or removal, the president of the senate to officiate, with the same powers, until another is elected. Supreme judicial officers to be appointed by the executive and the senate. The legislature to appoint courts in each state, so as to make the state governments unnecessary to it.

All state laws to be absolutely void which contravene the general laws. An officer to be appointed in each state to have a negative on all state laws. All the militia and the appointment of officers to be under the national government.

I confess that this plan and that from Virginia are very remote from the idea of the people. Perhaps the Jersey plan is nearest their expectation. But the people are gradually ripening in their opinions of government—they begin to be tired of an excess of democracy—and what even is the Virginia plan, but *pork still, with a little change of the sauce.*

Tuesday. June 26. in Convention

The duration of the 2d. branch under consideration.

Mr. Ghorum moved to fill the blank with "six years". one third of the members to go out every second year.

Mr. Wilson 2ded. the motion. . . .

MR. MADISON. In order to judge of the form to be given to this institution, it will be proper to take a view of the ends to be served by it. These were first to protect the people agst. their rulers: secondly to protect the people agst. the transient impressions into which they themselves might be led. A people deliberating in a temperate moment, and with the experience of other nations before them, on the plan of Govt. most likely to secure their happiness, would first be aware, that those chargd. with the public happiness, might betray their trust. An obvious precaution agst. this danger wd. be to divide the trust between different bodies of men, who might watch & check each other. In this they wd. be governed by the same prudence which has prevailed in organizing the subordinate departments of Govt. where all business liable to abuses is made to pass thro' separate hands, the one being a check on the other. It wd. next occur to such a people, that they themselves were liable to temporary errors, thro' want of information as to their true interest, and that men chosen for a short term, & employed but a small portion of that in public affairs, might err from the same cause. This reflection wd. naturally suggest that the Govt. be so constituted, as that one of its branches might have an oppy. of acquiring a competent knowledge of the public interests. Another reflection equally becoming a people on such an occasion, wd. be that they themselves, as well as a numerous body of Representatives, were liable to err also, from fickleness and passion. A necessary fence agst. this danger would be to select a portion of enlightened citizens, whose limited number, and firmness might seasonably interpose agst. impetuous counsels. It ought finally to occur to a people deliberating on a Govt. for themselves, that as different interests necessarily result from the liberty meant to be secured, the major interest might under sudden impulses be tempted to commit injustice on the minority. In all civilized Countries the people fall into different classes havg. a real or supposed difference of interests. There will be creditors & debtors, farmers, merchts. & manufacturers. There will be particularly the distinction of rich & poor. It was true as had been observd. by Mr Pinkney we had not among us those hereditary distinctions, of rank which were a great source of the contests in the ancient Govts. as well as the modern States of Europe, nor those extremes of wealth or poverty which characterize the latter. We cannot however be regarded even at this time, as one homogeneous mass, in which every thing that affects a part will affect in the same manner the whole.   In framing a system which we wish to last for ages, we shd. not lose sight of the changes which ages will produce.   An increase of population will of necessity increase the proportion of those who will labour under all the hardships of life, & secretly sigh for a more equal distribution of its blessings.   These may in time outnumber those who are placed above the feelings of indigence.   According to the equal laws of suffrage, the power will slide into the hands of the former.   No agrarian attempts have yet been made in this Country, but symptoms of a leveling spirit, as we have understood, have sufficiently appeared in a certain quarters to give notice of the future danger.   How is this danger to be guarded agst. on republican principles?   How is the danger in all cases of interested co-alitions to oppress the minority to be guarded agst.?   Among other means by the establishment of a body in the Govt. sufficiently respectable for its wisdom & virtue, to aid on such emergencies, the preponderance of justice by throwing its weight into that scale.   Such being the objects of the second branch in the proposed Govt. he thought a considerable duration ought to be given to it.   He did not conceive that the term of nine years could threaten any real danger; but in pursuing his particular ideas on the subject, he should require that the long term allowed to the 2d. branch should not commence till such a period of life as would render a perpetual disqualification to be re-elected little inconvenient either in a public or private view.   He observed that as it was more than probable we were now digesting a plan which in its operation wd. decide forever the fate of Republican Govt we ought not only to provide every guard to liberty that its preservation cd. require, but be equally careful to supply the defects which our own experience had particularly pointed out.

Mr. Sherman.   Govt. is instituted for those who live under it. It ought therefore to be so constituted as not to· be dangerous to their liberties.   The more permanency it has the worse if it be a bad Govt.   Frequent elections are necessary to preserve the good behavior of rulers.   They also tend to give permanency to the Government, by preserving that good behavior, because it ensures their re-election.   In Connecticut elections have been very frequent, yet great stability & uniformity both as to persons & measures have been experienced from its original establishmt. to the present time; a period of more than 130 years. He wished to have provision made for steadiness & wisdom in the system to be adopted; but he thought six or four years would be sufficient. He shd. be content with either.

Mr. Read wished it to be considered by the small States that it was their interest that we should become one people as much as possible, that State attachments shd. be extinguished as much as possible, that the Senate shd. be so constituted as to have the feelings of citizens of the whole.

Mr. Hamilton. He did not mean to enter particularly into the subject. He concurred with Mr. Madison in thinking we were now to decide for ever the fate of Republican Government; and that if we did not give to that form due stability and wisdom, it would be disgraced & lost among ourselves, disgraced & lost to mankind for ever. He acknowledged himself not to think favorably of Republican Government; but addressed his remarks to those who did think favorably of it, in order to prevail 'on them to tone their Government as high as possible. He professed himself to be as zealous an advocate for liberty as any man whatever, and trusted he should be as willing a martyr to it though he differed as to the form in which it was most eligible.— He concurred also in the general observations of Mr. Madison on the subject, which might be supported by others if it were necessary. It was certainly true that nothing like an equality of property existed: that an inequality would exist as long as liberty existed, and that it would unavoidably result from that very liberty itself. This inequality of property constituted the great & fundamental distinction in Society. When the Tribunitial power had levelled the boundary between the *patricians* & *plebians* what followed? The distinction between rich & poor was substituted. He meant not however to enlarge on the subject. He rose principally to remark that Mr. Sherman seemed not to recollect that one branch of the proposed Govt. was so formed, as to render it particularly the guardians of the poorer orders of citizens; nor to have adverted to the true causes of the stability which had been exemplified in Cont. Under the British system as well as the federal, many of the great powers appertaining to Govt. particularly all those relating to foreign Nations were not in the hands of the Govt. there. Their internal affairs also were extremely simple, owing to sundry causes many of which were peculiar to that Country. Of late the Governmt. had entirely given way to the people, and had in fact suspended many of its ordinary functions in order to prevent those turbulent scenes which had appeared elsewhere. . . . To those causes & not to the frequency of elections, the effect, as far as it existed ought to be chiefly ascribed.

Teusday August 7th. In Convention

.   .   .   .

"Art IV. Sect. 1.[1] taken up."

Mr. Govr. Morris moved to strike out the last member of the section beginning with the words "qualifications" of Electors." in order that some other provision might be substituted which wd. restrain the right of suffrage to freeholders.

Mr. Fitzsimmons 2ded. the motion

Mr. Williamson was opposed to it.

Mr. Wilson. This part of the Report was well considered by the Committee, and he did not think it could be changed for the better. It was difficult to form any uniform rule of qualifications for all the States. Unnecessary innovations he thought too should be avoided. It would be very hard & disagreeable for the same persons, at the same time, to vote for representatives in the State Legislature and to be excluded from a vote for those in the Natl. Legislature.

Mr. Govr. Morris. Such a hardship would be neither great nor novel. The people are accustomed to it and not dissatisfied with it, in several of the States. In some the qualifications are different for the choice of the Govr. & Representatives; In others for different Houses of the Legislature. Another objection agst. the clause as it stands is that it makes the qualifications of the Natl. Legislature depend on the will of the States, which he thought not proper.

Mr. Elseworth. thought the qualifications of the electors stood on the most proper footing. The right of suffrage was a tender point, and strongly guarded by most of the State Constitutions.

---

[1] Article IV, Sect. 1. "The members of the House of Representatives shall be chosen every second year, by the people of the several States comprehended within this Union. The qualifications of the electors shall be the same, from time to time, as those of the electors in the several States, of the most numerous branch of their own legislatures."

The people will not readily subscribe to the Natl. Constitution, if it should subject them to be disfranchised. The States are the best Judges of the circumstances and temper of their own people.

Col. Mason. The force of habit is certainly not attended to by those gentlemen who wish for innovations on this point. Eight or nine States have extended the right of suffrage beyond the freeholders. What will the people there say, if they should be disfranchised. A power to alter the qualifications would be a dangerous power in the hands of the Legislature.

Mr. Butler. There is no right of which the people are more jealous than that of suffrage Abridgments of it tend to the same revolution as in Holland, where they have at length thrown all power into the hands of the Senates, who fill up vacancies themselves, and form a rank aristocracy.

Mr. Dickenson. had a very different idea of the tendency of vesting the right of suffrage in the freeholders of the Country. He considered them as the best guardians of liberty; And the restriction of the right to them as a necessary defence agst. the dangerous influence of those multitudes without property & without principle, with which our Country like all others, will in time abound. As to the unpopularity of the innovation it was in his opinion chemirical. The great mass of our Citizens is composed at this time of freeholders, and will be pleased with it.

Mr Elseworth. How shall the freehold be defined? Ought not every man who pays a tax to vote for the representative who is to levy & dispose of his money? Shall the wealthy merchants and manufacturers, who will bear a full share of the public burdens be not allowed a voice in the imposition of them . . .

Mr. Govr. Morris. He had long learned not to be the dupe of words. The sound of Aristocracy therefore, had no effect on him. It was the thing, not the name, to which he was opposed, and one of his principal objections to the Constitution as it is now before us, is that it threatens this Country with an Aristocracy. The aristocracy will grow out of the House of Representatives. Give the votes to people who have no property, and they will sell them to the rich who will be able to buy them. We should not confine our attention to the present moment. The time is not distant when this Country will abound with mechanics & manufacturers who will receive their bread from their employers. Will such men be the secure & faithful

Guardians of liberty? Will they be the impregnable barrier agst. aristocracy?—He was as little duped by the association of the words, "taxation & Representation"—The man who does not give his vote freely is not represented. It is the man who dictates the vote. Children do not vote. Why? because they want prudence. because they have no will of their own. The ignorant & the dependent can be as little trusted with the public interest. He did not conceive the difficulty of defining "freeholders" to be insuperable. Still less that the restriction could be unpopular. 9/10 of the people are at present freeholders and these will certainly be pleased with it. As to Merchts. &c. if they have wealth & value the right they can acquire it. If not they don't deserve it.

Col. Mason. We all feel too strongly the remains of antient prejudices, and view things too much through a British Medium. A Freehold is the qualification in England, & hence it is imagined to be the only proper one. The true idea in his opinion was that every man having evidence of attachment to & permanent common interest with the Society ought to share in all its rights & privileges. Was this qualification restrained to freeholders? Does no other kind of property but land evidence a common interest in the proprietor? does nothing besides property mark a permanent attachment. Ought the merchant, the monied man, the parent of a number of children whose fortunes are to be pursued in their own Country, to be viewed as suspicious characters, and unworthy to be trusted with the common rights of their fellow Citizens

Mr. Madison. the right of suffrage is certainly one of the fundamental articles of republican Government, and ought not to be left to be regulated by the Legislature. A gradual abridgment of this right has been the mode in which Aristocracies have been built on the ruins of popular forms. Whether the Constitutional qualification ought to be a freehold, would with him depend much on the probable reception such a change would meet with in States where the right was now exercised by every description of people. In several of the States a freehold was now the qualification. Viewing the subject in its merits alone, the freeholders of the Country would be the safest depositories of Republican liberty. In future times a great majority of the people will not only be without landed, but any other sort of, property. These will either combine under the influence of their common situation; in which case, the rights of property & the public liberty, will not be secure in their hands: or which is more probable, they will become the tools of opulence & ambition, in which case there will be equal danger on another side. The example of England has been misconceived by Col Mason. A very small proportion of the Representatives are there chosen by freeholders. The greatest part are chosen by the Cities & boroughs, in many of which the qualification of suffrage is as low as it is in any one of the U. S. and it was in the boroughs & Cities rather than the Counties, that bribery most prevailed, & the influence of the Crown on elections was most dangerously exerted.

DOCR. FRANKLIN. It is of great consequence that we shd. not depress the virtue & public spirit of our common people; of which they displayed a great deal during the war, and which contributed principally to the favorable issue of it. He related the honorable refusal of the American seamen who were carried in great numbers into the British Prisons during the war, to redeem themselves from misery or to seek their fortunes, by entering on board the Ships of the Enemies to their Country; contrasting their patriotism with a contemporary instance in which the British seamen made prisoners by the Americans, readily entered on the ships of the latter on being promised a share of the prizes that might be made out of their own Country. This proceeded he said, from the different manner in which the common people were treated in America & G. Britain. He did not think that the elected had any right in any case to narrow the privileges of the electors. He quoted as arbitrary the British Statute setting forth the danger of tumultuous meetings, and under that pretext, narrowing the right of suffrage to persons having freeholds of a certain value; observing that this Statute was soon followed by another under the succeeding Parliamt. subjecting the people who had no votes to peculiar labors & hardships. He was persuaded also that such a restriction as was proposed would give great uneasiness in the populous States. The sons of a substantial farmer, not being themselves freeholders, would not be pleased at being disfranchised, and there are a great many persons of that description.

MR. MERCER. The Constitution is objectionable in many points, but in none more than the present. He objected to the footing on which the qualification was put, but particularly to the *mode of election* by the people. The people can not know & judge of the

Elections are not being held on sly. Candidates circulate and common people have some discretion.

Iron law of Oligarchies

characters of Candidates. The worse possible choice will be made. He quoted the case of the Senate in Virga. as an example in point— The people in Towns can unite their votes in favor of one favorite; & by that means always prevail over the people of the Country, who being dispersed will scatter their votes among a variety of candidates.

Mr. Rutlidge thought the idea of restraining the right of suffrage to the freeholders a very unadvised one. It would create division among the people & make enemies of all those who should be excluded. . . .

8. JAMES MADISON (1751–1836)

MADISON, called "father of the Constitution," was reared in the piedmont section of Virginia, where his father owned a large landed estate. A graduate of Princeton in 1771, he remained there another year to study Hebrew, ethics, and political philosophy. He held public office for over forty years. He was a member of the Orange County committee of safety (1775), the Virginia Constitutional Convention of 1776, House of Delegates, Governor's council, and the Continental Congress, Annapolis Convention, Congress of the Confederation, the Convention of 1787, and the Virginia ratifying convention. Under the Constitution he served four terms in the House of Representatives, and he was secretary of state (1801–09) and President (1809–17).

Madison wrote no book; but he was a methodical, accurate, and discerning student of political history, a skillful legislative draftsman, and a logical and persuasive political debater. He had leading parts in framing the first State constitution of Virginia, in drafting official notes in the Congress of the Confederation, and in promoting the adoption of Jefferson's liberal measures by the Virginia legislature. Most notable was his work in connection with framing, adopting, explaining, and putting into operation the Constitution. He helped promote the movement for assembling the Federal Convention, was its best informed member and one of its most influential debaters and committeemen, and he prepared the fullest record of its proceedings. He played an indispensable part in the movement for ratification of the Constitution—particularly in Virginia, where he had to overcome a powerful opposition led by Patrick Henry and George Mason, and in New York, where he was one of the authors of the "Federalist" letters in the newspapers.

The "immediate object" of these letters (written by Alexander Hamilton, Madison, and John Jay, from October, 1787, to May, 1788) was, said Madison, "to vindicate and recommend the new Constitution to the State of N. Y. whose ratification of the instrument, was doubtful as well as important." The letters were serious replies to more popular newspaper attacks; and it is doubtful how far they influenced either ordinary newspaper readers or the members of the New York convention. But they were widely copied in other papers, in New York and elsewhere, and were immediately accepted as expert expositions of the Constitution as well as able general discussions of government. They were collected and published in book form in 1788, under the title *The Federalist*, and there were revised reprints during the next few years. Jefferson called the collection "the best commentary on the principles of government which has ever been written." Probably no other work has been so frequently cited in discussions on doubtful points of constitutional interpretation. All the letters were signed "Publius" and the specific authorship of some of the numbers is in doubt. There is no doubt that Madison wrote "No. 10," copied below.

In the first Congress under the Constitution Madison helped steer through the House of Representatives the measures setting up the executive departments and a national revenue system. He was the author of the "Virginia Resolutions" against the Alien and Sedition Acts; and he was a member of the Virginia constitutional convention of 1829.

[See: Edward M. Burns, *James Madison, Philosopher of the Constitution* (1938); Edward G. Bourne, "Madison's Studies in the History of Federal Government," in *Essays in Historical Criticism* (1901), pp. 165–169; Gaillard Hunt, *The Life of James Madison* (1902); Paul Leicester Ford, "Editor's Introduction" and contemporary accounts, in his edition of *The Federalist*; letter of Madison to James K. Paulding, July 23, 1818, in *Writings*, ed. by Gaillard Hunt (9 vols., 1901–10), Vol. VIII, pp. 410–411; letter of Jefferson to Madison, in *Writings*, ed. by Ford (10 vols., 1892–99), Vol. V, pp. 52–56.]

THE FEDERALIST, NO. 10 (1787)[1]

To the People of the State of New York:

Among the numerous advantages promised by a well-constructed Union, none deserves to be more accurately developed than its tendency to break and control the violence of faction. The friend of popular governments never finds himself so much alarmed for their character and fate as when he contemplates their propensity to this dangerous vice. He will not fail, therefore, to set a due value on any plan which, without violating the principles to which he is attached, provides a proper cure for it. The instability, injustice, and confusion introduced into the public councils, have, in truth, been the mortal diseases under which popular governments have everywhere perished; as they continue to be the favorite and fruitful

[1] First appearing in the *New York Daily Advertiser*, Nov. 22, 1787. In *The Federalist*, ed. by Paul Leicester Ford (New York, 1898), pp. 54–63.

topics from which the adversaries to liberty derive their most specious declamations. The valuable improvements made by the American constitutions on the popular models, both ancient and modern, cannot certainly be too much admired; but it would be an unwarrantable partiality to contend that they have as effectually obviated the danger on this side as was wished and expected. Complaints are everywhere heard from our most considerate and virtuous citizens, equally the friends of public and private faith, and of public and personal liberty, that our governments are too unstable, that the public good is disregarded in the conflicts of rival parties, and that measures are too often decided, not according to the rules of justice and the rights of the minor party, but by the superior force of an interested and overbearing majority. However anxiously we may wish that these complaints had no foundation, the evidence of known facts will not permit us to deny that they are in some degree true. It will be found, indeed, on a candid review of our situation, that some of the distresses under which we labor have been erroneously charged on the operation of our governments; but it will be found, at the same time, that other causes will not alone account for many of our heaviest misfortunes; and, particularly, for that prevailing and increasing distrust of public engagements, and alarm for private rights, which are echoed from one end of the continent to the other. These must be chiefly, if not wholly, effects of the unsteadiness and injustice with which a factious spirit has tainted our public administrations.

By a faction, I understand a number of citizens, whether amounting to a majority or minority of the whole, who are united and actuated by some common impulse of passion, or of interest, adverse to the rights of other citizens, or to the permanent and aggregate interests of the community.

There are two methods of curing the mischiefs of faction: the one, by removing its causes; the other, by controlling its effects. There are again two methods of removing the causes of faction: the one, by destroying the liberty which is essential to its existence; the other, by giving to every citizen the same opinions, the same passions, and the same interests.

It could never be more truly said than of the first remedy, that it was worse than the disease. Liberty is to faction what air is to fire, an aliment without which it instantly expires. But it could not be less folly to abolish liberty, which is essential to political life because it nourishes faction, than it would be to wish the annihilation of air, which is essential to animal life, because it imparts to fire its destructive agency.

The second expedient is as impracticable as the first would be unwise. As long as the reason of man continues fallible, and he is at liberty to exercise it, different opinions will be formed. As long as the connection subsists between his reason and his self-love, his opinions and his passions will have a reciprocal influence on each other; and the former will be objects to which the latter will attach themselves. The diversity in the faculties of men, from which the rights of property originate, is not less an insuperable obstacle to a uniformity of interests. The protection of these faculties is the first object of government. From the protection of different and unequal faculties of acquiring property, the possession of different degrees and kinds of property immediately results; and from the influence of these on the sentiments and views of the respective proprietors, ensues a division of the society into different interests and parties.

The latent causes of faction are thus sown in the nature of man; and we see them everywhere brought into different degrees of activity, according to the different circumstances of civil society. A zeal for different opinions concerning religion, concerning government, and many other points, as well of speculation as of practice; an attachment to different leaders ambitiously contending for preeminence and power; or to persons of other descriptions whose fortunes have been interesting to the human passions, have, in turn, divided mankind into parties, inflamed them with mutual animosity, and rendered them much more disposed to vex and oppress each other than to co-operate for their common good. So strong is this propensity of mankind to fall into mutual animosities that, where no substantial occasion presents itself, the most frivolous and fanciful distinctions have been sufficient to kindle their unfriendly passions and excite their most violent conflicts. But the most common and durable source of factions has been the various and unequal distribution of property. Those who hold and those who are without property have ever formed distinct interests in society. Those who are creditors, and those who are debtors, fall under a like discrimination. A landed interest, a manufacturing interest, a mercantile interest, a moneyed interest, with many lesser interests, grow up of necessity in civilized nations, and divide them into different classes actuated by different sentiments and views. The regulation of these various and interfering interests forms the principal task of modern legislation, and involves the spirit of party and faction in the necessary and ordinary operations of the government.

No man is allowed to be a judge in his own cause, because his interest would certainly bias his judgment and, not improbably, corrupt his integrity. With equal, nay with greater reason, a body of men are unfit to be both judges and parties at the same time; yet what are many of the most important acts of legislation but so many judicial determinations, not indeed concerning the rights of single persons, but concerning the rights of large bodies of citizens? And what are the different classes of legislators but advocates and parties to the causes which they determine? Is a law proposed concerning private debts? It is a question to which the creditors are parties on one side and the debtors on the other. Justice ought to hold the balance between them. Yet the parties are, and must be, themselves the judges; and the most numerous party, or, in other words, the most powerful faction, must be expected to prevail. Shall domestic manufactures be encouraged, and in what degree, by restrictions on foreign manufactures? are questions which would be differently decided by the landed and the manufacturing classes, and probably by neither with a sole regard to justice and the public good. The apportionment of taxes on the various descriptions of property is an act which seems to require the most exact impartiality; yet there is, perhaps, no legislative act in which greater opportunity and temptation are given to a predominant party to trample on the rules of justice. Every shilling with which they overburden the inferior number is a shilling saved to their own pockets.

It is in vain to say that enlightened statesmen will be able to adjust these clashing interests, and render them all subservient to the public good. Enlightened statesmen will not always be at the helm. Nor in many cases can such an adjustment be made at all without taking into view indirect and remote considerations, which will rarely prevail over the immediate interest which one party may find in disregarding the rights of another or the good of the whole.

The inference to which we are brought is that the causes of faction cannot be removed, and that relief is only to be sought in the means of controlling its *effects*.

If a faction consists of less than a majority, relief is supplied by the republican principle, which enables the majority to defeat its sinister views by regular vote. It may clog the administration, it may convulse the society; but it will be unable to execute and mask its violence under the forms of the Constitution. When a majority is included in a faction, the form of popular government, on the other hand, enables it to sacrifice to its ruling passion or interest both the public good and the rights of other citizens. To secure the public good and private rights against the danger of such a faction, and at the same time to preserve the spirit and the form of popular government, is then the great object to which our inquiries are directed. Let me add that it is the great desideratum by which this form of government can be rescued from the opprobrium under which it has so long labored, and be recommended to the esteem and adoption of mankind.

By what means is this object attainable? Evidently by one of two only: Either the existence of the same passion or interest in a majority at the same time must be prevented, or the majority, having such coexistent passion or interest, must be rendered, by their number and local situation, unable to concert and carry into effect schemes of oppression. If the impulse and the opportunity be suffered to coincide, we well know that neither moral nor religious motives can be relied on as an adequate control. They are not found to be such on the injustice and violence of individuals, and lose their efficacy in proportion to the number combined together, that is, in proportion as their efficacy becomes needful.

From this view of the subject it may be concluded that a pure democracy, by which I mean a society consisting of a small number of citizens, who assemble and administer the government in person, can admit of no cure for the mischiefs of faction. A common passion or interest will, in almost every case, be felt by a majority of the whole; a communication and concert result from the form of government itself; and there is nothing to check the inducements to sacrifice the weaker party or an obnoxious individual. Hence it is that such democracies have ever been spectacles of turbulence and contention; have ever been found incompatible with personal security or the rights of property; and have in general been as short in

Executive & judicial control collapsed when Civil War broke out

their lives as they have been violent in their deaths. Theoretic politicians, who have patronized this species of government, have erroneously supposed that by reducing mankind to a perfect equality in their political rights, they would, at the same time, be perfectly equalized and assimilated in their possessions, their opinions, and their passions.

He intimates it is improbable that there will be large wieldy minorities as a result of repres. democracy.

A republic, by which I mean a government in which the scheme of representation takes place, opens a different prospect, and promises the cure for which we are seeking. Let us examine the points in which it varies from pure democracy, and we shall comprehend both the nature of the cure and the efficacy which it must derive from the Union.

The two great points of difference between a democracy and a republic are: first, the delegation of the government, in the latter, to a small number of citizens elected by the rest; secondly, the greater number of citizens, and greater sphere of country, over which the latter may be extended.

The effect of the first difference is, on the one hand, to refine and enlarge the public views, by passing them through the medium of a chosen body of citizens, whose wisdom may best discern the true interest of their country, and whose patriotism and love of justice will be least likely to sacrifice it to temporary or partial considerations. Under such a regulation, it may well happen that the public voice, pronounced by the representatives of the people, will be more consonant to the public good than if pronounced by the people themselves, convened for the purpose. On the other hand, the effect may be inverted. Men of factious tempers, of local prejudices, or of sinister designs, may, by intrigue, by corruption, or by other means, first obtain the suffrages, and then betray the interest, of the people. The question resulting is, whether small or extensive republics are more favorable to the election of proper guardians of the public weal; and it is clearly decided in favor of the latter by two obvious considerations:

In the first place, it is to be remarked that, however small the republic may be, the representatives must be raised to a certain number, in order to guard against the cabals of a few; and that, however large it may be, they must be limited to a certain number, in order to guard against the confusion of a multitude. Hence, the number of representatives in the two cases not being in proportion to that of the two constituents, and being proportionally greater in the small republic, it follows that, if the proportion of fit characters be not less in the large than in the small republic, the former will present a greater option, and consequently a greater probability of a fit choice.

In the next place, as each representative will be chosen by a greater number of citizens in the large than in the small republic, it will be more difficult for unworthy candidates to practice with success the vicious arts by which elections are too often carried; and the suffrages of the people, being more free, will be more likely to center in men who possess the most attractive merit and the most diffusive and established characters.

It must be confessed that in this, as in most other cases, there is a mean, on both sides of which inconveniences will be found to lie. By enlarging too much the number of electors, you render the representative too little acquainted with all their local circumstances and lesser interests; as by reducing it too much, you render him unduly attached to these, and too little fit to comprehend and pursue great and national objects. The federal Constitution forms a happy combination in this respect; the great and aggregate interests being referred to the national, the local and particular to the State legislatures.

The other point of difference is, the greater number of citizens and extent of territory which may be brought within the compass of republican than of democratic government; and it is this circumstance principally which renders factious combinations less to be dreaded in the former than in the latter. The smaller the society, the fewer probably will be the distinct parties and interests composing it; the fewer the distinct parties and interests, the more frequently will a majority be found of the same party; and the smaller the number of individuals composing a majority, and the smaller the compass within which they are placed, the more easily will they concert and execute their plans of oppression. Extend the sphere, and you take in a greater variety of parties and interests; you make it less probable that a majority of the whole will have a common motive to invade the rights of other citizens; or, if such a common motive exists, it will be more difficult for all who feel it to discover their own strength and to act in unison with each other. Besides other impediments, it may be remarked that where there is a consciousness of unjust or dishonorable purposes, communication is always checked by distrust in proportion to the number whose concurrence is necessary.

Hence it clearly appears that the same advantage which a republic has over a democracy, in controlling the effects of faction, is enjoyed by a large over a small republic, is enjoyed by the Union over the States composing it. Does the advantage consist in the substitution of representatives whose enlightened views and virtuous sentiments render them superior to local prejudices and to schemes of injustice? It will not be denied that the representation of the Union will be most likely to possess these requisite endowments. Does it consist in the great security afforded by a greater variety of parties against the event of any one party being able to outnumber and oppress the rest? In an equal degree does the increased variety of parties comprised within the Union increase this security. Does it, in fine, consist in the greater obstacles opposed to the concert and accomplishment of the secret wishes of an unjust and interested majority? Here, again, the extent of the Union gives it the most palpable advantage.

The influence of factious leaders may kindle a flame within their particular States, but will be unable to spread a general conflagration through the other States. A religious sect may degenerate into a political faction in a part of the Confederacy; but the variety of sects dispersed over the entire face of it must secure the national councils against any danger from that source. A rage for paper money, for an abolition of debts, for an equal division of property, or for any other improper or wicked project, will be less apt to pervade the whole body of the Union than a particular member of it; in the same proportion as such a malady is more likely to taint a particular county or district than an entire State.

In the extent and proper structure of the Union, therefore, we behold a republican remedy for the diseases most incident to republican government. And according to the degree of pleasure and pride we feel in being republicans ought to be our zeal in cherishing the spirit and supporting the character of Federalists.

PUBLIUS

9. BENJAMIN FRANKLIN (1706–90)

THE titles of biographies and special studies of Franklin indicate the wide scope of his interests and talents. He is called the "Many-sided," "Amazing," "First Civilized American," "The Apostle of Modern Times"; and there are books on his inventions, his contributions to medicine and science, his literary talents, and his educational, religious, economic, and political views. He was one of the organizers of the Academy for the Education of Youth (1751), which later became the University of Pennsylvania, and of the American Philosophical Society (1754), oldest of the greater learned societies of America. He was also a successful business man and an influential statesman.

At the age of seventeen he made his way from Boston, his native city, to Philadelphia, a poor boy seeking a job in a printing establishment. He rose rapidly to success in the printing and publishing business. At twenty-five, he bought the young *Pennsylvania Gazette* (now claimed as an ancestor by the *Saturday Evening Post*) and made it interesting by introducing editorials, weather reports, cartoons, and humorous comments. At forty-two he retired from active business in order to devote his time to scientific investigations and experiments, from which he acquired an international fame. But public affairs soon engaged his attention. He had served as a city councilman and a member of the State legislature. Now he was drawn into political life on a large scale. He served as delegate to the "Albany Congress" (1754); representative of Pennsylvania and other colonies on important missions to England; postmaster-general under the Second Continental Congress and a member of the committee to draft the Declaration of Independence; chief negotiator of the alliance with France and a member of the committee negotiating the terms of peace with England; president of the executive council of Pennsylvania; and member of the Convention of 1787. He was the oldest member of the Convention and enjoyed great prestige in it; he introduced few measures and made few speeches, but exercised a notable influence on the deliberations through his persuasiveness and tact in getting agreements by way of compromise.

Franklin wrote pamphlets on taxation, wages, monetary problems, international trade (advocating free trade), and population (anticipating Malthus). His occasional observations on problems of government were in his characteristic manner: avoiding irrelevant generalizations, and considering immediate ends from the standpoint of a practical sense of justice and a general confidence in the reasonableness and benevolence of ordinary men. His comments quoted below, on proposals to amend the Pennsylvania constitution in order to increase the political weight of men of wealth, were made in his eighty-fourth year.

[See: Carl Van Doren, *Benjamin Franklin* (1938); Carl L. Becker, "Benjamin Franklin," in *Dictionary of American Biography*; Paul Leicester Ford, *The Many-sided Franklin* (1899); William P. Trent, "Benjamin Franklin," in *McClure's Magazine*, Vol. VIII (1896–97), pp. 273–277.]

From QUERIES AND REMARKS RESPECTING ALTERATIONS IN THE CONSTITUTION OF PENNSYLVANIA (1789)[1]

III. ON THE LEGISLATIVE BRANCH

"*A plural Legislature* [quoting an anonymous writer in a newspaper] *is as necessary to good Government as a single Executive. It is not enough that your Legislature should be numerous; it should also be divided. Numbers alone are not a sufficient Barrier against the Impulses of Passion, the Combinations of Interest, the Intrigues of Faction, the Haste of Folly, or the Spirit of Encroachment. . . .*

"*Hence it is that the two Branches should be elected by Persons differently qualified; and in short, that, as far as possible, they should be made to represent different Interests. Under this Reasoning I would establish a Legislature of two Houses. The Upper should represent the Property; the Lower the Population of the State. The upper should be chosen by Freemen possessing in Lands and Houses one thousand Pounds; the Lower by all such as had resided four Years in the Country, and paid Taxes. The first should be chosen for four, the last for two years. They should in Authority be coequal.*"

Several Questions may arise upon this Proposition. 1st. What is the Proportion of Freemen possessing Lands and Houses of one thousand Pounds' value, compared to that of Freemen whose Possessions are inferior? Are they as one to ten? Are they even as one

[1] In *The Writings of Benjamin Franklin*, ed. by Albert Henry Smyth, 10 vols. (New York, 1905–07), Vol. X, pp. 54–60, at 55, 58–60.

to twenty? I should doubt whether they are as one to fifty. If this minority is to chuse a Body expressly to controul that which is to be chosen by the great Majority of the Freemen, what have this great Majority done to forfeit so great a Portion of their Right in Elections? Why is this Power of Controul, contrary to the spirit of all Democracies, to be vested in a Minority, instead of a Majority? Then is it intended, or is it not, that the Rich should have a Vote in the Choice of Members for the lower House, while those of inferior Property are deprived of the Right of voting for Members of the upper House? And why should the upper House, chosen by a Minority, have equal Power with the lower chosen by a Majority? Is it supposed that Wisdom is the necessary concomitant of Riches, and that one Man worth a thousand Pounds must have as much Wisdom as Twenty who have each only 999; and why is Property to be represented at all? Suppose one of our Indian Nations should now agree to form a civil Society; each Individual would bring into the Stock of the Society little more Property than his Gun and his Blanket, for at present he has no other. We know, that, when one of them has attempted to keep a few Swine, he has not been able to maintain a Property in them, his neighbours thinking they have a Right to kill and eat them whenever they want Provision, it being one of their Maxims that hunting is free for all; the accumulation therefore of Property in such a Society, and its Security to Individuals in every Society, must be an Effect of the Protection afforded to it by the joint Strength of the Society, in the Execution of its Laws. Private Property therefore is a Creature of Society, and is subject to the Calls of that Society, whenever its Necessities shall require it, even to its last Farthing; its Contributions therefore to the public Exigencies are not to be considered as conferring a Benefit on the Publick, entitling the Contributors to the Distinctions of Honour and Power, but as the Return of an Obligation previously received, or the Payment of a just Debt. The Combinations of Civil Society are not like those of a Set of Merchants, who club their Property in different Proportions for Building and Freighting a Ship, and may therefore have some Right to vote in the Disposition of the Voyage in a greater or less Degree according to their respective Contributions; but the important ends of Civil Society, and the personal Securities of Life and Liberty, these remain the same in every Member of the society; and the poorest continues to have an equal Claim to them with the most opulent, whatever Difference Time, Chance, or Industry may occasion in their Circumstances. On these Considerations, I am sorry to see the Signs this Paper I have been considering affords, of a Disposition among some of our People to commence an Aristocracy, by giving the Rich a predominancy in Government, a Choice peculiar to themselves in one half the Legislature to be proudly called the UPPER House, and the other Branch, chosen by the Majority of the People, degraded by the Denomination of the LOWER; and giving to this upper House a Permanency of four Years, and but two to the lower. I hope, therefore, that our Representatives in the Convention will not hastily go into these Innovations, but take the Advice of the Prophet, "Stand in the old ways, view the ancient Paths, consider them well, and be not among those that are given to Change."

The mass will fight property. To ignore them is folly.

There must be numerical equilibrium. There will be aristocracies by nature.

Aristocracies must exist within the framework of an all inclusive gov't.

It is no the law of nature that all are created equal; but it is a wise thing for the haves to conceed rights to life, liberty, + property if only to protect their interests.

10. JOEL BARLOW (1754–1812)

BARLOW was born in Redding, Connecticut, son of a small farmer. While a student at Yale he served in the Revolutionary army during vacations. After graduation he taught school for a short while, became joint publisher of a weekly newspaper (*The American Mercury,* 1784–85), read literature, philosophy, and law, and, with slight preparation, got a license to preach so that he might serve as an army chaplain. He was admitted to the bar in 1786, but found no success or satisfaction in that profession. He was a member of the literary group called "The Hartford Wits" (which included John Trumbull, Timothy and Theodore Dwight, Lemuel Hopkins, and others) and was one of the chief contributors to the *Anarchiad,* an "epic" poem produced by the group, satirizing popular government. His local reputation as a poet rested on his *Vision of Columbus* (1786–87), which he recast twenty years later into the longer *Columbiad,* glorifying popular government. He joined a company interested in selling Ohio land to Frenchmen and in 1788 went to France as an agent of the company. The venture collapsed almost immediately, but Barlow invested successfully in French consols and remained in Europe for fifteen years. There he became acquainted with leading literary intellectuals, observed and took part in some of the new political movements, arranged for the publication of Tom Paine's *Age of Reason* (while Paine was in prison), served briefly and successfully as United States consul in Algiers, and wrote poems and political essays. Returning to America in 1805, he set up a home, near Washington, D. C., which became a salon for liberals, and he prepared a project for a national university to be located at the capital. Madison appointed him minister to France in 1811, and he died the next year in Poland from an illness contracted while he was on his way to meet Napoleon in order to negotiate a trade treaty.

Barlow's two political essays are entitled: *Letter to the National Convention of France* (for which he was made a citizen of France) and *Advice to the Privileged Orders of Europe* (for which he was banished from England), both published in 1792. He took advanced stands in opposing the European class distinctions he thought the Federalists were trying to set up in America under the new Constitution. In order to secure actual equality of opportunity, Barlow proposed a system of public education; and to keep governmental authorities responsive to their broad social obligations he proposed easy methods of constitutional amendment, short terms of office, and a popular recall of elected officials. The passages below reveal some of his more general political ideas.

[See: *Brief Sketches of the Graduates of Yale College* (1907), Vol. IV, pp. 3–16; Stanley T. Williams and T. A. Zunder, in *Dictionary of American Biography*; Vernon L. Parrington, *Main Currents of American Thought*, Vol. I (1927), pp. 382–389.]

From ADVICE TO THE PRIVILEGED ORDERS IN THE SEVERAL STATES OF EUROPE (1792)[1]

Whether men are born to govern, or to obey, or to enjoy equal liberty, depends not on the original capacity of the mind, but on the *instinct of analogy*, or the *habit of thinking*. When children of the same family are taught to believe in the unconquerable distinctions of birth among themselves, they are completely fitted for a feudal government; because their minds are familiarised with all the gradations and degradations that such a government requires. The birth-right of domineering is not more readily claimed on the one hand, than it is acknowledged on the other; and the Jamaica planter is not more habitually convinced that an European is superior to an African, than he is that a lord is better than himself.

This subject deserves to be placed in a light, in which no writer, as far as I know, has yet considered it. When a person was repeating to Fontenelle the common adage *l'habitude est la seconde nature*, the philosopher replied, *Et faites moi la grace de me dire, quelle est la première*. When we assert that nature has established inequalities among men, and has thus given to some the right of governing others, or when we maintain the *contrary* of this position, we should be careful to define what sort of nature we mean, whether the *first* or *second nature*; or whether we mean that there is but one. A mere savage . . . would decide the question of equality by a trial of bodily strength, designating the man that could lift the heaviest beam to be the legislator; and unless all men could lift the same beam, they could not be equal in their rights. Aristotle would

[1] *Advice to the Privileged Orders in the Several States of Europe, Resulting from the Necessity and Propriety of a General Revolution in the Principle of Government* (London, 1792), pp. 26–39.

give the preference to him that excelled in mental capacity. Ulysses would make the decision upon a compound ratio of both. But there appears to me another step in this ladder, and that the *habit of thinking* is the only safe and universal criterion to which, in practice, the question can be referred. Indeed, when interest is laid aside, it is the only one to which, in civilized ages, it ever is referred. We never submit to a king, because he is stronger than we in bodily force, nor because he is superior in understanding or in information; but because we believe him born to govern, or at least, because a majority of the society believes it.

This *habit of thinking* has so much of nature in it, it is so undistinguishable from the indelible marks of the man, that it is a perfectly safe foundation for any system that we may choose to build upon it; indeed it is the *only* foundation, for it is the only point of contact by which men communicate as moral associates. As a practical position therefore, and as relating to almost all places and almost all times, in which the experiment has yet been made, Aristotle was as right in teaching, *That some are born to command, and others to be commanded,* as the national assembly was in declaring, *That men are born and always continue free and equal in respect to their rights.* The latter is as apparently false in the diet of Ratisbon, as the former is in the hall of the Jacobins.

Abstractedly considered, there can be no doubt of the unchangeable truth of the assembly's declaration; and they have taken the right method to make it a *practical* truth, by publishing it to the world for discussion. A general belief *that it is a truth,* makes it at once practical, confirms it in one nation, and extends it to others.

A due attention to the astonishing effects that are wrought in the world by *the habit of thinking,* will serve many valuable purposes. I cannot therefore dismiss the subject so soon as I intended; but will mention one or two instances of these effects, and leave the reflection of the reader to make the application to a thousand others.

First, It is evident that all the arbitrary systems in the world are founded and supported on this *second nature* of man, in counteraction of the *first.* Systems which distort and crush and subjugate every thing that we can suppose original and characteristic in man, as an undistorted being. It sustains the most absurd and abominable theories of religion, and honors them with as many martyrs as it does those that are the most peaceful and beneficent.

But *secondly*, we find for our consolation, that it will likewise support systems of equal liberty and national happiness. In the United States of America, the science of liberty is universally understood, felt and practised, as much by the simple as the wise, the weak as the strong. Their deep-rooted and inveterate habit of thinking is, that *all men are equal in their rights*, that *it is impossible to make them otherwise*; and this being their undisturbed belief, they have no conception how any man in his senses can entertain any other. This point once settled, every thing is settled. Many operations, which in Europe have been considered as incredible tales or dangerous experiments, are but the infallible consequences of this great principle. The first of these operations is *the business of election*, which with that people is carried on with as much gravity as their daily labor. There is no jealousy on the occasion, nothing lucrative in office; any man in society may attain to any place in the government, and may exercise its functions. They believe that there is nothing more difficult in the management of the affairs of a nation, than the affairs of a family; that it only requires more hands. They believe that it is the juggle of keeping up impositions to blind the eyes of the vulgar, that constitutes the intricacy of state. Banish the mysticism of inequality, and you banish almost all the evils attendant on human nature.

The people, being habituated to the election of all kinds of officers, the *magnitude* of the office makes no difficulty in the case. The president of the United States, who has more power while in office than some of the kings of Europe, is chosen with as little commotion as a churchwarden. There is a public service to be performed, and the people say who shall do it. The servant feels honored with the confidence reposed in him, and generally expresses his gratitude by a faithful performance.

Another of these operations is making every citizen a soldier, and every soldier a citizen; not only *permitting* every man to arm, but *obliging* him to arm. This fact, told in Europe previous to the French revolution, would have gained little credit; or at least it would have been regarded as a mark of an uncivilized people, extremely dangerous to a well ordered society. Men who build systems on an inversion of nature, are obliged to invert every thing that is to make part of that system. It is *because the people are civilized, that they are with safety armed*. It is an effect of their

conscious dignity, as citizens enjoying equal rights, that they wish
not to invade the rights of others. The danger (where there is any)
from armed citizens, is only to the *government*, not to the *society*;
and as long as they have nothing to revenge in the government
(which they cannot have while it is in their own hands) there are
many advantages in their being accustomed to the use of arms, and
no possible disadvantage.

Power, habitually in the hands of a whole community, loses all
the ordinary associated ideas of power. The exercise of power is a
relative term; it supposes an opposition,—something to operate
upon. We perceive no exertion of power in the motion of the
planetary system, but a very strong one in the movement of a whirlwind; it is because we see obstructions to the latter, but none to the
former. Where the government is *not* in the hands of the people,
there you find opposition, you perceive two contending interests,
and get an idea of the exercise of power; and whether this power be
in the hands of the government or of the people, or whether it
change from side to side, it is always to be dreaded. But the word
people in America has a different meaning from what it has in Europe. It there means the whole community, and comprehends
every human creature; here it means something else, more difficult
to define.

Another consequence of the habitual idea of equality, is the
facility of changing the structure of their government whenever and
as often as the society shall think there is any thing in it to amend.
As Mr. Burke has written no "reflections on the revolution" in
America, the people there have never yet been told that they had no
right "to frame a government for themselves;" they have therefore
done much of this business, without ever affixing to it the idea of
"sacrilege" or "usurpation," or any other term of rant to be found
in that gentleman's vocabulary.

Within a few years the fifteen states have not only framed each
its own state-constitution, and two successive federal constitutions;
but since the settlement of the present general government in the
year 1789, three of the states, Pennsylvania, South-Carolina and
Georgia, have totally new modeled their own. And all this is done
without the least confusion; the operation being scarcely known beyond the limits of the state where it is performed. Thus they are in
the habit of "*choosing their own governors*," of "*cashiering them for*

misconduct," of "framing a government for themselves," and all those abominable things, the mere naming of which, in Mr. Burke's opinion, has polluted the pulpit in the Old Jewry.

But it is said, These things will do very well for America, where the people are less numerous, less indigent, and better instructed; but they will not apply to Europe. This objection deserves a reply, not because it is solid, but because it is fashionable. It may be answered, that some parts of Spain, much of Poland, and almost the whole of Russia, are less peopled than the settled country in the United States; that poverty and ignorance are effects of slavery rather than its causes; but the best answer to be given, is the example of France. To the event of that revolution I will trust the argument. Let the people have time to become thoroughly and soberly grounded in the doctrine of equality, and there is no danger of oppression either from government or from anarchy. Very little instruction is necessary to teach a man his rights; and there is no person of common intellects in the most ignorant corner of Europe, but receives lessons enough, if they were of the proper kind. For writing and reading are not indispensible to the object; it is thinking right which makes them act right. Every child is taught to repeat about fifty Latin prayers, which set up the Pope, the Bishop, and the King, as the trinity of his adoration; he is taught that the powers that be are ordained of God, and therefore the soldier quartered in the parish has a right to cut his throat. Half this instruction, upon opposite principles, would go a great way; in that case Nature would be assisted, while here she is counteracted. Engrave it on the heart of a man, that all men are equal in rights, and that the government is their own, and then persuade him to sell his crucifix and buy a musquet,—and you have made him a good citizen.

Another consequence of a settled belief in the equality of rights, is, that under this belief there is no danger from Anarchy. This word has likewise acquired a different meaning in America from what we read of it in books. In Europe it means confusion, attended with mobs and carnage, where the innocent perish with the guilty. But it is very different where a country is used to a representative government, though it should have an interval of no government at all. Where the people at large feel and know that they can do every thing by themselves personally, they really do nothing by themselves personally. In the heat of the American revolution, when the people in some states were for a long time without the least shadow of law or government, they always acted by committees and representation. This they must call anarchy, for they know no other.

These are materials for the formation of governments, which need not be dreaded, though disjointed and laid asunder to make some repairs. They are deep-rooted habits of thinking, which almost change the moral nature of man; they are principles as much unknown to the ancient republics as to the modern monarchies of Europe.

We must not therefore rely upon systems drawn from the experimental reasonings of Aristotle, when we find them contradicted by what we feel to be the eternal truth of nature, and see brought to the test of our own experience. Aristotle was certainly a great politician; and Claudius Ptolemy was a great geographer; but the latter has said not a word of America, the largest quarter of the globe; nor the former, of representative republics, the resource of afflicted humanity.

Since I have brought these two great luminaries of science so near together, I will keep them in company a moment longer, to show the strange partiality that we may retain for one superstition after having laid aside another, though they are built on similar foundations. Ptolemy wrote a system of astronomy; in which he taught, among other things, that the earth was the centre of the universe, and that the heavenly bodies moved round it. This system is now taught (to the exclusion by anathema of all others) in Turkey, Arabia, Persia, Palestine, Egypt, and wherever the doctrines of Mahomet are taught; while at the same time, and with the same reverence, the politics of Aristotle are taught at the university of Oxford. The ground which supports the one is, that the sun stopt its course at the command of Joshua, which it could not have done, had it not been in motion; and the other, that *the powers that be are ordained of God.* Mention to a Mussulman the Copernican system, and you might as well speak to Mr. Burke about the rights of man; they both call you an atheist.

11. THOMAS JEFFERSON (1743–1826)

JEFFERSON was born in Albemarle County, Virginia, then near the western edge of colonial settlement. His paternal ancestors were of yeoman stock; his father, self-educated, had acquired a considerable landed estate and held various county offices. His mother was a Randolph, and this gave him an association with the first families of Virginia. He was graduated from William and Mary College in 1762, then read law (in the office of George Wythe, one of the most distinguished jurists of the day), and began a successful practice. His inheritance, in addition to the lands acquired through his wife, gave him an estate of about 10,000 acres and over a hundred slaves. His wife's lands were encumbered by debt, and this created a financial burden from which he was never able fully to rid himself.

Jefferson's varied interests and talents were manifested from early youth to old age. He learned foreign languages, ancient and modern; studied architecture; read history and the classics; made extensive collections of books, paintings, and sculpture; invented useful contrivances for the farm and home; and drew the plans and supervised the construction, continued for several decades, of his home ("Monticello"). He was president of the American Philosophical Society, from 1797 to 1815, and a member of important scientific societies of Europe. He held public office almost continuously from his middle twenties until his retirement from the presidency over forty years later: as county surveyor and justice of the peace; member of the Virginia House of Burgesses, of the Second Continental Congress, and of the House of Delegates under the first State constitution of Virginia; governor of Virginia; member of the Congress of the Confederation; minister to France (1785–89), first secretary of state of the United States (1790–93), vice-president (1797–1801), and President (1801–09).

Jefferson was not an orator and he made few speeches; but he was an expert legislative draftsman and committeeman and a skillful party leader. In the bitter controversies developing in President Washington's administrations, he soon superseded the younger James Madison as leader of the party of "Republicans," who opposed Hamilton's bills establishing the funding system, the United States Bank, and other "Federalist" measures tending to create a strong national authority under a liberal interpretation of constitutional grants of power to Congress. This interparty hostility was intensified by differences over foreign policy and by the general emotional opposition between the Jeffersonians' sympathy with the republicans of France and the Federalists' admiration for the more stable political and aristocratic system of England. Jefferson, moreover, became a special object of fear and hatred, because of the advanced stand he had taken in Virginia for religious freedom and other liberal objectives. Probably at no other time in our history has personal abuse in political conflict been so violent, particularly in the presidential campaign of 1800. Jefferson's opponents described him as coarse and vulgar and called him a deist, infidel, anarchist, and terrorist. Episcopalian ministers in Virginia and Puritan ministers in Connecticut called his measure disestablishing the church in Virginia an "atheist law." Other critics accused him of cowardice in public life and of dishonesty and cruelty in his business affairs. Perhaps the charge of deism was the least remote from the truth. Although reared in the Episcopal church, a fairly regular church attendant, and a contributor to churches of various denominations, Jefferson did not believe in miracles or the virgin birth, doubted the values of elaborate theological speculation, and strongly advocated religious toleration. He called himself "a real Christian, that is to say, a disciple of the doctrines of Jesus," and he prepared, with great care, two compendia of those doctrines.

Jefferson wrote only one complete book, the Notes on Virginia (1781–82), prepared in response to a series of questions submitted by the secretary of the French legation in Philadelphia, following an order from the French government to obtain miscellaneous facts about the American States. The book is a storehouse of information on the geography, resources, government, and social life of Virginia; and it contains major parts of Jefferson's social philosophy. Probably no other person has made such substantial contributions to the American political ideology: through this book; through the important declarations, bills, reports, and recommendations he prepared—the Preamble to the Virginia Constitution of 1776, the Declaration of Independence, bills in the Virginia legislature, reports in the Congress of the Confederation, and the "Kentucky Resolutions" against the Alien and Sedition Acts; and through his extensive correspondence. He nowhere set forth his ideas in a systematic form; and he is probably the most frequently misinterpreted of all American publicists. Yet perhaps no one in modern times has put forward a more comprehensive and well-balanced political program. For Jefferson was constantly concerned with the intellectual, spiritual, and economic aspects of democracy, as well as with its formal governmental machinery.

In Virginia, Jefferson prepared a series of bills, designed, he said to form "a system by which every fibre would be eradicated of ancient or future aristocracy, and a foundation laid for a government truly republican." His bills to abolish entails, to end primogeniture, and to disestablish the Church and grant religious toleration were enacted (in 1776, 1785, and 1786, respectively). He also drafted a general plan of public education—to enable citizens "to understand their rights, to maintain them, and to exercise with intelligence their parts in self-government." His "Bill for the More General Diffusion of Knowledge" (which was not enacted) provided for public schools, free to all children in the first three years and for the more capable in the higher grades, with the most capable sent free to William and Mary College for three years. He advocated the establishment of a free public library and the sending of newspapers through the mails at public expense, as further means of spreading information on civic affairs. He secured the enactment (in 1778) of a law prohibiting the further importation of slaves into Virginia and proposed other measures to check slavery. As "the last object for which I shall obtrude myself on the public observation," he brought about the establishment of the University of Virginia (chartered in 1819), for which he designed the architecture and the main lines of its administrative and educational policy. Jefferson himself prepared the familiar epitaph inscribed on the shaft above his grave at Monticello: "Here was buried Thomas Jefferson, author of the Declaration of American Independence, of the statute of Virginia for religious freedom, and father of the University of Virginia."

[See: Dumas Malone, "Thomas Jefferson," in *Dictionary of American Biography*, Vol. X (1933); Gilbert Chinard, *Thomas Jefferson, the Apostle of Americanism* (1929); Albert J. Nock, *Jefferson* (1926); David Muzzey, *Thomas Jefferson* (1918); Claude J. Bowers, *Jefferson and Hamilton* (1925); Charles M. Wiltse, *The Jeffersonian Tradition in America* (1935).]

From NOTES ON THE STATE OF VIRGINIA (1782)[1]

This constitution [the Virginia constitution of 1776] was formed when we were new and unexperienced in the science of government. It was the first, too, which was formed in the whole United States.

[1] NOTES on the state of VIRGINIA; *written in the year 1781, somewhat corrected and enlarged in the winter of 1782, for the use of a Foreigner of distinction, in answer to certain queries proposed by him respecting* (here follow headings for the different queries, relating to the geography, resources, government, and economic and cultural aspects of Virginia), in *The Writings of Thomas Jefferson*, ed. by Paul Leicester Ford, 10 vols. (New York, 1892–99), Vol. III, pp. 68–295, at 222–225, 229–233, 235, 251–255. The passages selected above are from Query XIII, *The constitution of the State and its several charters?*, and Query XIV, *The administration of justice and the description of the laws?*

No wonder then that time and trial have discovered very capital defects in it.

1. The majority of the men in the state, who pay and fight for its support, are unrepresented in the legislature, the roll of freeholders entitled to vote not including generally the half of those on the roll of the militia, or of the tax-gatherers.

2. Among those who share the representation, the shares are very unequal. Thus the county of Warwick, with only one hundred fighting men, has an equal representation with the county of Loudon, which has 1746. . . .

. . . It will appear at once that nineteen thousand men, living below the falls of the rivers, possess half of the senate, and want four members only of possessing a majority of the house of delegates; a want more than supplied by the vicinity of their situation to the seat of government, and of course the greater degree of convenience and punctuality with which their members may and will attend in the legislature. These nineteen thousand, therefore, living in one part of the country, give law to upwards of thirty thousand living in another, and appoint all their chief officers executive and judiciary. From the difference of their situation and circumstances, their interests will often be very different.

3. The senate is, by its constitution, too homogenous with the house of delegates. Being chosen by the same electors, at the same time, and out of the same subjects, the choice falls of course on men of the same description. The purpose of establishing different houses of legislation is to introduce the influence of different interests or different principles. Thus in Great Britain it is said their constitution relies on the house of commons for honesty, and the lords for wisdom; which would be a rational reliance, if honesty were to be bought with money, and if wisdom were hereditary. In some of the American States, the delegates and senators are so chosen, as that the first represent the persons, and the second the property of the State. But with us, wealth and wisdom have equal chance for admission into both houses. We do not, therefore, derive from the separation of our legislature into two houses, those benefits which a proper complication of principles is capable of producing, and those which alone can compensate the evils which may be produced by their dissensions.

4. All the powers of government, legislative, executive, and judi-

ciary, result to the legislative body. The concentrating these in the same hands is precisely the definition of despotic government. It will be no alleviation that these powers will be exercised by a plurality of hands, and not by a single one. 173 despots would surely be as oppressive as one. . . . An *elective despotism* was not the government we fought for, but one which should not only be founded on free principles, but in which the powers of government should be so divided and balanced among several bodies of magistracy, as that no one could transcend their legal limits, without being effectually checked and restrained by the others. For this reason that convention, which passed the ordinance of government, laid its foundation on this basis, that the legislative, executive and judiciary departments should be separate and distinct, so that no person should exercise the powers of more than one of them at the same time. But no barrier was provided between these several powers. The judiciary and executive members were left dependent on the legislative, for their subsistence in office, and some of them for their continuance in it. If therefore the legislature assumes executive and judiciary powers, no opposition is likely to be made; nor, if made, can it be effectual; because in that case they may put their proceedings into the form of an act of assembly, which will render them obligatory on the other branches. They have accordingly in many instances, decided rights which should have been left to judiciary controversy: and the direction of the executive, during the whole time of their session, is becoming habitual and familiar. And this is done with no ill intention. The views of the present members are perfectly upright. When they are led out of their regular province, it is by art in others, and inadvertence in themselves. And this will probably be the case for some time to come. But it will not be a very long time. Mankind soon learn to make interested uses of every right and power which they possess, or may assume. The public money and public liberty, intended to have been deposited with three branches of magistracy, but found inadvertently to be in the hands of one only, will soon be discovered to be sources of wealth and dominion to those who hold them; distinguished, too, by this tempting circumstance, that they are the instrument, as well as the object, of acquisition. With money we will get men, said Caesar, and with men we will get money. Nor should our assembly be deluded by the integrity of their own purposes, and conclude that these unlimited powers will never be abused, because themselves are not disposed to abuse them. They should look forward to a time, and that not a distant one, when a corruption in this, as in the country from which we derive our origin, will have seized the heads of government, and be spread by them through the body of the people; when they will purchase the voices of the people, and make them pay the price. Human nature is the same on every side of the Atlantic, and will be alike influenced by the same causes. The time to guard against corruption and tyranny, is before they shall have gotten hold of us. It is better to keep the wolf out of the fold, than to trust to drawing his teeth and talons after he shall have entered. To render these considerations the more cogent, we must observe in addition:

5. That the ordinary legislature may alter the constitution itself. . . . The other states in the union have been of opinion that to render a form of government unalterable by ordinary acts of assembly, the people must delegate persons with special powers. They have accordingly chosen special conventions to form and fix their governments. The individuals then who maintain the contrary opinion in this country, should have the modesty to suppose it possible that they may be wrong, and the rest of America right. . . .

6. That the assembly exercises a power of determining the quorum of their own body which may legislate for us. . . . The power, however, of fixing their own quorum has been avowed, and a precedent set. From forty it may be reduced to four, and from four to one; from a house to a committee, from a committee to a chairman or speaker, and thus an oligarchy or monarchy be substituted under forms supposed to be regular. . . . When, therefore, it is considered, that there is no legal obstacle to the assumption by the assembly of all the powers legislative, executive, and judiciary, and that these may come to the hands of the smallest rag of delegation, surely the people will say, and their representatives, while yet they have honest representatives, will advise them to say, that they will not acknowledge as laws any acts not considered and assented to by the major part of their delegates.

In enumerating the defects of the constitution, it would be wrong to count among them what is only the error of particular persons. In December 1776, our circumstances being much distressed, it was proposed in the house of delegates to create a *dictator*, invested with every power legislative, executive, and judiciary, civil and military, of life and of death, over our persons and over our properties: and in June 1781, again under calamity, the same proposition was repeated, and wanted a few votes only of being passed.—One who entered into this contest from a pure love of liberty, and a sense of injured rights, who determined to make every sacrifice, and to meet every danger, for the re-establishment of those rights on a firm basis, who did not mean to expend his blood and substance for the wretched purpose of changing this master for that, but to place the powers of governing him in a plurality of hands of his own choice, so that the corrupt will of no one man might in future oppress him, must stand confounded and dismayed when he is told, that a considerable portion of that plurality had meditated the surrender of them into a single hand, and, in lieu of a limited monarch, to deliver him over to a despotic one! How must he find his efforts and sacrifices abused and baffled, if he may still, by a single vote, be laid prostrate at the feet of one man! In God's name, from whence have they derived this power? Is it from our ancient laws? None such can be produced. Is it from any principle in our new constitution expressed or implied? Every lineament of that expressed or implied, is in full opposition to it. Its fundamental principle is, that the state shall be governed as a commonwealth. It provides a republican organization, proscribes under the name of prerogative the exercise of all powers undefined by the laws; places on this basis the whole system of our laws; and by consolidating them together, chooses that they shall be left to stand or fall together, never providing for any circumstances, nor admitting that such could arise, wherein either should be suspended; no, not for a moment. Our antient laws expressly declare, that those who are but delegates themselves shall not delegate to others powers which require judgment and integrity in their exercise.—Or was this proposition moved on a supposed right in the movers, of abandoning their posts in a moment of distress? The same laws forbid the abandonment of that post, even on ordinary occasions; and much more a transfer of their powers into other hands and other forms, without consulting the people. They never admit the idea that these, like sheep or cattle, may be given from hand to hand without an appeal to their own will.—Was it from the necessity of the case?

[handwritten marginalia:] proposed by body elected by people to delegate power granted them; power expressly resident in people only, and only to be redistributed on the people's word.

[handwritten marginalia:] amending conventions must have popular origin.

Anarchy is better than monarchy

Necessities which dissolve a government, do not convey its authority to an oligarchy or a monarchy. They throw back, into the hands of the people, the powers they had delegated, and leave them as individuals to shift for themselves. A leader may offer, but not impose himself, nor be imposed on them. Much less can their necks be submitted to his sword, their breath be held at his will or caprice. The necessity which should operate these tremendous effects should at least be palpable and irresistible. Yet in both instances, where it was feared, or pretended with us, it was belied by the event. . . . Our situation is indeed perilous, and I hope my countrymen will be sensible of it, and will apply, at a proper season, the proper remedy; which is a convention to fix the constitution,

Usurpation justifies rebellion.

to amend its defects, to bind up the several branches of government by certain laws, which, when they transgress, their acts shall become nullities; to render unnecessary an appeal to the people, or in other words a rebellion, on every infraction of their rights, on the peril that their acquiescence shall be construed into an intention to surrender those rights. . . .

Education

Another object of the revisal is, to diffuse knowledge more generally through the mass of the people. This bill proposes to lay off every country into small districts of five or six miles square, called hundreds and in each of them to establish a school for teaching, reading, writing, and arithmetic. The tutor to be supported by the hundred, and every person in it entitled to send their children three years gratis, and as much longer as they please, paying for it. These schools to be under a visitor who is annually to chuse the boy of best genius in the school, of those whose parents are too poor to give them further education, and to send him forward to one of the grammar schools, of which twenty are proposed to be erected in different parts of the country, for teaching Greek, Latin, geography, and the higher branches of numerical arithmetic. Of the boys thus sent in any one year, trial is to be made at the grammar schools one or two years, and the best genius of the whole selected, and continued six years, and the residue dismissed. By this means twenty of the best geniuses will be raked from the rubbish annually, and be instructed, at the public expence, so far as the grammar schools go. At the end of six years instruction, one half are to be discontinued (from among whom the grammar schools will probably be supplied with future masters); and the other half, who are to be chosen for the superiority of their parts and disposition, are to be sent and continued three years in the study of such sciences as they shall chuse, at William and Mary college, the plan of which is proposed to be enlarged, as will be hereafter explained, and extended to all the useful sciences. The ultimate result of the whole scheme of education would be the teaching all the children of the State reading, writing, and common arithmetic; turning out ten annually, of superior genius, well taught in Greek, Latin, geography, and the higher branches of arithmetic; turning out ten others annually, of still superior parts, who, to those branches of learning, shall have added such of the sciences as their genius shall have led them to; the furnishing to the wealthier part of the people convenient schools at which their children may be educated at their own expence.—The general objects of this law are to provide an education adapted to the years, to the capacity, and the condition of every one, and directed to their freedom and happiness. Specific details were not proper for the law. These must be the business of the visitors entrusted with its execution. The first stage of this education being the schools of the hundreds, wherein the great mass of the people will receive their instruction, the principal foundations of future order will be laid here. Instead, therefore, of putting the Bible and Testament into the hands of the children at an age when their judgments are not sufficiently matured for religious inquiries, their memories may here be stored with the most useful facts from Grecian, Roman, European, and American history. The first elements of morality too may be instilled into their minds; such as, when further developed as their judgments advance in strength, may teach them how to work out their own greatest happiness, by shewing them that it does not depend on the condition of life in which chance has placed them, but is always the result of a good conscience, good health, occupation, and freedom in all just pursuits.—Those whom either the wealth of their parents or the adoption of the state shall destine to higher degrees of learning, will go on to the grammar schools, which constitute the next stage, there to be instructed in the languages. . . . As soon as they are of sufficient age, it is supposed they will be sent on from the grammar schools to the university, which constitutes our third and last stage, there to study those sciences which may be adapted to their views. —By that part of our plan which prescribes the selection of the youths of genius from among the classes of the poor, we hope to avail the state of those talents which nature has sown as liberally among the poor as the rich, but which perish without use, if not sought for and cultivated.—But of all the views of this law none is more important, none more legitimate, than that of rendering the people the safe, as they are the ultimate, guardians of their own liberty. For this purpose the reading in the first stage, where *they* will receive their whole education, is proposed, as has been said, to be chiefly historical. History, by apprising them of the past, will enable them to judge of the future; it will avail them of the experience of other times and other nations; it will qualify them as judges of the actions and designs of men; it will enable them to know ambition under every disguise it may assume; and knowing it, to defeat its views. In every government on earth is some trace of human weakness, some germ of corruption and degeneracy, which cunning will discover, and wickedness insensibly open, cultivate and improve. Every government degenerates when trusted to the rulers of the people alone. The people themselves therefore are its only safe depositories. And to render even them safe, their minds must be improved to a certain degree. This indeed is not all that is necessary, though it be essentially necessary. An amendment of our constitution must here come in aid of the public education. The influence over government must be shared among all the people. If every individual which composes their mass participates of the ultimate authority, the government will be safe; because the corrupting the whole mass will exceed any private resources of wealth; and public ones cannot be provided but by levies on the people. In this case every man would have to pay his own price. The government of Great Britain has been corrupted, because but one man in ten has a right to vote for members of parliament. The sellers of the government, therefore, get nine-tenths of their price clear. It has been thought that corruption is restrained by confining the right of suffrage to a few of the wealthier of the people: but it would be more effectually restrained by an extension of that right to such numbers as would bid defiance to the means of corruption.

Lastly, it is proposed, by a bill in this revisal, to begin a public library and gallery, by laying out a certain sum annually in books, paintings, and statues.

From INAUGURAL ADDRESS (MARCH 4, 1801) [1]

During the contest of opinion through which we have passed the animation of discussions and of exertions has sometimes worn an aspect which might impose on strangers unused to think freely and to speak and to write what they think; but this being now decided by the voice of the nation, announced according to the rules of the Constitution, all will, of course, arrange themselves under the will of the law, and unite in common efforts for the common good. All, too, will bear in mind this sacred principle, that though the will of the majority is in all cases to prevail, that will to be rightful must be reasonable; that the minority possess their equal rights, which equal law must protect, and to violate would be oppression. Let us, then, fellow-citizens, unite with one heart and one mind. Let us restore to social intercourse that harmony and affection without which liberty and even life itself are but dreary things. And let us reflect that, having banished from our land that religious intolerance under which mankind so long bled and suffered, we have yet gained little if we countenance a political intolerance as despotic, as wicked, and capable of as bitter and bloody persecutions. During the throes and convulsions of the ancient world, during the agonizing spasms of infuriated man, seeking through blood and slaughter his long-lost liberty, it was not wonderful that the agitation of the billows should reach even this distant and peaceful shore; that this should be more felt and feared by some and less by others, and should divide opinions as to measures of safety. But every difference of opinion is not a difference of principle. We have called by different names brethren of the same principle. We are all Republicans, we are all Federalists. If there be any among us who would wish to dissolve this Union or to change its republican form, let them stand undisturbed as monuments of the safety with which error of opinion may be tolerated where reason is left free to combat it. I know, indeed, that some honest men fear that a republican government can not be strong, that this Government is not strong enough; but would the honest patriot, in the full tide of successful experiment,

Once tho Const has been ratified all should rally behind it.

[1] In A Compilation of the Messages and Papers of the Presidents, 1789–1902, ed. by James D. Richardson (20 vols., Washington, 1917), Vol. I, pp. 309–312, at 310–312.

abandon a government which has so far kept us free and firm on the theoretic and visionary fear that this Government, the world's best hope, may by possibility want energy to preserve itself? I trust not. I believe this, on the contrary, the strongest Government on earth. I believe it the only one where every man, at the call of the law, would fly to the standard of the law, and would meet invasions of the public order as his own personal concern. Sometimes it is said that man can not be trusted with the government of himself. Can he, then, be trusted with the government of others? Or have we found angels in the forms of kings to govern him? Let history answer this question.

great faith in common man.

Let us, then, with courage and confidence pursue our own Federal and Republican principles, our attachment to union and representative government. Kindly separated by nature and a wide ocean from the exterminating havoc of one quarter of the globe; too high-minded to endure the degradations of the others; possessing a chosen country, with room enough for our descendants to the thousandth and thousandth generation; entertaining a due sense of our equal right to the use of our own faculties, to the acquisitions of our own industry, to honor and confidence from our fellow-citizens, resulting not from birth, but from our actions and their sense of them; enlightened by a benign religion, professed, indeed, and practiced in various forms, yet all of them inculcating honesty, truth, temperance, gratitude, and the love of man; acknowledging and adoring an overruling Providence, which by all its dispensations proves that it delights in the happiness of man here and his greater happiness hereafter—with all these blessings, what more is necessary to make us a happy and a prosperous people? Still one thing more, fellow-citizens—a wise and frugal Government, which shall restrain men from injuring one another, shall leave them otherwise free to regulate their own pursuits of industry and improvement, and shall not take from the mouth of labor the bread it has earned. This is the sum of good government, and this is necessary to close the circle of our felicities.

faith in country opportunity

ingredient of religion

About to enter, fellow-citizens, on the exercise of duties which comprehend everything dear and valuable to you, it is proper you should understand what I deem the essential principles of our Government, and consequently those which ought to shape its Administration. I will compress them within the narrowest com-

pass they will bear, stating the general principle, but not all its
limitations. Equal and exact justice to all men, of whatever state
or persuasion, religious or political; peace, commerce, and honest
friendship with all nations, entangling alliances with none; the support of the State governments in all their rights, as the most competent administrations for our domestic concerns and the surest bul-
warks against antirepublican tendencies; the preservation of the
General Government in its whole constitutional vigor, as the sheet
anchor of our peace at home and safety abroad; a jealous care of
the right of election by the people—a mild and safe corrective of
abuses which are lopped by the sword of revolution where peaceable
remedies are unprovided; absolute acquiescence in the decisions of
the majority, the vital principle of republics, from which is no appeal but to force, the vital principle and immediate parent of despotism; a well-disciplined militia, our best reliance in peace and for
the first moments of war, till regulars may relieve them; the supremacy of the civil over the military authority; economy in the public
expense, that labor may be lightly burthened; the honest payment
of our debts and sacred preservation of the public faith; encouragement of agriculture, and of commerce as its handmaid; the diffusion
of information and arraignment of all abuses at the bar of the public
reason; freedom of religion; freedom of the press, and freedom of
person under the protection of the habeas corpus, and trial by juries
impartially selected. These principles form the bright constellation
which has gone before us and guided our steps through an age of
revolution and reformation. The wisdom of our sages and blood
of our heroes have been devoted to their attainment. They should
be the creed of our political faith, the text of civic instruction, the
touchstone by which to try the services of those we trust; and should
we wander from them in moments of error or of alarm, let us hasten
to retrace our steps and to regain the road which alone leads to
peace, liberty, and safety. . . . *THIS STATEMENT IS INCORRECT, THE
TENDENCIES IN SOCIETY ARE TOWARDS ARISTOCRACIES. THE
ARISTOCRATIC ARE NOT NECESSARILY VIRTUOUS. THEIR TALENTS*

From A LETTER TO JOHN ADAMS (OCTOBER 28, 1813)[1] *ARE GUISE
AND SOFT
WORDS.*

. . . I agree with you that there is a natural aristocracy among *THE BRILLANT
OFTEN LANGUIS*
men. The grounds of this are virtue and talents. Formerly, bodily
powers gave place among the aristoi. But since the invention of

[1] In Writings, Vol. IX, pp. 424–430.

(right margin) JEFFERSON CREDO.

gunpowder has armed the weak as well as the strong with missile death, bodily strength, like beauty, good humor, politeness and other accomplishments, has become but an auxiliary ground for distinction. There is also an artificial aristocracy, founded on wealth and birth, without either virtue or talents; for with these it would belong to the first class. The natural aristocracy I consider as the most precious gift of nature, for the instruction, the trusts, and government of society. And indeed, it would have been inconsistent in creation to have formed man for the social state, and not to have provided virtue and wisdom enough to manage the concerns of the society. May we not even say, that that form of government is the best, which provides the most effectually for a pure selection of these natural aristoi into the offices of government? The artificial aristocracy is a mischievous ingredient in government, and provision should be made to prevent its ascendency. On the question, what is the best provision, you and I differ; but we differ as rational friends, using the free exercise of our own reason, and mutually indulging its errors. You think it best to put the pseudo-aristoi into a separate chamber of legislation, where they may be hindered from doing mischief by their co-ordinate branches, and where, also, they may be a protection to wealth against the Agrarian and plundering enterprises of the majority of the people. I think that to give them power in order to prevent them from doing mischief, is arming them for it, and increasing instead of remedying the evil. For if the co-ordinate branches can arrest their action, so may they that of the co-ordinates. Mischief may be done negatively as well as positively. Of this, a cabal in the Senate of the United States has furnished many proofs. Nor do I believe them necessary to protect the wealthy; because enough of these will find their way into every branch of the legislation, to protect themselves. From fifteen to twenty legislatures of our own, in action for thirty years past, have proved that no fears of an equalization of property are to be apprehended from them. I think the best remedy is exactly that provided by all our constitutions, to leave to the citizens the free election and separation of the aristoi from the pseudo-aristoi, of the wheat from the chaff. In general they will elect the really good and wise. In some instances, wealth may corrupt, and birth blind them; but not in sufficient degree to endanger the society.

It is probable that our difference of opinion may, in some measure, be produced by a difference of character in those among whom we live. From what I have seen of Massachusetts and Connecticut myself, and still more from what I have heard, and the character given of the former by yourself, who know them so much better, there seems to be in those two States a traditionary reverence for certain families, which has rendered the offices of the government nearly hereditary in those families. I presume that from an early period of your history, members of those families happening to possess virtue and talents, have honestly exercised them for the good of the people, and by their services have endeared their names to them. . . . But although this hereditary succession to office with you, may, in some degree, be founded in real family merit, yet in a much higher degree, it has proceeded from your strict alliance of Church and State. These families are canonised in the eyes of the people on common principles, "you tickle me, and I will tickle you." In Virginia we have nothing of this. Our clergy, before the revolution, having been secured against rivalship by fixed salaries, did not give themselves the trouble of acquiring influence over the people. Of wealth, there were great accumulations in particular families, handed down from generation to generation, under the English law of entails. But the only object of ambition for the wealthy was a seat in the King's Council. All their court then was paid to the crown and its creatures; and they Philipised in all collisions between the King and the people. Hence they were unpopular; and that unpopularity continues attached to their names. A Randolph, a Carter, or a Burwell must have great personal superiority over a common competitor to be elected by the people even at this day. At the first session of our legislature after the Declaration of Independence, we passed a law abolishing entails. And this was followed by one abolishing the privilege of primogeniture, and dividing the lands of intestates equally among all their children, or other representatives. These laws, drawn by myself, laid the ax to the foot of pseudo-aristocracy. And had another which I prepared been adopted by the legislature, our work would have been complete. It was a bill for the more general diffusion of learning. This proposed to divide every county into wards of five or six miles square, like your townships; to establish in each ward a free school for reading, writing and common arithmetic; to provide for the annual selection of the best subjects from these schools, who might receive, at the public expense, a higher degree of education at a district school; and from these district schools to select a certain number of the most promising subjects to be completed at an University, where all the useful sciences should be taught. Worth and genius would thus have been sought out from every condition of life, and completely prepared by education for defeating the competition of wealth and birth for public trusts. My proposition had, for a further object, to impart to these wards those portions of self-government for which they are best qualified, by confiding to them the care of their poor, their roads, police, elections, the nomination of jurors, administration of justice in small cases, elementary exercises of militia; in short, to have made them little republics, with a warden at the head of each, for all those concerns which, being under their eye, they would better manage than the larger republics of the county or State. A general call of ward meetings by their wardens on the same day through the State, would at any time produce the genuine sense of the people on any required point, and would enable the State to act in mass, as your people have so often done, and with so much effect by their town meetings. The law for religious freedom, which made a part of this system, having put down the aristocracy of the clergy, and restored to the citizen the freedom of the mind, and those of entails and descents nurturing an equality of condition among them, this on education would have raised the mass of the people to the high ground of moral respectability necessary to their own safety, and to orderly government; and would have completed the great object of qualifying them to select the veritable aristoi, for the trusts of government, to the exclusion of the pseudalists . . . Although this law has not yet been acted on but in a small and inefficient degree, it is still considered as before the legislature, with other bills of the revised code, not yet taken up, and I have great hope that some patriotic spirit will, at a favorable moment, call it up, and make it the key-stone of the arch of our government.

With respect to aristocracy, we should further consider, that before the establishment of the American States, nothing was known to history but the man of the old world, crowded within limits either small or overcharged, and steeped in the vices which that situation generates. A government adapted to such men would be one thing; but a very different one, that for the man of these States.

Here every one may have land to labor for himself, if he chooses; or, preferring the exercise of any other industry, may exact for it such compensation as not only to afford a comfortable subsistence, but wherewith to provide for a cessation from labor in old age. Every one, by his property, or by his satisfactory situation, is interested in the support of law and order. And such men may safely and advantageously reserve to themselves a wholesome control over their public affairs, and a degree of freedom, which, in the hands *contrast* of the *canaille* of the cities of Europe, would be instantly perverted to the demolition and destruction of everything public and private. The history of the last twenty-five years of France, and of the last forty years in America, nay of its last two hundred years, proves the truth of both parts of this observation.

But even in Europe a change has sensibly taken place in the mind of man. Science had liberated the ideas of those who read and reflect, and the American example had kindled feelings of right in the people. An insurrection has consequently begun, of science, tal- *Science us birth* ents, and courage, against rank and birth, which have fallen into contempt. It has failed in its first effort, because the mobs of the cities, the instrument used for its accomplishment, debased by ignorance, poverty and vice, could not be restrained to rational action. But the world will recover from the panic of this first catastrophe. Science is progressive, and talents and enterprise on the alert. Resort may be had to the people of the country, a more governable power from their principles and subordination; and rank, and birth, and tinsel-aristocracy will finally shrink into insignificance, even there. This, however, we have no right to meddle with. It suffices for us, if the moral and physical condition of our own citizens qualifies them to select the able and good for the direction of their government, with a recurrence of elections at such short periods as will enable them to displace an unfaithful servant, before the mischief he meditates may be irremediable.

I have thus stated my opinion on a point on which we differ, not with a view to controversy, for we are both too old to change opinions which are the result of a long life of inquiry and reflection; but on the suggestions of a former letter of yours, that we ought not to die before we have explained ourselves to each other. We acted in perfect harmony, through a long and perilous contest for our liberty and independence. A constitution has been acquired, which, though neither of us thinks perfect, yet both consider as competent to render our fellow citizens the happiest and the securest on whom the sun has ever shone. If we do not think exactly alike as to its imperfections, it matters little to our country, which, after devoting to it long lives of disinterested labor, we have delivered over to our successors in life, who will be able to take care of it and of themselves.

12. JOHN ADAMS (1735–1826)

JOHN ADAMS was born in Braintree, Massachusetts, descended, on his father's side, from a long line of yeoman farmers. He was graduated from Harvard in 1755, taught school briefly, and then turned to the study of law, abandoning (because of doubts on "disputed points") what he said he "thought" had been an "inclination to preach." He practised law successfully in Braintree and later in Boston; but events soon drew him into political life. He was a leader in the agitation against England. The resolutions he prepared for the Braintree protest against the Stamp Act were taken as models by other Massachusetts towns. He served briefly in the State Assembly and Executive Council. He was a member of the first and second Continental Congresses and helped press through the Declaration of Independence. He was for a short time minister to the United Provinces, had part in the peace negotiations with England, and was minister to England from 1785 to 1788. The narrow margins by which he was chosen to the vice-presidency were due chiefly to the opposition of Alexander Hamilton, who considered him too vain, tactless, and stubborn to be accepted as a leader of the Federalists. Adams regarded the vice-presidency as "the most insignificant office . . . that ever the invention of man contrived," and said he could do "neither good nor evil" in it; yet he gave the office some significance, for, as presiding officer of the Senate, he cast the deciding votes on over twenty measures, several of which were of considerable importance. Hamilton's hostility again narrowed Adams' majority in his election to the Presidency in 1797, and a Hamilton-controlled cabinet contributed to the difficulties of his single term in that office. His most notable achievements as President were his avoidance of war, by skillfully maintaining a balance between extreme pro-British Federalists and pro-French Republicans, and his appointment of John Marshall as chief justice of the United States. Adams did not propose or actively advocate the famous Alien and Sedition Acts of 1798; but he signed them and later defended them as measures made necessary by threats of war.

During the quarter of a century following his term as President, Adams lived in retirement at Braintree, reading widely and carrying on an extensive correspondence. His important books and essays had been written during his active political life. In the Revolutionary period, he spoke as an advocate of equal and natural political and civil rights of men, and of popular rule moderated only by a governmental system of checks and balances.[1] Economic vagaries of the early State governments, political disorders of the post-Revolutionary period, and the excesses of the French Revolution, modified his views as to the best sort of government for America. He now placed chief importance on the necessity of preventing majority tyranny and safeguarding property rights by giving an important place in government to representatives of the rich, the well-born, and the educated; and he found these views confirmed by his readings from history and political philosophy. He set forth his views systematically in his *Defence of the Constitutions of Government of the United States of America* (3 vols., 1787–88), and his *Discourses on Davila* (1805)—first published (in 1790–91) as essays in the (Philadelphia) *Gazette of the United States.*

During the active political years of Jefferson and Adams, the Jeffersonians made somewhat exaggerated characterizations of Adams' criticisms of the popular democratic doctrine. In retirement the two chief protagonists renewed an old political friendship through a series of letters in which they reached a better understanding on points of agreement and disagreement between them. Both died on July 4, 1826.

[See: *The Life of John Adams*, by his grandson, Charles Francis Adams, (Vol. I of *The Works of John Adams*, Boston, 1850–56); Charles E. Merriam, *History of American Political Theories* (1903), ch. 3; Gilbert Chinard, *Honest John Adams* (1903).]

From A LETTER TO JAMES SULLIVAN (MAY 26, 1776)[2]

Our worthy friend, Mr. Gerry, has put into my hands a letter from you, of the sixth of May, in which you consider the principles of representation and legislation, and give us hints of some alterations, which you seem to think necessary, in the qualification of voters.

I wish, Sir, I could possibly find time to accompany you, in your investigation of the principles upon which a representative assembly stands, and ought to stand, and in your examination whether the

[1] These ideas were set forth in essays in the *Boston Gazette* in 1765, published two years later as a book entitled *A Dissertation on Canon and Feudal Law*; in letters to the *Boston Gazette* in 1774, in reply to letters of the Tory Daniel Leonard, later published (in 1819) as *Novanglus and Massachusettensis* (pseudonymns for Adams and Leonard); and in his *Thoughts on Government* (1776).

[2] In *The Works of John Adams*, ed. by Charles Francis Adams, 10 vols. (Boston, 1850–56), Vol. IX, pp. 375–378.

practice of our colony has been conformable to those principles. But, alas! Sir, my time is so incessantly engrossed by the business before me, that I cannot spare enough to go through so large a field; and as to books, it is not easy to obtain them here; nor could I find a moment to look into them, if I had them.

It is certain, in theory, that the only moral foundation of government is, the consent of the people. But to what an extent shall we carry this principle? Shall we say that every individual of the community, old and young, male and female, as well as rich and poor, must consent, expressly, to every act of legislation? No, you will say, this is impossible. How, then, does the right arise in the majority to govern the minority, against their will? Whence arises the right of the men to govern the women, without their consent? Whence the right of the old to bind the young, without theirs?

But let us first suppose that the whole community, of every age, rank, sex, and condition, has a right to vote. This community is assembled. A motion is made, and carried by a majority of one voice. The minority will not agree to this. Whence arises the right of the majority to govern, and the obligation of the minority to obey?

From necessity, you will say, because there can be no other rule. But why exclude women?

You will say, because their delicacy renders them unfit for practice and experience in the great businesses of life, and the hardy enterprises of war, as well as the arduous cares of state. Besides, their attention is so much engaged with the necessary nurture of their children, that nature has made them fittest for domestic cares. And children have not judgment or will of their own. True. But will not these reasons apply to others? Is it not equally true, that men in general, in every society, who are wholly destitute of property, are also too little acquainted with public affairs to form a right judgment, and too dependent upon other men to have a will of their own? If this is a fact, if you give to every man who has no property, a vote, will you not make a fine encouraging provision for corruption, by your fundamental law? Such is the frailty of the human heart, that very few men who have no property, have any judgment of their own. They talk and vote as they are directed by some man of property, who has attached their minds to his interest. . . .

Harrington has shown that power always follows property. This I believe to be as infallible a maxim in politics, as that action and reaction are equal, is in mechanics. Nay, I believe we may advance one step farther, and affirm that the balance of power in a society, accompanies the balance of property in land. The only possible way, then, of preserving the balance of power on the side of equal liberty and public virtue, is to make the acquisition of land easy to every member of society; to make a division of the land into small quantities, so that the multitude may be possessed of landed estates. If the multitude is possessed of the balance of real estate, the multitude will have the balance of power, and in that case the multitude will take care of the liberty, virtue, and interest of the multitude, in all acts of government.

I believe these principles have been felt, if not understood, in the Massachusetts Bay, from the beginning; and therefore I should think that wisdom and policy would dictate in these times to be very cautious of making alterations. Our people have never been very rigid in scrutinizing into the qualifications of voters, and I presume they will not now begin to be so. But I would not advise them to make any alteration in the laws, at present, respecting the qualifications of voters.

Your idea that those laws which affect the lives and personal liberty of all, or which inflict corporal punishment, affect those who are not qualified to vote, as well as those who are, is just. But so they do women, as well as men; children, as well as adults. What reason should there be for excluding a man of twenty years eleven months and twenty-seven days old, from a vote, when you admit one who is twenty-one? The reason is, you must fix upon some period in life, when the understanding and will of men in general, is fit to be trusted by the public. Will not the same reason justify the state in fixing upon some certain quantity of property, as a qualification?

The same reasoning which will induce you to admit all men who have no property, to vote, with those who have, for those laws which affect the person, will prove that you ought to admit women and children; for, generally speaking, women and children have as good judgments, and as independent minds, as those men who are wholly destitute of property; these last being to all intents and purposes as much dependent upon others, who will please to feed,

[handwritten marginalia:] ✓✓✓✓✓ Restrictions of children does not impede the oligarchical tendencies of society but doing so to men, who are egoistically speaking equally as motivated as those having money, makes them militant and constitutes a danger to life & property.

clothe, and employ them, as women are upon their husbands, or
children on their parents.

As to your idea of proportioning the votes of men, in money matters, to the property they hold, it is utterly impracticable. There is
no possible way of ascertaining, at any one time, how much every
man in a community is worth; and if there was, so fluctuating is
trade and property, that this state of it would change in half an
hour. The property of the whole community is shifting every hour,
and no record can be kept of the changes.

Society can be governed only by general rules. Government cannot accommodate itself to every particular case as it happens, nor
to the circumstances of particular persons. It must establish general comprehensive regulations for cases and persons. The only
question is, which general rule will accommodate most cases and
most persons.

Depend upon it, Sir, it is dangerous to open so fruitful a source of
controversy and altercation as would be opened by attempting to
alter the qualifications of voters; there will be no end of it. New
claims will arise; women will demand a vote; lads from twelve to
twenty-one will think their rights not enough attended to; and every
man who has not a farthing, will demand an equal voice with any
other, in all acts of state. It tends to confound and destroy all distinctions, and prostrate all ranks to one common level.

From A DEFENCE OF THE CONSTITUTIONS OF GOV-
ERNMENT OF THE UNITED STATES OF AMERICA
(1787–88) [1]

It is become a kind of fashion among writers, to admit, as a
maxim, that if you could be always sure of a wise, active, and virtuous prince, monarchy would be the best of governments. But this
is so far from being admissible, that it will forever remain true, that
a free government has a great advantage over a simple monarchy.
The best and wisest prince, by means of a freer communication with
his people, and the greater opportunities to collect the best advice
from the best of his subjects, would have an immense advantage in
a free state over a monarchy. A senate consisting of all that is most

[1] In Works, Vols. IV–VI, at Vol. IV, pp. 288–290, 579; Vol. VI, pp. 6–10,
57–59, 61–63, 87–90.

noble, wealthy, and able in the nation, with a right to counsel the crown at all times, is a check to ministers, and a security against abuses, such as a body of nobles who never meet, and have no such right, can never supply. Another assembly, composed of representatives chosen by the people in all parts, gives free access to the whole nation, and communicates all its wants, knowledge, projects, and wishes to government; it excites emulation among all classes, removes complaints, redresses grievances, affords opportunities of exertion to genius, though in obscurity, and gives full scope to all the faculties of man; it opens a passage for every speculation to the legislature, to administration, and to the public; it gives a universal energy to the human character, in every part of the state, such as never can be obtained in a monarchy. . . .

There can be no free government without a democratical branch in the constitution. Monarchies and aristocracies are in possession of the voice and influence of every university and academy in Europe. Democracy, simple democracy, never had a patron among men of letters. Democratical mixtures in government have lost almost all the advocates they ever had out of England and America. Men of letters must have a great deal of praise, and some of the necessaries, conveniences, and ornaments of life. Monarchies and aristocracies pay well and applaud liberally. The people have almost always expected to be served gratis, and to be paid for the honor of serving them; and their applauses and adorations are bestowed too often on artifices and tricks, on hypocrisy and superstition, on flattery, bribes, and largesses. It is no wonder then that democracies and democratical mixtures are annihilated all over Europe, except on a barren rock, a paltry fen, an inaccessible mountain, or an impenetrable forest. The people of England, to their immortal honor, are hitherto an exception; but, to the humiliation of human nature, they show very often that they are like other men. The people in America have now the best opportunity and the greatest trust in their hands, that Providence ever committed to so small a number, since the transgression of the first pair; if they betray their trust, their guilt will merit even greater punishment than other nations have suffered, and the indignation of Heaven. If there is one certain truth to be collected from the history of all ages, it is this; that the people's rights and liberties, and the democratical mixture in a constitution, can never be preserved without a strong executive, or, in other words, without separating the executive from the legislative power. If the executive power, or any considerable part of it, is left in the hands either of an aristocratical or a democratical assembly, it will corrupt the legislature as necessarily as rust corrupts iron, or as arsenic poisons the human body; and when the legislature is corrupted, the people are undone. . . .

By the authorities and examples already recited, you will be convinced that three branches of power have an unalterable foundation in nature; that they exist in every society natural and artificial; and that if all of them are not acknowledged in any constitution of government, it will be found to be imperfect, unstable, and soon enslaved; that the legislative and executive authorities are naturally distinct; and that liberty and the laws depend entirely on a separation of them in the frame of government; that the legislative power is naturally and necessarily sovereign and supreme over the executive; and, therefore, that the latter must be made an essential branch *checks* of the former, even with a negative, or it will not be able to defend itself, but will be soon invaded, undermined, attacked, or in some way or other totally ruined and annihilated by the former. . . .

Marchamont Nedham lays it down as a fundamental principle and an undeniable rule, "that the people, (that is, such as shall be successively chosen to represent the people,) are the best keepers of their own liberties, and that for many reasons. First, because they never think of usurping over other men's rights, but mind which way to preserve their own."

Our first attention should be turned to the proposition itself,— "The people are the best keepers of their own liberties."

But who are the people?

"Such as shall be successively chosen to represent them."

Here is a confusion both of words and ideas, which, though it may pass with the generality of readers in a fugitive pamphlet, or with a majority of auditors in a popular harangue, ought, for that very reason, to be as carefully avoided in politics as it is in philosophy or mathematics. If by *the people* is meant the whole body of a great nation, it should never be forgotten, that they can never act, consult, or reason together, because they cannot march five hundred miles, nor spare the time, nor find a space to meet; and, therefore, the proposition, that they are the best keepers of their own liberties, is not true. They are the worst conceivable; they are no keepers at all. They can neither act, judge, think, or will, as a body politic or corporation. If by *the people* is meant all the inhabitants of a single city, they are not in a general assembly, at all times, the best keepers of their own liberties, nor perhaps at any time, unless you separate from them the executive and judicial power, and temper their authority in legislation with the maturer counsels of the one and the few. If it is meant by *the people*, as our author explains himself, a representative assembly, "such as shall be successively chosen to represent the people," still they are not the best keepers of the people's liberties or their own, if you give them all the power, legislative, executive, and judicial. They would invade the liberties of the people, at least the majority of them would invade the liberties of the minority, sooner and oftener than an absolute monarchy, such as that of France, Spain, or Russia, or than a well-checked aristocracy, like Venice, Bern, or Holland.

An excellent writer has said, somewhat incautiously, that "a people will never oppress themselves, or invade their own rights." This compliment, if applied to human nature, or to mankind, or to any nation or people in being or in memory, is more than has been merited. If it should be admitted that a people will not unanimously agree to oppress themselves, it is as much as is ever, and more than is always, true. All kinds of experience show, that great numbers of individuals do oppress great numbers of other individuals; that parties often, if not always, oppress other parties; and majorities almost universally minorities. All that this observation can mean then, consistently with any color of fact, is, that the people will never unanimously agree to oppress themselves. But if one party agrees to oppress another, or the majority the minority, the people still oppress themselves, for one part of them oppress another.

"The people never think of usurping over other men's rights."

What can this mean? Does it mean that the people never unanimously think of usurping over other men's rights? This would be trifling; for there would, by the supposition, be no other men's rights to usurp. But if the people never, jointly nor severally, think of usurping the rights of others, what occasion can there be for any government at all? Are there no robberies, burglaries, murders, adulteries, thefts, nor cheats? Is not every crime a usurpation over other men's rights? Is not a great part, I will not say the greatest part, of men detected every day in some disposition or other, stronger or weaker, more or less, to usurp over other men's rights? There are some few, indeed, whose whole lives and conversations show that, in every thought, word, and action, they conscientiously respect the rights of others. There is a larger body still, who, in the general tenor of their thoughts and actions, discover similar principles and feelings, yet frequently err. If we should extend our candor so far as to own, that the majority of men are generally under the dominion of benevolence and good intentions, yet, it must be confessed, that a vast majority frequently transgress; and, what is more directly to the point, not only a majority, but almost all, confine their benevolence to their families, relations, personal friends, parish, village, city, county, province, and that very few, indeed, extend it impartially to the whole community. Now, grant but this truth, and the question is decided. If a majority are capable of preferring their own private interest, or that of their families, counties, and party, to that of the nation collectively, some provision must be made in the constitution, in favor of justice, to compel all to respect the common right, the public good, the universal law, in preference to all private and partial considerations.

The proposition of our author, then, should be reversed, and it should have been said, that they mind so much their own, that they never think enough of others. Suppose a nation, rich and poor, high and low, ten millions in number, all assembled together; not more than one or two millions will have lands, houses, or any personal property; if we take into the account the women and children, or even if we leave them out of the question, a great majority of every nation is wholly destitute of property, except a small quantity of clothes, and a few trifles of other movables. Would Mr. Nedham be responsible that, if all were to be decided by a vote of the majority, the eight or nine millions who have no property, would not think of usurping over the rights of the one or two millions who have? Property is surely a right of mankind as really as liberty. Perhaps, at first, prejudice, habit, shame or fear, principle or religion, would restrain the poor from attacking the rich, and the idle from usurping on the industrious; but the time would not be long before courage and enterprise would come, and pretexts be invented by degrees, to countenance the majority in dividing all the property among them, or at least, in sharing it equally with its present possessors. Debts would be abolished first; taxes laid heavy on the rich, and not at all on the others; and at last a downright equal division of every thing be demanded, and voted. What would be the consequence of this? The idle, the vicious, the intemperate, would rush into the utmost extravagance of debauchery, sell and spend all their share, and then demand a new division of those who purchased from them. The moment the idea is admitted into society, that property is not as sacred as the laws of God, and that there is not a force of law and public justice to protect it, anarchy and tyranny commence. If "THOU SHALT NOT COVET," and "THOU SHALT NOT STEAL," were not commandments of Heaven, they must be made inviolable precepts in every society, before it can be civilized or made free.

If the first part of the proposition, namely, that "the people never think of usurping over other men's rights," cannot be admitted, is the second, namely, "they mind which way to preserve their own," better founded?

There is in every nation and people under heaven a large proportion of persons who take no rational and prudent precautions to preserve what they have, much less to acquire more. Indolence is the natural character of man, to such a degree that nothing but the necessities of hunger, thirst, and other wants equally pressing, can stimulate him to action, until education is introduced in civilized societies, and the strongest motives of ambition to excel in arts, trades, and professions, are established in the minds of all men. Until this emulation is introduced, the lazy savage holds property in too little estimation to give himself trouble for the preservation or acquisition of it. In societies the most cultivated and polished, vanity, fashion, and folly prevail over every thought of ways to preserve their own. They seem rather to study what means of luxury, dissipation, and extravagance they can invent to get rid of it.

"The case is far otherwise among kings and grandees," says our author, "as all nations in the world have felt to some purpose."

That is, in other words, kings and grandees think of usurping over other men's rights, but do not mind which way to preserve their own. It is very easy to flatter the democratical portion of society, by making such distinctions between them and the monarchical and aristocratical; but flattery is as base an artifice, and as pernicious a vice, when offered to the people, as when given to the others. There is no reason to believe the one much honester or wiser than the other; they are all of the same clay; their minds and bodies are alike. The two latter have more knowledge and sagacity, derived from education, and more advantages for acquiring wisdom and virtue. As to usurping others' rights, they are all three equally guilty when unlimited in power. No wise man will trust either with an opportunity; and every judicious legislator will set all three to watch and control each other. We may appeal to every page of history we have hitherto turned over, for proofs irrefragable, that the people, when they have been unchecked, have been as unjust, tyrannical, brutal, barbarous, and cruel, as any king or senate possessed of uncontrollable power. The majority has eternally, and without one exception, usurped over the rights of the minority. . . .

Though we allow benevolence and generous affections to exist in the human breast, yet every moral theorist will admit the selfish passions in the generality of men to be the strongest. There are few who love the public better than themselves, though all may have some affection for the public. We are not, indeed, commanded to love our neighbor better than ourselves. Self-interest, private avidity, ambition, and avarice, will exist in every state of society, and under every form of government. A succession of powers and persons, by frequent elections, will not lessen these passions in any case, in a governor, senator, or representative; nor will the apprehension of an approaching election restrain them from indulgence if they have the power. The only remedy is to take away the power, by controlling the selfish avidity of the governor, by the senate and house; of the senate, by the governor and house; and of the house, by the governor and senate. Of all possible forms of government, a sovereignty in one assembly, successively chosen by the people, is perhaps the best calculated to facilitate the gratification of self-love, and the pursuit of the private interest of a few individuals; a few eminent conspicuous characters will be continued in their seats in the sovereign assembly, from one election to another, whatever changes are made in the seats around them; by superior art, address, and opulence, by more splendid birth, reputations, and connections, they will be able to intrigue with the people and their leaders, out of doors, until they worm out most of their opposers, and introduce their friends; to this end, they will bestow all offices, contracts, privileges in commerce, and other emoluments, on the latter and their connections, and throw every vexation and disappointment in the way of the former, until they establish such a system of hopes and fears throughout the state, as shall enable them to carry a majority in every fresh election of the house. The judges will be appointed by them and their party, and of consequence, will be obsequious enough to their inclinations. The whole judicial authority, as well as the executive, will be employed, perverted and prostituted to the purposes of electioneering. No justice will be attainable, nor will innocence or virtue be safe, in the judicial courts, but for the friends of the prevailing leaders; legal prosecutions will be instituted and carried on against opposers, to their vexation and ruin; and as they have the public purse at command, as well as the executive and judicial power, the public money will be expended in the same way. No favors will be attainable but by those who will court the ruling demagogues in the house, by voting for their friends and instruments; and pensions and pecuniary rewards and gratifications, as well as honors and offices of every kind, will be voted to friends and partisans. The leading minds and most influential characters among the clergy will be courted, and the views of the youth in this department will be turned upon those men, and the road to promotion and employment in the church will be obstructed against such as will not worship the general idol. Capital characters among the physicians will not be forgotten, and the means of acquiring reputation and practice in the healing art will be to get the state trumpeters on the side of youth. The bar, too, will be made so subservient, that a young gentleman will have no chance to obtain a character or clients, but by falling in with the views of the judges and their creators. Even the theatres, and actors and actresses, must become politicians, and convert the public pleasures into engines of popularity for the governing members of the house. The press, that great barrier and bulwark of the rights of mankind, when it is protected in its freedom by law, can now no longer be free; if the authors, writers, and printers, will not accept of the hire that will be offered them, they must submit to the ruin that will be denounced against them. The presses, with much secrecy and concealment, will be made the vehicles of calumny against the minority, and of panegyric and empirical applauses of the leaders of the majority, and no remedy can possibly be obtained. In one word, the whole system of affairs, and every conceivable motive of hope and fear, will be employed to promote the private interests of a few, and their obsequious majority; and there is no remedy but in arms. Accordingly we find in all the Italian republics the minority always were driven to arms in despair. . . .

. . . To expect self-denial from men, when they have a majority in their favor, and consequently power to gratify themselves, is to disbelieve all history and universal experience; it is to disbelieve Revelation and the Word of God, which informs us, the heart is deceitful above all things, and desperately wicked. There have been examples of self-denial, and will be again; but such exalted virtue never yet existed in any large body of men, and lasted long; and our author's argument requires it to be proved, not only that individuals, but that nations and majorities of nations, are capable, not only of a single act, or a few acts, of disinterested justice and exalted self-denial, but of a course of such heroic virtue for ages and generations; and not only that they are capable of this, but that it is probable they will practise it. There is no man so blind as not to see, that to talk of founding a government upon a supposition that nations and great bodies of men, left to themselves, will practise a course of self-denial, is either to babble like a new-born infant, or to deceive like an unprincipled impostor. . . .

It is pretended by some, that a sovereignty in a single assembly, annually elected, is the only one in which there is any responsibility for the exercise of power. In the mixed government we contend for, the ministers, at least of the executive power, are responsible for every instance of the exercise of it; and if they dispose of a single commission by corruption, they are responsible to a house of representatives, who may, by impeachment, make them responsible before a senate, where they may be accused, tried, condemned, and punished by independent judges. But in a single sovereign assembly, each member, at the end of his year, is only responsible to his constituents; and the majority of members who have been of one party, and carried all before them, are to be responsible only to their constituents, not to the constituents of the minority who have been overborne, injured, and plundered. And who are these constituents to whom the majority are accountable? Those very persons, to gratify whom they have prostituted the honors, rewards, wealth, and justice of the state. These, instead of punishing, will applaud; instead of discarding, will reëlect, with still greater eclat, and a more numerous majority; for the losing cause will be deserted by numbers. And this will be done in hopes of having still more injustice done, still more honors and profits divided among themselves, to the exclusion and mortification of the minority. It is then astonishing that such a simple government should be preferred to a mixed one, by any rational creature, on the score of responsibility.

There is, in short, no possible way of defending the minority, in such a government, from the tyranny of the majority, but by giving the former a negative on the latter,—the most absurd institution that ever took place among men. As the major may bear all possible relations of proportion to the minor part, it may be fifty-one against forty-nine in an assembly of a hundred, or it may be ninety-nine against one only. It becomes therefore necessary to give the negative to the minority, in all cases, though it be ever so small. Every member must possess it, or he can never be secure that himself and his constituents shall not be sacrificed by all the rest. This is the true ground and original of the *liberum veto* in Poland; but the consequence has been ruin to that noble but ill-constituted republic. One fool, or one knave, one member of the diet, which is a single sovereign assembly, bribed by an intriguing ambassador of some foreign power, has prevented measures the most essential to the defence, safety, and existence of the nation. Hence humiliations and partitions! This also is the reason on which is founded the law of the United Netherlands, that all the seven provinces must be unanimous in the assembly of the states-general; and all the cities and other voting bodies in the assemblies of the separate states. Having no sufficient checks in their uncouth constitution, nor any mediating power possessed of the whole executive, they have been driven to demand unanimity instead of a balance. And this must be done in every government of a single assembly, or the majority will instantly oppress the minority. But what kind of government would that be in the United States of America, or any one of them, that should require unanimity, or allow of the *liberum veto?* It is sufficient to ask the question, for every man will answer it alike. . . .

. . . It is agreed that the people in their assemblies, tempered by another coequal assembly and an executive coequal with either, are the best keepers of their liberties. But it is denied that in one assembly, collective or representative, they are the best keepers. It may be reasonably questioned, whether they are not the worst; be-

cause they are as sure to throw away their liberties, as a monarch or
a senate untempered are to take them; with this additional evil, that
they throw away their morals at the same time; whereas monarchs
and senates sometimes by severity preserve them in some degree.
In a simple democracy, the first citizen and the better sort of citizens are part of the people, and are equally "concerned" with any
others "in the point of liberty." But is it clear that in other forms
of government "the main interest and concernment, both of kings
and grandees, lies either in keeping the people in utter ignorance
what liberty is, or else in allowing and pleasing them only with the
name and shadow of liberty instead of the substance?" It is very
true that knowledge is very apt to make people uneasy under an
arbitrary and oppressive government. But a simple monarch or a
sovereign senate which is not arbitrary and oppressive, though absolute, if such cases can exist, would be interested to promote the
knowledge of the nation. It must, however, be admitted, that
simple governments will rarely if ever favor the dispersion of knowledge among the middle and lower ranks of people. But this is
equally true of simple democracy. The people themselves, if uncontrolled, will never long tolerate a freedom of inquiry, debate, or
writing; their idols must not be reflected on, nor their schemes and
actions scanned, upon pain of popular vengeance, which is not less
terrible than that of despots or sovereign senators.
. . . The way to secure liberty is to place it in the people's hands,
that is, to give them a power at all times to defend it in the legislature and in the courts of justice. But to give the people, uncontrolled, all the prerogatives and rights of supremacy, meaning the
whole executive and judicial power, or even the whole undivided
legislative, is not the way to preserve liberty. In such a government
it is often as great a crime to oppose or decry a popular demagogue,
or any of his principal friends, as in a simple monarchy to oppose a
king, or in a simple aristocracy the senators. The people will not
bear a contemptuous look or disrespectful word; nay, if the style of
your homage, flattery, and adoration, is not as hyperbolical as the
popular enthusiasm dictates, it is construed into disaffection; the
popular cry of envy, jealousy, suspicious temper, vanity, arrogance,
pride, ambition, impatience of a superior, is set up against a man,
and the rage and fury of an ungoverned rabble, stimulated under-
hand by the demagogic despots, breaks out into every kind of insult,

obloquy, and outrage, often ending in murders and massacres, like those of the De Witts, more horrible than any that the annals of despotism can produce.

It is indeed true, that "the interest of freedom is a virgin that every one seeks to deflour; and like a virgin it must be kept, or else (so great is the lust of mankind after dominion) there follows a rape upon the first opportunity." From this it follows, that liberty in the legislature is "more secure in the people's than in any other hands, because they are most concerned in it:" provided you keep the executive power out of their hands entirely, and give the property and liberty of the rich a security in a senate, against the encroachments of the poor in a popular assembly. Without this the rich will never enjoy any liberty, property, reputation, or life, in security. The rich have as clear a right to their liberty and property as the poor. It is essential to liberty that the rights of the rich be secured; if they are not, they will soon be robbed and become poor, and in their turn rob their robbers, and thus neither the liberty or property of any will be regarded. . . .

. . . Is it not an insult to common sense, for a people with the same breath to cry *liberty*, an *abolition of debts*, and *division of goods?* If debts are once abolished, and goods are divided, there will be the same reason for a fresh abolition and division every month and every day. And thus the idle, vicious, and abandoned, will live in constant riot on the spoils of the industrious, virtuous, and deserving. "Powerful and crafty underminers" have nowhere such rare sport as in a simple democracy or single popular assembly. Nowhere, not in the completest despotisms, does human nature show itself so completely depraved, so nearly approaching an equal mixture of brutality and devilism, as in the last stages of such a democracy, and in the beginning of that despotism that always succeeds it.

From A LETTER TO THOMAS BRAND-HOLLIS (JUNE 11, 1790)[1]

The great revolution in France is wonderful, but not supernatural. The hand of Providence is in it, I doubt not, working, however, by natural and ordinary means, such as produced the

[1] In *ibid.*, Vol. IX, pp. 569–571.

reformation in religion in the sixteenth century. That all men have one common nature, is a principle which will now universally prevail, and equal rights and equal duties will in a just sense, I hope, be inferred from it. But equal ranks and equal property never can be inferred from it, any more than equal understanding, agility, vigor, or beauty. Equal laws are all that ever can be derived from human equality. . . . The great and perpetual distinction in civilized societies, has been between the rich, who are few, and the poor, who are many. When the many are masters, they are too unruly, and then the few are too tame, and afraid to speak out the truth. When the few are masters, they are too severe, and then the many are too servile. This is the strict truth. The few have had most art and union, and therefore have generally prevailed in the end. The inference of wisdom from these premises is, that neither the poor nor the rich should ever be suffered to be masters. They should have equal power to defend themselves; and that their power may be always equal, there should be an independent mediator between them, always ready, always able, and always interested to assist the weakest. Equal laws can never be made or maintained without this balance. You see I still hold fast my scales, and weigh every thing in them. The French must finally become my disciples, or rather the disciples of Zeno, or they will have no equal laws, no personal liberty, no property, no lives. . . .

. . . In this country the pendulum has vibrated too far to the popular side, driven by men without experience or judgment, and horrid ravages have been made upon property by arbitrary multitudes or majorities of multitudes. France has severe trials to endure from the same cause. Both have found, or will find, that to place property at the mercy of a majority who have no property, is "committere agnum lupo." My fundamental maxim of government is, never to trust the lamb to the custody of the wolf. If you are not perfectly of my mind at present, I hereby promise and assure you that you will live to see that I am precisely right. Thus arrogantly concludes your assured friend.

From A LETTER TO SAMUEL ADAMS
(OCTOBER 18, 1790)[1]

. . . You agree, that there are undoubtedly principles of political architecture. But, instead of particularizing any of them, you seem to place all your hopes in the universal, or at least more general, prevalence of knowledge and benevolence. I think with you, that knowledge and benevolence ought to be promoted as much as possible; but, despairing of ever seeing them sufficiently general for the security of society, I am for seeking institutions which may supply in some degree the defect. If there were no ignorance, error, or vice, there would be neither principles nor systems of civil or political government.

I am not often satisfied with the opinions of Hume; but in this he seems well founded, that all projects of government, founded in the supposition or expectation of extraordinary degrees of virtue, are evidently chimerical. Nor do I believe it possible, humanly speaking, that men should ever be greatly improved in knowledge or benevolence, without assistance from the principles and system of government.

I am very willing to agree with you in fancying, that in the greatest improvements of society, government will be in the republican form. It is a fixed principle with me, that all good government is and must be republican. But, at the same time, your candor will agree with me, that there is not in lexicography a more fraudulent word. Whenever I use the word *republic* with approbation, I mean a government in which the people have collectively, or by representation, an essential share in the sovereignty. The republican forms of Poland and Venice are much worse, and those of Holland and Bern very little better, than the monarchical form in France before the late revolution. By the republican form, I know you do not mean the plan of Milton, Nedham, or Turgot. For, after a fair trial of its miseries, the simple monarchical form will ever be, as it has ever been, preferred to it by mankind. Are we not, my friend, in danger of rendering the word *republican* unpopular in this country by an indiscreet, indeterminate, and equivocal use of it? The people of England have been obliged to wean themselves

[1] In *ibid.*, Vol. VI, pp. 414–417.

from the use of it, by making it unpopular and unfashionable, because they found it was artfully used by some, and simply understood by others, to mean the government of their interregnum parliament. They found they could not wean themselves from that destructive form of government so entirely, as that a mischievous party would not still remain in favor of it, by any other means than by making the words *republic* and *republican* unpopular. They have succeeded to such a degree, that, with a vast majority of that nation, a republican is as unamiable as a witch, a blasphemer, a rebel, or a tyrant. If, in this country, the word *republic* should be generally understood, as it is by some, to mean a form of government inconsistent with a mixture of three powers, forming a mutual balance, we may depend upon it that such mischievous effects will be produced by the use of it as will compel the people of America to renounce, detest, and execrate it as the English do. With these explanations, restrictions, and limitations, I agree with you in your love of republican governments, but in no other sense.

With you, I have also the honor most perfectly to harmonize in your sentiments of the humanity and wisdom of promoting education in knowledge, virtue, and benevolence. But I think that these will confirm mankind in the opinion of the necessity of preserving and strengthening the dikes against the ocean, its tides and storms. Human appetites, passions, prejudices, and self-love will never be conquered by benevolence and knowledge alone, introduced by human means. The millennium itself neither supposes nor implies it. All civil government is then to cease, and the Messiah is to reign. That happy and holy state is therefore wholly out of this question. You and I agree in the utility of universal education; but will nations agree in it as fully and extensively as we do, and be at the expense of it? We know, with as much certainty as attends any human knowledge, that they will not. We cannot, therefore, advise the people to depend for their safety, liberty, and security, upon hopes and blessings which we know will not fall to their lot. If we do our duty then to the people, we shall not deceive them, but advise them to depend upon what is in their power and will relieve them.

Philosophers, ancient and modern, do not appear to me to have studied nature, the whole of nature, and nothing but nature. Lycurgus's principle was war and family pride; Solon's was what the

people would bear, &c. The best writings of antiquity upon government, those, I mean, of Aristotle, Zeno, and Cicero, are lost. We
have human nature, society, and universal history to observe and
study, and from these we may draw all the real principles which
ought to be regarded. Disciples will follow their masters, and interested partisans their chieftains; let us like it or not, we cannot
help it. But if the true principles can be discovered, and fairly,
fully, and impartially laid before the people, the more light increases, the more the reason of them will be seen, and the more
disciples they will have. Prejudice, passion, and private interest,
which will always mingle in human inquiries, one would think
might be enlisted on the side of truth, at least in the greatest number; for certainly the majority are interested in the truth, if they
could see to the end of all its consequences. "Kings have been
deposed by aspiring nobles." True, and never by any other.
"These" (the nobles, I suppose,) "have waged everlasting war against
the common rights of men." True, when they have been possessed
of the *summa imperii* in one body, without a check. So have the
plebeians; so have the people; so have kings; so has human nature, in
every shape and combination, and so it ever will. But, on the other
hand, the nobles have been essential parties in the preservation of
liberty, whenever and wherever it has existed. In Europe, they
alone have preserved it against kings and people, wherever it has
been preserved; or, at least, with very little assistance from the
people. One hideous despotism, as horrid as that of Turkey, would
have been the lot of every nation of Europe, if the nobles had not
made stands. By nobles, I mean not peculiarly an hereditary nobility, or any particular modification, but the natural and actual
aristocracy among mankind. The existence of this you will not
deny. You and I have seen four noble families rise up in Boston,—
the CRAFTS, GORES, DAWES, and AUSTINS. These are as really a nobility in our town, as the Howards, Somersets, Berties, &c., in England.
Blind, undistinguishing reproaches against the aristocratical part of
mankind, a division which nature has made, and we cannot abolish,
are neither pious nor benevolent. They are as pernicious as they are
false. They serve only to foment prejudice, jealousy, envy, animosity, and malevolence. They serve no ends but those of soph
istry, fraud, and the spirit of party. . . .

must be checks and balances in republican tripartite gov't. People are not educated enough to rule themselves. There must be limits at every turn.

From A LETTER TO JOHN TAYLOR (1814) [1]

I hope my last convinced you that democracy is as restless, as ambitious, as warlike and bloody, as aristocracy or monarchy.

You proceed to say, that I "ought to have placed right before us the effects of these three principles, namely,—democracy, aristocracy, and monarchy, commixed in the wars, rebellions, persecutions, and oppressions of the English form."

Pray, sir, what was the object of my book? [2] I was not writing a history of England, nor of the world. Inattention to this circumstance has been the cause of all the *honest* misapprehensions, misconstructions, and misrepresentations of the whole work. To see at one glance the design of the three volumes, you need only to look at the first page. M. Turgot "was not satisfied with the constitutions which had been formed for the different states of America. By most of them, the customs of England were imitated, without any particular motive. Instead of collecting all authority into one centre, that of the nation, they have established different bodies,— a body of representatives, a council, and a governor,—because there is in England a house of commons, a house of lords, and a king; they endeavor to balance these different powers."

This solemn opinion of M. Turgot, is the object of the whole of the three volumes. M. Turgot had seen only the constitutions of New York, Massachusetts, and Maryland, and the first constitution of Pennsylvania. His principal intention was to censure the three former. From these three the constitution of the United States was afterwards almost entirely drawn.

The drift of my whole work was, to vindicate these three constitutions against the reproaches of that great statesman, philosopher, and really excellent man, whom I well knew, and to defend them against his attacks, and only upon those points on which he had assaulted them. If this fact had been considered, it would have prevented a thousand witticisms and criticisms about the "misnomer," &c.

The points I had to illustrate and to prove, were,—

1. That the people of Massachusetts, New York, and Maryland

---

[1] In *ibid.*, Vol. VI, pp. 486–488, 494–495, 520–521.
[2] *Defence of the Constitutions of Government.*

were not to blame for instituting governors, councils, (or senates) and houses of representatives.

2. That they were not reprehensible for endeavoring to balance those different powers.

3. That they were to be applauded, not reproached, for not "collecting all authority into one centre, that of the nation," in whatever sense those dark, obscure, and incomprehensible words could be understood.

4. Construing these phrases, as it is believed they were intended, to recommend a sovereignty in a single assembly of representatives, that is, a representative of democracy, it was my duty to show that democracy was as unsteady, equally envious, ambitious, avaricious, vain, proud, cruel, and bloody, as aristocracy or monarchy.

5. That an equilibrium of those "different powers" was indispensably necessary to guard and defend the rights, liberties, and happiness of the people against the deleterious, contagious, and pestilential effects of those passions of vanity, pride, ambition, envy, revenge, lust, and cruelty, which domineer more or less in every government that has no BALANCE or an imperfect BALANCE.

6. That it was not an affected imitation of the English government, so much as an attachment to their old colonial forms, in every one of which there had been three branches,—a governor, a council, and a house of representatives,—which, added to the eternal reason and unalterable nature of things, induced the legislators of those three states to adopt their new constitutions.

The design of the three volumes, pursued from the first page of the first to the last page of the last, was to illustrate, elucidate, and demonstrate those six important truths. To illustrate and prove these truths, or to show them to be falsehoods, where can we look but into the heart of man and the history of his heart? In the heart were found those appetites, passions, prejudices, and selfish interests, which ought always to be controlled by reason, conscience, and social affections; but which are never perfectly so controlled, even by any individual, still less by nations and large bodies of men, and less and less, as communities grow larger and larger, more populous, more commercial, more wealthy, and more luxurious. In the history of his heart, a transient glance of the eye was cast over the most conspicuous, remarkable, and celebrated of those nations who had preserved any share of authority to the people, or who had approached the nearest to preserving all authority to the people, or who had mixed the authority of the people with that of patricians, or senates, or councils, or where the executive power had been separated from, or united with the legislative, or where the judicial power had been complicated with either, or separate from both. And it was endeavored to be shown, that those nations had been the happiest who had separated the legislative from the executive power, the judicial from both, and divided the legislative power itself into three branches, thereby producing a balance between the legislative and executive authority, a balance between the branches of the legislature, and a salutary check upon all these powers in the judicial, as had been done in the constitutions of Maryland, New York, and Massachusetts. I had nothing to do with despotisms or simple monarchies, unless it were incidentally, and by way of illustration. . . .

I find it difficult to understand you, when you say that "knowledge and ignorance are fluctuating." Knowledge is unchangeable; and ignorance cannot change, because it is nothing. It is a nonentity. Truth is one, uniform and eternal; knowledge of it cannot fluctuate any more than itself. Ignorance of truth, being a nonentity, cannot, surely, become entity and fluctuate and change like Proteus, or wind, or water. You sport away so merrily upon this topic, that I will have the pleasure of transcribing you. You say, "the aristocracy of superior abilities will be regulated by the extent of the space between knowledge and ignorance; as the space contracts or widens, it will be diminished or increased; and if aristocracy may be thus diminished, it follows that it may be thus destroyed."

What is the amount of this argument? Ignorance may be destroyed and knowledge increased ad infinitum. And do you expect that all men are to become omniscient, like the almighty and omniscient Hindoo, perfect Brahmins? Are your hopes founded upon an expectation that knowledge will one day be equally divided? Will women have as much knowledge as men? Will children have as much as their parents? If the time will never come when all men will have equal knowledge, it seems to follow, that some will know more than others; and that those who know most will have more influence than those who know least, or than those who know half way between the two extremes; and consequently will be aristocrats. "Superior abilities," comprehend abilities acquired by education and study, as well as genius and natural parts; and what a source of inequality and aristocracy is here! Suffer me to dilate a little in this place. Massachusetts has probably educated as many sons to letters, in proportion to her numbers, as any State in the Union, perhaps as any nation, ancient or modern. What proportion do the scholars bear to the whole number of people? I wish I had a catalogue of our Harvard University, that I might state exact numbers. Say that, in almost two hundred years, there have been three or four thousand educated, from perhaps two or three millions of people. Are not these aristocrats? or, in other words, have they not had more influence than any equal number of uneducated men? In fact, these men governed the province from its first settlement; these men have governed, and still govern, the state. These men, in schools, academies, colleges, and universities; these men, in the shape of ministers, lawyers, and physicians; these men, in academies of arts and sciences, in agricultural societies, in historical societies, in medical societies and in antiquarian societies, in banking institutions and in Washington benevolent societies, govern the state, at this twenty-sixth of December, 1814. The more you educate, without a balance in the government, the more aristocratical will the people and the government be. There never can be, in any nation, more than one fifth—no, not one tenth of the men, regularly educated to science and letters. I hope, then, you will acknowledge, that "abilities" form a DISTINCTION and confer a privilege, in fact, though they give no peculiar rights in society. . . .

And after all that can be done to disseminate knowledge, you never can equalize it. The number of laborers must, and will forever be so much more multitudinous than that of the students, that there will always be giants as well as pygmies, the former of which will have more influence than the latter; man for man, and head for head; and, therefore, the former will be aristocrats, and the latter democrats, if not Jacobins or *sans culottes.*

These morsels, and a million others analogous to them, which will easily occur to you, if you will be pleased to give them a careful mastication and rumination, must, I think, convince you, that no practicable or possible advancement of learning can ever equalize knowledge among men to such a degree, that some will not have more influence in society than others; and, consequently, that some will always be aristocrats, and others democrats. You may read the history of all the universities, academies, monasteries of the world, and see whether learning extinguishes human passions or corrects human vices. You will find in them as many parties and factions, as much jealousy and envy, hatred and malice, revenge and intrigue, as you will in any legislative assembly or executive council, the most ignorant city or village. Are not the men of letters,—philosophers, divines, physicians, lawyers, orators, and poets,—all over the world, at perpetual strife with one another? Knowledge, therefore, as well as genius, strength, activity, industry, beauty, and twenty other things, will forever be a natural cause of aristocracy.

From A LETTER TO THOMAS JEFFERSON
(JULY 13, 1813)[1]

It is very true, as you justly observe, I can say nothing new on this or any other subject of government. But when Lafayette harangued you, and me, and John Quincy Adams, through a whole evening, in your hotel in the *Cul de Sac,* at Paris, and developed the plans now in operation to reform France, though I was silent as you was, I then thought I could say something new to him. In plain truth, I was astonished at the grossness of his ignorance of government and history, as I had been for years before, at that of Turgot, Rochefoucauld, Condorcet, and Franklin. This gross ideology of them all first suggested to me the thought and the inclination, which I afterwards executed in London, of writing something upon aristocracy. I was restrained for years by many fearful considerations. Who and what was I? Why, a man of no name or consideration in Europe. The manual exercise of writing was painful and distressing to me, almost like a blow on the elbow or the knee; my style was habitually negligent, unstudied, unpolished; I should make enemies of all the French patriots, the Dutch patriots, the English republicans, dissenters, reformers, call them what you will; and, what came nearer home to my bosom than all the rest, I knew I should give offence to many, if not all, of my best friends in America, and, very probably, destroy all the little popularity I ever had in a country where popularity had more omnipotence than the British parliament assumed. Where should I get the necessary books? What printer or bookseller would undertake to print such hazardous writings? But,

[1] In *ibid.,* Vol. X, pp. 52–54.

when the French assembly of notables met, and I saw that Turgot's "government in one centre, and that centre the nation," a sentence as mysterious or as contradictory as the Athanasian creed, was about to take place; and when I saw that Shays's rebellion was breaking out in Massachusetts; and when I saw that even my obscure name was often quoted in France as an advocate for simple democracy; when I saw that the sympathies in America had caught the French flame, I was determined to wash my own hands as clear as I could of all this foulness. I had then strong forebodings that I was sacrificing all the emoluments of this life; and so it has happened, but not in so great a degree as I apprehended.

In truth, my "Defence of the Constitutions" and "Discourses on Davila," were the cause of that immense unpopularity which fell like the tower of Siloam upon me. Your steady defence of democratical principles, and your invariable favorable opinion of the French revolution, laid the foundation of your unbounded popularity. *Sic transit gloria mundi.*

Now, I will forfeit my life, if you can find one sentiment in my Defence of the Constitutions, or the Discourses on Davila, which, by a fair construction, can favor the introduction of hereditary monarchy or aristocracy into America. They were all written to support and strengthen the Constitution of the United States.

The wood-cutter on Mount Ida, though he was puzzled to find a tree to drop at first, I presume knew how to leave off when he was weary. But I never know when to cease when I begin to write to you.

He seems to have modified his earlier hope for having the Senate representing the moneyed interests (see p 112)

13. JOHN MARSHALL (1755–1835)

MARSHALL was born at Germantown, a small settlement in the frontier region of Virginia. His mother was a Randolph, first cousin of Jefferson's mother. His father, a man of culture and standing in the community, held local offices, served several terms in the Virginia legislature, and was a major in the Revolutionary War. John Marshall also had part in the war, reaching the rank of captain. In an interval of a few months in his military service he attended lectures by Chancellor George Wythe at William and Mary College, and he was admitted to the bar in 1780. He combined a successful practice with an active participation in public affairs. He served briefly as a member of the legislature and the Executive Council of Virginia. From the beginning of his career he was a strong nationalist and was one of the most effective debaters in the hard fight for ratification in the Virginia Convention. Against charges that the Constitution laid the foundations for an aristocracy, Marshall argued that it established only a "well-regulated democracy"; he gave an able exposition of the judiciary article, and in reply to complaints that the political departments of the federal government would assume oppressive powers, he stated (what the express terms of the Constitution did not make plain) that if the Congress should pass a law "not warranted by any of the powers enumerated," federal judges "would declare it void." Fifteen years later he had the opportunity (in *Marbury v. Madison*) to make that statement authoritative.

Marshall was a Federalist party leader in Virginia during the administrations of Washington and Adams. He declined Washington's proposal (in 1795) to appoint him attorney-general, and successive proposals by Adams to make him minister to France, associate justice of the Supreme Court, and secretary of war. He served as a member of the special mission to France to negotiate a settlement of disputes arising out of the French decrees against American shipping ("XYZ" mission of 1797). Late in Adams' presidential term he accepted two distinguished appointments and for over a month held both offices at the same time; for he was United States secretary of state from the summer of 1800 until the expiration of Adams' term the following March fourth, and he took office as chief justice of the United States on January 31, 1801.

Marshall had had no judicial experience prior to his appointment to the Supreme Court; and although he had been a brilliant and successful lawyer, he was, apparently, not widely read in common law and equity jurisprudence. Yet the opinions he rendered during his long term (1801–35) as chief justice, in cases hinging on interpretations of the Constitution, are almost as important as the Constitution itself in establishing the comprehensive system of law we know as "American Constitutional Law." Those decisions defined the places of Congress and the courts in the constitutional system and established now familiar doctrines concerning the Constitution as supreme law, the Supreme Court as final interpreter of the Constitution, and the wide discretion of Congress in choosing the means of executing powers enumerated in that instrument. He cited few precedents; indeed precedents had little bearing on most of the constitutional questions Marshall had to decide. His general method of exposition was that of logical deduction from the words of the Constitution, interpreted in the light of the ends for which the Constitution was instituted. Thus (he said late in his career) in deciding questions in dispute as to the division of powers, he only gave to Congress "those powers which the words of the grant, as usually understood, import, and which are consistent with the general views and objects of the instrument." [1]

Marshall's first important decision establishing the high position of the Supreme Court was delivered in the case of *Marbury v. Madison*. After the bitterly contested election of 1800, the Federalists, who lost control of both the Administration and Congress, decided to strengthen their position in the federal courts by creating a number of judicial offices, to which Federalists could be appointed before the Republicans came into office. One of two judiciary acts passed during the last month of Adams' administration (when Marshall was both chief justice and secretary of state) gave the President power to appoint any number he chose to be justices of the peace in the District of Columbia. President Adams made his nominations for these and the other new judicial offices ("midnight" appointments), the Senate confirmed them, and Marshall, as secretary of state, signed and sealed the commissions. Four of these commissions had not been delivered before Marshall's successor as secretary of state took office. Among these was that of William Marbury, who had been appointed a justice of the peace for the District of Columbia. Marbury and others appealed to the Supreme Court for a writ of mandamus to Secretary of State Madison to compel him to deliver the commissions. They were proceeding under a section of the Judiciary Act of 1789, empowering the Supreme Court to issue writs of mandamus to any "persons holding office, under the authority of the United States."

[1] *Gibbons v. Ogden*, United States Reports, 9 Wheaton 1 (1825), at p. 188.

Marshall's opinion shows how he was able to use the proceedings as a means of laying down constitutional principles giving power to the courts over both the President and Congress. The lower federal courts (although not the Supreme Court) may, Marshall held, be empowered to issue writs against the President's chief assistants; and the courts may nullify acts of Congress.

Lower federal courts had previously exercised the power of invalidating acts of Congress and there had been no widespread criticism of their action. Republican criticism of the action in the Marbury case was directed chiefly at Marshall's dictum that a cabinet officer was subject to mandamus, rather than at his opinion that the Court could invalidate an enactment of Congress. Later Republican criticisms of Marshall were directed against his invalidation of State statutes and against his "loose" construction of the Constitution in *sustaining* powers exercised by Congress. After *Marbury v. Madison* the Court held no enactment of Congress unconstitutional until over a half century later, in the famous Dred Scott case (decided in 1857).

It is of some interest to note that Marshall's predecessor as chief justice, Oliver Ellsworth, had not only had an important part, as a member of the Committee of Detail in the Convention of 1787, in drafting the Constitution, but had also had chief part, as chairman of the Senate Judiciary Committee, in framing the act of 1789, which Marshall's opinion held to be (in one section) violative of the Constitution. It is also of interest that the power of issuing writs of mandamus to officials of the United States government (a power which Marshall held could not be constitutionally exercised by the Supreme Court) had been exercised by the Court on two occasions prior to Marshall's appointment as chief justice.

[See: Edward S. Corwin, *John Marshall and the Constitution* (1919); R. E. Cushman, "Marshall and the Constitution," *Minnesota Law Review*, Vol. V (1920), pp. 1–31; William Draper Lewis, "John Marshall," in W. D. Lewis, ed. *Great American Lawyers*, Vol. II (1907), pp. 313–408; Albert J. Beveridge, *Life of John Marshall*, 4 vols. (1916–19).]

From OPINION OF THE COURT IN
MARBURY V. MADISON (1803)[1]

At the last term on the affidavits then read and filed with the clerk, a rule was granted in this case, requiring the secretary of state to show cause why a mandamus should not issue, directing him to

[1] United States Reports, 1 Cranch 137.

deliver to William Marbury his commission as a justice of the peace for the county of Washington, in the District of Columbia.

No cause has been shown, and the present motion is for a mandamus. The peculiar delicacy of this case, the novelty of some of its circumstances, and the real difficulty attending the points which occur in it, require a complete exposition of the principles on which the opinion to be given by the court is founded.

These principles have been, on the side of the applicant, very ably argued at the bar. In rendering the opinion of the court, there will be some departure in form, though not in substance, from the points stated in that argument.

In the order in which the court has viewed this subject, the following questions have been considered and decided.

1st. Has the applicant a right to the commission he demands?

2d. If he has a right, and that right has been violated, do the laws of his country afford him a remedy?

3d. If they do afford him a remedy, is it a *mandamus* issuing from this court?

The first object of the inquiry is,

1st. Has the applicant a right to the commission he demands?

His right originates in an act of congress passed in February, 1801, concerning the District of Columbia.

After dividing the district into two counties, the 11th section of this law enacts, "that there shall be appointed in and for each of the said counties, such number of discreet persons to be justices of the peace as the president of the United States shall, from time to time, think expedient, to continue in office for five years."

It appears, from the affidavits, that in compliance with this law, a commission for William Marbury, as a justice of the peace for the county of Washington, was signed by John Adams, then President of the United States; after which the seal of the United States was affixed to it; but the commission has never reached the person for whom it was made out.

In order to determine whether he is entitled to this commission, it becomes necessary to inquire whether he has been appointed to the office. For if he has been appointed, the law continues him in office for five years, and he is entitled to the possession of those evidences of office, which, being completed, became his property. . . .

The last act to be done by the president is the signature of the commission. He has then acted on the advice and consent of the senate to his own nomination. The time for deliberation has then passed. He has decided. His judgment, on the advice and consent of the senate concurring with his nomination, has been made, and the officer is appointed. This appointment is evidenced by an open, unequivocal act; and being the last act required from the person making it, necessarily excludes the idea of its being, so far as respects the appointment, an inchoate and incomplete transaction. . . .

It is, therefore, decidedly the opinion of the court, that when a commission has been signed by the President, the appointment is made; and that the commission is complete when the seal of the United States has been affixed to it by the Secretary of State. . . .

Mr. Marbury, then, since his commission was signed by the President, and sealed by the Secretary of State, was appointed; and as the law creating the office, gave the officer a right to hold for five years, independent of the executive, the appointment was not revocable, but vested in the officer legal rights, which are protected by the laws of his country.

To withhold his commission, therefore, is an act deemed by the court not warranted by law, but violative of a vested legal right.

This brings us to the second inquiry; which is,

2d. If he has a right, and that right has been violated, do the laws of his country afford him a remedy?

The very essence of civil liberty certainly consists in the right of every individual to claim the protection of the laws, whenever he receives an injury. One of the first duties of government is to afford that protection. . . .

The government of the United States has been emphatically termed a government of laws, and not of men. It will certainly cease to deserve this high appellation, if the laws furnish no remedy for the violation of a vested legal right.

If this obloquy is to be cast on the jurisprudence of our country, it must arise from the peculiar character of the case.

It behooves us, then, to inquire whether there be in its composition any ingredient which shall exempt it from legal investigation, or exclude the injured party from legal redress. In pursuing this inquiry the first question which presents itself is, whether this can be arranged with that class of cases which come under the description of *damnum absque injuria*—a loss without an injury.

This description of cases never has been considered, and it is believed never can be considered, as comprehending offices of trust, of honor, or of profit. The office of justice of peace in the District of Columbia is such an office; it is therefore worthy of the attention and guardianship of the laws. It has received that attention and guardianship. It has been created by special act of congress, and has been secured, so far as the laws can give security, to the person appointed to fill it, for five years. It is not, then, on account of the worthlessness of the thing pursued, that the injured party can be alleged to be without remedy.

Is it in the nature of the transaction? Is the act of delivering or withholding a commission to be considered as a mere political act, belonging to the executive department alone, for the performance of which entire confidence is placed by our constitution in the supreme executive; and for any misconduct respecting which, the injured individual has no remedy?

That there may be such cases is not to be questioned; but that every act of duty, to be performed in any of the great departments of government, constitutes such a case, is not to be admitted. . . .

The conclusion from this reasoning is, that where the heads of departments are the political or confidential agents of the executive, merely to execute the will of the President, or rather to act in cases in which the executive possesses a constitutional or legal discretion, nothing can be more perfectly clear than that their acts are only politically examinable. But where a specific duty is assigned by law, and individual rights depend upon the performance of that duty, it seems equally clear that the individual who considers himself injured, has a right to resort to the laws of his country for a remedy.

If this be the rule, let us inquire how it applies to the case under the consideration of the court.

The power of nominating to the senate, and the power of appointing the person nominated, are political powers, to be exercised by the President according to his own discretion. When he has made an appointment, he has exercised his whole power, and his discretion has been completely applied to the case. . . .

That question has been discussed, and the opinion is, that the latest point of time which can be taken as that at which the appointment was complete, and evidenced, was when, after the signature of the President, the seal of the United States was affixed to the commission.

It is, then, the opinion of the Court,

1st. That by signing the commission of Mr. Marbury, the President of the United States appointed him a justice of peace for the county of Washington, in the District of Columbia; and that the seal of the United States, affixed thereto by the Secretary of State, is conclusive testimony of the verity of the signature, and of the completion of the appointment; and that the appointment conferred on him a legal right to the office for the space of five years.

2d. That, having this legal title to the office, he has a consequent right to the commission; a refusal to deliver which is a plain violation of that right, for which the laws of his country afford him a remedy.

It remains to be inquired whether,

3d. He is entitled to the remedy for which he applies. This depends on,

1st. The nature of the writ applied for; and,

2d. The power of this court.

1st. The nature of the writ.

Blackstone, in the 3d volume of his Commentaries, page 110, defines a mandamus to be "a command issuing in the king's name from the court of king's bench, and directed to any person, corporation, or inferior court of judicature within the king's dominions, requiring them to do some particular thing therein specified, which appertains to their office and duty, and which the court of king's bench has previously determined, or at least supposes, to be consonant to right and justice." . . .

Still, to render the mandamus a proper remedy, the officer to whom it is to be directed, must be one to whom, on legal principles, such writ may be directed; and the person applying for it must be without any other specific and legal remedy.

1st. With respect to the officer to whom it would be directed. The intimate political relation subsisting between the President of the United States and the heads of departments, necessarily renders any legal investigation of the acts of one of those high officers peculiarly irksome, as well as delicate; and excites some hesitation with respect to the propriety of entering into such investigation. Impressions are often received without much reflection or examination, and it is not wonderful that in such a case as this the assertion, by an individual, of his legal claims in a court of justice, to which claims it is the duty of that court to attend, should at first view be considered by some, as an attempt to intrude into the cabinet, and to intermeddle with the prerogatives of the executive.

It is scarcely necessary for the court to disclaim all pretensions to such jurisdiction. An extravagance, so absurd and excessive, could not have been entertained for a moment. The province of the court is, solely, to decide on the rights of individuals, not to inquire how the executive, or executive officers, perform duties in which they have a discretion. Questions in their nature political, or which are, by the constitution and laws, submitted to the executive, can never be made in this court.

But, if this be not such a question; if, so far from being an intrusion into the secrets of the cabinet, it respects a paper which, according to law, is upon record, and to a copy of which the law gives a right, on the payment of ten cents; if it be no intermeddling with a subject over which the executive can be considered as having exercised any control; what is there in the exalted station of the officer, which shall bar a citizen from asserting, in a court of justice, his legal rights, or shall forbid a court to listen to the claim, or to issue a mandamus directing the performance of a duty, not depending on executive discretion, but on particular acts of congress, and the general principles of law?

If one of the heads of departments commits any illegal act, under colour of his office, by which an individual sustains an injury, it cannot be pretended that his office alone exempts him from being sued in the ordinary mode of proceedings, and being compelled to obey the judgment of the law. How, then, can his office exempt him from this particular mode of deciding on the legality of his conduct, if the case be such a case as would, were any other individual the party complained of, authorize the process?

It is not by the office of the person to whom the writ is directed, but the nature of the thing to be done, that the propriety or impropriety of issuing a mandamus is to be determined. Where the head of a department acts in a case in which executive discretion is to be exercised; in which he is the mere organ of executive will; it is again repeated, that any application to a court to control, in any respect, his conduct would be rejected without hesitation.

But where he is directed by law to do a certain act affecting the absolute rights of individuals, in the performance of which he is not placed under the particular direction of the President, and the performance of which the President cannot lawfully forbid, and therefore is never presumed to have forbidden; as for example, to record a commission, or a patent for land, which has received all the legal solemnities; or to give a copy of such record; in such cases, it is not perceived on what ground the courts of the country are further excused from the duty of giving judgment that right be done to an injured individual, than if the same services were to be performed by a person not the head of a department. . . .

This, then, is a plain case for a mandamus, either to deliver the commission, or a copy of it from the record; and it only remains to be inquired,

Whether it can issue from this court.

The act to establish the judicial courts of the United States authorizes the Supreme Court "to issue writs of mandamus in cases warranted by the principles and usages of law, to any courts appointed, or persons holding office, under the authority of the United States."

The Secretary of State, being a person holding an office under the authority of the United States, is precisely within the letter of the description, and if this court is not authorized to issue a writ of mandamus to such an officer, it must be because the law is unconstitutional, and therefore absolutely incapable of conferring the authority, and assigning the duties which its words purport to confer and assign.

The constitution vests the whole judicial power of the United States in one Supreme Court, and such inferior courts as congress shall, from time to time, ordain and establish. This power is expressly extended to all cases arising under the laws of the United States; and, consequently, in some form, may be exercised over the present case; because the right claimed is given by a law of the United States.

In the distribution of this power it is declared that "the Supreme Court shall have original jurisdiction in all cases affecting ambassadors, other public ministers and consuls, and those in which a state shall be a party. In all other cases, the Supreme Court shall have appellate jurisdiction."

It has been insisted, at the bar, that as the original grant of jurisdiction, to the Supreme and inferior courts, is general, and the clause, assigning original jurisdiction to the Supreme Court, contains no negative or restrictive words, the power remains to the legislature, to assign original jurisdiction to that court in other cases than those specified in the article which has been recited; provided those cases belong to the judicial power of the United States.

If it had been intended to leave it in the discretion of the legislature to apportion the judicial power between the supreme and inferior courts according to the will of that body, it would certainly have been useless to have proceeded further than to have defined the judicial power, and the tribunals in which it should be vested. The subsequent part of the section is mere surplusage, is entirely without meaning, if such is to be the construction. If congress remains at liberty to give this court appellate jurisdiction, where the constitution has declared their jurisdiction shall be original; and original jurisdiction where the constitution has declared it shall be appellate; the distribution of jurisdiction, made in the constitution, is form without substance.

Affirmative words are often, in their operation, negative of other objects than those affirmed; and in this case, a negative or exclusive sense must be given to them, or they have no operation at all.

It cannot be presumed that any clause in the constitution is intended to be without effect; and, therefore, such a construction is inadmissible, unless the words require it.

If the solicitude of the convention, respecting our peace with foreign powers, induced a provision that the Supreme Court should take original jurisdiction in cases which might be supposed to affect them; yet the clause would have proceeded no further than to provide for such cases, if no further restriction on the powers of congress had been intended. That they should have appellate jurisdiction in all other cases, with such exceptions as congress might make, is no restriction; unless the words be deemed exclusive of original jurisdiction.

When an instrument organizing fundamentally a judicial system, divides it into one supreme, and so many inferior courts as the legislature may ordain and establish; then enumerates its powers, and proceeds so far to distribute them, as to define the jurisdiction of the Supreme Court by declaring the cases in which it shall take original jurisdiction, and that in others it shall take appellate jurisdiction; the plain import of the words seems to be, that in one class of cases its jurisdiction is original, and not appellate; in the other it is appellate, and not original. If any other construction would render the clause inoperative, that is an additional reason for rejecting such other construction, and for adhering to their obvious meaning.

To enable this court, then, to issue a mandamus, it must be shown to be an exercise of appellate jurisdiction, or to be necessary to enable them to exercise appellate jurisdiction.

It has been stated at the bar that the appellate jurisdiction may be exercised in a variety of forms, and that if it be the will of the legislature that a mandamus should be used for that purpose, that will must be obeyed. This is true, yet the jurisdiction must be appellate, not original.

It is the essential criterion of appellate jurisdiction, that it revises and corrects the proceedings in a cause already instituted, and does not create that cause. Although, therefore, a mandamus may be directed to courts, yet to issue such a writ to an officer for the delivery of a paper, is in effect the same as to sustain an original action for that paper, and, therefore, seems not to belong to appellate, but to original jurisdiction. Neither is it necessary in such a case as this, to enable the court to exercise its appellate jurisdiction.

The authority, therefore, given to the Supreme Court, by the act establishing the judicial courts of the United States, to issue writs of mandamus to public officers, appears not to be warranted by the constitution; and it becomes necessary to inquire whether a jurisdiction so conferred can be exercised.

The question, whether an act, repugnant to the constitution, can become the law of the land, is a question deeply interesting to the United States; but, happily, not of an intricacy proportioned to its interest. It seems only necessary to recognize certain principles, supposed to have been long and well established, to decide it.

That the people have an original right to establish, for their future government, such principles, as, in their opinion, shall most conduce to their own happiness is the basis on which the whole American fabric has been erected. The exercise of this original right is a very great exertion; nor can it, nor ought it, to be frequently repeated. The principles, therefore, so established, are deemed fundamental. And as the authority from which they proceed is supreme, and can seldom act, they are designed to be permanent.

This original and supreme will organizes the government, and assigns to different departments their respective powers. It may either stop here, or establish certain limits not to be transcended by those departments.

The government of the United States is of the latter description. The powers of the legislature are defined and limited; and that those limits may not be mistaken, or forgotten, the constitution is written. To what purpose are powers limited, and to what purpose is that limitation committed to writing, if these limits may, at any time, be passed by those intended to be restrained? The distinction between a government with limited and unlimited powers is abolished, if those limits do not confine the persons on whom they are imposed, and if acts prohibited and acts allowed, are of equal obligation. It is a proposition too plain to be contested, that the constitution controls any legislative act repugnant to it; or, that the legislature may alter the constitution by an ordinary act.

Between these alternatives there is no middle ground. The constitution is either a superior paramount law, unchangeable by ordinary means, or it is on a level with ordinary legislative acts, and, like other acts, is alterable when the legislature shall please to alter it.

If the former part of the alternative be true, then a legislative act contrary to the constitution is not law: if the latter part be true, then written constitutions are absurd attempts, on the part of the people, to limit a power in its own nature illimitable.

Certainly all those who have framed written constitutions contemplate them as forming the fundamental and paramount law of the nation, and, consequently, the theory of every such government must be, that an act of the legislature, repugnant to the constitution, is void.

This theory is essentially attached to a written constitution, and, is consequently, to be considered, by this court, as one of the fundamental principles of our society. It is not therefore to be lost sight of in the further consideration of this subject.

If an act of the legislature, repugnant to the constitution, is void, does it, notwithstanding its invalidity, bind the courts, and oblige them to give it effect? Or, in other words, though it be not law, does it constitute a rule as operative as if it was a law? This would be to overthrow in fact what was established in theory; and would seem, at first view, an absurdity too gross to be insisted on. It shall, however, receive a more attentive consideration.

It is emphatically the province and duty of the judicial department to say what the law is. Those who apply the rule to particular cases, must of necessity expound and interpret that rule. If two laws conflict with each other, the courts must decide on the operation of each.

So if a law be in opposition to the constitution; if both the law and the constitution apply to a particular case, so that the court must either decide that case conformably to the law, disregarding the constitution; or conformably to the constitution, disregarding the law; the court must determine which of these conflicting rules governs the case. This is of the very essence of judicial duty.

If, then, the courts are to regard the constitution, and the constitution is superior to any ordinary act of the legislature, the constitution, and not such ordinary act, must govern the case to which they both apply.

Those, then, who controvert the principle that the constitution is to be considered, in court, as a paramount law, are reduced to the necessity of maintaining that courts must close their eyes on the constitution, and see only the law.

This doctrine would subvert the very foundation of all written constitution. It would declare that an act which, according to the principles and theory of our government, is entirely void, is yet, in practice, completely obligatory. It would declare that if the legislature shall do what is expressly forbidden, such act, notwithstanding the express prohibition, is in reality effectual. It would be giving to the legislature a practical and real omnipotence, with the same breath which professes to restrict their powers within narrow limits. It is prescribing limits, and declaring that those limits may be passed at pleasure.

That it thus reduces to nothing what we have deemed the greatest improvement on political institutions—a written constitution—would of itself be sufficient, in America, where written constitutions have been viewed with so much reverence, for rejecting the construction. But the peculiar expressions of the constitution of the United States furnish additional arguments in favour of its rejection.

The judicial power of the United States is extended to all cases arising under the constitution.

Could it be the intention of those who gave this power, to say that in using it the constitution should not be looked into? That a case arising under the constitution should be decided without examining the instrument under which it arises?

This is too extravagant to be maintained.

In some cases, then, the constitution must be looked into by the judges. And if they can open it at all, what part of it are they forbidden to read or to obey?

There are many other parts of the constitution which serve to illustrate this subject.

It is declared that "no tax or duty shall be laid on articles exported from any state." Suppose a duty on the export of cotton, of tobacco, or of flour; and a suit instituted to recover it. Ought judgment to be rendered in such a case? ought the judges to close their eyes on the constitution, and only see the law?

The constitution declares "that no bill of attainder or *ex post facto* law shall be passed."

If, however, such a bill should be passed, and a person should be prosecuted under it; must the court condemn to death those victims whom the constitution endeavours to preserve?

"No person," says the constitution, "shall be convicted of treason unless on the testimony of two witnesses to the same overt act, or on confession in open court."

Here the language of the constitution is addressed especially to the courts. It prescribes, directly for them, a rule of evidence not to be departed from. If the legislature should change that rule, and declare *one* witness, or a confession *out* of court, sufficient for conviction, must the constitutional principle yield to the legislative act?

From these, and many other selections which might be made, it is apparent, that the framers of the constitution contemplated that instrument as a rule for the government of *courts*, as well as of the legislature.

Why otherwise does it direct the judges to take an oath to support it? This oath certainly applies in an especial manner, to their conduct in their official character. How immoral to impose it on them, if they were to be used as the instruments, and the knowing instruments, for violating what they swear to support!

The oath of office, too, imposed by the legislature, is completely demonstrative of the legislative opinion on this subject. It is in these words: "I do solemnly swear that I will administer justice without respect to persons, and do equal right to the poor and to the rich; and that I will faithfully and impartially discharge all the duties incumbent on me as   , according to the best of my abilities and understanding, agreeably to the *constitution*, and laws of the United States."

Why does a judge swear to discharge his duties agreeably to the constitution of the United States, if that constitution forms no rule for his government? if it is closed upon him, and cannot be inspected by him?

If such be the real state of things, this is worse than solemn mockery. To prescribe, or to take this oath, becomes equally a crime.

It is also not entirely unworthy of observation, that in declaring what shall be the *supreme* law of the land, the *constitution* itself is first mentioned; and not the laws of the United States generally, but those only which shall be made in *pursuance* of the constitution, have that rank.

Thus, the particular phraseology of the constitution of the United States confirms and strengthens the principle, supposed to be essential to all written constitutions, that a law repugnant to the constitution is void; and that *courts*, as well as other departments, are bound by that instrument.

The rule must be discharged.

14. From *THOMAS JEFFERSON'S COMMENTS ON THE FEDERAL JUDICIARY IN LETTERS* (1807–21) *AND HIS AUTOBIOGRAPHY*

[Marshall's constitutional opinions, in *Marbury v. Madison* and later cases, raised important issues concerning the distribution of power among the three departments of government and evoked emphatic comments by the Jeffersonians, who charged that the sort of judicial supremacy established by Marshall's doctrine was not compatible with a genuinely democratic government.]

[To George Hay (June 2, 1807) [1]] While Burr's case [2] is depending before the court, I will trouble you, from time to time, with what occurs to me. I observe that the case of Marbury v. Madison has been cited, and I think it material to stop at the threshold the citing that case as authority, and to have it denied to be law. 1. Because the judges, in the outset, disclaimed all cognizance of the case, altho' they then went on to say what would have been their opinion, had they had cognizance of it. This, then, was confessedly an extrajudicial opinion, and, as such, of no authority. 2. Because, had it been judicially pronounced, it would have been against law; for to a commission, a deed, a bond, *delivery* is essential to give validity. Until, therefore, the commission is delivered out of the hands of the Executive & his agents, it is not his deed. He may withhold or cancel it at pleasure, as he might his private deed in the same situation. The Constitution intended that the three great branches of the government should be co-ordinate, & independent of each other. As to acts, therefore, which are to be done by either, it has given no controul to another branch. A judge, I presume, cannot sit on a bench without a commission, or a record of a commission; & the Constitution having given to the judiciary branch no means of compelling the executive either to *deliver* a commission, or to make a record of it, shews it did not intend to give the judiciary

[1] In *The Writings of Thomas Jefferson*. ed. by Paul Leicester Ford, Vol. IX, pp. 53–54.

[2] The trial of Aaron Burr for treason, before Chief Justice Marshall sitting as trial judge in the United States District Court.

that controul over the executive, but that it should remain in the power of the latter to do it or not. Where different branches have to act in their respective lines, finally & without appeal, under any law, they may give to it different and opposite constructions. . . .

On this construction I have hitherto acted; on this I shall ever act, and maintain it with the powers of the government, against any control which may be attempted by the judges, in subversion of the independence of the executive & Senate within their peculiar department. I presume, therefore, that in a case where our decision is by the Constitution the supreme one, & that which can be carried into effect, it is the constitutionally authoritative one, and that that by the judges was *coram non judice*, & unauthoritative, because it cannot be carried into effect. I have long wished for a proper occasion to have the gratuitous opinion in Marbury v. Madison brought before the public, & denounced as not law; & I think the present a fortunate one, because it occupies such a place in the public attention. I should be glad, therefore, if, in noticing that case, you could take occasion to express the determination of the executive, that the doctrines of that case were given extrajudicially & against law, and that their reverse will be the rule of action with the executive. If this opinion should not be your own, I would wish it to be expressed merely as that of the executive. If it is your own also, you would of course give to the arguments such a development as a case, incidental only, might render proper. I salute you with friendship and respect.

[To W. H. Torrance (June 11, 1815)[1]] . . . The . . . question, whether the judges are invested with exclusive authority to decide on the constitutionality of a law, has been heretofore a subject of consideration with me in the exercise of official duties. Certainly there is not a word in the constitution which has given that power to them more than to the executive or legislative branches. Questions of property, of character and of crime being ascribed to the judges, through a definite course of legal proceeding, laws involving such questions belong, of course, to them; and as they decide on them ultimately and without appeal, they of course decide *for themselves*. The constitutional validity of the law or laws again prescribing executive action, and to be administered by that branch ultimately and without appeal, the executive must de-

[1] In *ibid.*, Vol. IX, pp. 517–519.

we observe the law was passed with provisions which go beyond the constitution. Therefore we have no right to judge.

There is no situation provided for by guys who should be safeguarded by writs of mandamus.

Executive
is Judge

cide for *themselves* also, whether, under the constitution, they are valid or not. So also as to laws governing the proceedings of the legislature, that body must judge *for itself* the constitutionality of the law, and equally without appeal or control from its co-ordinate branches. And, in general, that branch which is to act ultimately, and without appeal, on any law, is the rightful expositor of the validity of the law, uncontrolled by the opinions of the other co-ordinate authorities. It may be said that contradictory decisions may arise in such case, and produce inconvenience. This is possible, and is a necessary failing in all human proceedings. Yet the prudence of the public functionaries, and authority of public opinion,

legislature
is
Judge

will generally produce accommodation. . . . But there is another opinion entertained by some men of such judgment and information as to lessen my confidence in my own. That is, that the legislature alone is the exclusive expounder of the sense of the constitution, in every part of it whatever. And they allege in its support, that this branch has authority to impeach and punish a member of

but see

Art II

sec 2

either of the others acting contrary to its declaration of the sense of the constitution. It may indeed be answered, that an act may still be valid although the party is punished for it, right or wrong. However, this opinion which ascribes exclusive exposition to the legislature, merits respect for its safety, there being in the body of the nation a control over them, which, if expressed by rejection on the subsequent exercise of their elective franchise, enlists public opinion against their exposition, and encourages a judge or executive on a future occasion to adhere to their former opinion. Between these two doctrines, every one has a right to choose, and I know of no third meriting any respect. . . .

[To Judge Spencer Roane (September 6, 1819) [1]] I had read in the Enquirer, and with great approbation, the pieces signed Hampden, and have read them again with redoubled approbation, in the copies you have been so kind as to send me. I subscribe to every tittle of them. They contain the true principles of the revolution of 1800, for that was as real a revolution in the principles of our government as that of 1776 was in its form; not effected indeed by the sword, as that, but by the rational and peaceable instrument of reform, the suffrage of the people. The nation declared its will by dismissing functionaries of one principle, and electing those of an-

[1] In *ibid.*, Vol. X, pp. 140–143.

other, in the two branches, executive and legislative, submitted to their election. Over the judiciary department, the constitution had deprived them of their control. That, therefore, has continued the reprobated system, and although new matter has been occasionally incorporated into the old, yet the leaven of the old mass seems to assimilate to itself the new, and after twenty years' confirmation of the federal system by the voice of the nation, declared through the medium of elections, we find the judiciary on every occasion, still driving us into consolidation.

In denying the right they usurp of exclusively explaining the constitution, I go further than you do, if I understand rightly your quotation from the Federalist, of an opinion that "the judiciary is the last resort in relation *to the other departments* of the government, but not in relation to the rights of the parties to the compact under which the judiciary is derived." If this opinion be sound, then indeed is our constitution a complete *felo de se*. For intending to establish three departments, co-ordinate and independent, that they might check and balance one another, it has given, according to this opinion, to one of them alone, the right to prescribe rules for the government of the others, and to that one too, which is unelected by, and independent of the nation. . . . The constitution, on this hypothesis, is a mere thing of wax in the hands of the judiciary, which they may twist and shape into any form they please. . . . My construction of the constitution is very different from that you quote. It is that each department is truly independent of the others, and has an equal right to decide for itself what is the meaning of the constitution in the cases submitted to its action; and especially, where it is to act ultimately and without appeal. . . .

[To William Charles Jarvis (September 28, 1820) [1]] I thank you, Sir, for the copy of your Republican which you have been so kind as to send me . . . You seem, in pages 84 and 148, to consider the judges as the ultimate arbiters of all constitutional questions; a very dangerous doctrine indeed, and one which would place us under the despotism of an oligarchy. Our judges are as honest as other men, and not more so. They have, with others, the same passions for party, for power, and the privilege of their corps. Their maxim is "*boni judicis est ampliare jurisdictionem*," and their power the more dangerous as they are in office for life, and not responsible, as

[1] In *ibid.*, Vol. X, pp. 160–161.

the other functionaries are, to the elective control. The constitution has erected no such single tribunal, knowing that to whatever hands confided, with the corruptions of time and party, its members would become despots. It has more wisely made all the departments co-equal and co-sovereign within themselves. If the legislature fails to pass laws for a census, for paying the judges and other officers of government, for establishing a militia, for naturalization as prescribed by the constitution, or if they fail to meet in congress, the judges cannot issue their mandamus to them; if the President fails to supply the place of a judge, to appoint other civil or military officers, to issue requisite commissions, the judges cannot force him. They can issue their mandamus or distringas to no executive or legislative officer to enforce the fulfilment of their official duties, any more than the president or legislature may issue orders to the judges or their officers. . . . I know no safe depository of the ultimate powers of the society but the people themselves; and if we think them not enlightened enough to exercise their control with a wholesome discretion, the remedy is not to take it from them, but to inform their discretion by education. This is the true corrective of abuses of constitutional power. . . .

[To Thomas Ritchie (December 25, 1820) [1]] On my return home after a long absence, I find here your favor of November the 23d, with Colonel Taylor's "Construction Construed," which you have been so kind as to send me, in the name of the author as well as yourself. . . . If there be anything amiss . . . in the present state of our affairs, as the formidable deficit lately unfolded to us indicates, I ascribe it to the inattention of Congress to their duties, to their unwise dissipation and waste of the public contributions. They seemed, some little while ago, to be at a loss for objects whereon to throw away the supposed fathomless funds of the treasury. . . .

But it is not from this branch of government we have most to fear. Taxes and short elections will keep them right. The judiciary of the United States is the subtle corps of sappers and miners constantly working under ground to undermine the foundations of our confederated fabric. They are construing our constitution from a co-ordination of a general and special government to a general and supreme one alone. . . . Having found, from experience, that im-

[1] In *ibid.*, Vol. X, pp. 169–171.

peachment is an impracticable thing, a mere scare-crow, they consider themselves secure for life; they sculk from responsibility to public opinion, the only remaining hold on them . . . A judiciary independent of a king or executive alone, is a good thing; but independence of the will of the nation is a solecism, at least in a republican government. . . .

[*Autobiography*[1]] But there was another amendment [*i.e.* a provision which Jefferson, in 1821, believed the Convention of 1787 should have incorporated in the Constitution] of which none of us thought at the time and in the omission of which lurks the germ that is to destroy this happy combination of National powers in the General government for matters of National concern, and independent powers in the states for what concerns the states severally. In England it was a great point gained at the Revolution, that the commissions of the judges, which had hitherto been during pleasure, should thenceforth be made during good behavior. A Judiciary dependent on the will of the King had proved itself the most oppressive of all tools in the hands of that Magistrate. Nothing then could be more salutary than a change there to the tenure of good behavior; and the question of good behavior left to the vote of a simple majority in the two houses of parliament. Before the revolution we were all good English Whigs, cordial in their free principles, and in their jealousies of their executive Magistrate. These jealousies are very apparent in all our state constitutions; and, in the general government in this instance, we have gone even beyond the English caution, by requiring a vote of two thirds in one of the Houses for removing a judge; a vote so impossible where any defence is made, before men of ordinary prejudices & passions, that our judges are effectually independent of the nation. But this ought not to be. I would not indeed make them dependant on the Executive authority, as they formerly were in England; but I deem it indispensable to the continuance of this government that they should be submitted to some practical & impartial controul: and that this, to be imparted, must be compounded of a mixture of state and federal authorities. It is not enough that honest men are appointed judges. All know the influence of interest on the mind of man, and how unconsciously his judgment is warped by that influence. To this bias add that of the esprit de corps, of their peculiar maxim and

[1] In *ibid.*, Vol. I, pp. 111–114.

creed that "it is the office of a good judge to enlarge his jurisdiction," and the absence of responsibility, and how can we expect impartial decision between the General government, of which they are themselves so eminent a part, and an individual state from which they have nothing to hope or fear. We have seen too that, contrary to all correct example, they are in the habit of going out of the question before them, to throw an anchor ahead and grapple further hold for future advances of power. They are then in fact the corps of sappers & miners, steadily working to undermine the independant rights of the States, & to consolidate all power in the hands of that government in which they have so important a freehold estate. But it is not by the consolidation, or concentration of powers, but by their distribution, that good government is effected. Were not this great country already divided into states, that division must be made, that each might do for itself what concerns itself directly, and what it can so much better do than a distant authority. Every state again is divided into counties, each to take care of what lies within it's local bounds; each county again into townships or wards, to manage minuter details; and every ward into farms, to be governed each by it's individual proprietor. Were we directed from Washington when to sow, & when to reap, we should soon want bread. It is by this partition of cares, descending in gradation from general to particular, that the mass of human affairs may be best managed for the good and prosperity of all. I repeat that I do not charge the judges with wilful and ill-intentioned error; but honest error must be arrested where it's toleration leads to public ruin. As, for the safety of society, we commit honest maniacs to Bedlam, so judges should be withdrawn from their bench, whose erroneous biases are leading us to dissolution. It may indeed injure them in fame or in fortune; but it saves the republic, which is the first and supreme law.

15. FISHER AMES (1758–1808)

AMES was born in Dedham, Massachusetts, son of Nathaniel Ames, an innkeeper, physician, and publisher of a famous almanac. He was graduated from Harvard in his sixteenth year, taught in the local school for a few years, read widely, studied law, and was admitted to the bar in 1781. He soon became more interested in public affairs than in the practice of law. Alarmed by Shays' Rebellion (1786–87) and by what he considered to be reckless policies of the new State governments, he expressed his views in long essays in the Boston newspapers, pointing out the threats of popular government to public order and the security of private property. He was a member of the Massachusetts ratifying convention, served a year in the State legislature, and was a member of the House of Representatives in the first four terms of Congress. A brilliant debater, he ably advocated Federalist measures on the floor of the House, particularly in his famous speech supporting appropriations for the execution of the Jay treaty of 1794.

He retired from political office voluntarily in 1797 and a few years later declined the presidency of Harvard. He continued his incisive discussion of public affairs. He warmly defended the Sedition Act of 1798, denounced the foreign policies of Jefferson and Madison, and after Jefferson's election in 1800, warned of the imminence of anarchy. He had a vivid and emphatic style, drew his illustrations widely from ancient and modern history, and was regarded as a leading theoretical spokesman for the Federalists.

[See: John Quincy Adams, *Review of the Works of Fisher Ames* (1809); Samuel E. Morison, "Squire Ames and Doctor Ames," *New England Quarterly*, Vol. I (1928), pp. 3–31; Seth Ames, bibliographical note in *Works of Fisher Ames* (1854), Vol. I, pp. 1–28; Vernon L. Parrington, *Main Currents of American Thought*, Vol. II (1927), pp. 279–288.]

From THE DANGERS OF AMERICAN LIBERTY (1805)[1]

I fear that the future fortunes of our country no longer depend on counsel. We have persevered in our errors too long to change our

[1] In *The Works of Fisher Ames*, ed. by Seth Ames, 2 vols. (Boston, 1854), Vol. II, pp. 344–399; at 345–348, 361, 393–395, 397–399. By courtesy of Little, Brown & Company.

propensities by now enlightening our convictions. The political sphere, like the globe we tread upon, never stands still, but with a silent swiftness accomplishes the revolutions which, we are too ready to believe, are effected by our wisdom, or might have been controlled by our efforts. There is a kind of fatality in the affairs of republics, that eludes the foresight of the wise as much as it frustrates the toils and sacrifices of the patriot and the hero. Events proceed, not as they were expected or intended, but as they are impelled by the irresistible laws of our political existence. Things inevitable happen, and we are astonished, as if they were miracles, and the course of nature had been overpowered or suspended to produce them. Hence it is, that, till lately, more than half our countrymen believed our public tranquillity was firmly established, and that our liberty did not merely rest upon dry land, but was wedged, or rather rooted high above the flood in the rocks of granite, as immovably as the pillars that prop the universe. They, or at least the discerning of them, are at length no less disappointed than terrified to perceive that we have all the time floated, with a fearless and unregarded course, down the stream of events, till we are now visibly drawn within the revolutionary suction of Niagara, and every thing that is liberty will be dashed to pieces in the descent. . . .

There is of course a large portion of our citizens who will not believe, even on the evidence of facts, that any public evils exist, or are impending. They deride the apprehensions of those who foresee that licentiousness will prove, as it ever has proved, fatal to liberty. They consider her as a nymph, who need not be coy to keep herself pure, but that on the contrary, her chastity will grow robust by frequent scuffles with her seducers. They say, while a faction is a minority it will remain harmless by being outvoted; and if it should become a majority, all its acts, however profligate or violent, are then legitimate. For with the democrats the people is a sovereign who can do no wrong, even when he respects and spares no existing right, and whose voice, however obtained or however counterfeited, bears all the sanctity and all the force of a living divinity.

Where, then, it will be asked, in a tone both of menace and of triumph, can the people's dangers lie, unless it be with the persecuted federalists. They are the partisans of monarchy, who propagate their principles in order, as soon as they have increased

[handwritten margin note:] There must be restraint

[handwritten note at bottom:] Is it worse to have a rampant majority to a king.

their sect, to introduce a king; for by this only avenue they foretell his approach. Is it possible the people should ever be their own enemies? If all government were dissolved to-day, would they not reëstablish it to-morrow, with no other prejudice to the public liberty than some superfluous fears of its friends, some abortive projects of its enemies? Nay, would not liberty rise resplendent with the light of fresh experience, and coated in the sevenfold mail of constitutional amendments?

These opinions are fiercely maintained, not only as if there were evidence to prove them, but as if it were a merit to believe them, by men who tell you that in the most desperate extremity of faction or usurpation we have an unfailing resource in the good sense of the nation. They assure us there is at least as much wisdom in the people as in these ingenious tenets of their creed.

For any purpose, therefore, of popular use or general impression, it seems almost fruitless to discuss the question, whether our public liberty can subsist, and what is to be the condition of that awful futurity to which we are hastening. The clamors of party are so loud, and the resistance of national vanity is so stubborn, it will be impossible to convince any but the very wise, (and in every state they are the very few,) that our democratic liberty is utterly untenable; that we are devoted to the successive struggles of factions, who will rule by turns, the worst of whom will rule last, and triumph by the sword. But for the wise this unwelcome task is, perhaps, superfluous: they, possibly, are already convinced.

All such men are, or ought to be, agreed that simple governments are despotisms; and of all despotisms a democracy, though the least durable, is the most violent. It is also true, that all the existing governments we are acquainted with are more or less mixed, or balanced and checked, however imperfectly, by the ingredients and principles that belong to the other simple sorts. It is nevertheless a fact, that there is scarcely any civil constitution in the world, that, according to American ideas, is so mixed and combined as to be favorable to the liberty of the subject—none, absolutely none, that an American patriot would be willing to adopt for, much less to impose on, his country. Without pretending to define that liberty, which writers at length agree is incapable of any precise and comprehensive definition, all the European governments, except the British, admit a most formidable portion of arbitrary power; whereas in America no plan of government, without a large and preponderating commixture of democracy, can for a moment possess our confidence and attachment.

It is unquestionable that the concern of the people in the affairs of such a government tends to elevate the character, and enlarge the comprehension, as well as the enjoyments of the citizens; and supposing the government wisely constituted, and the laws steadily and firmly carried into execution, these effects, in which every lover of mankind must exult, will not be attended with a corresponding depravation of the public manners and morals. I have never yet met with an American of any party who seemed willing to exclude the people from their temperate and well-regulated share of concern in the government. Indeed it is notorious, that there was scarcely an advocate for the federal Constitution who was not anxious, from the first, to hazard the experiment of an unprecedented, and almost unqualified proportion of democracy, both in constructing and administering the government, and who did not rely with confidence, if not blind presumption on its success. This is certain, the body of the federalists were always, and yet are, essentially democratic in their political notions. The truth is, the American nation, with ideas and prejudices wholly democratic, undertook to frame, and expected tranquilly and with energy and success to administer, a republican government. . . .

The theory of a democracy supposes that the will of the people ought to prevail, and that, as the majority possess not only the better right, but the superior force, of course it will prevail. A greater force, they argue, will inevitably overcome a less. When a constitution provides, with an imposing solemnity of detail, for the collection of the opinions of a majority of the citizens, every sanguine reader not only becomes assured that the will of the people must prevail, but he goes further, and refuses to examine the reasons, and to excuse the incivism and presumption of those who can doubt of this inevitable result. Yet common sense and our own recent experience have shown, that a combination of a very small minority can effectually defeat the authority of the national will. The votes of a majority may sometimes, though not invariably, show what ought to be done; but to awe or subdue the force of a thousand men, the government must call out the superior force of two thousand men. It is therefore established the very instant it is brought

we have a licentious democracy that would have to use force to have its will; but not doing so fails.

to the test, that the mere will of a majority is inefficient and without authority.   And as to employing a superior force to procure obedience, which a democratic government has an undoubted right to do, and so indeed has every other, it is obvious that the admitted necessity of this resort completely overthrows all the boasted advantages of the democratic system.   For if obedience cannot be procured by reason, it must be obtained by compulsion; and this is exactly what every other government will do in a like case. . . .

They are certainly blind who do not see that we are descending from a supposed orderly and stable republican government into a licentious democracy, with a progress that baffles all means to resist, and scarcely leaves leisure to deplore its celerity.   The institutions and the hopes that Washington raised are nearly prostrate; and his name and memory would perish, if the rage of his enemies had any power over history.   But they have not—history will give scope to her vengeance, and posterity will not be defrauded.

But if our experience had not clearly given warning of our approaching catastrophe, the very nature of democracy would inevitably produce it.

A government by the passions of the multitude, or, no less correctly, according to the vices and ambition of their leaders, is a democracy.   We have heard so long of the indefeasible sovereignty of the people, and have admitted so many specious theories of the rights of man, which are contradicted by his nature and experience, that few will dread at all, and fewer still will dread as they ought, the evils of an American democracy.   They will not believe them near, or they will think them tolerable or temporary.   Fatal delusion! . . .

The people, as a body, cannot deliberate.   Nevertheless, they will feel an irresistible impulse to act, and their resolutions will be dictated to them by their demagogues.   The consciousness, or the opinion, that they possess the supreme power, will inspire inordinate passions; and the violent men, who are the most forward to gratify those passions, will be their favorites.   What is called the government of the people is in fact too often the arbitrary power of such men.   Here, then, we have the faithful portrait of democracy.   What avails the boasted power of individual citizens? or of what value is the will of the majority, if that will is dictated by a committee of demagogues, and law and right are in fact at the mercy of a victorious faction? To make a nation free, the crafty must be kept in awe, and the violent in restraint. The weak and the simple find their liberty arise not from their own individual sovereignty, but from the power of law and justice over all. It is only by the due restraint of others, that I am free.

Popular sovereignty is scarcely less beneficent than awful, when it resides in their courts of justice; there its office, like a sort of human providence, is to warn, enlighten, and protect; when the people are inflamed to seize and exercise it in their assemblies, it is competent only to kill and destroy. Temperate liberty is like the dew, as it falls unseen from its own heaven; constant without excess, it finds vegetation thirsting for its refreshment, and imparts to it the vigor to take more. All nature, moistened with blessings, sparkles in the morning ray. But democracy is a water-spout that bursts from the clouds, and lays the ravaged earth bare to its rocky foundations. The labors of man lie whelmed with his hopes beneath masses of ruin, that bury not only the dead but their monuments.

It is the almost universal mistake of our countrymen, that democracy would be mild and safe in America. They charge the horrid excesses of France not so much to human nature, which will never act better, when the restraints of government, morals, and religion are thrown off, but to the characteristic cruelty and wickedness of Frenchmen.

The truth is, and let it humble our pride, the most ferocious of all animals, when his passions are roused to fury and are uncontrolled, is man; and of all governments, the worst is that which never fails to excite, but was never found to restrain those passions, that is, democracy. It is an illuminated hell, that in the midst of remorse, horror, and torture, rings with festivity; for experience shows, that one joy remains to this most malignant description of the damned, the power to make others wretched. When a man looks round and sees his neighbors mild and merciful, he cannot feel afraid of the abuse of their power over him; and surely if they oppress me, he will say, they will spare their own liberty, for that is dear to all mankind. It is so. The human heart is so constituted, that a man loves liberty as naturally as himself. Yet liberty is a rare thing in the world, though the love of it is so universal. . . .

Faction will inevitably triumph. Where the government is both stable and free, there may be parties. There will be differences of opinion, and the pride of opinion will be sufficient to generate contests, and to inflame them with bitterness and rancor. There will be rivalships among those whom genius, fame, or station have made great, and these will deeply agitate the state without often hazarding its safety. Such parties will excite alarm, but they may be safely left, like the elements, to exhaust their fury upon each other.

The object of their strife is to get power *under* the government; for, where that is constituted as it should be, the power *over* the government will not seem attainable, and, of course, will not be attempted.

But in democratic states there will be factions. The sovereign power being nominally in the hands of all, will be effectively within the grasp of a few; and therefore, by the very laws of our nature, a few will combine, intrigue, lie, and fight to engross it to themselves. All history bears testimony, that this attempt has never yet been disappointed.

Who will be the associates? Certainly not the virtuous, who do not wish to control the society, but quietly to enjoy its protection. The enterprising merchant, the thriving tradesman, the careful farmer, will be engrossed by the toils of their business, and will have little time or inclination for the unprofitable and disquieting pursuits of politics. It is not the industrious, sober husbandman, who will plough that barren field; it is the lazy and dissolute bankrupt, who has no other to plough. The idle, the ambitious, and the needy will band together to break the hold that law has upon them, and then to get hold of law. Faction is a Hercules, whose first labor is to strangle this lion, and then to make armor of his skin. In every democratic state, the ruling faction will have law to keep down its enemies; but it will arrogate to itself an undisputed power over law. If our ruling faction has found any impediments, we ask, which of them is now remaining? And is it not absurd to suppose that the conquerors will be contented with half the fruits of victory?

We are to be subject, then, to a despotic faction, irritated by the resistance that has delayed, and the scorn that pursues their triumph, elate with the insolence of an arbitrary and uncontrollable domination, and who will exercise their sway, not according to the rules of integrity or national policy, but in conformity with their own exclusive interests and passions.

This is a state of things which admits of progress, but not of ref-

Progress isn't a priori in world.

ormation; it is the beginning of a revolution, which must advance. Our affairs, as first observed, no longer depend on counsel. The opinion of a majority is no longer invited or permitted to control our destinies, or even to retard their consummation. The men in power may, and no doubt will give place to some other faction, who will succeed, because they are abler men, or possibly, in candor we say it, because they are worse. Intrigue will for some time answer instead of force, or the mob will supply it. But by degrees force only will be relied on by those who are *in*, and employed by those who are *out*. The vis major will prevail, and some bold chieftain will conquer liberty, and triumph and reign in her name.

Yet it is confessed, we have hopes that this event is not very near. We have no cities as large as London or Paris; and of course the ambitious demagogues may find the ranks of their standing army too thin to rule by them alone. It is also worth remark, that our mobs are not, like those of Europe, excitable by the cry of no bread. The dread of famine is everywhere else a power of political electricity, that glides through all the haunts of filth, and vice, and want in a city, with incredible speed, and in times of insurrection rives and scorches with a sudden force, like heaven's own thunder. Accordingly, we find the sober men of Europe more afraid of the despotism of the rabble than of the government.

But as in the United States we see less of this description of low vulgar, and as in the essential circumstance alluded to, they are so much less manageable by their demagogues, we are to expect that our affairs will be long guided by courting the mob, before they are violently changed by employing them. While the passions of the multitude can be conciliated to confer power and to overcome all impediments to its action, our rulers have a plain and easy task to perform. It costs them nothing but hypocrisy. As soon, however, as rival favorites of the people may happen to contend by the practice of the same arts, we are to look for the sanguinary strife of ambition. Brissot will fall by the hand of Danton, and he will be supplanted by Robespierre. The revolution will proceed in exactly the same way, but not with so rapid a pace, as that of France.

16. JOHN TAYLOR (1753–1824)

JOHN TAYLOR of CAROLINE" was born in Caroline County, in the piedmont section of Virginia. He spent two years at William and Mary College, was admitted to the bar in 1774, served in the Continental Army, reaching the rank of major, and was a lieutenant-colonel in the Virginia militia in the last year of the Revolutionary War. He married his cousin, daughter of a wealthy planter and lawyer (John Penn of North Carolina, signer of the Declaration of Independence). He served eight years in the Virginia Assembly and three brief terms, by appointment, in the United States Senate (1792–94, 1803–05, 1822–24). He was a thoroughgoing libertarian, agrarian, States'-rights democrat. In the Virginia legislature he supported Jefferson's measures for religious freedom and advocated constitutional changes to equalize suffrage and the apportionment of representation. He opposed ratification of the Federal Constitution on the ground that it transferred too much power from the States to the general government and inadequately safeguarded individual rights against the latter. He wrote pamphlets against Hamilton's fiscal and commercial measures and introduced into the Virginia legislature the "Resolutions" against the Sedition Act of 1798. Although he defended the Louisiana Purchase, he opposed the later Jefferson-Madison foreign policy and warned that war in 1812 would bring about a greater concentration of power in Washington. He held protective tariffs to be unconstitutional as well as economically unnatural and dangerous, criticized Marshall's nationalistic constructions of the Constitution, and denied that there was any constitutional right of appeal from State courts to the United States Supreme Court. On one occasion he suggested that the States had the right forcibly to resist encroachments on their constitutional prerogatives. American historians have called Taylor "the statesman of agrarianism," "the philosopher of Jeffersonian democracy," and the "prophet of secession."

Taylor's general political and economic doctrines are set forth in four influential works: *An Inquiry into the Principles and Policy of the Government of the United States* (1814); *Construction Construed and Constitutions Vindicated* (1820); *Tyranny Unmasked* (1822); and *New Views of the Constitution of the United States* (1823). These contain a comprehensive exposition of Jefferson's social philosophy, and of the

173

whole Jeffersonian movement as a defense of agrarian democracy against the "moneyed," "paper," aristocracy envisaged in Hamilton's policies, Marshall's constitutional doctrines, and John Adams' political theory. His *Inquiry* was begun as a reply to Adams' *Defence of the Constitutions of Government of the United States.* He was actively interested in his own farms and wrote popular articles on methods for the improvement of farming and on the difficulties of an agricultural community in a country controlled by a business aristocracy. The articles were published as a book, *Arator* (1813), which was a popular and influential work in the South for many years. Jefferson said (in 1820) that he and Taylor had "rarely, if ever, differed in any political principle of importance." [1]

[See: Benjamin F. Wright, Jr., "The Philosopher of Jeffersonian Democracy," *American Political Science Review*, Vol. XXII (1928), pp. 870–892; Charles A. Beard, *Economic Origins of Jeffersonian Democracy* (1915), pp. 196–211, 322–352; William E. Dodd, "John Taylor, of Caroline, Prophet of Secession," in *John B. Branch Historical Papers of Randolph-Macon College*, Vol. II (1905–08), pp. 214–252; Henry H. Simms, *Life of John Taylor* (1932).]

From INQUIRY INTO THE PRINCIPLES AND POLICY OF THE GOVERNMENT OF THE UNITED STATES (1814) [2]

The reader will be pleased to recollect the question in debate. Mr. Adams asserts, that an aristocratical body of men is necessary, as being natural. Having thus gotten it, he admits that it will be ambitious and dangerous to liberty. Being ambitious and dangerous, he infers, that it ought to be controlled. And this, he says, can only be effected by a king over it, and a house of commons under it; thus placing it between two fires, on account of its strength, danger and ambition.

The entire hypothesis rests upon a single foundation, "that aristocracy is natural and inevitable;" and therefore this ground-work ought to be well examined.

The contrivance for erecting a system, by asserting and setting out from the will of God, or from nature, is not new. Most of those systems of government, to which Mr. Adams refers us for instruction, resorted to it; and therefore the propriety of reviving the prin-

[1] *Writings* (Ford ed.), Vol. X, p. 170.
[2] (Fredericksburg, 1814), pp. 11–12, 15–16, 20–30.

ciple, upon which these ancient systems were generally or universally founded, to revive its effects, must be admitted. "It is the will of Jupiter," exclaimed some artful combination of men. "The will of Jupiter is inevitable," responded the same combination to itself; and ignorance submitted to a fate, manufactured by human fraud.

Whenever it is impossible to prove a principle, which is necessary to support a system, a reference to an inevitable power, calling it God or nature, is preferable to reasoning; because every such principle is more likely to be exploded, than established by reasoning. For instance; it would be difficult to convince us, that we ought to erect an aristocracy spontaneously; the folly of which, Mr. Adams unwarily admits, by insisting upon the great danger to be apprehended from it, to enhance the merit of his system, in meeting this danger with a king and a house of commons. And therefore the short and safe expedient is, to tell us that nature has settled the question, by declaring that we shall have an aristocracy; being induced to believe and concede this, the difficulty is over; and the whole system, bottomed upon the concession, becomes irrefutable.

Hence have been derived, the sanctity of oracles, the divinity of kings, and the holiness of priests; and now that these bubbles have become the scoff of common sense, experiment is to decide, whether there remains in America a stock of superstition, upon which can be ingrafted, "an aristocracy from nature." . . .

As the aristocracies of priestcraft and conquest decayed, that of patronage and paper stock grew; not the rival, but the instrument of a king; without rank or title; regardless of honor; of insatiable avarice; and neither conspicuous for virtue and knowledge, or capable of being collected into a legislative chamber. Differing in all its qualities from Mr. Adams's natural aristocracy, and defying his remedy, it is condensed and combined by an interest, exclusive, and inimical to public good.

Why has Mr. Adams written volumes to instruct us how to manage an order of nobles, sons of the Gods, of exclusive virtue, talents and wealth, and attended by the pomp and fraud of superstition; or one of feudal barons, holding great districts of unalienable country, warlike, high spirited, turbulent and dangerous; now that these orders are no more? Whilst he passes over in silence the aristocracy of paper and patronage, more numerous, more burdensome, unexposed to public jealousy by the badge of title, and not too honorable or high spirited to use and serve executive power, for the sake of pillaging the people. Are these odious vices, to be concealed under apprehensions of ancient aristocracies, which, however natural, are supplanted by this modern one? . . .

For the sake of perspicuity, I shall call the ancient aristocracy, chiefly created and supported by superstition, "the aristocracy of the first age;" that produced by conquest, known by the title of the feudal system, "the aristocracy of the second age;" and that erected by paper and patronage, "the aristocracy of the third or present age." If aristocracy is the work of nature, by deserting her accustomed constancy, and slily changing the shape of her work, she has cunningly perplexed our defensive operations . . .

Suppose the people of England should attempt to abolish monarchy. Both the aristocracy of the present age, and the nobility would arrange themselves in its defence. Which would be most formidable? The remnant or hieroglyphick of the feudal system, would indeed display a ridiculous pomp, and imbecile importance; it would appear armed with title, ribbon and symbol, and evince its weakness by tottering under shadows. But the real aristocracy of the present age; neither begotten by the Gods, the curse of conquest, nor the offspring of nature; the aristocracy of patronage and paper would draw out its fleets, armies, public debt, corporate bodies and civil offices. Which species of aristocracy, I ask again, would be the strongest auxiliary for despotism, and the most dangerous enemy to the nation? And yet Mr. Adams has written three volumes, to excite our jealousy against the aristocracy of motto and blazon, without disclosing the danger from the aristocracy of paper and patronage; that political hydra of modern invention, whose arms embrace a whole nation, whose ears hear every sound, whose eyes see all objects, and whose hands can reach every purse and every throat. . . .

Every society, in Mr. Adams's opinion, will naturally produce a class of men minor in number, but superior to the major class in virtue, abilities and wealth; and hence, important, dangerous and ambitious. That they may be watched and controlled, they must be thrown into a separate legislative body, and balanced by a king on one side, and a house of Commons on the other; otherwise they will usurp the government.

This assertion depends upon a plain computation. Can a class of men, capable of being condensed in a legislative chamber, under the eye of the king and the Commons, be found in Great Britain, possessing more virtue, wisdom and wealth, than the rest of the nation; or even a portion sufficiently exclusive, to render it important, dangerous and ambitious? And if such a class could have been found, would not its importance and ambition presently become victims to printing, alienation and commerce?

If it be admitted, that the mass of virtue, wisdom and wealth, remaining with the people of Great Britain, infinitely exceeds that collected into the present house of lords, Mr. Adams's system contains the palpable error, of providing against the importance, danger and ambition of a diminutive portion of the virtue, wisdom and wealth of a nation, and of not providing against the importance, danger and ambition of the great mass of these qualities. This great mass, it may be answered, will be prevented from doing harm to the nation, by the representative principle to be found in the house of commons. If that principle is capable of managing the great mass of virtue, wisdom and wealth, it is also capable of managing an inconsiderable portion of this mass; and hence results the propriety of an elective, and the impropriety of an hereditary senate, upon Mr. Adams's own principles.

In this argument, Mr. Adams's definition of aristocracy is adhered to; he makes it to consist in a dangerous share of virtue, wisdom and wealth, held by a number of individuals, so few, as to be capable of constituting a legislative branch. The difference between us is, that his computation to make out a fact analagous to his system, must refer to the period of feudal aristocracy; mine takes the fact now existing, as the best foundation for political inferences, to be now applied.

But his definition undoubtedly possesses a considerable share of truth, and suggests an observation extremely plain. The possession by a few, of the major part of the whole stock of renown, talents or wealth, within the compass of a society, was the moral cause which supported the aristocracies of the first and second ages; when the cause ceased, the effects ceased also; and the aristocracies of superstition and the feudal system disappeared. But this effect may be revived by reviving its cause. A monopoly by a few, of renown, talents or wealth, may be reproduced, by superstition, conquest or fraud; and the question is, whether this would be advisable, for the sake of trying the efficacy of his system. . . .

We are ready to acknowledge that extraordinary virtue, talents and wealth united, will govern, and ought to govern; and yet it is denied that this concession is reconcileable with the system of king, lords and commons. If a body of men which possesses the virtue, talents and wealth of a nation, ought to govern; it follows, that a body of men, which does not possess these attributes, ought not to govern. . . .

Having thus conceded to Mr. Adams, that wherever a few possess the mass of the renown, virtue, talents and wealth of a nation, that they will become an aristocracy, and probably ought to do so; it would be a concession, strictly reciprocal, to admit, that wherever no such body is to be found, an aristocracy ought not to be created by legal assignments of wealth and poverty. As the first species of minority will govern, because of the power arising from such monopolies only, so no other species can, without these sources of power. Where its sources are, power will be found; and hence the great mass of wealth, created by the system of paper and patronage, has annihilated the power of the didactick and titled peerage of England; because it has not a sufficient mass of virtue, renown, talents or wealth, to oppose against stock and patronage.

The aristocracies of the first and second ages were indebted for their power to ignorance, fraud and superstition; now reason, sincerity and truth, are demanded by the human mind. It disdains to worship a pageant or fear a phantom, and is only to be guided by views of interest or happiness. This change in the human character indicates an impossibility of reviving the principles which sustained the aristocracies of the first and second age, when mankind believed in the Gods of a pantheon, and in the prophetic powers of convulsed women.

Talents and virtue are now so widely distributed, as to have rendered a monopoly of either, equivalent to that of antiquity, impracticable; and if an aristocracy ought to have existed, whilst it possessed such a monopoly, it ought not also to exist, because this monopoly is irretrievably lost. The distribution of wealth produced by commerce and alienation, is equal to that of knowledge of virtue, produced by printing; but as the first distribution might be artificially counteracted, with a better prospect of success than the latter, aristocracy has abandoned a reliance on a monopoly of virtue, renown and abilities, and resorted wholly to a monopoly of wealth, by the system of paper and patronage. Modern taxes and frauds to collect money, and not ancient authors, will therefore afford the best evidence of its present character.

A distribution of knowledge, virtue and wealth, produced public opinion, which ought now to govern for the reason urged by Mr. Adams in favour of aristocracy. It is the declaration of the mass of national wealth, virtue and talents. Power, in Mr. Adams's opinion, ought to follow this mass in the hands of a few, because it is the ornament of society. It is unimportant whether an aristocracy is a natural, physical or moral effect, if its cause, by means, natural, physical or moral, may be lost or transferred. Whenever the mass of wealth, virtue and talents, is lost by a few and transferred to a great portion of a nation, an aristocracy no longer retains the only sanctions of its claim; and wherever these sanctions deposit themselves, they carry the interwoven power. By spreading themselves so generally throughout a nation, as to be no longer compressible into a legislative chamber, or inheritable by the aid of perpetuity and superstition, these antient sanctions of aristocracy, become the modern sanctions of public opinion. And as its will (now the rightful sovereign upon the self-same principle, urged in favor of the best founded aristocracy) can no longer be obtained through the medium of an hereditary order, the American invention of applying the doctrine of responsibility to magistrates, is the only one yet discovered for effecting the same object, which was effected by an aristocracy, holding the mass of national virtue, talents and wealth. This mass governed through such an aristocracy. This mass cannot now govern through any aristocracy. This mass has searched for a new organ, as a medium for exercising the sovereignty, to which it is on all sides allowed to be entitled; and this medium is representation.

17. DANIEL WEBSTER (1782–1852)

WEBSTER was born in the frontier village of Salisbury, New Hampshire, where his parents had recently settled as farmers. His father had served as a captain in the Revolutionary army and later held public offices, as member of the New Hampshire legislature and of the State ratifying convention of 1788 and as lay judge on the bench of the local court of common pleas. As a boy Daniel showed signs of inferior physical stamina and superior intellectual tastes and capacities; and his family, at some sacrifice, arranged for him to attend Phillips Exeter Academy, and Dartmouth College, from which he was graduated in 1801. He read law, was admitted to the bar in 1805, and soon attained success and prestige in his practice, first at Portsmouth and later in Boston. In a considerable number of important cases he was the attorney for manufacturing and trading concerns, and he came to be regarded as the most effective spokesman, before the courts and in deliberative bodies, for the mercantile and industrial interests of the northeast. His arguments in celebrated cases before the Supreme Court (the "Dartmouth College case," *McCulloch v. Maryland, Gibbons v. Ogden,* and others) were undoubtedly of assistance to Chief Justice Marshall in establishing a method of loose constitutional interpretation favorable to the protection of private economic interests against State interferences and to the validation of positive acts by the national government in the promotion of those interests.

Webster held important national political offices during most of his life after his early thirties. He was a member of the House of Representatives (1813–17, 1823–27), United States senator (1827–41, 1845–50), and secretary of state (1841–43, 1850–52), and he was an active member of the Massachusetts constitutional convention of 1820–21. His Senate and Court speeches as well as his popular orations—notably at Plymouth in celebration of the two hundredth anniversary of the landing of the Pilgrims, and at the laying of the cornerstone of Bunker Hill monument —gave him the designation (which still survives) as "America's greatest orator." He was acquainted with some of the modern classics of political theory and found in them justification for the position he had taken in his legal and political arguments: that property interests should and do play a predominant part in determining the policies of government and the distribution of political power. His published writings on these and other matters are chiefly enlarged or revised versions of his speeches. His speech in the Massachusetts convention, against removing the provision in the State constitution apportioning legislative representation according to the amount of taxes paid by the several districts, contains typical ideas of conservatives of that period on the interrelation of government and property.[1]

The original State constitutions (1776–80) had been adopted in the midst of a revolutionary movement inspired by solemn assertions of the natural rights of all men to have equal voices in their governments; the movement had gained popular support because of the expectations by many common people that the achievement of independence from England would destroy some of the political privileges of wealthy planters, merchants, and other minority groups at home. Thus the preambles and bills of rights of the new constitutions proclaimed the political rights of "the whole people." Yet all the constitutions retained old colonial regulations that denied political rights to most of the ordinary male white citizens, and they distributed those rights unequally. They confined voting rights to property owners and apportioned representation in the State legislatures in such a way as to give the older, wealthier districts in the east a disproportionate number of representatives. As soon as independence was won there began to be insistent demands for the removal of these disqualifications and discriminations; and the movements of events were favorable to their claims. The rapid settlement of the west and the increase of the industrial wage-earning population of eastern cities nourished a democratic spirit that could not be ignored. Of the nine new States admitted to the Union between 1789 and 1830, all but two (Maine and Vermont) were on the western frontier. The constitutions of these States and constitutional amendments in most of the original States put an end to property requirements for voting; by 1840 a male, adult, white citizenship suffrage had been approximately achieved throughout the country. Other constitutional changes abolished high property qualifications for office holding and increased the number and shortened the terms of the elective State officials.

In some of the eastern States there was stubborn resistance to these changes, manifested notably in the constitutional conventions of Massachusetts (1820), New York (1820–21), and Virginia (1829–30), where leading statesmen of the nation took part in the debates, generally on the conservative side. In the Massachusetts convention, former President John Adams, Supreme Court Justice Joseph Story, and Daniel Webster

[1] For further ideas of Webster on this subject, see below, pp. 504ff.

strongly defended the principle that private property should be given a special voice in the determination of public questions. The Massachusetts constitution then in force restricted voting rights to owners of freeholds of the annual value of three pounds or of other estates worth sixty pounds; and it provided that the legislature, "in assigning the numbers [of senators] to be elected by the respective districts, shall govern themselves by the proportion of the public taxes paid by the said districts." [1] Webster spoke in defense of that provision.

[See: Arthur C. Cole, "Daniel Webster," in *Dictionary of American Biography*; Vernon L. Parrington, *Main Currents of American Thought*, Vol. II (1927), pp. 306–316; Claude M. Fuess, *Daniel Webster*, 2 vols. (1930); Gamaliel Bradford, in *As God Made Them* (1929), pp. 3–42.]

From SPEECH ON "APPORTIONMENT OF THE SENATE"; IN THE MASSACHUSETTS STATE CONSTITUTIONAL CONVENTION OF 1820–21 [2]

MR. WEBSTER spoke in substance as follows:

I know not, sir, whether it be probable that any opinions or votes of mine are ever likely to be of more permanent importance, than those which I may give in the discharge of my duties in this body. And of the questions which may arise here, I anticipate no one of greater consequence than the present. I ask leave therefore to submit a few remarks to the consideration of the committee.

The subject before us, is the manner of constituting the legislative department of government. We have already decided that the legislative power shall exist, as it has heretofore existed, in two separate and distinct branches, a senate and a house of representatives. We propose also, at least I have heard no intimation of a contrary opinion, that these branches shall, in form, possess a negative on each other. And I presume I may take it for granted, that the members of both these houses are to be chosen annually. The immediate question, now under discussion is, *in what manner* shall the senators be elected? They are to be chosen in districts; but shall they be chosen, in proportion to the *number of inhabitants* in each

[1] Massachusetts Constitution of 1780, Ch. I, Sect. II, Art. I.

[2] In *Journal of Debates and Proceedings in the Convention . . . to Revise the Constitution of Massachusetts*, 1820–21 (Boston, 1853), pp. 304–321, at 304, 306–309, 312–317. For speeches of Adams and Story on the same subject, see *ibid.*, pp. 277–279, 283–295.

district, or, in other words, *in proportion to the part which each district bears in the public burdens of the State*. The latter is the existing provision of the constitution; and to this I give my support. . . .

I understand the reason of *checks* and *balances*, in the legislative power, to arise from the truth that, in representative governments, that department is the leading and predominating power; and if its will may be, at any time, suddenly and hastily expressed, there is great danger that it may overthrow all other powers. Legislative bodies naturally feel strong, because they are numerous, and because they consider themselves as the immediate representatives of the people. They depend on public opinion to sustain their measures, and they undoubtedly possess great means of influencing public opinion. With all the guards which can be raised by constitutional provisions, we are not likely to be too well secured against cases of improper, or hasty, or intemperate legislation. It may be observed, also, that the executive power, so uniformly the object of jealousy to republics, has become, in the states of this Union, deprived of the greatest part, both of its importance and its splendor, by the establishment of the general government. . . . Even the power of appointment, so exclusively, one would think, an executive power, is, in very many of the states, held or controlled by the legislature; that department either making the principal appointments, itself, or else surrounding the chief executive magistrate with a council of its own election, possessing a negative upon his nominations.

Nor has it been found easy, nor in all cases possible, to preserve the judicial department from the progress of legislative encroachment. Indeed, in some of the states all judges are appointed by the legislature; in others, although appointed by the executive, they are removable at the pleasure of the legislature. In all, the provision for their maintenance is necessarily to be made by the legislature. As if Montesquieu had never demonstrated the necessity of separating the departments of government; as if Mr. Adams had not done the same thing, with equal ability, and more clearness, in his defence of the American Constitution; as if the sentiments of Mr. Hamilton and Mr. Madison were already forgotten; we see, all around us, a tendency to extend the legislative power over the proper sphere of the other departments. And as the legislature, from the very nature of things, is the most powerful department, it becomes necessary to provide, in the mode of forming it, some check which shall ensure deliberation and caution in its measures. If all legislative power rested in one house, it is very problematical, whether any proper independence could be given, either to the executive or the judiciary. Experience does not speak encouragingly on that point. If we look through the several constitutions of the states, we shall perceive that generally the departments are most distinct and independent, where the legislature is composed of two houses, with equal authority, and mutual checks. If all legislative power be in one popular body, all other power, sooner or later, will be there also.

I wish now, sir, to correct a most important mistake, in the manner in which this question has been stated. It has been said, that we propose to give to property, merely as such, a control over the people numerically considered. But this I take not to be at all the true nature of the proposition. The senate is not to be a check on the *people*, but on the *house of representatives*. It is the case of an authority, given to *one* agent, to check or control the acts of *another*. The people, having conferred on the house of representatives, powers which are great, and, from their nature, liable to abuse, require for their own security another house, which shall possess an effectual negative on the first. This does not limit the power of the people; but only the authority of their agents. It is not a restraint on their rights, but a restraint on that power which they have delegated. It limits the authority of agents, in making laws to bind their principles. And if it be wise to give one agent the power of checking or controlling another, it is equally wise, most manifestly, that there should be some difference of character, sentiment, feeling, or origin, in that agent, who is to possess this control. Otherwise, it is not at all probable that the control will ever be exercised. To require the consent of two agents to the validity of an act, and yet to appoint agents so similar, in all respects, as to create a moral certainty that what one does the other will do also, would be inconsistent and nugatory. There can be no effectual control without some difference of origin, or character, or interest, or feeling, or sentiment. And the great question, in this country, has been, where to find, or how to create this difference, in governments entirely elective and popular? . . .

. . . The best authority for the support of a particular principle or provision in government, is experience; and, of all experience, our own, if it have been long enough to give the principle a fair trial, should be most decisive. This provision has existed for forty years; and while so many gentlemen contend that it is wrong in theory, no one has shown that it has been either injurious or inconvenient in practice. No one pretends that it has caused a bad law to be enacted or a good one to be rejected. To call on us, then, to strike out this provision, because we should be able to find no authority for it in any book on government, would seem to be like requiring a mechanic to abandon the use of an implement, which had always answered all the purposes designed by it, because he could find no model of it in the patent office.

But, sir, I take the *principle* to be well established by writers of the greatest authority. In the first place, those who have treated of natural law have maintained, as a principle of that law, that, as far as the object of society is the protection of something in which the members possess unequal shares, it is just that the weight of each person in the common councils, should bear a relation and proportion to his interest. Such is the sentiment of Grotius, and he refers, in support of it, to several institutions among the ancient states.

Those authors, who have written more particularly on the subject of political institutions, have, many of them, maintained similar sentiments. Not, indeed, that every man's power should be in exact proportion to his property, but that, in a general sense, and in a general form, property, as such, should have its weight and influence in political arrangement. . . . One of the most ingenious of political writers is Mr. Harrington, an author not now read so much as he deserves. It is his leading object, in his "Oceana," to prove, that power *naturally* and *necessarily* follows property. He maintains that a government, founded on property, is legitimately founded; and that a government founded on the disregard of property is founded in injustice, and can only be maintained by military force. "If one man," says he, "be sole landlord, like the grand seignior, his empire is absolute. If a few possess the land, this makes the gothic or feudal constitution. If the *whole* people be landlords, then is it a Commonwealth." "It is strange," says Mr. Pope, in one of his recorded conversations, "that Harrington should be the first man to find out so evident and demonstrable a truth, as that of property being the true basis and *measure* of power." In truth he was not the first: the idea is as old as political science itself. It may be found in Aristotle, Lord Bacon, Sir Walter Raleigh, and other writers. Harrington seems, however, to be the first writer who has illustrated and expanded the principle, and given to it the effect and prominence which justly belong to it. To this sentiment, sir, I entirely agree. It seems to me to be plain, that, in the absence of military force, political power naturally and necessarily goes into the hands which hold the property. In my judgment, therefore, a republican form of government rests not more on political constitutions than on those laws which regulate the descent and transmission of property. . . .

If the nature of our institutions be to found government on property, and that it should look to those who hold property for its protection, it is entirely just that property should have its due weight and consideration in political arrangements. Life and personal liberty are, no doubt, to be protected by law; but property is also to be protected by law, and is the fund out of which the means for protecting life and liberty are usually furnished. We have no experience that teaches us, that any other rights are safe, where property is not safe. Confiscation and plunder are generally, in revolutionary commotions, not far before banishment, imprisonment and death. It would be monstrous to give even the name of government, to any association, in which the rights of property should not be competently secured. The disastrous revolutions which the world has witnessed; those political thunder-storms and earthquakes which have overthrown the pillars of society from their very deepest foundations, have been revolutions *against property*. Since the honorable member from Quincy (President ADAMS) has alluded, on this occasion, to the history of the ancient states, it would be presumption, in me, to dwell upon it. It may be truly said, however, I think, that Rome herself is an example of the mischievous influence of the popular power, when disconnected with property, and in a corrupt age. It is true, the arm of Caesar prostrated her liberty; but Caesar found his support within her very walls. Those who were profligate, and necessitous, and factious, and desperate, and capable, therefore, of being influenced by bribes and largesses, which were distributed with the utmost prodigality, outnumbered and outvoted, in the tribes and centuries, the substantial, sober, prudent and faithful citizens. Property was in the hands of one description of men, and power in those of another; and the balance of the constitution was destroyed. Let it never be forgotten that it was the popular magistrates, elevated to office where the bad outnumbered the good, where those who had no stake in the Commonwealth, by clamor, and noise, and numbers, drowned the voice of those who had, that laid the neck of Rome at the foot of her conqueror. When Caesar, manifesting a disposition to march his army into Italy, approached that little stream, which has become so memorable from its association with his character and conduct, a decree was proposed in the senate, declaring him a public enemy, if he did not disband his troops. To this decree the popular tribunes, the sworn protectors of the people, interposed their negative; and thus opened the high road of Italy, and the gates of Rome herself, to the approach of her conqueror.

The English revolution of 1688 was a revolution *in favor of property*, as well as of other rights. It was brought about by the men of property, for their security; and our own immortal revolution was undertaken, not to shake or plunder property, but to protect it. The acts of which the country complained, were such as violated rights of property. An immense majority of all those who had an interest in the soil were in favor of the revolution; and they carried it through, looking to its results for the security of their possessions. It was the property of the frugal yeomanry of New-England, hard earned, but freely given, that enabled her to act her proper part, and perform her full duty, in achieving the independence of the country. . . .

I will beg leave to ask, sir, whether property may not be said to *deserve* this portion of respect and power in the government? It pays, at this moment, I think, *five sixths* of all the public taxes; *one sixth* only being raised on persons. Not only, sir, do these taxes support those burdens, which all governments require, but we have, in New-England, from early times holden property to be subject to *another* great public use;—I mean the support of SCHOOLS. . . .

. . . Does any history show property more beneficently applied? Did any government ever subject the property of those who have estates, to a burden, for a purpose more favorable to the poor, or more useful to the whole community? Sir, *property* and the power which the law exercises over it, for the purpose of instruction, is the basis of the system. It is entitled to the respect and protection of government, because, in a very vital respect, it aids and sustains government. . . . If we take away from the towns the power of assessing taxes on property, will the school houses remain open? If we deny to the poor, the benefit which they now derive from the property of the rich, will their children remain on their forms, or will they not, rather, be in the streets, in idleness and in vice?

I might ask, again, sir, how is it with religious instruction? Do not the towns and parishes raise money, by vote of the majority, assessed on property, for the maintenance of religious worship? Are not the poor, as well as the rich, benefited by the means of attending on public worship, and do they not, equally with the rich, possess a voice and vote, in the choice of the minister, and in all other parish concerns? Does any man, sir, wish to try the experiment of striking out of the constitution the regard which it has hitherto maintained for property, and of foregoing also the extraordinary benefit which society among us, for near two centuries, has derived, from laying the burden of religious and literary instruction of all classes upon property? Does any man wish to see those only worshipping God, who are able to build churches and maintain ministers for themselves; and those children only educated, whose parents possess the means of educating them? Sir, it is as unwise as it is unjust to make property an object of jealousy. Instead of being, in any just sense, a popular course, such a course would be most injurious and destructive to the best interest of the people. The nature of our laws sufficiently secures us against any dangerous accumulations; and, used and diffused, as we have it, the whole operation of property is in the highest degree useful, both to the rich and to the poor. I rejoice, sir, that every man in this community may call all property his own, so far as he has occasion for it, to furnish for himself and his children the blessings of religious instruction and the elements of knowledge. This celestial, and this earthly light, he is entitled to by the fundamental laws. It is every poor man's undoubted birthright, it is the great blessing which this constitution has secured to him, it is his solace in life, and it may well be his consolation in death, that his country stands pledged by the faith which it has plighted to all its citizens, to protect his children from ignorance, barbarism and vice. . . .

As to the *right* of apportioning senators upon this principle, I do not understand how there can be a question about it. All government is a modification of general principles and general truths, with a view to practical utility. Personal liberty, for instance, is a clear right, and is to be provided for; but it is not a clearer right than the right of property, though it may be more important. It is therefore entitled to protection. But property is also to be protected; and when it is remembered how great a portion of the people of this State possess property, I cannot understand how its protection or its influence is hostile to their rights and privileges.

For these reasons, sir, I am in favor of maintaining that *check* in the constitution of the Legislature, which has so long existed there.

18. JAMES KENT (1763–1847)

KENT was born in Fredericksburgh, New York, grandson of a Presbyterian minister. He was graduated from Yale in 1781. During an interruption in his residence at the college, caused by the presence of the Revolutionary armies, he came upon a copy of Blackstone's *Commentaries*. He read the four volumes and said that the work impressed him so much that he "fondly determined to be a lawyer." He came to be known as "The American Blackstone." He read law in lawyers' offices and started practice in Poughkeepsie, removing to New York City in 1793 (following his defeat as Federalist candidate for Congress by his Democratic brother-in-law). A few years earlier he had been elected to the New York Assembly, where he served three terms. He was subsequently a justice of the State supreme court for sixteen years (chief justice for eight years) and he was chancellor for nine years. He was an outspoken political conservative, and his judicial career was brought to an end by a provision in the new State constitution of 1821 (drafted by a Democratically controlled convention) requiring the retirement of judges at the age of sixty.

Kent held the first professorship of law at Columbia College, from 1794 to 1798, and he occupied the chair again for three years following his retirement from the chancellorship. He drew few students; but he rewrote and enlarged his lectures, which were published as the *Commentaries on American Law* in eight volumes (1826–30), covering international law, constitutional law, municipal law, and basic fields of private law.[1] His renown as one of the greatest American jurists rests chiefly on the parts of the *Commentaries* dealing with the English common law in its American applications, and on his work on the bench. He introduced into the New York courts the practice of handing down written opinions. As commentator and supreme court justice he brought into American law much of the eighteenth-century English common law, greatly needed in the rapidly developing commercial economy. His work as chancellor

---

[1] Five subsequent editions appeared during Kent's lifetime. A twelfth edition was edited by Oliver Wendell Holmes, Jr., sixteen years after Kent's death. The part on international law (subsequently published separately) was the first important American work in that field; and his commentary on the Constitution was the ablest on that subject, until the appearance of Story's *Commentaries* a few years later.

(together with Story's writing and teaching in the same period) laid the foundations of equity jurisprudence in the United States.

Kent was a member of the New York constitutional convention of 1821, and his speech against liberalizing the suffrage is one of the ablest statements of the conservative position in that period.

[See: William Kent, *Memoirs and Letters of James Kent* (1898); Frederick C. Hicks, *Men and Books Famous in the Law* (1921), pp. 136–158; James Brown Scott, "James Kent," in *Great American Lawyers* (ed. by William Lewis, 1907–09), pp. 491–533.]

SPEECH ON THE ELECTIVE FRANCHISE
(SEPTEMBER 22, 1821) [1]

CHANCELLOR KENT. I am in favour of the amendment which has been submitted by my honourable colleague from Albany; and I must beg leave to trespass for a few moments upon the patience of the committee, while I state the reasons which have induced me to wish, that the senate should continue, as heretofore, the representative of the landed interest, and exempted from the control of universal suffrage. I hope what I may have to say will be kindly received, for it will be well intended. But, if I thought otherwise, I should still prefer to hazard the loss of the little popularity which I might have in this house, or out of it, than to hazard the loss of the approbation of my own conscience.

I have reflected upon the report of the select committee with attention and with anxiety. We appear to be disregarding the principles of the constitution, under which we have so long and so happily lived, and to be changing some of its essential institutions. I cannot but think that the considerate men who have studied the history of republics, or are read in lessons of experience, must look with concern upon our apparent disposition to vibrate from a well balanced government, to the extremes of the democratic doctrines. Such a broad proposition as that contained in the report, at the distance of ten years past, would have struck the public mind with

[1] Delivered in New York State Constitutional Convention, on September 22, 1821, in support of a proposal to retain a property qualification for voters for state senators (the proposal having been submitted as an amendment to a pending proposal to remove the property qualification for all voters). In *Reports of the Proceedings and Debates of the Convention of 1821, Assembled for the Purpose of Amending the Constitution of the State of New-York* (Albany, 1821), pp. 219–222.

astonishment and terror. So rapid has been the career of our vibration.

Let us recall our attention, for a moment, to our past history.

This state has existed for forty-four years under our present constitution, which was formed by those illustrious sages and patriots who adorned the revolution. It has wonderfully fulfilled all the great ends of civil government. During that long period, we have enjoyed in an eminent degree, the blessings of civil and religious liberty. We have had our lives, our privileges, and our property, protected. We have had a succession of wise and temperate legislatures. The code of our statute law has been again and again revised and corrected, and it may proudly bear a comparison with that of any other people. We have had, during that period, (though I am, perhaps, not the fittest person to say it) a regular, stable, honest, and enlightened administration of justice. All the peaceable pursuits of industry, and all the important interests of education and science, have been fostered and encouraged. We have trebled our numbers within the last twenty-five years, have displayed mighty resources, and have made unexampled progress in the career of prosperity and greatness.

Our financial credit stands at an enviable height; and we are now successfully engaged in connecting the great lakes with the ocean by stupendous canals, which excite the admiration of our neighbours, and will make a conspicuous figure even upon the map of the United States.

These are some of the fruits of our present government; and yet we seem to be dissatisfied with our condition, and we are engaged in the bold and hazardous experiment of remoddelling the constitution. Is it not fit and discreet: I speak as to wise men; is it not fit and proper that we should pause in our career, and reflect well on the immensity of the innovation in contemplation? Discontent in the midst of so much prosperity, and with such abundant means of happiness, looks like ingratitude, and as if we were disposed to arraign the goodness of Providence. Do we not expose ourselves to the danger of being deprived of the blessings we have enjoyed?—When the husbandman has gathered in his harvest, and has filled his barns and his graneries with the fruits of his industry, if he should then become discontented and unthankful, would he not have reason to apprehend, that the Lord of the harvest might come in his wrath, and with his lightning destroy them?

The senate has hitherto been elected by the farmers of the state —by the free and independent lords of the soil, worth at least $250 in freehold estate, over and above all debts charged thereon. The governor has been chosen by the same electors, and we have hith-erto elected citizens of elevated rank and character. Our assembly has been chosen by freeholders, possessing a freehold of the value of $50, or by persons renting a tenement of the yearly value of $5, and who have been rated and actually paid taxes to the state. By the report before us, we propose to annihilate, at one stroke, all those property distinctions and to bow before the idol of universal suffrage. That extreme democratic principle, when applied to the legislative and executive departments of government, has been re-garded with terror, by the wise men of every age, because in every European republic. ancient and modern, in which it has been tried, it has terminated disastrously, and been productive of corruption, injustice, violence, and tyranny. And dare we flatter ourselves that we are a peculiar people, who can run the career of history, ex-empted from the passions which have disturbed and corrupted the rest of mankind? If we are like other races of men, with similar follies and vices, then I greatly fear that our posterity will have reason to deplore in sackcloth and ashes, the delusion of the day.

It is not my purpose at present to interfere with the report of the committee, so far as respects the qualifications of electors for governor and members of assembly. I shall feel grateful if we may be permitted to retain the stability and security of a senate, bot-tomed upon the freehold property of the state. Such a body, so constituted, may prove a sheet anchor amidst the future factions and storms of the republic. The great leading and governing in-terest of this state, is, at present, the agricultural; and what mad-ness would it be to commit that interest to the winds. The great body of the people, are now the owners and actual cultivators of the soil. With that wholesome population we always expect to find moderation, frugality, order, honesty, and a due sense of inde-pendence, liberty, and justice. It is impossible that any people can lose their liberties by internal fraud or violence, so long as the country is parcelled out among freeholders of moderate possessions, and those freeholders have a sure and efficient control in the affairs of the government. Their habits, sympathies, and employments, necessarily inspire them with a correct spirit of freedom and justice; they are the safest guardians of property and the laws: We certainly cannot too highly appreciate the value of the agricultural interest: It is the foundation of national wealth and power. According to the opinion of her ablest political economists, it is the surplus produce of the agriculture of England, that enables her to support her vast body of manufacturers, her formidable fleets and armies, and the crowds of persons engaged in the liberal professions, and the cultivation of the various arts.

Now, sir, I wish to preserve our senate as the representative of the landed interest. I wish those who have an interest in the soil, to retain the exclusive possession of a branch in the legislature, as a strong hold in which they may find safety through all the vicissitudes which the state may be destined, in the course of Providence, to experience. I wish them to be always enabled to say that their freeholds cannot be taxed without their consent. The men of no property, together with the crowds of dependants connected with great manufacturing and commercial establishments, and the motley and undefinable population of crowded ports, may, perhaps, at some future day, under skilful management, predominate in the assembly, and yet we should be perfectly safe if no laws could pass without the free consent of the owners of the soil. That security we at present enjoy; and it is that security which I wish to retain.

The apprehended danger from the experiment of universal suffrage applied to the whole legislative department, is no dream of the imagination. It is too mighty an excitement for the moral constitution of men to endure. The tendency of universal suffrage, is to jeopardize the rights of property, and the principles of liberty. There is a constant tendency in human society, and the history of every age proves it; there is a tendency in the poor to covet and to share the plunder of the rich; in the debtor to relax or avoid the obligation of contracts; in the majority to tyranize over the minority, and trample down their rights; in the indolent and the profligate, to cast the whole burthens of society upon the industrious and the virtuous; and *there is a tendency in ambitious and wicked men, to inflame these combustible materials.* It requires a vigilant government, and a firm administration of justice, to counteract that tendency. Thou shalt not covet; thou shalt not steal; are divine injunctions induced by this miserable depravity of our nature. Who can undertake to calculate with any precision, how many millions of people, this great state will contain in the course of this and the next century, and who can estimate the future extent and magnitude of our commercial ports? The disproportion between the men of property, and the men of no property, will be in every society in a ratio to its commerce, wealth, and population. We are no longer to remain plain and simple republics of farmers, like the New-England colonists, or the Dutch settlements on the Hudson. We are fast becoming a great nation, with great commerce, manufactures, population, wealth, luxuries, and with the vices and miseries that they engender. One seventh of the population of the city of Paris at this day subsists on charity, and one third of the inhabitants of that city die in the hospitals; what would become of such a city with universal suffrage? France has upwards of four, and England upwards of five millions of manufacturing and commercial labourers without property. Could these kingdoms sustain the weight of universal suffrage? The radicals in England, with the force of that mighty engine, would at once sweep away the property, the laws, and the liberties of that island like a deluge.

The growth of the city of New-York is enough to startle and awaken those who are pursuing the *ignis fatuus* of universal suffrage.

In	1773	it had	21,000	souls.
	1801	"	60,000	do.
	1806	"	76,000	do.
	1820	"	123,000	do.

It is rapidly swelling into the unwieldly population, and with the burdensome pauperism, of an European metropolis. New-York is destined to become the future London of America; and in less than a century, that city, with the operation of universal suffrage, and under skilful direction, will govern this state.

The notion that every man that works a day on the road, or serves an idle hour in the militia, is entitled as of right to an equal participation in the whole power of the government, is most unreasonable, and has no foundation in justice. We had better at once discard from the report such a nominal test of merit. If such persons have an equal share in one branch of the legislature, it is surely as much as they can in justice or policy demand. Society is an association for the protection of property as well as of life, and the individual who contributes only one cent to the common stock, ought not to have the same power and influence in directing the property concerns of the partnership, as he who contributes his thousands. He will not have the same inducements to care, and diligence, and fidelity. His inducements and his temptation would be to divide the whole capital upon the principles of an agrarian law.

Liberty, rightly understood, is an inestimable blessing, but liberty without wisdom, and without justice, is no better than wild and savage licentiousness. The danger which we have hereafter to apprehend, is not the want, but the abuse, of liberty. We have to apprehend the oppression of minorities, and a disposition to encroach on private right—to disturb chartered privileges—and to weaken, degrade, and overawe the administration of justice; we have to apprehend the establishment of unequal, and consequently, unjust systems of taxation, and all the mischiefs of a crude and mutable legislation. A stable senate, exempted from the influence of universal suffrage, will powerfully check these dangerous propensities, and such a check becomes the more necessary, since this Convention has already determined to withdraw the watchful eye of the judicial department from the passage of laws.

We are destined to become a great manufacturing as well as commercial state. We have already numerous and prosperous factories of one kind or another, and one master capitalist with his one hundred apprentices, and journeymen, and agents, and dependents, will bear down at the polls an equal number of farmers of small estates in his vicinity, who cannot safely unite for their common defence. Large manufacturing and mechanical establishments, can act in an instant with the unity and efficacy of disciplined troops. It is against such combinations, among others, that I think we ought to give to the freeholders, or those who have interest in land, one branch of the legislature for their asylum and their comfort. Universal suffrage once granted, is granted forever, and never can be recalled. There is no retrograde step in the rear of democracy. However mischievous the precedent may be in its consequences, or however fatal in its effects, universal suffrage never can be recalled or checked, but by the strength of the bayonet. We stand, therefore, this moment, on the brink of fate, on the very edge of the precipice. If we let go our present hold on the senate, we commit our proudest hopes and our most precious interests to the waves.

It ought further to be observed, that the senate is a court of justice in the last resort. It is the last depository of public and private rights; of civil and criminal justice. This gives the subject an awful consideration, and wonderfully increases the importance of securing that house from the inroads of universal suffrage. Our country freeholders are exclusively our jurors in the administration of justice, and there is equal reason that none but those who have an interest in the soil, should have any concern in the composition of that court. As long as the senate is safe, justice is safe, property is safe, and our liberties are safe. But when the wisdom, the integrity, and the independence of that court is lost, we may be certain that the freedom and happiness of this state, are fled forever.

I hope, sir, we shall not carry desolation through all the departments of the fabric erected by our fathers. I hope we shall not put forward to the world a new constitution, as will meet with the scorn of the wise, and the tears of the patriot.

19. NON-FREEHOLDERS' MEMORIAL TO THE VIRGINIA CONSTITUTIONAL CONVENTION OF 1829–30

QUESTIONS concerning suffrage and the apportionment of representation were major issues in the Virginia constitutional convention of 1829–30. All shades of opinion on the question were represented: Jacksonian radicals from the western counties demanded full manhood suffrage and representation according to population; conservatives of the east opposed any change; and there were intermediate groups. The constitution of 1776, then in force, provided "that all men, having sufficient evidence of permanent common interest with, and attachment to, the community, have the right of suffrage," and "the right of suffrage shall remain as exercised at present." This meant that qualifications laid down in a colonial statute of 1762 still prevailed: in order to vote, one must own a freehold estate of fifty acres, or twenty-five acres of cultivated land with a house of designated size, or a town lot and house. These requirements caused considerable dissatisfaction within the State and were said to keep out or drive out just the type of men who were needed to help develop the State's rich natural resources.

The convention was an assembly of notables. Chief among the speakers opposing change were the governor of the State (William B. Giles, formerly a disciple of Jefferson), former Presidents Madison and Monroe, Chief Justice Marshall, John Randolph of Roanoke, A. P. Upshur (a justice of the Virginia supreme court), Littleton W. Tazewell (United States senator), and Benjamin W. Leigh (a distinguished lawyer). They argued that the eastern counties were entitled to a disproportionate representation in the legislature because they paid a disproportionate share of the taxes; and that landowners should have a prevailing voice in government not only because they were politically wiser but also because they were, through their lands, definitely and permanently tied to the community and had a greater and more enduring stake in a just and efficient administration of the affairs of the community. They carried the day; the convention settled on minor modifications of the suffrage qualifications.[1]

[1] Under the new provisions the voter had to own an estate worth twenty-five dollars annually, or occupy a house worth twenty dollars annually, or be a tax-paying father of a family. The constitution adopted in 1850 removed all property qualifications.

Obscurer members of the convention had vigorously answered their distinguished colleagues. They warned against the smugness of the office-holding, landowning, groups; and they protested against the injustice of disqualifying many hard-working, tax-paying citizens, merely on the ground that they owned no lands or other sizable estates. Said one member:

> The consequence is, that many of our citizens, virtuous, intelligent, industrious men, forego all their attachments to their native soil, their house, and the scenes of their youthful sports, and pass away into some of those Western States, where they can enjoy the privileges appertaining to freemen, by right of nature, not by purchase. . . .
>
> I have seen the respectable young men of the country—the mechanic, the merchant, the farmer, of mature age, of intelligence superior to that of one half the freeholders, and glowing with a patriotism which would make them laugh at death in defence of their country: I have seen such commanded to stand back from the polls, to give way to the owner of a petty freehold.[1]

The most impressive statement of the democratic case came from a group outside the convention, and is printed below.

From MEMORIAL OF THE NON-FREEHOLDERS OF THE CITY OF RICHMOND (1829) [2]

Mr. Marshall of Richmond said, that he was charged with a memorial from a numerous and respectable body of citizens, the non-freeholders of the city of Richmond. The object sought in the memorial, was an extension of the right of suffrage. The language of the memorial was respectful, and the petitioners accompanied their request with such arguments, as to them appeared convincing, in support of the object in view.

The memorial was thereupon received, and read as follows:

The Memorial of the Non-Freeholders of the City of Richmond, respectfully addressed to the Convention, now assembled to deliberate on amendments to the State Constitution:

Your memorialists, as their designation imports, belong to that class of citizens, who, not having the good fortune to possess a certain portion of land, are, for that cause only, debarred from the

[1] *Proceedings and Debates,* pp. 353–354.

[2] Addressed to the Virginia State Constitutional Convention. In *Proceedings and Debates of the Virginia State Convention of 1829–30* (Richmond, 1830),. at pp. 25–31.

enjoyment of the right of suffrage. Experience has but too clearly evinced, what, indeed, reason had always foretold, by how frail a tenure they hold every other right, who are denied this, the highest prerogative of freemen. The want of it has afforded both the pretext and the means of excluding the entire class, to which your memorialists belong, from all participation in the recent election of the body, they now respectfully address. Comprising a very large part, probably a majority of male citizens of mature age, they have been passed by, like aliens or slaves, as if destitute of interest, or unworthy of a voice, in measures involving their future political destiny: whilst the freeholders, sole possessors, under the existing Constitution, of the elective franchise, have, upon the strength of that possession alone, asserted and maintained in themselves, the exclusive power of new-modelling the fundamental laws of the State: in other words, have seized upon the sovereign authority.

It cannot be necessary, in addressing the Convention now assembled, to expatiate on the momentous importance of the right of suffrage, or to enumerate the evils consequent upon its unjust limitation. Were there no other than that your memorialists have brought to your attention, and which has made them feel with full force their degraded condition, well might it justify their best efforts to obtain the great privilege they now seek, as the only effectual method of preventing its recurrence. To that privilege, they respectfully contend, they are entitled equally with its present possessors. Many are bold enough to deny their title. None can show a better. It rests upon no subtle or abstruse reasoning; but upon grounds simple in their character, intelligible to the plainest capacity, and such as appeal to the heart, as well as the understanding, of all who comprehend and duly appreciate the principles of free Government. Among the doctrines inculcated in the great charter handed down to us, as a declaration of the rights pertaining to the good people of Virginia and their posterity, "as the basis and foundation of Government," we are taught,

"That all men are by nature equally free and independent, and have certain inherent rights, of which, when they enter into a state of society, they cannot, by any compact, deprive or divest their posterity: namely, the enjoyment of life and liberty, with the means of acquiring and possessing property, and pursuing and obtaining happiness and safety.

"That all power is vested in, and consequently derived from, the people.

"That a majority of the community hath an indubitable, unalienable, and indefeasible right to reform, alter or abolish the Government.

"That no man, nor set of men, are entitled to exclusive or separate emoluments or privileges, but in consideration of public services.

"That all men, having sufficient evidence of permanent common interest with, and attachment to, the community, have a right of suffrage, and cannot be taxed, or deprived of their property, without their consent, or that of their representative, nor bound by any law, to which they have not, in like manner, assented, for the public good."

How do the principles thus proclaimed, accord with the existing regulation of suffrage? A regulation, which, instead of the equality nature ordains, creates an odious distinction between members of the same community; robs of all share, in the enactment of the laws, a large portion of the citizens, bound by them, and whose blood and treasure are pledged to maintain them, and vests in a favoured class, not in consideration of their public services, but of their private possessions, the highest of all privileges; one which, as is now in flagrant proof, if it does not constitute, at least is held practically to confer, absolute sovereignty. Let it not be urged, that the regulation complained of and the charter it violates, sprung from the same honored source. The conflict between them is not on that account the less apparent. Nor does it derogate from the fair fame of the Convention of '76, that they should not have framed a Constitution perfect in all its parts. Deliberating amid the din of arms, not merely on a plan of Government, but on the necessary means for conducting a most unequal struggle for national existence, it was not to be expected, that the relative rights of the citizens, could be maturely considered, or adjusted in detail. From any change of the regulation, in regard to suffrage, a subject prolific, always, of much dissention, they might have feared to generate feuds among those, upon whose harmony of feeling and concert of action, depended the salvation of their country. They left it, therefore, as they found it. The non-freeholders, moreover, unrepresented in the Convention, and for the most part, probably, engaged in resisting the common enemy, it is fair to infer, in the actual condition of the country, had neither the opportunity nor the inclination to press their claims. Nor should it be forgotten, that the Convention having been chosen by the freeholders, whose political power was derived from the abrogated Government, many of our wisest Statesmen regarded the Constitution itself, as wanting in authority, or at least as repealable by a succeeding Legislature: and, accordingly, it has, in point of fact, since undergone a material change, in the very provision now in question, touching the right of suffrage.

If the Bill of Rights may not challenge respect, the opinions of any individual, however eminent, will be still more lightly regarded. Yet your memorialists cannot but exult in the countenance their cause has received from him, who was ever foremost to assert the rights of his fellow men; the venerated author of the Declaration of Independence, and of the Act of Religious Freedom. When those rights are brought in question, they know of none whose sentiments are worthy of higher estimation. To none among the founders of our Republic, are we indebted for more in its institutions, that is admirable in theory, or valuable in practice. His name is identified with the independence of his country; with all that is liberal and enlightened in her policy. Never had liberty an advocate of more unaffected zeal; of more splendid abilities; of purer principles. Nor is there in ancient or modern times, an example to be found of one, who in his life and conduct, more strongly exemplified the sincerity of his faith, or more brightly illustrated the beauty of its tenets. . . .

But not to the authority of great names merely, does the existing restriction upon suffrage stand opposed: reason and justice equally condemn it. The object, it is presumed, meant to be attained, was, as far as practicable, to admit the meritorious, and reject the unworthy. And had this object really been attained, whatever opinions might prevail as to the mere right, not a murmur probably would have been heard. Surely it were much to be desired that every citizen should be qualified for the proper exercise of all his rights, and the due performance of all his duties. But the same qualifications that entitle him to assume the management of his private affairs, and to claim all other privileges of citizenship, equally entitle him, in the judgment of your memorialists, to be entrusted with this, the dearest of all his privileges, the most important of all his concerns. But if otherwise, still they cannot discern in the possession of land any evidence of peculiar merit, or superior title. To ascribe to a landed possession, moral or intellectual endowments, would truly be regarded as ludicrous, were it not for the gravity with which the proposition is maintained, and still more for the grave consequences flowing from it. Such possession no more proves him who has it, wiser or better, than it proves him taller or stronger, than him who has it not. That cannot be a fit criterion for the exercise of any right, the possession of which does not indicate the existence, nor the want of it the absence, of any essential qualification.

But this criterion, it is strenuously insisted, though not perfect, is yet the best human wisdom can devise. It affords the strongest, if not the only evidence of the requisite qualifications; more particularly of what are absolutely essential, "permanent common interest with, and attachment to, the community." Those who cannot furnish this evidence, are therefore deservedly excluded.

Your memorialists do not design to institute a comparison; they fear none that can be fairly made between the privileged and the proscribed classes. They may be permitted, however, without disrespect, to remark, that of the latter, not a few possess land: many, though not proprietors, are yet cultivators of the soil: others are engaged in avocations of a different nature, often as useful, presupposing no less integrity, requiring as much intelligence, and as fixed a residence, as agricultural pursuits. Virtue, intelligence, are not among the products of the soil. Attachment to property, often a sordid sentiment, is not to be confounded with the sacred flame of patriotism. The love of country, like that of parents and offspring, is engrafted in our nature. It exists in all climates, among all classes, under every possible form of Government. Riches oftener impair it than poverty. Who has it not is a monster.

Your memorialists feel the difficulty of undertaking calmly to repel charges and insinuations involving in infamy themselves, and so large a portion of their fellow-citizens. To be deprived of their rightful equality, and to hear as an apology that they are too ignorant and vicious to enjoy it, is no ordinary trial of patience. Yet they will suppress the indignant emotions these sweeping denunciations are well calculated to excite. The freeholders themselves know them to be unfounded: Why, else, are arms placed in the hands of a body of disaffected citizens, so ignorant, so depraved, and so numerous? In the hour of danger, they have drawn no invidious distinctions between the sons of Virginia. The muster rolls have undergone no scrutiny, no comparison with the land books, with a view to expunge those who have been struck from the ranks of freemen. If the landless citizens have been ignominiously driven from the polls, in time of peace, they have at least been generously summoned, in war, to the battle-field. Nor have they disobeyed the summons, or, less profusely than others, poured out their blood in the defence of that country which is asked to disown them. Will it be said they owe allegiance to the Government that gives them protection? Be it so: and if they acknowledge the obligation; if privileges are really extended to them in defence of which they may reasonably be required to shed their blood, have they not motives, irresistible motives, of attachment to the community? Have they not an interest, a deep interest, in perpetuating the blessings they enjoy, and a right, consequently, to guard those blessings, not from foreign aggression merely, but from domestic encroachment?

But, it is said, yield them this right, and they will abuse it: property, that is, landed property, will be rendered insecure, or at least overburthened, by those who possess it not. The freeholders, on the contrary, can pass no law to the injury of any other class, which will not more injuriously affect themselves. The alarm is sounded too, of danger from large manufacturing institutions, where one corrupt individual may sway the corrupt votes of thousands. It were a vain task to attempt to meet all the flimsy pretexts urged, to allay all the apprehensions felt or feigned by the enemies of a just and liberal policy. The danger of abuse is a dangerous plea. Like *necessity*, the detested plea of the tyrant, or the still more detestible plea of the Jesuit, *expediency*; it serves as an ever-ready apology for all oppression. If we are sincerely republican, we must give our confidence to the pri[n]ciples we profess. We have been taught by our fathers, that all power is vested in, and derived from, the people; not the freeholders: that the majority of the community, in whom abides the physical force, have also the political right of creating and remoulding at will, their civil institutions. Nor can this right be any where more safely deposited. The generality of mankind, doubtless, desire to become owners of property: left free to reap the fruit of their labours, they will seek to acquire it honestly. It can never be their interest to overburthen, or render precarious, what they themselves desire to enjoy in peace. But should they ever prove as base as the argument supposes, force alone; arms, not votes, could effect their designs; and when that shall be attempted, what virtue is there in Constitutional restrictions, in mere wax and paper, to withstand it? To deny to the great body of the people all share in the Government; on suspicion that they may deprive others of their property, to rob them, in advance of their rights; to look to a privileged order as the fountain and depository of all power; is to depart from the fundamental maxims, to destroy the chief beauty, the characteristic feature, indeed, of Republican Government. . . .

The right of suffrage, however, it seems, is not a natural right. If by natural, is meant what is just and reasonable, then, nothing is more reasonable than that those whose purses contribute to maintain, whose lives are pledged to defend the country, should participate in all the privileges of citizenship. But say it is not a natural right. Whence did the freeholders derive it? How become its exclusive possessors? Will they arrogantly tell us they own the country, because they hold the land? The right by which they hold their land is not itself a natural right, and by consequence, nothing claimed as incidental to it. Whence then did they derive this privilege? From grant or conquest? Not from the latter. No war has ever been waged to assert it. If from the former, by whom was it conferred? They cannot, if they would, recur to the Royal Instructions of that English monarch, of infamous memory, who enjoined it upon the Governor of the then Colony of Virginia, "to take care that the members of the Assembly be elected *only by the freeholders*, as being more agreeable to the custome of England:" he might have added more congenial also with monarchical institutions. If Colonial regulations might properly be looked to, then the right, not of freeholders merely, but of *freemen*, to vote, may be traced to a more distant antiquity, and a less polluted source. But, by our ever-glorious revolution, the Government whence these regulations emanated, was annulled, and with it all the political privileges it had conferred, swept away. Will they rely on the Constitutional provision? That was the act of men delegated by themselves. They exercised the very right in question in appointing the body from whom they profess to derive it, and indeed gave to that body all the power it possessed. What is this but to say they generously conferred the privilege upon themselves? Perhaps they may rely on length of time to forestal enquiry. We acknowledge no act of limitations against the oppressed. Or will they disdain to shew any title; and, clinging to power, rest on force, the last argument of Kings, as its source and its defence? This were, doubtless, the more politic course.

Let us concede that the right of suffrage is a social right; that it must of necessity be regulated by society. Still the question recurs, is the existing limitation proper? For obvious reasons, by almost universal consent, women and children, aliens and slaves, are excluded. It were useless to discuss the propriety of a rule that scarcely admits of diversity of opinion. What is concurred in by those who constitute the society, the body politic, must be taken to be right. But the exclusion of these classes for reasons peculiarly applicable to them, is no argument for excluding others to whom no one of those reasons applies.

It is said to be *expedient*, however, to exclude non-freeholders also. Who shall judge of this expediency? The society: and does that embrace the proprietors of certain portions of land only? Expedient, for whom? for the freeholders. A harsh appellation would he deserve, who, on the plea of expediency, should take from another his property: what, then, should be said of him who, on that plea, takes from another his rights, upon which the security, not of his property only, but of his life and liberty depends?

But the non-freeholders are condemned for pursuing an abstract right, whose privation occasions no practical injury.

Your memorialists do not, perhaps, sufficiently comprehend the precise import of this language, so often used. The enjoyment of all other rights, whether of person or property, they will not deny, may be as perfect among those deprived of the privilege of voting, as among those possessing it. It may be as great under a despotism, as under any other form of Government. But they alone deserve to be called free, or have a guarantee for their rights, who participate in the formation of their political institutions, and in the control of those who make and administer the laws. To such as may be disposed to surrender this, or any other immunity, to the keeping of others, no practical mischief may ensue from its abandonment; or if any, none that will not be justly merited. Not so with him who feels as a freeman should; who would think for himself and speak what he thinks; who would not commit his conscience or his liberty to the uncontrolled direction of others. To him the privation of right, of that especially, which is the only safeguard of freedom, is practically wrong. So thought the fathers of the republic. It was not the oppressive weight of the taxes imposed by England on America: it was the assertion of a right to impose any burthens whatever upon those who were not represented; to bind by laws those who had no share, personal or delegated, in their enactment, that roused this continent to arms. . . .

20. JOHN C. CALHOUN (1782–1850)

CALHOUN, leading constitutional and theoretical spokesman for the South in its stand on slavery and States Rights, was born in western South Carolina in a family recently arrived from piedmont Virginia. The father, of moderate means and little schooling but prominent in the new community, sent his son to Yale to enter the Junior class. After graduation in 1804, John went on to study law in the new school at Litchfield, Connecticut, and then returned south to practise in his native county. He acquired a considerable estate, through marriage to a cousin from the "low country," and set up a large plantation near his birthplace. He was elected to the State legislature in his twenty-sixth year and to Congress two years later. Thenceforth he held office at Washington continuously (save for two years) until his death. He was member of the House of Representatives (1811–17), secretary of war (1817–25), vice-president (1825–32), and senator (1833–43, 1845–50).

In his earlier years at Washington, Calhoun was predominantly a nationalist in his political views. He supported protective tariffs, internal improvements, and the United States Bank. With his growing realization of the effects of the tariffs on the South, under the increasing rates demanded by Northern industrialists, and with the intensification of differences between North and South over the slavery question, he radically changed his position. In the *Exposition of 1828* (prepared for the State legislature) and in his Senate speeches, he stated the South Carolina doctrine of nullification, which was put forth as a constitutional foundation of an attack on the high tariffs. He wrote two works to supply a general political theory for his constitutional doctrine of the "concurrent majority" (see below, pp. 374–384) and his defense of slavery; they are the *Disquisition on Government* and the *Discourses on Government*. The latter was not completed.

In defending slavery, Calhoun set forth, in the *Disquisition* and in private letters and Senate speeches, the Southern aristocratic theory in its most comprehensive form. Among even freemen, he maintained, there are ineradicable differences in mind and character; property inevitably gets into the hands of the abler minority; an unequal division of political and social authority rightly follows an unequal distribution of wealth;

the doctrine that men have natural rights to liberty and equality tends to destroy social order and economic security; and history has not shown a single "civilized society in which one portion of the community did not, in point of fact, live on the labor of the other."

[See: *Correspondence of John C. Calhoun*, ed. by J. Franklin Jameson (1899), Vol. II, pp. 367, 758; "Speech on the Abolition Petitions," in the Senate, Feb. 6, 1837, in *Works* (ed. by Richard K. Crallé), Vol. II, pp. 625–633; Ulrich B. Phillips, in *Dictionary of American Biography* (1929); Charles E. Merriam, *American Political Theories* (1903), ch. 6; Gaillard Hunt, *John C. Calhoun* (1908); Charles M. Wiltse, "Calhoun's Democracy," *Journal of Politics*, Vol. III (1941), pp. 210–223; William M. Meigs, *The Life of John Caldwell Calhoun* (2 vols., 1917).]

From A DISQUISITION ON GOVERNMENT (1848–50)[1]

There is another error, not less great and dangerous, usually associated with the one which has just been considered [viz. that all people are equally entitled to liberty[2]]. I refer to the opinion, that liberty and equality are so intimately united, that liberty cannot be perfect without perfect equality.

That they are united to a certain extent,—and that equality of citizens, in the eyes of the law, is essential to liberty in a popular government, is conceded. But to go further, and make equality of condition essential to liberty, would be to destroy both liberty and progress. The reason is, that inequality of condition, while it is a necessary consequence of liberty, is, at the same time, indispensable to progress. In order to understand why this is so, it is necessary to bear in mind, that the main spring to progress is, the desire of individuals to better their condition; and that the strongest impulse which can be given to it is, to leave individuals free to exert themselves in the manner they may deem best for that purpose, as far at least as it can be done consistently with the ends for which government is ordained,—and to secure to all the fruits of their exertions. Now, as individuals differ greatly from each other, in intelligence, sagacity, energy, perseverance, skill, habits of industry and economy, physical power, position and opportunity,—the necessary effect of leaving all free to exert themselves to better their

[1] In *The Works of John C. Calhoun*, ed. by Richard K. Crallé, 6 vols. (Charleston, S. C., 1851), Vol. I, pp. 56–59.
[2] See below, p. 384.

condition, must be a corresponding inequality between those who may possess these qualities and advantages in a high degree, and those who may be deficient in them. The only means by which this result can be prevented are, either to impose such restrictions on the exertions of those who may possess them in a high degree, as will place them on a level with those who do not; or to deprive them of the fruits of their exertions. But to impose such restrictions on them would be destructive of liberty,—while, to deprive them of the fruits of their exertions, would be to destroy the desire of bettering their condition. It is, indeed, this inequality of condition between the front and rear ranks, in the march of progress, which gives so· strong an impulse to the former to maintain their position, and to the latter to press forward into their files. This gives to progress its greatest impulse. To force the front rank back to the rear, or attempt to push forward the rear into· line with the front, by the interposition of the government, would put an end to the impulse, and effectually arrest the march of progress.

These great and dangerous errors have their origin in the prevalent opinion that all men are born free and equal;—than which nothing can be more unfounded and false. It rests upon the assumption of a fact, which is contrary to universal observation, in whatever light it may be· regarded. It is, indeed, difficult to explain how an opinion so destitute of all sound reason, ever could have been so extensively entertained, unless we regard it as being confounded with another, which has some semblance of truth;—but which, when properly understood, is not less false and dangerous. I refer to the assertion, that all men are equal in the state of nature; meaning, by a state of nature, a state of individuality, supposed to have existed prior to the social and political state; and in which men lived apart and independent of each other. If such a state ever did exist, all men would have been, indeed, free and equal in it; that is, free to do as they pleased, and exempt from the authority or control of others—as, by supposition, it existed anterior to society and government. But such a state is purely hypothetical. It never did, nor can exist; as it is inconsistent with the preservation and perpetuation of the race. It is, therefore, a great misnomer to call it *the state of nature*. Instead of being the natural state of man, it is, of all conceivable states, the most opposed to his nature —most repugnant to his feelings, and most incompatible with his wants. His natural state, is the social and political—the one for which his Creator made him, and the only one in which he can preserve and perfect his race. As, then, there never was such a state as the, so called, state of nature, and never can be, it follows, that men, instead of being born in it, are born in the social and political state; and of course, instead of being born free and equal, are born subject, not only to parental authority, but to the laws and institutions of the country where born, and under whose protection they draw their first breath.

21. WALT WHITMAN (1819–92)

WHITMAN was born in Huntington, Long Island; his father was a farmer and carpenter. The family moved to Brooklyn and here Whitman had his formal schooling, which ended in his twelfth year. He then worked as office boy, typesetter, schoolteacher (for five years), editor of local Long Island newspapers, editor for two years (1846–48) of the Brooklyn *Daily Eagle*, editorial writer (for brief periods) on several New York papers and magazines, and manager of a paper in New Orleans for a few months. In 1855 there appeared the first edition of his *Leaves of Grass*, of which there were ten later editions during his lifetime, each edition longer than its predecessor. During most of the Civil War he worked as a nurse in army hospitals near Washington; and he remained in Washington for several years holding small governmental jobs. From the early seventies until his death he lived with a brother in Camden, New Jersey, in a somewhat eccentric style and in precarious health. His numerous poems, composed with new devices of form and subject matter, gained him bitter critics and admiring friends. Many distinguished writers visited him; but, his biographers say, he was read hardly at all by plain people of the sort he had exalted in his poems.

Whitman had some part in the political life of his day. In his twenties he was a stump speaker for the Democratic party. As an editorial writer he took a strong stand against the territorial extension of slavery and in favor of gradual emancipation; it was a fiery editorial on the slavery question that caused his dismissal from the Brooklyn *Eagle*. He attacked monopolies and high tariffs and advocated labor legislation, prison reform, the abolition of capital punishment, the improvement of public education, and the extension of the territorial domain of the United States in fulfillment of a world mission. In numerous places he expressed his faith in the exalted destiny of democracy and democratic America. His general democratic faith had essentially the same philosophical basis as that of Emerson (who, Whitman said, "brought me to boil"). He shared Emerson's belief in the all-pervading Reason, God, "Over-soul," in Man. But there were wider social implications in his conception of equality ("I want to encourage in young men the spirit that does not know what it is to feel that it stands in the presence of superiors"). He attached more importance than Emerson did to the benevolent, fraternal, and secular aspects of equality, and he insisted more on positive action to achieve the democratic goal. He believed in the perfectibility of man, yet acknowledged also the baser and cruder aspects of man's nature. The latter disturbed him less basically than it did other philosophical democrats of his day; and he scorned all aristocratic criticism of political democracy. Common people in America, he said, might be as dirty as Matthew Arnold considered them, but everything worth while "comes out of the dirt." His longest prose work, *Democratic Vistas* (1871), was his attempt to rationalize that faith.

[For Whitman's political ideas, see (besides the selection below), in his *Leaves of Grass,* "For You O Democracy" (1860), "One's Self I Sing" (1867), "Thou Mother with Thy Equal Brood" (1872); also "The Eighteenth Presidency" (1856?), in Clifton J. Furness ed., *Walt Whitman's Workshop: a Collection of Unpublished Manuscripts* (1928); "Notes for Lectures on Democracy and 'Adhesiveness' " (1855?), *ibid.,* pp. 54–64. See also: Vernon L. Parrington, *Main Currents of American Thought,* Vol. III (1930), pp. 69–86; Ralph H. Gabriel, *The Course of American Democratic Thought* (1940), ch. 11; Bliss Perry, *Walt Whitman: His Life and Work* (1906); F. O. Matthiessen, *American Renaissance* (1941), pp. 517–625, 649–652.]

From DEMOCRATIC VISTAS (1870)[1]

. . . I will not gloss over the appalling dangers of universal suffrage in the United States. In fact, it is to admit and face these dangers I am writing. To him or her within whose thought rages the battle, advancing, retreating, between democracy's convictions, aspirations, and the people's crudeness, vice, caprices, I mainly write this essay. I shall use the words America and democracy as convertible terms. Not an ordinary one is the issue. The United States are destined either to surmount the gorgeous history of feudalism, or else prove the most tremendous failure of time. Not the least doubtful am I on any prospects of their material success. The triumphant future of their business, geographic and productive departments, on larger scales and in more varieties than ever, is certain. In those respects the republic must soon (if she does not already) outstrip all examples hitherto afforded, and dominate the world.

[1] In Walt Whitman, *Complete Prose Works* (New York, 1914), pp. 197–250, at 198–200, 207–208, 211–213, 216–218. By courtesy of Mitchell Kennerley.

Admitting all this, with the priceless value of our political institutions, general suffrage, (and fully acknowledging the latest, widest opening of the doors,) I say that, far deeper than these, what finally and only is to make of our western world a nationality superior to any hither known, and out-topping the past, must be vigorous, yet unsuspected Literatures, perfect personalities and sociologies, original, transcendental, and expressing (what, in highest sense, are not yet express'd at all,) democracy and the modern. With these, and out of these, I promulge new races of Teachers, and of perfect Women, indispensable to endow the birth-stock of a New World. For feudalism, caste, the ecclesiastic traditions, though palpably retreating from political institutions, still hold essentially, by their spirit, even in this country, entire possession of the more important fields, indeed the very subsoil, of education, and of social standards and literature.

I say that democracy can never prove itself beyond cavil, until it founds and luxuriantly grows its own forms of art, poems, schools, theology, displacing all that exists, or that has been produced anywhere in the past, under opposite influences. It is curious to me that while so many voices, pens, minds, in the press, lecture-rooms, in our Congress, &c., are discussing intellectual topics, pecuniary dangers, legislative problems, the suffrage, tariff and labor questions, and the various business and benevolent needs of America, with propositions, remedies, often worth deep attention, there is one need, a hiatus the profoundest, that no eye seems to perceive, no voice to state. Our fundamental want to-day in the United States, with closest, amplest reference to present conditions, and to the future, is of a class, and the clear idea of a class, of native authors, literatuses, far different, far higher in grade than any yet known, sacerdotal, modern, fit to cope with our occasions, lands, permeating the whole mass of American mentality, taste, belief, breathing into it a new breath of life, giving it decision, affecting politics far more than the popular superficial suffrage, with results inside and underneath the elections of Presidents or Congresses—radiating, begetting appropriate teachers, schools, manners, and, as its grandest result, accomplishing, (what neither the schools nor the churches and their clergy have hitherto accomplish'd, and without which this nation will no more stand, permanently, soundly, than a house will stand without a substratum,) a religious and moral character beneath the political and productive and intellectual bases of the States. . . .

For after the rest is said—after the many time-honor'd and really true things for subordination, experience, rights of property, &c., have listen'd to and acquiesced in—after the valuable and well-settled statement of our duties and relations in society is thoroughly conn'd over and exhausted—it remains to bring forward and modify everything else with the idea of that Something a man is, (last precious consolation of the drudging poor,) standing apart from all else, divine in his own right, and a woman in hers, sole and untouchable by any canons of authority, or any rule derived from precedent, state-safety, the acts of legislatures, or even from what is called religion, modesty, or art. The radiation of this truth is the key of the most significant doings of our immediately preceding three centuries, and has been the political genesis and life of America. Advancing visibly, it still more advances invisibly. Underneath the flunctuations of the expressions of society, as well as the movements of the politics of the leading nations of the world, we see steadily pressing ahead and strengthening itself, even in the midst of immense tendencies toward aggregation, this image of completeness in separatism, of individual personal dignity, of a single person, either male or female, characterized in the main, not from extrinsic acquirements or position, but in the pride of himself or herself alone; and, as an eventual conclusion and summing up, (or else the entire scheme of things is aimless, a cheat, a crash,) the simple idea that the last, best dependence is to be upon humanity itself, and its own inherent, normal, full-grown qualities, without any superstitious support whatever. This idea of perfect individualism it is indeed that deepest tinges and gives character to the idea of the aggregate. For it is mainly or altogether to serve independent separatism that we favor a strong generalization, consolidation. As it is to give the best vitality and freedom to the rights of the States, (every bit as important as the right of nationality, the union,) that we insist on the identity of the Union at all hazards.

The purpose of democracy—supplanting old belief in the necessary absoluteness of establish'd dynastic rulership, temporal, ecclesiastical, and scholastic, as furnishing the only security against chaos, crime, and ignorance—is, through many transmigrations, and amid endless ridicules, arguments, and ostensible failures, to illustrate, at all hazards, this doctrine or theory that man, properly train'd in sanest, highest freedom, may and must become a law, and series of laws, unto himself, surrounding and providing for, not only his own personal control, but all his relations to other individuals, and to the State; and that, while other theories, as in the past histories of nations, have proved wise enough, and indispensable perhaps for their conditions, *this*, as matters now stand in our civilized world, is the only scheme worth working from, as warranting results like those of Nature's laws, reliable, when once establish'd, to carry on themselves. . . .

Meantime, general humanity, (for to that we return, as, for our purposes, what it really is, to bear in mind,) has always, in every department, been full of perverse maleficence, and is so yet. In downcast hours the soul thinks it always will be—but soon recovers from such sickly moods. I myself see clearly enough the crude, defective streaks in all the strata of the common people; the specimens and vast collections of the ignorant, the credulous, the unfit and uncouth, the incapable, and the very low and poor. . . . The point is a formidable one, and there will doubtless always be numbers of solid and reflective citizens who will never get over it. Our answer is general, and is involved in the scope and letter of this essay. We believe the ulterior object of political and all other government, (having, of course, provided for the police, the safety of life, property, and for the basic statute and common law, and their administration, always first in order,) to be among the rest, not merely to rule, to repress disorder, &c., but to develop, to open up to cultivation, to encourage the possibilities of all beneficent and manly outcroppage, and of that aspiration for independence, and the pride and self-respect latent in all characters. (Or, if there be exceptions, we cannot, fixing our eyes on them alone, make theirs the rule for all.)

I say the mission of government, henceforth, in civilized lands, is not repression alone, and not authority alone, not even of law, nor by that favorite standard of the eminent writer, the rule of the best men, the born heroes and captains of the race, (as if such ever, or one time out of a hundred, get into the big places, elective or dynastic)—but higher than the highest arbitrary rule, to train communities through all their grades, beginning with individuals and ending there again, to rule themselves. What Christ appear'd for in the moral-spiritual field for human-kind, namely, that in respect to the absolute soul, there is in the possession of such by each single individual, something so transcendent, so incapable of gradations, (like life,) that, to that extent, it places all beings on a common level, utterly regardless of the distinctions of intellect, virtue, station, or any height or lowliness whatever—is tallied in like manner, in this other field, by democracy's rule that men, the nation, as a common aggregate of living identities, affording in each a separate and complete subject for freedom, worldly thrift and happiness, and for a fair chance for growth, and for protection in citizenship, &c., must, to the political extent of the suffrage or vote, if no further, be placed, in each and in the whole, on one broad, primary, universal, common platform.

The purpose is not altogether direct; perhaps it is more indirect. For it is not that democracy is of exhaustive account, in itself. Perhaps, indeed, it is, (like Nature,) of no account in itself. It is that, as we see, it is the best, perhaps only, fit and full means, formulater, general caller-forth, trainer, for the million, not for grand material personalities only, but for immortal souls. To be a voter with the rest is not so much; and this, like every institute, will have its imperfections. But to become an enfranchised man, and now, impediments removed, to stand and start without humiliation, and equal with the rest; to commence, or have the road clear'd to commence, the grand experiment of development, whose end, (perhaps requiring several generations,) may be the forming of a full-grown man or woman—that is something. To ballast the State is also secured, and in our times is to be secured, in no other way.

We do not, (at any rate I do not,) put it either on the ground that the People, the masses, even the best of them, are, in their latent or exhibited qualities, essentially sensible and good—nor on the ground of their rights; but that good or bad, rights or no rights, the demoratic formula is the only safe and preservative one for coming times. We endow the masses with the suffrage for their own sake, no doubt; then, perhaps still more, from another point of view, for community's sake. Leaving the rest to the sentimentalists, we present freedom as sufficient in its scientific aspect, cold as ice, reasoning, deductive, clear and passionless as crystal. . . .

Political democracy, as it exists and practically works in America, with all its threatening evils, supplies a training-school for making first-class men. It is life's gymnasium, not of good only, but of all. We try often, though we fall back often. A brave delight, fit for freedom's athletes, fills these arenas, and fully satisfies, out of the action in them, irrespective of success. Whatever we do not attain, we at any rate attain the experiences of the fight, the hardening of the strong campaign, and throb with currents of attempt at least. Time is ample. Let the victors come after us. Not for nothing does evil play its part among us. Judging from the main portions of the history of the world, so far, justice is always in jeopardy, peace walks amid hourly pitfalls, and of slavery, misery, meanness, the craft of tyrants and the credulity of the populace, in some of their protean forms, no voice can at any time say, They are not. The clouds break a little, and the sun shines out—but soon and certain the lowering darkness falls again, as if to last forever. Yet is there an immortal courage and prophecy in every sane soul that cannot, must not, under any circumstances, capitulate. Vive, the attack— the perennial assault! Vive, the unpopular cause—the spirit that audaciously aims—the never-abandon'd efforts, pursued the same amid opposing proofs and precedents.

Once, before the war, (alas! I dare not say how many times the mood has come!) I, too, was fill'd with doubt and gloom. A foreigner, an acute and good man, had impressively said to me, that day—putting in form, indeed, my own observations: "I have travel'd much in the United States, and watch'd their politicians, and listen'd to the speeches of the candidates, and read the journals, and gone into the public houses, and heard the unguarded talk of men. And I have found your vaunted America honeycomb'd from top to toe with infidelism, even to itself and its own programme. I have mark'd the brazen hell-faces of secession and slavery gazing defiantly from all the windows and doorways. I have everywhere found, primarily, thieves and scalliwags arranging the nominations to offices, and sometimes filling the offices themselves. I have found the north just as full of bad stuff as the south. Of the holders of public office in the Nation or the States or their municipalities, I have found that not one in a hundred has been chosen by any spontaneous selection of the outsiders, the people, but all have been nominated and put through by little or large caucuses of the politicians, and have got in by corrupt rings and electioneering, not capacity or desert. I have noticed how the millions of sturdy farmers and mechanics are thus the helpless supplejacks of comparatively few politicians. And I have noticed more and more, the alarming spectacle of parties usurping the government, and openly and shamelessly wielding it for party purposes."

Sad, serious, deep truths. Yet are there other, still deeper, amply confronting, dominating truths. Over those politicians and great and little rings, and over all their insolence and wiles, and over the powerfulest parties, looms a power, too sluggish maybe, but ever holding decisions and decrees in hand, ready, with stern process, to execute them as soon as plainly needed—and at times, indeed, summarily crushing to atoms the mightiest parties, even in the hour of their pride.

In saner hours far different are the amounts of these things from what, at first sight, they appear. Though it is no doubt important who is elected governor, mayor, or legislator, (and full of dismay when incompetent or vile ones get elected, as they sometimes do,) there are other, quieter contingencies, infinitely more important. Shams, &c., will always be the show, like ocean's scum; enough, if waters deep and clear make up the rest. Enough, that while the piled embroider'd shoddy gaud and fraud spreads to the superficial eye, the hidden warp and weft are genuine, and will wear forever. Enough, in short, that the race, the land which could raise such as the late rebellion, could also put it down.

The average man of a land at last only is important. He, in these States, remains immortal owner and boss, deriving good uses, somehow, out of any sort of servant in office, even the basest; (certain universal requisites, and their settled regularity and protection, being first secured,) a nation like ours, in a sort of geological formation state, trying continually new experiments, choosing new delegations, is not served by the best men only, but sometimes more by those that provoke it—by the combats they arouse. Thus national rage, fury, discussions, &c., better than content. Thus, also, the warning signals, invaluable for after times.

What is more dramatic than the spectacle we have seen repeated, and doubtless long shall see—the popular judgment taking the successful candidates on trial in the offices—standing off, as it were, and observing them and their doings for a while, and always giving, finally, the fit, exactly due reward? I think, after all, the sublimest part of political history, and its culmination, is currently issuing from the American people. I know nothing grander, better exercise, better digestion, more positive proof of the past, the triumphant result of faith in human-kind, than a well-contested American national election.

22. E. L. GODKIN (1831–1902)

EDWIN LAWRENCE GODKIN was born in southeastern Ireland, son of a Presbyterian minister, who was also, at times, a newspaper publisher, newspaper correspondent, and political speaker. Godkin was educated at preparatory schools in England and at Queens College, Belfast. He studied law briefly at Lincoln's Inn, worked awhile in a London publishing house (which published a history of Hungary by him), and spent two years in the Crimea as correspondent of the London *Daily News* and a few months as editorial writer on a Belfast paper. In his twenty-sixth year, he moved to the United States, which he had pictured as the place in which his dream of a modern educated democracy would come true. Here he traveled, read American political history, made the acquaintance of publicists and literary men, and soon came to know the American political scene. During the Civil War he was correspondent again of the London *Daily News*, giving his reports a pro-Unionist slant. Shortly after the close of the war, a group of his acquaintances raised funds for a new weekly journal of "politics, literature, science, and art"; they named it *The Nation*, and the first issue appeared on July 6, 1865, with Godkin as editor. It had a small circulation but enjoyed wide prestige among the most prominent writers of the day and among college graduates generally. When, in 1870, Harvard offered Godkin a professorship of history, distinguished friends urged him to decline the offer, on the ground that it was easier to find another Harvard professor than another editor good enough for *The Nation*. In 1881, *The Nation* was taken over by the New York *Evening Post*, owned by Henry Villard, *The Nation* being issued as a weekly edition of the *Post*; and two years later (after the retirement of Carl Shurz), Godkin became editor-in-chief of the combined periodicals. The two journals (owned by Villard, who was born and educated in Germany, and edited by Godkin, born in Ireland of English ancestry and educated in England and Ireland) were accepted as leading organs of American intellectual liberalism.

Godkin's editorials were clear, informed, reasonable, fluent, and emphatic. He was tied to no particular group. Persistently he advocated a lowering of tariff rates, civil service reform, clean elections, and the improvement of city government, and he opposed carpetbag government in the south, cheap money, imperialism, favors to big business, and a too stringent regulation of business. He defended American democracy against its aristocratic critics in England, yet cautioned Americans against either remaining too frontier or becoming too proletarian in their governmental and social policy. His political ideal for America was a genuinely democratic electorate choosing educated and high-minded public officials through a free and honest electoral system. The growth of a "venal" and "trivial" press and other features of the "gilded age," led him in his latter years to fear that he might see "the America of my youthful dreams vanish . . . and the commencement on this continent of the old story." Although he continued to point out the more favorable signs, such as the vast expansion and improvement of elementary and higher education, he still thought that the business, journalistic, and political-party follies of American democracy, in 1895, might be the signs of the beginning throughout the world generally of "a long period of decline like that which followed the fall of the Roman empire and then a recrudescence under some other form of society."

[See: Rollo Ogden, *Life and Letters of Edwin Lawrence Godkin*, 2 vols. (1907); James Ford Rhodes, "Edwin Lawrence Godkin," in *Historical Essays* (1909), pp. 265–297; Vernon L. Parrington, *Main Currents of American Thought*, Vol. III (1930), pp. 154–168.]

From THE REAL PROBLEMS OF DEMOCRACY (1896) [1]

All authors who touch at all on democracy in our day recognize in it a new and potent force, destined before long to effect very serious changes in the social structure, and to alter, in many important respects, the way in which men have looked at human society since the foundation of Christianity. But they handle it very much as we handle electricity; that is to say, tentatively. They admit they are dealing with a very mysterious power, of which they know as yet but little, and on the future manifestations of which they cannot pronounce with any confidence. . . . Every man, or nearly every man, who takes up a pen to examine the questions what democracy is, and what effect it is likely to have on the race, is himself either an earnest advocate or an earnest opponent of it. He sees in it either the regeneration of mankind or the ruin of our civilization. This is true of nearly every writer of eminence who

[1] In Edwin Lawrence Godkin, *Problems of Modern Democracy* (3rd ed., New York, 1907), pp. 275–310, at 276–277, 281–290, 292–302, 305–308. By special arrangement with Charles Scribner's Sons.

has touched on it since the French Revolution. The most moderate of its enemies seldom admits more on its behalf than his own ignorance of what it promises. Its defenders are, as a rule, too enthusiastic to make their predictions of much philosophic value. . . .

. . . For my part, I never read a description of the evils of democracy at the present day without inquiring with what state of society or with what kind of government the writer compares it. When and where was the polity from observation of which he has formed his standard? When and where was the state of things, the "good estate," from which we have declined or are declining? This is extremely important, for all we know or can say about government must be the result of actual observation. "Ideal government," as it is called, such as is described in Plato's "Republic," or More's "Utopia," or Bellamy's "Looking Backward," is interesting to read about, as the play of an individual mind, but no one considers any of these books very helpful to those who are actually contending with the problems of to-day.

To enable any reformer to make his impress on the age in which he lives, or to win any considerable number of his countrymen over to his way of thinking, the state of things he seeks to bring about must commend itself to his contemporaries as capable of realization. He must have some model in his mind's eye, not too far removed, either in time or in distance, from the popular imagination. This is an essential condition of the advance of all great multitudes. Every man's standard of civilization is drawn from what he has seen, or thinks he may readily reach. Nearly all differences touching governments, between various peoples or between various classes of the same society, came from differences of standards. Some are extremely content with a state of things that others think impossible. An Indian, for instance, cannot understand the white man's eagerness to get him to give up the tepee, in which he has been so happy, for the log cabin or the frame house. The spoils politician is puzzled by the Mugwump's passion for competitive examinations, and government based on party distribution of the offices as spoils seems to him most natural and thoroughly successful. Probably few or no Tammany men can to this day quite understand the objection of reformers to their style of government. They see that tens of thousands apparently like it and are satisfied with it. What is the need of a change? The cause of all the discussion is that the Mugwump has a different standard of government from the politician, and is not satisfied until the government he lives under comes up to it. In like manner, when a monarchist or conservative begins to complain to a democrat of the defects of his system and of the gloominess of its prospects, in order to produce any effect he must point out from what period or from what system there has been a falling away. When and where were things any better, taken as a whole? And how much better were they? This is a question which every writer on democracy is bound to answer at the outset.

. . . When we undertake to compare one régime with another, old with new times, it does not do to fasten on one feature of either. In our day this is sure to be ineffective. If we judge American society, for instance, solely from the point of view of legislative purity and ability, it will certainly suffer in comparison with that of Great Britain. If we judge it from the point of view of judicial learning and independence, we shall probably reach the same conclusion. It would be quite easy to point out certain losses which it sustains from the absence of an aristocracy, as contrasted with any European country. . . . To produce any real effect the comparison has to be complete. You have to compare the general happiness from all causes. You have to treat the two contrasted communities as places for the poor and friendless man, or for the industrious, enterprising, and thrifty man, to live in, as well as for the wealthy and cultivated man. Otherwise you make no headway. Every reader will think instantly of the things you have overlooked. . . .

The truth is that democracy is simply an experiment in the application of the principle of equality to the management of the common affairs of the community. It is the principle of equality which has conquered the world. That one man is as good as another is an outgrowth of what may be called social consciousness, and as soon as it has got possession of the State, democratic government follows as a matter of course. The theory of the social contract is an offspring of it. This theory made no impression on the masses when Locke preached it. It did not reach the people till Rousseau took it up, in the middle of the last century. Since then it has made great strides. Rulers have become the mere hired servants of the mass of the community, and criticism of them has come naturally with the employment of them as agents. The notion that all men are alike, and are entitled to an equal voice in the management of the common affairs, is democracy. It is the effort of all to assert this, and to see how the thing can be done, which forms the democratic experiment that is being tried in so many countries.

Many things have occurred which seem to warrant the belief that it will not succeed. What constitutes the success of a government? The very first answer to this question is that we cannot tell whether a government is successful or not without seeing how long it lasts. The first duty of a government is to last. A government, however good, which does not last is a failure. The Athenian republic, the Roman republic and empire, the Venetian republic, the French monarchy, the English monarchy, and the American republic, have all to be tried by this test. To say that a government is a very good government, but that it was overthrown or changed in a few years, is almost a contradiction in terms. All we know of any value about any government is derived from observation of its working. It must be confessed, therefore, that nearly all that we read in our day about democracy is pure speculation. No democracy has lasted long enough to enable one to write a treatise on it of much value. . . .

The men who first began to write on democracy, toward the close of the last century and the beginning of this, had really a very small notion of its working on the scale which the modern world witnesses. Their only opportunities of observation lay in the history of the small Greek communities, of early Rome, of Venice and the minor Swiss cantons, and of the early New England States. They had not for a moment pictured to themselves the government by universal suffrage of communities numbering tens of millions. Their democracies all met in the forum or market-place; their leading men were known to every citizen. Nothing seemed easier than to fill the public offices by a mere show of hands. Every man was supposed to be intensely occupied with public affairs, to be eager to vote on them, and to be quite able to vote intelligently. The work of management had not a prominent place in any former democratic scheme. The "demagogue"—that is, the man who leads people astray by specious schemes, by hostility to the rich, or eagerness for war, or profuse prodigality, or winning eloquence—was well known. But the man who does not speak, who makes no public impression, who is not rich or eloquent or in any manner distinguished, yet who leads the voters and holds legislation in the hollow of his hand, had still to make his appearance.

In the new, unforeseen, enormous democracy, 40,000,000 to 100,000,000 in England, or France, or America, he is indispensable. In these large democracies, the work of bringing the popular will to bear in filling the offices of the government, or in performing any act of government, is one of great difficulty, which needs almost constant attention from a large army of "workers." To influence, persuade, or inform this immense body of persons is no easy matter, as two antagonistic forces are always engaged in pulling it in different directions. The diffusion among it of any one view of anything would be a serious task. To insure the triumph of either view is still more serious. Then, a very large proportion of the voters are not interested in public questions at all, or their feeble interest has to be aroused and kept awake. Another large proportion do not desire to give themselves the trouble to vote. They have to be, in some manner, induced to go to the polls, or have to be prepared to go by numerous visits. The business of what is called the "canvass" in modern democracy is, in fact, something unlooked for and unprovided for by theoretical democrats. It has produced a profession whose sole occupation is to get people to vote in a particular way. As the mass of voters increases, this profession, of course, becomes larger and more important. In my own opinion, its importance constitutes the strongest argument against woman suffrage. The doubling of the number of votes to be influenced or managed in any community is a very grave consideration; for not only have you to find such workers, with the certainty that their character will not be very high, but you have to pay them, and no provision for their payment has ever been made in any scheme of democratic government. The duty of remunerating them is thrown on the victorious parties at elections; in America, for a long time, this duty was discharged by distributing among them the smaller offices. There has been an escape from it here by what is called civil service reform, or, in other words, by competitive examination. In England, the aristocracy, finding the government patronage passing out of their hands, judiciously introduced the merit system, in time to save it from the incoming democracy, but in France and Italy the tendency is still in the direction of "spoils." The passion for government places is strong, and the difficulty of getting anything done for the State, except in return for a place, grows apace, on the whole. If I said that the reluctance of a democracy to vote at all, or to vote right, was not foreseen by the early democratic advocates, and that they made no provision for it in their system, I should not be very far wrong. This was the greatest mistake of the theoretic democrats. They never foresaw the big democracies. The working of democracy in America is something of which they had no conception. They did not anticipate the necessity of organizing and directing the suffrage, nor of the intervention of the boss and his assistants. . . .

Another new phenomenon which has greatly affected the development of democratic government, and has received no attention, is the growth of corporations. These aggregations of capital in a few hands have created a new power in the State, whose influence on government has been very grave. They employ a vast number of voters, over whom their influence is paramount; a single railroad company has in its service thousands of men. They own immense sums of money, which they think it but right to use freely for their own protection. In some States, men make a livelihood in the legislature by "striking" them,—that is, threatening them with hostile legislation, and getting themselves bought off by the agent of the corporation; for each corporation is apt to keep an agent at the seat of government to meet these very demands, and makes no secret of it. Latterly the bosses have taken charge of this business themselves. They receive the money, and see that the legislature is properly managed in return. The companies have, in fact, created a code of morality to meet this exigency. The officers say that they are the custodians of large amounts of other people's property, which they are bound to defend, by whomsoever attacked. That wrong does exist in the State is not their affair. The reform of the legislature or of the State is not their affair. It is their business to keep safely what has been placed in their charge. Indeed, the levying of blackmail on companies, either as a contribution to campaign expenses or as fees to pay for protection, is now one of the principal sources of a boss's revenue, and, in States like New York, goes a good way toward enabling him to defy hostile sentiment. It furnishes him with funds for subsidizing the legislature and the press. How to bring these corporations under the law, and at the

same time protect them from unjust attacks, is one of the most
serious problems of democratic government. . . .

This brings me naturally to two other serious and significant
changes which have occurred within fifty years in democratic societies. I mean the decline of the legislatures, and the transfer of
power, or rather of the work of government, from the rich to the
poor.

That this decline of the legislatures is not a mere decline in manners seems to me undeniable. It is a decline in the quality of the
members in general respect, in education, in social position, in morality, in public spirit, in care and deliberation, and, I think I must
add, in integrity, also. Legislation is more hasty and more voluminous, is drafted with less care, and enacted with less deliberation
and with much greater indifference to public opinion, particularly
to instructed and thoughtful public opinion. This is said to be
true of France and Italy, and in some degree of England, but it is
especially true of America. Congress and the State legislatures are
not what they were forty years ago. Both the Senate and the
House contain fewer men of prominence and ability. The members are more slenderly instructed, but much more eagerly interested, in questions of political economy, finance, and taxation than
they used to be, and more disposed to turn to account what they
conceive to be their knowledge. They are more difficult to lead,
and yet are more under the domination of their own cliques or
sets. In the State legislatures, the boss is far more powerful than
he was. But little legislation originates with the members themselves. It is generally concocted outside and passed under orders.
Few of the members are really chosen and elected by the people.
They are suggested and returned by the boss of the State or district.
They feel accountable to him, and not to the public. The old machinery of agitation, the public meeting and the press, produces
little effect on them. Their motives are rarely made known. Many
of their acts, if not corrupt, are open to the suspicion of corruption;
some of them are bold attempts to extort money. All this is true,
as I have said, in some degree or other, of all the countries in which
democratic institutions have taken or begun to take root. These
bodies have not answered the earlier expectations of democratic
philosophers. The men who were expected to go to them do not
go to them. The men who have served the public well in them do

not return to the service. The influence on them of the intellectual, cultivated, or instructed world is small.

To account for this, or to say how it is to be mended, is, I admit,
very difficult. Few subjects have done more to baffle reformers and
investigators. It is the great puzzle of the heartiest friends of democracy. The matter is growing more serious in America as society is becoming richer and more complicated. As commerce
increases, credit expands and interests multiply, of course the machinery of government increases in delicacy. Derangement becomes easier, repair more difficult. The effect, for instance, of
instability in taxation, or of adventures in foreign policy, upon
foreign trade, or upon investment and the movements of capital,
is very great; so that already merchants, bankers, and dealers in
money are beginning to ask themselves whether it will be long
possible to carry on the financial affairs of a great nation under a
government so unskilful, and possessed of so little knowledge of
the machinery of credit, as democratic governments generally are.
This gives great importance to the question, What prospect is
there of any change for the better? What sign is there of anything
of the kind? As to this I confess I think the dependence of the
optimist, if he descends to argument at all, must be on the general
progress of the race in self-restraint, in love of order, and in a better
knowledge, through experience, of the conditions of successful government. Any such process must necessarily be slow, and no results can be looked for until after the trial and failure of many experiments.

In other words, I do not look for the improvement of democratic legislatures in quality within any moderate period. What I
believe democratic societies will do, in order to improve their government and make better provision for the protection of property
and the preservation of order, is to restrict the power of these assemblies and shorten their sittings, and to use the referendum more
freely for the production of really important laws. I have very
little doubt that, before many years elapse, the American people
will get their government more largely from constitutional conventions, and will confine the legislatures within very narrow limits
and make them meet at rare intervals. The tendencies all over the
Union are in this direction, and Switzerland, the most democratic
country in Europe, is showing the way distinctly toward less law-

making and more frequent consultation of the people at large. I believe, for instance, that after a few years' experience of the transfer of the currency question, which has now begun, to the management of popular suffrage, the legal tender quality of money, which is now behind the whole trouble, will be abolished, and the duty of the government will be confined simply to weighing and stamping. The usefulness of the legal tender now is ludicrously disproportioned to the noise made about it. Except as a rule for fixing the denomination in which debtors must pay their debts in the absence of an agreement—which rarely causes any dispute—and for enabling debtors to cheat their creditors by paper money or the adulteration of coin—which is not infrequent—it is difficult to see what good purpose legal tender serves. It is almost certain that the day will come when it will be seen that no democratic government is fit to be entrusted with the power of giving any substance legal tender quality, and that the very best solution of the money problem is to be found in letting people make their own bargains —a solution which will be hastened by the increasing tendency to settle contracts, make purchases, and pay debts by check or draft.

The other corrective of which I see signs, though of less importance, is the increasing ability or willingness of business men to separate their business from their politics, and to refuse any longer to put money into the hands of party agents to do as they please with it. This use of money, especially since the growth of the tariff question in importance, has been one of the great sources of the degradation of American politics, because it supports the excesses or abuses of the nominating system by strengthening the hands of the boss; for it is he who generally receives the funds. But it would be absurd to build great hopes of progress on the mere cessation of an abuse. It is a thing to be noted rather than dwelt on. All that we can say with certainty is that no Western society is likely, in modern times, to let itself run completely down, as the ancient societies often did, without vigorous attempts at recovery and improvement. The general belief in progress which now prevails, the greatly increased desire to extract comfort out of life (and comfort includes quiet and order), the more scientific spirit of the time, the disposition of all classes to assume social responsibility, and the sense of what the French call "solidarity" diffused by the press, assure us that every means of progress will be tried, that no defect will be submitted to indefinitely; but what means of improvement will be most effective, and what safeguards will be found most reliable, he would be a rash man who would venture to predict in detail.

As to the transfer of the government to the poor, it should be remembered that, except during very short periods in ancient democracies, the world has been governed by rich men; that is, by the great landholders or the great merchants. This is true of all the ancient republics and of all the modern monarchies. The unfitness of poor men for the important offices of legislation and administration has been generally acted on in the modern world, as a State doctrine. Every government has been a rich man's government. It is only in some of the smaller Swiss cantons that departures from this rule have been made. But, as a rule, in democratic societies in our day, government has been transferred to poor men. These poor men find themselves in possession of very great power over rich communities. Through the taxing power rich corporations and rich individuals are at their mercy. They are not restrained by tradition; they are often stimulated by envy or other anti-social passions. If it were not for the restrictions imposed in American States by the Constitution, the lives of rich men and of companies would be full of difficulty. There has grown up around this change the foreshadowing of a code of morality in which men's right to be rich is called in question, and the spoliation of them, if done under forms of law, is not an offense against morality. This, again, is counterbalanced or neutralized by the general popular tendency to make the accumulation of wealth the one sign of worldly success, and to estimate men by the size of their income, from whatever source derived. There is probably in America to-day a nearer approach to a literal rendering of the English term "worth," as measuring a man's possessions, than ever occurred elsewhere; that is, the term is more fully descriptive of the fact than it has ever been. Inevitably, there has appeared side by side with this a certain distrust of the opinions of persons who have not made money, which has naturally had an injurious effect on the government, and has, along with several other causes, contributed to the exclusion of the learned or professional class from the work of administration. A faithful description of the position of the wealthy class in America to-day would probably say that the accumulation of wealth by a man's own exertion is admired by the public, and greatly respected if he gives it fully to public objects, but that his attempt to participate in the work of government is viewed with a certain jealousy, while contributions for party purposes are eagerly received by the bosses, and offices are occasionally given in return for them by regular bargain. It is in this way, in fact, as well as through lower forms of corruption, that individual wealth protects itself against the consequences of the change to which I have already called attention, the transfer of the government to the poor and obscure. Property still has weight in public affairs, but not open weight, and the power of persuading the legislators has been taken from the public orator, or writer, who wielded it in the beginning of the century, and turned over to the successful man of affairs, who has schemes to carry out, but cannot waste time in arguing about them with anybody. . . .

What is most serious of all is that we have not, as England or France or Germany has, one great capital, in which all the philosophers and speculators, and in fact men of education, live and make a philosophical or political atmosphere, are influenced by each other's opinions, enjoy each other's society, profit by each other's criticism, and transmit to the provinces, as from a court of last resort, final judgments on literature, art, and politics, and snap their fingers at country denunciation and grumbling. Our thinkers are scattered all over the country, hundreds or thousands of miles away from their congeners. They brood rather than speculate. They live among "plain people." They have a human desire to be comfortable and happy with their neighbors, to receive their approval and respect. They have but few opportunities of intercourse with their fellows in other parts of the country. Even in cases like the Venezuelan affair, or like the greenback or silver "craze," it is so easy to fall in with the crowd, or still easier to be silent, so hard to be generally denounced as "unpatriotic" or as a "Mugwump," or to be accused of foreign tastes or leanings, that attempts to point out a "more excellent way" are somewhat under a cloud. Only men of marked ability or strong character make them, and even for these the work is wearisome and a little disheartening. In short, the influence of the scholarly, thinking, philosophical class is not felt in American progress nearly as much as it ought to be.

This is the more regrettable because no rational observer can suppose that the government of the United States is destined to retain indefinitely its present form. It is sure, like all governments which have preceded it, to change, and probably change from century to century. The history of all republics and of all monarchies, like the history of man himself, is one of incessant change. . . .

For these reasons and many others, all disquisition on the phe-nomena of modern democracy in any community as final, or as certain to result in despotism or in any other great calamity, appears to me exceedingly inadequate. Democracy in America, like democracy and monarchy elsewhere, is following the course of other political societies. It is suffering from unforeseen evils, as well as enjoying unforeseen blessings. It will probably be worse before it is better. It is trying a great many experiments in laws and manners, of which some, doubtless, will be hideous failures. The régime of "crazes" through which it is now passing is very discouraging, but it is engaged, like most other civilized societies, in a search after remedies.

23. FREDERICK JACKSON TURNER (1861–1932)

TURNER was born in a frontier town of Wisconsin. He was a professor of American history at the University of Wisconsin and later at Harvard University and was president of the American Historical Association (1909–10). In 1893, he read a paper before the latter body on "The Significance of the Frontier in American History." His thesis was that "The existence of an area of free land, its continuous recession, and the advance of American settlement westward, explain American development": inherited ideas and institutions, brought over from Europe or copied by one generation from an earlier American generation, have played a relatively minor part in that development; and "American social development has been continually beginning over again on the frontier." This theory was almost immediately recognized as a new and valuable type of historical interpretation and research, at least for American history. Turner's later writings, as well as numerous works by other historians, have applied the theory to different geographical sections and to different periods and phases of American life; and Turner's approach initiated or strengthened a general trend towards economic and environmental interpretations of significant events and ideas in American history.

[See: Frederick J. Turner, *The Frontier in American History* (1920), ch. 1; Carl Becker, "Frederick Jackson Turner," in Howard W. Odum, ed., *American Masters of Social Science* (1927), pp. 273–318; Merle Curti, "The Section and the Frontier in American History: the Methodological Concepts of F. J. Turner," in Stuart A. Rice ed., *Methods in Social Science* (1931), pp. 353–367; Frederick L. Paxon, "A Generation of the Frontier Hypothesis, 1893–1932," *Pacific Historical Review*, Vol. II (1933), pp. 34–41; Benjamin F. Wright, Jr., "American Democracy and the Frontier," *Yale Review*, N. S. Vol. XX (1930–31), pp. 349–365.]

From CONTRIBUTIONS OF THE WEST TO AMERICAN DEMOCRACY (1903)[1]

Political thought in the period of the French Revolution tended to treat democracy as an absolute system applicable to all times

[1] Appearing originally in the *Atlantic Monthly* (January, 1903), reprinted in Turner's *The Frontier in American History* (New York, 1920), pp. 243–268. By special arrangement with Henry Holt.

and to all peoples, a system that was to be created by the act of the people themselves on philosophical principles. Ever since that era there has been an inclination on the part of writers on democracy to emphasize the analytical and theoretical treatment to the neglect of the underlying factors of historical development.

If, however, we consider the underlying conditions and forces that create the democratic type of government, and at times contradict the external forms to which the name democracy is applied, we shall find that under this name there have appeared a multitude of political types radically unlike in fact.

The careful student of history must, therefore, seek the explanation of the forms and changes of political institutions in the social and economic forces that determine them. To know that at any one time a nation may be called a democracy, an aristocracy, or a monarchy, is not so important as to know what are the social and economic tendencies of the state. These are the vital forces that work beneath the surface and dominate the external form. It is to changes in the economic and social life of a people that we must look for the forces that ultimately create and modify organs of political action. For the time, adaptation of political structure may be incomplete or concealed. Old organs will be utilized to express new forces, and so gradual and subtle will be the change that it may hardly be recognized. The pseudo-democracies under the Medici at Florence and under Augustus at Rome are familiar examples of this type. Or again, if the political structure be rigid, incapable of responding to the changes demanded by growth, the expansive forces of social and economic transformation may rend it in some catastrophe like that of the French Revolution. In all these changes both conscious ideals and unconscious social reorganization are at work.

These facts are familiar to the student, and yet it is doubtful if they have been fully considered in connection with American democracy. For a century at least, in conventional expression, Americans have referred to a "glorious Constitution" in explaining the stability and prosperity of their democracy. We have believed as a nation that other peoples had only to will our democratic institutions in order to repeat our own career.

In dealing with Western contributions to democracy, it is essential that the considerations which have just been mentioned shall be kept in mind. Whatever these contributions may have been, we find ourselves at the present time in an era of such profound economic and social transformation as to raise the question of the effect of these changes upon the democratic institutions of the United States. Within a decade four marked changes have occurred in our national development; taken together they constitute a revolution.

First, there is the exhaustion of the supply of free land and the closing of the movement of Western advance as an effective factor in American development. The first rough conquest of the wilderness is accomplished, and that great supply of free lands which year after year has served to reinforce the democratic influences in the United States is exhausted. It is true that vast tracts of government land are still untaken, but they constitute the mountain and arid regions, only a small fraction of them capable of conquest, and then only by the application of capital and combined effort. The free lands that made the American pioneer have gone.

In the second place, contemporaneously with this there has been such a concentration of capital in the control of fundamental industries as to make a new epoch in the economic development of the United States. The iron, the coal, and the cattle of the country have all fallen under the domination of a few great corporations with allied interests, and by the rapid combination of the important railroad systems and steamship lines, in concert with these same forces, even the breadstuffs and the manufactures of the nation are to some degree controlled in a similar way. This is largely the work of the last decade. The development of the greatest iron mines of Lake Superior occurred in the early nineties, and in the same decade came the combination by which the coal and the coke of the country, and the transportation systems that connect them with the iron mines, have been brought under a few concentrated managements. Side by side with this concentration of capital has gone the combination of labor in the same vast industries. The one is in a certain sense the concomitant of the other, but the movement acquires an additional significance because of the fact that during the past fifteen years the labor class has been so recruited by a tide of foreign immigration that this class is now largely made up of persons of foreign parentage, and the lines of cleavage which begin to appear in this country between capital and labor have been accentuated by distinctions of nationality.

A third phenomenon connected with the two just mentioned is the expansion of the United States politically and commercially into lands beyond the seas. A cycle of American development has been completed. Up to the close of the War of 1812, this country was involved in the fortunes of the European state system. The first quarter of a century of our national existence was almost a continual struggle to prevent ourselves being drawn into the European wars. At the close of that era of conflict, the United States set its face toward the West. It began the settlement and improvement of the vast interior of the country. Here was the field of our colonization, here the field of our political activity. This process being completed, it is not strange that we find the United States again involved in world-politics. The revolution that occurred four years ago, when the United States struck down that ancient nation under whose auspices the New World was discovered, is hardly yet more than dimly understood. The insular wreckage of the Spanish War, Porto Rico and the Philippines, with the problems presented by the Hawaiian Islands, Cuba, the Isthmian Canal, and China, all are indications of the new direction of the ship of state, and while we thus turn our attention overseas, our concentrated industrial strength has given us a striking power against the commerce of Europe that is already producing consternation in the Old World. Having completed the conquest of the wilderness, and having consolidated our interests, we are beginning to consider the relations of democracy and empire.

And fourth, the political parties of the United States now tend to divide on issues that involve the question of Socialism. The rise of the Populist party in the last decade, and the acceptance of so many of its principles by the Democratic party under the leadership of Mr. Bryan, show in striking manner the birth of new political ideas, the reformation of the lines of political conflict. . . .

From the beginning of the settlement of America, the frontier regions have exercised a steady influence toward democracy. In Virginia, to take an example, it can be traced as early as the period of Bacon's Rebellion, a hundred years before our Declaration of Independence. The small landholders, seeing that their powers

were steadily passing into the hands of the wealthy planters who
controlled Church and State and lands, rose in revolt. A generation later, in the governorship of Alexander Spotswood, we find a
contest between the frontier settlers and the property-holding
classes of the coast. The democracy with which Spotswood had to
struggle, and of which he so bitterly complained, was a democracy
made up of small landholders, of the newer immigrants, and of in-
dented servants, who at the expiration of their time of servitude
passed into the interior to take up lands and engage in pioneer
farming. The "War of the Regulation," just on the eve of the
American Revolution, shows the steady persistence of this struggle
between the classes of the interior and those of the coast. The
Declaration of Grievances which the back counties of the Carolinas
then drew up against the aristocracy that dominated the politics of
those colonies exhibits the contest between the democracy of the
frontier and the established classes who apportioned the legislature in such fashion as to secure effective control of government.
Indeed, in a period before the outbreak of the American Revolution, one can trace a distinct belt of democratic territory extending
from the back country of New England down through western
New York, Pennsylvania, and the South.

In each colony this region was in conflict with the dominant
classes of the coast. It constituted a quasi-revolutionary area before
the days of the Revolution, and it formed the basis on which the
Democratic party was afterwards established. It was, therefore,
in the West, as it was in the period before the Declaration of
Independence, that the struggle for democratic development first
revealed itself, and in that area the essential ideas of American
democracy had already appeared. Through the period of the Revolution and of the Confederation a similar contest can be noted.
On the frontier of New England, along the western border of
Pennsylvania, Virginia, and the Carolinas, and in the communities
beyond the Alleghany Mountains, there arose a demand of the
frontier settlers for independent statehood based on democratic
provisions. There is a strain of fierceness in their energetic petitions demanding self-government under the theory that every
people have the right to establish their own political institutions
in an area which they have won from the wilderness. Those revolutionary principles based on natural rights, for which the seaboard

colonies were contending, were taken up with frontier energy in an attempt to apply them to the lands of the West. No one can read their petitions denouncing the control exercised by the wealthy landholders of the coast, appealing to the record of their conquest of the wilderness, and demanding the possession of the lands for which they have fought the Indians, and which they had reduced by their ax to civilization, without recognizing in these frontier communities the cradle of a belligerent Western democracy. "A fool can sometimes put on his coat better than a wise man can do it for him,"—such is the philosophy of its petitioners. In this period also came the contests of the interior agricultural portion of New England against the coast-wise merchants and property-holders, of which Shays' Rebellion is the best known, although by no means an isolated instance.

By the time of the constitutional convention, this struggle for democracy had effected, a fairly well-defined division into parties. Although these parties did not at first recognize their interstate connections, there were similar issues on which they split in almost all the States. The demands for an issue of paper money, the stay of execution against debtors, and the relief against excessive taxation were found in every colony in the interior agricultural regions. The rise of this significant movement wakened the apprehensions of the men of means, and in the debates over the basis of suffrage for the House of Representatives in the constitutional convention of 1787 leaders of the conservative party did not hesitate to demand that safeguards to the property should be furnished the coast against the interior. The outcome of the debate left the question of suffrage for the House of Representatives dependent upon the policy of the separate States. This was in effect imposing a property qualification throughout the nation as a whole, and it was only as the interior of the country developed that these restrictions gradually gave way in the direction of manhood suffrage.

All of these scattered democratic tendencies Jefferson combined, in the period of Washington's presidency, into the Democratic-Republican party. Jefferson was the first prophet of American democracy, and when we analyse the essential features of his gospel, it is clear that the Western influence was the dominant element. Jefferson himself was born in the frontier region of Virginia, on the edge of the Blue Ridge, in the middle of the eighteenth century.

His father was a pioneer. Jefferson's "Notes on Virginia" reveal clearly his conception that democracy should have an agricultural basis, and that manufacturing development and city life were dangerous to the purity of the body politic. Simplicity and economy in government, the right of revolution, the freedom of the individual, the belief that those who win the vacant lands are entitled to shape their own government in their own way,—these are all parts of the platform of political principles to which he gave his adhesion, and they are all elements eminently characteristic of the Western democracy into which he was born.

In the period of the Revolution he had brought in a series of measures which tended to throw the power of Virginia into the hands of the settlers in the interior rather than of the coastwise aristocracy. The repeal of the laws of entail and primogeniture would have destroyed the great estates on which the planting aristocracy based its power. The abolition of the Established Church would still further have diminished the influence of the coastwise party in favor of the dissenting sects of the interior. His scheme of general public education reflected the same tendency, and his demand for the abolition of slavery was characteristic of a representative of the West rather than of the old-time aristocracy of the coast. His sympathy with the Western expansion culminated in the Louisiana Purchase. In short, the tendencies of Jefferson's legislation were to replace the dominance of the planting aristocracy by the dominance of the interior class, which had sought in vain to achieve its liberties in the period of Bacon's Rebellion.

Nevertheless, Thomas Jefferson was the John the Baptist of democracy, not its Moses. Only with the slow setting of the tide of settlement farther and farther toward the interior did the democratic influence grow strong enough to take actual possession of the government. The period from 1800 to 1820 saw a steady increase in these tendencies. . . .

Even the newly created States of the Southwest showed the tendency. The wind of democracy blew so strongly from the West, that even in the older States of New York, Massachusetts, Connecticut, and Virginia, conventions were called, which liberalized their constitutions by strengthening the democratic basis of the State. In the same time the labor population of the cities began to assert its power and its determination to share in government.

Of this frontier democracy which now took possession of the nation, Andrew Jackson was the very personification. He was born in the backwoods of the Carolinas in the midst of the turbulent democracy that preceded the Revolution, and he grew up in the frontier State of Tennessee. In the midst of this region of personal feuds and frontier ideals of law, he quickly rose to leadership. The appearance of this frontiersman on the floor of Congress was an omen full of significance. He reached Philadelphia at the close of Washington's administration, having ridden on horseback nearly eight hundred miles to his destination. . . . At last the frontier in the person of its typical man had found a place in the Government. This six-foot backwoodsman, with blue eyes that could blaze on occasion, this choleric, impetuous, self-willed Scotch-Irish leader of men, this expert duelist, and ready fighter, this embodiment of the tenacious, vehement, personal West, was in politics to stay. The frontier democracy of that time had the instincts of the clansman in the days of Scotch border warfare. Vehement and tenacious as the democracy was, strenuously as each man contended with his neighbor for the spoils of the new country that opened before them, they all had respect for the man who best expressed their aspirations and their ideas. Every community had its hero. In the War of 1812 and the subsequent Indian fighting Jackson made good his claim, not only to the loyalty of the people of Tennessee, but of the whole West, and even of the nation. He had the essential traits of the Kentucky and Tennessee frontier. It was a frontier free from the influence of European ideas and institutions. The men of the "Western World" turned their backs upon the Atlantic Ocean, and with a grim energy and self-reliance began to build up a society free from the dominance of ancient forms.

The Westerner defended himself and resented governmental restrictions. The duel and the blood-feud found congenial soil in Kentucky and Tennessee. The idea of the personality of law was often dominant over the organized machinery of justice. That method was best which was most direct and effective. The backwoodsman was intolerant of men who split hairs, or scrupled over the method of reaching the right. In a word, the unchecked development of the individual was the significant product of this frontier democracy. It sought rather to express itself by choosing a man of the people, than by the formation of elaborate govern-mental institutions.

It was because Andrew Jackson personified these essential West-ern traits that in his presidency he became the idol and the mouth-piece of the popular will. In his assault upon the Bank as an engine of aristocracy, and in his denunciation of nullification, he went directly to his object with the ruthless energy of a frontiers-man. For formal law and the subleties of State sovereignty he had the contempt of a backwoodsman. Nor is it without significance that this typical man of the new democracy will always be as-sociated with the triumph of the spoils system in national politics. To the new democracy of the West, office was an opportunity to exercise natural rights as an equal citizen of the community. Rota-tion in office served not simply to allow the successful man to punish his enemies and reward his friends, but it also furnished the training in the actual conduct of political affairs which every Amer-ican claimed as his birthright. Only in a primitive democracy of the type of the United States in 1830 could such a system have existed without the ruin of the State. National government in that period was no complex and nicely adjusted machine, and the evils of the system were long in making themselves fully apparent.

The triumph of Andrew Jackson marked the end of the old era of trained statesmen for the Presidency. With him began the era of the popular hero. Even Martin Van Buren, whom we think of in connection with the East, was born in a log house under conditions that were not unlike parts of the older West. Harrison was the hero of the Northwest, as Jackson had been of the South-west. Polk was a typical Tennesseean, eager to expand the nation, and Zachary Taylor was what Webster called a "frontier colonel." During the period that followed Jackson, power passed from the region of Kentucky and Tennessee to the border of the Mississippi. The natural democratic tendencies that had earlier shown them-selves in the Gulf States were destroyed, however, by the spread of cotton culture, and the development of great plantations in that region. What had been typical of the democracy of the Revolu-tionary frontier and of the frontier of Andrew Jackson was now to be seen in the States between the Ohio and the Mississippi. As Andrew Jackson is the typical democrat of the former region, so Abraham Lincoln is the very embodiment of the pioneer period of the Old Northwest. Indeed, he is the embodiment of the democracy of the West. . . .

The pioneer life from which Lincoln came differed in important respects from the frontier democracy typified by Andrew Jackson. Jackson's democracy was contentious, individualistic, and it sought the ideal of local self-government and expansion. Lincoln represents rather the pioneer folk who entered the forest of the great Northwest to chop out a home, to build up their fortunes in the midst of a continually ascending industrial movement. In the democracy of the Southwest, industrial development and city life were only minor factors, but to the democracy of the Northwest they were its very life. To widen the area of the clearing, to contend with one another for the mastery of the industrial resources of the rich provinces, to struggle for a place in the ascending movement of society, to transmit to one's offspring the chance for education, for industrial betterment, for the rise in life which the hardships of the pioneer existence denied to the pioneer himself, these were some of the ideals of the region to which Lincoln came. The men were commonwealth builders, industry builders. Whereas the type of hero in the Southwest was militant, in the Northwest he was industrial. It was in the midst of these "plain people," as he loved to call them, that Lincoln grew to manhood. As Emerson says: "He is the true history of the American people in his time." The years of his early life were the years when the democracy of the Northwest came into struggle with the institution of slavery which threatened to forbid the expansion of the democratic pioneer life in the West. In President Eliot's essay on "Five American Contributions to Civilization," he instances as one of the supreme tests of American democracy its attitude upon the question of slavery. But if democracy chose wisely and worked effectively toward the solution of this problem, it must be remembered that Western democracy took the lead. The rail-splitter himself became the nation's President in that fierce time of struggle, and armies of the woodsmen and pioneer farmers recruited in the Old Northwest made free the Father of Waters, marched through Georgia, and helped to force the struggle to a conclusion at Appomattox. The free pioneer democracy struck down the slaveholding aristocracy on its march to the West.

The last chapter in the development of Western democracy is

the one that deals with its conquest over the vast spaces of the new West. At each new stage of Western development, the people have had to grapple with larger areas, with bigger combinations. The little colony of Massachusetts veterans that settled at Marietta received a land grant as large as the State of Rhode Island. The band of Connecticut pioneers that followed Moses Cleaveland to the Connecticut Reserve occupied a region as large as the parent State. The area which settlers of New England stock occupied on the prairies of northern Illinois surpassed the combined area of Massachusetts, Connecticut, and Rhode Island. Men who had become accustomed to the narrow valleys and the little towns of the East found themselves out on the boundless spaces of the West dealing with units of such magnitude as dwarfed their former experience. The Great Lakes, the Prairies, the Great Plains, the Rocky Mountains, the Mississippi and the Missouri, furnished new standards of measurement for the achievement of this industrial democracy. Individualism began to give way to coöperation and to governmental activity. Even in the earlier days of the democratic conquest of the wilderness, demands had been made upon the government for support in internal improvements, but this new West showed a growing tendency to call to its assistance the powerful arm of national authority. In the period since the Civil War, the vast public domain has been donated to the individual farmer, to States for education, to railroads for the construction of transportation lines.

Moreover, with the advent of democracy in the last fifteen years upon the Great Plains, new physical conditions have presented themselves which have accelerated the social tendency of Western democracy. The pioneer farmer of the days of Lincoln could place his family on a flatboat, strike into the wilderness, cut out his clearing, and with little or no capital go on to the achievement of industrial independence. Even the homesteader on the Western prairies found it possible to work out a similar independent destiny, although the factor of transportation made a serious and increasing impediment to the free working-out of his individual career. But when the arid lands and the mineral resources of the Far West were reached, no conquest was possible by the old individual pioneer methods. Here expensive irrigation works must be constructed, coöperative activity was demanded in utilization of the water supply, capital beyond the reach of the small farmer was required. In a word, the physiographic province itself decreed that the destiny of this new frontier should be social rather than individual.

Magnitude of social achievement is the watchword of the democracy since the Civil War. From petty towns built in the marshes, cities arose whose greatness and industrial power are the wonder of our time. The conditions were ideal for the production of captains of industry. The old democratic admiration for the self-made man, its old deference to the rights of competitive individual development, together with the stupendous natural resources that opened to the conquest of the keenest and the strongest, gave such conditions of mobility as enabled the development of the large corporate industries which in our own decade have marked the West.

Thus, in brief, have been outlined the chief phases of the development of Western democracy in the different areas which it has conquered. There has been a steady development of the industrial ideal, and a steady increase of the social tendency, in this later movement of Western democracy. While the individualism of the frontier, so prominent in the earliest days of the Western advance, has been preserved as an ideal, more and more these individuals struggling each with the other, dealing with vaster and vaster areas, with larger and larger problems, have found it necessary to combine under the leadership of the strongest. This is the explanation of the rise of those preëminent captains of industry whose genius has concentrated capital to control the fundamental resources of the nation. If now in the way of recapitulation, we try to pick out from the influences that have gone to the making of Western democracy the factors which constitute the net result of this movement, we shall have to mention at least the following:—

Most important of all has been the fact that an area of free land has continually lain on the western border of the settled area of the United States. Whenever social conditions tended to crystallize in the East, whenever capital tended to press upon labor or political restraints to impede the freedom of the mass, there was this gate of escape to the free conditions of the frontier. These free lands promoted individualism, economic equality, freedom to rise, democracy. Men would not accept inferior wages and a permanent position of social subordination when this promised land of freedom and equality was theirs for the taking. Who would rest content under oppressive legislative conditions when with a slight effort he might reach a land wherein to become a co-worker in the building of free cities and free States on the lines of his own ideal? In a word, then, free lands meant free opportunities. Their existence has differentiated the American democracy from the democracies which have preceded it, because ever, as democracy in the East took the form of highly specialized and complicated industrial society, in the West it kept in touch with primitive conditions, and by action and reaction these two forces have shaped our history.

In the next place, these free lands and this treasury of industrial resources have existed over such vast spaces that they have demanded of democracy increasing spaciousness of design and power of execution. Western democracy is contrasted with the democracy of all other times in the largeness of the tasks to which it has set its hand, and in the vast achievements which it has wrought out in the control of nature and of politics. It would be difficult to over-emphasize the importance of this training upon democracy. Never before in the history of the world has a democracy existed on so vast an area and handled things in the gross with such success, with such largeness of design, and such grasp upon the means of execution. In short, democracy has learned in the West of the United States how to deal with the problem of magnitude. The old historic democracies were but little states with primitive economic conditions.

But the very task of dealing with vast resources, over vast areas, under the conditions of free competition furnished by the West, has produced the rise of those captains of industry whose success in consolidating economic power now raises the question as to whether democracy under such conditions can survive. For the old military type of Western leaders like George Rogers Clark, Andrew Jackson, and William Henry Harrison have been substituted such industrial leaders as James J. Hill, John D. Rockefeller, and Andrew Carnegie.

The question is imperative, then, What ideals persist from this democratic experience of the West; and have they acquired sufficient momentum to sustain themselves under conditions so radically unlike those in the days of their origin?   In other words, the question put at the beginning of this discussion becomes pertinent. Under the forms of the American democracy is there in reality evolving such a concentration of economic and social power in the hands of a comparatively few men as may make political democracy an appearance rather than a reality?   The free lands are gone.   The material forces that gave vitality to Western democracy are passing away.   It is to the realm of the spirit, to the domain of ideals and legislation, that we must look for Western influence upon democracy in our own days.

Western democracy has been from the time of its birth idealistic. The very fact of the wilderness appealed to men as a fair, blank page on which to write a new chapter in the story of man's struggle for a higher type of society.   The Western wilds, from the Alleghanies to the Pacific, constituted the richest free gift that was ever spread out before civilized man.   To the peasant and artisan of the Old World, bound by the chains of social class, as old as custom and as inevitable as fate, the West offered an exit into a free life and greater well-being among the bounties of nature, into the midst of resources that demanded manly exertion, and that gave in return the chance for indefinite ascent in the scale of social advance.   "To each she offered gifts after his will."   Never again can such an opportunity come to the sons of men.   It was unique, and the thing is so near us, so much a part of our lives, that we do not even yet comprehend its full significance.   The existence of this land of opportunity has made America the goal of idealists from the days of the Pilgrim Fathers.   With all the materialism of the pioneer movements, this idealistic conception of the vacant lands as an opportunity for a new order of things is unmistakably present. . . .

If the later West offers few such striking illustrations of the relation of the wilderness to idealistic schemes, and if some of the designs were fantastic and abortive, none the less the influence is a fact.   Hardly a Western State but has been the Mecca of some sect or band of social reformers, anxious to put into practice their ideals, in vacant land, far removed from the checks of a settled form of social organization.   Consider the Dunkards, the Icarians, the Fourierists, the Mormons, and similar idealists who sought our Western wilds.   But the idealistic influence is not limited to the dreamers' conception of a new State. It gave to the pioneer farmer and city builder a restless energy, a quick capacity for judgment and action, a belief in liberty, freedom of opportunity, and a resistance to the domination of class which infused a vitality and power into the individual atoms of this democratic mass. Even as he dwelt among the stumps of his newly-cut clearing, the pioneer had the creative vision of a new order of society. In imagination he pushed back the forest boundary to the confines of a mighty Commonwealth; he willed that log cabins should become the lofty buildings of great cities. He decreed that his children should enter into a heritage of education, comfort, and social welfare, and for this ideal he bore the scars of the wilderness. Possessed with this idea he ennobled his task and laid deep foundations for a democratic State. Nor was this idealism by any means limited to the American pioneer.

To the old native democratic stock has been added a vast army of recruits from the Old World. There are in the Middle West alone four million persons of German parentage out of a total of seven millions in the country. Over a million persons of Scandinavian parentage live in the same region. The democracy of the newer West is deeply affected by the ideals brought by these immigrants from the Old World. To them America was not simply a new home; it was a land of opportunity, of freedom, of democracy. It meant to them, as to the American pioneer that preceded them, the opportunity to destroy the bonds of social caste that bound them in their older home, to hew out for themselves in a new country a destiny proportioned to the powers that God had given them, a chance to place their families under better conditions and to win a larger life than the life that they had left behind. He who believes that even the hordes of recent immigrants from southern Italy are drawn to these shores by nothing more than a dull and blind materialism has not penetrated into the heart of the problem. The idealism and expectation of these children of the Old World, the hopes which they have formed for a newer and freer life across the seas, are almost pathetic when one considers how far they are from the possibility of fruition. He who would take stock of American democracy must not forget the accumulation of human purposes and ideals which immigration has added to the American populace.

In this connection it must also be remembered that these democratic ideals have existed at each stage of the advance of the frontier, and have left behind them deep and enduring effects on the thinking of the whole country. Long after the frontier period of a particular region of the United States has passed away, the conception of society, the ideals and aspirations which it produced, persist in the minds of the people. So recent has been the transition of the greater portion of the United States from frontier conditions to conditions of settled life, that we are, over the large portion of the United States, hardly a generation removed from the primitive conditions of the West. If, indeed, we ourselves were not pioneers, our fathers were, and the inherited ways of looking at things, the fundamental assumptions of the American people, have all been shaped by this experience of democracy on its westward march. This experience has been wrought into the very warp and woof of American thought.

Even those masters of industry and capital who have risen to power by the conquest of Western resources came from the midst of this society and still profess its principles. John D. Rockefeller was born on a New York farm, and began his career as a young business man in St. Louis. Marcus Hanna was a Cleveland grocer's clerk at the age of twenty. Claus Spreckles, the sugar king, came from Germany as a steerage passenger to the United States in 1848. Marshall Field was a farmer boy in Conway, Massachusetts, until he left to grow up with the young Chicago. Andrew Carnegie came as a ten-year-old boy from Scotland to Pittsburgh, then a distinctively Western town. He built up his fortunes through successive grades until he became the dominating factor in the great iron industries, and paved the way for that colossal achievement, the Steel Trust. Whatever may be the tendencies of this corporation, there can be little doubt of the democratic ideals of Mr. Carnegie himself. With lavish hand he has strewn millions through the United States for the promotion of libraries. The effect of this library movement in perpetuating the democracy that comes from an intelligent and self-respecting people can hardly be measured. In his "Triumphant Democracy," published in 1886, Mr. Carnegie, the ironmaster, said, in reference to the mineral wealth of the United States: "Thank God, these treasures are in the hands of an intelligent people, the Democracy, to be used for the general good of the masses, and not made the spoils of monarchs, courts, and aristocracy, to be turned to the base and selfish ends of a privileged hereditary class." It would be hard to find a more rigorous assertion of democratic doctrine that the celebrated utterance, attributed to the same man, that he should feel it a disgrace to die rich.

In enumerating the services of American democracy, President Eliot included the corporation as one of its achievements, declaring that "freedom of incorporation, though no longer exclusively a democratic agency, has given a strong support to democratic institutions." In one sense this is doubtless true, since the corporation has been one of the means by which small properties can be aggregated into an effective working body. Socialistic writers have long been fond of pointing out also that these various concentrations pave the way for and make possible social control. From this point of view it is possible that the masters of industry may prove to be not so much an incipient aristocracy as the pathfinders for democracy in reducing the industrial world to systematic consolidation suited to democratic control. The great geniuses that have built up the modern industrial concentration were trained in the midst of democratic society. They were the product of these democratic conditions. Freedom to rise was the very condition of their existence. Whether they will be followed by successors who will adopt the exploitation of the masses, and who will be capable of retaining under efficient control these vast resources, is one of the questions which we shall have to face.

This, at least, is clear: American democracy is fundamentally the outcome of the experiences of the American people in dealing with the West. Western democracy through the whole of its earlier period tended to the production of a society of which the most distinctive fact was the freedom of the individual to rise under conditions of social mobility, and whose ambition was the liberty and well-being of the masses. This conception has vitalized all American democracy, and has brought it into sharp contrasts with the democracies of history, and with those modern efforts of Europe to create an artificial democratic order by legislation. The problem of the United States is not to create democracy, but to conserve democratic institutions and ideals. In the later period of its development, Western democracy has been gaining experience in the problem of social control. It has steadily enlarged the sphere of its action and the instruments for its perpetuation. By its system of public schools, from the grades to the graduate work of the great universities, the West has created a larger single body of intelligent plain people than can be found elsewhere in the world. Its political tendencies, whether we consider Democracy, Populism, or Republicanism, are distinctly in the direction of greater social control and the conservation of the old democratic ideals.

To these ideals the West adheres with even a passionate determination. If, in working out its mastery of the resources of the interior, it has produced a type of industrial leader so powerful as to be the wonder of the world, nevertheless, it is still to be determined whether these men constitute a menace to democratic institutions, or the most efficient factor for adjusting democratic control to the new conditions.

Whatever shall be the outcome of the rush of this huge industrial modern United States to its place among the nations of the earth, the formation of its Western democracy will always remain one of the wonderful chapters in the history of the human race. Into this vast shaggy continent of ours poured the first feeble tide of European settlement. European men, institutions, and ideas were lodged in the American wilderness, and this great American West took them to her bosom, taught them a new way of looking upon the destiny of the common man, trained them in adaptation to the conditions of the New World, to the creation of new institutions to meet new needs; and ever as society on her eastern border grew to resemble the Old World in its social forms and its industry, ever, as it began to lose faith in the ideals of democracy, she opened new provinces, and dowered new democracies in her most distant domains with her material treasures and with the ennobling influence that the fierce love of freedom, the strength that came from hewing out a home, making a school and a church, and creating a higher future for his family, furnished to the pioneer.

She gave to the world such types as the farmer Thomas Jefferson, with his Declaration of Independence, his statute for religious toleration, and his purchase of Louisiana. She gave us Andrew Jackson, that fierce Tennessee spirit who broke down the traditions of conservative rule, swept away the privacies and privileges of officialdom, and, like a Gothic leader, opened the temple of the nation to the populace. She gave us Abraham Lincoln, whose gaunt frontier form and gnarled, massive hand told of the conflict with the forest, whose grasp of the ax-handle of the pioneer was no firmer than his grasp of the helm of the ship of state as it breasted the seas of civil war. She has furnished to this new democracy her stores of mineral wealth, that dwarf of those of the Old World, and her provinces that in themselves are vaster and more productive than most of the nations of Europe. Out of her bounty has come a nation whose industrial competition alarms the Old World, and the masters of whose resources wield wealth and power vaster than the wealth and power of kings. Best of all, the West gave, not only to the American, but to the unhappy and oppressed of all lands, a vision of hope, and assurance that the world held a place where were to be found high faith in man and the will and power to furnish him the opportunity to grow to the full measure of his own capacity. Great and powerful as are the new sons of her loins, the Republic is greater than they. The paths of the pioneer have widened into broad highways. The forest clearing has expanded into affluent commonwealths. Let us see to it that the ideals of the pioneer in his log cabin shall enlarge into the spiritual life of a democracy where civic power shall dominate and utilize individual achievement for the common good.

24. H. L. MENCKEN (1880–   )

HENRY LOUIS MENCKEN, born in Baltimore, was educated in private schools and the Baltimore Polytechnic. He has held editorial positions on Baltimore newspapers, usually the "Sun-papers," since 1903. He was associated with the *Smart Set* as literary critic and later co-editor (1908–23) and with *The Nation* as contributing editor (1921–32); and he was a founder (with George Jean Nathan) and editor of the *American Mercury* (1924–33). He has written poems, plays, literary criticism, a definitive work on common American speech (*The American Language*, 1918, latest edition 1936), and numerous works discussing American morals and politics—notably the six volumes of *Prejudices* (between 1919 and 1927), *Notes on Democracy* (1926), *Treatise on Gods* (1930), and *Treatise on Right and Wrong* (1934). He is regarded as a "realist" and an iconoclast in his discussions of contemporary American society. His trenchant attacks on the common-man's moral, cultural, and political standards have been applauded, now by "liberals," now by "conservatives."

From NOTES ON DEMOCRACY (1926)[1]

DEMOCRATIC MAN

1. *His Appearance in the World*

Democracy came into the Western World to the tune of sweet, soft music. There was, at the start, no harsh bawling from below; there was only a dulcet twittering from above. Democratic man thus began as an ideal being, full of ineffable virtues and romantic wrongs—in brief, as Rousseau's noble savage in smock and jerkin, brought out of the tropical wilds to shame the lords and masters of the civilized lands. The fact continues to have important consequences to this day. It remains impossible, as it was in the Eighteenth Century, to separate the democratic idea from the theory that there is a mystical merit, an esoteric and ineradicable

[1] (New York, 1926) at pp. 3–11, 15–21, 43–46, 48–56, 64–68. By special arrangement with Alfred A. Knopf.

rectitude, in the man at the bottom of the scale—that inferiority, by some strange magic, becomes a sort of superiority—nay, the superiority of superiorities. Everywhere on earth, save where the enlightenment of the modern age is confessedly in transient eclipse, the movement is toward the completer and more enamoured enfranchisement of the lower orders. Down there, one hears, lies a deep, illimitable reservoir of righteousness and wisdom, unpolluted by the corruption of privilege. What baffles statesmen is to be solved by the people, instantly and by a sort of seraphic intuition. Their yearnings are pure; they alone are capable of a perfect patriotism; in them is the only hope of peace and happiness on this lugubrious ball. The cure for the evils of democracy is more democracy!

This notion, as I hint, originated in the poetic fancy of gentlemen on the upper levels—sentimentalists who, observing to their distress that the ass was over-laden, proposed to reform transport by putting him into the cart. A stale Christian bilge ran through their veins, though many of them, as it happened, toyed with what is now called Modernism. They were the direct ancestors of the more saccharine Liberals of to-day, who yet mouth their tattered phrases and dream their preposterous dreams. I can find no record that these phrases, in the beginning, made much impression upon the actual objects of their rhetoric. Early democratic man seems to have given little thought to the democratic ideal, and less veneration. What he wanted was something concrete and highly materialistic—more to eat, less work, higher wages, lower taxes. He had no apparent belief in the acroamatic virtue of his own class, and certainly none in its capacity to rule. His aim was not to exterminate the baron, but simply to bring the baron back to a proper discharge of baronial business. When, by the wild shooting that naturally accompanies all mob movements, the former end was accidentally accomplished, and men out of the mob began to take on baronial airs, the mob itself quickly showed its opinion of them by butchering them deliberately and in earnest. Once the pikes were out, indeed, it was a great deal more dangerous to be a tribune of the people than to be an ornament of the old order. The more copiously the blood gushed, the nearer that old order came to resurrection. The Paris proletariat, having been misled into killing its King in 1793, devoted the next two years to killing those who had misled it, and by the middle of 1796 it had another King in fact, and in three years more he was King *de jure*, with an attendant herd of barons, counts, marquises and dukes, some of them new but most of them old, to guard, symbolize and execute his sovereignty.   And he and they were immensely popular—so popular that half France leaped to suicide that their glory might blind the world.

Meanwhile, of course, there had been a certain seeping down of democratic theory from the metaphysicians to the mob—obscured by the uproar, but still going on.   Rhetoric, like a stealthy plague, was doing its immemorial work.   Where men were confronted by the harsh, exigent realities of battle and pillage, as they were everywhere on the Continent, it got into their veins only slowly, but where they had time to listen to oratory, as in England and, above all, in America, it fetched them more quickly.   Eventually, as the world grew exhausted and the wars passed, it began to make its effects felt everywhere.   Democratic man, contemplating himself, was suddenly warmed by the spectacle.   His condition had plainly improved.   Once a slave, he was now only a serf.   Once condemned to silence, he was now free to criticize his masters, and even to flout them, and the ordinances of God with them.   As he gained skill and fluency at that sombre and fascinating art, he began to heave in wonder at his own merit.   He was not only, it appeared, free to praise and damn, challenge and remonstrate; he was also gifted with a peculiar rectitude of thought and will, and a high talent for ideas, particularly on the political plane.   So his wishes, in his mind, began to take on the dignity of legal rights, and after a while, of intrinsic and natural rights, and by the same token the wishes of his masters sank to the level of mere ignominious lusts. By 1828 in America and by 1848 in Europe the doctrine had arisen that all moral excellence, and with it all pure and unfettered sagacity, resided in the inferior four-fifths of mankind.   In 1867 a philosopher out of the gutter pushed that doctrine to its logical conclusion.   He taught that the superior minority had no virtues at all, and hence no rights at all—that the world belonged exclusively and absolutely to those who hewed its wood and drew its water.   In less than half a century he had more followers in the world, open and covert, than any other sophist since the age of the Apostles.

Since then, to be sure, there has been a considerable recession from that extreme position. The dictatorship of the proletariat, tried here and there, has turned out to be—if I may venture a prejudiced judgment—somewhat impracticable. Even the most advanced Liberals, observing the thing in being, have been moved to cough sadly behind their hands. But it would certainly be going beyond the facts to say that the underlying democratic dogma has been abandoned, or even appreciably overhauled. To the contrary, it is now more prosperous than ever before. The late war was fought in its name, and it was embraced with loud hosannas by all the defeated nations. Everywhere in Christendom it is now official, save in a few benighted lands where God is temporarily asleep. Everywhere its fundamental axioms are accepted: (a) that the great masses of men have an inalienable right, born of the very nature of things, to govern themselves, and (b) that they are competent to do it. Are they occasionally detected in gross and lamentable imbecilities? Then it is only because they are misinformed by those who would exploit them: the remedy is more education. Are they, at times, seen to be a trifle naughty, even swinish? Then it is only a natural reaction against the oppressions they suffer: the remedy is to deliver them. The central aim of all the Christian governments of to-day, in theory if not in fact, is to further their liberation, to augment their power, to drive ever larger and larger pipes into the great reservoir of their natural wisdom. That government is called good which responds most quickly and accurately to their desires and ideas. That is called bad which conditions their omnipotence and puts a question mark after their omniscience.

2. Varieties of Homo Sapiens

So much for the theory. It seems to me, and I shall here contend, that all the known facts lie flatly against it—that there is actually no more evidence for the wisdom of the inferior man, nor for his virtue, than there is for the notion that Friday is an unlucky day. There was, perhaps, some excuse for believing in these phantasms in the days when they were first heard of in the world, for it was then difficult to put them to the test, and what cannot be tried and disproved has always had a lascivious lure for illogical man. But now we know a great deal more about the content and character of the human mind than we used to know, both on high levels and on low levels, and what we have learned has pretty well disposed of the old belief in its congenital intuitions and inherent benevolences. It is, we discover, a function, at least mainly, of purely physical and chemical phenomena, and its development and operation are subject to precisely the same natural laws which govern the development and operation, say, of the human nose or lungs. There are minds which start out with a superior equipment, and proceed to high and arduous deeds; there are minds which never get any further than a sort of insensate sweating, like that of a kidney. We not only observe such differences; we also begin to chart them with more or less accuracy. Of one mind we may say with some confidence that it shows an extraordinary capacity for function and development—that its possessor, exposed to a suitable process of training, may be trusted to acquire the largest body of knowledge and the highest skill at ratiocination to which *Homo sapiens* is adapted. Of another we may say with the same confidence that its abilities are sharply limited—that no conceivable training can move it beyond a certain point. In other words, men differ inside their heads as they differ outside. There are men who are naturally intelligent and can learn, and there are men who are naturally stupid and cannot. . . .

3. *The New Psychology*

The concept of arrested development has caused an upheaval in psychology, and reduced the arduous introspections of the old-time psychologists to a series of ingenious but unimportant fancies. Men are *not* alike, and very little can be learned about the mental processes of a congressman, an ice-wagon driver or a cinema actor by studying the mental processes of a genuinely superior man. The difference is not only qualitative; it is also, in important ways, quantitative. One thus sees the world as a vast field of greased poles, flying gaudy and seductive flags. Up each a human soul goes shinning, painfully and with many a slip. Some climb eventually to the high levels; a few scale the dizziest heights. But the great majority never get very far from the ground. There they struggle for a while, and then give it up. The effort is too much for them; it doesn't seem to be worth its agonies. Golf is easier; so is joining Rotary; so is Fundamentalism; so is osteopathy; so is Americanism.

In an aristocratic society government is a function of those who have got relatively far up the poles, either by their own prowess or by starting from the shoulders of their fathers—which is to say, either by God's grace or by God's grace. In a democratic society it is the function of all, and hence mainly of those who have got only a few spans from the ground. Their eyes, to be sure, are still thrown toward the stars. They contemplate, now bitterly, now admiringly, the backsides of those who are above them. They are bitter when they sense anything rationally describable as actual superiority; they admire when what they see is fraud. Bitterness and admiration, interacting, form a complex of prejudices which tends to cast itself into more or less stable forms. Fresh delusions, of course, enter into it from time to time, usually on waves of frantic emotion, but it keeps its main outlines. This complex of prejudices is what is known, under democracy, as public opinion. It is the glory of democratic states.

Its content is best studied by a process of analysis—that is, by turning from the complex whole to the simpler parts. What does the mob think? It thinks, obviously, what its individual members think. And what is that? It is, in brief, what somewhat sharp-nosed and unpleasant children think. The mob, being composed, in the overwhelming main, of men and women who have not got beyond the ideas and emotions of childhood, hovers, in mental age, around the time of puberty, and chiefly below it. If we would get at its thoughts and feelings we must look for light to the thoughts and feelings of adolescents. The old-time introspective psychology offered little help here. It concerned itself almost exclusively with the mental processes of the more reflective, and hence the superior sort of adults; it fell into the disastrous fallacy of viewing a child as simply a little man. Just as modern medicine, by rejecting a similar fallacy on the physical plane, has set up the science and art of pediatrics, so the new behaviourist psychology has given a new dignity and autonomy to the study of the child mind. The first steps were very difficult. The behaviourists not only had to invent an entirely new technique, like the pediatricians before them; they also had to meet the furious opposition of the orthodox psychologists, whose moony speculations they laughed at and whose authority they derided. But they persisted, and the problems before them turned out, in the end, to be relatively simple, and by no means difficult to solve. By observing attentively what was before everyone's nose they quickly developed facts which left the orthodox psychologists in an untenable and absurd position. One by one, the old psychological categories went overboard, and with them a vast mass of vague and meaningless psychological terminology.

On the cleared ground remained a massive discovery: that the earliest and most profound of human emotions is fear. Man comes into the world weak and naked, and almost as devoid of intelligence as an oyster, but he brings with him a highly complex and sensitive susceptibility to fear. He can tremble and cry out in the first hours of his life—nay, in the first minute. Make a loud noise behind an infant just born, and it will shake like a Sunday-school superintendent taken in adultery. Take away its support—that is, make it believe that it is falling—and it will send up such a whoop as comes from yokels when the travelling tooth-puller has at them. These fears, by their character, suggest that they have a phylogenic origin—that is, that they represent inherited race experience, out of the deep darkness and abysm of time. . . . And all the evidence indicates that every other emotion is subordinate to it. None other shows itself so soon, and none other enters so powerfully into the first functioning of the infant mind. And to the primeval and yet profoundly rational fears that it brings into the world it quickly adds others that depart farther and farther from rationality. It begins to fear ideas as well as things, strange men as well as hostile nature. It picks up dreads and trepidations from its mother, from its nurse, from other children. At the age of three years, as Dr. Watson shows, its mental baggage is often little more than a vast mass of such things. It has anxieties, horrors, even superstitions. And as it increases in years it adds constantly to the stock.

The process of education is largely a process of getting rid of such fears. It rehearses, after a fashion, the upward struggle of man. The ideal educated man is simply one who has put away as foolish the immemorial fears of the race—of strange men and strange ideas, of the powers and principalities of the air. He is sure of himself in the world; no dread of the dark rides him; he is serene. To produce such men is the central aim of every rational system of education; even under democracy it is one of the aims, though perhaps only a subordinate one. What brings it to futility is simply the fact that the vast majority of men are congenitally incapable of any such intellectual progress. They cannot take in new ideas, and they cannot get rid of old fears. They lack the logical sense; they are unable to reason from a set of facts before them, free from emotional distraction. But they also lack something more fundamental: they are incompetent to take in the bald facts themselves. . . .

7. Liberty and Democratic Man

. . . All the revolutions in history have been started by hungry city mobs. The fact is, indeed, so plain that it has attracted the notice even of historians, and some of them deduce from it the doctrine that city life breeds a love of liberty. It may be so, but certainly that love is not visible in the lower orders. I can think of no city revolution that actually had liberty for its object, in any rational sense. The ideas of freedom that prevail in the world to-day were first formulated by country gentlemen, aided and abetted by poets and philosophers, with occasional help from an eccentric king. One of the most valid of them—that of free speech —was actually given its first support in law by the most absolute monarch of modern times, to wit, Frederick the Great. When the city mob fights it is not for liberty, but for ham and cabbage. When it wins, its first act is to destroy every form of freedom that is not directed wholly to that end. And its second is to butcher all professional libertarians. If Thomas Jefferson had been living in Paris in 1793 he would have made an even narrower escape from the guillotine than Thomas Paine made.

The fact is that liberty, in any true sense, is a concept that lies quite beyond the reach of the inferior man's mind. He can imagine and even esteem, in his way, certain false forms of liberty— for example, the right to choose between two political mountebanks, and to yell for the more obviously dishonest—but the reality is incomprehensible to him. And no wonder, for genuine liberty demands of its votaries a quality he lacks completely, and that is courage. The man who loves it must be willing to fight for it; blood, said Jefferson, is its natural manure. More, he must be able to endure it—an even more arduous business. Liberty means self-reliance, it means resolution, it means enterprise, it means the capacity for doing without. The free man is one who has won a small and precarious territory from the great mob of his inferiors, and is prepared and ready to defend it and make it support him. All around him are enemies, and where he stands there is no friend. He can hope for little help from other men of his own kind, for they have battles of their own to fight. He has made of himself a sort of god in his little world, and he must face the responsibilities of a god, and the dreadful loneliness. Has *Homo boobiens* any talent for this magnificent self-reliance? He has the same talent for it that he has for writing symphonies in the manner of Ludwig van Beethoven, no less and no more. That is to say, he has no talent whatsoever, nor even any understanding that such a talent exists. Liberty is unfathomable to him. He can no more comprehend it than he can comprehend honour. What he mistakes for it, nine times out of ten, is simply the banal right to empty hallelujahs upon his oppressors. He is an ox whose last proud, defiant gesture is to lick the butcher behind the ear. . . .

Thus the lower orders of men, however grandiloquently they may talk of liberty to-day, have actually had but a short and highly deceptive experience of it. It is not in their blood. The grandfathers of at least half of them were slaves, and the great-grandfathers of three-fourths, and the great-great-grandfathers of seven-eighths, and the great-great-great-grandfathers of practically all. The heritage of freedom belongs to a small minority of men, descended, whether legitimately or by adultery, from the old lords of the soil or from the patricians of the free towns. It is my contention that such a heritage is necessary in order that the concept of liberty, with all its disturbing and unnatural implications, may be so much as grasped—that such ideas cannot be implanted in the mind of man at will, but must be bred in as all other basic ideas are bred in. The proletarian may mouth the phrases, as he did in Jefferson's day, but he cannot take in the underlying realities, as was also demonstrated in Jefferson's day. What his great-great-grandchildren may be capable of I am not concerned with here; my business is with the man himself as he now walks the world. Viewed thus, it must be obvious that he is still incapable of bearing the pangs of liberty. They make him uncomfortable; they alarm him; they fill him with a great loneliness. There is no high adventurousness in him, but only fear. He not only doesn't long for liberty; he is quite unable to stand it. What he longs for is something wholly different, to wit, security. He needs protection. He is afraid of getting hurt. All else is affectation, delusion, empty words.

The fact, as we shall see, explains many of the most puzzling political phenomena of so-called free states. The great masses of men, though theoretically free, are seen to submit supinely to oppression and exploitation of a hundred abhorrent sorts. Have they no means of resistance? Obviously they have. The worst tyrant, even under democratic plutocracy, has but one throat to slit. The moment the majority decided to overthrow him he would be overthrown. But the majority lacks the resolution; it cannot imagine taking the risk. So it looks for leaders with the necessary courage, and when they appear it follows them slavishly, even after their courage is discovered to be mere buncombe and their altruism only a cloak for more and worse oppressions. Thus it oscillates eternally between scoundrels, or, if you would take them at their own valuation, heroes. Politics becomes the trade of playing upon its natural poltroonery—of scaring it half to death, and then proposing to save it. There is in it no other quality of which a practical politician, taking one day with another, may be sure. Every theoretically free people wonders at the slavishness of all the others. But there is no actual difference between them.

8. *The Effects Upon Progress*

It follows that the inferior man, being a natural slave himself, is quite unable to understand the desire for liberty in his superiors. If he apprehends that desire at all it is only as an appetite for a good of which he is himself incapable. He thus envies those who harbour it, and is eager to put them down. Justice, in fact, is always unpopular and in difficulties under democracy, save perhaps that false form of so-called social justice which is designed solely to get the laborer more than his fair hire. The wars of extermination that are waged against heretical minorities never meet with any opposition on the lower levels. The proletarian is always ready to help destroy the rights of his fellow proletarian, as was revealed brilliantly by the heroic services of the American Legion in the pogrom against Reds, just after the late war, and even more brilliantly by the aid that the American Federation of Labour gave to the same gallant crusade. The city workman, oppressed by

Prohibition, mourns the loss of his beer, not the loss of his liberty. He is ever willing to support similar raids upon the liberty of the other fellow, and he is not outraged when they are carried on in gross violation of the most elemental principles of justice and common decency. When, in a democratic state, any protest against such obscenities is heard at all, it comes from the higher levels. There a few genuine believers in liberty and justice survive, huddled upon a burning deck. Is it to be marvelled at that most of them, on inspection, turn out to be the grandsons of similar heretics of earlier times? I think not. It takes quite as long to breed a libertarian as it takes to breed a race-horse. Neither may be expected to issue from a farm mare.

The whole progress of the world, even in the direction of ameliorating the lot of the masses, is always opposed by the masses. The notion that their clamour brought about all the governmental and social reforms of the last century, and that those reforms were delayed by the superior minority, is sheer nonsense; even Liberals begin to reject it as absurd. Consider, for example, the history of the American Department of Agriculture. Whatever the corruptions and imbecilities of this department in democratic hands, it must be plain to everyone that the net effect of its work over many years has been a series of immense benefits to the American farmer—benefits that have at once reduced his labour and augmented his profits. Nevertheless, it is a matter of history that the farmers of the United States, when the Department began as a bureau of the Patent Office in 1830, opposed it almost unanimously, and that for years their bitter derision kept it feeble. Without leaving the United States one may go even farther back. When John Adams, during his presidency, proposed to set up a Weather Bureau, he was denounced as an idiot and a scoundrel, as Henry Adams has set forth in the introduction to "The Decay of Democratic Dogma." Examples from our own time are so numerous and notorious that it is needless to direct attention to them. It is axiomatic that all measures for safeguarding the public health are opposed by the majority, and that getting them upon the books is mainly a matter of deceiving and checkmating it. What happened in Los Angeles when a vaccination ordinance was submitted to a popular referendum is typical of what would happen anywhere under the same circumstances. The ordinance was rejected, and smallpox spread in the town. The prole-

tariat, alarmed, then proceeded against it by going to Christian
Scientists, osteopaths and chiropractors. Precisely the same thing
happened in Switzerland.

Turn now to Germany, a country lately delivered from despotism
by the arms of altruistic heroes. The social legislation of that country, for more than half a century, afforded a model to all other
countries. All the workingmen's insurance, minimum wage, child
labour and other such acts of the United States are bald imitations
of it, and in England, before the war, the mountebank Lloyd-
George borrowed his whole bag of tricks from it. Well, Dr. Hans
Delbrück, in his "Regierung und Volkswille," tells us that this legislation was fought step by step at home, and with the utmost
ferocity, by the beneficiaries of it. When Bismarck formulated it
and essayed to get it through the Reichstag he was opposed by
every mob-master in the Empire, save only his kept Socialist, Ferdi-
nand Lassalle. The common people were so heavily against him
for several years that he had to carry on the government without
the consent of the Reichstag—that is, unconstitutionally, and at the
risk of his head. If the proletariat had been able to get control of
the German courts, as it had got control of the Reichstag, it would
have deposed him from office and condemned him to death for
high treason. His treason consisted in trying to formulate a code
of legislation designed to restore its old rights under the Prussian
common law, destroyed by the rise of the industrial system, and
to grant it many new and valuable benefits.

"Let any competently instructed person," says Sir Henry Maine,
"turn over in his mind the great epochs of scientific invention and
social change during the past two centuries, and consider what
would have occurred if universal suffrage had been established at
any one of them." Here, obviously, Sir Henry speaks of universal
suffrage that is genuinely effective—suffrage that registers the actual will of the people accurately and automatically. As we shall
see, no such thing exists in the world to-day, save in limited areas.
Public policies are determined and laws are made by small minorities playing upon the fears and imbecilities of the mob—sometimes
minorities of intelligent and honest men, but usually minorities of
rogues. But the fact does not disturb the validity of Maine's argument. "Universal suffrage," he goes on, "would certainly have prohibited the spinning-jenny and the power loom. It would certainly

have forbidden the threshing-machine. It would have prevented the adoption of the Gregorian Calender; it would have restored the Stuarts. It would have proscribed the Roman Catholics, with the mob which burned Lord Mansfield's house and library in 1780; and it would have proscribed the Dissenters, with the mob which burned Dr. Priestley's house and library in 1791." So much for England. What of the United States? I point briefly to the anti-evolution acts which now begin to adorn the statute-books of the Hookworm Belt, all of them supported vociferously by the lower orders. I point to the anti-vivisection and anti-contraception statutes, to the laws licensing osteopaths and other such frauds, and to the multitude of acts depriving relatively enlightened minorities of the common rights of free assemblage and free speech. They increase in proportion as *vox populi* is the actual voice of the state; they run with that "more democracy" which Liberals advocate. . . .

9. *The Eternal Mob*

Such is man on the nether levels. Such is the pet and glory of democratic states. Human progress passes him by. Its aims are unintelligible to him and its finest fruits are beyond his reach: what reaches him is what falls from the tree, and is shared with his four-footed brothers. He has changed but little since the earliest recorded time, and that change is for the worse quite as often as it is for the better. He still believes in ghosts, and has only shifted his belief in witches to the political sphere. He is still a slave to priests, and trembles before their preposterous magic. He is lazy, improvident and unclean. All the durable values of the world, though his labour has entered into them, have been created against his opposition. He can imagine nothing beautiful and he can grasp nothing true. Whenever he is confronted by a choice between two ideas, the one sound and the other not, he chooses almost infallibly, and by a sort of pathological compulsion, the one that is not. Behind all the great tyrants and butchers of history he has marched with loud hosannas, but his hand is eternally against those who seek to liberate the spirit of the race. He was in favour of Nero and Torquemada by instinct, and he was against Galileo and Savonarola by the same instinct. When a Cagliostro dies he is ready for a Danton; from the funeral of a Barnum he rushes to the triumph of a Bryan. The world gets nothing from him save his brute labour, and even that he tries to evade. It owes nothing to him that has any solid dignity or worth, not even democracy. In two thousand years he has moved an inch: from the sports of the arena to the lynching-party—and another inch: from the obscenities of the Saturnalia to the obscenities of the Methodist revival. So he lives out his life in the image of Jahveh. What is worth knowing he doesn't know and doesn't want to know; what he knows is not true. The cardinal articles of his credo are the inventions of mountebanks; his heroes are mainly scoundrels.

Do I forget his central virtue—at least in Christendom? Do I forget his simple piety, his touching fidelity to the faith? I forget nothing: I simply answer, What faith? Is it argued by any rational man that the debased Christianity cherished by the mob in all the Christian countries of to-day has any colourable likeness to the body of ideas preached by Christ? If so, then let us have a better teaching of the Bible in the public-schools. The plain fact is that this bogus Christianity has no more relation to the system of Christ than it has to the system of Aristotle. It is the invention of Paul and his attendant rabble-rousers—a body of men exactly comparable to the corps of evangelical pastors of to-day, which is to say, a body devoid of sense and lamentably indifferent to common honesty. The mob, having heard Christ, turned against Him, and applauded His crucifixion. His theological ideas were too logical and too plausible for it, and his ethical ideas were enormously too austere. What it yearned for was the old comfortable balderdash under a new and gaudy name, and that is precisely what Paul offered it. He borrowed from all the wandering dervishes and soul-snatchers of Asia Minor, and flavoured the stew with remnants of the Greek demonology. The result was a code of doctrines so discordant and so nonsensical that no two men since, examining it at length, have ever agreed upon its precise meaning. But Paul knew his mob: he had been a travelling labour leader. He knew that nonsense was its natural provender—that the unintelligible soothed it like sweet music. He was the *Stammvater* of all the Christian mob-masters of to-day, terrorizing and enchanting the mob with their insane damnations, eating their seven fried chickens a week, passing the diligent plate, busy among the women. Once the early church emerged from the Roman catacombs and began to yield to that reorganization of society which was forced upon the ancient world by the barbarian invasions, Paul was thrown over-board as Methodists throw Wesley overboard when they acquire the means and leisure for golf, and Peter was put in his place. Peter was a blackguard, but he was at least free from any taint of Little Bethel. The Roman Church, in the aristocratic feudal age, pro-moted him *post mortem* to the Papacy, and then raised him to the mystical dignity of Rock, a rank obviously quasi-celestial. But Paul remained the prophet of the sewers. He was to emerge cen-turies later in many incarnations—Luther, Calvin, Wesley, and so on. He remains to-day the arch-theologian of the mob. His turgid and witless metaphysics make Christianity bearable to men who would be repelled by Christ's simple and magnificent reduction of the duties of man to the duties of a gentleman.

25. E. G. CONKLIN (1863–)

EDWIN GRANT CONKLIN was born in Waldo, Ohio. He was graduated from Ohio Wesleyan University and gained the degree of Doctor of Philosophy at Johns Hopkins University. He was a professor of biology at Ohio Wesleyan University and professor of zoology successively at Northwestern University, the University of Pennsylvania, and Princeton University (1908–33). He is the author of numerous biological and zoological works, including studies of the mechanism of heredity and evolution, the direction of human evolution, and the applications of biological doctrines to social and political questions.

From EVOLUTION AND DEMOCRACY (1922)[1]

The Biological Bases of Democracy

There have been, and still are, many kinds of democracy in many fields, and it is therefore difficult to draw a very sharp and discriminating definition of what is meant by this term. But it will be admitted, I think, that democracy in the widest sense means much more than a form of government, that it is indeed a system of social organization affecting almost every relation of man to man. *It is a system which, ideally at least, attempts to equalize the opportunities and responsibilities of individuals in society.* As thus defined it would apply not merely to government and the administration of justice but also to education and individual development, to industry and its reward, property.

But this ideal of absolute equality has never been, and can never be, fully realized in human society because nature has made men unequal in every respect—physically, intellectually, and morally—and there is no possible way in which such natural inequalities can be wholly eradicated. Furthermore, the very nature of organization, that is, specialization and co-operation, implies inequalities and limitations; without these there could be no such thing as so-

[1] Pt. ii of *The Direction of Human Evolution* (rev. ed. New York, 1934), at pp. 100–105, 108–111, 127–139, 145–153, 155–156. By special arrangement with Charles Scribner's Sons.

ciety or progress. A society in which every individual is absolutely free and equal would be not only an impossibility but also a contradiction in terms.

Looked at merely as a system of government, a democracy in which all the people rule directly, as in ancient Greece, is an impossibility in any populous state. Instead, modern democracies are representative governments, in which the people as a whole choose their representatives to administer the government for them. General policy may be determined by the people, but the details of carrying out of any policy must be left to chosen leaders. Further, it has been found necessary to hedge about even such a modified democracy as this by limiting suffrage to adult persons, not feeble-minded, insane, or criminal; and it is perfectly evident that higher intellectual qualifications are necessary. . . .

When it is remembered that mental capacity is inherited, that parents of low intelligence generally produce children of low intelligence and that on the average they have more children than persons of high intelligence, and, furthermore, when we consider that the intellectual capacity or "mental age" can be changed very little by education we are in a position to appreciate the very serious condition which confronts us as a nation.

We have always recognized that the success of democracy depends upon the intelligence of the people, but we have never before had any adequate conception of the very low level of the average intelligence of the nation. Furthermore, we have generally assumed that intelligence depended upon education and that general compulsory education would solve all our problems. Education is still one of our greatest needs, but, alas, it is not the magical panacea that was once supposed. Education can only bring to development the qualities which are potentially present; it cannot increase those potentialities or capacities; and the attempt to educate a person of D grade beyond the fifth year of the elementary schools is usually wasted effort.

Undoubtedly the ultimate standing and success of any popular government must depend upon the intelligence of its citizens, and yet owing to the larger families of the unintelligent and to the great influx of foreigners of low mental capacity, our average intelligence has probably been declining for the past twenty-five years at least.

There is some demand, especially on the part of police authorities, that finger-prints be made of every person in the nation for purposes of identification; how much more desirable it is that every person be classified mentally! By this means we could avoid untold waste of time and effort in trying to give higher education to those incapable of profiting by it and in trying to fit the wrong persons into particular positions. And at the same time we should greatly increase the happiness and contentment of the people concerned, for nothing is so productive of unrest and discontent as the putting of men and women into positions which they are incapable of filling, or, worse still, of assigning persons of high capacity to low-grade work. Let us have the finger-prints, but before everything else let us have a mental classification of all children of school age. When once this has been done perhaps the least intelligent group can ultimately be denied the suffrage as are imbeciles, insane, and criminals at present. . . .

. . . We hear much of the tyranny, inefficiency, ignorance, and corruption of democracies and unfortunately much of this is only too true. Democracy is charged with being responsible for all these sins, whereas in many instances they are due to some of the worst types of autocracy which are merely shielding themselves under the name of democracy. We do not change the nature of anything by merely changing its name and an autocracy, oligarchy, or aristocracy that calls itself a democracy cannot be used to disprove the value of real democracy.

Again many of the faults which are charged up against democracy such as emotionalism, irrationalism, blind partisanship, and selfishness are found under every other form of social organization and cannot properly be attributed to democracy but belong rather to human nature; the most that can be said of these is that democracy no more than other systems has been able to eliminate them.

No system of government lives up to its best ideals and no single system is universally adapted to all people. No doubt democracy operates best with those in whom superior intelligence is associated with high morality, in whom the love of freedom is associated with a compelling desire for social order and justice. No doubt it is generally better for parents to govern young children than to make them absolutely self-governing; no doubt people of superior intelligence and morality can govern primitive people more efficiently than they can govern themselves; no doubt a wise and beneficent autocracy can accomplish many desirable things which an ignorant and corrupt democracy cannot. The question which lies back of all this is, What is the ultimate purpose of government? In the case of children, is it not to bring them to a condition where they can wisely govern themselves? Is the ultimate purpose different in the case of primitive peoples, or of the masses in a democracy? Is not the ultimate aim of government the highest possible development of the individual, the nation, and the race? Is not the educative power of democracy its greatest virtue?

These great problems of the hour should be viewed not only in the light of human history, but also in the long perspective of the history of living things upon the earth. Undoubtedly the fundamental concepts of biology apply to man no less than to other organisms, but it must be admitted that the application of biological principles to specific problems of social organization is often of doubtful value. Thus we find that biological sanction has been claimed for wholly antagonistic opinions, as, for example, for and against war, communism, woman's suffrage, polygamy, etc. Those who are searching for biological analogies to support almost any preconceived theory in philosophy, sociology, education, or government can usually find them, for the living world is large and extraordinarily varied, and almost every possible human condition has its parallel somewhere among lower organisms, where we find many kinds of degeneration as well as progress.

This uncertainty and ambiguity in the application of biological principles to man and his institutions, has brought this whole process of reasoning into disrepute among those who look upon man as a being who stands wholly outside the realm of biology, but in spite of the uncertainties of biological analogies when applied to minor phases and problems of human society, no one who has felt the force and sweep of the great doctrine of evolution, can doubt that biological principles underlie the physical, intellectual, and social evolution of man—that biology is a torch-bearer not merely into the dark backgrounds of human history, but also into the still more obscure regions of the future development of the race.

The Declaration of Independence is, in many respects, the charter of our democracy. Adopted at a time when it was necessary to secure the utmost co-operation of the Colonies and of the world, it made its appeal directly to the social instincts, as well as to the intelligence of men, to their love of freedom, justice, and equality. The rights of man have ever been the foundation-stones of democracy. The Declaration held "these truths to be self-evident; that all men are created equal; that they are endowed by their Creator with certain inalienable rights; that among these rights are life, liberty, and the pursuit of happiness. That to accomplish these purposes, governments are instituted among men, deriving all their just powers from the consent of the governed." Here are the foundation principles of democracy, which are summarized more concisely in the motto of France—"Liberty, Equality, Fraternity."

What is the teaching of biology regarding these principles of democracy? How can we harmonize individual liberty and social organization, democratic equality and hereditary inequality, universal fraternity, and national and class hostility? Or to put the question in a more practical form—How can we develop social organization in spite of individual liberty, democratic equality in spite of hereditary inequality, universal fraternity in spite of national and class antagonisms? These are great problems, and the student of animal organization and evolution can do no more than to offer a few biological suggestions as to their solution. . . .

Democratic Equality vs. Hereditary Inequality

Equality is one of the most important factors in producing social harmony. It is the dearest one of the democratic graces. 'And now abideth Liberty, Fraternity, Equality, but the greatest of these is Equality.' The creed of democracy has generally been that all men are created equal, and that the inequalities which exist are due to environment, education, or opportunity.

And yet nothing is more evident than the inequalities of personality, intelligence, usefulness, and influence; and the inequalities of heredity are greater even than those of environment. Recent work on development and evolution shows that the influence of environment is relatively slight, that of heredity overwhelming. Not only poets, but also scholars, statesmen, leaders, and laborers are born and not made. Hereditary inequality has always been the strong fortress of aristocracy, and scientific studies of heredity seem on first thought to support the contentions of aristocracy in this respect rather than those of democracy.

How shall we harmonize the teachings of biology with those of democracy; the proven inequalities of heredity with the assumed equality of man? Shall we revise our ideas of heredity, or of democracy? I have sometimes been asked: "Do you believe in heredity; how then can you believe in democracy? Do you believe in equality; how then can you believe in heredity?"

Aristocracy is founded upon an obsolete idea of heredity, namely the "law of entail." It confuses social and biological inheritance. A son may inherit the property of his father but not his personality; under the law of primogeniture the oldest son inherits the kingdom, titles, privileges of his father in their entirety, but not his intelligence, character, and personality. In natural or biological inheritance the germinal causes of the traits of the parents are separated and are redistributed to their offspring so· that the latter are "mosaics" of ancestral traits. These germinal causes of traits, which are called genes, are transmitted unchanged, but in the fertilization of the egg one-half of the genes from each parent is lost and is replaced by half from the other parent. So numerous are these genes that the combinations of them in the offspring are rarely, if ever, the same in two individuals, and so complex is their influence upon one another and upon the process of development, that no two sexually produced individuals are ever exactly alike. Consequently the best traits may appear in parents and be lost in their offspring; genius in an ancestor, may be replaced by incompetence, imbecility, or insanity in a descendant. As each generation must start life anew from the germ cells, so in every person there is a new distribution of hereditary factors or genes. Every person has a new hereditary deal, if not always a square one.

Owing to the fact that some traits, or rather their genes, are dominant and others recessive, certain of the latter may be carried along for several generations in a latent condition only to appear in some later offspring in which the dominant gene is not ·present. Feeble-mindedness, for example, is a recessive character, and East has calculated that it is present in a recessive form in one person out of fourteen of the entire population of this country, but it does not actually appear unless two of these recessive genes come together in a fertilized egg. On the other hand, feeble-mindedness and other recessive characters become latent when mated with normal and dominant characters. The later history of the famous, or rather infamous, "Jukes family" shows that many of the descendants are normal and useful citizens probably because their parents married into normal families.

This is the great law of heredity discovered by Mendel, and it differs fundamentally from the law of entail. Property may be entailed, but not personality; titles and privileges, but not character and ability. With the law of entail in mind, it is not surprising that strict hereditarians should have questioned the reputed parentage of Jesus, or Shakespeare, or Lincoln, or that lovers of democracy should have refused to believe in this kind of heredity; but the law of entail is of man's making, while, so far as we know, the law of Mendel is the only law of natural inheritance.

Think of the great men of unknown lineage, and the unknown men of great lineage; think of the close relationship of all persons of the same race; of the wide distribution of good and bad traits in the whole population; of incompetence and even feeble-mindedness in great families, and of genius and greatness in unknown families, and say whether natural inheritance supports the claims of aristocracy or of democracy.

When we remember that most of the great leaders of mankind came of humble parents; that many of the greatest geniuses had the most lowly origin; that Shakespeare was the son of a bankrupt butcher and an ignorant woman who could not write her name, that as a youth he is said to have been known more for poaching than for scholarship, and that his acquaintance with the London theatres began by his holding horses for their patrons; that Beethoven's mother was a consumptive, the daughter of a cook, and his father a confirmed drunkard; that Schubert's father was a peasant by birth and his mother a domestic servant; that Faraday, perhaps the greatest scientific discoverer of any age, was born over a stable, his father a poor sick blacksmith, his mother an ignorant drudge, and his only education obtained in selling newspapers on the streets of London and later in working as apprentice to a bookbinder; that the great Pasteur was the son of a tanner; that Lincoln's parents were accounted "poor white trash" and his early surroundings and education most unpromising; and so on through the long list of names in which democracy glories—when we remember these we may well ask whether aristocracy can show a better record. The law of entail is aristocratic, but the law of Mendel is democratic. . . .

It may be objected that I have ended by denying that there is any inheritance, at least so far as intellectual and social qualities are concerned, but this is not the case. While it is true that good and bad hereditary traits are widely distributed among all classes and conditions of men, they are not equally distributed. On the contrary the chances of good or bad traits appearing in offspring are much higher in some families than in others, but no family has a monopoly of good or bad traits, and no social system can afford to ignore the great personages that appear in obscure families, or to exalt nonentities to leadership because they belong to great families. In short, preferment and distinction should depend upon individual worth and not upon family name or position. This is orthodox democratic doctrine, but not the faith or practice of aristocracy.

Finally democratic equality does not now mean, and has never in the past meant, that all men are equal in personality. It is not a denial of personal inequalities, but is the only genuine recognition of them. On the other hand, rigid family and class distinctions are denials of individual distinctions. Democratic equality does not mean equality of heredity, environment, education, or possessions; least of all does it mean equality of intelligence, usefulness, or influence.

It does mean equality before the law, equal justice for all, no special privileges due merely to birth, freedom to find one's work and place in society. In short it means that every man shall be measured by his own merits, and not by the merits of some ancestor whose good traits may have passed to a collateral line.

Democracy alone permits a natural classification of men with respect to social value, as contrasted with all artificial and conventional classifications. It contributes more than any other system of government to the contentment, happiness, stability, and peace of a nation. It brings a message of justice, and hope, and inspiration to people in all walks of life. . . .

Universal Fraternity vs. National and Class Antagonisms

Evolution shows that we are all cousins if not brothers. The lines of descent from innumerable ancestors converge in us, and will radiate from us to innumerable descendants. Genealogists picture descent as a tree in which the trunk represents some single ancestor and the branches all of his descendants, but such a representation is wholly at variance with biological facts because in sexual reproduction every person has two parents. The "genealogical tree" is the result of an attempt to trace descent back to some one distinguished ancestor while ignoring all others. The various branches of a family do not trace back to a single trunk, but rather to an increasing number of branches. A graphic representation of descent is not a tree but a net in which every individual is represented by a knot formed by the union of two lines which may be traced backward and forward to an ever-increasing number of knots and lines until all are united in this vast genealogical net of humanity. If the number of our ancestors doubled in each ascending generation, as it would do if the marriage of cousins of various degrees did not take place, each of us would be descended from more than a billion ancestors of a thousand years ago, let us say in the reign of William the Conqueror. Even allowing for numerous intermarriages of relatives it is highly probable that all people of English or French or German stock are descended from common ancestors of a thousand years ago.

A book has been published recently in which several of our Presidents, heads of universities, and captains of industry and finance are shown to be descended from Charlemagne. This distinction is one which they share with probably more than half of the citizens of this Republic. Einhard, the contemporary biographer of Charlemagne, says that he had nine wives, besides many concubines, and although he was fond of his children he never knew how many he had. If it were possible to trace our genealogies far enough into the past and through all their ramifications it would be found that all of us are literally descendants of royalty, of Alfred and Charlemagne and William the Conqueror and of any and every other person of one thousand or more years ago who left many descendants—including nonentities and worse; we hunt up our noble ancestors and forget the others. . . .

But while our lines of descent lead back to practically all people of the same race and country of a thousand or more years ago, we have inherited our traits of character from only a very small number of these ancestors. It is known that inheritance passes from one generation to the next in the germ cells, and more specifically in the chromosomes or deeply staining threads found in the nuclei of those cells.

The number of chromosomes is constant for every species, and typically each chromosome has come down in unbroken lineage from previous generations. But in the formation of the germ cells one-half of the specific number is thrown away and when egg and sperm unite the specific number is again restored.

In man there are probably forty-eight chromosomes, twenty-four from the father and twenty-four from the mother; but these are usually derived in unequal numbers from the four grandparents; for example, sixteen may come from the paternal grandfather and eight from the paternal grandmother, four from the maternal grandfather and twenty from the maternal grandmother, or the number which comes from each grandparent may vary all the way from twenty-four to naught. One or more of the eight great-grand-parents may have furnished no chromosomes and no inherited traits to the great-grandchild, and finally no one in the world can inherit chromosomes (or traits) from more than forty-eight con-temporary ancestors, assuming that the chromosomes preserve their identity, since no one has more than forty-eight chromosomes. Consequently, although each of us has had thousands of ancestors, he has had only a small number of transmitters. Many a person bears the name of some distinguished ancestor but does not have a single one of his chromosomes or hereditary traits, whereas others who do not bear his name, and are usually reckoned as collateral descendants, have received his chromosomes and are his true in-heritors.

There has been much foolish talk and loose thinking regarding old families and length of descent. As Tennyson says:

> "The gardener Adam and his wife
> Smile at the claims of long descent."

In length of descent we are all equal, and in community of descent we are all cousins if not brothers. Our lines stretch out to all our race. Each individual or family is not a separate and independent entity, but merely a minor unit in the great organism of mankind. Biology and the Bible agree that "God hath made of one blood all nations of men." There are no really pure lines of human descent, and few isolated stocks, and these owe their origin to geographical isolation rather than to anything else. There has been, and still is, abundant interbreeding among all minor varieties and races of men, and as a result mankind is a hopelessly mongrel species. Indeed, in this respect man is like any other wide-ranging species. He has no such claim to ancestral purity as has any pure breed of domesticated animals and plants. Man is indeed a wild species and cannot be domesticated because there is no one to domesticate him.

As a result of this common descent the resemblances between all types of men are vastly more numerous and important than the differences. This fact is especially evident to the biologist, for even the types which differ most widely, such as the white, yellow, and black races, are evidently only varieties or subspecies of *Homo sapiens*, while no other existing creature can be placed in the same zoological genus or family with man. When I reflect upon the resemblances between all men and the differences which separate man from all other animals, I think I can understand the words of a prayer which I used to hear when I was a boy: "We thank thee, Lord, that thou hast made us men." . . .

Hereditary social classes such as exist in many parts of Europe are the antithesis of democracy. That which is hereditary in such classes is not necessarily personal merit, but purely environmental advantages or disadvantages. Such artificial distinctions largely ignore the natural abilities or disabilities of men and are fundamentally unjust and undemocratic. On the other hand, classes such as are found in schools, which are based upon personal merit, and in which every one is free to pass from one class to another depending upon his ability, are not only wholly democratic, but are absolutely necessary to a well-organized society.

Means says: "The perfect democracy will be a state in which there will be classes absolutely rigid as to their functions for society but absolutely fluid as to the individuals who compose them. A man's or a woman's position in society will, in such a state, be determined by his or her peculiar aptitude and talents, not by hereditary position, nor by nepotism, nor by human authority, but solely by individual merit."

What could be more wasteful, absurd, and tragic than a system of artifical class distinctions which condemns low-born genius to the humblest work and puts well-born blockheads in exalted places? All persons enjoy most the work which they are led to believe that they can do best, and that nation will be most contented and most efficient whose people are free to find the places in the social system for which they are best fitted. This is one of the strongest arguments against hereditary classes, and in favor of a genuine democracy—not that in such a democracy all men are equal, but that all are free from purely artificial restraints in finding their own levels. One of the most beneficial influences of the Great War, and of wars in general, is the breaking up of rigid class distinctions, the elimination of stupid lords and junkers and military officers, and the elevation of men of genius to exalted places, irrespective of birth or social position.

Bateson, the English naturalist, has tentatively expressed the opinion that hereditary classes are desirable from the standpoint of eugenics, basing this opinion no doubt upon the fact that intellectual and social qualities are often, though, as he sadly admits, not always, characteristic of certain families. No doubt the best biological and social results would obtain if intermarriage occurred only between individuals of similar hereditary types. Such a segregation takes place naturally and normally where instinct and inclination are not interfered with by purely artificial restrictions and conventions. But even the oldest royal families, and much more our modern aristocracies and pseudo-aristocracies, are of such mixed lineage that their children vary greatly in ability, and it is contrary to instinct and to good breeding for a woman of talent to marry the stupid son of a distinguished family, or for a man of genius to marry a shallow-minded heiress. It would be good for society in general, and for its individual members in particular, if every person were free to find his or her proper level both in occupation and marriage, irrespective of family obscurity or pride. In democratic America we all rejoice when some divinely gifted rail-splitter becomes by his own merits the greatest figure of his generation, and we ought to rejoice, though of course regretfully, when the ungifted son of a railroad president finds his proper place working on the track, or when the low-minded heiress elopes with the coachman.

When we turn from the more personal aspects of fixed social classes to their control of governments and of public affairs in general, we find that the evidence of their disruptive and antisocial influences are worst of all. The world has had experience of many kinds of exclusive class rule—absolute monarchy, aristocracy, middle class, and proletariat—and though some of these have proved better than others, they have all been bad, for they have endangered or destroyed social unity and harmony, and have ended sooner or later in disaster. Russia has recently gone from one of these extremes to the other, and the end of the tyranny of the proletariat cannot long be delayed. An autocracy or aristocracy may be progressive and efficient, but it is always dangerous, for no person or class is wise or good enough to rule other classes or persons without their participation or consent. Not only do governments derive all their just powers from the consent of the governed, but they derive their safety and stability from this source as well. What a demonstration have the greatest military autocracies of Europe furnished the world of their utter weakness and helplessness against an aroused people!

The strength and stability of democracies are proportional to their inclusiveness, their breadth of base, whereas autocracies are inverted pyramids. Equal universal suffrage and majority rule are the only self-regulating and self-preserving mechanisms which have been discovered as yet for harmonizing conflicting interest in governments; they are the safety-valves of society. Theoretically, there is danger that majority rule may end in tyranny over minorities, but the social instincts of justice and fair play are wide-spread among men, and experience has generally shown that in the long run majorities may be counted upon to be just to minorities that play fair. The more intelligent members of society always have an immense advantage over the more ignorant, and even in a genuine democracy the danger is not so much that ignorant and venal majorities may oppress the better elements in society, as that intelligent but unscrupulous minorities may exercise tyranny over the mass of the people in spite of their numbers.

Majority rule would level society down to general mediocrity were it not for the instinct of the people to follow leaders. Modern democracy is not the rule of the people as a whole, of ignorant masses, of "the blind god of numbers." A democracy, no less than an autocracy, is a government by leaders, but in the former case these leaders are chosen by the people and are responsible to them and in the latter they are not. Leaders in a democracy have great power, and in crises such as war, their powers may be temporarily greatly increased, but they are not autocrats, for they must render to the people an account of their stewardship. In no modern form of government do the people as a whole make plans for war or peace, for taxation or legislation or even party platforms. These things are determined by leaders, and in general the mass of the people hold them responsible only for results. Government, no less than personal behavior, proceeds by the principle of "trial and error," and the majority in a democracy decide only whether the results are failures or successes. Furthermore a democracy is much more sensitive to this test than is any other form of government, for a failure is quickly abandoned and its authors repudiated. The contrast between democracy and autocracy is not between "numbers and rightness," but it is between rightness as measured by the effect upon the majority or on only a small minority of the people. . . .

One of the charges which has been brought against democracy is that it fails to develop capable leaders. For example, Cram says: "Democratic government for the last twenty-five years has neither desired nor created leaders of an intellectual or moral capacity above that of the general mass of voters, and when by chance they appear they are abandoned for a type that is not of the numerical average but below it, and the standard has been lowering itself for a generation."

Means quotes this approvingly and points out that our people are showing a general decay of morals. He says he has seen, in a certain Eastern city, "young men and women, who had ancestors among that splendid group of men who signed the Declaration of Independence, acting like drunkards and prostitutes"; and he attributes this lower tone of morals to "the newcomers whose origin was in heaven knows what gutter."

Every period has its Jeremiahs, who get joy and satisfaction from pointing out how much worse this degenerate age is than the "good old times" of the past. To some people the sunset of yesterday was much more beautiful than the sunrise of to-day, and this is especially true of those who never get up to see the sun rise. Is there not every reason to believe that coming generations will look upon Roosevelt and Wilson as this generation looks upon the great

political leaders of former times? And as to the moral degeneration of those descendants of the Signers, is it certain that the young
blades of the Revolutionary period drank less alcohol and led more
chaste lives than those of the present day? And does it seem probable that these descendants of our first families were led astray by
"gutter-born" immigrants, generally poor, ignorant and hard-working?

Such condemnations of the present, as compared with the past,
are not critical nor judicious. They are an expression of emotion
rather than reason, of sentiment rather than evidence. They are
characteristic of those who see in history a record of deterioration
rather than of progress, who place the golden age in the distant
past and engage in ancestor-worship. But the evidences of social
and moral progress are all about us, and those who take the long
view of human history will not mistake marginal eddies for the
main stream.

The greatest danger that confronts democracy is not its lack of
specialization, its slowness and inefficiency, its levelling down to
mediocrity, or its lack of capable leaders, but the fact that unscrupulous leaders may pervert and misdirect the normal social instincts
of the people in order to accomplish selfish and partisan purposes.
During the war there was a wide-spread and highly organized cultivation of emotions of hate, suspicion, chauvinism. In some instances leaders, newspapers, and organizations did their best to
work the people up to a frenzy, little realizing or caring how dangerous this process is. At present a similar propaganda is being
waged against Japan and Mexico, and unless it can be met by
reason and common sense it will in time get beyond peaceful
bounds. It is this appeal of unscrupulous or ignorant leaders to
primitive instincts and emotions rather than to reason which makes
possible blind prejudice and hatred between classes and races and
nations; it is this which provokes wars and destroys peace and
progress. . . .

Conclusion

Can democracy save itself from the serious faults and dangers
which threaten it? Can the people, as a whole, be trusted to choose
wisely their leaders and policies? Can the democratic ideals of
liberty, equality, and fraternity bring about that rational co-opera-

tion upon which the further progress of society must depend? No man can now answer these questions with certainty, but at least it can be said that no other system of social organization which has yet been tried holds so much promise of success.

The rational powers of the masses of mankind are not very great, and if the success of democracy depended upon human reason alone the prospect would not be very encouraging. Although Lincoln's saying is true that "You can fool all of the people some of the time, and some of the people all of the time, but you cannot fool all of the people all of the time," nevertheless if a majority of the people can be fooled most of the time the outlook for future democracy would not be very bright, if progress depended solely upon the rational powers of mankind.

But the firm foundations upon which democracy rests go·deeper than the intellect and reason of man; they go down to the instincts and emotions and moral judgments which underlie all social evolution. Upon these foundations the rational organization of society stands as a splendid but still insecure superstructure.

The moral judgments of men may be no better than their practical judgments, but judgment which is founded upon much experience, even it be based on so low a level as "trial and error," is generally sound. Out of the conflict of opinions and ideals of multitudes of persons in all walks and circumstances of life there comes at last a compromise or adjustment which we call "common sense" and which has the pragmatic quality of viability.

Although we cannot always trust the rational processes of the people as a whole, it is the creed of democracy that we can trust their social instincts and moral judgments. Their instincts of service and sympathy, and their judgments as to right and wrong, as to justice and injustice, are the bases upon which the ideals of liberty, equality, and fraternity rest. These instincts and judgments are so deep-seated and so wide-spread, that they form a firm foundation for democracy.

II. POLITICAL AUTHORITY AND CIVIL LIBERTIES

1. JOHN WINTHROP (1588-1649) [1]

From *A DEFENCE OF AN ORDER OF COURT MADE IN THE YEAR 1637* [2]

IN THE midst of the Antinomian controversy in Massachusetts Bay in 1637, the general court adopted an order providing that no immigrants should be allowed to reside in the colony without first having obtained the permission of one of the magistrates. According to Winthrop's account, the object of the order was "to keep out all persons as might be dangerous to the commonwealth." The actual aim appears to have been to prevent the Antinomians from bringing in recruits for their party. The order aroused considerable criticism in Boston and there were unfriendly demonstrations against Winthrop as Governor. Sir Henry Vane, who had just been defeated for election to the governorship, called the order "an act of tyranny." Winthrop prepared a formal statement in defense of the order, as follows:

> A *Declaration of the Intent and Equitye of the Order made at the last Court, to this effect, that none should be received to inhabite within this Jurisdiction but such as should be allowed by some of the Magistrates.*

For clearing of such scruples as have arisen about his order, it is to be considered, first, what is the essentiall forme of a common weale or body politic such as this is, which I conceive to be this— The consent of a certaine companie of people, to cohabite together, under one government for their mutual safety and welfare. . . .

It is clearly agreed, by all, that the care of safety and wellfare was the original cause or occasion of common weales and of many familyes subjecting themselves to rulers and laws; for no man hath lawfull power over another, but by birth or consent, so likewise, by the law of proprietye, no man can have just interest in that which belongeth to another, without his consent.

---

[1] For a sketch of Winthrop, see pp. 15–16 above.

[2] In Thomas Hutchinson, *A Collection of Original Papers Relative to the History of the Colony of Massachusets-Bay* (Boston, 1769), pp. 67–71.

From the premises will arise these conclusions.

1. No common weale can be founded but by free consent.

2. The persons so incorporating have a public and relative interest each in other, and in the place of their cohabitation and goods, and laws, &c. and in all the means of their wellfare so as none other can claime priviledge with them but by free consent.

3. The nature of such an incorporation tyes every member thereof to seeke out and entertaine all means that may conduce to the wellfare of the bodye, and to keepe off whatsoever doth appeare to tend to theire damage.

4. The wellfare of the whole is to be put to apparent hazard for the advantage of any particular members.

From these conclusions I thus reason.

1. If we heere be a corporation established by free consent, if the place of our cohabitation be our owne, then no man hath right to come into us &c. without our consent.

2. If no man hath right to our lands, our government priviledges, &c. but by our consent, then it is reason we should take notice of before we conferre any such upon them.

3. If we are bound to keepe off whatsoever appears to tend to our ruine or damage, then may we lawfully refuse to receive such whose dispositions suite not with ours and whose society (we know) will be hurtfull to us, and therefore it is lawfull to take knowledge of all men before we receive them.

4. The churches take liberty (as lawfully they may) to receive or reject at their discretion; yea particular towns make orders to the like effect; why then should the common weale be denied the like liberty and the whole more restrained than any parte?

5. If it be sinne in us to deny some men place &c. among us, then it is because of some right they have to this place &c. for to deny a man that which he hath no right unto is neither sinne nor injury.

6. If strangers have right to our houses or lands, &c. then it is either of justice or of mercye; if of justice let them plead it, and we shall know what to answer: but if it be only in way of mercye, or by the rule of hospitality, &c. then I answer 1st, A man is not a fit object of mercye except he be in miserye. 2d, We are not bound to exercise mercye to others to the ruine of ourselves. 3d, There are few that stand in neede of mercye at theire first coming hither.

As for hospitality, that rule doth not bind further than for some present occasion, not for continual residence.

7. A family is a little common wealth, and a common wealth is a greate family. Now as a family is not bound to entertaine all comers, no not every good man (otherwise than by way of hospitality) no more is a common wealth.

8. It is a generall received rule, *turpius ejicitur quam non admittitur hospes*, it is worse to receive a man whom we must cast out againe, than to denye him admittance.

9. The rule of the Apostle, John 2. 10. is, that such as come and bring not the true doctrine with them should not be received to house, and by the same reason not into the common weale.

10. Seeing it must be granted that there may come such persons (suppose Jesuits, &c.) which by consent of all ought to be rejected, it will follow that this law (being only for notice to be taken of all that come to us, without which we cannot avoyd such as indeed are to be kept out) is no other but just and needfull, and if any should be rejected that ought to be received, that is not to be imputed to the law, but to those who are betrusted with the execution of it. And herein is to be considered, what the intent of the law is, and by consequence, by what rule they are to walke, who are betrusted with the keeping of it. The intent of the law is to preserve the wellfare of the body; and for this ende to have none received into any fellowship with it who are likely to disturbe the same, and this intent (I am sure) is lawful and good. Now then, if such to whom the keeping of this law is committed, be persuaded in theire judgments that such a man is likely to disturbe and hinder the publick weale, but some others who are not in the same trust, judge otherwise, yet they are to follow theire owne judgments, rather then the judgments of others who are not alike interested: As in tryall of an offender by a jury; the twelve men are satisfied in their consciences, upon the evidence given, that the party deserves death: but there are 20 or 40 standers by, who conceive otherwise, yet is the jury bound to condemn him according to their owne consciences, and not to acquit him upon the different opinion of other men, except theire reasons can convince them of the errour of theire consciences, and this is according to the rule of the Apostle, Rom. 14. 5. Let every man be fully persuaded in his own mynde.

From COMMENTS ON A POPULAR PETITION
(MAY 22, 1639)[1]

WINTHROP'S election to the governorship for the seventh time
in 1639 was not altogether harmonious. There were fears among
a considerable number of the people that the governor and magistrates
were striving to keep themselves in office permanently and at the same
time release themselves from effective limitation by the deputies elected
from the towns. The passages below from Winthrop's Journal give an
account of some of these fears and reveal Winthrop's views on the
extent to which private citizens may properly petition the authorities
for the repeal of a law.

The court of elections was; at which time there a small eclipse
of the sun. Mr. Winthrop was chosen governour again, though
some laboring had been, by some of the elders and others, to have
changed, not out of any dislike of him (for they all loved and esteemed him,) but out of their fear lest it might make way for having a governour for life, which some had propounded as most agreeable to God's institution and the practice of all well ordered states.
But neither the governour nor any other attempted the thing;
though some jealousies arose which were increased by two occasions. The first was, there being want of assistants, the governour
and other magistrates thought fit (in the warrant for the court)
to propound three, amongst which Mr. Downing, the governour's
brother-in-law, was one, which they conceived to be done to
strengthen his party, and therefore, though he were known to be a
very able man, etc., and one who had done many good offices for
the country for these ten years, yet the people would not choose
him. Another occasion of their jealousy was, the court, finding
the number of deputies to be much increased by the addition of
new plantations, thought fit, for the ease both of the country and
the court, to reduce all towns to two deputies. This occasioned
some to fear, that the magistrates intended to make themselves
stronger, and the deputies weaker, and so, in time, to bring all
power into the hands of the magistrates; so as the people in some

---

[1] In A Journal of the Transactions and Occurrences in the Settlement of Massachusetts and the Other New England Colonies, from the Year 1630 to 1644, ed. by
James Savage, new ed., 2 vols. (Boston, 1853), Vol. I, pp. 360–363.

towns were much displeased with their deputies for yielding to such an order. Whereupon, at the next session, it was propounded to have the number of deputies restored; and allegations were made, that it was an infringement of their liberty; so as, after much debate, and such reasons given for diminishing the number of deputies, and clearly proved that their liberty consisted not in the number, but in the thing, divers of the deputies, who came with intent to reverse the last order, were, by force of reason, brought to uphold it; so that, when it was put to the vote, the last order for two deputies only was confirmed. Yet, the next day, a petition was brought to the court from the freemen of Roxbury, to have the third deputy restored. Whereupon the reasons of the court's proceedings were set down in writing, and all objections answered, and sent to such towns as were unsatisfied with this advice, that, if any could take away those reasons, or bring us better for what they did desire, we should be ready, at the next court, to repeal the said order.

The hands of some of the elders (learned and godly men) were to this petition, though suddenly drawn in, and without due consideration, for the lawfulness of it may well be questioned: for when the people have chosen men to be their rulers, and to make their laws, and bound themselves by oath to submit thereto, now to combine together (a lesser part of them) in a public petition to have any order repealed, which is not repugnant to the law of God, savors of resisting an ordinance of God; for the people, having deputed others, have no power to make or alter laws, but are to be subject; and if any such order seem unlawful or inconvenient, they were better prefer some reason, etc., to the court, with manifestation of their desire to move them to a review, than peremptorily to petition to have it repealed, which amounts to a plain reproof of those whom God hath set over them, and putting dishonor upon them, against the tenor of the fifth commandment. . . .

From A SPEECH TO THE GENERAL COURT
(JULY 3, 1645)[1]

IN 1645 the general court held a long session, largely occupied with a "trial" of Winthrop, then deputy-governor, for having participated with other magistrates in an act in excess of authority. The matter arose out of a dispute over the appointment of the captain of a militia company in the town of Hingham. The townspeople had chosen one Allen to replace one Emes who had recently been the captain after having previously served as lieutenant of the company. Allen's appointment was submitted to the magistrates for confirmation. The magistrates, "considering the injury that would hereby accrue to Emes, refused to allow of Allen, but willed both sides to return home, and every officer to keep his place . . . until the court should take further order." A majority of the townsmen voted to defy the magistrates' action and selected Allen for the post. A long, complicated, and tumultuous controversy ensued. The matter finally came before the general court, where the deputies voted, by a small majority, "that the magistrates exercised too much power, and that the people's liberty was thereby in danger." Winthrop defended himself, and there was a debate followed by a vote of acquittal for Winthrop —a conclusion apparently reached not on the merits of the case but because of a threat by the magistrates that they would appeal an adverse decision to an arbitrating board of clergymen, who would almost certainly overrule a decision against Winthrop. The court also voted to fine the chief petitioners and rioters. Winthrop then asked and was given "leave for a little speech." The speech has been called "the classical expression of Puritan political theory."

The great questions that have troubled the country, are about the authority of the magistrates and the liberty of the people. It is yourselves who have called us to this office, and being called by you, we have our authority from God, in way of an ordinance, such as hath the image of God eminently stamped upon it, the contempt and violation whereof hath been vindicated with examples of divine vengeance. I entreat you to consider, that when you choose magistrates, you take them from among yourselves, men subject to like passions as you are. Therefore when you see infirmities in us, you should reflect upon your own, and that would make you bear the more with us, and not be severe censurers of the failings of your

[1] In *ibid.*, Vol. II, pp. 280–282.

magistrates, when you have continual experience of the like infirmities in yourselves and others.   We account him a good servant,
who breaks not his covenant.   The covenant between you and us
is the oath you have taken of us, which is to this purpose, that we
shall govern you and judge your causes by the rules of God's laws
and our own, according to our best skill.   When you agree with a
workman to build you a ship or house, etc., he undertakes as well
for his skill as for his faithfulness, for it is his profession, and you
pay him for both.   But when you call one to be a magistrate, he
doth not profess nor undertake to have sufficient skill for that
office, nor can you furnish him with gifts, etc., therefore you must
run the hazard of his skill and ability.   But if he fail in faithfulness,
which by his oath he is bound unto, that he must answer for.   If
it fall out that the case be clear to common apprehension, and the
rule clear also, if he transgress here, the error is not in the skill, but
in the evil of the will: it must be required of him.   But if the case
be doubtful, or the rule doubtful, to men of such understanding
and parts as your magistrates are, if your magistrates should err here,
yourselves must bear it.

For the other point concerning liberty, I observe a great mistake
in the country about that.   There is a twofold liberty, natural (I
mean as our nature is now corrupt) and civil or federal.   The first
is common to man with beasts and other creatures.   By this, man,
as he stands in relation to man simply, hath liberty to do what he
lists; it is a liberty to evil as well as to good.   This liberty is incompatible and inconsistent with authority, and cannot endure the
least restraint of the most just authority.   The exercise and maintaining of this liberty makes men grow more evil, and in time to
be worse than brute beasts: omnes sumus licentia deteriores.[1]   This
is that great enemy of truth and peace, that wild beast, which all
the ordinances of God are bent against, to restrain and subdue it.
The other kind of liberty I call civil or federal, it may also be
termed moral, in reference to the covenant between God and man,
in the moral law, and the politic covenants and constitutions,
amongst men themselves.   This liberty is the proper end and object
of authority, and cannot subsist without it; and it is a liberty to
that only which is good, just, and honest.   This liberty you are to
stand for, with the hazard (not only of your goods, but) of your

---

[1] "Without restraint, we are all worse" [than beasts].

lives, if need be. Whatsoever crosseth this, is not authority, but a distemper thereof. This liberty is maintained and exercised in a way of subjection to authority; it is of the same kind of liberty wherewith Christ hath made us free. ·The woman's own choice makes such a man her husband; yet being so chosen, he is her lord, and she is to be subject to him, yet in a way of liberty, not of bondage; and a true wife accounts her subjection her honor and freedom, and would not think her condition safe and free, but in her subjection to her husband's authority. Such is the liberty of the church under the authority of Christ, her king and husband; his yoke is so easy and sweet to her as a bride's ornaments; and if through frowardness or wantonness, etc., she shake it off, at any time, she is at no rest in her spirit, until she take it up again; and whether her lord smiles upon her, and embraceth her in his arms, or whether he frowns, or rebukes, or smites her, she apprehends the sweetness of his love in all, and is refreshed, supported, and instructed by every such dispensation of his authority over her. On the other side, ye know who they are that complain of this yoke, and say, let us break their bands, etc., we will not have this man to rule over us. Even so, brethren, it will be between you and your magistrates. If you stand for your natural corrupt liberties, and will do what is good in your own eyes, you will not endure the least weight of authority, but will murmur, and oppose, and be always striving to shake off that yoke; but if you will be satisfied to enjoy such civil and lawful liberties, such as Christ allows you, then will you quietly and cheerfully submit unto that authority which is set over you, in all the administrations of it, for your good. Wherein, if we fail at any time, we hope we shall be willing (by God's assistance) to hearken to good advice from any of you, or in any other way of God; so shall your liberties be preserved, in upholding the honor and power of authority amongst you. . . .

2. NATHANIEL WARD (c. 1578–1652)

NATHANIEL WARD was born in Haverhill, England. His father, two of his brothers, and one of his sons were Puritan ministers. Nathaniel practised law for fifteen years after leaving Emmanuel College, Cambridge, where he had received the baccalaureate and master's degrees. On a trip to Prussia he became acquainted with the Calvinist theologian, David Pareus, and at the latter's urging entered the ministry, in about his thirtieth year. He preached Puritain doctrines and was excommunicated and dismissed by Archbishop Laud in 1633. He had taken part in the formation of the Massachusetts Bay Company, and in 1634 (in his late fifties) he migrated to the colony, where he remained for twelve years. He held the pastorate at the new settlement of "Agawam" (later called Ipswich), but resigned after three or four years on the ground of ill-health. His two principal achievements in the colony were his contribution (in his early sixties) to the first code of laws adopted in America and his authorship, five years later, of a unique political pamphlet.

Ward had reached the colony when the deputies elected from the towns were beginning to insist on the prerogatives of the general court as a representative governing organ. One of their first demands was that a body of laws be framed to guide and limit the magistrates ("assistants") in the discharge of their judicial duties. "The people," John Winthrop recorded in his Journal, "thought their condition very unsafe, while so much power rested in the discretion of magistrates." The assistants were for delay, arguing that experience in the colony had been too brief for any such undertaking and that a codification of law by the colonists might be taken as a defiance of the laws of England. Committees were set up in 1635 and 1636, but they accomplished nothing, except that in the latter year John Cotton submitted a compilation, which Winthrop called "Moses His Judicials" (see p. 21, above). In 1639, the general court appointed another committee, which submitted, as alternative choices, both Cotton's code and a new compilation prepared principally by Ward. The document finally adopted, in November, 1641, as the "Body of Liberties," contained provisions from both compilations, but was chiefly the work of Ward. This code is based generally on the English common law, although it contains some innovations (such as the provision for

the congregational form of church government, the prohibition of monopolies, and the interdiction of any sort of payment for legal assistance
in court proceedings), and some of its criminal law is taken from the
Bible. It was soon displaced by more extensive compilations. It is of
interest to note that these earliest American codes, designed to secure a
government of laws rather than of men, were adopted as checks on judges
rather than on legislators.

Ward's political treatise, *The Simple Cobler of Aggawam*, was written
during his last two years in the colony (published in London, over the
pseudonymn "Theodore de la Guard" in 1647, the year of Ward's return
to England). The author writes in the character of a cobbler in a new
world looking back on the political and religious troubles of the old
world. The cobbler drew only occasional illustrations from his vocation
and did not hesitate to display a considerable knowledge of law, theology,
and the classics. Ward wrote in an eccentric style; but his views on
"polypiety" (quoted below) represent very well the stand on religious
toleration taken by the early Puritan leaders of Massachusetts Bay. The
work contains a mild protest against arbitrary authority in non-religious
matters and a plea for a better balanced and more clearly defined distribution of powers between King, Lords, and Commons in the government
of England. There is also a long and humorous digression ridiculing
current fashions in women's dress in England and the Bay colony.

[See: John Ward Dean, *A Memoir of the Rev. Nathaniel Ward* (1868);
Samuel E. Morison, *Builders of the Bay Colony* (1930), ch. 7; Vernon L.
Parrington, *Main Currents of American Thought*, Vol. I (1927), pp. 76–81.]

From THE SIMPLE COBLER OF AGGAWAM IN AMERICA (1647) [1]

Either I am in Apoplexy, or that man is in a Lethargy, who doth
not now sensibly feel God shaking the Heavens over his head, and
the Earth under his feet: The Heavens so, as the Sun begins to
turn into darkness, the Moon into blood, the Stars to fall down to
the ground; So that little Light of Comfort or Counsel is left to
the Sons of Men: The Earth so, as the foundations are failing, the
righteous scarce know where to find rest, the inhabitants stagger
like drunken men: it is in a manner dissolved both in Religions and

[1] Text from "The Fifth Edition, with some Amendments," in *Tracts and Other
Papers Relating . . . to the Origin, Settlement, and Progress of the Colonies in
North America*, ed. by Peter Force (Washington, 1844), Vol. III, no. 8, at pp. 5
(beginning of the text) –9, 17–18.

Relations: And no marvel; for, they have defiled it by transgressing the Laws, changing the Ordinances, and breaking the Everlasting Covenant. The Truths of God are the Pillars of the World, whereon States and Churches may stand quiet if they will; if they will not, He can easily shake them off into delusions, and distractions enough. . . .

. . . Too many men having not laid their foundations sure, nor ballasted their Spirits deep with humility and fear, are prest enough of themselves to evaporate their own apprehensions. Those that are acquainted with Story know, it hath ever been so in new Editions of Churches: Such as are least able, are most busy to pudder in the rubbish, and to raise dust in the eyes of more steady Repayrers. Civil Commotions make room for uncivil practises: Religious mutations, for irreligious opinions: Change of Air, discovers corrupt bodies: Reformation of Religion, unsound minds. He that hath any well-faced phansy in his Crown, and doth not vent it now, fears the pride of his own heart will dub him dunce for ever. Such a one will trouble the whole *Israel* of God with his most untimely births, though he makes the bones of his vanity stick up, to the view and grief of all that are godly wise. The devil desires no better sport than to see light heads handle their heels, and fetch their carreers in a time, when the Roof of Liberty stands open.

The next perplexed Question, with pious and ponderous men, will be: What should be done for the healing of these comfortless exulcerations. I am the unablest adviser of a thousand, the unworthiest of ten thousand; yet I hope I may presume to assert what follows without just offence.

First, such as have given or taken any unfriendly reports of us *New-English*, should doe well to recollect themselves. We have been reputed a Colluvies of wild Opinionists, swarmed into a remote wilderness to find elbow-room for our Phanatic Doctrines and practises; I trust our diligence past, and constant sedulity against such persons and courses, will plead better things for us. I dare take upon me, to be the Herauld of *New-England* so far, as to proclaim to the World, in the name of our Colony, that all Familists, Antinomians, Anabaptists, and other Enthusiasts shall have free Liberty to keep away from us, and such as will come to be gone as fast as they can, the sooner the better.

Secondly, I dare aver, that God doth no where in his word tolerate Christian States, to give Tolerations to such adversaries of his Truth, if they have power in their hands to suppress them.

Here is lately brought us an Extract of a *Magna Charta*, so called, compiled between the Sub-planters of a *West-Indian* Island; whereof the first Article of constipulation, firmly provides free stable-room and litter for all kind of Consciences, be they never so dirty or jadish; making it actionable, yea, treasonable, to disturb any man in his Religion, or to discommend it, whatever it be. We are very sorry to see such professed Prophaneness in *English* Pro- fessors, as industriously to lay their Religious foundations on the ruine of true Religion; which strictly binds every Conscience to *contend earnestly for the Truth: to preserve unity of Spirit, Faith and Ordinances, to be all like minded, of one accord; every man to take his Brother into his Christian care, to stand fast with one spirit, with one mind, striving together for the faith of the Gospel;* and by no means to permit Heresies or Erronious Opinions: But God abhorring such loathsome beverages, hath in his righteous judgment blasted that enterprize, which might otherwise have pros- pered well, for ought I know; I presume their case is generally known ere this.

If the Devil might have his free option, I believe he would ask nothing else, but liberty to enfranchize all false Religions, and to embondage the true; nor should he need: It is much to be feared that lax Tolerations upon State-pretences and planting necessities, will be the next subtle Stratagem he will spread to distate the Truth of God, and supplant the Peace of the Churches. Tolerations in things tolerable, exquisitely drawn out by the lines of the Scripture, and pensil of the Spirit, are the sacred favours of Truth, the due latitudes of Love, the fair Compartments of Christian fraternity: but irregular dispensations, dealt forth by the facilities of men, are the frontiers of error, the redoubts of Schisme, the perillous irrita- ments of carnal and spiritual enmity.

My heart hath naturally detested four things: The standing of the Apocrypha in the Bible; Forainers dwelling in my Country, to crowd out Native Subjects into the corners of the Earth; Alchy- mized Coines; Tolerations of divers Religions, or of one Religion in segregant shapes: He that willingly assents to the last, if he ex- amines his heart by day-light, his Conscience will tell him, he is either an Atheist, or an Heretick, or an Hypocrite, or at best a captive to some Lust: Poly-piety is the greatest impiety in the World. . . .

Not to tolerate things meerly indifferent to weak Consciences, argues a Conscience too strong: pressed uniformity in these, causes much disunity: To tolerate more than indifferents, is not to deal indifferently with God: He that doth it, takes his Scepter out of his hand, and bids him stand by. Who hath to do to institute Religion but God. The power of all Religion and Ordinances, lies in their Purity: their Purity in their Simplicity: then are mixtures pernicious. I lived in a City, where a Papist Preached in one Church, a Lutheran in another, a Calvinist in a third; a Lutheran one part of the day, a Calvinist the other, in the same Pulpit: the Religion of that Place was but motly and meagre, their affections Leopard-like.

If the whole Creature should conspire to do the Creator a mischief, or offer him an insolency, it would be in nothing more, than in erecting untruths against his Truth, or by sophisticating his Truths with humane medleyes: the removing of some one iota in Scripture, may draw out all the life, and traverse all the Truth of the whole Bible: but to authorise an untruth, by a Toleration of State, is to build a sconce against the walls of Heaven, to batter God out of his Chair: To tell a practical lye, is a great Sin, but yet transient; but to set up a Theorical untruth, is to warrant every lye that lyes from its root to the top of every branch it hath, which are not a few. . . .

He that is willing to tolerate any Religion, or discrepant way of Religion, besides his own, unless it be in matters meerly indifferent, either doubts of his own, or is not sincere in it.

He that is willing to tolerate any unsound Opinion, that his own may also be tolerated, though never so sound, will for a need hang God's Bible at the Devils girdle.

Every toleration of false Religions, or Opinions hath as many Errors and Sins in it, as all the false Religions and Opinions it tolerates, and one sound one more.

That State that will give Liberty of Conscience in matters of Religion, must give Liberty of Conscience and Conversation in their Moral Laws, or else the Fiddle will be out of Tune, and some of the strings crack.

He that will rather make an irreligious quarel with other Religions than try the Truth of his own by valuable Arguments, and peaceable Sufferings; either his Religion, or himself is irreligious.

Experience will teach Churches and Christians, that it is far better to live in a State united, though a little Corrupt, than in a State, whereof some Part is incorrupt, and all the rest divided. . . .

Hence it is, that God is so jealous of his Truths, that he hath taken order in his due justice: First, that no practical Sin is so Sinful as some error in judgment; no man so accursed with indelible infamy and dedolent impenitency, as Authors of Heresie. Secondly, that the least Error, if grown sturdy and pressed, shall set open the Spittle-door of all the squint-ey'd, wry-necked and brasenfaced Errors that are or ever were of that litter; if they be not enough to serve its turn, it will beget more, though it hath not one crust of reason to maintain them. Thirdly, that that State which will permit Errors in Religion, shall admit Errors in Policy unavoidably. Fourthly, that that Policy which will suffer irreligious Errors, shall suffer the loss of so much Liberty in one kind or other. . . .

. . . How all Religions should enjoy their liberty, Justice its due regularity, Civil cohabitation moral honesty, in one and the same Jurisdiction, is beyond the Artique of my comprehension. If the whole conclave of Hell can so compromise, exadverse, and diametrical contradictions, as to compolitize such a multimonstrous maufrey of heteroclytes and quicquidlibets quietly; I trust I may say with all humble reverence, they can do more than the Senate of Heaven. . . .

It is greatly to be lamented, to observe the wanton fearlessness of this Age, especially of Younger Professors, to greet new Opinions and Opinionists: as if former truths were grown Superannuate, and Sapless, if not altogether antiquate. *Non senescet veritas.*[1] No man ever saw a gray hair on the head or beard of any Truth, wrinckle, or morphew on its face: The bed of Truth is green all the year long. He that cannot solace himself with any saving truth, as affectionately as at the first acquaintance with it, hath not only a fastidious, but an adulterous Heart. . . .

[1] "The truth does not become too old."

3. ROGER WILLIAMS (1603–82)

ROGER WILLIAMS, earliest advocate of religious toleration in America, was the son of a London merchant tailor. In his youth he learned shorthand and took notes on proceedings in the Star Chamber court, thereby attracting the attention of Sir Edward Coke, who helped him through Pembroke College, Cambridge. He stayed on at Cambridge to prepare for the ministry and took orders in the Church of England. He came increasingly under Puritan influences, however, and late in 1630 migrated to Massachusetts Bay (two years ahead of John Cotton and Thomas Hooker, who soon took the lead in getting him out of the colony). His arrival was regarded as an important event by the colonists; but he had gone beyond the Puritan beliefs and he rejected a call from the Boston church, which he regarded as not sufficiently separated from the Anglican church. Accepting a call from Plymouth, he found that his views were even too advanced for the Separatists there. He found a sympathetic hearing at Salem, where he remained until forced out by the Boston magistrates, over the protests of his parishioners.

The clerical and political leaders of the colony, troubled by Williams' insistence on separation from the Church of England, were definitely alarmed by other views he was spreading abroad. He was "teaching publickly" that the royal grants of land to the colonists (under titles claimed by right of first discovery by a Christian ruler, a claim which Williams called "a solemn public lie") were "unjust usurpations upon others possessions," since there had been no voluntary sale by the Indian owners and no payment to them. He opposed the colony's rule that every resident take an oath to submit to the laws and orders of the general court and to report speedily any plots against the government; and he denied that civil magistrates had any power to enforce purely religious commandments. He was tried before the general court in October, 1635, convicted for spreading "newe and dangerous opinions, against the aucthoritie of magistrates," and sentenced to leave the colony within six weeks. Cotton and Williams gave conflicting explanations of the essential reasons for the prosecution: Cotton contending that Williams' main offenses were his criticism of the land patents and his opposition to the oath of fidelity; Williams maintaining that opposition to him was based chiefly on his assertion that civil power "extended only to the bodies, and goods, and outward state of men." Contemporary accounts by Winthrop and others appear to support Williams' explanation.

Before the expiration of the six-months period, the court modified its sentence to allow Williams to remain until Spring, provided he would not go about trying to "draw others to his opinions." But when the magistrates heard reports that he continued to declare his views to those who came to his home and that he was planning a settlement outside of Massachusetts, they ordered him deported to England. Williams, warned by the somewhat sympathetic Winthrop, evaded the order of arrest, and he and a number of his followers escaped to lands of the Narragansett Indians. Here he bought a large tract from the Indians, associated other heads of families with him in a land company, and drew up a covenant for a government—"only in civill things"; and royal charters (in 1644 and 1663) gave official sanction to this experiment with liberty of conscience and separation of church and state.

Williams' ideas on religious and political liberty were set forth most extensively in several works written in the course of a long controversy with Cotton; the most important of these, *The Bloudy Tenent of Persecution* (written and published in London in 1644), was burned by the common hangman in execution of an order of Parliament.

Williams' settlement (which he called "Providence Plantations," because of "God's mercefull providence unto me in my destresse") drew adherents from numerous sects, and they were well treated. Some of the newcomers were occasions of trouble in the colony, however; for they pushed their own claims to liberty so far as to protest vigorously against the execution of judgments on them in some ordinary civil and criminal cases. On returning from one of his trips to England, Williams found that there had been considerable dissension and disorder during his absence. Whereupon he wrote a *Letter to the Town of Providence* (1655) in order to lay down lines distinguishing freedom of religion and conscience from a disturbance of the public peace and an obstruction to the administration of justice.

[See: Cotton Mather, *Magnalia Christi Americana* (1702, ed. of 1853–55), Vol. II, pp. 455–459; Samuel H. Brockunier, *The Irrepressible Democrat,* Roger Williams (1940); James E. Ernst, *The Political Thought of Roger Williams* (1929); Vernon L. Parrington, *Main Currents of American Thought,* Vol. I (1927), pp. 62–75.]

From THE BLOUDY TENENT OF PERSECUTION (1644)[1]

First, That the blood of so many hundred thousand soules of *Protestants* and *Papists,* spilt in the *Wars* of *present* and *former Ages,* for their respective *Consciences,* is not *required* nor *accepted* by *Jesus Christ* the *Prince* of *Peace.*

Secondly, Pregnant *Scripturs* and *Arguments* are throughout the *Worke* proposed against the *Doctrine* of *persecution* for *cause* of *Conscience.*

Thirdly, Satisfactorie Answers are given to *Scriptures,* and objections produced by Mr. *Calvin, Beza,* Mr. *Cotton,* and the Ministers of the New English Churches and others former and later, tending to prove the *Doctrine* of *persecution* for cause of *Conscience.*

Fourthly, The *Doctrine* of *persecution* for cause of *Conscience,* is proved guilty of all the *blood* of the *Soules* crying for *vengeance* under the *Altar.*

Fifthly, All *Civill States* with their *Officers* of *justice* in their respective *constitutions* and *administrations* are proved *essentially Civill,* and therefore not *Judges, Governours* or *Defendours* of the *Spirituall* or *Christian state* and *Worship.*

Sixtly, It is the will and command of God, that (since the comming of his *Sonne* the *Lord Jesus*) a *permission* of the most *Paganish, Jewish, Turkish,* or *Antichristian* consciences and *worships,* bee granted to *all* men in all *Nations* and *Countries:* and they are onely to bee *fought* against with that *Sword* which is only (in *Soule* matters) *able* to conquer, to wit, the *Sword* of *Gods Spirit,* the *Word* of *God.*

Seventhly, The *state* of the Land of *Israel,* the *Kings* and *people* thereof in *Peace* & *War,* is proved *figurative* and *ceremoniall,* and no *patterne* nor *president* for any *Kingdome* or *civill state* in the *world* to follow.

Eightly, *God* requireth not an *uniformity* of *Religion* to be *inacted* and *inforced* in any *civill state;* which *inforced uniformity* (sooner or later) is the greatest occasion of *civill Warre,* ravishing

[1] The Bloudy Tenent, of Persecution, for cause of Conscience, discussed, in A Conference betweene Truth and Peace (1644), ed. by Samuel L. Caldwell, in *Publications of the Narragansett Club (First Series),* Vol. III (Providence, 1867), pp. 3–4, 177, 178–179.

of *conscience, persecution* of *Christ Jesus* in his servants, and of the *hypocrisie* and *destruction* of *millions* of *souls*.

Ninthly, In holding an inforced *uniformity* of *Religion* in a *civill state*, wee must necessarily *disclaime* our desires and hopes of the *Iewes* conversion to *Christ*.

Tenthly, An inforced *uniformity* of *Religion* throughout a *Nation* or *civill state*, confounds the *Civill* and *Religious*, denies the principles of Christianity and civility, and that *Jesus Christ* is come in the Flesh.

Eleventhly, The permission of other *consciences* and *worships* then a state professeth, only can (according to God) procure a firme and lasting *peace*, (good *assurance* being taken according to the *wisedome* of the *civill state* for uniformity of *civill obedience* from all sorts.)

Twelfthly, lastly, true *civility* and *Christianity* may both flourish in a *state* or *Kingdome*, notwithstanding the *permission* of divers and contrary *consciences*, either of *Iew* or *Gentile*.

CHAP. LIX.

Unto those excellent and famous speeches of those Princes worthy to be written in *golden letters* or *rows* of *Diamonds* upon all the gates of all the Cities and Palaces in the World, the Answerer (without any particular reply) returnes two things.

Truth. First, that Princes profession and practice is no rule of *conscience:* unto this as all men will subscribe, so may they also observe how the Answerer deales with Princes.

One while they are the nursing Fathers of the Church, not only to feed, but also to correct, and therefore consequently bound to judge what is true *feeding* and *correcting:* and consequently *all men* are bound to submit to their *feeding* and *correcting*.

Another while, when Princes crosse Mr. *Cottons* judgement and practice, then it matters not what the *profession* and *practice* of Princes is; for (saith he) their *profession* and *practice* is no Rule to *Conscience*.

I aske then, unto what *Magistrates* or *Princes* will themselves or any so perswaded submit, as unto keepers of both *Tables*, as unto the *Antitypes* of the *Kings* of *Israel* and *Judah*, and nursing *Fathers* and *Mothers* of the *Church?*

First, will it not evidently follow, that by these Tenents they ought not to submit to any Magistrates in the world in these cases, but to Magistrates just of their owne *conscience:* and

Secondly, that all other *Consciences* in the world (except their owne) must be persecuted by such their Magistrates? . . .

CHAP. LX.

Truth. In the second place hee saith that *Princes* out of *State policy* tolerate what suits not with *Christianity,* and out of State *necessity* tolerate (as *David* did *Joab*) against their wils.

To which I answer,

First, that although with him in the first I confesse that *Princes* may tolerate that out of *State policy* which will not stand with *Christianity,* yet in the second he must acknowledge with me, that there is a *necessity* sometime of *State Toleration,* as in the case of *Ioab,* and so his former *affirmation* generally laid downe (*viz.* that it is evill to tolerate *seducing Teachers,* or *scandalous livers*) was not duly waighed in the *Balance* of the *Sanctuary,* and is too light.

Secondly, I affirme that that State policy and State necessity, which (for the *peace* of the *State* and preventing of Rivers of *civill Blood*) permits the *Consciences* of men, will bee found to agree most punctually with the *Rules* of the best *Politician* that ever the World saw, the *King* of *Kings,* and *Lord* of *Lords,* in comparison of whom *Salomon* himselfe had but a *drop* of *wisedome,* compared to *Christs* Ocean, and was but a *Farthing Candle* compared with the *All* and *Ever glorious Son* of *Rightcousnesse.* . . .

LETTER TO THE TOWN OF PROVIDENCE
(*JANUARY, 1655*) [1]

That ever I should speak or write a tittle, that tends to such an infinite liberty of conscience, is a mistake, and which I have ever disclaimed and abhorred. To prevent such mistakes, I shall at present only propose this case: There goes many a ship to sea, with many hundred souls in one ship, whose weal and woe is common, and is a true picture of a commonwealth, or a human combination or society. It hath fallen out sometimes, that both papists and protestants, Jews and Turks, may be embarked in one ship; upon

---

[1] In *Letters of Roger Williams, 1632–1682,* ed. by John Russell Bartlett, in *ibid.* Vol. VI (Providence, 1874), pp. 278–279.

which supposal I affirm, that all the liberty of conscience, that ever
I pleaded for, turns upon these two hinges—that none of the
papists, protestants, Jews, or Turks, be forced to come to the ship's
prayers or worship, nor compelled from their own particular prayers
or worship, if they practice any. I further add, that I never denied,
that notwithstanding this liberty, the commander of this ship ought
to command the ship's course, yea, and also command that justice,
peace and sobriety, be kept and practiced, both among the seamen
and all the passengers. If any of the seamen refuse to perform their
services, or passengers to pay their freight; if any refuse to help, in
person or purse, towards the common charges or defence; if any
refuse to obey the common laws and orders of the ship, concerning
their common peace or preservation; if any shall mutiny and rise
up against their commanders and officers; if any should preach or
write that there ought to be no commanders or officers, because all
are equal in Christ, therefore no masters nor officers, no laws nor
orders, nor corrections nor punishments;—I say, I never denied,
but in such cases, whatever is pretended, the commander or commanders may judge, resist, compel and punish such transgressors,
according to their deserts and merits. This if seriously and honestly
minded, may, if it so please the Father of lights, let in some light to
such as willingly shut not their eyes.

I remain studious of your common peace and liberty.

ROGER WILLIAMS

4. JOHN CALLENDER (1706–48)

SOON after Roger Williams founded his Providence settlement he announced himself to be a Baptist. That sect had been established in England in 1608 and one of its main principles was complete separation of church and state. Williams and several of his associates established a Baptist church at Providence, in 1639. Williams soon withdrew and proclaimed himself to be only a "Seeker," accepting no particular creed except that of belief in the fundamentals of Christianity. Recent Baptist historians express doubts as to the complete Baptist orthodoxy of the original Providence group. There is no doubt, however, that Rhode Island soon became one of the strongest Baptist centers in America; and Baptists, who suffered persecution in other New England colonies, took a prominent part in the struggle for religious liberty in colonial America.

A hundred years after the founding of Rhode Island, John Callender, a Baptist minister in Newport, wrote an impressive account of religious liberty in Rhode Island, in a brief book reviewing important events and policies of the colony during its first century. Born in Boston and a graduate of Harvard, Callender held pastorates in Baptist churches in Swansea, Massachusetts, and, from 1731 until his death, in Newport. Popular and respected in the community, he took a stand in advance of his denomination in advocating the admission of non-Baptists to participation in communion in Baptist churches. Besides his *Historical Discourse*, he collected information (used by later writers) on the history of the Baptists in America.

[See: Romeo Elton, "Memoirs of the Rev. John Callender, A.M.," in the second edition (1838) of Callender's *Historical Discourse on the Civil and Religious Affairs of the Colony of Rhode-Island and Providence Plantations*.]

From AN HISTORICAL DISCOURSE, ON . . . RHODE-ISLAND (1739) [1]

Almost all the first settlers of New-England were Puritans. The people at Plymouth were generally of that sort called Separatists,

[1] *An Historical Discourse on the Civil and Religious Affairs of the Colony of Rhode-Island*, ed. by Romeo Elton (2d rev. ed., Providence, 1838), at pp. 68–71, 80–82, 103–109.

and those of Boston generally had lived in the communion of the Church of England, though they scrupled conforming to some of the ceremonies. But these being come to so great a distance from the Bishops' power, could well enough agree in the same forms of worship, and method of discipline with the church at Plymouth, and a mixed form of church government was generally set up. Though they had seemed well enough united, by the common zeal against the ceremonies, yet now they were removed from the ecclesiastical courts, with a patent which gave them liberty of conscience, a variety of opinions as to several points, before not so much regarded, and perhaps not thought of, now began to be visible, and operate with considerable effects. It is no wonder such differences in opinion arose among them, as had been the case before among the Protestants in general. . . .

. . . the chief leaders, and the major part of the people, soon discovered themselves as fond of uniformity, and as loath to allow liberty of conscience to such as differed from themselves, as those from whose power they had fled. Notwithstanding all their sufferings and complaints in England, they seemed incapable of mutual forbearance; perhaps they were afraid of provoking the higher powers at home, if they countenanced other sects; and perhaps those who differed from them took the more freedom, in venting and pressing their peculiar opinions, from the safety and protection they expected, under a charter that had granted liberty of conscience.

In reality, the true grounds of liberty of conscience were not then known, or embraced by any sect or party of Christians; all parties seemed to think that as they only were in the possession of the truth, so they alone had a right to restrain, and crush all other opinions, which they respectively called error and heresy, where they were the most numerous and powerful; and in other places they pleaded a title to liberty and freedom of their consciences. And yet, at the same time, all would disclaim persecution for conscience sake, which has something in it so unjust and absurd, so cruel and impious, that all men are ashamed of the least imputation of it. A pretence of the public peace, the preservation of the Church of Christ from infection, and the obstinacy of the heretics, are always made use of, to excuse and justify that, which, stripped of all disguises, and called by its true name, the light of nature, and the laws of Christ Jesus condemn and forbid, in the most plain and solemn manner. . . . These were not the only people who thought they were doing God good service, when smiting their brethren and fellow-servants. All other christian sects acted generally, as if they thought this was the very best service they could do to God, and the most effectual way to promote the gospel of peace, and prove themselves the true and genuine disciples of Jesus Christ—of Jesus Christ, who hath declared, his kingdom was not of this world, who had commanded his disciples to call no man master on earth, who had forbidden them to exercise lordship over each other's consciences, who had required them to let the tares grow with the wheat till the harvest, and who had, in fine, given mutual love, peace, long-suffering, and kindness, as the badge and mark of his religion. . . .

. . . The public affairs of town and Colony were affected by these contentions, and the Governor and Assistants put in and out, as the one or the other side prevailed. The whole people unhappily run into factions and parties, in such a manner, as if contention and every evil work had not been evidences incontestible, that the wisdom from which they proceeded could not be from above. But so it is, where men differ about religion, their contentions are usually the most sharp, and carried on with the most irreligious heat and animosity: even though they differ about the smallest matters, or when, as was the case here, they differ from each other but in a very little.

A great part of the body of the people, and I am apt to think, at the first, the majority of the town of Boston, were of the same side the question with those people who afterwards came here. It is certain, the synod and the court were both held at New-Town, because of the disaffection of the people of Boston. The deputies of the town, at least some of them, openly espoused that party. The town, at least many of them, petitioned in their favor. And Mr. Cotton, the chief oracle then of both town and country, was confidently believed by them to be of the opinion they contended for. To which I might add the number of the people in that town, that were censured at the court.

Those who came away, were most of them long esteemed as brethren of the church, and never censured by the church at all; nay, that church did long retain some particularities, as to the brethren's power in church affairs, and their liberty to exercise their gifts in private or family meetings, and as to the subjects of infant baptism. It is certain, Mr. Wheelwright, minister to a branch of that church, at a place since called Braintree, (where the town had some lands,) was eager and zealous against the covenant of works; and was banished by the court for what was then called sedition, by the same rule which will make every dissent from, or opposition to, a majority in any religious affairs, to be sedition, and an iniquity to be punished by the judge. The minor part must always be seditious, if it be sedition to defend their own religious opinions, and endeavor to confute the contrary. This maxim, once allowed, must chain men down under errors and falsehoods wherever they prevail, and even rivet their chains. On this foot, what will become of the glorious martyrs for the gospel in the first ages of it, and the holy apostles, who turned the world upside down, who turned men from darkness to light, from the gods of the nations, whom they called vanities, to the living and true God? Nay, what shall we say of our blessed Saviour himself, who says he came to send division on earth? How shall we excuse the Protestants, nay, how shall we justify the Puritans themselves, if it be seditious to oppose any religious opinions we think are false or erroneous, when the major part of the society happen to think otherwise? . . .

I take it to have been no dishonor to the Colony, that Christians, of every denomination, were suffered to lead quiet and peaceable lives, without any fines or punishments for their speculative opinions, or for using those external forms of worship they believed God had appointed, and would accept. Bigots may call this confusion and disorder, and it may be so, according to their poor worldly notions of religion, and the kingdom of Christ. But the pretended order of human authority, assuming the place and prerogatives of Jesus Christ, and trampling on the consciences of his subjects, is, as Mr. R. Williams most justly calls it, "monstrous disorder."

Though it be very certain, that a public worship of God is very necessary, even to civilize mankind, who would be likely to lose all sense of religion without it; yet it will not follow, that the civil magistrate, as such, has authority to appoint the rites of worship, and constrain all his subjects to use them, much less to punish them for using any other. What has been forever the consequences of his pretending to such authority, and using his power to support it? What glory doth it bring to God, and what good can it do to men, to force them to attend a worship they disapprove?   It can only make them hypocrites, and God abhors such worshippers.

Notwithstanding our constitution left every one to his own liberty, and his conscience; and notwithstanding the variety of opinions that were entertained, and notwithstanding some may have contracted too great an indifference to any social worship, yet I am well assured there scarce ever was a time, the hundred years past, in which there was not a weekly public worship of God, attended by Christians, on this Island and in the other first towns of the Colony.

It is no ways unlikely, some odd and whimsical opinions may have been broached; the liberty enjoyed here, would tempt persons distressed for their opinions in the neighboring governments, to retire to this Colony as an asylum.   It is no ways unlikely, that some persons of a very different genius and spirit from the first settlers, might intrude themselves, and use this liberty as an occasion to the flesh; but the first set of men who came here, were a pious generation, men of virtue and godliness, notwithstanding their tincture of enthusiasm, which was not peculiar to them; and notwithstanding their peculiar opinions of justification, and the nature and rights of the Christian church.   They had not so many great and wise men among them, perhaps, as were in some of the other Colonies; but their whole number was very small, in comparison with the other Colonies.   Nevertheless, they had some very considerable men, and of superior merit.   It is true, likewise, their form of government was too feeble; their first Patent left them without sufficient authority in their civil officers, to check any popular humors; but yet, they did, and that as early as the Massachusetts Colony, form a body of good laws, by which all vice, and every immorality, was discouraged or punished.   And throughout the whole history of the Island and Colony, there is manifestly an aim and endeavor to prevent or suppress all disorders and immoralities, and to promote universal peace, virtue, godliness, and charity.

I do not pretend to defend all the opinions that were entertained by any of them; much less, all the extravagant notions that were unjustly ascribed to some of them; nor yet to justify every word or action that might be the effect of heated zeal, or raised indignation

and resentment. That man, who will go about to justify or condemn a party, in the gross, and without distinction, shall never be
approved or imitated by me; much less can it be expected, I should
defend all the opinions of so many different religious parties, as
were here united in civil peace. However, I dare say it after Mr. J.
Clark, that "notwithstanding the different consciences and understandings among them, they agreed to maintain civil justice and
judgments; neither were there such outrages committed among
them, as in other parts of the country were frequently seen."
(*Clark's Nar. Introd.*) And I bear them witness, they had a zeal
for God: If it were not according to knowledge in every article, yet
they lay open to instruction, desirous to find out and discover the
whole mind and will of God; which cannot so truly be said of all
places, where yet men are not more infallible. If there were any
of them, who made shipwreck of faith and a good conscience, perhaps it would be as easy, as it would be invidious, to find parallels
enough in other places, to shew there are other dangerous rocks, besides liberty of conscience. It is an unaccountable humor that has
prevailed among too many Christian sects, to make religion and the
gospel consist in their own peculiar and distinguishing tenets . . .

It must be a mean, contracted way of thinking, to confine the
favor of God and the power of godliness, to one set of speculative
opinions, or any particular external forms of worship. How hard
must it be, to imagine all other Christians but ourselves must be
formal and hypocritical, and destitute of the grace of God, because
their education or capacity differs from ours, or that God has given
them more or less light than to us, though we cannot deny, they give
the proper evidence of their fearing God, by their working righteousness; and shew their love to him, by keeping what they understand he has commanded; and though their faith in Christ Jesus
purifies their hearts, and works by love, and overcomes the world.
It would be hard to shew, why liberty of conscience, mutual forbearance and good will, why brotherly kindness and charity, is not
as good a center of unity, as a constrained uniformity in external
ceremonies, or a forced subscription to ambiguous articles. Experience has dearly convinced the world, that unanimity in judgment
and affection cannot be secured by penal laws. Who can tell, why
the unity of the spirit in the bonds of peace, is not enough for
Christians to aim at? And who can assign a reason, why they may

not love one another, though abounding in their own several senses? And why, if they live in peace, the God of love and peace may not be with them?

Indulgence to tender consciences, might be a reproach to the Colony, an hundred years ago, but a better way of thinking prevails in the Protestant part of the Christian church at present. It is now a glory to the Colony, to have avowed such sentiments so long ago, while blindness in this article happened in other places, and to have led the way as an example to others, and to have first put the theory into practice.

Liberty of conscience is more fully established and enjoyed now, in the other New-English Colonies; and our mother Kingdom grants a legal toleration to all peaceable and conscientious dissenters from the parliamentary establishment. Greater light breaking into the world and the church, and especially all parties by turns experiencing and complaining aloud of the hardships of constraint, they are come to allow as reasonable to all others, what they want and challenge for themselves. And there is no other bottom but this to rest upon, to leave others the liberty we should desire ourselves, the liberty wherewith Christ hath made them free. This is doing as we would be done by, the grand rule of justice and equity . . .

5. SAMUEL ADAMS (1722–1803)

SAMUEL ADAMS (a second cousin of John Adams) was born in Boston, went through Harvard, and prepared for the law. He made no success in the practice of law, mismanaged affairs in local governmental offices, and lost a sizable business left him by his father. A patient wife and other relatives and friends saved him from domestic financial worries and he devoted his energies to public affairs. He organized meetings of protest against the British policies, helped organize the non-importation associations and the intimidating "Sons of Liberty" and "Boston Tea Party," and played the chief part in inaugurating the "committees of correspondence"—extra-legal bodies set up to coordinate the activities of patriotic groups and facilitate their propaganda. He held public office for over thirty years. When we refer to him as "The Father of the American Revolution" (in some instances he has even been given Washington's title of "Father of His Country") we usually have in mind his successful activities in instigating mass protests and originating the new agencies to combat the British policies. But he did more than that. He prepared several of the most important of the formal statements of the colonial position. As soon as he had taken his seat as a member of the Massachusetts house of representatives (in which he served from 1765 to 1774) he introduced a set of resolutions intended to be a guide for the policy of all the colonies. These "Massachusetts Resolves" (adopted October 29, 1765) affirmed the colonists' claims not only as "essential rights of the British Constitution" but also as "rights founded in the law of God and nature," to be denied, therefore, by "no law of society" anywhere. Ridiculed in England as "the ravings of a parcel of wild enthusiasts," the Resolves were widely applauded and copied in the colonies.

More significant was the report Adams prepared for a Boston meeting, in connection with the creation of the first of the committees of correspondence. The Boston Town Records report a motion adopted on November 2, 1772, as follows:

> It was then moved by Mr. Samuel Adams, that a committee of correspondence be appointed, to consist of twenty-one persons, to state the rights of the Colonists and of this province in particular, as men and Christians and as subjects; and to communicate and publish the same to the

several towns and to the world as the sense of this town, with the infringements and violations thereof that have been, or from time to time may be, made.

Adams was assigned the task of drawing up the statement on the rights of the colonists; two others prepared the list of grievances and the letters to be sent to the several towns. A meeting at Faneuil Hall on November 20 approved the three reports. Adams' statement (adopted over three and a half years before the Declaration of Independence) is given in full below. It sets forth, in clearer theoretical form than other documents of the period, a general explanation and justification of the civil liberties claimed by the colonists. Samuel Adams, said Jefferson, was "the fountain of the most important measures" of the Revolutionary period.

Adams' public career continued a quarter of a century longer. He was a member of the Continental Congresses, where he signed the Declaration of Independence, seconded John Adams' motion to make Washington commander-in-chief, and proposed conferring dictatorial powers on Washington. He was a member of the Massachusetts constitutional convention (1779–80) and served in the new State government as member of the senate and executive council, as lieutenant-governor, and as governor (1794–97.) As a result of this active experience in administering the new government Adams (whom Governor Thomas Hutchinson had called "the Grand Incendiary of the Province") now admitted the need for strong government; or at least he excluded economic grievances as just grounds for resisting the governmental authority of a republic. When farmers in western and central Massachusetts organized and armed themselves in order to stop the foreclosure of mortgages on their properties and prevent imprisonment for debts arising out of the high taxes after the Revolution ("Shays' Rebellion," 1786–87), Adams denounced the movement and urged the governor to use strong measures in suppressing it. "Now that we have regular and constitutional government," he said, "popular committees and county conventions are not only useless but dangerous. They served an excellent purpose and were highly necessary when they were set up, and I shall not repent the small share I then took in them. . . . In monarchies the crime of treason and rebellion may admit of being pardoned or lightly punished; but the man who dares to rebel against the laws of a republic ought to suffer death." As governor, he vetoed a bill for the repeal of a prohibition on opening a theatre in Boston.

[See: William V. Wells, *The Life and Public Services of Samuel Adams* (3 vols., 1865); James K. Hosmer, *Samuel Adams* (1885); *The Writings of Samuel Adams* (4 vols., 1904–08), Vol. II, pp. 13–26; Vol. IV, pp. 183–187.]

THE RIGHTS OF THE COLONISTS (1772)[1]

Adopted by the Town of Boston, November 20, 1772

The Committee appointed by the Town the second Instant "to State the Rights of the Colonists and of this Province in particular, as Men, as Christians, and as Subjects; to communicate and publish the same to the several Towns in this Province and to the World as the sense of this Town with the Infringements and Violations thereof that have been, or from Time to Time may be made. Also requesting of each Town a free Communication of their Sentiments Reported—

First, a State of the Rights of the Colonists and of this Province in particular—

Secondly, A List of the Infringements, and Violations of those Rights.—

Thirdly, A Letter of Correspondence with the other Towns.—

1st. Natural Rights of the Colonists as Men.—

Among the Natural Rights of the Colonists are these First. a Right to Life; Secondly to Liberty; thirdly to Property; together with the Right to support and defend them in the best manner they can—Those are evident Branches of, rather than deductions from the Duty of Self Preservation, commonly called the first Law of Nature—

All Men have a Right to remain in a State of Nature as long as they please: And in case of intollerable Oppression, Civil or Religious, to leave the Society they belong to, and enter into another.—

When Men enter into Society, it is by voluntary consent; and they have a right to demand and insist upon the performance of such conditions, And previous limitations as form an equitable original compact.—

Every natural Right not expressly given up or from the nature of a Social Compact necessarily ceded remains.—

All positive and civil laws, should conform as far as possible, to the Law of natural reason and equity.—

[1] In The Writings of Samuel Adams, ed. by Harry Alonzo Cushing, 4 vols. (1904–08), Vol. II, pp. 350–359.

As neither reason requires, nor religeon permits the contrary, every Man living in or out of a state of civil society, has a right peaceably and quietly to worship God according to the dictates of his conscience.—

"Just and true liberty, equal and impartial liberty" in matters spiritual and temporal, is a thing that all Men are clearly entitled to, by the eternal and immutable laws Of God and nature, as well as by the law of Nations, & all well grounded municipal laws, which must have their foundation in the former.—

In regard to Religeon, mutual tolleration in the different professions thereof, is what all good and candid minds in all ages have ever practiced; and both by precept and example inculcated on mankind: And it is now generally agreed among christians that this spirit of toleration in the fullest extent consistent with the being of civil society "is the chief characteristical mark of the true church" & In so much that M^r. Lock has asserted, and proved beyond the possibility of contradiction on any solid ground, that such toleration ought to be extended to all whose doctrines are not subversive of society. The only Sects which he thinks ought to be, and which by all wise laws are excluded from such toleration, are those who teach Doctrines subversive of the Civil Government under which they live. The Roman Catholicks or Papists are excluded by reason of such Doctrines as these "that Princes excommunicated may be deposed, and those they call *Hereticks* may be destroyed without mercy; besides their recognizing the Pope in so absolute a manner, in subversion of Government, by introducing as far as possible into the states, under whose protection they enjoy life, liberty and property, that solecism in politicks, Imperium in imperio leading directly to the worst anarchy and confusion, civil discord, war and blood shed—

The natural liberty of Men by entring into society is abridg'd or restrained so far only as is necessary for the Great end of Society the best good of the whole—

In the state of nature, every man is under God, Judge and sole Judge, of his own rights and the injuries done him: By entering into society, he agrees to an Arbiter or indifferent Judge between him and his neighbours; but he no more renounces his original right, than by taking a cause out of the ordinary course of law, and leaving the decision to Referees or indifferent Arbitrations. In the last case he must pay the Referees for time and trouble; he should be also willing to pay his Just quota for the support of government, the law and constitution; the end of which is to furnish indifferent and impartial Judges in all cases that may happen, whether civil ecclesiastical, marine or military.—

"The natural liberty of man is to be free from any superior power on earth, and not to be under the will or legislative authority of man; but only to have the law of nature for his rule."—

In the state of nature men may as the *Patriarchs* did, employ hired servants for the defence of their lives, liberty and property: and they should pay them reasonable wages. Government was instituted for the purposes of common defence; and those who hold the reins of government have an equitable natural right to an honourable support from the same principle "that the labourer is worthy of his hire" but then the same community which they serve, ought to be assessors of their pay: Governors have no right to seek what they please; by this, instead of being content with the station assigned them, that of honourable servants of the society, they would soon become Absolute masters, Despots, and Tyrants. Hence as a private man has a right to say, what wages he will give in his private affairs, so has a Community to determine what they will give and grant of their Substance, for the Administration of publick affairs. And in both cases more are ready generally to offer their Service at the proposed and stipulated price, than are able and willing to perform their duty.—

In short it is the greatest absurdity to suppose it in the power of one or any number of men at the entering into society, to renounce their essential natural rights, or the means of preserving those rights when the great end of civil government from the very nature of its institution is for the support, protection and defence of those very rights: the principal of which as is before observed, are life liberty and property. If men through fear, fraud or mistake, should *in terms* renounce and give up any essential natural right, the eternal law of reason and the great end of society, would absolutely vacate such renunciation; the right to freedom being *the gift* of God Almighty, it is not in the power of Man to alienate this gift, and voluntarily become a slave—

2ᵈ. *The Rights of the Colonists as Christians*—

These may be best understood by reading—and carefully studying the institutes of the great Lawgiver and head of the Christian Church: which are to be found closely written and promulgated in the New Testament—

By the Act of the British Parliament commonly called the Toleration Act, every subject in England Except Papists &c was restored to, and re-established in, his natural right to worship God according to the dictates of his own conscience. And by the Charter of this Province it is granted ordained and established (that it is declared as an original right) that there shall be liberty of conscience allowed in the worship of God, to all christians except Papists, inhabiting or which shall inhabit or be resident within said Province or Territory. Magna Charta itself is in substance but a constrained Declaration, or proclamation, and promulgation in the name of King, Lord, and Commons of the sense the latter had of their original inherent, indefeazible natural Rights, as also those of free Citizens equally perdurable with the other. That great author that great jurist, and even that Court writer Mr. Justice Blackstone holds that this recognition was justly obtained of King John sword in hand: and peradventure it must be one day sword in hand again rescued and preserved from total destruction and oblivion.—

3d. *The Rights of the Colonists as Subjects*

A Common Wealth or state is a body politick or civil society of men, united together to promote their mutual safety and prosperity, by means of their union.

The *absolute Rights* of Englishmen, and all freemen in or out of Civil society, are principally, *personal security personal liberty* and *private property.*

All Persons born in the British American Colonies are by the laws of God and nature, and by the Common law of England, ex-*clusive of all charters from the Crown,* well Entitled, and by the Acts of the British Parliament are declared to be entitled to all the natural essential, inherent & inseperable Rights Liberties and Privileges of Subjects born in Great Britain, or within the Realm. Among those Rights are the following; which no men or body of men, consistently with their own rights as men and citizens or members of society, can for themselves give up, or take away from others.

First, "The first fundamental positive law of all Commonwealths or States, is the establishing the legislative power; as the first fundamental *natural* law also, which is to govern even the legislative power itself, is the preservation of the Society."

Secondly, The Legislative has no right to absolute arbitrary power over the lives and fortunes of the people: Nor can mortals assume a prerogative, not only too high for men, but for Angels; and therefore reserved for the exercise of the *Deity* alone.—

"The Legislative cannot Justly *assume* to itself a power to rule by extempore arbitrary decrees; but it is bound to see that Justice is dispensed, and that the rights of the subjects be decided, by promulgated, standing and known laws, and authorized *independent Judges;"* that is independent as far as possible of Prince or People. *"There shall be one rule of Justice for rich and poor; for the favorite in Court, and the Countryman at the Plough."*

Thirdly, The supreme power cannot Justly take from any man, any part of his property without his consent, in person or by his Representative.—

These are some of the first principles of natural law & Justice, and the great Barriers of all free states, and of the British Constitution in particular. It is utterly irreconcileable to these principles, and to many other fundamental maxims of the common law, common sense and reason, that a British house of commons, should have a right, at pleasure, to give and grant the property of the Colonists. That these Colonists are well entitled to all the essential rights, liberties and privileges of men and freemen, born in Britain, is manifest, not only from the Colony charter, in general, but acts of the British Parliament. The statute of the 13th of George 2. c. 7 naturalizes even foreigners after seven years residence. The words of the Massachusetts Charter are these, "And further our will and pleasure is, and we do hereby for us, our heirs and successors, grant establish and ordain, that all and every of the subjects of us, our heirs and successors, which shall go to and inhabit within our said province or territory and every of their children which shall happen to be born there, or on the seas in going thither, or returning from thence shall have and enjoy, all liberties and immunities of free and natural subjects within any of the dominions of us, our heirs and successors, to all intents constructions & purposes whatsoever as if they and every of them were born within this our Realm of England." Now what liberty can there be, where property is taken away without consent? Can it be said with any colour of truth and

Justice, that this Continent of three thousand miles in length, and of a breadth as yet unexplored, in which however, its supposed, there are five millions of people, has the least voice, vote or influence in the decisions of the British Parliament? Have they, all together, any more right or power to return a single number to that house of commons, who have not inadvertently, but deliberately assumed a power to dispose of their lives, Liberties and properties, then to choose an Emperor of China! Had the Colonists a right to return members to the british parliament, it would only be hurtfull; as from their local situation and circumstances it is impossible they should be ever truly and properly represented there. The inhabitants of this country in all probability in a few years will be more numerous, than those of Great Britain and Ireland together; yet it is absurdly expected by the promoters of the present measures, that these, with their posterity to all generations, should be easy while their property, shall be disposed of by a house of commons at three thousand miles distant from them; and who cannot be supposed to have the least care or concern for their real interest: Who have not only no natural care for their interest, but must be in effect bribed against it; as every burden they lay on the colonists is so much saved or gained to themselves. Hitherto many of the Colonists have been free from Quit Rents; but if the breath of a british house of commons can originate an act for taking away all our money, our lands will go next or be subject to rack rents from haughty and relentless landlords who will ride at ease, while we are trodden in the dirt. The Colonists have been branded with the odious names of traitors and rebels, only for complaining of their grievances; How long such treatment will, or ought to be born is submitted.

6. DANIEL LEONARD (1740–1829)

THE ablest American defender of the British cause in the period of the Revolution was Daniel Leonard, member of a family of the high provincial aristocracy. He was the son of a wealthy ironmonger of Norton, Massachusetts. A graduate of Harvard, he practised law at Taunton and was King's attorney for Bristol County. In 1770 he was elected to the general court, where he took a strong stand on the colonists' side. However, Governor Thomas Hutchinson (last royal governor of the colony) "exercised his blandishments" and Leonard became a staunch Loyalist. His patriotic neighbors then attacked his home and he fled to Boston where he was made solicitor to the customs commissioners. In a series of letters to the *Massachusetts Gazette* (1774–75), over the pen name "Massachusettensis," he set forth in detail a legal and moral justification of the Crown's dealings with the colonies and warned the colonists of the disasters they would suffer from any revolutionary attempt. The selections below are from the particular letters in which he discussed more generally the need for strong authoritarian government and the moral wrong and practical dangers of seditious activities. John Adams replied to these letters with his "Novanglus" letters in the *Boston Gazette*.

After the Declaration of Independence Taunton authorities seized Leonard's properties and forbade his return to the town. When the British officials withdrew from Boston, he made his way to England, where he continued to carry on Loyalist propaganda. In 1780 he was indirectly associated with a plan devised by Massachusetts Loyalists to set up in Maine a separate colony in which he would be chief justice. The plan was abandoned when Wedderburn, attorney general, ruled that the region was a part of the original territory of Massachusetts Bay. After serving as chief justice of Bermuda (1782–1806) Leonard returned to London, where he became a leader of the bar.

[See: Ralph Davol, *Two Men of Taunton* (1912), *passim*; Moses Coit Tyler, *Literary History of the American Revolution* (1897), Vol. I, ch. 16; Edward A Jones, *The Loyalists of Massachusetts* (1930), pp. 129–131; Vernon L. Parrington, *Main Currents of American Thought*, Vol. I (1927), pp. 87–91.]

From "MASSACHUSETTENSIS" LETTERS (1774–75) [1]

MASSACHUSETTENSIS

ADDRESSED

To the Inhabitants of the Province of Massachusetts Bay,

December 12, 1774

My Dear Countrymen,

When a people, by what means soever, are reduced to such a situation, that every thing they hold dear, as men and citizens, is at stake, it is not only excuseable, but even praiseworthy for an individual to offer to the public any thing, that he may think has a tendency to ward off the impending danger; nor should he be restrained from an apprehension that what he may offer will be unpopular, any more than a physician should be restrained from prescribing a salutary medicine, through fear it might be unpalatable to his patient.

The press, when open to all parties and influenced by none, is a salutary engine in a free state, perhaps a necessary one to preserve the freedom of that state; but, when a party has gained the ascendancy so far as to become the licensers of the press, either by an act of government, or by playing off the resentment of the populace against printers and authors, the press itself becomes an engine of oppression or licentiousness, and is as pernicious to society, as otherwise it would be beneficial. It is too true to be denied, that ever since the origin of our controversy with Great Britain, the press, in this town, has been much devoted to the partizans of liberty; they have been indulged in publishing what they pleased, fas vel nefas, while little has been published on the part of government. The effect this must have had upon the minds of the people in general is obvious; they must have formed their opinion upon a partial view of the subject, and of course it must have been in some degree erroneous. In short, the changes have been rung so often upon oppression, tyranny and slavery, that, whether sleeping or waking,

[1] Novanglus, and Massachusettensis; or Political Essays, Published in the Years 1774 and 1775, on the Principal Points of Controversy, Between Great Britain and Her Colonies (Boston, 1819), at pp. 141–142, 145–146, 152–153, 187–188, 226–227. "Novanglus" is John Adams.

they are continually vibrating in our ears; and it is now high time to ask ourselves, whether we have not been deluded by sound only.

My dear countrymen, let us divest ourselves of prejudice, take a view of our present wretched situation, contrast it with our former happy one, carefully investigate the cause, and industriously seek some means to escape the evils we now feel, and prevent those that we have reason to expect.

We have been so long advancing to our present state, and by such gradations, that perhaps many of us are insensible of our true state and real danger. Should you be told that acts of high treason are flagrant through the country, that a great part of the province is in actual rebellion, would you believe it true? Should you not deem the person asserting it, an enemy to the province? Nay, should you not spurn him from you with indignation? Be calm, my friends; it is necessary to know the worst of a disease, to enable us to provide an effectual remedy. Are not the bands of society cut asunder, and the sanctions that hold man to man, trampled upon? Can any of us recover a debt, or obtain compensation for an injury, by law? Are not many persons, whom once we respected and revered, driven from their homes and families, and forced to fly to the army for protection, for no other reason but their having accepted commissions under our king? Is not civil government dissolved? Some have been made to believe that nothing short of attempting the life of the king, or fighting his troops, can amount to high treason or rebellion. If, reader, you are one of those, apply to an honest lawyer, (if such an one can be found) and enquire what kind of offence it is for a number of men to assemble armed, and forcibly to obstruct the course of justice, even to prevent the king's courts from being held at their stated terms; for a body of people to seize upon the king's provincial revenue; I mean the monies collected by virtue of grants made by the general court to his majesty for the support of his government, within this province; for a body of men to assemble without being called by authority, and to pass governmental acts; or for a number of people to take the militia out of the hands of the king's representative, or to form a new militia, or to raise men and appoint officers for a public purpose, without the order or permission of the king, or his representative; or for a number of men to take to their arms, and march with a professed design of opposing the king's troops; ask, reader, of such a lawyer, what is the crime, and what the punishment; and if, perchance, thou art one that hast been active in these things, and art not insensibility itself, his answer will harrow up thy soul. . . .

. . . Upon a superficial view we might imagine that this province was nearly unanimous; but the case is far different. A very considerable part of the men of property in this province, are at this day firmly attached to the cause of government; bodies of men, compelling persons to disavow their sentiments, to resign commissions, or to subscribe leagues and covenants, has wrought no change in their sentiments; it has only attached them more closely to government, and caused them to wish more fervently, and to pray more devoutly, for its restoration. These, and thousands beside, if they fight at all, will fight under the banners of loyalty. I can assure you that associations are now forming in several parts of this province, for the support of his majesty's government and mutual defence; and let me tell you, whenever the royal standard shall be set up, there will be such a flocking to it, as will astonish the most obdurate. And now, in God's name, what is it that has brought us to this brink of destruction? Has not the government of Great Britain been as mild and equitable in the colonies, as in any part of her extensive dominions? Has not she been a nursing mother to us, from the days of our infancy to this time? Has she not been indulgent almost to a fault? Might not each one of us at this day have sat quietly under his own vine and fig-tree, and there have been none to make us afraid, were it not for our own folly? Will not posterity be amazed, when they are told that the present distraction took its rise from a three penny duty on tea, and call it a more unaccountable frenzy, and more disgraceful to the annals of America, than that of the witchcraft? . . .

December 26, 1774

The bulk of the people are generally but little versed in matters of state. Want of inclination or opportunity to figure in public life, makes them content to rest the affairs of government in the hands, where accident or merit has placed them. Their views and employments are confined to the humbler walks of business or retirement. There is a latent spark however, in their breasts, capable of being kindled into a flame; to do this has always been the employment of the disaffected. They begin by reminding the people of the elevated rank they hold in the universe, as men; that all men by nature are equal; that kings are but the ministers of the people; that their authority is delegated to them by the people for their good, and they have a right to resume it, and place it in other hands, or keep it themselves, whenever it is made use of to oppress them. Doubtless there have been instances where these principles have been inculcated to obtain a redress of real grievances, but they have been much oftener perverted to the worst of purposes. No government, however perfect in theory, is administered in perfection; the frailty of man does not admit of it. A small mistake, in point of policy, often furnishes a pretence to libel government, and persuade the people that their rulers are tyrants, and the whole government a system of oppression. Thus the seeds of sedition are usually sown, and the people are led to sacrifice real liberty to licentiousness, which gradually ripens into rebellion and civil war. And what is still more to be lamented, the generality of the people, who are thus made the dupes of artifice, and the mere stilts of ambition, are sure to be losers in the end. The best they can expect, is to be thrown neglected by, when they are no longer wanted; but they are seldom so happy; if they are subdued, confiscation of estate and ignominious death are their portion; if they conquer, their own army is often turned upon them, to subjugate them to a more tyrannical government than that they rebelled against. History is replete with instances of this kind; we can trace them in remote antiquity, we find them in modern times, and have a remarkable one in the very country from which we are derived. It is an universal truth, that he that would excite a rebellion, whatever professions of philanthropy he may make, when he is insinuating and worming himself into the good graces of the people, is at heart as great a tyrant as ever wielded the iron rod of oppression. I shall have occasion hereafter to consider this matter more fully, when I shall endeavour to convince you how little we can gain, and how much we may lose, by this unequal, unnatural, and desperate contest. . . .

February 6, 1775

Rebellion is the most atrocious offence, that can be perpetrated by man, save those which are committed more immediately against the supreme Governor of the Universe, who is the avenger of his own cause. It dissolves the social band, annihilates the security resulting from law and government; introduces fraud, violence, rapine, murder, sacrilege, and the long train of evils, that riot, uncontrouled, in a state of nature. Allegiance and protection are reciprocal. The subject is bound by the compact to yield obedience to government, and in return, is entitled to protection from it; thus the poor are protected against the rich; the weak against the strong; the individual against the many; and this protection is guaranteed to each member, by the whole community. But when government is laid prostrate, a state of war, of all against all commences; might overcomes right; innocence itself has no security, unless the individual sequesters himself from his fellowmen, inhabits his own cave, and seeks his own prey. This is what is called a state of nature. I once thought it chimerical.

The punishment inflicted upon rebels and traitors, in all states, bears some proportion to the aggravated crime. By our law, the punishment is, "That the offender be drawn to the gallows, and not be carried, or walk; that he be hanged by the neck, and then cut down alive; that his entrails be taken out and burned while he is yet alive; that his head be cut off; that his body be divided into four parts; that his head and quarters be at the king's disposal." The consequences of attainder, are forfeiture and corruption of blood. . . .

April 3, 1775

Do you expect to conquer in war? War is no longer a simple, but an intricate science, not to be learned from books or two or three campaigns, but from long experience. You need not be told that his majesty's generals, Gage and Haldimand, are possessed of every talent requisite to great commanders, matured by long experience in many parts of the world, and stand high in military fame: that many of the officers have been bred to arms from their infancy, and a large proportion of the army *now* here, have already reaped immortal honors in the iron harvest of the field.—Alas! My friends, you have nothing to oppose to this force, but a militia unused to service, impatient of command, and destitute of resources. Can your officers depend upon the privates, or the privates upon the officers? Your war can be but little more than mere tumultary rage: and besides, there is an awful disparity between troops that fight the battles of their sovereign, and those that follow the standard of rebellion. These reflections may arrest you in an hour that you think not of, and come too late to serve you. Nothing short of a miracle could gain you one battle; but could you destroy all the British troops that are now here, and burn the men of war that command our coast, it would be but the beginning of sorrow; and yet without a decisive battle, one campaign would ruin you. This province does not produce its necessary provision, when the husbandman can pursue his calling without molestation: what then must be your condition, when the demand shall be increased, and the resource in a manner cut off? Figure to yourselves what must be your distress, should your wives and children be driven from such places, as the king's troops shall occupy, into the interior parts of the province, and they as well as you, be destitute of support. I take no pleasure in painting these scenes of distress. The whigs affect to divert you from them by ridicule; but should war commence, you can expect nothing but its severities. Might I hazard an opinion, but few of your leaders ever intended to engage in hostilities, but they may have rendered inevitable what they intended for intimidation. Those that unsheath the sword of rebellion may throw away the scabbard, they cannot be treated with, while in arms; and if they lay them down, they are in no other predicament than conquered rebels. The conquered in other wars do not forfeit the rights of men, nor all the rights of citizens, even their bravery is rewarded by a generous victor; far different is the case of a routed rebel host. My dear countrymen, you have before you, at your election, peace or war, happiness or misery. May the God of our forefathers direct you in the way that leads to peace and happiness, before your feet stumble on the dark mountains, before the evil days come, wherein you shall say, we have no pleasure in them.

MASSACHUSETTENSIS

7. JEFFERSON'S FIGHT FOR RELIGIOUS FREEDOM

AFTER the adoption of the original Virginia constitution in 1776, Jefferson resigned from the Congress of the Confederation in order, as we have seen, to return to Virginia where, as a member of the lower house of the legislature, he could most effectively promote the enactment of the recently enunciated liberal principles into law. He took his seat on October 7, 1776 and immediately began this work. In his *Notes on Virginia* (1782) he reviewed previous legislation affecting religious matters in Virginia and set forth his reasons for advocating complete freedom. After a long fight the act for religious freedom was adopted in 1786. Jefferson regarded this as one of his most important achievements and later selected it as one of the three accomplishments to be recorded on his tombstone. It was the first law of its sort to be enacted by an independent commonwealth, and it formed a precedent that was followed, generally or in part, in the other States.

From NOTES ON THE STATE OF VIRGINIA (1782) [1]

QUERY XVII. *The different religions received into that state?*

The first settlers in this country were emigrants from England, of the English church, just at a point of time when it was flushed with complete victory over the religious of all other persuasions. Possessed, as they became, of the powers of making, administering and executing the laws, they shewed equal intolerance in this country with their Presbyterian brethren, who had emigrated to the nothern government. The poor Quakers were flying from persecution in England. They cast their eyes on these new countries as asylums of civil and religious freedom; but they found them free only for the reigning sect. Several acts of the Virginia assembly of 1659, 1662, and 1693, had made it penal in parents to refuse to have their children baptized; had prohibited the unlawful assem-

[1] In *The Writings of Thomas Jefferson*, ed. by Paul Leicester Ford, Vol. III, pp. 261–266. For the life of Jefferson, see above, pp. 99–101.

bling of Quakers; had made it penal for any master of a vessel to bring a Quaker into the state; had ordered those already here, and such as should come thereafter, to be imprisoned till they should abjure the country; provided a milder punishment for their first and second return, but death for their third; had inhibited all persons from suffering their meetings in or near their houses, entertaining them individually, or disposing of books which supported their tenets. If no capital execution took place here, as did in New-England, it was not owing to the moderation of the church, or spirit of the legislature, as may be inferred from the law itself; but to historical circumstances which have not been handed down to us. The Anglicans retained full possession of the country about a century. Other opinions began then to creep in, and the great care of the government to support their own church, having begotten an equal degree of indolence in its clergy, two thirds of the people had become dissenters at the commencement of the present revolution. The laws indeed were still oppressive on them, but the spirit of the one party had subsided into moderation, and of the other had risen to a degree of determination which commanded respect.

The present state of our laws on the subject of religion is this. The convention of May 1776, in their declaration of rights, declared it to be a truth, and a natural right, that the exercise of religion should be free; but when they proceeded to form on that declaration the ordinance of government, instead of taking up every principle declared in the bill of rights, and guarding it by legislative sanction, they passed over that which asserted our religious rights, leaving them as they found them. The same convention, however, when they met as a member of the general assembly in October 1776, repealed all *acts of parliament* which had rendered criminal the maintaining any opinions in matters of religion, the forbearing to repair to church, and the exercising any mode of worship; and suspended the laws giving salaries to the clergy, which suspension was made perpetual in October 1779. Statutory oppressions in religion being thus wiped away, we remain at present under those only imposed by the common law, or by our own acts of assembly. At the common law, *heresy* was a capital offence, punishable by burning. Its definition was left to the ecclesiastical judges, before whom the conviction was, till the statute of the 1 El. c. 1. circumscribed it, by declaring that nothing should be deemed heresy but what had been so determined by authority of the canonical scriptures, or by one of the four first general councils, or by some other council having for the grounds of their declaration the express and plain words of the scriptures. Heresy, thus circumscribed, being an offence at the common law, our act of assembly of October 1777, c. 17 gives cognizance of it to the general court, by declaring that the jurisdiction of that court shall be general in all matters at the common law. . . . By our own act of assembly of 1705, c. 30, if a person brought up in the christian religion denies the being of a God, or the trinity, or asserts there are more Gods than one, or denies the christian religion to be true, or the scriptures to be of divine authority, he is punishable on the first offence by incapacity to hold any office or employment ecclesiastical, civil, or military; on the second by disability to sue, to take any gift or legacy, to be guardian, executor or administrator, and by three years imprisonment, without bail. A father's right to the custody of his own children being founded in law on his right of guardianship, this being taken away, they may of course be severed from him and put, by the authority of a court, into more orthodox hands. This is a summary view of that religious slavery under which a people have been willing to remain who have lavished their lives and fortunes for the establishment of their civil freedom. The error seems not sufficiently eradicated, that the operations of the mind, as well as the acts of the body, are subject to the coercion of the laws. But our rulers can have authority over such natural rights, only as we have submitted to them. The rights of conscience we never submitted, we could not submit. We are answerable for them to our God. The legitimate powers of government extend to such acts only as are injurious to others. But it does me no injury for my neighbor to say there are twenty gods, or no god. It neither picks my pocket nor breaks my leg. If it be said his testimony in a court of justice cannot be relied on, reject it then, and be the stigma on him. Constraint may make him worse by making him a hypocrite, but it will never make him a truer man. It may fix him obstinately in his errors, but will not cure them. Reason and free inquiry are the only effectual agents against error. Give a loose to them, they will support the true religion by bringing every false one to their tribunal, to the test of their investigation. They are the natural enemies of error, and of error only. Had not the Roman government permitted free inquiry, christianity could never have been introduced. Had not free inquiry been indulged, at the aera of the reformation, the corruptions of christianity could not have been purged away. If it be restrained now, the present corruptions will be protected, and new ones encouraged. Was the government to prescribe to us our medicine and diet, our bodies would be in such keeping as our souls are now. Thus in France the emetic was once forbidden as a medicine, and the potatoe as an article of food. Government is just as infallible, too, when it fixes systems in physics. Galileo was sent to the inquisition for affirming that the earth was a sphere; the government had declared it to be as flat as a trencher, and Galileo was obliged to abjure his error. This error however at length prevailed, the earth became a globe, and Descartes declared it was whirled round its axis by a vortex. The government in which he lived was wise enough to see that this was no question of civil jurisdiction, or we should all have been involved by authority in vortices. In fact the vortices have been exploded, and the Newtonian principle of gravitation is now more firmly established, on the basis of reason, than it would be were the government to step in and to make it an article of necessary faith. Reason and experiment have been indulged, and error has fled before them. It is error alone which needs the support of government. Truth can stand by itself. Subject opinion to coercion: whom will you make your inquisitors? Fallible men; men governed by bad passions, by private as well as public reasons. And why subject it to coercion? To produce uniformity. But is uniformity of opinion desireable? No more than of face and stature. Introduce the bed of Procrustes then, and as there is danger that the large men may beat the small, make us all of a size, by lopping the former and stretching the latter. Difference of opinion is advantageous in religion. The several sects perform the office of a Censor morum over each other. Is uniformity attainable? Millions of innocent men, women and children, since the introduction of Christianity, have been burnt, tortured, fined, imprisoned: yet we have not advanced one inch towards uniformity. What has been the effect of coercion? To make one half the world fools, and the other half hypocrites. To support roguery and error all over the earth. Let us reflect that it is inhabited by a thousand millions of people. That these profess probably a thousand different systems of religion. That ours is but one of that thousand. That if there be but one right, and ours that one, we should wish to see the 999 wandering sects gathered into the fold of truth. But against such a majority we cannot effect this by force. Reason and persuasion are the only practicable instruments. To make way for these, free inquiry must be indulged; and how can we wish others to indulge it while we refuse it our selves. But every state, says an inquisitor, has established some religion. "No two, say I, have established the same." Is this a proof of the infallibility of establishments? Our sister states of Pennsylvania and New York, however, have long subsisted without any establishment at all. The experiment was new and doubtful when they made it. It has answered beyond conception. They flourish infinitely. Religion is well supported; of various kinds indeed, but all good enough; all sufficient to preserve peace and order: or if a sect arises whose tenets would subvert morals, good sense has fair play, and reasons and laughs it out of doors, without suffering the state to be troubled with it. They do not hang more malefactors than we do. They are not more disturbed with religious dissentions. On the contrary, their harmony is unparallelled, and can be ascribed to nothing but their unbounded tolerance, because there is no other circumstance in which they differ from every nation on earth. They have made the happy discovery, that the way to silence religious disputes, is to take no notice of them. Let us too give this experiment fair play, and get rid, while we may, of those tyrannical laws. It is true we are as yet secured against them by the spirit of the times. I doubt whether the people of this country would suffer an execution for heresy, or a three years imprisonment for not comprehending the mysteries of the trinity. But is the spirit of the people an infallible, a permanent reliance? Is it government? Is this the kind of protection we receive in return for the rights we give up? Besides, the spirit of the times may alter, will alter. Our rulers will become corrupt, our people careless. A single zealot may commence persecuter, and better men be his victims. It can never be too often repeated, that the time for fixing every essential right on a legal basis is while our rulers are honest, and ourselves united. From the conclusion of this war we shall be going down hill. It will not then be necessary to resort every moment to the people for support. They will be forgotten therefore, and their rights disregarded. They will forget themselves, but in the sole faculty of making money, and will never think of uniting to effect a due respect for their rights. The shackles, therefore, which shall not be knocked off at the conclusion of this war, will remain on us long, will be made heavier and heavier, till our rights shall revive or expire in a convulsion.

AN ACT FOR ESTABLISHING RELIGIOUS FREEDOM VIRGINIA (1786) [1]

SECTION I. Whereas Almighty God hath created the mind free; that all attempts to influence it by temporal punishments or burthens, or by civil incapacitations, tend only to beget habits of hypocrisy and meanness, and are a departure from the plan of the Holy Author of our religion, who being Lord both of body and mind, yet chose not to propagate it by coercions on either, as was in his Almighty power to do; that the impious presumption of Legislators and rulers, civil as well as ecclesiastical, who being themselves but fallible and uninspired men, have assumed dominion over the faith of others, setting up their own opinions and modes of thinking as the only true and infallible, and as such endeavouring to impose them on others, hath established and maintained false religions over the greatest part of the world, and through all time; that to compel a man to furnish contributions of money for the propagation of opinions which he disbelieves, is sinful and tyrannical; that even the forcing him to support this or that teacher of his own religious persuasion, is depriving him of the comfortable liberty of giving his contributions to the particular pastor, whose morals he would make his pattern, and whose powers he feels most persuasive to righteousness, and is withdrawing from the ministry those temporary rewards, which proceeding from an approbation of their personal conduct, are an additional incitement to earnest and unremitting labours for the instruction of mankind; that our civil rights have no dependence on our religious opinions, any more than our opinions in physics or geometry; that therefore the proscribing any citizen as unworthy the public confidence, by laying upon him an incapacity of being called to the offices of trust and emolument, unless he profess or renounce this or that religious

[1] Ch. XXXIV of Acts Passed at a General Assembly of the Commonwealth of Virginia, October session, 1785 (Richmond, [1786]).

opinion, is depriving him injuriously of those privileges and advantages to which in common with his fellow-citizens he has a natural right; that it tends only to corrupt the principles of that religion it is meant to encourage, by bribing with a monopoly of worldly honours and emoluments, those who will externally profess and conform to it; that though indeed these are criminal who do not withstand such temptation, yet neither are those innocent who lay the bait in their way; that to suffer the civil Magistrate to intrude his powers into the field of opinion, and to restrain the profession or propagation of principles on supposition of their ill tendency, is a dangerous fallacy, which at once destroys all religious liberty, because he being of course judge of that tendency will make his opinions the rule of judgment, and approve or condemn the sentiments of others only as they shall square with or differ from his own; that it is time enough for the rightful purposes of civil government, for its officers to interfere when principles break out into overt acts against peace and good order; and finally, that truth is great and will prevail if left to herself, that she is the proper and sufficient antagonist to error, and has nothing to fear from the conflict, unless by human interposition disarmed of her natural weapons, free argument and debate, errors ceasing to be dangerous when it is permitted freely to contradict them:

SECT. II. *BE it enacted by the General Assembly,* That no man shall be compelled to frequent or support any religious worship, place, or Ministry whatsoever, nor shall be enforced, restrained, molested, or burthened in his body or goods, nor shall otherwise suffer on account of his religious opinions or belief; but that all men shall be free to profess, and by argument to maintain, their opinions in matters of religion, and that the same shall in no wise diminish, enlarge, or affect their civil capacities.

SECT. III. AND though we well know this Assembly elected by the people for the ordinary purposes of legislation only, have no power to restrain the Acts of succeeding Assemblies, constituted with powers equal to our own, and that therefore to declare this Act to be irrevocable, would be of no effect in law; yet we are free to declare, and do declare, that the rights hereby asserted, are of the natural rights of mankind, and that if any Act shall be hereafter passed to repeal the present, or to narrow its operation, such Act will be an infringement of natural right.

8. ELBRIDGE GERRY (1744–1814)

IN CONNECTION with the framing, adoption, and early operation of the Federal Constitution, sharp differences of opinion
arose (as all text-books point out) as to the advantages and the disadvantages and dangers in setting up a strong central government. The
pamphlet quoted below, by Elbridge Gerry, reveals very well the views
of those who opposed ratification on the ground that the Constitution
conferred dangerously unlimited powers on the federal government.

Gerry's life was characterized by an unusual combination of apparently contradictory interests and ideas. He was born in Marblehead,
Massachusetts; his father (master of a sailing vessel) had recently migrated from England and married the daughter of a Boston merchant.
After graduating from Harvard, Elbridge joined his father's shipping and
mercantile business, made money as a trader and privateer during the
Revolutionary War, retired from business with a moderate fortune in
1786, and devoted most of the rest of his life to public affairs. He had
been elected to the Massachusetts legislature in 1772, allied himself
with Samuel Adams in the agitation against England, rendered valuable
administrative services on committees of correspondence and in the
Second Continental Congress, signed the Declaration of Independence,
and was a member of the Congress of the Confederation. He was also
a member of the Convention of 1787, where he had somewhat vacillating notions on what the new constitution should be. He wanted both
a broad suffrage and effective checks on the popularly elected representatives; a government empowered to deal positively with the fiscal and
commercial needs of the nation, yet strongly restrained against oppressive action. He vehemently opposed ratifying the Constitution because
he believed it created an undemocratic and inadequately limited central
government, and he was an Anti-Federalist member of the first House
of Representatives; yet he gave strong support to Hamilton's centralizing
policies.

Gerry was sole Republican member of the "XYZ" commission to
France in 1787 and exasperated his Federalist colleagues by proposing
conciliatory measures. He served two terms as Republican governor of
Massachusetts and became responsible, in his turbulent second term,
for a new word, "gerrymandering," by proposing a rearrangement of the
State senatorial districts (to the advantage of the Republicans) that

resulted in the creation of one of the districts in the shape (according to a contemporary cartoon) of a salamander. He was elected vice-president in 1813 and died in office two years later.

Gerry was not a member of the Massachusetts ratifying convention, but he attended by invitation in order to answer questions on disputed issues. His pamphlet opposing ratification was widely distributed by opponents of ratification in Massachusetts and New York; although one Anti-Federalist group in upper New York thought Gerry's style "too sublime and florid" for the people of that region.

[See: James T. Austin, The Life of Elbridge Gerry, 2 vols. (1828–29); S. E. Morrison, "Elbridge Gerry, Gentleman-Democrat," in New England Quarterly, Vol. II (1929), pp. 6–33.]

From OBSERVATIONS ON THE NEW CONSTITUTION (1788)[1]

. . . On these shores freedom has planted her standard, diped in the purple tide that flowed from the veins of her martyred heroes; and here every uncorrupted American yet hopes to see it supported by the vigour, the justice, the wisdom and unanimity of the people, in spite of the deep-laid plots, the secret intrigues, or the bold effrontery of those interested and avaricious adventurers for placc, who intoxicated with the ideas of distinction and preferment have prostrated every worthy principle beneath the shrine of ambition. Yet these are the men who tell us republicanism is dwindled into theory—that we are incapable of enjoying our liberties—and that we must have a master. . . .

All writers on government agree, and the feelings of the human mind witness the truth of these political axioms, that man is born free and possessed of certain unalienable rights—that government is instituted for the protection, safety and happiness of the people, and not for the profit, honour, or private interest of any man, family, or class of men—That the origin of all power is in the people, and that they have an incontestible right to check the creatures of their own creation, vested with certain powers to guard the life, liberty and property of the community: And if certain selected bodies of men, deputed on these principles, determine contrary

[1] Observations On the new Constitution, and on the Federal and State Conventions. By a Columbian Patriot, in Pamphlets on the Constitution of the United States . . . 1787–1788, ed. by Paul Leicester Ford (Brooklyn, 1888), pp. 1–23, at 5–13.

to the wishes and expectations of their constituents, the people have an undoubted right to reject their decisions, to call for a revision of their conduct, to depute others in their room, or if they think proper, to demand further time for deliberation on matters of the greatest moment: it therefore is an unwarrantable stretch of authority or influence, if any methods are taken to preclude this peaceful and reasonable mode of enquiry and decision. And it is with inexpressible anxiety, that many of the best friends of the Union of the States—to the peaceable and equal participation of the rights of nature, and to the glory and dignity of this country, behold the insiduous arts, and the strenuous efforts of the partisans of arbitrary power, by their vague definitions of the best established truths, endeavoring to envelope the mind in darkness the concomitant of slavery, and to lock the strong chains of domestic despotism on a country, which by the most glorious and successful struggles is but newly emancipated from the spectre of foreign dominion.—But there are certain seasons in the course of human affairs, when Genius, Virtue, and Patriotism, seems to nod over the vices of the times, and perhaps never more remarkably, than at the present period; or we should not see such a passive disposition prevail in some, who we must candidly suppose, have liberal and enlarged sentiments; while a supple multitude are paying a blind and idolatrous homage to the opinions of those who by the most precipitate steps are treading down their dear bought privileges; and who are endeavouring by all the arts of insinuation, and influence, to betray the people of the United States, into an acceptance of a most complicated system of government; marked on the one side with the *dark, secret* and *profound intrigues*, of the statesman, long practised in the purlieus of despotism; and on the other, with the ideal projects of *young ambition*, with its wings just expanded to soar to a summit, which imagination has painted in such gawdy colours as to intoxicate the *inexperienced votary*, and to send *him* rambling from State to State, to collect materials to construct the ladder of preferment.

. . . Some gentlemen, with laboured zeal, have spent much time in urging the necessity of government, from the embarrassments of trade—the want of respectability abroad and confidence of the public engagements at home:—These are obvious truths which no one denies; and there are few who do not unite in the general wish for the restoration of public faith, the revival of commerce, arts, agriculture, and industry, under a lenient, peaceable and energetick government: But the most sagacious advocates for the party have not by fair discusion, and rational argumentation, evinced the necessity of adopting this many headed monster; of such motley mixture, that its enemies cannot trace a feature of Democratick or Republican extract; nor have its friends the courage to denominate a Monarchy, an Aristocracy, or an Oligarchy, and the favoured bantling must have passed through the short period of its existence without a name, had not Mr. *Wilson*, in the fertility of his genius, suggested the happy epithet of a *Federal Republic*. . . .

2.[1] There is no security in the profered system, either for the rights of conscience or the liberty of the Press: Despotism usually while it is gaining ground, will suffer men to think, say, or write what they please; but when once established, if it is thought necessary to subserve the purposes, of arbitrary power, the most unjust restrictions may take place in the first instance, and an *imprimatur* on the Press in the next, may silence the complaints, and forbid the most decent remonstrances of an injured and oppressed people.

3. There are no well defined limits of the Judiciary Powers, they seem to be left as a boundless ocean, that has broken over the chart of the Supreme Lawgiver, "*thus far shalt thou go and no further*," and as they cannot be comprehended by the clearest capacity, or the most sagacious mind, it would be an Herculean labour to attempt to describe the dangers with which they are replete.

4. The Executive and the Legislative are so dangerously blended as to give just cause of alarm, and everything relative thereto, is couched in such ambiguous terms—in such vague and indefinite expression, as is a sufficient ground without any objection, for the reprobation of a system, that the authors dare not hazard to a clear investigation.

5. The abolition of trial by jury in civil causes.—This mode of trial the learned Judge Blackstone observes, "has been coeval with the first rudiments of civil government, that property, liberty and life, depend on maintaining in its legal force the constitutional trial by jury." . . .

6. Though it has been said by Mr. *Wilson* and many others, that a Standing-Army is necessary for the dignity and safety of

[1] Gerry has no paragraph numbered "1."

America, yet freedom revolts at the idea, when the Divan, or the Despot, may draw out his dragoons to suppress the murmurs of a few, who may yet cherish those sublime principles which call forth the exertions, and lead to the best improvements of the human mind. It is hoped this country may yet be governed by milder methods than are usually displayed beneath the bannerets of military law.—Standing armies have been the nursery of vice and the bane of liberty from the Roman legions to the establishment of the artful Ximenes, and from the ruin of the Cortes of Spain, to the planting of the British cohorts in the capitals of America:—By the edicts of an authority vested in the sovereign power by the proposed constitution, the militia of the country, the bulwark of defence, and the security of national liberty if no longer under the controul of civil authority; but at the rescript of the Monarch, or the aristocracy, they may either be employed to extort the enormous sums that will be necessary to support the civil list—to maintain the regalia of power—and the splendour of the most useless part of the community, or they may be sent into foreign countries for the fulfilment of treaties, stipulated by the President and two-thirds of the Senate.

7. Notwithstanding the delusory promise to guarantee a Republican form of government to every State in the Union—If the most discerning eye could discover any meaning at all in the engagement, there are no resources left for the support of internal government, or the liquidation of the debts of the State. Every source of revenue is in the monopoly of Congress, and if the several legislatures in their enfeebled state, should against their own feelings be necessitated to attempt a dry tax for the payment of their debts, and the support of internal police, even this may be required for the purposes of the general government.

8. As the new Congress are empowered to determine their own salaries, the requisitions for this purpose may not be very moderate, and the drain for public moneys will probably rise past all calculation . . .

9. There is no provision for a rotation, nor anything to prevent the perpetuity of office in the same hands for life; which by a little well timed bribery, will probably be done, to the exclusion of men of the best abilities from their share in the offices of government.— By this neglect we lose the advantages of that check to the over-

bearing insolence of office, which by rendering him ineligible at certain periods, keeps the mind of man in equilibrio, and teaches him the feelings of the governed, and better qualifies him to govern in his turn.

10. The inhabitants of the United States, are liable to be draged from the vicinity of their own country, or state, to answer the litigious or unjust suit of an adversary, on the most distant borders of the Continent: in short the appelate jurisdiction of the Supreme Federal Court, includes an unwarrantable stretch of power over the liberty, life, and property of the subject, through the wide Continent of America.

11. One Representative to thirty thousand inhabitants is a very inadequate representation; and every man who is not lost to all sense of freedom to his country, must reprobate the idea of Congress altering by law, or on any pretence whatever, interfering with any regulations for time, places, and manner of choosing our own Representatives.

12. If the sovereignty of America is designed to be elective, the surcumscribing the votes to only ten electors in this State, and the same proportion in all the others, is nearly tantamount to the exclusion of the voice of the people in the choice of their first magistrate. It is vesting the choice solely in an aristocratic junto, who may easily combine in each State to place at the head of the Union the most convenient instrument for despotic sway.

13. A Senate chosen for six years will, in most instances, be an appointment for life, as the influence of such a body over the minds of the people will be coequal to the extensive powers with which they are vested, and they will not only forget, but be forgotten by their constituents—a branch of the Supreme Legislature thus set beyond all responsibility is totally repugnant to every principle of a free government.

14. There is no privision by a bill of rights to guard against the dangerous encroachments of power in too many instances to be named . . . We are told by a gentleman of too much virtue and real probity to suspect he has a design to deceive—"that the whole constitution is a declaration of rights,"—but mankind must think for themselves, and to many very judicious and discerning characters, the whole constitution with very few exceptions appears a perversion of the rights of particular states, and of private citizens.

—But the gentleman goes on to tell us, "that the primary object is the general government, and that the rights of individuals are only incidentally mentioned, and that there was a clear impropriety in being very particular about them." But, asking pardon for dissenting from such respectable authority, who has been led into several mistakes, more from his prediliction in favour of certain modes of government, than from a want of understanding or veracity. The rights of individuals ought to be the primary object of all government, and cannot be too securely guarded by the most explicit declarations in their favor. . . .

9. ALEXANDER HAMILTON (1757–1804)

D URING the "Critical Period" after the Revolution, Alexander Hamilton, more than anyone else, was convinced of the supreme necessity of establishing a central government that would be empowered to restore economic stability and public order and promote national prosperity by strong and positive action.

Hamilton was born in the British West Indies. Both of his parents were apparently of families of good social standing; but in his boyhood the death of his mother and the bankruptcy of his father threw him upon relatives. He gave early signs of intellectual brilliance and an ability to write. He was accordingly sent to America in 1773 and entered Kings College (now Columbia) in New York City. Almost immediately he joined in the agitation against England. He made speeches and wrote newspaper articles and pamphlets (notably, at the age of seventeen, *The Farmer Refuted*). Like the other pamphleteers, he took his stand on the colonial charters, the English Constitution, and the "natural . . . sacred rights of mankind." Even at that age, however, he stood for orderliness in protest: he condemned the raids on Tory newspapers and helped protect from a mob the Tory president of his college. He studied artillery warfare and was made captain of a volunteer artillery company early in 1776. Soon he was appointed secretary and then (at the age of twenty) aide-de-camp to General Washington, whom he ably served by preparing correspondence and orders and giving advice on military administration. He saw military service again and took part in the expedition to Yorktown. In the previous year he had married the daughter of Gen. Philip Schuyler, and thereby became associated with a rich and prominent New York family.

After the war he read law and in a few months was admitted to the bar. He had a thriving practice, but continued his active participation in public affairs. He was one of the first to see the impossibility of obtaining adequate reform by ordinary amendment of the Articles of Confederation. In the Annapolis Convention of 1786 he secured the adoption of the proposal for a Constitutional Convention and as a member of the New York legislature he pushed through a resolution urging Congress to support the proposal. He was a member of the Convention. Early in its proceedings he submitted proposals for an upper legislative

343

chamber and a president, both to be chosen by property-owners and to hold office during "good behavior," and for a wide transfer of powers from the States to the central government, the latter to appoint the State governors and to exercise a veto power over State legislation in order to prevent conflict with federal legislation. He rarely attended the Convention after the first few weeks: his ideas were too extreme for most of his colleagues; the vote of his State, on issues he deemed critical, would be determined by his two Anti-Federalist colleagues, Robert Yates and John Lansing; and he had a thriving law practice. Yet at the close of the Convention he pled for unanimous support of the document and was the only signer from New York. He initiated the "Publius" newspaper letters of 1787-88 (the "Federalist" papers), wrote over half of them, and led the fight for ratification on the floor of the New York convention. As first secretary of the treasury (1790-95) he prepared the reports and wrote the laws that contributed so much to the establishment of the new government on stable economic bases; and he was Washington's chief administrative and political adviser. He had considerable justification for his later statement (in 1802) that "perhaps no man in the United States has sacrificed or done more for the present Constitution than myself." [1]

Hamilton was also an able political orator and an energetic party leader—not always to the best effect. After his return to private life and a successful legal practice, he endeavored to keep control of the Federalist party and to convince public opinion of the grave dangers in Republican policies. His ruthless intra-party intrigues against John Adams caused serious trouble in the latter's presidential administration and contributed to the Federalist defeat in 1800. He fought his Republican opponents with extreme bitterness. Rumors of remarks he made about Aaron Burr led to the latter's challenge to the duel that ended Hamilton's life.

Hamilton's three decades in America had been a period of intense political activity—insurrection, war, and the sudden construction of new governments. He had had no experience with longer-standing efforts to safeguard popular liberties. From the beginning of his life in this country he had been impressed with the social and political unreliability of ordinary men and with the supreme need for establishing strong and efficient government. He was never as reactionary as his opponents painted him and was usually willing to make some concessions to prevailing desires for representative government. The year before he died he explained that he had always been in favor of having one legislative chamber popularly elected: in the Convention, he said, he had proposed only a good-behavior, not a life, tenure for President and senators, and

[1] Letter to Gouverneur Morris, Feb. 27, 1802, in Works (ed. by Lodge, 1904 ed.), Vol. X, p. 425.

had expected that these officials would in some way be made politically responsible in the exercise of their powers. But the agrarian Republicans appeared to him to have no conception of the constant need for competent and authoritative government. In his efforts to prevent a Republican victory in the election of 1800 he urged the governor of New York (John Jay) to call a special session of the legislature in order to revise the method of appointing presidential electors in such a way that it would be difficult for Jefferson to carry that State. "In times like these," he said, "it will not do to be over-scrupulous; . . . scruples of delicacy and propriety . . . ought to yield to the extraordinary nature of the crisis" and "ought not to hinder the taking of a *legal* and *constitutional* step to prevent an atheist in religion, and fanatic in politics, from getting possession of the helm of state." The outcome of the election filled him with forebodings; and after a year of Jefferson's administration he concluded that "this American world was not meant for me," and he retained only a vague hope that some day the people would be ready "to recover the Constitution." [1]

In Washington's second administration, Hamilton had taken the initiative in securing a forceful assertion of authority by the federal government. The excise law of 1791 imposed a heavy tax on whiskey. The tax was particularly burdensome on inhabitants of western communities, where whiskey was the most economically transportable and barterable commodity. The farmers of western Pennsylvania adopted resolutions declaring, in terms like those of the Stamp Act protests of 1765, that an internal tax on articles for consumption was a destruction of liberty, and they engaged in boycotts and applied tar and feathers to officials attempting to enforce the law. Hamilton persuaded Washington to assemble an army of the State militia to occupy the western counties and put down the insurrection by force. He accompanied the expedition in a supervisory capacity; and he wrote letters to the newspapers in order to inform the public of the significance of the affair. Opponents charged that he had deliberately helped provoke the resistance in order to create an occasion for a conspicuous demonstration of the efficiency and power of the central government under Federalist control.

When the Republicans took control of Congress and the Executive in March, 1801, they soon directed their attention to the new federal judgeships which the preceding Congress had created in its last days and to which President Adams had made appointments, from Federalist party-members, during the last hours of his administration ("midnight appointments"). Congress finally got rid of the newly appointed judges by repealing the statutes that had created their offices. While the mat-

[1] Letters of Sept. 18, 1803, May 7, 1800, and Feb. 27, 1802, in *ibid.*, Vol. X, pp. 446–448, 372–373, 425–426.

ter was under debate, Hamilton wrote a letter vigorously assailing that method of evading the constitutional provision establishing a "good-behavior" tenure for federal judges. His letter is a general contention that in popular governments it is the legislative bodies, not the executives or courts, that are most likely to act oppressively, and that courts, if they are made independent of the other departments, are the least dangerous and most indispensable guardians of civil liberty.

[See: William G. Sumner, *Alexander Hamilton* (1890); Henry Cabot Lodge, *Alexander Hamilton* (1882).]

A LETTER ON THE "WHISKEY REBELLION" (AUGUST 28, 1794)[1]

If it were to be asked, What is the most sacred duty, and the greatest source of security in a republic? the answer would be, An inviolable respect for the Constitution and laws—the first growing out of the last. It is by this, in a great degree, that the rich and the powerful are to be restrained from enterprises against the common liberty—operated upon by the influence of a general sentiment, by their interest in the principle, and by the obstacles which the habit it produces erects against innovation and encroachment. It is by this, in a still greater degree, that caballers, intriguers, and demagogues are prevented from climbing on the shoulders of faction to the tempting seats of usurpation and tyranny.

Were it not that it might require too long a discussion, it would not be difficult to demonstrate that a large and well-organized republic can scarcely lose its liberty from any other cause than that of anarchy, to which a contempt of the laws is the high-road.

But without entering into so wide a field, it is sufficient to present to your view a more simple and a more obvious truth, which is this: that a sacred respect for the constitutional law is the vital principle, the sustaining energy, of a free government.

Government is frequently and aptly classed under two descriptions—a government of FORCE, and a government of LAWS; the first is the definition of despotism—the last, of liberty. But how can a government of laws exist when the laws are disrespected and disobeyed? Government supposes control. It is that POWER by which individuals in society are kept from doing injury to each other, and

[1] In *The Works of Alexander Hamilton*, ed. by Henry Cabot Lodge, 12 vols. (New York, 1904), Vol. VI, pp. 418–424.

are brought to cooperate to a common end. The instruments by which it must act are either the AUTHORITY of the laws or FORCE. If the first be destroyed, the last must be substituted; and where this becomes the ordinary instrument of government, there is an end to liberty!

Those, therefore, who preach doctrines, or set examples which undermine or subvert the authority of the laws, lead us from freedom to slavery; they incapacitate us for a GOVERNMENT of LAWS, and consequently prepare the way for one of FORCE, for mankind must have GOVERNMENT OF ONE SORT OR ANOTHER. There are, indeed, great and urgent cases where the bounds of the Constitution are manifestly transgressed, or its constitutional authorities so exercised as to produce unequivocal oppression on the community, and to render resistance justifiable. But such cases can give no color to the resistance by a comparatively inconsiderable part of a community, of constitutional laws distinguished by no extraordinary features of rigor or oppression, and acquiesced in by the body of the community.

Such a resistance is treason against society, against liberty, against every thing that ought to be dear to a free, enlightened, and prudent people. To tolerate it, were to abandon your most precious interests. Not to subdue it, were to tolerate it. Those who openly or covertly dissuade you from exertions adequate to the occasion, are your worst enemies. They treat you either as fools or cowards, too weak to perceive your interest or your duty, or too dastardly to pursue them. They therefore merit and will, no doubt, meet your contempt. To the plausible but hollow harangue of such conspirators you cannot fail to reply, How long, ye Catilines, will ye abuse our patience?

To urge the execution of that system would manifest, it is said, an intemperate spirit; and to excite your disapprobation of that course, you are threatened with the danger of a civil war, which is called the consummation of human evil.

To crown the outrage upon your understandings, the insurgents are represented as men who understand the principles of freedom, and know the horrors and distresses of anarchy, and who, therefore, must have been tempted to hostility against the laws by a RADICAL DEFECT, EITHER in the government or in those intrusted with its administration. How *thin* the partition which divides the insinuation from the assertion, that the government is in fault, and the insurgents in the right!

Fellow-citizens: A name, a sound, has too often had influence on the affairs of nations; an EXCISE has too long been the successful watchword of party. It has even sometimes led astray well-meaning men. The experiment is now to be tried whether there be any spell in it of sufficient force to unnerve the arm which may be found necessary to be raised in defence of law and order.

The jugglers who endeavor to cheat us with the sound, have never dared to venture into the fair fields of argument. They are conscious that it is easier to declaim than to reason on the subject. They know it to be better to play a game with the passions and prejudices, than to engage seriously with the understanding of the auditory. You have already seen that the merits of excise laws are immaterial to the question to be decided, that you have prejudged the point by a solemn constitutional act, and that until you shall have revoked or modified that act, resistance to its operation is a criminal infraction of the social compact, an inversion of the fundamental principles of republican government, and a daring attack upon YOUR sovereignty, which you are bound, by every motive of duty and self-preservation, to withstand and defeat. The matter might safely be suffered to rest here; but I shall take a future opportunity to examine the reasonableness of the prejudice which is inculcated against excise laws, and which has become the pretext for excesses tending to dissolve the bands of society.

Fellow-citizens: You are told that it will be intemperate to urge the execution of the laws which are resisted. What? Will it be indeed intemperate in your Chief Magistrate, sworn to maintain the Constitution, charged faithfully to execute the laws, and authorized to employ for that purpose force, when the ordinary means fail—will it be intemperate in him to exert that force, when the Constitution and the laws are opposed by force? Can he answer it to his conscience, to you, not to exert it?

Yes, it is said; because the execution of it will produce civil war—the consummation of human evil.

Fellow-citizens: Civil war is, undoubtedly, a great evil. It is one that every good man would wish to avoid, and will deplore if inevitable. But it is incomparably a less evil than the destruction of government. The first brings with it serious but temporary and partial ills; the last undermines the foundations of our security and happiness. And where should we be if it were once to grow into a maxim, that force is not to be used against the seditious combinations of parts of the community to resist the laws? This would be to give a CARTE BLANCHE to ambition, to licentiousness, to foreign intrigue, to make you the prey of the gold of other nations—the sport of the passions and vices of individuals among yourselves. The hydra Anarchy would rear its head in every quarter. The goodly fabric you have established would be rent asunder, and precipitated into the dust. You knew how to encounter civil war rather than surrender your liberty to foreign domination; you will not hesitate now to brave it rather than to surrender your sovereignty to the tyranny of a faction; you will be as deaf to the apostles of anarchy now as you were to the emissaries of despotism then. Your love of liberty will guide you now as it did then; you know that the POWER of the majority and LIBERTY are inseparable. Destroy that, and this perishes. But, in truth, that which properly can be called civil war is not to be apprehended—unless from the act of those who endeavor to fan the flame, by rendering the government odious. A civil war is a contest between two GREAT parts of the same empire. The exertion of the strength of the nation to suppress resistance to its laws, by a sixtieth part of itself, is not of that description.

After endeavoring to alarm you with the horrors of civil war, an attempt is made to excite your sympathy in favor of the armed faction, by telling you that those who compose it are men who understand the principles of freedom, and know the horrors and distresses of anarchy, and must therefore have been prompted to hostility against the laws by a radical defect EITHER in the government OR in its administration. Fellow-citizens, for an answer to this you have only to consult your senses. The natural consequences of radical defect in a government, or in its administration, are national distress and suffering. Look around you—where is it? Do you feel it? Do you see it?

Go in quest of it beyond the Alleghany, and instead of it you will find that there also a scene of unparalleled prosperity upbraids the ingratitude and madness of those who are endeavoring to cloud the bright face of our political horizon, and to mar the happiest lot that beneficent Heaven ever indulged to undeserving mortals.

When you have turned your eyes towards that scene, examine well the men whose knowledge of the principles of freedom is so emphatically vaunted—where did they get their better knowledge of those principles than that which you possess? How is it that you have been so blind or tame as to remain quiet, while they have been goaded into hostility against the laws by a RADICAL DEFECT in the government or its administration? Are you willing to yield them the palm of discernment, of patriotism, or of courage?

From LETTER ON THE INDEPENDENT JUDICIARY (MARCH 2, 1802)[1]

Can [the proposal to remove judges by abolishing their offices] be . . . defended by any principle of constitutional policy?

To establish the affirmative of this question, it has been argued that if the judges hold their offices by a title absolutely independent of the legislative will, the judicial department becomes a colossal and overbearing power, capable of degenerating into a permanent tyranny; at liberty, if audacious and corrupt enough, to render the authority of the Legislature nugatory by expounding away the laws, and to assume a despotic control over the rights of persons and property.

To this argument (which supposes the case of a palpable abuse of power) a plain and conclusive answer is, that the Constitution has provided a complete safeguard in the authority of the House of Representatives to impeach, of the Senate to condemn. The judges are in this way amenable to public justice for misconduct, and, upon conviction, removable from office. In the hands of the Legislature itself is placed the weapon by which they may be put down and the other branches of the government protected. The pretended danger, therefore, is evidently imaginary—the security perfect.

Reverse the medal. Concede to the Legislature a legal discretion to abolish the judges, where is the defence? where the security for the judicial department? There is absolutely none. This most valuable member of the government, when rightly constituted the surest guardian of person and property, of which stability is a prime characteristic, losing at once its most essential attributes, and

[1] In *ibid*, Vol. VIII, pp. 330–337, at 331–336.

doomed to fluctuate with the variable tide of faction, degenerates into a disgusting mirror of all the various malignant and turbulent humors of party spirit.

Let us not be deceived. The real danger is on the side of that foul and fatal doctrine, which emboldens its votaries, with daring front and unhallowed step, to enter the holy temple of justice and pluck from their seats the venerable personages, who, under the solemn sanction of the Constitution, are commissioned to officiate there—to guard that sacred compact with jealous vigilance—to dispense the laws with a steady and impartial hand—unmoved by the storms of faction, unawed by its powers, unseduced by its favors—shielding right and innocence from every attack—resisting and repressing violence from every quarter. 'T is from the triumph of that execrable doctrine that we may have to date the downfall of our government, and, with it, of the whole fabric of republican liberty. Who will have the folly to deny that the definition of despotism is the concentration of all the powers of government in one person or in one body? Who is so blind as not to see that the right of the Legislature to abolish the judges at pleasure, destroys the independence of the judicial department, and swallows it up in the impetuous vortex of legislative influence? Who is so weak as to hope that the Executive, deprived of so powerful an auxiliary, will long survive? What dispassionate man can withstand the conviction that the boundaries between the departments will be thenceforth nominal, and that there will be no longer more than one active and efficient department?

It is a fundamental maxim of free government, that the three great departments of power, *legislative, executive,* and *judiciary,* shall be essentially distinct and independent, the one of the other. This principle, very influential in most of our State constitutions, has been particularly attended to in the Constitution of the United States; which, in order to give effect to it, has adopted a precaution peculiar to itself, in the provisions that forbid the Legislature to vary in any way the compensation of the *President,* or to diminish that of a *judge.*

It is a principle equally sound, that though in a government like that of Great Britain, having an hereditary chief with vast prerogatives, the danger to liberty, by the predominance of one department over the other, is on the side of the executive; yet in popular forms of government, this danger is chiefly to be apprehended from the legislative branch.

The power of legislation is, in its own nature, the most comprehensive and potent of the three great subdivisions of sovereignty. It is the will of the government; it prescribes universally the rule of action, and the sanctions which are to enforce it. It creates and regulates the public force, and it commands the public purse. If deposited in an elective representative of the people, it has, in most cases, the body of the nation for its auxiliary, and generally acts with all the momentum of popular favor. In every such government it is consequently an organ of immense strength. But when there is an hereditary chief magistrate, clothed with dazzling prerogatives and a great patronage, there is a powerful counterpoise, which, in most cases, is sufficient to preserve the equilibrium of the government; in some cases, to incline the scale too much to its own side.

In governments wholly popular or representative, there is no adequate counterpoise. Confidence in the most numerous, or legislative department, and jealousy of the executive chief, form the genius of every such government. That jealousy, operating in the constitution of the executive, causes this organ to be intrinsically feeble; and witholding in the course of administration accessory means of force and influence, is for the most part vigilant to continue it in a state of impotence. The result is that the legislative body, in this species of government, possesses additional resources of power and weight; while the executive is rendered much too weak for competition; almost too weak for self-defence.

A third principle, not less well founded than the other two, is that the judiciary department is naturally the weakest of the three. The sources of strength to the legislative branches have been briefly delineated. The executive, by means of its several active powers, of the dispensation of honors and emoluments, and of the direction of the public force, is evidently the second in strength. The judiciary, on the other hand, can ordain nothing. It commands neither the purse nor the sword. It has scarcely any patronage. Its functions are not active but deliberative. Its main province is to declare the meaning of the laws; and, in extraordinary cases, it must even look up to the executive aid for the execution of its decisions. Its chief strength is in the veneration which it is able to inspire by the wisdom and rectitude of its judgments.

This character of the judiciary clearly indicates that it is not only the weakest of the three departments of power, but, also, as it regards the security and preservation of civil liberty, by far the safest. In a conflict with the other departments, it will be happy if it can defend itself—to annoy them is beyond its power. In vain would it singly attempt enterprises against the rights of the citizen. The other departments could quickly arrest its arm and punish its temerity. It can only, then, become an effectual instrument of oppression, when it is combined with one of the more active and powerful organs; and against a combination of this sort, the true and best guard is a complete independence of each and both of them. Its dependence on either will imply and involve a subserviency to the views of the department on which it shall depend. Its independence of both will render it a powerful check upon the others, and a precious shield to the rights of persons and property. Safety, liberty, are therefore inseparably connected with the real and substantial independence of the courts and judges.

10. FISHER AMES ON THE DANGERS OF POPULAR LIBERTIES

MANY conservatives (from among bankers, speculators, and the larger merchants) in the early days of independence believed that the first State governments were both too weak and too strong: too conciliatory in dealing with disorderly demands for reform, too arbitrary in dealing with the interests of property-owners. Although the Revolution had been primarily a revolt against British policy and a movement for home rule, it drew strong support from many in the poorer sections of the population because of their hope for changes that would give them a greater voice in government at home and some relief from the burden of their debts. Several of the early State legislatures enacted measures for the benefit of these groups, as by issuing paper money that was made legal tender for the payment of debts, or by authorizing the payment of debts in goods instead of money. More moderate groups regained control in most of the States shortly after the close of the War; but the insistent demands of debtor groups could not be entirely ignored. In Massachusetts, as we have seen, a small-farmer group, defeated at the polls and rendered desperate over debts, high taxes, and threats of mortgage foreclosures, arose in revolt ("Shays' Rebellion," 1786–87). State authorities suppressed the revolt but dealt leniently with the revolters; and during the next few years Massachusetts and other States enacted moderate measures for the protection of debtors. All this greatly increased the conservative fears of popular majorities and led to demands for new safeguards for public order and economic stability. The major business of government, according to the conservative view, was to protect property and preserve order. On the one hand, in keeping "in due subjection to law and order the dangerous mass of the poor and vicious" (to use Fisher Ames' expression), a government should act authoritatively, even to the extent of abrogating ordinary civil liberties. On the other hand, in dealing with property rights, a legislature should act only under strict constitutional limitations applied by courts far removed from popular control. Both of these ideas appear in the sections below from Fisher Ames, who, as we have seen, was a leading spokesman for conservative Federalists.[1] The

[1] See above, p. 165.

first was written at the time of Shays' Rebellion, the second after nearly twenty years more of experience under the government of popular majorities. His references to the "Constitution" and "Supreme Court" are to the constitution and supreme court of Massachusetts.

From A LETTER TO THE "INDEPENDENT CHRONICLE" (OCTOBER 12, 1786) [1]

Many friends of the government seem to think it a duty to practise a little well-intended hypocrisy, when conversing on the subject of the late commotions in the Commonwealth. They seem to think it prudent and necessary to conceal from the people, and even from themselves, the magnitude of the present danger. They affect to hope, that there is not any real disaffection to government among the rioters, and that reason will soon dispel the delusion which has excited them to arms. But the present crisis is too important, and appearances too menacing, to admit of pusillanimous councils, and half-way measures. Every citizen has a right to know the truth. It is time to speak out, and to rouse the torpid patriotism of men, who have every thing to lose by the subversion of an excellent Constitution. . . .

It will be necessary to consider the nature and probable consequences of the late riots, in order to determine, whether this alternative, to surrender or to defend the Constitution, is now the question before the General Court.

The crime of high treason has not been always supposed to imply the greatest moral turpitude and corruption of mind; but it has ever stood first on the list of civil crimes. In European states, the rebellion of a small number of persons can excite but little apprehension, and no danger; an armed force is there kept up, which can crush tumults almost as soon as they break out; or if a rebellion prevails, the conqueror succeeds to the power and titles of his vanquished competitor. The head of the government is changed; but the government remains.

The crime of levying war against the state is attended with particular aggravations and dangers in this country. Our government has no armed force; it subsists by the supposed approbation of the

[1] Signed "Lucius Junius Brutus"; in The Works of Fisher Ames, ed. by Seth Ames, Vol. II, pp. 91–97. By courtesy of Little, Brown & Company.

majority; the first murmurs of sedition excite doubts of that approbation; timid, credulous, and ambitious men concur to magnify the
danger. In such a government, the danger is real, as soon as it is
dreaded. No sooner is the standard of rebellion displayed, than
men of desperate principles and fortunes resort to it; the pillars of
government are shaken; the edifice totters from its centre; the foot
of a child may overthrow it; the hands of giants cannot rebuild it.
For if our government should be destroyed, what but the total destruction of civil society must ensue? A more popular form could
not be contrived, nor could it stand; one less popular would not be
adopted. The people then, wearied by anarchy, and wasted by
intestine war, must fall an easy prey to foreign or domestic tyranny.
Besides, our Constitution is the free act of the people; they stand
solemnly pledged for its defence, and treason against such a Constitution implies a high degree of moral depravity. . . .

. . . This crime against a free Commonwealth, which has no
standing military force, will be repeated if it is not punished; witness the increase of insolence and numbers, with which the late
riots have succeeded each other. The certainty of punishment is
the truest security against crimes; but if a number of individuals
are allowed, with impunity, to support by arms their disapprobation
of public measures, though the Constitution should remain, yet we
shall be cursed with a government by men, and not by laws. The
plans of an enlightened and permanent national policy may be
defeated by, and in fact must depend upon, the desperate ambition
of the worst men in the Commonwealth; upon the convenience of
bankrupts and sots, who have gambled or slept away their estates;
upon the sophisms of wrong-headed men of some understanding;
and upon the prejudices, caprice, and ignorant enthusiasm of a
multitude of tavern-haunting politicians, who have none at all. The
supreme power of the State will be found to reside with such men;
and in making laws, the object will not be the general good, but the
will and interest of the vile legislators. This will be a government
by men, and the worst of men; and such men, actuated by the
strongest passions of the heart, having nothing to lose, and, hoping
from the general confusion to reap a copious harvest, will acquire
in every society a larger share of influence, than equal property and
abilities will give to better citizens. The motives to refuse obedience to government are many and strong; impunity will multiply

and enforce them. Many men would rebel, rather than be ruined; but they would rather not rebel than be hanged. The English government may sometimes treat insurrections with lenity, for they dare to punish. But who will impute our forbearance either to prudence or magnanimity?

It need not be observed, that it is rebellion to oppose any of the courts of justice; but opposing the Supreme Court, whose justices are so revered for their great learning and integrity, is known to be high treason by every individual who has mingled with the mob. Many of them have been deluded with the pretence of grievances; but they well know that the method of redress which they have sought is treasonable; they dare to commit the offence, because they believe that government have not the power and spirit to punish them.

This seems therefore to be the time, and perhaps the only time, to revive just ideas of the criminality and danger of treason; for our government to govern; for our rulers to vindicate the violated majesty of a free Commonwealth; to convince the advocates of democracy, that the Constitution may yet be defended, and that it is worth defending; that the supreme power is really held by the legal representatives of the people; that the county conventions and riotous assemblies of armed men shall no longer be allowed to legislate, and to form an *imperium in imperio*; and that the protection of government shall yet be effectually extended to every citizen of the Commonwealth.

In a free government, the reality of grievances is no kind of justification of rebellion. . . .

It may be very proper to use arguments, to publish addresses, and fulminate proclamations against high treason; but the man who expects to disperse a mob of a thousand men, by ten thousand arguments, has certainly never been in one. I have heard it remarked, that men are not to be reasoned out of an opinion that they have not reasoned themselves into. The case, though important, is simple. Government does not subsist by making proselytes to sound reason, or by compromise and arbitration with its members; but by the power of the community compelling the obedience of individuals. If that is not done, who will seek its protection, or fear its vengeance? Government may prevail in the argument, and yet we may lose the Constitution. . . .

But should government resolve that a measure which is morally wrong is politically right; that it is necessary to sacrifice its friends and advocates to buy a truce from its foes; will those foes, having tasted the sweets of ruling, intermit their enterprises, while there is a remnant of authority left in the State to inflict punishments and to impose taxes, and that authority is no longer formidable by the support of those men whose rights have been already surrendered? Did cowardice, did injustice, ever save a sinking state? Did any man, by giving up a portion of his just right, because he had not courage to maintain it, ever save the residue? The insolence of the aggressor is usually proportioned to the tameness of the sufferer. Every individual has a right to tell his rulers, "I am one of the parties to the constitutional contract. I promised allegiance, and I require protection for my life and property. I am ready to risk both in your defence. I am competent to make my own contracts; and when they are violated to seek their interpretation and redress in the judicial courts. I never gave you a right to interpose in them. Without my consent, or a crime committed, neither you, nor any individual, have a right to my property. I refuse my consent; I am innocent of any crime. I solemnly protest against the transfer of my property to my debtor. An act making paper or swine a tender, is a confiscation of my estate, and a breach of that compact under which I thought I had secured protection. If ye say that the people are distressed, I ask is the proposed relief less distressing? Relieve distress from your own funds; exercise the virtues of charity and compassion at your own charge, as I do. Am I to lose my property, and to be involved in distress, to relieve persons whom I never saw, and who are unworthy of compassion if they accept the dishonest relief? If your virtues lead you to oppress me, what am I to expect from your vices? But if ye will suffer my life to depend upon the mercy of the mob, and my property upon their opinion of the expediency of my keeping it, at least restore me the right which I renounced when I became a citizen, of vindicating my own rights, and avenging my own injuries."

In fine, the public will be convinced that the designs of the rioters are subversive of government; that they have knowingly incurred the penalties of high treason; that arguments will not reach them; will not be understood; if understood will not convince them; and after having gone such lengths, conviction will not disarm them; that if government should reason and deliberate when they ought to act; should choose committees, publish addresses, and do nothing; we shall see our free Constitution expire, the state of nature restored, and our rank among savages taken somewhere below the Oneida Indians. If government should do worse than nothing, should make paper money or a tender act, all hopes of seeing the people quiet and property safe, are at an end. Such an act would be the legal triumph of treason.

But, before we make such a sacrifice, let us consider our force to defend the State. And to direct that force, at the head of the government is a magistrate whose firmness, integrity, and ability are well known. The senate and house have hitherto deserved the public confidence. Every man of principle and property will give them his most zealous aid. A select corps of militia may easily be formed, of such men as may be trusted; the force of the United States may be relied upon, if needed. The insurgents, without leaders, and without resources, will claim the mercy of the government as soon as vigorous counsels are adopted.

But if the Constitution must fall, let us discharge our duty, and attempt its defence. Let us not furnish our enemies with a triumph, nor the dishonored page of history with evidence that it was formed with too much wisdom to be valued, and required too much virtue to be maintained by its members.

From "THE DANGERS OF AMERICAN LIBERTY" (1805) [1]

The great object, then, of political wisdom in framing our Constitution, was to guard against licentiousness, that inbred malady of democracies, that deforms their infancy with gray hairs and decrepitude.

The federalists relied much on the efficiency of an independent judiciary, as a check on the hasty turbulence of the popular passions. They supposed the senate, proceeding from the states, and chosen for six years, would form a sort of balance to the democracy, and realize the hope that a federal republic of states might subsist. They counted much on the information of the citizens; that they would

[1] In The Works of Fisher Ames, ed. by Seth Ames, Vol. II, pp. 344–399, 349–350, 355–359, 363–364. 367–369. By courtesy of Little, Brown & Company.

give their unremitted attention to public affairs; that either dissensions would not arise in our happy country, or if they should, that the citizens would remain calm, and would walk, like the three Jews in Nebuchadnezzar's furnace, unharmed amidst the fires of party. . . .

What is there left that can check its excesses or retard the velocity of its fall? Not the control of the several states, for they already whirl in the vortex of faction; and of consequence, not the senate, which is appointed by the states. Surely not the judiciary, for we cannot expect the office of the priesthood from the victim at the altar. Are we to be sheltered by the force of ancient manners? Will this be sufficient to control the two evil spirits of license and innovation? Where is any vestige of those manners left, but in New England? And even in New England their authority is contested and their purity debased. Are our civil and religious institutions to stand so firmly as to sustain themselves and so much of the fabric of the public order as is propped by their support? On the contrary, do we not find the ruling faction in avowed hostility to our religious institutions? In effect, though not in form, their protection is abandoned by our laws and confided to the steadiness of sentiment and fashion; and if they are still powerful auxiliaries of lawful authority, it is owing to the tenaciousness with which even a degenerate people maintain their habits, and to a yet remaining, though impaired veneration for the maxims of our ancestors. We are changing, and if democracy triumphs in New England, it is to be apprehended that in a few years we shall be as prone to disclaim our great progenitors, as they, if they should return again to the earth, with grief and shame to disown their degenerate descendants.

Is the turbulence of our democracy to be restrained by preferring to the magistracy only the grave and upright, the men who profess the best moral and religious principles, and whose lives bear testimony in favor of their profession, whose virtues inspire confidence, whose services, gratitude, and whose talents command admiration? Such magistrates would add dignity to the best government, and disarm the malignity of the worst. But the bare moving of this question will be understood as a sarcasm by men of both parties. The powers of impudence itself are scarcely adequate to say that our magistrates are such men. . . .

Although it does not appear that the science of good government

has made any advances since the invention of printing, it is nevertheless the opinion of many that this art has risen, like another sun
in the sky, to shed new light and joy on the political world. The
press, however, has left the understanding of the mass of men just
where it found it; but by supplying an endless stimulus to their
imagination and passions, it has rendered their temper and habits
infinitely worse. It has inspired ignorance with presumption, so
that those who cannot be governed by reason are no longer to be
awed by authority. The many, who before the art of printing never
mistook in a case of oppression, because they complained from their
actual sense of it, have become susceptible of every transient enthusiasm, and of more than womanish fickleness of caprice. Public
affairs are transacted now on a stage where all the interest and passions grow out of fiction, or are inspired by the art, and often controlled at the pleasure of the actors. The press is a new, and certainly a powerful, agent in human affairs. It will change, but it is
difficult to conceive how, by rendering men indocile and presump-
tuous, it can change societies for the better. They are pervaded by
its heat, and kept forever restless by its activity. While it has impaired the force that every just government can employ in self-
defence, it has imparted to its enemies the secret of that wildfire
that blazes with the most consuming fierceness on attempting to
quench it.

Shall we then be told that the press will constitute an adequate
check to the progress of every species of tyranny? Is it to be denied
that the press has been the base and venal instrument of the very
men whom it ought to gibbet to universal abhorrence? While they
were climbing to power it aided their ascent; and now they have
reached it, does it not conceal or justify their abominations? Or,
while it is confessed that the majority of citizens form their ideas
of men and measures almost solely from the light that reaches them
through the magic-lantern of the press, do our comforters still depend on the all-restoring, all-preserving power of general information? And are they not destitute of all this, or rather of any better
information themselves, if they can urge this vapid nonsense in the
midst of a yet spreading political delusion, in the midst of the "palpable obscure" that settles on the land, from believing what is false,
and misconstruing what is true? Can they believe all this, when
they consider how much truth is impeded by party on its way to the

public understanding, and even after having reached it, how much it still falls short of its proper mark, while it leaves the envious, jealous, vindictive will unconquered? . . .

It is undoubtedly a salutary labor to diffuse among the citizens of a free state, as far as the thing is possible, a just knowledge of their public affairs. But the difficulty of this task is augmented exactly in proportion to the freedom of the state; for the more free the citizens, the bolder and more profligate will be their demagogues, the more numerous and eccentric the popular errors, and the more vehement and pertinacious the passions that defend them.

Yet, as if there were neither vice nor passion in the world, one of the loudest of our boasts, one of the dearest of all the tenets of our creed is, that we are a sovereign people, self-governed—it would be nearer truth to say, self-conceited. For in what sense is it true that any people, however free, are self-governed? If they have in fact no government but such as comports with their ever-varying and often inordinate desires, then it is anarchy; if it counteracts those desires, it is compulsory. The individual who is left to act according to his own humor is not governed at all; and if any considerable number, and especially any combination of individuals, find or can place themselves in this situation, then the society is no longer free. For liberty obviously consists in the salutary restraint, and not in the uncontrolled indulgence of such humors. Now of all desires, none will so much need restraint, or so impatiently endure it, as those of the ambitious, who will form factions, first to elude, then to rival, and finally to usurp the powers of the state; and of the sons of vice, who are the enemies of law, because no just law can be their friend. The first want to govern the state; and the others, that the state should not govern them. A sense of common interest will soon incline these two original factions of every free state to coalesce into one. . . .

It is not however the faction of debtors only that is to be expected to arise under a democracy. Every bad passion that dreads restraint from the laws will seek impunity and indulgence in faction. The associates will not come together in cold blood. They will not, like their federal adversaries, yawn over the contemplation of their cause, and shrink from the claim of its necessary perils and sacrifices. They will do all that can possibly be done, and they will attempt more. They will begin early, persevere long, ask no respite for themselves, and are sure to triumph if their enemies take any. Suppose at first their numbers to be exceedingly few, their efforts will for that reason be so much the greater. They will call themselves the people; they will in their name arraign every act of government as wicked and weak; they will oblige the rulers to stand forever on the defensive, as culprits at the bar of an offended public. With a venal press at command, concealing their number and their infamy, is it to be doubted that the ignorant will soon or late unite with the vicious? Their union is inevitable; and, when united, those allies are powerful enough to strike terror into the hearts of the firmest rulers. It is in vain, it is indeed childish to say, that an enlightened people will understand their own affairs, and thus the acts of a faction will be baffled. No people on earth are or can be so enlightened as to the details of political affairs. To study politics, so as to know correctly the force of the reasons for a large part of the public measures, would stop the labor of the plough and the hammer; and how are these million of students to have access to the means of information? . . .

. . . In a tyranny individuals are nothing. Conscious of their nothingness, the spirit of liberty is torpid or extinct. But in a free state there is, necessarily, a great mass of power left in the hands of the citizens, with the spirit to use and the desire to augment it. Hence will proceed an infinity of clubs and associations, for purposes often laudable or harmless, but not unfrequently factious. It is obvious, that the combination of some hundreds or thousands for political ends will produce a great aggregate stock or mass of power. As by combining they greatly augment their power, for that very reason they will combine; and as magistrates would seldom like to devolve their authority upon volunteers who might offer to play the magistrate in their stead, there is almost nothing left for a band of combined citizens to do, but to discredit and obstruct the government and laws. The possession of power by the magistrate is not so sure to produce respect as to kindle envy; and to the envious it is a gratification to humble those who are exalted. But the ambitious find the public discontent a passport to office—then they must breed or inflame discontent. We have the example before our eyes. . . .

As property is the object of the great mass of every faction, the rules that keep it sacred will be annulled, or so far shaken, as to bring enough of it within the grasp of the dominant party to reward their partisans with booty. But the chieftains, thirsting only for dominion, will search for the means of extending or establishing it. They will, of course, innovate, till the vestiges of private right, and of restraints on public authority, are effaced; until the real people are stripped of all privilege and influence, and become even more abject and spiritless than weak. The many may be deluded, but the success of a faction is ever the victory of a few; and the power of the few can be supported by nothing but force. This catastrophe is fatal. . . .

Is this catastrophe too distant to be viewed, or too improbable to be dreaded? I should not think it so formidably near as I do, if in the short interval of impending fate, in which alone it can be of any use to be active, the heart of every honest man in the nation, or even in New England, was penetrated with the anxiety that oppresses my own. Then the subversion of the public liberty would at least be delayed, if it could not be prevented. Her maladies might be palliated, if not cured. She might long drag on the life of an invalid, instead of soon suffering the death of a martyr. . . .

11. JOHN QUINCY ADAMS (1767–1848)

MORE moderate warnings of the tendencies of popular majorities to over-ride minority rights were expressed by John Adams and his eldest son, John Quincy. The latter was born in Braintree (now Quincy), Massachusetts. He attended preparatory schools in Europe and at the age of sixteen he was secretary to his father in the peace negotiations with England. Graduated from Harvard in 1787, he was admitted to the bar three years later, but had little opportunity for practice. He was in public office for about half a century: as minister to Berlin, member of the State senate, United States senator, minister to Russia, member of the peace commission after the War of 1812, secretary of state (under Monroe), President (1825–29), and member of the House of Representatives (1831–48)—the only ex-President who has served in the House. He was an informed, forthright, and skillful diplomat. He played an influential part in the negotiations of the Treaty of Ghent (1814); as secretary of state he managed successfully the difficult negotiations with Spain over Florida; and historians give him a large share of credit for the formulation of the Monroe Doctrine. He was nonpartisan and independent in his stands on domestic issues. Elected to the United States Senate (in 1803) as a Federalist, he became an apostate in the eyes of Massachusetts Federalists when he supported Jefferson's measures against British interferences with American commerce. As President he kept in office active followers of his political opponents and rivals. In the House of Representatives he gave strong support to President Jackson (a bitter political enemy) in the nullification controversy, and he was a persistent and adroit and (for much of the time) a lone spokesman for antislavery groups.

In 1791 Adams wrote a series of newspaper letters replying to Tom Paine's *Rights of Man*; in these he attacked the claims he found in the current democratic doctrines, in France and America, that the rights of a popular government extended as far as its power. Half a century later, in the House of Representatives, he took a strong stand in defense of minority rights of petition and discussion. On May 26, 1836, the House adopted (under a motion for the previous question) a resolution providing that all petitions or other papers relating in any way to slavery should, "without being either printed or referred, be laid upon the table, and that no further action whatever shall be had thereon." Adams set himself doggedly to undo that "gag" rule. At the opening of each session of Congress for eight years, he moved the repeal of the rule. In 1838 he occupied most of the "morning hour" every day for three weeks, speaking (despite many parliamentary maneuvers to upset him) on the rights of petition and of freedom of debate. His annual motions were defeated by decreasing majorities, until on December 3, 1844 (in his seventy-eighth year), the rule was repealed by a vote of 108 to 80. Adams wrote in his diary that night: "Blessed, forever blessed, be the name of God."

[See: *Speech of John Quincy Adams . . . upon the Right of People, Men and Women, to Petition* (Washington, 1838); John T. Morse, Jr., *John Quincy Adams* (1898).]

From "LETTERS OF PUBLICOLA" (1791)[1]

SIR, The late Revolution in France has opened an extensive field of speculation to the philosopher and to the politician. An event so astonishing and unexpected in its nature, and so important in its consequences, naturally arrested the peculiar attention of the whole civilized world. The friends of liberty and of man have seen with pleasure the temples of despotism levelled with the ground, and the Genius of Freedom rising suddenly in his collected and ir-resistible strength, and snapping in an instant all the cords with which, for centuries, he had been bound. Upon the downfall of the arbitrary system of government in France, there appears to have been but one sentiment, and that sentiment of exultation; but while the friends of humanity have rejoiced at the emancipation of so many millions of their fellow creatures, they have waited with anxious expectation to see upon what foundations they would at-tempt to establish their newly-acquired liberty. The proceedings of their Representative Assembly have been contemplated in very different points of view, by men of names equally illustrious, and of characters equally favourable to the cause of liberty. Among the publications which have appeared upon the subject, two pam-phlets, founded upon very different principles, appear to have been received with the greatest avidity, and seem calculated to leave the

[1] Published in the *Columbian Centinel*, June 8 to July 27; in *The Writings of John Quincy Adams*, ed. by Worthington C. Ford, 7 vols. (New York, 1913–1917), Vol. I, pp. 65–110, at 65–67, 70–73, 91–94.

deepest impression. The one written by Mr. Burke, which is one continued invective upon almost all the proceedings of the National Assembly since the Revolution, and which passes a severe and indiscriminating censure upon almost all their transactions: The other the production of Mr. Paine, containing a defence of the Assembly, and approving every thing they have done, with applause as undistinguishing as is the censure of Mr. Burke. . . .

. . . As to the right, he scruples not to say, "that which a whole nation chuses to do, it has a right to do." This proposition is a part of what Mr. Paine calls a system of principles in opposition to those of Mr. Burke, and it is laid down without any sort of qualification. It is not my intention to defend the principles of Mr. Burke; truth is the only object of my pursuit, and I shall without hesitation refuse my assent to every principle inconsistent with that, whether it proceeds from Mr. Burke, Mr. Paine, or even from the illustrious National Assembly of France. This principle, that a whole nation has a right to do whatever it pleases, cannot in any sense whatever be admitted as true. The eternal and immutable laws of justice and of morality are paramount to all human legislation. The violation of those laws is certainly within the power, but it is not among the rights of nations. The power of a nation is the collected power of all the individuals which compose it. The rights of a nation are in like manner the collected rights of its individuals; and it must *follow* from thence, that the powers of a nation are more extensive than its rights, in the very same proportion with those of individuals. It is somewhat remarkable that, in speaking of the exercise of the particular right of forming a Constitution, Mr. Paine himself denies to a nation that omnipotence which he had before so liberally bestowed. For this same nation, which has a right to do whatever it pleases, has no right to establish a Government in *hereditary succession*. It is of infinite consequence, that the distinction between *power* and *right* should be fully acknowledged, and admitted as one of the fundamental principles of Legislators. A whole nation, such as France, England, or America, can act only by representation; and the acts of the representative body must be considered as the acts of the nation. We must go farther, and say, that the acts of the majority in the Representative Assembly are the acts of the whole body, and consequently of the whole nation. If, therefore, a majority thus constituted are bound by no law human or divine, and have no other rule but their sovereign will and pleasure to direct them, what possible security can any citizen of the nation have for the protection of his unalienable rights? The principles of liberty must still be the sport of arbitrary power, and the hideous form of despotism must lay aside the diadem and the scepter, only to assume the party-colored garments of democracy. . . .

The people of England have, in common with other nations, a natural and unalienable right to form a Constitution of Government, not because a whole nation has a right to do whatever it chooses to do, but because Government being instituted for the common security of the natural rights of every individual, it must be liable to alterations whenever it becomes incompetent for that purpose. The right of a people to legislate for succeeding generations derives all its authority from the consent of that posterity who are bound by their laws; and therefore the expressions of perpetuity used by the Parliament of 1688, contain no absurdity; and expressions of a similar nature may be found in all the Constitutions of the United States.

But, Sir, when this right is thus admitted in its fullest latitude, it must also be admitted, that it ought never to be exercised but in cases of extreme urgency: Every nation has a right as unquestionable to dissolve the bands of civil society, by which they are united, and to return to that state of individual imbecility in which man is supposed to have existed, previous to the formation of the social compact. The people of America have been compelled, by an unaccountable necessity, distressing in its operation, but glorious in its consequences, to exercise this right; and whenever a nation has no other alternative but the degradation of slavery, or the formidable conflict of a Revolution, the generous spirit of freedom will not hesitate a moment in the choice. . . .

The Constitution of the United States appears to me to unite all the advantages, both of the French and of the English, while it has avoided the evils of both. By that Constitution, the people have delegated the power of alteration, by vesting it in the Congress, together with the State Legislatures; while at the same time it has provided for alterations by the people themselves in their original character, whenever it shall evidently appear to be the wish of the people to make them. This article appears to be replete with wisdom; I believe it will stand the test of the severest examination, though, according to the ideas emanating from Mr. Paine, and coming to us, at the same time, by reflection from the Secretary of State, it contains a very dangerous political heresy.

It is a maxim which will not, I trust, be disputed, that no Government, of which the people is not a constituent part, can secure their equal rights; but where this is the case, to cramp the operations of their own Government with unnecessary restrictions, and forbid themselves to enact useful laws, what is it but to defeat the purposes of society by the very act which gives it a permanent existence; to tie their own hands from an imaginary apprehension, that if left at liberty, they would administer poison to the body which nourishes them.

It is in the distribution of the national powers, it is in the independent spirit of the people, and not in the manuscript limitations of the legislative authority, that a nation is to secure the protection of its liberties. In this commonwealth we have a Constitution, most parts of which are unalterable by our ordinary Legislatures; it has existed but ten years: and already its operation has convinced us all, that several alterations in the system would be highly expedient. Our Legislative body would be fully competent to the purpose, and, if they had the power, would readily make such alterations as might suit the convenience of the people; but they have no authority to act in these cases for the benefit of the people; and as the inconveniences to which this injudicious jealousy has subjected us, are not at this time of such importance, as to render the alterations of immediate or absolute necessity, we must wait our appointed time, and patiently submit to the operation of bad laws, because we have not chosen to invest our Legislature with the power of making good ones. Let us not be frightened, however, from the pursuit of our common interest by the words arbitrary power. Distribute the whole of your power in such a manner, as will necessarily prevent any one man, or body of men, or any possible combination of individual interests, from being arbitrary, but do not incumber your own representatives with shackles, prejudicial to your own interests; nor suffer yourselves, like the Spanish Monarch of ridiculous memory, to be roasted to death, by denying to your servants the power of removing the fire from before you.

But although a Constitution, professedly unalterable by the common legislative authority, is of weight sufficient to prevent the enacting of many good laws, yet it will not always operate as a check upon your legislature. Such is the poverty of all human labors, that even a whole nation cannot express themselves upon paper with so much accuracy and precision, as not to admit of much latitude of explanation and construction. The Legislature must always be allowed to judge of the intentions with which the instrument was formed, and to construe and explain accordingly the expressions which it contains. They some times think proper to violate the letter of the Constitution by adhering to its spirit, and at other times they sacrifice the spirit by adhering strictly to the letter. But when your Legislature undertakes to decide that the spirit of the Constitution is directly contrary to its express letter, where is the power in the nation that should control them? The same power which will always be sufficient to control a Legislature, of which the people are a constituent part; it is the spirit of the people. Let your legislative and executive authorities be so constituted, as to prevent every essential, or dangerous abuse of the powers delegated, but depend upon the honest and enlightened spirit of the people for a security which you never will obtain, by merely withholding your powers, unless that spirit should be constantly kept up. Divide your power so that every part of it may at all times be used for your advantage, but in such a manner, that your rights may never depend upon the will of any one man or body of men; entrust even the power of altering your Constitution itself, because occasion may arise, when the use even of that power may be absolutely necessary for your own welfare; when, at the same time, it may be impossible for you to act in your original character, with the expedition necessary for your salvation: but reserve to yourselves a concurrent power of altering the Constitution in your own persons, because by the decay to which all the works of man are liable, it is possible that your Legislature may become incompetent to make such alterations as may be necessary. But when the people are constantly represented in the Legislature, I believe they will never find it necessary to recur to their original character, in order to make any alterations, which they may deem expedient, unless they deny the power of making them to their Legislature.

12. From A LETTER FROM JOHN ADAMS TO
JOHN TAYLOR (1814)[1]

You say, sir, that I have gravely counted up several victims "of popular rage, as proofs that democracy is more pernicious than monarchy or aristocracy." This is not my doctrine, Mr. Taylor. My opinion is, and always has been, that absolute power intoxicates alike despots, monarchs, aristocrats, and democrats, and jacobins, and *sans culottes*. I cannot say that democracy has been more pernicious, on the whole, than any of the others. Its atrocities have been more transient; those of the others have been more permanent. The history of all ages shows that the caprice, cruelties, and horrors of democracy have soon disgusted, alarmed, and terrified themselves. They soon cry, "this will not do; we have gone too far! We are all in the wrong! We are none of us safe! We must unite in some clever fellow, who can protect us all,—Caesar, Bonaparte, who you will! Though we distrust, hate, and abhor them all; yet we must submit to one or another of them, stand by him, cry him up to the skies, and swear that he is the greatest, best, and finest man that ever lived!"

It has been my fortune, good or bad, to live in Europe ten years, from 1778 to 1788, in a public character. This destiny, singular in America, forced upon my attention the course of events in France, Holland, Geneva, and Switzerland, among many other nations; and this has irresistibly attracted my thoughts more than has been for my interest. The subject cannot have escaped you. What has been the conduct of the democratic parties in all those nations? How horribly bloody in some! Has it been steady, consistent, uniform, in any? Has it not leaped from democracy to aristocracy, to oligarchy, to military despotism, and back again to monarchy, as often, and as easily, as the birds fly to the lower, the middle, or the

[1] In The Works of John Adams, ed. by Charles Francis Adams, Vol. VI, pp. 447–521, at 477–478, 484–485, 495–496.

upper limbs of a tree, or leap from branch to branch, or hop from spray to spray?

Democracy, nevertheless, must not be disgraced; democracy must not be despised. Democracy must be respected; democracy must be honored; democracy must be cherished; democracy must be an essential, an integral part of the sovereignty, and have a control over the whole government, or moral liberty cannot exist, or any other liberty. I have been always grieved by the gross abuses of this respectable word. One party speak of it as the most amiable, venerable, indeed, as the sole object of its adoration; the other, as the sole object of its scorn, abhorrence, and execration. Neither party, in my opinion, know what they say. Some of them care not what they say, provided they can accomplish their own selfish purposes. These ought not to be forgiven. . . .

You say, I "might have exhibited millions of plebeians sacrificed to the pride, folly, and ambition of monarchy and aristocracy." This is very true. And I might have exhibited as many millions of plebeians sacrificed by the pride, folly, and ambition of their fellow-plebeians and their own, in proportion to the extent and duration of their power. Remember, democracy never lasts long. It soon wastes, exhausts, and murders itself. There never was a democracy yet that did not commit suicide. It is in vain to say that democracy is less vain, less proud, less selfish, less ambitious, or less avaricious than aristocracy or monarchy. It is not true, in fact, and nowhere appears in history. Those passions are the same in all men, under all forms of simple government, and when unchecked, produce the same effects of fraud, violence, and cruelty. When clear prospects are opened before vanity, pride, avarice, or ambition, for their easy gratification, it is hard for the most considerate philosophers and the most conscientious moralists to resist the temptation. Individuals have conquered themselves. Nations and large bodies of men, never. . . .

And here, sir, permit me, by way of digression, to remark another discouragement to honest political literature, and the progress of real political science. If a *well-meant* publication appears, it is instantly searched for an unpopular word, or one that can be made so by misconstruction, misrepresentation, or by any credible and imposing deception. Some ambitious, popular demagogue gives the alarm,—"heresy?" Holy, democratical church has decreed that word to be "heresy!" Down with him! And, if there was no check to their passions, and no balance to their government, they would say, *à la lanterne! à la guillotine! roast him! bake him! boil him! fry him!* The Inquisition in Spain would not celebrate more joyfully an *auto-da-fé*. . . .

13 JOHN C. CALHOUN (1782–1850)

CALHOUN'S doctrine of the "concurrent majority" is a significant and distinctive attempt to devise a constitutional scheme for reconciling majority rule with the protection of minority groups. Calhoun was primarily concerned with protecting the slave-holding South as a coherent group having certain interests distinct from those of the rest of the nation. His theory, that political justice and stability can be secured only by according a defensive veto to each of the principal territorial divisions of a federal union, is essentially similar to other doctrines advocating governmental devices to give a special voice in government to each of the principal economic groups making up a political community. (Compare John Adams, above, pp. 121–123, 130–131, 134–135, 138.)

[See: William S. Carpenter, *The Development of American Political Thought* (1930), pp. 143–152; Vernon L. Parrington, *Main Currents in American Thought*, Vol. II (1927), pp. 69–82; Charles E. Merriam, *American Political Theories* (1903), ch. 7; Christopher Hollis, *The American Heresy* (1930), pp. 82–117.]

From A DISQUISITION ON GOVERNMENT (1848–50)[1]

In order to have a clear and just conception of the nature and object of government, it is indispensable to understand correctly what that constitution or law of our nature is, in which government originates; or, to express it more fully and accurately,—that law, without which government would not, and with which, it must necessarily exist. Without this, it is as impossible to lay any solid foundation for the science of government, as it would be to lay one for that of astronomy, without a like understanding of that constitution or law of the material world, according to which the several bodies composing the solar system mutually act on each other, and by which they are kept in their respective spheres. The first

---

[1] In *The Works of John C. Calhoun*, ed. by Richard K. Crallé, 6 vols. (Charleston, S. C., 1851), Vol. I, pp. 1–9, 12–16, 24–29, 35–36, 55–56.

question, accordingly, to be considered is,—What is that constitution or law of our nature, without which government would not exist, and with which its existence is necessary?

In considering this, I assume, as an incontestable fact, that man is so constituted as to be a social being. His inclinations and wants, physical and moral, irresistibly impel him to associate with his kind; and he has, accordingly, never been found, in any age or country, in any state other than the social. In no other, indeed, could he exist; and in no other,—were it possible for him to exist,—could he attain to a full development of his moral and intellectual faculties, or raise himself, in the scale of being, much above the level of the brute creation.

I next assume, also, as a fact not less incontestable, that, while man is so constituted as to make the social state necessary to his existence and the full development of his faculties, this state itself cannot exist without government. The assumption rests on universal experience. In no age or country has any society or community ever been found, whether enlightened or savage, without government of some description.

Having assumed these, as unquestionable phenomena of our nature, I shall, without further remark, proceed to the investigation of the primary and important question,—What is that constitution of our nature, which, while it impels man to associate with his kind, renders it impossible for society to exist without government?

The answer will be found in the fact, (not less incontestable than either of the others,) that, while man is created for the social state, and is accordingly so formed as to feel what affects others, as well as what affects himself, he is, at the same time, so constituted as to feel more intensely what affects him directly, than what affects him indirectly through others; or, to express it differently, he is so constituted, that his direct or individual affections are stronger than his sympathetic or social feelings. I intentionally avoid the expression, *selfish* feelings, as applicable to the former; because, as commonly used, it implies an unusual excess of the individual over the social feelings, in the person to whom it is applied; and, consequently, something depraved and vicious. My object is, to exclude such inference, and to restrict the inquiry exclusively to facts in their bearings on the subject under consideration, viewed as mere phenomena appertaining to our nature,—constituted as it is; and which are as

unquestionable as is that of gravitation, or any other phenomenon
of the material world.

In asserting that our individual are stronger than our social feelings, it is not intended to deny that there are instances, growing out
of peculiar relations,—as that of a mother and her infant,—or resulting from the force of education and habit over peculiar constitutions, in which the latter have overpowered the former; but these
instances are few, and always regarded as something extraordinary.
The deep impression they make, whenever they occur, is the strongest proof that they are regarded as exceptions to some general and
well understood law of our nature; just as some of the minor powers
of the material world are apparently to gravitation.

I might go farther, and assert this to be a phenomenon, not of
our nature only, but of all animated existence, throughout its entire
range, so far as our knowledge extends. It would, indeed, seem to
be essentially connected with the great law of self-preservation
which pervades all that feels, from man down to the lowest and
most insignificant reptile or insect. In none is it stronger than in
man. His social feelings may, indeed, in a state of safety and
abundance, combined with high intellectual and moral culture,
acquire great expansion and force; but not so great as to overpower
this all-pervading and essential law of animated existence.

But that constitution of our nature which makes us feel more
intensely what affects us directly than what affects us indirectly
through others, necessarily leads to conflict between individuals.
Each, in consequence, has a greater regard for his own safety or
happiness, than for the safety or happiness of others; and, where
these come in opposition, is ready to sacrifice the interests of others
to his own. And hence, the tendency to a universal state of conflict, between individual and individual; accompanied by the connected passions of suspicion, jealousy, anger and revenge,—followed
by insolence, fraud and cruelty;—and, if not prevented by some controlling power, ending in a state of universal discord and confusion,
destructive of the social state and the ends for which it is ordained.
This controlling power, wherever vested, or by whomsoever exercised, is GOVERNMENT.

It follows, then, that man is so constituted, that government is
necessary to the existence of society, and society to his existence,
and the perfection of his faculties. It follows, also, that govern-

ment has its origin in this twofold constitution of his nature; the sympathetic or social feelings constituting the remote,—and the individual or direct, the proximate cause. . . .

But government, although intended to protect and preserve society, has itself a strong tendency to disorder and abuse of its powers, as all experience and almost every page of history testify. The cause is to be found in the same constitution of our nature which makes government indispensable. The powers which it is necessary for government to possess, in order to repress violence and preserve order, cannot execute themselves. They must be administered by men in whom, like others, the individual are stronger than the social feelings. And hence, the powers vested in them to prevent injustice and oppression on the part of others, will, if left unguarded, be by them converted into instruments to oppress the rest of the community. That, by which this is prevented, by whatever name called, is what is meant by CONSTITUTION, in its most comprehensive sense, when applied to GOVERNMENT. . . .

With these remarks, I proceed to the consideration of the important and difficult question: How is this tendency of government to be counteracted? Or, to express it more fully,—How can those who are invested with the powers of government be prevented from employing them, as the means of aggrandizing themselves, instead of using them to protect and preserve society? It cannot be done by instituting a higher power to control the government, and those who administer it. This would be but to change the seat of authority, and to make this higher power, in reality, the government; with the same tendency, on the part of those who might control its powers, to pervert them into instruments of aggrandizement. Nor can it be done by limiting the powers of government, so as to make it too feeble to be made an instrument of abuse; for, passing by the difficulty of so limiting its powers, without creating a power higher than the government itself to enforce the observance of the limitations, it is a sufficient objection that it would, if practicable, defeat the end for which government is ordained, by making it too feeble to protect and preserve society. The powers necessary for this purpose will ever prove sufficient to aggrandize those who control it, at the expense of the rest of the community. . . .

How government, then, must be constructed, in order to counteract, through its organism, this tendency on the part of those who make and execute the laws to oppress those subject to their operation, is the next question which claims attention.

There is but one way in which this can possibly be done; and that is, by such an organism as will furnish the ruled with the means of resisting successfully this tendency on the part of the rulers to oppression and abuse. Power can only be resisted by power,—and tendency by tendency. Those who exercise power and those subject to its exercise,—the rulers and the ruled,—stand in antagonistic relations to each other. The same constitution of our nature which leads rulers to oppress the ruled,—regardless of the object for which government is ordained,—will, with equal strength, lead the ruled to resist, when possessed of the means of making peaceable and effective resistance. Such an organism, then, as will furnish the means by which resistance may be systematically and peaceably made on the part of the ruled, to oppression and abuse of power on the part of the rulers, is the first and indispensable step towards *forming* a constitutional government. And as this can only be effected by or through the right of suffrage,—(the right on the part of the ruled to choose their rulers at proper intervals, and to hold them thereby responsible for their conduct,)—the responsibility of the rulers to the ruled, through the right of suffrage, is the indispensable and primary principle in the *foundation* of a constitutional government. When this right is properly guarded, and the people sufficiently enlightened to understand their own rights and the interests of the community, and duly to appreciate the motives and conduct of those appointed to make and execute the laws, it is all-sufficient to give to those who elect, effective control over those they have elected.

I call the right of suffrage the indispensable and primary principle; for it would be a great and dangerous mistake to suppose, as many do, that it is, of itself, sufficient to form constitutional governments. To this erroneous opinion may be traced one of the causes, why so few attempts to form constitutional governments have succeeded; and why, of the few which have, so small a number have had durable existence. It has led, not only to mistakes in the attempts to form such governments, but to their overthrow, when they have, by some good fortune, been correctly formed. So far from being, of itself, sufficient,—however well guarded it might be, and however enlightened the people,—it would, unaided by other provisions, leave the government as absolute, as it would be in the hands of irresponsible rulers; and with a tendency, at least as strong, towards oppression and abuse of its powers; as I shall next proceed to explain.

The right of suffrage, of itself, can do no more than give complete control to those who elect, over the conduct of those they have elected. In doing this, it accomplishes all it possibly can accomplish. This is its aim,—and when this is attained, its end is fulfilled. It can do no more, however enlightened the people, or however widely extended or well guarded the right may be. The sum total, then, of its effects, when most successful, is, to make those elected, the true and faithful representatives of those who elected them,—instead of irresponsible rulers,—as they would be without it; and thus, by converting it into an agency, and the rulers into agents, to divest government of all claims to sovereignty, and to retain it unimpaired to the community. But it is manifest that the right of suffrage, in making these changes, transfers, in reality, the actual control over the government, from those who make and execute the laws, to the body of the community; and, thereby, places the powers of the government as fully in the mass of the community, as they would be if they, in fact, had assembled, made, and executed the laws themselves, without the intervention of representatives or agents. The more perfectly it does this, the more perfectly it accomplishes its ends; but in doing so, it only changes the seat of authority, without counteracting, in the least, the tendency of the government to oppression and abuse of its powers.

If the whole community had the same interests, so that the interests of each and every portion would be so affected by the action of the government, that the laws which oppressed or impoverished one portion, would necessarily oppress and impoverish all others,— or the reverse,—then the right of suffrage, of itself, would be all-sufficient to counteract the tendency of the government to oppression and abuse of its powers; and, of course, would form, of itself, a perfect constitutional government. The interest of all being the same, by supposition, as far as the action of the government was concerned, all would have like interests as to what laws should be made, and how they should be executed. All strife and struggle would cease as to who should be elected to make and execute them. The only question would be, who was most fit; who the wisest and most capable of understanding the common interest of the whole. This decided, the election would pass off quietly, and without party discord; as no one portion could advance its own peculiar interest without regard to the rest, by electing a favorite candidate.

But such is not the case. On the contrary, nothing is more difficult than to equalize the action of the government, in reference to the various and diversified interests of the community; and nothing more easy than to pervert its powers into instruments to aggrandize and enrich one or more interests by oppressing and impoverishing the others; and this too, under the operation of laws, couched in general terms;—and which, on their face, appear fair and equal. Nor is this the case in some particular communities only. It is so in all; the small and the great,—the poor and the rich,—irrespective of pursuits, productions, or degrees of civilization;—with, however, this, difference, that the more extensive and populous the country, the more diversified the condition and pursuits of its population, and the richer, more luxurious, and dissimilar the people, the more difficult is it to equalize the action of the government,—and the more easy for one portion of the community to pervert its powers to oppress, and plunder the other.

Such being the case, it necessarily results, that the right of suffrage, by placing the control of the government in the community must, from the same constitution of our nature which makes government necessary to preserve society, lead to conflict among its different interests,—each striving to obtain possession of its powers, as the means of protecting itself against the others;—or of advancing its respective interests, regardless of the interests of others. For this purpose, a struggle will take place between the various interests to obtain a majority, in order to control the government. If no one interest be strong enough, of itself, to obtain it, a combination will be formed between those whose interests are most alike; —each conceding something to the others, until a sufficient number is obtained to make a majority. The process may be slow, and much time may be required before a compact, organized majority can be thus formed; but formed it will be in time, even without preconcert or design, by the sure workings of that principle or constitution of our nature in which government itself originates. When once formed, the community will be divided into two great parties, —a major and minor,—between which there will be incessant struggles on the one side to retain, and on the other to obtain the majority,—and, thereby, the control of the government and the advantages it confers. . . .

As, then, the right of suffrage, without some other provision, cannot counteract this tendency of government, the next question for consideration is—What is that other provision? This demands the most serious consideration; for of all the questions embraced in the science of government, it involves a principle, the most important, and the least understood; and when understood, the most difficult of application in practice. It is, indeed, emphatically, that principle which makes the constitution, in its strict and limited sense.

From what has been said, it is manifest, that this provision must be of a character calculated to prevent any one interest, or combination of interests, from using the powers of government to aggrandize itself at the expense of the others. Here lies the evil: and just in proportion as it shall prevent, or fail to prevent it, in the same degree it will effect, or fail to effect the end intended to be accomplished. There is but one certain mode in which this result can be secured; and that is, by the adoption of some restriction or limitation, which shall so effectually prevent any one interest, or combination of interests, from obtaining the exclusive control of the government, as to render hopeless all attempts directed to that end. There is, again, but one mode in which this can be effected; and that is, by taking the sense of each interest or portion of the community, which may be unequally and injuriously affected by the action of the government, separately, through its own majority, or in some other way by which its voice may be fairly expressed; and to require the consent of each interest, either to put or to keep the government in action. This, too, can be accomplished only in one way,—and that is, by such an organism of the government,—and, if necessary for the purpose, of the community also,—as will, by dividing and distributing the powers of government, give to each division or interest, through its appropriate organ, either a concurrent voice in making and executing the laws, or a veto on their execution. It is only by such an organism, that the assent of each can be made necessary to put the government in motion; or the power made effectual to arrest its action, when put in motion;— and it is only by the one or the other that the different interests, orders, classes, or portions, into which the community may be divided, can be protected, and all conflict and struggle between them prevented,—by rendering it impossible to put or to keep it in action, without the concurrent consent of all.

Such an organism as this, combined with the right of suffrage, constitutes, in fact, the elements of constitutional government. The one, by rendering those who make and execute the laws responsible to those on whom they operate, prevents the rulers from oppressing the ruled; and the other, by making it impossible for any one interest or combination of interests or class, or order, or portion of the community, to obtain exclusive control, prevents any one of them from oppressing the other. It is clear, that oppression and abuse of power must come, if at all, from the one or the other quarter. From no other can they come. It follows, that the two, suffrage and proper organism combined, are sufficient to counteract the tendency of government to oppression and abuse of power; and to restrict it to the fulfilment of the great ends for which it is ordained. . . .

It may be readily inferred, from what has been stated, that the effect of organism is neither to supersede nor diminish the importance of the right of suffrage; but to aid and perfect it. The object of the latter is, to collect the sense of the community. The more fully and perfectly it accomplishes this, the more fully and perfectly it fulfils its end. But the most it can do, of itself, is to collect the sense of the greater number; that is, of the stronger interests, or combination of interests; and to assume this to be the sense of the community. It is only when aided by a proper organism, that it can collect the sense of the entire community,—of each and all its interests; of each, through its appropriate organ, and of the whole, through all of them united. This would truly be the sense of the entire community; for whatever diversity each interest might have within itself,—as all would have the same interest in reference to the action of the government, the individuals composing each would be fully and truly represented by its own majority or appropriate organ, regarded in reference to the other interests. In brief, every individual of every interest might trust, with confidence, its majority or appropriate organ, against that of every other interest.

It results, from what has been said, that there are two different modes in which the sense of the community may be taken; one, simply by the right of suffrage, unaided; the other, by the right through a proper organism. Each collects the sense of the majority. But one regards numbers only, and considers the whole community as a unit, having but one common interest throughout; and collects the sense of the greater number of the whole, as that of the community. The other, on the contrary, regards interests as well as numbers;—considering the community as made up of different and conflicting interests, as far as the action of the government is concerned; and takes the sense of each, through its majority or appropriate organ, and the united sense of all, as the sense of the entire community. The former of these I shall call the numerical, or absolute majority; and the latter, the concurrent, or constitutional majority. I call it the constitutional majority, because it is an essential element in every constitutional government,—be its form what it may. So great is the difference, politically speaking, between the two majorities, that they cannot be confounded, without leading to great and fatal errors; and yet the distinction between them has been so entirely overlooked, that when the term *majority* is used in political discussions, it is applied exclusively to designate the numerical,—as if there were no other. Until this distinction is recognized, and better understood, there will continue to be great liability to error in properly constructing constitutional governments, especially of the popular form, and of preserving them when properly constructed. . . .

The necessary consequence of taking the sense of the community by the concurrent majority is, as has been explained, to give to each interest or portion of the community a negative on the others. It is this mutual negative among its various conflicting interests, which invests each with the power of protecting itself;—and places the rights and safety of each, where only they can be securely placed, under its own guardianship. Without this there can be no systematic, peaceful, or effective resistance to the natural tendency of each to come into conflict with the others: and without this there can be no constitution. It is this negative power,—the power of preventing or arresting the action of the government,—be it called by what term it may,—veto, interposition, nullification, check, or balance of power,—which, in fact, forms the constitution. They are all but different names for the negative power. In all its forms, and under all its names, it results from the concurrent majority. Without this there can be no negative; and, without a negative, no constitution. The assertion is true in reference to all constitutional governments, be their forms what they may. It is, indeed, the negative power which makes the constitution,—and the positive which makes the government. The one is the power of acting;—and the other the power of preventing or arresting action. The two, combined, make constitutional governments. . . .

Liberty, indeed, though among the greatest of blessings, is not so great as that of protection; inasmuch, as the end of the former is the progress and improvement of the race,—while that of the latter is its preservation and perpetuation. And hence, when the two come into conflict, liberty must, and ever ought, to yield to protection; as the existence of the race is of greater moment than its improvement.

It follows, from what has been stated, that it is a great and dangerous error to suppose that all people are equally entitled to liberty. It is a reward to be earned, not a blessing to be gratuitously lavished on all alike;—a reward reserved for the intelligent, the patriotic, the virtuous and deserving;—and not a boon to be bestowed on a people too ignorant, degraded and vicious, to be capable either of appreciating or of enjoying it. Nor is it any disparagement to liberty, that such is, and ought to be the case. On the contrary, its greatest praise,—its proudest distinction is, that an all-wise Providence has reserved it, as the noblest and highest reward for the development of our faculties, moral and intellectual. A reward more appropriate than liberty could not be conferred on the deserving;—nor a punishment inflicted on the undeserving more just, than to be subject to lawless and despotic rule. This dispensation seems to be the result of some fixed law;—and every effort to disturb or defeat it, by attempting to elevate a people in the scale of liberty, above the point to which they are entitled to rise, must ever prove abortive, and end in disappointment. The progress of a people rising from a lower to a higher point in the scale of liberty, is necessarily slow;—and by attempting to precipitate, we either retard, or permanently defeat it. . . .

14. HENRY DAVID THOREAU (1817–62)

IN THE middle decades of the nineteenth century some distinguished writers and statesmen took an extreme stand on questions concerning the rights of private individuals to resist or disobey governmental authority. Their attitude was associated in part with their hostility to slavery and their exasperation over what they regarded as the compromising policy of the federal government in dealing with that evil institution. Their views, however, had a broader theoretical basis and reflected prevailing humanitarian, individualistic, ideas associated with the philosophical and ethical creed of transcendentalism.

Thoreau was born in Concord, Massachusetts, and spent most of his life in or near that village, where his father carried on successfully a pencil manufactory in the home, with the aid of all the family. In early youth he began his pursuits as nature lover, naturalist, and moralist: roving in the woods and fields for pleasure as well as to gather specimens for scientific study and to see what nature had to teach about satisfactory ways of living. He went to Harvard, completing the requirements for graduation but declining a diploma. He and a brother conducted a private school in Concord until it was ended after four years by the brother's ill-health. For a while he lived in Ralph Waldo Emerson's home, as handyman and companion, and in the home of Emerson's brother, as a tutor. At Emerson's he got to know other "Transcendentalists," including Bronson Alcott and Margaret Fuller, and he came to share some of their views on self-culture, high thinking, and plain living, their critical attitude towards conventional society, and their desire to demonstrate their views through mild forms of social experimentation. He contributed to the Transcendentalist quarterly, the *Dial*; and there and in other writings he strongly assailed Southern slavery, Northern exploitation of wage labor, and what he regarded generally as the cant, vulgarity, and callousness of American society.

In his late twenties Thoreau built cheaply (aided by a supply of materials from friends and relatives) a house on Walden Pond and for over two years lived in it alone (with food supplied from the Thoreau and Emerson households). His account of his experiences, published several years later (*Walden*, 1854), contains many emphatic and eloquent comments on the moral and spiritual values of living close to nature. In other works (most of them published posthumously) on his trips on the Concord and Merrimack rivers and his rural travels, in Maine, New York, and Canada, he again mixed descriptions of nature with moral, religious, and literary observations.

Thoreau was not a hermit or a philosophical anarchist. Although he did not vote, he ordinarily paid his taxes, worked (at various brief jobs) for his living, and associated and exchanged favors with his neighbors. On some occasions also he warmly praised attempts to right social wrongs by violent group action (e.g., John Brown's attempt at Harper's Ferry). Moreover, he acknowledged that there were certain social needs which only an organized political community could supply. But he had a general dislike for authority and force and disparaged many social conventions. Apart from his genuine belief in the moral and aesthetic values of solitude, he believed that some of the coercive restrictions of society were so destructive of man's moral integrity that a conscientious individual must resist them by following some form of non-cooperation or disobedience. Thus in order to show positively his hostility to a society that protected slavery and was moving into a war to extend slave territory, he refused to pay a tax and for this spent a night in jail. (He was freed next day when a relative paid the tax.) This event was the occasion for his well-known essay on "Resistance to Civil Government," later called "Civil Disobedience."

[See: Ralph Waldo Emerson, "Thoreau" (1863), an enlargement of an address at Thoreau's funeral, in *Lectures and Biographical Sketches* (1884), pp. 421–452; Henry Seidel Canby, *Thoreau* (1939); Vernon L. Parrington, *Main Currents of American Thought*, Vol. II (1927), pp. 400–413; F. O. Matthiessen, *American Renaissance* (1941), pp. 76–99.]

From CIVIL DISOBEDIENCE (1849)[1]

I heartily accept the motto, "That government is best which governs least;" and I should like to see it acted up to more rapidly and systematically. Carried out, it finally amounts to this, which also I believe,—"That government is best which governs not at all;" and when men are prepared for it, that will be the kind of government which they will have. Government is at best but an expedient; but most governments are usually, and all governments are sometimes, inexpedient. The objections which have been brought

[1] In *The Writings of Henry David Thoreau*, 20 vols. (Boston, c. 1906), Vol. IV, pp. 356–387, at 356–361, 367, 369–372, 375–376, 383–387. By courtesy of Houghton Mifflin Company.

against a standing army, and they are many and weighty, and deserve to prevail, may also at last be brought against a standing government. The standing army is only an arm of the standing government. The government itself, which is only the mode which the people have chosen to execute their will, is equally liable to be abused and perverted before the people can act through it. Witness the present Mexican war, the work of comparatively a few individuals using the standing government as their tool; for, in the outset, the people would not have consented to this measure.

This American government,—what is it but a tradition, though a recent one, endeavoring to transmit itself unimpaired to posterity, but each instant losing some of its integrity? It has not the vitality and force of a single living man; for a single man can bend it to his will. It is a sort of wooden gun to the people themselves. But it is not the less necessary for this; for the people must have some complicated machinery or other, and hear its din, to satisfy that idea of government which they have. Governments show thus how successfully men can be imposed on, even impose on themselves, for their own advantage. It is excellent, we must all allow. Yet this government never of itself furthered any enterprise, but by the alacrity with which it got out of its way. *It* does not keep the country free. *It* does not settle the West. *It* does not educate. The character inherent in the American people has done all that has been accomplished; and it would have done somewhat more, if the government had not sometimes got in its way. For government is an expedient by which men would fain succeed in letting one another alone; and, as has been said, when it is most expedient, the governed are most let alone by it. Trade and commerce, if they were not made of india-rubber, would never manage to bounce over the obstacles which legislators are continually putting in their way; and, if one were to judge these men wholly by the effects of their actions and not partly by their intentions, they would deserve to be classed and punished with those mischievous persons who put obstructions on the railroads.

But, to speak practically and as a citizen, unlike those who call themselves no-government men, I ask for, not at once no government, but *at once a better government.* Let every man make known what kind of government would command his respect, and that will be one step toward obtaining it.

After all, the practical reason why, when the power is once in the hands of the people, a majority are permitted, and for a long period continue, to rule is not because they are most likely to be in the right, nor because this seems fairest to the minority, but because they are physically the strongest. But a government in which the majority rule in all cases cannot be based on justice, even as far as men understand it. Can there not be a government in which majorities do not virtually decide right and wrong, but conscience? —in which majorities decide only those questions to which the rule of expediency is applicable? Must the citizen ever for a moment, or in the least degree, resign his conscience to the legislator? Why has every man a conscience, then? I think that we should be men first, and subjects afterward. It is not desirable to cultivate a respect for the law, so much as for the right. The only obligation which I have a right to assume is to do at any time what I think right. It is truly enough said that a corporation has no conscience; but a corporation of conscientious men is a corporation *with* a conscience. Law never made men a whit more just; and, by means of their respect for it, even the well-disposed are daily made the agents of injustice. A common and natural result of an undue respect for law is, that you may see a file of soldiers, colonel, captain, corporal, privates, powder-monkeys, and all, marching in admirable order over hill and dale to the wars, against their wills, ay, against their common sense and consciences, which makes it very steep marching indeed, and produces a palpitation of the heart. They have no doubt that it is a damnable business in which they are concerned; they are all peaceably inclined. Now, what are they? Men at all? or small movable forts and magazines, at the service of some unscrupulous man in power? Visit the Navy-Yard, and behold a marine, such a man as an American government can make, or such as it can make a man with its black arts,—a mere shadow and reminiscence of humanity, a man laid out alive and standing, and already, as one may say, buried under arms with funeral accompaniments, though it may be,—

> Not a drum was heard, not a funeral note,
>   As his corse to the rampart we hurried;
> Not a soldier discharged his farewell shot
>   O'er the grave where our hero we buried.

The mass of men serve the state thus, not as men mainly, but as machines, with their bodies. They are the standing army, and the militia, jailers, constables, *posse comitatus*, etc. In most cases there is no free exercise whatever of the judgment or of the moral sense; but they put themselves on a level with wood and earth and stones; and wooden men can perhaps be manufactured that will serve the purpose as well. Such command no more respect than men of straw or a lump of dirt. They have the same sort of worth only as horses and dogs. Yet such as these even are commonly esteemed good citizens. Others—as most legislators, politicians, lawyers, ministers, and office-holders—serve the state chiefly with their heads; and, as they rarely make any moral distinctions, they are as likely to serve the devil, without *intending* it, as God. A very few—as heroes, patriots, martyrs, reformers in the great sense, and *men*—serve the state with their consciences also, and so necessarily resist it for the most part; and they are commonly treated as enemies by it. . . .

How does it become a man to behave toward this American government to-day? I answer, that he cannot without disgrace be associated with it. I cannot for an instant recognize that political organization as *my* government which is the *slave's* government also.

All men recognize the right of revolution; that is, the right to refuse allegiance to, and to resist, the government, when its tyranny or its inefficiency are great and unendurable. But almost all say that such is not the case now. But such was the case, they think, in the Revolution of '75. If one were to tell me that this was a bad government because it taxed certain foreign commodities brought to its ports, it is most probable that I should not make an ado about it, for I can do without them. All machines have their friction; and possibly this does enough good to counterbalance the evil. At any rate, it is a great evil to make a stir about it. But when the friction comes to have its machine, and oppression and robbery are organized, I say, let us not have such a machine any longer. In other words, when a sixth of the population of a nation which has undertaken to be the refuge of liberty are slaves, and a whole country is unjustly overrun and conquered by a foreign army, and subjected to military law, I think that it is not too soon for honest men to rebel and revolutionize. What makes this duty the more urgent is the fact that the country so overrun is not our own, but ours is the invading army. . . .

Unjust laws exist: shall we be content to obey them, or shall we endeavor to amend them, and obey them until we have succeeded, or shall we transgress them at once? Men generally, under such a government as this, think that they ought to wait until they have persuaded the majority to alter them. They think that, if they should resist, the remedy would be worse than the evil. But it is the fault of the government itself that the remedy *is* worse than the evil. *It* makes it worse. Why is it not more apt to anticipate and provide for reform? Why does it not cherish its wise minority? Why does it cry and resist before it is hurt? Why does it not encourage its citizens to be on the alert to point out its faults, and *do* better than it would have them? Why does it always crucify Christ, and excommunicate Copernicus and Luther, and pronounce Washington and Franklin rebels? . . .

I do not hesitate to say, that those who call themselves Abolitionists should at once effectually withdraw their support, both in person and property, from the government of Massachusetts, and not wait till they constitute a majority of one, before they suffer the right to prevail through them. I think that it is enough if they have God on their side, without waiting for that other one. Moreover, any man more right than his neighbors constitutes a majority of one already.

I meet this American government, or its representative, the State government, directly, and face to face, once a year—no more —in the person of its tax-gatherer; this is the only mode in which a man situated as I am necessarily meets it; and it then says distinctly, Recognize me; and the simplest, the most effectual, and, in the present posture of affairs, the indispensablest mode of treating with it on this head, of expressing your little satisfaction with and love for it, is to deny it then. My civil neighbor, the tax-gatherer, is the very man I have to deal with,—for it is, after all, with men and not with parchment that I quarrel,—and he has voluntarily chosen to be an agent of the government. How shall he ever know well what he is and does as an officer of the government, or as a man, until he is obliged to consider whether he shall treat me, his neighbor, for whom he has respect, as a neighbor and well-disposed man, or as a maniac and disturber of the peace, and see if he can get over this obstruction to his neighborliness without a ruder and more impetuous thought or speech corresponding with his action. I know this well, that if one thousand, if one hundred, if ten men whom I could name,—if then *honest* men only,—ay, if *one* HONEST man, in this State of Massachusetts, *ceasing to hold slaves*, were actually to withdraw from this copartnership, and be locked up in the county jail therefor, it would be the abolition of slavery in America. For it matters not how small the beginning may seem to be: what is once well done is done forever. But we love better to talk about it: that we say is our mission. Reform keeps many scores of newspapers in its service, but not one man. If my esteemed neighbor, the State's ambassador, who will devote his days to the settlement of the question of human rights in the Council Chamber, instead of being threatened with the prisons of Carolina, were to sit down the prisoner of Massachusetts, that State which is so anxious to foist the sin of slavery upon her sister,—though at present she can discover only an act of inhospitality to be the ground of a quarrel with her,—the Legislature would not wholly waive the subject the following winter.

Under a government which imprisons any unjustly, the true place for a just man is also a prison. The proper place to-day, the only place which Massachusetts has provided for her freer and less desponding spirits, is in her prisons, to be put out and locked out of the State by her own act, as they have already put themselves out by their principles. It is there that the fugitive slave, and the Mexican prisoner on parole, and the Indian come to plead the wrongs of his race should find them; on that separate, but more free and honorable, ground, where the State places those who are not *with* her, but *against* her,—the only house in a slave State in which a free man can abide with honor. If any think that their influence would be lost there, and their voices no longer afflict the ear of the State, that they would not be as an enemy within its walls, they do not know by how much truth is stronger than error, nor how much more eloquently and effectively he can combat injustice who has experienced a little in his own person. Cast your whole vote, not a strip of paper merely, but your whole influence. A minority is powerless while it conforms to the majority; it is not even a minority then; but it is irresistible when it clogs by its whole weight. If the alternative is to keep all just men in prison, or give up war and slavery, the State will not hesitate which to choose. If a thousand men were not to pay their tax-bills this year, that would not be a violent and bloody measure, as it would be to pay them, and enable the State to commit violence and shed innocent blood. This is, in fact, the definition of a peaceable revolution, if any such is possible. If the tax-gatherer, or any other public officer, asks me, as one has done, "But what shall I do?" my answer is, "If you really wish to do anything, resign your office." When the subject has refused allegiance, and the officer has resigned his office, then the revolution is accomplished. But even suppose blood should flow. Is there not a sort of blood shed when the conscience is wounded? Through this wound a man's real manhood and immortality flow out, and he bleeds to an everlasting death. I see this blood flowing now. . . .

I have paid no poll-tax for six years. I was put into a jail once on this account, for one night; and, as I stood considering the walls of solid stone, two or three feet thick, the door of wood and iron, a foot thick, and the iron grating which strained the light, I could not help being struck with the foolishness of that institution which treated me as if I were mere flesh and blood and bones, to be locked up. I wondered that it should have concluded at length that this was the best use it could put me to, and had never thought to avail itself of my services in some way. I saw that, if there was a wall of stone between me and my townsmen, there was a still more difficult one to climb or break through before they could get to be as free as I was. I did not for a moment feel confined, and the walls seemed a great waste of stone and mortar. I felt as if I alone of all my townsmen had paid my tax. They plainly did not know how to treat me, but behaved like persons who are underbred. In every threat and in every compliment there was a blunder; for they thought that my chief desire was to stand the other side of that stone wall. I could not but smile to see how industriously they locked the door on my meditations, which followed them out again without let or hindrance, and *they* were really all that was dangerous. As they could not reach me, they had resolved to punish my body; just as boys, if they cannot come at some person against whom they have a spite, will abuse his dog. I saw that the State was half-witted, that it was timid as a lone woman with her silver spoons, and that it did not know its friends from its foes, and I lost all my remaining respect for it, and pitied it.

Thus the State never intentionally confronts a man's sense, intellectual or moral, but only his body, his senses. It is not armed with superior wit or honesty, but with superior physical strength. I was not born to be forced. I will breathe after my own fashion. Let us see who is the strongest. What force has a multitude? They only can force me who obey a higher law than I. They force me to become like themselves. I do not hear of *men* being *forced* to live this way or that by masses of men. What sort of life were that to live? When I meet a government which says to me, "Your money or your life," why should I be in haste to give it my money? It may be in a great strait, and not know what to do: I cannot help that. It must help itself; do as I do. It is not worth the while to snivel about it. I am not responsible for the successful working of the machinery of society. I am not the son of the engineer. I perceive that, when an acorn and a chestnut fall side by side, the one does not remain inert to make way for the other, but both obey their own laws, and spring and grow and flourish as best they can, till one, perchance, overshadows and destroys the other. If a plant cannot live according to its nature, it dies; and so a man. . . .

I know that most men think differently from myself; but those whose lives are by profession devoted to the study of these or kindred subjects content me as little as any. Statesmen and legislators, standing so completely within the institution, never distinctly and nakedly behold it. They speak of moving society, but have no resting-place without it. They may be men of a certain experience and discrimination, and have no doubt invented ingenious and even useful systems, for which we sincerely thank them; but all their wit and usefulness lie within certain not very wide limits. They are wont to forget that the world is not governed by policy and expediency. Webster never goes behind government, and so cannot speak with authority about it. His words are wisdom to those legislators who contemplate no essential reform in the existing government; but for thinkers, and those who legislate for all time, he never once glances at the subject. I know of those whose serene and wise speculations on this theme would soon reveal the limits of his mind's range and hospitality. Yet, compared with the cheap professions of most reformers, and the still cheaper wisdom and eloquence of politicians in general, his are almost the only sensible and valuable words, and we thank Heaven for him. Comparatively, he is always strong, original, and, above all, practical. Still, his quality is not wisdom, but prudence. The lawyer's truth is not Truth, but consistency or a consistent expediency. Truth is always in harmony with herself, and is not concerned chiefly to reveal the justice that may consist with wrong-doing. He well deserves to be called, as he has been called, the Defender of the Constitution. There are really no blows to be given by him but defensive ones. He is not a leader, but a follower. His leaders are the men of '87. "I have never made an effort," he says, "and never propose to make an effort; I have never countenanced an effort, and never mean to countenance an effort, to disturb the arrangement as originally made, by which the various States came into the Union." Still thinking of the sanction which the Constitution gives to slavery, he says, "Because it was a part of the original compact,—let it stand." Notwithstanding his special acuteness and ability, he is unable to take a fact out of its merely political relations, and behold it as it lies absolutely to be disposed of by the intellect,—what, for instance, it behooves a man to do here in America to-day with regard to slavery. . . .

The authority of government, even such as I am willing to submit to,—for I will cheerfully obey those who know and can do better than I, and in many things even those who neither know nor can do so well,—is still an impure one: to be strictly just, it must have the sanction and consent of the governed. It can have no pure right over my person and property but what I concede to it. The progress from an absolute to a limited monarchy, from a limited monarchy to a democracy, is a progress toward a true respect for the individual. Even the Chinese philosopher was wise enough to regard the individual as the basis of the empire. Is a democracy, such as we know it, the last improvement possible in government? Is it not possible to take a step further towards recognizing and organizing the rights of man? There will never be a really free and enlightened State until the State comes to recognize the individual as a higher and independent power, from which all its own power and authority are derived, and treats him accordingly. I please myself with imagining a State at last which can afford to be just to all men, and to treat the individual with respect as a neighbor; which even would not think it inconsistent with its own repose if a few were to live aloof from it, not meddling with it, nor embraced by it, who fulfilled all the duties of neighbors and fellow-men. A State which bore this kind of fruit, and suffered it to drop off as fast as it ripened, would prepare the way for a still more perfect and glorious State, which also I have imagined, but not yet anywhere seen.

15. DANIEL WEBSTER (1782–1852)

THERE were some among the genuine opponents of slavery who strongly condemned all resistance to or non-compliance with the enforcement of laws duly enacted to protect the constitutional rights of slave-owners; and who disparaged all agitation for radical measures against slavery that would tend to disrupt national unity and interfere with the harmonious consideration of more pressing public questions.

Daniel Webster was the most forceful and eloquent Congressional advocate of strong nationalism and constitutionalism in the pre-Civil War debates on the nature of the union. At the beginning of his political career he had shown some signs that he might align himself with the opposite school. In his first term in the House of Representatives he opposed high protective tariffs and recommended limitations on the Bank of the United States. And in opposing the War of 1812 as useless and reckless, he took a constitutional position not essentially different from that of the South Carolina nullificationists against whom he spoke so forcefully in the Senate a decade and a half later. He denounced the 1812 proposal for conscription as arbitrary and despotic and declared that if the proposal should be adopted, "it will be the solemn duty of the State Governments to protect their own authority over their own militia, and to interpose between their citizens and arbitrary power. They are among the objects for which the State Governments exist; and their highest obligations bind them to the preservation of their own rights and the liberties of their people." [1] He soon reversed his position and defended nationalist economic policies and the nationalist constitutional doctrine. He supported high tariffs and national expenditures for internal improvements, and championed the Bank against President Jackson's assaults. His Senate speeches on the nature of the union, in the famous Webster-Hayne debate of 1830 and the later debates with Calhoun, are regarded as containing the most powerful of all statements of the nationalist constitutional doctrine: that a union of the American people came into existence before the States, and that the federal Constitution was framed by representatives of the American people (not by the States) and was, therefore, not a contract between States but the fundamental law of a government which was

---

[1] *Writings and Speeches* (1903), Vol. XIV, p. 68.

supreme, within the range of powers granted it by the Constitution, over the States.

Webster's famous "Seventh of March Speech" (to which he gave the title "The Constitution and the Union") was delivered in support of Henry Clay's "Compromise" measures (of 1850) for the settlement of issues between North and South over the slavery question. It was a carefully elaborated, eloquent plea for the composing of differences over slavery in order to prevent disunion and enable Congress to proceed more effectively in settling problems of the tariff and other economic matters. It was regarded as having done more than any other speech to insure the enactment of Clay's measures and as having thereby delayed the outbreak of the war. It evoked extreme denunciation in the North. Rev. Theodore Parker likened Webster's speech to "the act of Benedict Arnold"; Horace Mann called Webster a "fallen star, Lucifer descending from heaven"; and Emerson, Lowell, Whittier, Thoreau, Channing, Charles Sumner, Mrs. Stowe, Margaret Fuller, and other abolitionists, extreme and moderate, characterized his speech in generally similar terms.[1]

From SPEECH IN THE SENATE ON "THE CONSTITU- TION AND THE UNION" (MARCH 7, 1850) [2]

MR. PRESIDENT, in the excited times in which we live, there is found to exist a state of crimination and recrimination between the North and South. There are lists of grievances produced by each; and those grievances, real or supposed, alienate the minds of one portion of the country from the other, exasperate the feelings, and subdue the sense of fraternal affection, patriotic love, and mutual regard. I shall bestow a little attention, Sir, upon these various grievances existing on the one side and on the other. I begin with complaints of the South. I will not answer, further than I have, the general statements of the honorable Senator from South Carolina, that the North has prospered at the expense of the South in consequence of the manner of administering this government, in the collecting of its revenues, and so forth. These are disputed topics, and I have no inclination to enter into them. But I will allude to other complaints of the South, and especially to one which has in my opinion just foundation; and that is, that there

[1] For further items on Webster, see above, pp. 180–182.
[2] In *The Works of Daniel Webster*, 6 vols. (1st ed., Boston, 1851), Vol. V, pp. 324–367, at 353–354, 355, 357–358. By courtesy of Little, Brown & Company.

has been found at the North, among individuals and among legislators, a disinclination to perform fully their constitutional duties
in regard to the return of persons bound to service who have escaped
into the free States. In that respect, the South, in my judgment, is
right, and the North is wrong. Every member of every Northern
legislature is bound by oath, like every other officer in the country,
to support the Constitution of the United States; and the article of
the Constitution which says to these States that they shall deliver up
fugitives from service is as binding in honor and conscience as any
other article. No man fulfils his duty in any legislature who sets
himself to find excuses, evasions, escapes from this constitutional
obligation. I have always thought that the Constitution addressed
itself to the legislatures of the States or to the States themselves.
It says that those persons escaping to other States "shall be delivered
up," and I confess I have always been of the opinion that it was an
injunction upon the States themselves. When it is said that a
person escaping into another State, and coming therefore within the
jurisdiction of that State, shall be delivered up, it seems to me the
import of the clause is, that the State itself, in obedience to the
Constitution, shall cause him to be delivered up. That is my judgment. I have always entertained that opinion, and I entertain it
now. But when the subject, some years ago, was before the Supreme Court of the United States, the majority of the judges held
that the power to cause fugitives from service to be delivered up
was a power to be exercised under the authority of this government.
I do not know, on the whole, that it may not have been a fortunate
decision. My habit is to respect the result of judicial deliberations
and the solemnity of judicial decisions. . . . And I desire to call
the attention of all sober-minded men at the North, of all conscientious men, of all men who are not carried away by some fanatical idea or some false impression, to their constitutional obligations.
I put it to all the sober and sound minds at the North as a question
of morals and a question of conscience. What right have they, in
their legislative capacity or any other capacity, to endeavor to get
round this Constitution, or to embarrass the free exercise of the
rights secured by the Constitution to the persons whose slaves
escape from them? None at all; none at all. Neither in the forum
of conscience, nor before the face of the Constitution, are they, in
my opinion, justified in such an attempt. Of course it is a matter

for their consideration. They probably, in the excitement of the times, have not stopped to consider of this. They have followed what seemed to be the current of thought and of motives, as the occasion arose, and they have neglected to investigate fully the real question, and to consider their constitutional obligations; which, I am sure, if they did consider, they would fulfil with alacrity. I repeat, therefore, Sir, that here is a well-founded ground of complaint against the North, which ought to be removed, which it is now in the power of the different departments of this government to remove; which calls for the enactment of proper laws authorizing the judicature of this government, in the several States, to do all that is necessary for the recapture of fugitive slaves and for their restoration to those who claim them. Wherever I go, and whenever I speak on the subject, and when I speak here I desire to speak to the whole North, I say that the South has been injured in this respect, and has a right to complain; and the North has been too careless of what I think the Constitution peremptorily and emphatically enjoins upon her as a duty. . . .

Then, Sir, there are the Abolition societies, of which I am unwilling to speak, but in regard to which I have very clear notions and opinions. I do not think them useful. I think their operations for the last twenty years have produced nothing good or valuable. At the same time, I believe thousands of their members to be honest and good men, perfectly well-meaning men. They have excited feelings; they think they must do something for the cause of liberty; and, in their sphere of action, they do not see what else they can do than to contribute to an Abolition press, or an Abolition society, or to pay an Abolition lecturer. I do not mean to impute gross motives even to the leaders of these societies, but I am not blind to the consequences of their proceedings. I cannot but see what mischiefs their interference with the South has produced. And is it not plain to every man? Let any gentleman who entertains doubts on this point recur to the debates in the Virginia House of Delegates in 1832, and he will see with what freedom a proposition made by Mr. Jefferson Randolph for the gradual abolition of slavery was discussed in that body. Every one spoke of slavery as he thought; very ignominious and disparaging names and epithets were applied to it. The debates in the House of Delegates on that occasion, I believe, were all published. They were read by every colored man who

could read, and to those who could not read, those debates were
read by others. At that time Virginia was not unwilling or afraid
to discuss this question, and to let that part of her population know
as much of the discussion as they could learn. That was in 1832.
As has been said by the honorable member from South Carolina,
these Abolition societies commenced their course of action in 1835.
It is said, I do not know how true it may be, that they sent incendiary publications into the slave States; at any rate, they attempted to
arouse, and did arouse, a very strong feeling; in other words, they
created great agitation in the North against Southern slavery.
Well, what was the result? The bonds of the slaves were bound
more firmly than before, their rivets were more strongly fastened.
Public opinion, which in Virginia had begun to be exhibited against
slavery, and was opening out for the discussion of the question,
drew back and shut itself up in its castle. I wish to know whether
any body in Virginia can now talk openly as Mr. Randolph, Governor McDowell, and others talked in 1832, and sent their remarks
to the press? We all know the fact, and we all know the cause; and
every thing that these agitating people have done has been, not to
enlarge, but to restrain, not to set free, but to bind faster, the slave
population of the South. . . .

16. WILLIAM H. SEWARD (1801–72)

SEWARD was born in Orange County, New York, and was graduated from Union College in Schenectady. He was a successful lawyer, as far as he had time to be. He had a long political career, serving as State senator, State governor, United States senator for two terms (1848–60), and secretary of state in the cabinets of Presidents Lincoln and Johnson. He entered politics as an Anti-Mason, became a leader of the Whigs after 1838, joined the Republicans on the slavery question, and was the outstanding leader of that party in the later 1850's. He vigorously opposed the compromises of 1850, joined in denouncing the Dred Scott decision as a political plot, and, in an address at Rochester in 1858, coined the phrase "irrepressible conflict" in characterizing the controversy between North and South. He was a spokesman for the idea of the "manifest destiny" of the United States; as secretary of state he negotiated the purchase of Alaska and recommended the acquisition of Hawaii, the Dominican Republic, and forts of the Danish West Indies. On a few occasions he advocated compromise on the slavery question, partly under the pressures of political opportunism and partly because of a belief in the justice and practicality of a policy of moderation. Generally, however, he was one of the most outspoken among the political antislavery leaders. After the war he advocated moderation in dealing with the South and supported President Johnson in the latter's struggles with the Radical Republicans over reconstruction.

It was in the course of the Senate debate of 1850 that Seward delivered his famous "Eleventh of March Speech," in which he denounced the fugitive-slave bill, predicted that it could not be enforced and that the fall of slavery was inevitable, and called on his colleagues to follow their moral convictions in deciding how to vote on Clay's proposals. His appeal to a "higher law" was taken up enthusiastically by radical anti-slavery agitators as a plea for action in defiance of the Constitution and statutes where these were applied in blocking efforts to get rid of slavery. Neither in Seward's speech nor in later explanations of it did he make clear what forms of practical action he had in mind in his appeal to a law higher than the Constitution.

[See: Frederick Bancroft, *The Life of William H. Seward* (2 vols., 1900).]

From A SPEECH IN THE UNITED STATES SENATE
(MARCH 11, 1850) [1]

We deem the principle of the law for the recapture of fugitives, therefore unjust, unconstitutional, and immoral; and thus, while patriotism withholds its approbation, the consciences of our people condemn it.

You will say that these convictions of ours are disloyal. Grant it for the sake of argument. They are, nevertheless, honest; and the law is to be executed among us, not among you; not by us, but by the Federal authority. Has any Government ever succeeded in changing the moral convictions of its subjects by force? But these convictions imply no disloyalty. We reverence the Constitution, although we perceive this defect, just as we acknowledge the splendor and the power of the sun, although its surface is tarnished with here and there an opaque spot.

Your Constitution and laws convert hospitality to the refugee, from the most degrading oppression on earth, into a crime, but all mankind except you esteem that hospitality a virtue. The right of extradition of a fugitive from justice, is not admitted by the law of nature and of nations, but rests in voluntary compacts. I know of only two compacts found in diplomatic history that admitted EX-TRADITION OF SLAVES. Here is one of them. It is found in a treaty of peace made between Alexander Comnenus and Leontine, Greek Emperors, at Constantinople, and Oleg, King of Russia, in the year 902, and is in these words:

> If a Russian slave take flight, or even if he is carried away by any one under pretence of having been bought, his master shall have the right and power to pursue him, and hunt for and capture him wherever he shall be found; and any person who shall oppose the master in the execution of this right, shall be deemed guilty of violating this treaty, and be punished accordingly.

This was in the year of grace 902, in the period called the "Dark Ages," and the contracting Powers were despotisms. And here is the other:

> No person held to service or labor in one State, under the laws thereof, escaping into another, shall, in consequence of any law or regulation

[1] In *Congressional Globe* (Vol. XXII, pt. i), 31st Cong., 1st Sess., Appendix, pp. 260–269.

therein, be discharged from such service or labor, but shall be delivered up, on claim of the party to whom such service or labor is due.

This is from the Constitution of the United States in 1787, and the parties were the republican States of this Union. The law of nations disavows such compacts; the law of nature, written on the hearts and consciences of freemen, repudiates them. Armed power could not enforce them, because there is no public conscience to sustain them. I know that there are laws of various sorts which regulate the conduct of men. There are constitutions and statutes, codes mercantile and codes civil; but when we are legislating for States, especially when we are founding States, all these laws must be brought to the standard of the laws of God, and must be tried by that standard, and must stand or fall by it. This principle was happily explained by one of the most distinguished political philosophers of England, in these emphatic words:

There is but one law for all—namely, that law which governs all law—the law of our Creator—the law of humanity, justice, equity—the law of nature and of nations. So far as any laws fortify this primeval law, and give it more precision, more energy, more effect, by their declarations, such laws enter into the sanctuary and participate in the sacredness of its character; but the man who quotes as precedents the abuses of tyrants and robbers, pollutes the very fountains of justice, destroys the foundations of all law, and therefore removes the only safeguard against evil men, whether governors or governed—the guard which prevents governors from becoming tyrants, and the governed from becoming rebels. . . .

. . . It is true, indeed, that the national domain is ours; it is true, it was acquired by the valor and with the wealth of the whole nation; but we hold, nevertheless, no arbitrary power over it. We hold no arbitrary authority over anything, whether acquired lawfully, or seized by usurpation. The Constitution regulates our stewardship; the Constitution devotes the domain to union, to justice, to defence, to welfare, and to liberty.

But there is a higher law than the Constitution, which regulates our authority over the domain, and devotes it to the same noble purposes. The territory is a part—no inconsiderable part—of the common heritage of mankind, bestowed upon them by the Creator of the universe. We are his stewards, and must so discharge our trust as to secure, in the highest attainable degree, their happiness. . . .

17. THEODORE PARKER (1810–60)

PARKER was born in Lexington, Massachusetts, son of a farmer and mechanic. He had three or four years of formal schooling, passed the Harvard examinations without attending courses, and, after teaching school for a few years in order to earn the means for further study, entered the Harvard Divinity School, from which he was graduated in his twenty-sixth year. He was an assiduous reader and became a scholarly theologian and linguist. He aligned himself with the Transcendentalists, and he assumed leadership of liberal Congregationalist protests against both the old Calvinist orthodoxy (which held for predestination, man's depravity, and God's wrath) and the new Unitarian orthodoxy (which still doubted God's desire and man's ability to improve man's lot on earth). Parker maintained that vice, poverty, and ignorance were products of society's mistakes rather than of an innate viciousness or incompetence in man, that mankind had moved towards higher and happier forms of civilization, and that "toil and thought" were essential factors in that development. Accordingly he urged that churches and other voluntary societies should take part in movements for improving the lot of the poor. He was an uncompromising opponent of slavery, denounced Webster and the other respectable New England Whigs for their compromises, gave advice to leading antislavery statesmen, and was arrested for assisting in the escape of a fugitive slave; he was promptly released, because his sermons had made him a man of power in his community. He preached and lectured energetically and eloquently for the rights of women and of workingmen, for prison reform, and for organized action to improve the character and competence of the poor. He was prevailingly skeptical of reforms by governmental action, and he was emphatic in urging protest, and, in extreme cases, resistance, where a government imposed unjust commands and restraints.

[See: Theodore Parker, "Some Account of My Ministry" (1852), in the collection of his *Additional Speeches* (Boston, 1855), Vol. II, pp. 295–370; John Weiss, *Life and Correspondence of Theodore Parker* (2 vols., 1864); Vernon L. Parrington, *Main Currents of American Thought*, Vol. II (1927), pp. 414–425; Henry Steele Commager, *Theodore Parker* (1936).]

From "THE LAW OF GOD AND THE STATUTES OF MEN" (1854) [1]

Now see the relation of the individual to the Statutes of men. There is a natural duty to obey every statute which is just. It is so before the thing becomes a statute. The legislator makes a decree; it is a declaration that certain things must be done, or certain other things not done. If the things commanded are just, the statute does not make them just; does not make them any more morally obligatory than they were before. The legislator may make it very uncomfortable for me to disobey his command, when that is wicked; he cannot make it right for me to keep it when wicked. All the moral obligation depends on the justice of the statute, not on its legality; not on its constitutionality; but, the fact that it is a part of the natural Law of God, the natural mode of operation of man. The statute no more makes it a moral duty to love men and not hate them, than the multiplication table makes twice two four: the multiplication table declares this; it does not make it. If a statute announces, "Thou shalt hate thy neighbor, not love him," it does not change the natural moral duty, more than the multiplication table would alter the fact if it should declare that twice two is three. Geometry proves that the three angles of a triangle are equal to two right angles: it does not make the equality between the two.

Now then, as it is a moral duty to obey a just statute because it is just, so it is a moral duty to disobey any statute which is unjust. If the statute squares with the Law of God, if the constitution of Morocco corresponds with the Constitution of the Universe, which God writ in my heart,—then I am to keep the constitution of Morocco; if not, disobey it, as a matter of conscience.

Here in disobedience, there are two degrees. First, there is Passive Disobedience, non-obedience, the doing nothing for the statute; and second, there is Active Disobedience, which is resistance, the doing something, not for the statute, but something against it. Sometimes the moral duty is accomplished by the passive disobedience, doing nothing; sometimes, to accomplish the

[1] "A Sermon Preached . . . in Boston . . . June 18, 1854"; in *Additional Speeches*, 2 vols. (Boston, 1855), Vol. II, pp. 179–212, at 197–205, 208–211. By courtesy of Little, Brown & Company.

moral duty, it is requisite to resist, to do something against the statute. However, we are to resist wrong by right, not wrong by wrong.

There are many statutes which relate mainly to matters of convenience. They are rules of public conduct indeed, but only rules of prudence, not of morals. Such are the statutes declaring that a man shall not vote till twenty-one; that he shall drive his team on the right hand side of the street; that he may take six per cent. per annum as interest, and not sixty; that he may catch Alewives in Taunton River on Fridays, and not on Thursdays or Saturdays. It is necessary that there should be such rules of prudence as these; and while they do not offend the conscience every good man will respect them; it is not immoral to keep them. . . .

When the foremost moral men make a statute in advance of the people, and then attempt to enforce that law against the consent of the majority of the people, it is an effort in the right direction and is educational; then I suppose the best men will try to execute the law, and will appeal to the best motives in the rest of men. But even in such a case, if ever this is attempted, it should always be done with the greatest caution, lest the leader go too fast for his followers, undertaking to drag the nation instead of leading them. You may drag dead oxen, drive living oxen; but a nation is not to be dragged, not to be driven, even in the right direction; it is to be led. A grown father, six feet high, does not walk five miles the hour with his child two years old; if he does, he must drag his boy; if he wants to lead him he must go by slow and careful steps, now and then taking him over the rough places in his arms. That must be done when the lawmaker is very far in advance of the people; he must lead them gently to the right end.

But when a wicked statute is made by the hindmost men in morals, men far in the rear of the average of the people, and urging them in the wrong direction; when the statute offends the conscience of the people, and the rulers undertake by violence to enforce the statute, then it can be only mean men who will desire its execution, and they must appeal to the lowest motives which animate mean men, and will thus debase the people further and further.

The priest makes a creed against the mind of the people, and says, "There is no truth above my creed! Down with your reason!

it asks terrible questions." So the Catholic is always taught by authority. The priest does not aim to convince the reason; not at all! He says to the philosophers, "This is the Doctrine of the Church. It is a true doctrine, and you must believe it, not because it is true,—you have no right to ask questions,—but because the church says so." The tyrant makes a statute, and says, "There is no Law above this." The subject is not to ask, "Is the statute right? does it conform to the Constitution of the Universe, to God's will reflected in my conscience?" He is only to inquire, "Is it a statute-law? what does the judge say? There is no Higher Law."

That is the doctrine which is taught to-day in almost every political newspaper in this country, Whig and Democratic; and in many of the theological newspapers. But the theological newspapers do not teach it as a Principle and all at once; they teach it in detail, as a Measure, telling us that this or that particular statute is to be observed, say conscience what it may. It is assumed that the legislator is not amenable to the rules of natural justice He is only to be checked by the constitution of the land, not the Constitution of the Universe.

See how the principle once worked. Pharaoh made a statute that all of the new-born boys of Hebrew parentage should be killed as soon as they were born. That was the statute; and instructions were given to the nurses, "If it be a son, then ye shall kill him." Did it become the moral duty of Nurse Shiprah and Nurse Puah to drown every new-born Hebrew baby in the River Nile? Was it the moral duty of Amran and Jochebed to allow Moses to be killed? It is only a legitimate application of the principle laid down by "the highest authorities" in America,—what are called the highest, though I reckon them among the lowest. . . .

King Herod ordered all the young children in Bethlehem to be slain. Was it right for the magistrates to execute the order? for the Justices of the Peace to kill the babies? for the fathers and mothers to do nothing against the massacre of those innocents? The person who wrote the account of it seems to have been of rather a different opinion.

King Henry the Eighth of England, ordered that no man should read the English Bible. Reading the Bible in the Kingdom was made a felony,—punishable with death, without benefit of clergy. Was it the duty of Dr. Franklin's humble fathers to refuse to read their Bibles? They did read them, and your fathers and mine also, I trust. King Pharaoh, Darius, Herod, Henry the Eighth, could not make a wrong thing right. If a mechanic puts his wheel on the upper side of the dam, do you suppose the Merrimack is going to run up into New Hampshire to turn his mill? Just as soon as the great God will undo his own moral work to accommodate a foolish and wicked legislator.

Suppose it was not the king, a one-headed legislator, but the majority of the nation, a legislator with many heads, who made the statutes, would that alter the case? Once, when France was democratic, the democracy ordered the butchery of thousands of men and women. Was it a moral duty to massacre the people?

I know very well it is commonly taught that it is the moral duty of the officers of government to execute every statute, and of the people to submit thereto, no matter how wicked the statute may be. This is the doctrine of the Supreme Court of the United States of America, of the Executive of the United States; I know very well it is the doctrine of the majority of the Legislature in both Houses of Congress; it is the doctrine of the churches of Commerce;—God be praised, it is not the doctrine of the churches of Christianity, and there are such in every denomination, in many a town; even in the great centres of commerce there are ministers of many denominations, earnest, faithful men, who declare openly that they will keep God's Law, come what will of man's statute. This is practical piety; the opposite is practical atheism. I have known some speculative atheists. I abhor their doctrines; but the speculative atheists that I have known, all recognize a Law higher than men's passions and calculations; the Law of some Power which makes the Universe and sways it for noble purposes and to a blessed end.

Then comes the doctrine:—While the statute is on the books it must be enforced: it is not only the Right of the legislator to make any constitutional statute he pleases, but it is the moral and religious Duty of the magistrate to enforce the statute; it is the duty of the people to obey. So in Pharaoh's time it was a moral duty to drown the babies in the Nile; in Darius' time to pray to King Darius, and him only; in Herod's time to massacre the children of Bethlehem; in Henry the Eighth's time to cast your Bible to the flames. Iscariot only did a disagreeable duty. . . .

But the notion that every statute must be enforced is historically false. Who enforces the Sunday law in Massachusetts? Every daily newspaper you will read to-morrow morning violates the statutes of Massachusetts to-day. It would not be possible to enforce them. Of all the sixty millions of bank capital in Massachusetts, within twelve months, every dollar has violated the statute against Usury. Nobody enforces these acts. Half the statutes of New England are but sleeping lions to wait for the call of the people; nobody wakes them up every day. Some have been so long fast asleep that they are dead.

When the nation will accept every creed which the priest makes, because it is made for them, then they are tools for the priest, intellectually dead; and they are fit to have Catholic tyrants rule over them in the church. When the nation is willing to accept a statute which violates the nation's conscience, the nation is rotten. If a statute is right, I will ask how I can best obey it. When it is wrong, I will ask how I can best disobey it,—most safely, most effectually, with the least violence. When we make the priest the keeper of our creed, the State the master of our conscience, then it is all over with us. . . .

Religion is the only basis for every thing. It must go everywhere, into the man's shop, into the seamstress' work-room, must steer the sailor's ship. Reverence for the Infinite Mind, and Conscience, and Heart, and Soul, who is Cause and Providence of this world,—that must go up to the highest heights of our speculation, down to the lowest deeps of our practice. Take that away, and there is nothing on which you can depend, even for your money; or for your liberty and life. Without a reverence for the Higher Law of God every thing will be ruled by interest or violence. The Church will collapse into nothing, the State will go down to ruin!

18. ABRAHAM LINCOLN ON SLAVERY

BORN in a log cabin in the backwoods of Kentucky, Lincoln knew little of his ancestry. His mother, who died in his tenth year, appears to have been completely illiterate, and he said that his father "grew up literally without education." Lincoln himself had very little schooling. Looking back in 1860, he said he thought that all his schooling "did not amount to one year" and that whatever education he had was "'picked up"; he "borrowed books . . . and went at it in good earnest." His father was never prosperous and the family moved frequently, residing in Indiana a while, and moving finally to Illinois in Lincoln's twenty-second year. Here Lincoln worked briefly at various jobs—in a mill, in a store (which soon "winked out"), as a surveyor, as postmaster at New Salem, and as a captain in the Black Hawk Indian war, where, he said, he was "in no battle."

Lincoln rapidly made friends in Illinois. He entered politics as a Whig, ran unsuccessfully for the lower house of the State legislature in 1832, was elected two years later and re-elected for three terms, with increasing majorities, and became minority floor leader. He had been using his spare time in reading law and was admitted to the bar in 1836. The following year he moved to Springfield, where he practised successfully in partnership with lawyers of local prominence. In 1846 he was elected to the national House of Representatives. Here he joined in the party attack on the Mexican War, charging that the war had been "unnecessarily and unconstitutionally commenced" by President Polk and that the President had misrepresented the real aims of the war. He was not a candidate for re-election and held no further public office until his inauguration as President of the United States twelve years later. But, along with his extensive legal practice, he continued to play an influential part in political affairs, as party counselor, committeeman, and campaign speaker. He joined the new Republican party and was soon recognized as leading spokesman for the party in Illinois. He ran unsuccessfully for the United States Senate in 1858. In the famous series of debates between Lincoln and Stephen A. Douglass in that campaign, the chief issue was the relative clarity and consistency of the rivals' views on the powers and obligations of Congress in dealing with slavery.

Lincoln's views on the slavery question were reasonably consistent throughout his career. In 1837 he and a fellow member of the Illinois legislature had joined in a protest against certain anti-abolitionist resolutions that had passed both houses of the legislature. They defined their position as follows:

They believe that the institution of slavery is founded on injustice and bad policy, but that the promulgation of abolition doctrines tends rather to increase than abate its evils.

They believe that the Congress of the United States has no power under the Constitution to interfere with the institution of slavery in the different States.

They believe that the Congress of the United States has the power, under the Constitution, to abolish slavery in the District of Columbia, but that the power ought not to be exercised unless at the request of the people of the District.

In Congress, twelve years later, Lincoln introduced resolutions to exclude slavery from the District, provided a majority of its resident citizens should so vote. At various times he advocated a policy of gradual emancipation in the slave States, with compensation to the owners. He urged compliance with the fugitive-slave laws, but stood emphatically for the power of Congress to exclude slavery from the territories. His bitter denunciation of the action of the United States Supreme Court in the Dred Scott case was directed against the Court's delay (for political reasons, according to Lincoln) in announcing its decision, and against its holdings that a free Negro could not become a citizen and that neither Congress nor a territorial government could exclude slavery from the territories. In 1860 he declared that he held to the position he had defined in his statement of 1837, "so far as it goes." His Emancipation Proclamation (January 1, 1863), freeing slaves in the regions under the control of the Confederacy, was issued as a war measure.

Several months before the end of the war, Lincoln made clear the general lines of the moderate policy he would advocate for the restoration of the Southern States after the war. In his Second Inaugural Address (March 4, 1865), in his last public address (April 11), and in his last cabinet meeting (April 14, the day of his assassination), he continued to urge leniency in dealing with the Southern States.

[See: Lincoln's "Short Autobiography Written . . . to use in Preparing a Popular Campaign Biography in the Election of 1860" (June, 1860), in *Complete Works* (ed. by Nicolay and Hay, 1905), Vol. VI, pp. 24–38; Carl Sandburg, *Abraham Lincoln, the Prairie Years* (2 vols., 1926), and *Abraham Lincoln, the War Years* (4 vols., 1939); James G. Randall, in *Dictionary of American Biography*.

[For Lincoln's statements on his views on slavery, see the following passages from his *Complete Works:* Vol. VI, pp. 33–34 (Statement in the Illinois legislature in 1837); Vol. III, pp. 1–15 (Speech Delivered at Springfield, June 16, 1858); Vol. V, pp. 293–328 (Speech at Cooper Union, Feb. 27, 1860); Vol. VIII, pp. 161–164 (Final Emancipation Proclamation, January 1, 1863); Vol. XI, pp. 44–47 (Second Inaugural Address, March 4, 1865); Vol. XI, pp. 84–92 ("Last Public Address," April 11, 1865).]

A LETTER TO H. L. PIERCE AND OTHERS
(APRIL 6, 1859) [1]

Your kind note inviting me to attend a festival in Boston, on the 28th instant, in honor of the birthday of Thomas Jefferson, was duly received. My engagements are such that I cannot attend.

Bearing in mind that about seventy years ago two great political parties were first formed in this country, that Thomas Jefferson was the head of one of them and Boston the headquarters of the other, it is both curious and interesting that those supposed to descend politically from the party opposed to Jefferson should now be celebrating his birthday in their own original seat of empire, while those claiming political descent from him have nearly ceased to breathe his name everywhere.

Remembering, too, that the Jefferson party was formed upon its supposed superior devotion to the personal rights of men, holding the rights of property to be secondary only, and greatly inferior, and assuming that the so-called Democracy of to-day are the Jefferson, and their opponents the anti-Jefferson, party, it will be equally interesting to note how completely the two have changed hands as to the principle upon which they were originally supposed to be divided. The Democracy of to-day hold the liberty of one man to be absolutely nothing, when in conflict with another man's right of property; Republicans, on the contrary, are for both the man and the dollar, but in case of conflict the man before the dollar. . . .

But . . . it is now no child's play to save the principles of Jefferson from total overthrow in this nation. One would state with great confidence that he could convince any sane child that the simpler propositions of Euclid are true; but nevertheless he would fail, utterly, with one who should deny the definitions and axioms.

---

[1] In *Complete Works of Abraham Lincoln*, ed. by John G. Nicolay and John Hay, new and enl. ed. (New York, 1894, 1905), Vol. V, pp. 124–127. By courtesy of D. Appleton-Century Company.

The principles of Jefferson are the definitions and axioms of free society. And yet they are denied and evaded, with no small show of success. One dashingly calls them "glittering generalities." Another bluntly calls them "self-evident lies." And others insidiously argue that they apply to "superior races." These expressions, differing in form, are identical in object and effect—the supplanting the principles of free government, and restoring those of classification, caste, and legitimacy. They would delight a convocation of crowned heads plotting against the people. They are the vanguard, the miners and sappers of returning despotism. We must repulse them, or they will subjugate us. This is a world of compensation; and he who would be no slave must consent to have no slave. Those who deny freedom to others deserve it not for themselves, and, under a just God, cannot long retain it. All honor to Jefferson—to the man, who, in the concrete pressure of a struggle for national independence by a single people, had the coolness, forecast, and capacity to introduce into a merely revolutionary document an abstract truth, applicable to all men and all times, and so to embalm it there that to-day and in all coming days it shall be a rebuke and a stumbling-block to the very harbingers of reappearing tyranny and oppression.

Your obedient servant,
A. LINCOLN

19. CIVIL LIBERTIES IN WARTIME

THE CIVIL WAR

A STATE of war frequently brings on unusual limitations upon freedom of assembly, speech, and publication, and a suspension of some of the customary guarantees of fair trials, before the courts. An inescapable obligation of a government is to keep a country safe from attack or defeat; and the accomplishment of that obligation in time of war may demand a vigor and speed of action not ordinarily required for the discharge of the peacetime duties of governments.

In the Civil War the limitations or suspensions of certain liberties were accomplished by executive rather than legislative action. Early in the war, Congress enacted two measures to strengthen the laws against treason and to provide new penalties for conspiracies in opposition to the activities of the government (Acts of July 31, 1861 and July 17, 1862); but little was done under these measures. The more aggressive steps in pursuit of the war were taken by the President. Even before Congress had recognized the existence of a state of war, Lincoln had, without statutory authority, raised a volunteer army, added to the regular army, paid out unappropriated funds, excluded certain correspondence ·from the mails, and proclaimed a blockade of southern ports. On September 24, 1862, he issued a proclamation (still without statutory authorization) providing that during the "insurrection" all persons discouraging enlistment, resisting the draft, or guilty of any disloyal practice, were subject to martial law and liable to trial by courts-martial or military commissions; and authorizing the suspension of the privilege of the writ of habeas corpus in the arrests of such persons. Thousands of persons were arrested without the opportunity for a hearing on the grounds of arrest and imprisoned without trial before the ordinary courts. Newspapers in New York (the *World* and the *Journal of Commerce*), Louisville, New Orleans, Baltimore, and Philadelphia were suppressed or suspended by military orders.

Several famous controversies emerged from arrests under the suspension of the writ of habeas corpus. An order of a general caused the arrest of one Merryman, a citizen of Maryland, on the charge that he was associated with an organization in avowed hostility to the government of the United States; and he was confined in a military fort. The chief justice of the United States (Taney), acting as a trial judge on circuit duty, issued a writ directing the general to produce the prisoner in court so that the cause of his imprisonment might be judicially examined. The general declined to do this, citing the President's suspension of the privilege of the writ. The chief justice issued an attachment for contempt against the general; the marshall seeking to serve the writ was refused admission to the fort. The chief justice then delivered an opinion, which he laid before the President, holding that only Congress had the power to authorize a suspension of the privilege of the writ of habeas corpus. He stated his view that it was the President's duty to execute the court's judgment and release the prisoner. Lincoln did not reply and Merryman remained in prison.

Vallandigham, a Congressman from Ohio, was arrested under a military order, tried by a military commission, and sentenced to close confinement for the duration of the war, because he had made a speech advocating a negotiated peace and accusing the President of needlessly prolonging a bloody war, and had thereby violated a military order against declarations of sympathy for the enemy. The Supreme Court refused to review this case, on the ground that it had no authority, under the Constitution or the judiciary act, to hear appeals from the proceedings of a military commission. Lincoln commuted Vallandigham's sentence to banishment into Confederate territory. Congress finally passed a law (March 3, 1863) providing that "during the present rebellion, the President . . . whenever, in his judgment, the public safety may require it, is authorized to suspend the privilege of the writ of habeas corpus in any case throughout the United States, or any part thereof." One Milligan, a citizen of Indiana, was arrested, under order of a military officer, and confined in a military prison on charges of conspiracy against the government of the United States, inciting insurrection, etc.; having been engaged, according to the charge, in a plot to release rebel prisoners and unite them with a newly formed expedition against federal forces. He was tried, convicted, and sentenced to death by a military commission. A year after the close of the war the Supreme Court held that Milligan's trial by a military commission was illegal. Associate Justice Davis, speaking for the majority of the court, said that Congress had not authorized and had no power to authorize the trial, even in wartime, of a civilian by court martial, in loyal territory where the civil courts were in full and normal operation.

"The Constitution of the United States," said Justice Davis, "is a law for rulers and people, equally in war and in peace, and covers with the shield of its protection all classes of men, at all times, and under all circumstances. No doctrine, involving more pernicious consequences, was ever invented by the wit of man than that any of its provisions can be suspended during any of the great exigencies of government. Such a doctrine leads directly to anarchy or despotism, but the theory of necessity on which it is based is false; for the government, within the Constitution, has all the powers granted to it which are necessary to preserve its existence; as has been happily proved by the result of the great effort to throw off its just authority."

Milligan was released from prison after the Supreme Court's decision in his favor; he then brought action against the general under whose order he had been arrested and received an award of nominal damages. Most of those who were imprisoned served only short terms of confinement. Hundreds of newspapers abused the Administration without governmental interference. Various abolitionists, political rivals, and despairers of a Unionist victory, assailed Lincoln as a usurper and a despot. Prominent members of his party admonished him that "the authority of Congress must be respected" and that a President should "confine himself to his executive duties."

[See: James G. Randall, Constitutional Problems under Lincoln (1926); Arthur C. Cole, "Lincoln and the American Tradition of Civil Liberty," Journal of Illinois State Historical Society, Vol. XIX (1926–27), pp. 102– 114; John A. Marshall, American Bastille: a History of the Illegal Arrests and Imprisonments during the late Civil War (1869); Ex parte Merryman, Federalist Case No. 9, 487 (1861); Ex parte Vallandigham, 1 Wallace 243 (1863); Ex parte Milligan, 4 Wallace 2 (1866).]

From LETTERS OF LINCOLN (1863–64)

To Erastus Corning and others (June 12, 1863) [1] Your letter of May 19, inclosing the resolutions of a public meeting held at Albany, New York, on the 16th of the same month, was received several days ago.

The resolutions, as I understand them, are resolvable into two propositions—first, the expression of a purpose to sustain the cause of the Union, to secure peace through victory, and to support the administration in every constitutional and lawful measure to suppress the rebellion; and, secondly, a declaration of censure upon the administration for supposed unconstitutional action, such as the

[1] In Complete Works of Abraham Lincoln, ed. by John G. Nicolay and John Hay, new and enl. ed. (New York, 1894, 1905), Vol. VIII, pp. 298–314.

making of military arrests. And from the two propositions a third is deduced, which is that the gentlemen composing the meeting are resolved on doing their part to maintain our common government and country, despite the folly or wickedness, as they may conceive, of any administration. This position is eminently patriotic and as such I thank the meeting, and congratulate the nation for it. My own purpose is the same; so that the meeting and myself have a common object, and can have no difference, except in the choice of means or measures for effecting that object.

And here I ought to close this paper, and would close it, if there were no apprehension that more injurious consequences than any merely personal to myself might follow the censures systematically cast upon me for doing what, in my view of duty, I could not forbear. The resolutions promise to support me in every constitutional and lawful measure to suppress the rebellion; and I have not knowingly employed, nor shall knowingly employ, any other. But the meeting, by their resolutions, assert and argue that certain military arrests and proceedings following them, for which I am ultimately responsible are unconstitutional. I think they are not. The resolutions quote from the Constitution the definition of treason, and also the limiting safeguards and guarantees therein provided for the citizen on trials for treason, and on his being held to answer for capital or otherwise infamous crimes, and in criminal prosecutions his right to a speedy and public trial by an impartial jury. They proceed to resolve "that these safeguards of the rights of the citizen against the pretensions of arbitrary power were intended more especially for his protection in times of civil commotion." . . . I, too, am devotedly for them after civil war and before civil war, and at all times, "except when, in cases of rebellion or invasion, the public safety may require" their suspension. . . . But these provisions of the Constitution have no application to the case we have in hand, because the arrests complained of were not made for treason—that is, not for the treason defined in the Constitution, and upon the conviction of which the punishment is death—nor yet were they made to hold persons to answer for any capital or otherwise infamous crimes; nor were the proceedings following, in any constitutional or legal sense, "criminal prosecutions." The arrests were made on totally different grounds, and the proceedings following accorded with the grounds of the arrests. Let us consider the real

case with which we are dealing, and apply to it the parts of the
Constitution plainly made for such cases.

Prior to my installation here it had been inculcated that any
State had a lawful right to secede from the national Union, and
that it would be expedient to exercise the right whenever the dev-
otees of the doctrine should fail to elect a president to their own
liking. I was elected contrary to their liking; and, accordingly, so
far as it was legally possible, they had taken seven States out of the
Union, had seized many of the United States forts, and had fired
upon the United States flag, all before I was inaugurated, and, of
course, before I had done any official act whatever. The rebellion
thus begun soon ran into the present civil war; and, in certain respects, it began on very unequal terms between the parties. The
insurgents had been preparing for it more than thirty years, while
the government had taken no steps to resist them. The former
had carefully considered all the means which could be turned to
their account. It undoubtedly was a well-pondered reliance with
them that in their own unrestricted effort to destroy Union, Constitution and law, all together, the government would, in great degree, be restrained by the same Constitution and law from arresting their progress. Their sympathizers pervaded all departments of
the government and nearly all communities of the people. From
this material, under cover of "liberty of speech," "liberty of the
press," and "*habeas corpus*," they hoped to keep on foot amongst
us a most efficient corps of spies, informers, suppliers and aiders and
abettors of their cause in a thousand ways. They knew that in
times such as they were inaugurating, by the Constitution itself the
"*habeas corpus*" might be suspended; but they also knew they had
friends who would make a question as to who was to suspend it;
meanwhile their spies and others might remain at large to help on
their cause. Or if, as has happened, the Executive should suspend
the writ without ruinous waste of time, instances of arresting innocent persons might occur, as are always likely to occur in such
cases; and then a clamor could be raised in regard to this, which
might be at least of some service to the insurgent cause. It needed
no very keen perception to discover this part of the enemy's program, so soon as by open hostilities their machinery was fairly put
in motion. Yet, thoroughly imbued with a reverence for the guaranteed rights of individuals, I was slow to adopt the strong measures

which by degrees I have been forced to regard as being within the exceptions of the Constitution, and as indispensable to the public safety. Nothing is better known to history than that courts of justice are utterly incompetent to such cases. Civil courts are organized chiefly for trials of individuals, or, at most, a few individuals acting in concert—and this in quiet times, and on charges of crimes well defined in the law. Even in times of peace bands of horse-thieves and robbers frequently grow too numerous and powerful for the ordinary courts of justice. But what comparison, in numbers, have such bands ever borne to the insurgent sympathizers even in many of the loyal States? Again, a jury too frequently has at least one member more ready to hang the panel than to hang the traitor. And yet again, he who dissuades one man from volunteering, or induces one soldier to desert, weakens the Union cause as much as he who kills a Union soldier in battle. Yet this dissuasion or inducement may be so conducted as to be no defined crime of which any civil court would take cognizance.

Ours is a case of rebellion—so called by the resolutions before me—in fact, a clear, flagrant, gigantic case of rebellion; and the provision of the Constitution that "the privilege of the writ of *habeas corpus* shall not be suspended unless when, in cases of rebellion or invasion, the public safety may require it," is the provision which specially applies to our present case. This provision plainly attests the understanding of those who made the Constitution that ordinary courts of justice are inadequate to "cases of rebellion"—attests their purpose that, in such cases, men may be held in custody whom the courts, acting on ordinary rules, would discharge. *Habeas corpus* does not discharge men who are proved to be guilty of defined crime; and its suspension is allowed by the Constitution on purpose that men may be arrested and held who cannot be proved to be guilty of defined crime, "when, in cases of rebellion or invasion, the public safety may require it."

This is precisely our present case—a case of rebellion wherein the public safety does require the suspension. Indeed, arrests by process of courts and arrests in cases of rebellion do not proceed altogether upon the same basis. The former is directed at the small percentage of ordinary and continuous perpetration of crime, while the latter is directed at sudden and extensive uprisings against the government, which, at most, will succeed or fail in no great length of time. In the latter case arrests are made not so much for what has been done, as for what probably would be done. The latter is more for the preventive and less for the vindictive than the former. In such cases the purposes of men are much more easily understood than in cases of ordinary crime. . . .

By the third resolution the meeting indicate their opinion that military arrests may be constitutional in localities where rebellion actually exists, but that such arrests are unconstitutional in localities where rebellion or insurrection does not actually exist. They insist that such arrests shall not be made "outside of the lines of necessary military occupation and the scenes of insurrection." Inasmuch, however, as the Constitution itself makes no such distinction, I am unable to believe that there is any such constitutional distinction. I concede that the class of arrests complained of can be constitutional only when, in cases of rebellion or invasion, the public safety may require them; and I insist that in such cases they are constitutional wherever the public safety does require them, as well in places to which they may prevent the rebellion extending, as in those where it may be already prevailing; as well where they may restrain mischievous interference with the raising and supplying of armies to suppress the rebellion, as where the rebellion may actually be; as well where they may restrain the enticing men out of the army, as where they would prevent mutiny in the army; equally constitutional at all places where they will conduce to the public safety, as against the dangers of rebellion or invasion. Take the particular case mentioned by the meeting. It is asserted in substance, that Mr. Vallandigham was, by a military commander, seized and tried "for no other reason than words addressed to a public meeting in criticism of the course of the administration, and in condemnation of the military orders of the general." Now, if there be no mistake about this, if this assertion is the truth and the whole truth, if there was no other reason for the arrest, then I concede that the arrest was wrong. But the arrest, as I understand, was made for a very different reason. Mr. Vallandigham avows his hostility to the war on the part of the Union; and his arrest was made because he was laboring, with some effect, to prevent the raising of troops, to encourage desertions from the army, and to leave the rebellion without an adequate military force to suppress it. He was not arrested because he was damaging the political prospects of the administration or the personal interests of the commanding general but because he was damaging the army, upon the existence and vigor of which the life of the nation depends. He was warring upon the military, and this gave the military constitutional jurisdiction to lay hands upon him. If Mr. Vallandigham was not damaging the military power of the country, then his arrest was made on mistake of fact, which I would be glad to correct on reasonably satisfactory evidence. . . .

One of the resolutions expresses the opinion of the meeting that arbitrary arrests will have the effect to divide and distract those who should be united in suppressing the rebellion and I am specifically called on to discharge Mr. Vallandigham. I regard this as, at least, a fair appeal to me on the expediency of exercising a constitutional power which I think exists. In response to such appeal I have to say, it gave me pain when I learned that Mr. Vallandigham had been arrested (that is, I was pained that there should have seemed to be a necessity for arresting him), and that it will afford me great pleasure to discharge him so soon as I can by any means believe the public safety will not suffer by it.

I further say that, as the war progresses, it appears to me, opinion and action, which were in great confusion at first, take shape and fall into more regular channels, so that the necessity for strong dealing with them gradually decreases. I have every reason to desire that it should cease altogether, and far from the least is my regard for the opinions and wishes of those who, like the meeting at Albany, declare their purpose to sustain the government in every constitutional and lawful measure to suppress the rebellion. Still, I must continue to do so much as may seem to be required by the public safety.

A. LINCOLN

To A. G. Hodges (April 4, 1864) [1] You ask me to put in writing the substance of what I verbally said the other day in your presence, to Governor Bramlette and Senator Dixon. It was about as follows:

"I am naturally antislavery. If slavery is not wrong, nothing is wrong. I cannot remember when I did not so think and feel, and yet I have never understood that the presidency conferred upon me

[1] In *ibid.*, Vol. X, pp. 65–68.

an unrestricted right to act officially upon this judgment and feeling. It was in the oath I took that I would, to the best of my ability, preserve, protect, and defend the Constitution of the United States. I could not take the office without taking the oath. Nor was it my view that I might take an oath to get power, and break the oath in using the power. I understood, too, that in ordinary civil administration this oath even forbade me to practically indulge my primary abstract judgment on the moral question of slavery. I had publicly declared this many times and in many ways. And I aver that, to this day, I have done no official act in mere deference to my abstract judgment and feeling on slavery. I did understand, however, that my oath to preserve the Constitution to the best of my ability imposed upon me the duty of preserving, by every indispensable means, that government—that nation, of which that Constitution was the organic law. Was it possible to lose the nation and yet preserve the Constitution? By general law, life and limb must be protected, yet often a limb must be amputated to save a life; but a life is never wisely given to save a limb. I felt that measures otherwise unconstitutional might become lawful by becoming indispensable to the preservation of the Constitution through the preservation of the nation. Right or wrong, I assumed this ground, and now avow it. I could not feel that, to the best of my ability, I had even tried to preserve the Constitution, if, to save slavery or any minor matter, I should permit the wreck of government, country, and Constitution all together. When, early in the war, General Frémont attempted military emancipation, I forbade it, because I did not then think it an indispensable necessity. When, a little later, General Cameron, then Secretary of War, suggested the arming of the blacks, I objected because I did not yet think it an indispensable necessity. When, still later, General Hunter attempted military emancipation, I again forbade it, because I did not yet think the indispensable necessity had come. When in March and May and July, 1862, I made earnest and successive appeals to the border States to favor compensated emancipation, I believed the indispensable necessity for military emancipation and arming the blacks would come unless averted by that measure. They declined the proposition, and I was, in my best judgment, driven to the alternative of either surrendering the Union, and with it the Constitution, or of laying strong hand upon the colored element. I chose the latter. In choosing it, I hoped for greater gain than loss; but of this, I was not entirely confident. More than a year of trial now shows no loss by it in our foreign relations, none in our home popular sentiment, none in our white military force—no loss by it anyhow or anywhere. On the contrary it shows a gain of quite a hundred and thirty thousand soldiers, seamen, and laborers. These are palpable facts, about which, as facts, there can be no caviling. We have the men; and we could not have had them without the measure.

"And now let any Union man who complains of the measure test himself by writing down in one line that he is for subduing the rebellion by force of arms; and in the next, that he is for taking these hundred and thirty thousand men from the Union side, and placing them where they would be but for the measure he condemns. If he cannot face his case so stated, it is only because he cannot face the truth."

I add a word which was not in the verbal conversation. In telling this tale I attempt no compliment to my own sagacity. I claim not to have controlled events, but confess plainly that events have controlled me. Now, at the end of three years' struggle, the nation's condition is not what either party, or any man, devised or expected. God alone can claim it. Whither it is tending seems plain. If God now wills the removal of a great wrong, and wills also that we of the North, as well as you of the South, shall pay fairly for our complicity in that wrong, impartial history will find therein new cause to attest and revere the justice and goodness of God.

Yours truly,

A. LINCOLN

THE WORLD WAR (1914-17)

IN THE World War I Congress took action to restrict the exercise of some of the ordinary civil liberties. An act of June, 1917 (the "Espionage Act") prohibited the willful making of statements intended to obstruct recruiting or enlistment, to interfere with the operation of the military or naval forces, or to cause insubordination or refusal of duty in the armed forces; and authorized the postmaster-general to refuse mailing privileges to any paper or person he believed to be using the mails to violate the act. Another measure, passed in May of the following year (the "Sedition Act"), provided severe penalties for words or acts intended to interfere with the sale of liberty bonds or the production of war necessities, or to incite resistance to the United States, or to aid the enemy; it also punished the use of "disloyal, profane, scurrilous, or abusive language" about our military forces or form of government, Constitution, flag, or uniform, or language intended to bring any of these into "contempt, scorn, contumely, or disrepute." Both acts were sustained by the Supreme Court in so far as any of the provisions were in question in cases arising under the acts. In no case was it necessary for the Court to pass on the validity of the clause of the Sedition Act dealing with abusive or contemptuous language about the constitution or form of government, etc. The Supreme Court unanimously sustained the Espionage Act in a case (the first, under the act, to come before that court) involving a charge of using words intended to obstruct recruitment and enlistment. Speaking for the court, Justice Holmes said (in part):

> We admit that in many places and in ordinary times the defendants in saying all that was said in the circular would have been within their constitutional rights. But the character of every act depends upon the circumstances in which it is done. . . . The most stringent protection of free speech would not protect a man in falsely shouting fire in a theatre and causing a panic. . . . The question in every case is whether the words used are used in such circumstances and are of such a nature as to create a clear and present danger that they will bring about the substantive evils that Congress has a right to prevent. It is a question of proximity and degree. When a nation is at war many things that might be said in time of peace are such a hindrance to its effort that their utterance will not be endured so long as men fight and that no Court could regard them as protected by any constitutional right.[1]

In some other cases sharp differences of opinion appeared among the Supreme Court justices on questions as to when utterances fell within the valid prohibitions of the espionage and sedition acts. Justice Holmes and Brandeis contended (in dissenting opinions) that for a conviction there must be sufficient evidence of an intention to produce the consequences stated in the acts; and that the court should hold to the test laid down in the Schenck case (quoted above), requiring proof of "a clear and present danger" in the circumstances in which the words were uttered. The justices in the majority were content with a showing of a probable knowledge, on the part of the defendant, of the consequences of his words; or with a showing of a "tendency" of the words to

[1] Schenck v. U. S., 249 U. S. 47 (1919).

produce the consequences stated in the acts. Some two thousand proceedings were brought under the two acts; there were nearly a thousand convictions and imprisonments; and agents of the Department of Justice made a number of arbitrary arrests.

In both the Civil War and the first World War, opponents of the war policies called the government of the United States a despotism and a dictatorship. In neither war, however, was there any suppression of the ordinary machinery of legislation or any general censorship of speech or publication. In both wars there was, within Congress, in the press and on public platforms, widespread criticism of the government's aims and methods. In the latter war, moreover, persons accused of violating the war statutes were tried before the regular courts and according to the regular judicial procedure; most of the persons arrested were released on bail while awaiting trial and (if convicted) while awaiting the outcome of appeals to higher courts.

[See Zechariah Chaffee, *Freedom of Speech* (1920); Carl B. Swisher, "Civil Liberties in War Time," *Political Science Quarterly*, Vol. LV (1940), pp. 321–347.]

MAJORITY AND MINORITY OPINIONS IN ABRAMS v. UNITED STATES (1919) [1]

MR. JUSTICE CLARKE delivered the opinion of the court.

On a single indictment, containing four counts, the five plaintiffs in error, hereinafter designated the defendants, were convicted of conspiring to violate provisions of the Espionage Act of Congress (§ 3, Title I, of Act approved June 15, 1917, as amended May 16, 1918, 40 Stat. 553).

Each of the first three counts charged the defendants with conspiring, when the United States was at war with the Imperial Government of Germany, to unlawfully utter, print, write and publish: In the first count, "disloyal, scurrilous and abusive language about the form of Government of the United States;" in the second count, language "intended to bring the form of Government of the United States into contempt, scorn, contumely and disrepute;" and in the third count, language "intended to incite, provoke and encourage resistance to the United States in said war." The charge in the fourth count was that the defendants conspired "when the United

[1] 250 United States Reports 616.

States was at war with the Imperial German Government, . . . un-lawfully and wilfully, by utterance, writing, printing and publica-tion, to urge, incite and advocate curtailment of production of things and products, to wit, ordnance and ammunition, necessary and essential to the prosecution of the war." The offenses were charged in the language of the act of Congress.

It was charged in each count of the indictment that it was part of the conspiracy that the defendants would attempt to accomplish their unlawful purpose by printing, writing and distributing in the City of New York many copies of a leaflet or circular, printed in the English language, and of another printed in the Yiddish lan-guage, copies of which, properly identified, were attached to the in-dictment.

All of the five defendants were born in Russia. They were intelli-gent, had considerable schooling, and at the time they were ar-rested they had lived in the United States terms varying from five to ten years, but none of them had applied for naturalization. Four of them testified as witnesses in their own behalf and of these, three frankly avowed that they were "rebels," "revolutionists," "anarch-ists," that they did not believe in government in any form, and they declared that they had no interest whatever in the Government of the United States. The fourth defendant testified that he was a "socialist" and believed in "a proper kind of government, not capi-talistic," but in his classification the Government of the United States was "capitalistic."

It was admitted on the trial that the defendants had united to print and distribute the described circulars and that five thousand of them had been printed and distributed about the 22d day of August, 1918. The group had a meeting place in New York City, in rooms rented by defendant Abrams, under an assumed name, and there the subject of printing the circulars was discussed about two weeks before the defendants were arrested. The defendant Abrams, although not a printer, on July 27, 1918, purchased the printing out-fit with which the circulars were printed and installed it in a base-ment room where the work was done at night. The circulars were distributed some by throwing them from a window of a building where one of the defendants was employed and others secretly, in New York City.

The defendants pleaded "not guilty," and the case of the Government consisted in showing the facts we have stated, and in introducing in evidence copies of the two printed circulars attached to the indictment, a sheet entitled "Revolutionists Unite for Action," written by the defendant Lipman, and found on him when he was arrested, and another paper, found at the headquarters of the group, and for which Abrams assumed responsibility.

Thus the conspiracy and the doing of the overt acts charged were largely admitted and were fully established.

On the record thus described it is argued, somewhat faintly, that the acts charged against the defendants were not unlawful because within the protection of that freedom of speech and of the press which is guaranteed by the First Amendment to the Constitution of the United States, and that the entire Espionage Act is unconstitutional because in conflict with that Amendment. . . .

The first of the two articles attached to the indictment is conspicuously headed, "The Hypocrisy of the United States and her Allies." After denouncing President Wilson as a hypocrite and a coward because troops were sent into Russia, it proceeds to assail our Government in general, saying:

"His [the President's] shameful, cowardly silence about the intervention in Russia reveals the hypocrisy of the plutocratic gang in Washington and vicinity."

It continues:

"He [the President] is too much of a coward to come out openly and say: 'We capitalistic nations cannot afford to have a proletarian republic in Russia.'"

Among the capitalistic nations Abrams testified the United States was included.

Growing more inflammatory as it proceeds, the circular culminates in:

"The Russian Revolution cries: Workers of the World! Awake! Rise! Put down your enemy and mine!

"Yes! friends, there is only one enemy of the workers of the world and that is CAPITALISM."

This is clearly an appeal to the "workers" of this country to arise and put down by force the Government of the United States which they characterize as their "hypocritical," "cowardly" and "capitalistic" enemy.

It concludes:

"Awake! Awake, you Workers of the World!

"REVOLUTIONISTS."

The second of the articles was printed in the Yiddish language and in the translation is headed, "Workers—Wake up." After referring to "his Majesty, Mr. Wilson, and the rest of the gang; dogs of all colors!", it continues:

"Workers, Russian emigrants, you who had the least belief in the honesty of our Government," which defendants admitted referred to the United States Government, "must now throw away all confidence, must spit in the face the false, hypocritic, military propaganda which has fooled you so relentlessly, calling forth your sympathy, your help, to the prosecution of the war."

The purpose of this obviously was to persuade the persons to whom it was addressed to turn a deaf ear to patriotic appeals in behalf of the Government of the United States, and to cease to render it assistance in the prosecution of the war.

It goes on:

"With the money which you have loaned, or are going to loan them, they will make bullets not only for the Germans, but also for the Workers Soviets of Russia. *Workers in the ammunition factories, you are producing bullets, bayonets, cannon, to murder not only the Germans, but also your dearest, best, who are in Russia and are fighting for freedom.*"

It will not do to say, as is now argued, that the only intent of these defendants was to prevent injury to the Russian cause. Men must be held to have intended, and to be accountable for, the effects which their acts were likely to produce. Even if their primary purpose and intent was to aid the cause of the Russian Revolution, the plan of action which they adopted necessarily involved, before it could be realized, defeat of the war program of the United States, for the obvious effect of this appeal, if it should become effective, as they hoped it might, would be to persuade persons of character such as those whom they regarded themselves as addressing, not to aid government loans and not to work in ammunition factories, where their work would produce "bullets, bayonets, cannon" and other munitions of war, the use of which would cause the "murder" of Germans and Russians.

Again, the spirit becomes more bitter as it proceeds to declare that—

"America and her Allies have betrayed (the Workers). Their robberish aims are clear to all men. The destruction of the Russian Revolution, that is the politics of the march to Russia.

"Workers, our reply to the barbaric intervention has to be a general strike! An open challenge only will let the Government know that not only the Russian Worker fights for freedom, but also here in America lives the spirit of Revolution."

This is not an attempt to bring about a change of administration by candid discussion, for no matter what may have incited the outbreak on the part of the defendant anarchists, the manifest purpose of such a publication was to create an attempt to defeat the war plans of the Government of the United States, by bringing upon the country the paralysis of a general strike, thereby arresting the production of all munitions and other things essential to the conduct of the war.

This purpose is emphasized in the next paragraph, which reads:

"Do not let the Government scare you with their wild punishment in prisons, hanging and shooting. We must not and will not betray the splendid fighters of Russia. *Workers, up to fight.*"

After more of the same kind, the circular concludes:

"Woe unto those who will be in the way of progress. Let solidarity live!"

It is signed, "The Rebels."

That the interpretation we have put upon these articles, circulated in the greatest port of our land, from which great numbers of soldiers were at the time taking ship daily, and in which great quantities of war supplies of every kind were at the time being manufactured for transportation overseas, is not only the fair interpretation of them, but that it is the meaning which their authors consciously intended should be conveyed by them to others is further shown by the additional writings found in the meeting place of the defendant group and on the person of one of them. One of these circulars is headed: "Revolutionists! Unite for Action!"

After denouncing the President as "Our Kaiser" and the hypocrisy of the United States and her Allies, this article concludes:

"Socialists, Anarchists, Industrial Workers of the World, Socialists, Labor party men and other revolutionary organizations *Unite for action* and let us save the Workers' Republic of Russia!

"*Know you lovers of freedom that in order to save the Russian revolution, we must keep the armies of the allied countries busy at home.*"

Thus was again avowed the purpose to throw the country into a state of revolution if possible and to thereby frustrate the military program of the Government.

The remaining article, after denouncing the President for what is characterized as hostility to the Russian revolution, continues:

"We, the toilers of America, who believe in real liberty, shall *pledge ourselves*, in case the United States will participate in that bloody conspiracy against Russia, *to create so great a disturbance that the autocrats of America shall be compelled to keep their armies at home, and not be able to spare any for Russia.*"

It concludes with this definite threat of armed rebellion:

"If they will use arms against the Russian people to enforce their standard of order, *so will we use arms*, and they shall never see the ruin of the Russian Revolution."

These excerpts sufficiently show, that while the immediate occasion for this particular outbreak of lawlessness, on the part of the defendant alien anarchists, may have been resentment caused by our Government sending troops into Russia as a strategic operation against the Germans on the eastern battle front, yet the plain purpose of their propaganda was to excite, at the supreme crisis of the war, disaffection, sedition, riots, and, as they hoped, revolution, in this country for the purpose of embarrassing and if possible defeating the military plans of the Government in Europe. A technical distinction may perhaps be taken between disloyal and abusive language applied to the *form* of our government or language intended to bring the *form* of our government into contempt and disrepute, and language of like character and intended to produce like results directed against the President and Congress, the agencies through which that form of government must function in time of war. But it is not necessary to a decision of this case to consider whether such distinction is vital or merely formal, for the language of these circulars was obviously intended to provoke and to encourage resistance to the United States in the war, as the third count runs, and, the defendants, in terms, plainly urged and advocated a resort to a general strike of workers in ammunition factories for the purpose of curtailing the production of ordnance and munitions necessary and essential to the prosecution of the war as is charged in the fourth count. Thus it is clear not only that some evidence but that much persuasive evidence was before the jury tending to prove that the defendants were guilty as charged in both the third and fourth counts of the indictment and under the long established rule of law hereinbefore stated the judgment of the District Court must be

Affirmed.

MR. JUSTICE HOLMES dissenting. . . .

No argument seems to me necessary to show that these pronunciamentos in no way attack the form of government of the United States, or that they do not support either of the first two counts. What little I have to say about the third count may be postponed until I have considered the fourth. With regard to that it seems too plain to be denied that the suggestion to workers in the ammunition factories that they are producing bullets to murder their dearest, and the further advocacy of a general strike, both in the second leaflet, do urge curtailment of production of things necessary to the prosecution of the war within the meaning of the Act of May 16, 1918, c. 75, 40 Stat. 553, amending § 3 of the earlier Act of 1917. But to make the conduct criminal that statute requires that it should be "with intent by such curtailment to cripple or hinder the United States in the prosecution of the war." It seems to me that no such intent is proved.

I am aware of course that the word intent as vaguely used in ordinary legal discussion means no more than knowledge at the time of the act that the consequences said to be intended will ensue. Even less than that will satisfy the general principle of civil and criminal liability. A man may have to pay damages, may be sent to prison, at common law might be hanged, if at the time of his act he knew facts from which common experience showed that the consequences would follow, whether he individually could foresee them or not. But, when words are used exactly, a deed is not done with intent to produce a consequence unless that consequence is the aim of the deed. It may be obvious, and obvious to the actor, that the consequence will follow, and he may be liable for it even if he regrets it, but he does not do the act with intent to produce it unless the aim to produce it is the proximate motive of the specific act, although there may be some deeper motive behind.

It seems to me that this statute must be taken to use its words in a strict and accurate sense. They would be absurd in any other. A patriot might think that we were wasting money on aeroplanes, or making more cannon of a certain kind than we needed, and might advocate curtailment with success, yet even if it turned out that the curtailment hindered and was thought by other minds to have been obviously likely to hinder the United States in the prosecution of the war, no one would hold such conduct a crime. I admit that my illustration does not answer all that might be said but it is enough to show what I think and to let me pass to a more important aspect of the case. I refer to the First Amendment to the Constitution that Congress shall make no law abridging the freedom of speech.

. . . I do not doubt for a moment that by the same reasoning that would justify punishing persuasion to murder, the United States constitutionally may punish speech that produces or is intended to produce a clear and imminent danger that it will bring about forthwith certain substantive evils that the United States constitutionally may seek to prevent. The power undoubtedly is greater in time of war than in time of peace because war opens dangers that do not exist at other times.

But as against dangers peculiar to war, as against others, the principle of the right to free speech is always the same. It is only the present danger of immediate evil or an intent to bring it about that warrants Congress in setting a limit to the expression of opinion where private rights are not concerned. Congress certainly cannot forbid all effort to change the mind of the country. Now nobody can suppose that the surreptitious publishing of a silly leaflet by an unknown man, without more, would present any immediate danger that its opinions would hinder the success of the government arms or have any appreciable tendency to do so. Publishing those opinions for the very purpose of obstructing however, might indicate a greater danger and at any rate would have the quality of an attempt. So I assume that the second leaflet if published for the purposes alleged in the fourth count might be punishable. But it seems pretty clear to me that nothing less than that would bring these papers within the scope of this law. An actual intent in the sense that I have explained is necessary to constitute an attempt, where a further act of the same individual is required to complete the substantive crime . . .

I do not see how anyone can find the intent required by the statute in any of the defendants' words. The second leaflet is the only one that affords even a foundation for the charge, and there, without invoking the hatred of German militarism expressed in the former one, it is evident from the beginning to the end that the only object of the paper is to help Russia and stop American intervention there against the popular government—not to impede the United States in the war that it was carrying on. To say that two phrases taken literally might import a suggestion of conduct that would have interference with the war as an indirect and probably undesired effect seems to me by no means enough to show an attempt to produce that effect. . . .

In this case sentences of twenty years imprisonment have been imposed for the publishing of two leaflets that I believe the defendants had as much right to publish as the Government has to publish the Constitution of the United States now vainly invoked by them. Even if I am technically wrong and enough can be squeezed from these poor and puny anonymities to turn the color of legal litmus paper; I will add, even if what I think the necessary intent were shown; the most nominal punishment seems to me all that possibly could be inflicted, unless the defendants are to be made to suffer not for what the indictment alleges but for the creed that they avow—a creed that I believe to be the creed of ignorance and immaturity when honestly held, as I see no reason to doubt that it was held here, but which, although made the subject of examination at the trial, no one has a right even to consider in dealing with the charges before the Court.

Persecution for the expression of opinions seems to me perfectly logical. If you have no doubt of your premises or your power and want a certain result with all your heart you naturally express your wishes in law and sweep away all opposition. To allow opposition by speech seems to indicate that you think the speech impotent, as when a man says that he has squared the circle, or that you do not care whole-heartedly for the result, or that you doubt either your power or your premises. But when men have realized that time has upset many fighting faiths, they may come to believe even more than they believe the very foundations of their own conduct that the ultimate good desired is better reached by free trade in ideas—that the best test of truth is the power of the thought to get itself accepted in the competition of the market, and that truth is the only ground upon which their wishes safely can be carried out. That at any rate is the theory of our Constitution. It is an experiment, as all life is an experiment. Every year if not every day we have to wager our salvation upon some prophecy based upon imperfect knowledge. While that experiment is part of our system I think that we should be eternally vigilant against attempts to check the expression of opinions that we loathe and believe to be fraught with death, unless they so imminently threaten immediate interference with the lawful and pressing purposes of the law that an immediate check is required to save the country. I wholly disagree with the argument of the Government that the First Amendment left the common law as to seditious libel in force. History seems to me against the notion. I have conceived that the United States through many years had shown its repentance for the Sedition Act of 1798, by repaying fines that it imposed. Only the emergency that makes it immediately dangerous to leave the correction of evil counsels to time warrants making any exception to the sweeping command, "Congress shall make no law . . . abridging the freedom of speech." Of course I am speaking only of expressions of opinion and exhortations, which were all that were uttered here, but I regret that I cannot put into more impressive words my belief that in their conviction upon this indictment the defendants were deprived of their rights under the Constitution of the United States.

MR. JUSTICE BRANDEIS concurs with the foregoing opinion.

20. RECENT JUDICIAL INTERPRETATION OF CONSTITUTIONAL GUARANTEES OF CIVIL LIBERTY

THE constitutional guarantees of civil liberties in the first ten amendments have been uniformly held by the United States Supreme Court to apply only to the federal government. This was definitely established in 1833 when the Court held (in Barron v. Baltimore, 7 Peters 243, Chief Justice Marshall delivering the opinion) that the provision of the fifth amendment that "no person shall be deprived of life, liberty, or property without due process of law" did not apply to the States and the local units within the States. The fourteenth amendment (adopted in 1868) expressly applied a due process of law clause to the States, and its effect is to impose on the States certain limitations identical with or substantially equivalent to some of the specific guarantees of the first amendments. Thus although the express provision of the sixth amendment guaranteeing to an accused person the right "to have the assistance of counsel for his defense" does not apply to the States, yet a neglect by a State to assure that right is, the courts held, a deprivation of liberty without due process of law. The court has wavered somewhat in its holdings as to the applicability of some of the other limitations of the first amendments. As late as 1922, it held (in Prudential Insurance Company v. Cheek, 259 U. S. 530) that "neither the Fourteenth Amendment nor any other provision of the Constitution . . . imposes upon the states any restriction about 'freedom of speech.'" Three years later the court (in the Gitlow case below) definitely abandoned that position. Accordingly, the States, as well as Congress, are now clearly bound by the federal Constitution not to make any law prohibiting the free exercise of religion or abridging the freedom of speech, the press or peaceable assembly.

In 1902, a few years after the assassination of President McKinley in Buffalo, by a man who called himself an anarchist, the New York legislature enacted a law for the punishment of "criminal anarchy." About two decades later nearly half of the States passed laws against "criminal syndicalism." These later laws (and the active enforcement of laws against anarchism) were induced, in the first instance, by the growth of the Industrial Workers of the World, a labor group that had been organized in 1905 in opposition to the craft unionism and conservative tactics of the American Federation of Labor. The "I.W.W." proclaimed the "destruction of capitalism" as its ultimate aim, rejected collective bargaining, and advocated "direct action," through general strikes and "sabotage," as its chief means of contention. It reached its peak of membership in 1912 and during the next few years carried on somewhat conspicuous activities in various parts of the country. Idaho passed a law against "criminal syndicalism" in 1917, and a few States followed her example during the next year. The more rapid spread of the legislation was hastened by post-war fears of social upheaval, occasioned particularly by the Bolshevik revolution in Russia in 1917 and the formal organization of a Communist party in the United States two years later. By the end of 1919, twenty-one States had passed statutes imposing severe penalties on the advocacy, by speech or publication, of doctrines that recommended or endorsed violence or other unlawful action as methods of agitation for political or economic change. During the next five years, the period of most active enforcement of these measures, there were numerous indictments and convictions, with prison sentences running from one to fourteen years. The State courts uniformly upheld the validity of the statutes, adjudging them not to be violative of either the State constitutional guarantees of freedom of speech and assembly or of State and federal guarantees against a deprivation of liberty without due process of law. Most of the State courts held that mere membership in an organization that had been formed to advocate the doctrines named in the acts was a sufficient basis for conviction. The holdings of the United States Supreme Court on that question are reviewed in the opinion in De Jonge v. Oregon, the second case recorded below.

Differences between the majority and minority opinions in the Gitlow case hinge again (as in the Abrams case above) in part on the distinction between a "bad tendency" and "a clear and present danger" as the proper test for determining whether the words in question are validly restrained by legislation.

MAJORITY AND MINORITY OPINIONS IN
GITLOW v. NEW YORK (1925) [1]

MR. JUSTICE SANFORD delivered the opinion of the Court.

Benjamin Gitlow was indicted in the Supreme Court of New York, with three others, for the statutory crime of criminal anarchy. . . .

[1] 268 United States Reports 652.

The contention here is that the statute, by its terms and as applied in this case, is repugnant to the due process clause of the Fourteenth Amendment. Its material provisions are:

"§ 160. *Criminal anarchy defined.* Criminal anarchy is the doctrine that organized government should be overthrown by force or violence, or by assassination of the executive head or of any of the executive officials of government, or by any unlawful means. The advocacy of such doctrine either by word of mouth or writing is a felony.

"§ 161. *Advocacy of criminal anarchy.* Any person who:

"1. By word of mouth or writing advocates, advises or teaches the duty, necessity or propriety of overthrowing or overturning organized government by force or violence, or by assassination of the executive head or of any of the executive officials of government, or by any unlawful means; or,

"2. Prints, publishes, edits, issues or knowingly circulates, sells, distributes or publicly displays any book, paper, document, or written or printed matter in any form, containing or advocating, advising or teaching the doctrine that organized government should be overthrown by force, violence or any unlawful means . . . ,

"Is guilty of a felony and punishable" by imprisonment or fine, or both.

The indictment was in two counts. The first charged that the defendant had advocated, advised and taught the duty, necessity and propriety of overthrowing and overturning organized government by force, violence and unlawful means, by certain writings therein set forth entitled "The Left Wing Manifesto"; the second that he had printed, published and knowingly circulated and distributed a certain paper called "The Revolutionary Age," containing the writings set forth in the first count advocating, advising and teaching the doctrine that organized government should be overthrown by force, violence and unlawful means.

The following facts were established on the trial by undisputed evidence and admissions: The defendant is a member of the Left Wing Section of the Socialist Party, a dissenting branch or faction of that party formed in opposition to its dominant policy of "moderate Socialism." Membership in both is open to aliens as well as citizens. The Left Wing Section was organized nationally at a conference in New York City in June, 1919, attended by ninety delegates from twenty different States. The conference elected a National Council, of which the defendant was a member, and left to it the adoption of a "Manifesto." This was published in The Revolutionary Age, the official organ of the Left Wing. The defendant was on the board of managers of the paper and was its business manager. He arranged for the printing of the paper and took to the printer the manuscript of the first issue which contained the Left Wing Manifesto, and also a Communist Program and a Program of the Left Wing that had been adopted by the conference. Sixteen thousand copies were printed, which were delivered at the premises in New York City used as the office of the Revolutionary Age and the headquarters of the Left Wing, and occupied by the defendant and other officials. These copies were paid for by the defendant, as business manager of the paper. Employees at this office wrapped and mailed out copies of the paper under the defendant's direction; and copies were sold from this office. It was admitted that the defendant signed a card subscribing to the Manifesto and Program of the Left Wing, which all applicants were required to sign before being admitted to membership; that he went to different parts of the State to speak to branches of the Socialist Party about the principles of the Left Wing and advocated their adoption; and that he was responsible for the Manifesto as it appeared, that "he knew of the publication, in a general way and he knew of its publication afterwards, and is responsible for its circulation."

There was no evidence of any effect resulting from the publication and circulation of the Manifesto.

No witnesses were offered in behalf of the defendant.

Extracts from the Manifesto are set forth in the margin. Coupled with a review of the rise of Socialism, it condemned the dominant "moderate Socialism" for its recognition of the necessity of the democratic parliamentary state; repudiated its policy of introducing Socialism by legislative measures; and advocated, in plain and unequivocal language, the necessity of accomplishing the "Communist Revolution" by a militant and "revolutionary Socialism", based on "the class struggle" and mobilizing the "power of the proletariat in action," through mass industrial revolts developing into mass political strikes and "revolutionary mass action", for the purpose of conquering and destroying the parliamentary state and establishing in its place, through a "revolutionary dictatorship of the proletariat", the system of Communist Socialism. The then recent strikes in Seattle and Winnipeg were cited as instances of a development already verging on revolutionary action and suggestive of proletarian dictatorship, in which the strike-workers were "trying to usurp the functions of municipal government"; and revolutionary Socialism, it was urged, must use these mass industrial revolts to broaden the strike, make it general and militant, and develop it into mass political strikes and revolutionary mass action for the annihilation of the parliamentary state. . . .

The court, among other things, charged the jury, in substance, that they must determine what was the intent, purpose and fair meaning of the Manifesto; that its words must be taken in their ordinary meaning, as they would be understood by people whom it might reach; that a mere statement or analysis of social and economic facts and historical incidents, in the nature of an essay, accompanied by prophecy as to the future course of events, but with no teaching, advice or advocacy of action, would not constitute the advocacy, advice or teaching of a doctrine for the overthrow of government within the meaning of the statute; that a mere statement that unlawful acts might accomplish such a purpose would be insufficient, unless there was a teaching, advising and advocacy of employing such unlawful acts for the purpose of overthrowing government; and that if the jury had a reasonable doubt that the Manifesto did teach, advocate or advise the duty, necessity or propriety of using unlawful means for the overthrowing of organized government, the defendant was entitled to an acquittal. . . .

The precise question presented, and the only question which we can consider under this writ of error, then is, whether the statute, as construed and applied in this case by the state courts, deprived the defendant of his liberty of expression in violation of the due process clause of the Fourteenth Amendment.

The statute does not penalize the utterance or publication of abstract "doctrine" or academic discussion having no quality of incitement to any concrete action. It is not aimed against mere historical or philosophical essays. It does not restrain the advocacy of changes in the form of government by constitutional and lawful means. What it prohibits is language advocating, advising or teaching the overthrow of organized government by unlawful means. These words imply urging to action. Advocacy is defined in the Century Dictionary as: "1. The act of pleading for, supporting, or recommending; active espousal." It is not the abstract "doctrine" of overthrowing organized government by unlawful means which is denounced by the statute, but the advocacy of action for the accomplishment of that purpose. It was so construed and applied by the trial judge, who specifically charged the jury that: "A mere grouping of historical events and a prophetic deduction from them would neither constitute advocacy, advice or teaching of a doctrine for the overthrow of government by force, violence or unlawful means. [And] if it were a mere essay on the subject, as suggested by counsel, based upon deductions from alleged historical events, with no teaching, advice or advocacy of action, it would not constitute a violation of the statute. . . ."

The Manifesto, plainly, is neither the statement of abstract doctrine nor, as suggested by counsel, mere prediction that industrial disturbances and revolutionary mass strikes will result spontaneously in an inevitable process of evolution in the economic system. It advocates and urges in fervent language mass action which shall progressively foment industrial disturbances and through political mass strikes and revolutionary mass action overthrow and destroy organized parliamentary government. It concludes with a call to action in these words: "The proletariat revolution and the Communist reconstruction of society—*the struggle for these*—is now indispensable. . . . The Communist International calls the proletariat of the world to the final struggle!" This is not the expression of philosophical abstraction, the mere prediction of future events; it is the language of direct incitement.

The means advocated for bringing about the destruction of organized parliamentary government, namely, mass industrial revolts usurping the functions of municipal government, political mass strikes directed against the parliamentary state, and revolutionary mass action for its final destruction, necessarily imply the use of force and violence, and in their essential nature are inherently unlawful in a constitutional government of law and order. That the jury were warranted in finding that the Manifesto advocated not merely the abstract doctrine of overthrowing organized government by force, violence and unlawful means, but action to that end, is clear.

For present purposes we may and do assume that freedom of speech and of the press—which are protected by the First Amendment from abridgment by Congress—are among the fundamental personal rights and "liberties" protected by the due process clause of the Fourteenth Amendment from impairment by the States. . . .

It is a fundamental principle, long established, that the freedom of speech and of the press which is secured by the Constitution, does not confer an absolute right to speak or publish, without responsibility, whatever one may choose, or an unrestricted and unbridled license that gives immunity for every possible use of language and prevents the punishment of those who abuse this freedom. . . .

That a State in the exercise of its police power may punish those who abuse this freedom by utterances inimical to the public welfare, tending to corrupt public morals, incite to crime, or disturb the public peace, is not open to question. . . .

And, for yet more imperative reasons, a State may punish utterances endangering the foundations of organized government and threatening its overthrow by unlawful means. These imperil its own existence as a constitutional State. Freedom of speech and press . . . does not protect disturbances to the public peace or the attempt to subvert the government. It does not protect publications or teachings which tend to subvert or imperil the government or to impede or hinder it in the performance of its governmental duties. . . . It does not protect publications prompting the overthrow of government by force; the punishment of those who publish articles which tend to destroy organized society being essential to the security of freedom and the stability of the State. . . . And a State may penalize utterances which openly advocate the overthrow of the representative and constitutional form of government of the United States and the several States, by violence or other unlawful means. . . . In short this freedom does not deprive a State of the primary and essential right of self preservation; which, so long as human governments endure, they cannot be denied. . . .

By enacting the present statute the State has determined, through its legislative body, that utterances advocating the overthrow of organized government by force, violence and unlawful means, are so inimical to the general welfare and involve such danger of substantive evil that they may be penalized in the exercise of its police power. . . . That utterances inciting to the overthrow of organized government by unlawful means, present a sufficient danger of substantive evil to bring their punishment within the range of legislative discretion, is clear. Such utterances, by their very nature, involve danger to the public peace and to the security of the State. They threaten breaches of the peace and ultimate revolution. And the immediate danger is none the less real and substantial, because the effect of a given utterance cannot be accurately foreseen. The State cannot reasonably be required to measure the danger from every such utterance in the nice balance of a jeweler's scale. A single revolutionary spark may kindle a fire that, smouldering for a time, may burst into a sweeping and destructive conflagration. It cannot be said that the State is acting arbitrarily or unreasonably when in the exercise of its judgment as to the measures necessary to protect the public peace and safety, it seeks to extinguish the spark without waiting until it has enkindled the flame or blazed into the conflagration. It cannot reasonably be required to defer the adoption of measures for its own peace and safety until the revolutionary utterances lead to actual disturbances of the public peace or imminent and immediate danger of its own destruction; but it may, in the exercise of its judgment, suppress the threatened danger in its incipiency. . . .

We cannot hold that the present statute is an arbitrary or unreasonable exercise of the police power of the State unwarrantably infringing the freedom of speech or press; and we must and do sustain its constitutionality.

. . . In other words, when the legislative body has determined generally, in the constitutional exercise of its discretion, that utterances of a certain kind involve such danger of substantive evil that they may be punished, the question whether any specific utterance coming within the prohibited class is likely, in and of itself, to bring about the substantive evil, is not open to consideration. . . .

Mr. Justice Holmes, dissenting.

Mr. Justice Brandeis and I are of opinion that this judgment should be reversed. The general principle of free speech, it seems to me, must be taken to be included in the Fourteenth Amendment, in view of the scope that has been given to the word 'liberty' as there used, although perhaps it may be accepted with a somewhat larger latitude of interpretation than is allowed to Congress by the sweeping language that governs or ought to govern the laws of the United States. If I am right, then I think that the criterion sanctioned by the full Court in Schenck v. United States, 249 U.S. 47, 52, applies. "The question in every case is whether the words used are used in such circumstances and are of such a nature as to create a clear and present danger that they will bring about the substantive evils that [the State] has a right to prevent." . . . If what I think the correct test is applied, it is manifest that there was no present danger of an attempt to overthrow the government by force on the part of the admittedly small minority who shared the defendant's views. It is said that this manifesto was more than a theory, that it was an incitement. Every idea is an incitement. It offers itself for belief and if believed it is acted on unless some other belief outweighs it or some failure of energy stifles the movement at its birth. The only difference between the expression of an opinion and an incitement in the narrower sense is the speaker's enthusiasm for the result. Eloquence may set fire to reason. But whatever may be thought of the redundant discourse before us it had no chance of starting a present conflagration. If in the long run the beliefs expressed in proletarian dictatorship are destined to be accepted by the dominant forces of the community, the only meaning of free speech is that they should be given their chance and have their way.

If the publication of this document had been laid as an attempt to induce an uprising against government at once and not at some indefinite time in the future it would have presented a different question. The object would have been one with which the law might deal, subject to the doubt whether there was any danger that the publication could produce any result, or in other words, whether it was not futile and too remote from possible consequences. But the indictment alleges the publication and nothing more.

OPINION OF THE COURT IN
DE JONGE v. OREGON (1937) [1]

Mr. Chief Justice Hughes delivered the opinion of the Court.

Appellant, Dirk De Jonge, was indicted in Multnomah County, Oregon, for violation of the Criminal Syndicalism Law of that

[1] 299 United States Reports 353.

State. The Act . . . defines "criminal syndicalism" as "the doctrine which advocates crime, physical violence, sabotage or any unlawful acts or methods as a means of accomplishing or effecting industrial or political change or revolution." With this preliminary definition the Act proceeds to describe a number of offenses, embracing the teaching of criminal syndicalism, the printing or distribution of books, pamphlets, etc., advocating that doctrine, the organization of a society or assemblage which advocates it, and presiding at or assisting in conducting a meeting of such an organization, society or group. The prohibited acts are made felonies, punishable by imprisonment for not less than one year nor more than ten years, or by a fine of not more than $1,000, or by both.

We are concerned with but one of the described offenses and with the validity of the statute in this particular application. The charge is that appellant assisted in the conduct of a meeting which was called under the auspices of the Communist Party, an organization advocating criminal syndicalism. The defense was that the meeting was public and orderly and was held for a lawful purpose; that while it was held under the auspices of the Communist Party, neither criminal syndicalism nor any unlawful conduct was taught or advocated at the meeting either by appellant or by others. Appellant moved for a direction of acquittal, contending that the statute as applied to him, for merely assisting at a meeting called by the Communist Party at which nothing unlawful was done or advocated, violated the due process clause of the Fourteenth Amendment of the Constitution of the United States.

This contention was overruled. Appellant was found guilty as charged and was sentenced to imprisonment for seven years. The judgment was affirmed by the Supreme Court of the State, which considered the constitutional question and sustained the statute as thus applied. . . . The case comes here on appeal.

The record does not present the evidence adduced at the trial. The parties have substituted a stipulation of facts, which was made and filed after the decision of the Supreme Court of the State and after the Chief Justice of that court had allowed the appeal and had directed transmission here of a certified transcript of the record. We do not approve of that practice, where it does not appear that the stipulation has received the approval of the court, as we think that adherence to our rule as to the preparation of records is important for the protection of the court whose decision is under review as well as of this Court. See Rule 10. But as the question presented in this instance does not turn upon an appreciation of the facts on any disputed point, we turn to the merits.

The stipulation, after setting forth the charging part of the indictment, recites in substance the following: That on July 27, 1934, there was held in Portland, a meeting which had been advertised by handbills issued by the Portland section of the Communist Party; that the number of persons in attendance was variously estimated at from 150 to 300; that some of those present, who were members of the Communist Party, estimated that not to exceed ten to fifteen per cent. of those in attendance were such members; that the meeting was open to the public without charge and no questions were asked of those entering, with respect to their relation to the Communist Party; that the notice of the meeting advertised it as a protest against illegal raids on workers' halls and homes and against the shooting of striking longshoremen by Portland police; that the chairman stated that it was a meeting held by the Communist Party; that the first speaker dwelt on the activities of the Young Communist League; that the defendant De Jonge, the second speaker, was a member of the Communist Party and went to the meeting to speak in its name; that in his talk he protested against conditions in the county jail, the action of city police in relation to the maritime strike then in progress in Portland and numerous other matters; that he discussed the reason for the raids on the Communist headquarters and workers' halls and offices; that he told the workers that these attacks were due to efforts on the part of the steamship companies and stevedoring companies to break the maritime longshoremen's and seamen's strike; that they hoped to break the strike by pitting the longshoremen and seamen against the Communist movement; that there was also testimony to the effect that defendant asked those present to do more work in obtaining members for the Communist Party and requested all to be at the meeting of the party to be held in Portland on the following evening and to bring their friends to show their defiance to local police authority and to assist them in their revolutionary tactics; that there was also testimony that defendant urged the purchase of certain communist literature which was sold at the meeting; that while the meeting was still in progress it was raided by the police;

that the meeting was conducted in an orderly manner; that defendant and several others who were actively conducting the meeting were arrested by the police and that on searching the hall the police found a quantity of communist literature.

The stipulation then set forth various extracts from the literature of the Communist Party to show its advocacy of criminal syndicalism. The stipulation does not disclose any activity by the defendant as a basis for his prosecution other than his participation in the meeting in question. Nor does the stipulation show that the communist literature distributed at the meeting contained any advocacy of criminal syndicalism or of any unlawful conduct. It was admitted by the Attorney General of the State in his argument at the bar of this Court that the literature distributed in the meeting was not of that sort and that the extracts contained in the stipulation were taken from communist literature found elsewhere. Its introduction in evidence was for the purpose of showing that the Communist Party as such did advocate the doctrine of criminal syndicalism, a fact which is not disputed on this appeal.

While the stipulation of facts is but a condensed statement, still much of it is irrelevant in the light of the particular charge of the indictment as construed by the Supreme Court. The indictment charged as follows:

"The said Dirk De Jonge, Don Cluster, Edward R. Denny and Earl Stewart on the 27th day of July, A.D., 1934, in the county of Multnomah and State of Oregon, then and there being, did then and there unlawfully and feloniously preside at, conduct and assist in conducting an assemblage of persons, organization, society and group, to-wit: The Communist Party, a more particular description of which said assemblage of persons, organization, society and group is to this grand jury unknown, which said assemblage of persons, organization, society and group did then and there unlawfully and feloniously teach and advocate the doctrine of criminal syndicalism and sabotage, contrary to the statutes in such cases made and provided, and against the peace and dignity of the State of Oregon."

On the theory that this was a charge that criminal syndicalism and sabotage were advocated at the meeting in question, defendant moved for acquittal insisting that the evidence was insufficient to warrant his conviction. The trial court denied his motion and error in this respect was assigned on appeal. The Supreme Court of the State put aside that contention by ruling that the indictment did not charge that criminal syndicalism or sabotage was advocated at the meeting described in the evidence, either by defendant or by anyone else. The words of the indictment that "said assemblage of persons, organization, society and group did then and there unlawfully and feloniously teach and advocate the doctrine of criminal syndicalism and sabotage," referred not to the meeting in question, or to anything then and there said or done by defendant or others, but to the advocacy of criminal syndicalism and sabotage by the Communist Party in Multnomah County. The ruling of the state court upon this point was precise. The court said (152 Ore. p. 330):

"Turning now to the grounds for a directed verdict set forth in defendant's motion therefor, we note that he asserts and argues that the indictment charges the assemblage at which he spoke with unlawfully and feloniously teaching and advocating the doctrine of criminal syndicalism and sabotage, and elsewhere in the same motion he contends that the indictment charges the defendant with unlawfully and feloniously teaching and advocating said doctrine at said meeting. The indictment does not, however, charge the defendant, nor the assemblage at which he spoke, with teaching or advocating at said meeting at 68 Southwest Alder street, in the city of Portland, the doctrine of criminal syndicalism or sabotage. What the indictment does charge, in plain and concise language, is that the defendant presided at, conducted and assisted in conducting an assemblage of persons, organization, society and group, to-wit, the Communist party, which said assemblage of persons, organization, society and group was unlawfully teaching and advocating in Multnomah county the doctrine of criminal syndicalism and sabotage."

In this view, lack of sufficient evidence as to illegal advocacy or action at the meeting became immaterial. Having limited the charge to defendant's participation in a meeting called by the Communist Party, the state court sustained the conviction upon that basis regardless of what was said or done at the meeting.

We must take the indictment as thus construed. Conviction upon a charge not made would be sheer denial of due process. It thus appears that, while defendant was a member of the Communist Party, he was not indicted for participating in its organization, or for joining it, or for soliciting members or for distributing its literature. He was not charged with teaching or advocating criminal syndicalism or sabotage or any unlawful acts, either at the meeting or elsewhere. He was accordingly deprived of the benefit of evidence as to the orderly and lawful conduct of the meeting and that it was not called or used for the advocacy of criminal syndicalism or sabotage or any unlawful action. His sole offense as charged, and for which he was convicted and sentenced to imprisonment for seven years, was that he had assisted in the conduct of a public meeting, albeit otherwise lawful, which was held under the auspices of the Communist Party.

The broad reach of the statute as thus applied is plain. While defendant was a member of the Communist Party, that membership was not necessary to conviction on such a charge. A like fate might have attended any speaker, although not a member who "assisted in the conduct" of the meeting. However innocuous the object of the meeting, however lawful the subjects and tenor of the addresses, however reasonable and timely the discussion, all those assisting in the conduct of the meeting would be subject to imprisonment as felons if the meeting were held by the Communist Party. This manifest result was brought out sharply at this bar by the concessions which the Attorney General made, and could not avoid, in the light of the decision of the state court. Thus if the Communist Party had called a public meeting in Portland to discuss the tariff, or the foreign policy of the Government, or taxation, or relief, or candidacies for the offices of President, members of Congress, Governor, or state legislators, every speaker who assisted in the conduct of the meeting would be equally guilty with the defendant in this case, upon the charge as here defined and sustained. The list of illustrations might be indefinitely extended to every variety of meetings under the auspices of the Communist Party although held for the discussion of political issues or to adopt protests and pass resolutions of an entirely innocent and proper character.

While the States are entitled to protect themselves from the abuse of the privileges of our institutions through an attempted substitution of force and violence in the place of peaceful political action in order to effect revolutionary changes in government, none of our decisions go to the length of sustaining such a curtailment of the right of free speech and assembly as the Oregon statute demands in its present application.   In *Gitlow v. New York*, 268 U. S. 652, under the New York statute defining criminal anarchy, the defendant was found to be responsible for a "manifesto" advocating the overthrow of the government by violence and unlawful means. *Id.*, pp. 656, 662, 663.   In *Whitney v. California*, 274 U. S. 357, under the California statute relating to criminal syndicalism, the defendant was found guilty of wilfully and deliberately assisting in the forming of an organization for the purpose of carrying on a revolutionary class struggle by criminal methods.   The defendant was convicted of participation in what amounted to a conspiracy to commit serious crimes. . . .

Freedom of speech and of the press are fundamental rights which are safeguarded by the due process clause of the Fourteenth Amendment of the Federal Constitution. . . .   The right of peaceable assembly is a right cognate to those of free speech and free press and is equally fundamental. . . .   The First Amendment of the Federal Constitution expressly guarantees that right against abridgment by Congress.   But explicit mention there does not argue exclusion elsewhere.   For the right is one that cannot be denied without violating those fundamental principles of liberty and justice which lie at the base of all civil and political institutions,—principles which the Fourteenth Amendment embodies in the general terms of its due process clause. . . .

These rights may be abused by using speech or press or assembly in order to incite to violence and crime.   The people through their legislatures may protect themselves against that abuse.   But the legislative intervention can find constitutional justification only by dealing with the abuse.   The rights themselves must not be curtailed.   The greater the importance of safeguarding the community from incitements to the overthrow of our institutions by force and violence, the more imperative is the need to preserve inviolate the constitutional rights of free speech, free press and free assembly in order to maintain the opportunity for free political discussion, to the end that government may be responsive to the will of the people and that changes, if desired, may be obtained by peaceful means. Therein lies the security of the Republic, the very foundation of constitutional government.

It follows from these considerations that, consistently with the Federal Constitution, peaceable assembly for lawful discussion cannot be made a crime. The holding of meetings for peaceable political action cannot be proscribed. Those who assist in the conduct of such meetings cannot be branded as criminals on that score. The question, if the rights of free speech and peaceable assembly are to be preserved, is not as to the auspices under which the meeting is held but as to its purpose; not as to the relations of the speakers, but whether their utterances transcend the bounds of the freedom of speech which the Constitution protects. If the persons assembling have committed crimes elsewhere, if they have formed or are engaged in a conspiracy against the public peace and order, they may be prosecuted for their conspiracy or other violation of valid laws. But it is a different matter when the State, instead of prosecuting them for such offenses, seizes upon mere participation in a peaceable assembly and a lawful public discussion as the basis for a criminal charge.

We are not called upon to review the findings of the state court as to the objectives of the Communist Party. Notwithstanding those objectives, the defendant still enjoyed his personal right of free speech and to take part in a peaceable assembly having a lawful purpose, although called by that Party. The defendant was none the less entitled to discuss the public issues of the day and thus in a lawful manner, without incitement to violence or crime, to seek redress of alleged grievances. That was of the essence of his guaranteed personal liberty.

We hold that the Oregon statute as applied to the particular charge as defined by the state court is repugnant to the due process clause of the Fourteenth Amendment. The judgment of conviction is reversed and the cause is remanded for further proceedings not inconsistent with this opinion.

Reversed.

The unanimous opinion in De Jonge v. Oregon is in line with a strongly prevailing trend in the decisions of the United States Supreme Court since 1935, in cases in which the constitutionality of State and local regulations have been in question, in reference to the due process clause of the fourteenth amendment. The court has rendered a remarkable series of decisions protecting rights of free speech, free association, and fair trials before the courts. In some twenty-five cases during a six-year period, from 1935 through 1940, only two of the decisions were against the claims of civil rights violated: a unanimous decision upholding the right of a State university to expel a student on the ground of his refusal to take compulsory military service; and a decision, with one dissent, upholding the authority of a local school board to exclude children who had refused on religious grounds to salute the United States flag. In four cases the court reversed convictions obtained against Negroes in States where Negroes were persistently excluded from membership on grand and trial juries; in another case it reversed the conviction of a Negro who had been, in effect, denied the right of counsel. In all the other cases the court has sustained the claims of the complaining individuals. In one case the court nullified the barring of Negroes from party primaries and in another the denial of their admission to the law school of a State university. Three times the court reversed convictions where confessions had been obtained through torture. In one case the court nullified a State statute that was aimed, indirectly but obviously, at suppressing newspapers opposed to the political faction then in control of the State. In three cases the court nullified efforts to prevent peaceful picketing. Finally, the court in seven cases reversed convictions for distributing literature or holding meetings without the permission of public authorities or for participating in the public meetings or distributing the literature of radical groups.

III. GOVERNMENT AND PROPERTY RIGHTS

INTRODUCTION

FOR AN adequate perspective of the American tradition concerning the fundamental problems of Democracy and of Political Authority it was essential to begin with a consideration of the first settlers. In the case of the no less fundamental problem of Property Rights, however, this is unnecessary. Indeed until the end of the colonial period there was little significant analysis of the nature of "property" or reflection upon the governmental issues to which differing conceptions of ownership and possession might give rise. Down to the Revolution there was a general consensus of opinion on basic matters touching the nature of property. It was taken for granted, for example, that one of the primary reasons for the very existence of government was the protection and regulation of private ownership; and, likewise, that to base political representation on property qualifications was both a natural and a reasonable procedure.

This, of course, does not imply that the colonies were free from controversy regarding these matters. Political disputes about actual governmental policies were frequent, as to both the representation and the regulation of property. As the colonies expanded and prospered, the economic interests involved became far too numerous and complicated to allow of even the appearance of integrated harmony such as mercantilist ideas of the time presupposed. Certain economic group conflicts in the colonies were inevitable. Tenants were often opposed to landlords, yeomen farmers to plantation owners, shopkeepers and small farmers to bankers and merchants. Their differences ranged over a wide area, covering questions of monetary policy, rules of tenure and inheritance, taxation methods and the perennial issues that have beset all the colonies of the English-speaking world, such as property qualifications for franchise and office and the apportionment of representation among the different kinds of property-holders.

But the groups opposed to one another over such questions were concerned with immediate and concrete issues, not with generalized conceptions of the ideally best or rationally necessary form of eco-

455

nomic organization. Even in the eighteenth-century disputes between the colonies and the mother country, which arose out of Parliament's economic policy under the Georges, the arguments were developed in terms of imperial constitutional law rather than in terms of a body of economic doctrine to be applied in America. Such a body of doctrine, indeed, was entirely lacking on both sides of the Atlantic. In Britain, mercantilism was already in process of rapid disintegration both as a theory and as a policy; and on this side, economic speculation had been merely casual, incidental to other purposes. Benjamin Franklin has sometimes been called America's first economic theorist, and it is true that during more than half a century (from the 1720's to the 1770's) he wrote a number of thoughtful and informed essays on such subjects as wages, money, credit, and the like, often supporting his practical suggestions with more generalized conceptions pertaining to exchange value, the population problem, and the distribution of wealth. But he made no attempt to unify such ideas into a coherent system. On the contrary, his various theoretical observations remain not only dispersed but often mutually contradictory.

Our first significant debates relating to theories of public economic policy, therefore, date from the early days of independence; they are to be found notably in the writings of Jefferson, Hamilton, John Adams and John Taylor. There were several reasons for the appearance now of more generalized considerations of the problem of property. The Revolutionary struggle had upset our foreign trade, disrupted much of our agriculture and industry, and displaced many of the men who had directed economic policy. Debates upon fundamental economic principles were thus almost inevitable. Moreover, the colonists were now charged with the determination of their economic as well as their political destiny. No longer could resentment and blame be directed against a remote and external Parliament. Disharmonies had now to be solved from within; and that meant a search for guiding principles. In politics the idiom had changed from "the rights of Englishmen" to "the rights of man." A similar ideological shift was inevitable in the sphere of economic assumptions.

In the early days of independence old domestic differences between agrarian and mercantile interests broke out anew; the lines between them were now more sharply drawn; and writers were

driven to relate such rivalries to more general ideas concerning the
forms and powers of government on the one hand and the scope
and methods of governmental action in relation to property interests on the other. Both groups associated high moral and practical values with private property, and attacked policies, national or
State, that threatened the rights and interests of owners. But they
had in mind different conceptions of moral and practical ends and
were concerned with different sorts of owners. The issue of fundamental economic ideas was thus clearly set by the force of circumstances and the search for directional principles was begun. Since
then American writers have almost continually defended particular
economic programs in terms of general conceptions of a society
ideally best for America, or in relation to general theories about the
moral and psychological nature of man.

1. THOMAS JEFFERSON

From *NOTES ON THE STATE OF VIRGINIA* (1782)[1]

QUERY XIX. *The present state of manufactures, commerce, interior and exterior trade?*

We never had an interior trade of any importance. Our exterior commerce has suffered very much from the beginning of the present contest. During this time we have manufactured within our families the most necessary articles of cloathing. Those of cotton will bear some comparison with the same kinds of manufacture in Europe; but those of wool, flax and hemp are very coarse, unsightly, and unpleasant: and such is our attachment to agriculture, and such our preference for foreign manufactures, that be it wise or unwise, our people will certainly return as soon as they can, to the raising raw materials, and exchanging them for finer manufactures than they are able to execute themselves.

The political oeconomists of Europe have established it as a principle, that every State should endeavour to manufacture for itself; and this principle, like many others, we transfer to America, without calculating the difference of circumstance which should often produce a difference of result. In Europe the lands are either cultivated, or locked up against the cultivator. Manufacture must therefore be resorted to, of necessity, not of choice, to support the surplus of their people. But we have an immensity of land courting the industry of the husbandman. Is it best then that all our citizens should be employed in its improvement, or that one half should be called off from that to exercise manufactures and handicraft arts for the other? Those who labour in the earth are the chosen people of God, if ever he had a chosen people, whose breasts he has made his peculiar deposit for substantial and genuine virtue. It is the focus in which he keeps alive that sacred fire, which otherwise might escape from the face of the earth. Corruption of morals in the mass of cultivators is a phaenomenon of which no

[1] In *The Writings of Thomas Jefferson*, ed. by Paul Leicester Ford, Vol. III, pp. 268–269.

458

age nor nation has furnished an example. It is the mark set on those, who not looking up to heaven, to their own soil and industry, as does the husbandman, for their subsistence, depend for it on casualties and caprice of customers. Dependance begets subservience and venality, suffocates the germ of virtue, and prepares fit tools for the designs of ambition. This, the natural progress and consequence of the arts, has sometimes perhaps been retarded by accidental circumstances: but, generally speaking the proportion which the aggregate of the other classes of citizens bears in any state to that of its husbandmen, is the proportion of its unsound to its healthy parts, and is a good enough barometer whereby to measure its degree of corruption. While we have land to labour then, let us never wish to see our citizens occupied at a work-bench, or twirling a distaff. Carpenters, masons, smiths, are wanting in husbandry: but, for the general operations of manufacture, let our work-shops remain in Europe. It is better to carry provisions and materials to workmen there, than bring them to the provisions and materials, and with them their manners and principles. The loss by the transportation of commodities across the Atlantic will be made up in happiness and permanence of government. The mobs of great cities add just so much to the support of pure government, as sores do to the strength of the human body. It is the manners and spirit of a people which preserve a republic in vigour. A degeneracy in these is a canker which soon eats to the heart of its laws and constitution.

From A LETTER TO REV. JAMES MADISON (OCTOBER 28, 1785)[1]

Fontainbleau Oct. 28. 1795

Dear Sir,—Seven o'clock, and retired to my fireside, I have determined to enter into conversation with you. This is a village of about 5000 inhabitants. . . . This being the first trip I set out yesterday morning to take a view of the place. . . . As soon as I had got clear of the town I fell in with a poor woman walking at

[1] In *ibid.*, Vol. VII, pp. 33–36. Rev. James Madison, a cousin of President James Madison, was president of William and Mary College; Jefferson carried on an extensive correspondence with him. Jefferson dated this letter 1795 but the contents of the letter make it obvious that he wrote it in 1785.

the same rate with myself & going the same course. . . . She told me she was a day labourer, at 8. sous or 4ᵈ sterling the day; that she had two children to maintain, & to pay a rent of 30 livres for her house, (which would consume the hire of 75 days) that often she could get no emploiment, and of course was without bread. As we had walked together near a mile & she had so far served me as a guide, I gave her, on parting, 24 sous. She burst into tears of a gratitude which I could perceive was unfeigned because she was unable to utter a word. . . . This little attendrissement, with the solitude of my walk led me into a train of reflections on that unequal division of property which occasions the numberless instances of wretchedness which I had observed in this country & is to be observed all over Europe. The property of this country is absolutely concentrated in a very few hands, having revenues of from half a million of guineas a year downwards. These employ the flower of the country as servants, some of them having as many as 200 domestics, not labouring. They employ also a great number of manufacturers, & tradesmen, & lastly the class of labouring husbandmen. But after all there comes the most numerous of all the classes, that is, the poor who cannot find work. I asked myself what could be the reason that so many should be permitted to beg who are willing to work, in a country where there is a very considerable proportion of uncultivated lands? These lands are undisturbed only for the sake of game. It should seem then that it must be because of the enormous wealth of the proprietors which places them above attention to the encrease of their revenues by permitting these lands to be laboured. I am conscious that an equal division of property is impracticable. But the consequences of this enormous inequality producing so much misery to the bulk of mankind, legislators cannot invent too many devices for subdividing property, only taking care to let their subdivisions go hand in hand with the natural affections of the human mind. The descent of property of every kind therefore to all the children, or to all the brothers & sisters, or other relations in equal degree is a politic measure, and a practicable one. Another means of silently lessening the inequality of property is to exempt all from taxation below a certain point, & to tax the higher portions of property in geometrical progression as they rise. Whenever there is in any country, uncultivated lands and unemployed poor, it is clear that the laws of property have been so far extended as to violate natural right. The earth is given as a common stock for man to labour & live on. If for the encouragement of industry we allow it to be appropriated, we must take care that other employment be provided to those excluded from the appropriation. If we do not the fundamental right to labour the earth returns to the unemployed. It is too soon yet in our country to say that every man who cannot find employment but who can find uncultivated land shall be at liberty to cultivate it, paying a moderate rent. But it is not too soon to provide by every possible means that as few as possible shall be without a little portion of land. The small land holders are the most precious part of a state.

From *LETTER TO BENJAMIN AUSTIN (JANUARY 9, 1816)*[1]

You tell me I am quoted by those who wish to continue our dependence on England for manufactures. There was a time when I might have been so quoted with more candor, but within the thirty years which have since elapsed, how are circumstances changed! We were then in peace. Our independent place among nations was acknowledged. A commerce which offered the raw material in exchange for the same material after receiving the last touch of industry, was worthy of welcome to all nations. It was expected that those especially to whom manufacturing industry was important, would cherish the friendship of such customers by every favor, by every inducement, and particularly cultivate their peace by every act of justice and friendship. Under this prospect the question seemed legitimate, whether, with such an immensity of unimproved land, courting the hand of husbandry, the industry of agriculture, or that of manufactures, would add most to the national wealth? And the doubt was entertained on this consideration chiefly, that to the labor of the husbandman a vast addition is made by the spontaneous energies of the earth on which it is employed: for one grain of wheat committed to the earth, she renders twenty, thirty, and even fifty fold, whereas to the labor of the manufacturer nothing is added. Pounds of flax, in his hands, yield, on the contrary, but pennyweights of lace. This exchange, too, laborious as it might

[1] In *The Writings of Thomas Jefferson*, ed. by Paul Leicester Ford, Vol. X, pp. 7-11, at 8-10.

seem, what a field did it promise for the occupations of the ocean; what a nursery for that class of citizens who were to exercise and maintain our equal rights on that element? This was the state of things in 1785, when the "Notes on Virginia" were first printed; when, the ocean being open to all nations, and their common right in it acknowledged and exercised under regulations sanctioned by the assent and usage of all, it was thought that the doubt might claim some consideration. But who in 1785 could foresee the rapid depravity which was to render the close of that century the disgrace of the history of man? Who could have imagined that the two most distinguished in the rank of nations, for science and civilization, would have suddenly descended from that honorable eminence, and setting at defiance all those moral laws established by the Author of nature between nation and nation, as between man and man, would cover earth and sea with robberies and piracies, merely because strong enough to do it with temporal impunity; and that under this disbandment of nations from social order, we should have been despoiled of a thousand ships, and have thousands of our citizens reduced to Algerine slavery. . . . Thus were we completely excluded from the ocean. Compare this state of things with that of '85, and say whether an opinion founded in the circumstances of that day can be fairly applied to those of the present. We have experienced what we did not then believe, that there exists both profligacy and power enough to exclude us from the field of interchange with other nations: that to be independent for the comforts of life we must fabricate them ourselves. We must now place the manufacturer by the side of the agriculturist. The former question is suppressed, or rather assumes a new form. Shall we make our own comforts, or go without them, at the will of a foreign nation? He, therefore, who is now against domestic manufacture, must be for reducing us either to dependence on that foreign nation, or to be clothed in skins, and to live like wild beasts in dens and caverns. I am not one of these; experience has taught me that manufactures are now as necessary to our independence as to our comfort; and if those who quote me as of a different opinion, will keep pace with me in purchasing nothing foreign where an equivalent of domestic fabric can be obtained, without regard to difference of price, it will not be our fault if we do not soon have a supply at home equal to our demand, and wrest that weapon of distress from the hand which has wielded it. If it shall be proposed to go beyond our own supply, the question of '85 will then recur, will our *surplus* labor be then most beneficially employed in the culture of the earth, or in the fabrications of art? We have time yet for consideration, before that question will press upon us; and the maxim to be applied will depend on the circumstances which shall then exist; for in so complicated a science as political economy, no one axiom can be laid down as wise and expedient for all times and circumstances, and for their contraries. . . .

2. JOHN ADAMS

From A DEFENCE OF THE CONSTITUTIONS OF GOVERNMENT OF THE UNITED STATES OF AMERICA
(1787–88)[1]

Property is surely a right of mankind as really as liberty. Perhaps, at first, prejudice, habit, shame or fear, principle or religion, would restrain the poor from attacking the rich, and the idle from usurping on the industrious; but the time would not be long before courage and enterprise would come, and pretexts be invented by degrees, to countenance the majority in dividing all the property among them, or at least, in sharing it equally with its present possessors. Debts would be abolished first; taxes laid heavy on the rich, and not at all on the others; and at last a downright equal division of every thing be demanded, and voted. What would be the consequence of this? The idle, the vicious, the intemperate, would rush into the utmost extravagance of debauchery, sell and spend all their share, and then demand a new division of those who purchased from them. The moment the idea is admitted into society, that property is not as sacred as the laws of God, and that there is not a force of law and public justice to protect it, anarchy and tyranny commence. . . .

From A LETTER TO HENRY MARCHANT
(AUGUST 18, 1789)[2]

I have received your kind and obliging letter of the 16th of July, and am sorry that the extreme heat of the weather, and a constant attendance on the duties of an office which is somewhat laborious and fatiguing, have prevented my giving it an earlier answer. The approbation you are pleased to express of my public conduct, is a great satisfaction to me. It is true that I have run through a course

[1] In Works, Vols. IV–VI, at Vol. VI, pp. 8–9.
[2] In The Works of John Adams, ed. by Charles Francis Adams, Vol. IX, pp. 559–561.

of dangers, hardships, and fatigues, by sea and land, and a series of perplexed negotiations among various nations, and at different courts, which have never fallen to the lot of any other American, and scarcely to any other man. But although I may flatter myself that under the favor of Heaven I have had as much success as could have been rationally expected, yet I find myself obliged with you to lament that our countrymen have not availed themselves of the advantages which Providence has placed in their power. After a generous contest for liberty, of twenty years' continuance, Americans forgot wherein liberty consisted. After a bloody war in defence of property, they forgot that property was sacred. After an arduous struggle for the freedom of commerce, they voluntarily shackled it with arbitrary trammels. After fighting for justice as the end of government, they seemed determined to banish that virtue from the earth. Rhode Island has carried all these errors to their extremes, but there is not any State in the Union which is wholly free from the same mistakes. I should denominate this conduct guilty as well as erroneous, if I were not sensible that it has been owing to the loss of that balance in our government which can alone preserve wisdom or virtue in society.

From DISCOURSES ON DAVILA (1789–90)[1]

The great question will forever remain, who shall work? Our species cannot all be idle. Leisure for study must ever be the portion of a few. The number employed in government must forever be very small. Food, raiment, and habitations, the indispensable wants of all, are not to be obtained without the continual toil of ninety-nine in a hundred of mankind. As rest is rapture to the weary man, those who labor little will always be envied by those who labor much, though the latter in reality be probably the most enviable. With all the encouragements, public and private, which can ever be given to general education, and it is scarcely possible they should be too many or too great, the laboring part of the people can never be learned. The controversy between the rich and the poor, the laborious and the idle, the learned and the ignorant, distinctions as old as the creation, and as extensive as the globe,

[1] *Discourses on Davila; a Series of Papers on Political History*, in *ibid*., Vol. VI, pp. 221–403, at 279–281.

distinctions which no art or policy, no degree of virtue or philosophy can ever wholly destroy, will continue, and rivalries will spring out of them. These parties will be represented in the legislature, and must be balanced, or one will oppress the other. There will never probably be found any other mode of establishing such an equilibrium, than by constituting the representation of each an independent branch of the legislature, and an independent executive authority, such as that in our government, to be a third branch and a mediator or an arbitrator between them. Property must be secured, or liberty cannot exist. But if unlimited or unbalanced power of disposing property, be put into the hands of those who have no property, France will find, as we have found, the lamb committed to the custody of the wolf. In such a case, all the pathetic exhortations and addresses of the national assembly to the people, to respect property, will be regarded no more than the warbles of the songsters of the forest. The great art of lawgiving consists in balancing the poor against the rich in the legislature, and in constituting the legislative a perfect balance against the executive power, at the same time that no individual or party can become its rival. The essence of a free government consists in an effectual control of rivalries.

From A LETTER TO JOHN TAYLOR (APRIL, 1814) [1]

That the first want of man is his dinner, and the second his girl, were truths well known to every democrat and aristocrat, long before the great philosopher Malthus arose, to think he enlightened the world by the discovery.

It has been equally well known that the second want is frequently so impetuous as to make men and women forget the first, and rush into rash marriages, leaving both the first and second wants, their own as well as those of their children and grandchildren, to the chapter of accidents. The most religious very often leave the consideration of these wants to him who supplies the young ravens when they cry.

The natural, necessary, and unavoidable consequence of all this is, that the multiplication of the population so far transcends the multiplication of the means of subsistence, that the constant labor

[1] In *ibid.*, Vol. VI, pp. 516–517.

of nine tenths of our species will forever be necessary to prevent all of them from starving with hunger, cold, and pestilence. Make all men Newtons, or, if you will, Jeffersons, or Taylors, or Randolphs, and they would all perish in a heap! . . .

The modern improvers of society,—ameliorators of the condition of mankind, instructors of the human species,—have assumed too much. They have not only condemned all the philosophy and policy of all ages of men, but they have undertaken to build a new universe, to ameliorate the system of eternal wisdom and benevolence. . . .

3. ALEXANDER HAMILTON

A S FIRST secretary of the treasury Hamilton submitted a series of
reports that were of significant influence on congressional action.
These included: (1) a report (January, 1790) recommending that the
federal government assume the State debts incurred during the Revolution and that both national and State debts be refunded at par; (2) a
report (December, 1790) proposing an excise tax to provide revenue for
the federal government and also to impress ordinary citizens with the
existence of that government; (3) a report (December, 1790) recommending the establishment of a Bank of the United States, to be incorporated by Congress, with the federal government owning one-fifth of
the capital stock; and (4) a report, issued December 5, 1791, advocating
duties on imports in order to promote American manufactures, especially
those that would make this country "independent on foreign nations, for
military or economic supplies." The famous Report on Manufactures
presents an exceptionally able exposition of the policy of a diversified and
well-balanced economy; and it has exercised profound influence later on
defenses, in America and elsewhere, of the system of protective tariffs.

From REPORT ON MANUFACTURES (1791)[1]

The Secretary of the Treasury, in obedience to the order of the
House of Representatives, of the 15th day of January, 1790, has
applied his attention, at as early a period as his other duties would
permit, to the subject of Manufactures, and particularly to the
means of promoting such as will tend to render the United States
independent on foreign nations for military and other essential
supplies; and he thereupon respectfully submits the following report:

The expediency of encouraging manufactures in the United
States, which was not long since deemed very questionable, appears at this time to be pretty generally admitted. The embarrassments which have obstructed the progress of our external trade,

[1] To the House of Representatives, December 5, 1791; in *The Works of Alexander
Hamilton*, ed. by Henry Cabot Lodge, Vol. IV, pp. 70–198, at 70–74, 86–107,
193–198.

have led to serious reflections on the necessity of enlarging the sphere of our domestic commerce. The restrictive regulations, which, in foreign markets, abridge the vent of the increasing surplus of our agricultural produce, serve to beget an earnest desire that a more extensive demand for that surplus may be created at home; and the complete success which has rewarded manufacturing enterprise in some valuable branches, conspiring with the promising symptoms which attend some less mature essays in others, justify a hope that the obstacles to the growth of this species of industry are less formidable than they were apprehended to be, and that it is not difficult to find, in its further extension, a full indemnification for any external disadvantages, which are or may be experienced, as well as an accession of resources, favorable to national independence and safety.

There are still, nevertheless, respectable patrons of opinions unfriendly to the encouragement of manufactures. The following are, substantially, the arguments by which these opinions are defended:

"In every country (say those who entertain them) agriculture is the most beneficial and productive object of human industry. This position, generally if not universally true, applies with peculiar emphasis to the United States, on account of their immense tracts of fertile territory, uninhabited and unimproved. Nothing can afford so advantageous an employment for capital and labor, as the conversion of this extensive wilderness into cultivated farms. Nothing, equally with this, can contribute to the population, strength, and real riches of the country.

"To endeavor, by the extraordinary patronage of government, to accelerate the growth of manufactures, is, in fact, to endeavor, by force and art, to transfer the natural current of industry from a more to a less beneficial channel. Whatever has such a tendency, must necessarily be unwise; indeed, it can hardly ever be wise in a government to attempt to give a direction to the industry of its citizens. This, under the quick-sighted guidance of private interest, will, if left to itself, infallibly find its own way to the most profitable employment; and it is by such employment, that the public prosperity will be most effectually promoted. To leave industry to itself, therefore, is, in almost every case, the soundest as well as the simplest policy.

"This policy is not only recommended to the United States, by considerations which affect all nations; it is, in a manner, dictated to them by the imperious force of a very peculiar situation. The smallness of their population compared with their territory; the constant allurements to emigration from the settled to the unsettled parts of the country; the facility with which the less independent condition of an artisan can be exchanged for the more independent condition of a farmer;—these, and similar causes, conspire to produce, and, for a length of time, must continue to occasion, a scarcity of hands for manufacturing occupation, and dearness of labor generally. To these disadvantages for the prosecution of manufactures, a deficiency of pecuniary capital being added, the prospect of a successful competition with the manufactures of Europe, must be regarded as little less than desperate. Extensive manufactures can only be the offspring of a redundant, at least of a full, population. Till the latter shall characterize the situation of this country, 't is vain to hope for the former.

"If, contrary to the natural course of things, an unseasonable and premature spring can be given to certain fabrics, by heavy duties, prohibitions, bounties, or by other forced expedients, this will only be to sacrifice the interests of the community to those of particular classes. Besides the misdirection of labor, a virtual monopoly will be given to the persons employed on such fabrics; and an enhancement of price, the inevitable consequence of every monopoly, must be defrayed at the expense of the other parts of society. It is far preferable, that those persons should be engaged in the cultivation of the earth, and that we should procure, in exchange for its productions, the commodities with which foreigners are able to supply us in greater perfection and upon better terms."

This mode of reasoning is founded upon facts and principles which have certainly respectable pretensions. If it had governed the conduct of nations more generally than it has done, there is room to suppose that it might have carried them faster to prosperity and greatness than they have attained by the pursuit of maxims too widely opposite. Most general theories, however, admit of numerous exceptions, and there are few, if any, of the political kind, which do not blend a considerable portion of error with the truths they inculcate.

. . . In order to an accurate judgment how far that which has been just stated ought to be deemed liable to a similar imputation, it is necessary to advert carefully to the considerations which plead in favor of manufactures, and which appear to recommend the special and positive encouragement of them in certain cases and under certain reasonable limitations.

It ought readily be conceded that the cultivation of the earth, as the primary and most certain source of national supply, as the immediate and chief source of subsistence to a man, as the principal source of those materials which constitute the nutriment of other kinds of labor, as including a state most favorable to the freedom and independence of the human mind—one, perhaps, most conducive to the multiplication of the human species, has intrinsically a strong claim to pre-eminence over every other kind of industry.

But, that it has a title to any thing like an exclusive predilection, in any country, ought to be admitted with great caution; that it is even more productive than every other branch of industry, requires more evidence than has yet been given in support of the position. That its real interests, precious and important as, without the help of exaggeration, they truly are, will be advanced, rather than injured, by the due encouragement of manufactures, may, it is believed, be satisfactorily demonstrated. And it is also believed that the expediency of such encouragement, in a general view, may be shown to be recommended by the most cogent and persuasive motives of national policy. . . .

It is now proper to proceed a step further, and to enumerate the principal circumstances from which it may be inferred that manufacturing establishments not only occasion a positive augmentation of the produce and revenue of the society, but that they contribute essentially to rendering them greater than they could possibly be without such establishments. These circumstances are:

1. The division of labor.
2. An extension of the use of machinery.
3. Additional employment to classes of the community not ordinarily engaged in the business.
4. The promoting of emigration from foreign countries.
5. The furnishing greater scope for the diversity of talents and dispositions, which discriminate men from each other.
6. The affording a more ample and various field for enterprise.
7. The creating, in some instances, a new, and securing, in all, a

more certain and steady demand for the surplus produce of the soil.

Each of these circumstances has a considerable influence upon the total mass of industrious effort in a community; together, they add to it a degree of energy and effect which is not easily conceived. Some comments upon each of them, in the order in which they have been stated, may serve to explain their importance.

1. As to the division of labor.

It has justly been observed, that there is scarcely any thing of greater moment in the economy of a nation than the proper division of labor. The separation of occupations causes each to be carried to a much greater perfection than it could possibly acquire if they were blended. This arises principally from three circumstances:

1st. The greater skill and dexterity naturally resulting from a constant and undivided application to a single object. It is evident that these properties must increase in proportion to the separation and simplification of objects, and the steadiness of the attention devoted to each; and must be less in proportion to the complication of objects, and the number among which the attention is distracted.

2d. The economy of time, by avoiding the loss of it, incident to a frequent transition from one operation to another of a different nature. This depends on various circumstances: the transition itself, the orderly disposition of the implements, machines, and materials employed in the operation to be relinquished, the preparatory steps to the commencement of a new one, the interruption of the impulse which the mind of the workman acquires from being engaged in a particular operation, the distractions, hesitations, and reluctances which attend the passage from one kind of business to another.

3d. An extension of the use of machinery. A man occupied on a single object will have it more in his power, and will be more naturally led to exert his imagination, in devising methods to facilitate and abridge labor, than if he were perplexed by a variety of independent and dissimilar operations. Besides this the fabrication of machines, in numerous instances, becoming itself a distinct trade, the artist who follows it has all the advantages which have been enumerated, for improvement in his particular art; and, in both ways, the invention and application of machinery are extended.

And from these causes united, the mere separation of the occupation of the cultivator from that of the artificer, has the effect of augmenting the productive powers of labor, and with them, the total mass of the produce or revenue of a country. In this single view of the subject, therefore, the utility of artificers or manufacturers, towards promoting an increase of productive industry, is apparent.

2. As to an extension of the use of machinery, a
   point which, though partly anticipated, requires
   to be placed in one or two additional lights.

The employment of machinery forms an item of great importance in the general mass of national industry. It is an artificial force brought in aid of the natural force of man; and, to all the purposes of labor, is an increase of hands, an accession of strength, unencumbered too by the expense of maintaining the laborer. May it not, therefore, be fairly inferred, that those occupations which give greatest scope to the use of this auxiliary, contribute most to the general stock of industrious effort, and, in consequence, to the general product of industry?

It shall be taken for granted, and the truth of the position referred to observation, that manufacturing pursuits are susceptible, in a greater degree, of the application of machinery, than those of agriculture. If so, all the difference is lost to a community which, instead of manufacturing for itself, procures the fabrics requisite to its supply from other countries. The substitution of foreign for domestic manufactures is a transfer to foreign nations of the advantages accruing from the employment of machinery, in the modes in which it is capable of being employed with most utility and to the greatest extent.

The cotton-mill, invented in England, within the last twenty years, is a signal illustration of the general proposition which has been just advanced. In consequence of it, all the different processes for spinning cotton are performed by means of machines, which are put in motion by water, and attended chiefly by women and children—and by a smaller number of persons, in the whole, than are requisite in the ordinary mode of spinning. And it is an advantage of great moment, that the operations of this mill continue with convenience during the night as well as through the day.

The prodigious effect of such a machine is easily conceived. To this invention is to be attributed, essentially, the immense progress which has been so suddenly made in Great Britain, in the various fabrics of cotton.

> 3. *As to the additional employment of classes of the community not originally engaged in the particular business.*

This is not among the least valuable of the means by which manufacturing institutions contribute to augment the general stock of industry and production. In places where those institutions prevail, besides the persons regularly engaged in them, they afford occasional and extra employment to industrious individuals and families, who are willing to devote the leisure resulting from the intermissions of their ordinary pursuits to collateral labors, as a resource for multiplying their acquisitions or their enjoyments. The husbandman himself experiences a new source of profit and support from the increased industry of his wife and daughters, invited and stimulated by the demands of the neighboring manufactories.

Besides this advantage of occasional employment to classes having different occupations, there is another, of a nature allied to it, and of a similar tendency. This is the employment of persons who would otherwise be idle, and in many cases a burthen on the community, either from the bias of temper, habit, infirmity of body, or some other cause, indisposing or disqualifying them for the toils of the country. It is worthy of particular remark that, in general, women and children are rendered more useful, and the latter more early useful, by manufacturing establishments, than they would otherwise be. Of the number of persons employed in the cotton manufactories of Great Britain, it is computed that four sevenths, nearly, are women and children, of whom the greatest proportion are children, and many of them of a tender age.

And thus it appears to be one of the attributes of manufactures, and one of no small consequence, to give occasion to the exertion of a greater quantity of industry, even by the same number of persons, where they happen to prevail, than would exist if there were no such establishments.

4. As to the promoting of emigration from foreign countries.

Men reluctantly quit one course of occupation and livelihood for another, unless invited to it by very apparent and proximate advantages. Many who would go from one country to another, if they had a prospect of continuing with more benefit the callings to which they have been educated, will often not be tempted to change their situation by the hope of doing better in some other way. Manufacturers who, listening to the powerful invitations of a better price for their fabrics or their labor, of greater cheapness of provisions and raw materials, of an exemption from the chief part of the taxes, burthens, and restraints which they endure in the Old World, of greater personal independence and consequence, under the operation of a more equal government, and of what is far more precious than mere religious toleration, a perfect equality of religious privileges, would probably flock from Europe to the United States, to pursue their own trades or professions, if they were once made sensible of the advantages they would enjoy, and were inspired with an assurance of encouragement and employment, will, with difficulty, be induced to transplant themselves, with a view to becoming cultivators of land.

If it be true, then, that it is the interest of the United States to open every possible avenue to emigration from abroad, it affords a weighty argument for the encouragement of manufactures; which, for the reasons just assigned, will have the strongest tendency to multiply the inducements to it.

Here is perceived an important resource, not only for extending the population, and with it the useful and productive labor of the country, but likewise for the prosecution of manufactures, without deducting from the number of hands which might otherwise be drawn to tillage, and even for the indemnification of agriculture for such as might happen to be diverted from it. Many, whom manufacturing views would induce to emigrate, would, afterwards, yield to the temptations which the particular situation of this country holds out to agricultural pursuits. And while agriculture would, in other respects, derive many signal and unmingled advantages from the growth of manufactures, it is a problem whether it would gain or lose, as to the article of the number of persons employed in carrying it on.

> 5. As to the furnishing greater scope for the diver-
> sity of talents and dispositions, which discrimi-
> nate men from each other.

This is a much more powerful means of augmenting the fund of national industry, than may at first sight appear. It is a just observation, that minds of the strongest and most active powers for their proper objects, fall below mediocrity, and labor without effect, if confined to uncongenial pursuits. And it is thence to be inferred, that the results of human exertion may be immensely increased by diversifying its objects. When all the different kinds of industry obtain in a community, each individual can find his proper element, and can call into activity the whole vigor of his nature. And the community is benefited by the services of its respective members, in the manner in which each can serve it with most effect.

If there be any thing in a remark often to be met with, namely, that there is, in the genius of the people of this country, a peculiar aptitude for mechanic improvements, it would operate as a forcible reason for giving opportunities to the exercise of that species of talent, by the propagation of manufactures.

> 6. As to the affording a more ample and various
> field for enterprise.

This also is of greater consequence in the general scale of national exertion than might, perhaps, on a superficial view be supposed, and has effects not altogether dissimilar from those of the circumstance last noticed. To cherish and stimulate the activity of the human mind, by multiplying the objects of enterprise, is not among the least considerable of the expedients by which the wealth of a nation may be promoted. Even things in themselves not positively advantageous sometimes become so, by their tendency to provoke exertion. Every new scene which is opened to the busy nature of man to rouse and exert itself, is the addition of a new energy to the general stock of effort.

The spirit of enterprise, useful and prolific as it is, must necessarily be contracted or expanded, in proportion to the simplicity or variety of the occupations and productions which are to be found in a society. It must be less in a nation of mere cultivators, than in a nation of cultivators and merchants; less in a nation of cultivators and merchants, than in a nation of cultivators, artificers, and merchants.

> 7. As to the creating, in some instances, a new, and
> securing, in all, a more certain and steady de-
> mand for the surplus produce of the soil.

This is among the most important of the circumstances which have been indicated. It is a principal means by which the establishment of manufactures contributes to an augmentation of the produce or revenue of a country, and has an immediate and direct relation to the prosperity of agriculture.

It is evident that the exertions of the husbandman will be steady or fluctuating, vigorous or feeble, in proportion to the steadiness or fluctuation, adequateness or inadequateness, of the markets on which he must depend for the vent of the surplus which may be produced by his labor; and that such surplus, in the ordinary course of things, will be greater or less in the same proportion.

For the purpose of this vent, a domestic market is greatly to be preferred to a foreign one; because it is, in the nature of things, far more to be relied upon.

It is a primary object of the policy of nations, to be able to supply themselves with subsistence from their own soils; and manufacturing nations, as far as circumstances permit, endeavor to procure from the same source the raw materials necessary for their own fabrics. This disposition, urged by the spirit of monopoly, is sometimes even carried to an injudicious extreme. It seems not always to be recollected, that nations who have neither mines nor manufactures can only obtain the manufactured articles of which they stand in need, by an exchange of the products of their soils; and that if those who can best furnish them with such articles are unwilling to give a due course to this exchange, they must, of necessity, make every possible effort to manufacture for themselves; the effect of which is, that the manufacturing nations abridge the natural advantages of their situation, through an unwillingness to permit the agricultural countries to enjoy the advantages of theirs, and sacrifice the interests of a mutually beneficial intercourse to the vain project of selling every thing and buying nothing.

But it is also a consequence of the policy which has been noted, that the foreign demand for the products of agricultural countries is, in a great degree, rather casual and occasional, than certain or constant. . . .

. . . The differences of seasons in the countries which are the consumers, make immense differences in the produce of their own soils, in different years; and consequently in the degrees of their necessity for foreign supply. . . .

Considering how fast and how much the progress of new settlements in the United States must increase the surplus produce of the soil, and weighing seriously the tendency of the system which prevails among most of the commercial nations of Europe, whatever dependence may be placed on the force of natural circumstances to counteract the effects of an artificial policy, there appear strong reasons to regard the foreign demand for that surplus as too uncertain a reliance, and to desire a substitute for it in an extensive domestic market.

To secure such a market there is no other expedient than to promote manufacturing establishments. Manufacturers, who constitute the most numerous class, after the cultivators of land, are for that reason the principal consumers of the surplus of their labor.

This idea of an extensive domestic market for the surplus produce of the soil, is of the first consequence. It is, of all things, that which most effectually conduces to a flourishing state of agriculture. . . .

It merits particular observation, that the multiplication of manufactories not only furnishes a market for those articles which have been accustomed to be produced in abundance in a country, but it likewise creates a demand for such as were either unknown or produced in inconsiderable quantities. . . .

. . . Previously to a further discussion of the objections to the encouragement of manufactures, which have been stated, it will be of use to see what can be said, in reference to the particular situation of the United States, against the conclusions appearing to result from what has been already offered.

It may be observed, and the idea is of no inconsiderable weight, that however true it might be that a state which, possessing large tracts of vacant and fertile territory, was, at the same time, secluded from foreign commerce, would find its interest and the interest of agriculture in diverting a part of its population from tillage to manufactures, yet it will not follow, that the same is true of a state which, having such vacant and fertile territory, has, at the same time, ample opportunity of procuring from abroad, on good terms, all the fabrics of which it stands in need, for the supply of its inhabitants. . . .

To these observations, the following appears to be a satisfactory answer:

1st. If the system of perfect liberty to industry and commerce were the prevailing system of nations, the arguments which dissuade a country, in the predicament of the United States, from the zealous pursuit of manufactures, would doubtless have great force. It will not be affirmed that they might not be permitted, with few exceptions, to serve as a rule of national conduct. In such a state of things, each country would have a full benefit of its peculiar advantages to compensate for its deficiencies or disadvantages. If one nation were in a condition to supply manufactured articles on better terms than another, that other might find an abundant indemnification in a superior capacity to furnish the produce of the soil. And a free exchange, mutually beneficial, of the commodities which each was able to supply, on the best terms, might be carried on between them, supporting, in full vigor, the industry of each. And though the circumstances which have been mentioned, and others which will be unfolded hereafter, render it probable that nations, merely agricultural, would not enjoy the same degree of opulence, in proportion to their numbers, as those which united manufactures with agriculture, yet the progressive improvement of the lands of the former might, in the end, atone for an inferior degree of opulence in the meantime; and in a case in which opposite considerations are pretty equally balanced, the option ought, perhaps, always be in favor of leaving industry to its own direction.

But the system which has been mentioned is far from characterizing the general policy of nations. The prevalent one has been regulated by an opposite spirit. The consequence of it is, that the United States are, to a certain extent, in the situation of a country precluded from foreign commerce. They can, indeed, without difficulty, obtain from abroad the manufactured supplies of which they are in want; but they experience numerous and very injurious impediments to the emission and vent of their own commodities. Nor is this the case in reference to a single foreign nation only.

The regulations of several countries, with which we have the most extensive intercourse, throw serious obstructions in the way of the principal staples of the United States.

In such a position of things, the United States cannot exchange with Europe on equal terms; and the want of reciprocity would render them the victim of a system which should induce them to confine their views to agriculture, and refrain from manufactures. A constant and increasing necessity, on their part, for the commodities of Europe, and only a partial and occasional demand for their own, in return, could not but expose them to a state of impoverishment, compared with the opulence to which their political and natural advantages authorize them to aspire. . . .

2d. The conversion of their waste into cultivated lands is certainly a point of great moment in the political calculations of the United States. But the degree in which this may possibly be retarded by the encouragement of manufactories, does not appear to countervail the powerful inducements to afford that encouragement.

An observation made in another place is of a nature to have great influence upon this question. If it cannot be denied, that the interests, even of agriculture, may be advanced more by having such of the lands of a State as are occupied, under good cultivation, than by having a greater quantity occupied under a much inferior cultivation; and if manufactories, for the reasons assigned, must be admitted to have a tendency to promote a more steady and vigorous cultivation of the lands occupied than would happen without them, it will follow that they are capable of indemnifying a country for a diminution of the progress of new settlements, and may serve to increase both the capital value and the income of its lands, even though they should abridge the number of acres under tillage.

But it does by no means follow, that the progress of new settlements would be retarded by the extension of manufactures. The desire of being an independent proprietor of land is founded on such strong principles in the human breast, that, where the opportunity of becoming so is as great as it is in the United States, the proportion will be small of those whose situations would otherwise lead to it, who would be diverted from it toward manufactures. And it is highly probable, as already intimated, that the accession of foreigners, who, originally drawn over by manufacturing views, would afterward abandon them for agricultural, would be more than an equivalent for those of our own citizens who might happen to be detached from them.

The remaining objections to a particular encouragement of manufactures in the United States now require to be examined.

One of these turns on the proposition, that industry, if left to itself, will naturally find its way to the most useful and profitable employment. Whence it is inferred that manufactures, without the aid of government, will grow up as soon and as fast as the natural state of things and the interest of the community may require.

Against the solidity of this hypothesis, in the full latitude of the terms, very cogent reasons may be offered. These have relation to the strong influence of habit and the spirit of imitation; the fear of want of success in untried enterprises; the intrinsic difficulties incident to first essays towards a competition with those who have previously attained to perfection in the business to be attempted; the bounties, premiums, and other artificial encouragements with which foreign nations second the exertions of their own citizens, in the branches in which they are to be rivalled.

Experience teaches, that men are often so much governed by what they are accustomed to see and practise, that the simplest and most obvious improvements, in the most ordinary occupations, are adopted with hesitation, reluctance, and by slow gradations. The spontaneous transition to new pursuits, in a community long habituated to different ones, may be expected to be attended with proportionably greater difficulty. When former occupations ceased to yield a profit adequate to the subsistence of their followers, or when there was an absolute deficiency of employment in them, owing to the superabundance of hands, changes would ensue; but these changes would be likely to be more tardy than might consist with the interest either of individuals or of the society. In many cases they would not happen, while a bare support could be insured by an adherence to ancient courses, though a resort to a more profitable employment might be practicable. To produce the desirable changes as early as may be expedient may therefore require the incitement and patronage of government.

The apprehension of failing in new attempts is, perhaps, a more serious impediment. There are dispositions apt to be attracted by the mere novelty of an undertaking; but these are not always those best calculated to give it success. To this it is of importance that the confidence of cautious, sagacious capitalists, both citizens and foreigners, should be excited. And to inspire this description of persons with confidence, it is essential that they should be made to see in any project which is new—and for that reason alone, if for no other, precarious—the prospect of such a degree of countenance and support from government, as may be capable of overcoming the obstacles inseparable from first experiments.

The superiority antecedently enjoyed by nations who have pre-occupied and perfected a branch of industry, constitutes a more formidable obstacle than either of those which have been mentioned, to the introduction of the same branch into a country in which it did not before exist. To maintain, between the recent establishments of one country, and the long-matured establishments of another country, a competition upon equal terms, both as to quality and price, is, in most cases, impracticable. The disparity, in the one, or in the other, or in both, must necessarily be so considerable, as to forbid a successful rivalship, without the extraordinary aid and protection of government.

But the greatest obstacle of all to the successful prosecution of a new branch of industry in a country in which it was before unknown, consists, as far as the instances apply, in the bounties, premiums, and other aids which are granted, in a variety of cases, by the nations in which the establishments to be imitated are previously introduced. It is well known (and particular examples, in the course of this report, will be cited) that certain nations grant bounties on the exportation of particular commodities, to enable their own workmen to undersell and supplant all competitors in the countries to which those commodities are sent. Hence the undertakers of a new manufacture have to contend, not only with the natural disadvantages of a new undertaking, but with the gratuities and remunerations which other governments bestow. To be enabled to contend with success, it is evident that the interference and aid of their own governments are indispensable.

Combinations by those engaged in a particular branch of business in one country, to frustrate the first efforts to introduce it into another, by temporary sacrifices, recompensed, perhaps, by extraordinary indemnifications of the government of such country, are believed to have existed, and are not to be regarded as destitute of probability. The existence or assurance of aid from the government of the country in which the business is to be introduced, may be essential to fortify adventurers against the dread of such combinations; to defeat their efforts, if formed; and to prevent their being formed, by demonstrating that they must in the end prove fruitless.

Whatever room there may be for an expectation that the industry of a people, under the direction of private interest, will, upon equal terms, find out the most beneficial employment for itself, there is none for a reliance that it will struggle against the force of unequal terms, or will, of itself, surmount all the adventitious barriers to a successful competition which may have been erected, either by the advantages naturally acquired from practice and previous possession of the ground, or by those which may have sprung from positive regulations and an artificial policy. This general reflection might alone suffice as an answer to the objection under examination, exclusively of the weighty considerations which have been particularly urged. . . .

The foregoing heads comprise the most important of the several kinds of manufactures which have occurred as requiring, and, at the same time, as most proper for public encouragement; and such measures for affording it as have appeared best calculated to answer the end, have been suggested.

The observations which have accompanied this delineation of objects, supersede the necessity of many supplementary remarks. One or two, however, may not be altogether superfluous.

Bounties are, in various instances, proposed as one species of encouragement.

It is a familiar objection to them that they are difficult to be managed, and liable to frauds. But neither that difficulty nor this danger seems sufficiently great to countervail the advantages of which they are productive when rightly applied. And it is presumed to have been shown that they are, in some cases, particularly in the infancy of new enterprises, indispensable.

It will, however, be necessary to guard, with extraordinary circumspection, the manner of dispensing them. The requisite precautions have been thought of, but to enter into the detail would swell this report, already voluminous, to a size too inconvenient.

If the principle shall not be deemed inadmissible, the means of avoiding an abuse of it will not be likely to present unsurmountable obstacles. There are useful guides from practice in other quarters.

It shall, therefore, only be remarked here, in relation to this point, that any bounty which may be applied to the manufacture of an article, cannot, with safety, extend beyond those manufactories at which the making of the article is a regular trade. It would be impossible to annex adequate precautions to a benefit of that nature, if extended to every private family in which the manufacture was incidentally carried on; and, being a merely incidental occupation which engages a portion of time that would otherwise be lost, it can be advantageously carried on without so special an aid.

The possibility of a diminution of the revenue may also present itself as an objection to the arrangements which have been submitted.

But there is no truth which may be more firmly relied upon, than that the interests of the revenue are promoted by whatever promotes an increase of national industry and wealth.

In proportion to the degree of these, is the capacity of every country to contribute to the public treasury; and where the capacity to pay is increased, or even is not decreased, the only consequence of measures which diminish any particular resource, is a change of the object. If, by encouraging the manufacture of an article at home, the revenue which has been wont to accrue from its importation should be lessened, an indemnification can easily be found, either out of the manufacture itself, or from some other object which may be deemed more convenient.

The measures, however, which have been submitted, taken aggregately, will, for a long time to come, rather augment than decrease the public revenue.

There is little room to hope, that the progress of manufactures will so equally keep pace with the progress of population, as to prevent even a gradual augmentation of the product of the duties on imported articles.

As, nevertheless, an abolition in some instances, and a reduction in others, of duties which have been pledged for the public debt, is proposed, it is essential that it should be accompanied with a competent substitute. In order to this, it is requisite that all the additional duties which shall be laid, be appropriated, in the first instance, to replace all defalcations which may proceed from any such abolition or diminution. It is evident, at first glance, that they will not only be adequate to this, but will yield a considerable surplus. This surplus will serve:

First. To constitute a fund for paying the bounties which shall have been decreed.

Secondly. To constitute a fund for the operations of a board to be established, for promoting arts, agriculture, manufactures, and commerce. Of this institution, different intimations have been given in the course of this report. An outline of a plan for it shall now be submitted.

Let a certain annual sum be set apart, and placed under the management of commissioners, not less than three, to consist of certain officers of the government and their successors in office.

Let these commissioners be empowered to apply the fund confided to them, to defray the expenses of the emigration of artists and manufacturers in particular branches of extraordinary importance; to induce the prosecution and introduction of useful discoveries, inventions, and improvements, by proportionate rewards, judiciously held out and applied; to encourage by premiums, both honorable and lucrative, the exertions of individuals and of classes, in relation to the several objects they are charged with promoting; and to afford such other aids to those objects as may be generally designated by law.

The commissioners to render to the Legislature an annual account of their transactions and disbursements; and all such sums as shall not have been applied to the purposes of their trust, at the end of every three years, to revert to the treasury. It may, also, be enjoined upon them not to draw out the money, but for the purpose of some specific disbursement.

It may, moreover, be of use to authorize them to receive voluntary contributions, making it their duty to apply them to the particular objects for which they may have been made, if any shall have been designated by the donors.

There is reason to believe that the progress of particular manufactures has been much retarded by the want of skilful workmen. And it often happens, that the capitals employed are not equal to the purposes of bringing from abroad workmen of a superior kind. Here, in cases worthy of it, the auxiliary agency of government would, in all probability, be useful. There are also valuable workmen in every branch, who are prevented from emigrating, solely, by the want of means. Occasional aids to such persons, properly administered, might be a source of valuable acquisitions to the country.

The propriety of stimulating by rewards the invention and introduction of useful improvements, is admitted without difficulty. But the success of attempts in this way must evidently depend much on the manner of conducting them. It is probable that the placing of the dispensation of those rewards under some proper discretionary direction, where they may be accompanied by collateral expedients, will serve to give them the surest efficacy. It seems impracticable to apportion, by general rules, specific compensations for discoveries of unknown and disproportionate utility.

The great use which may be made of a fund of this nature, to procure and import foreign improvements, is particularly obvious. Among these, the article of machines would form a most important item.

The operation and utility of premiums have been adverted to, together with the advantages which have resulted from their dispensation, under the direction of certain public and private societies. Of this, some experience has been had, in the instance of the Pennsylvania Society for the promotion of manufactures and useful arts; but the funds of that association have been too contracted to produce more than a very small portion of the good to which the principles of it would have led. It may confidently be affirmed, that there is scarcely any thing which has been devised, better calculated to excite a general spirit of improvement than the institutions of this nature. They are truly invaluable.

In countries where there is great private wealth, much may be effected by the voluntary contributions of patriotic individuals; but in a community situated like that of the United States, the public purse must supply the deficiency of private resource. In what can it be so useful, as in prompting and improving the efforts of industry?

All which is humbly submitted.

ALEXANDER HAMILTON,
Secretary of the Treasury.

4. FLETCHER v. PECK (1810)

A QUESTION of property rights was involved in the first case in which the United States Supreme Court declared invalid an act of a State legislature. In 1795 the legislature of Georgia passed an act granting twenty million acres of the public lands of the State (the "Yazoo lands") to four land-speculating companies, for a total sum of $500,000. There was clear evidence that passage of the act had been secured through fraud and bribery; most of the legislators voting for the act had stock in the purchasing companies. Public opinion was aroused; the question was a major issue in the next election, and nearly every candidate elected had promised to remove the fraud. Accordingly in 1796 the new legislature adopted a law repealing the act of 1795 and expunging from the records all evidence of its passage. In 1802 Georgia ceded to the United States its claims to the recovered lands. Meanwhile the lands had passed into the hands of innocent purchasers, whose spokesmen sought for several years to secure from Congress compensation for the lands they would lose as a result of the act of 1796. Failing in this effort, they resorted to the federal courts. One Peck had conveyed his lands to Fletcher, with a covenant that the title had not been impaired by the 1796 act. In a "made-up" case Fletcher sued Peck for breach of this warranty of title. The trial court decided in favor of Peck, thereby upholding the titles under the 1795 act. Fletcher appealed to the Supreme Court, which affirmed the decision and declared the 1796 act null and void. The decision raised another storm of protest. Georgia congressmen complained that the court had thwarted efforts of the people of Georgia to right a wrong committed by its own faithless representatives. States' rights advocates everywhere were aroused by the federal court's assertion of a right to pass on the validity of the acts of a State.

Chief Justice Marshall's opinion in the case is of particular significance because of (1) his holding that the provision of the federal Constitution (Art. I, sec. 10) forbidding a State to pass any law impairing the obligation of contracts applied to property grants by a State as well as to contracts between private individuals; and (2) his intimation that not only the Constitution but also "the nature of society and government" set limits to the power of a legislature over private property. "Marshall's opinion," said his leading biographer, "did more than

487

affect the controversy in Congress over the Yazoo lands. It announced fundamental principles for the guidance of the States and the stabilizing of American business."

[See: Albert J. Beveridge, *The Life of John Marshall* (4 vols., 1919), Vol. III, ch. 10; Charles Warren, *The Supreme Court in United States History* (1932), Vol. I, pp. 392–399.]

From THE OPINION OF THE COURT [1]

March 16, 1810. MARSHALL, Ch. J., delivered the opinion of the court as follows . . .

The lands in controversy vested absolutely in James Gunn and others, the original grantees, by the conveyance of the governor, made in pursuance of an act of assembly to which the legislature was fully competent. Being thus in full possession of the legal estate, they, for a valuable consideration, conveyed portions of the land to those who were willing to purchase. If the original transaction was infected with fraud, these purchasers did not participate in it, and had no notice of it. They were innocent. Yet the legislature of Georgia has involved them in the fate of the first parties to the transaction, and, if the act be valid, has annihilated their rights also.

The legislature of Georgia was a party to this transaction; and for a party to pronounce its own deed invalid, whatever cause may be assigned for its invalidity, must be considered as a mere act of power which must find its vindication in a train of reasoning not often heard in courts of justice. . . .

If the legislature of Georgia was not bound to submit its pretensions to those tribunals which are established for the security of property, and to decide on human rights, if it might claim to itself the power of judging in its own case, yet there are certain great principles of justice, whose authority is universally acknowledged, that ought not to be entirely disregarded. . . .

In this case the legislature may have had ample proof that the original grant was obtained by practices which can never be too much reprobated, and which would have justified its abrogation so far as respected those to whom crime was imputable. But the grant, when issued, conveyed an estate in fee-simple to the grantee, clothed with all the solemnities which law can bestow. This estate was

[1] United States Reports, 6 Cranch 87, at pp. 132–139.

transferable; and those who purchased parts of it were not stained by that guilt which infected the original transaction. Their case is not distinguishable from the ordinary case of purchasers of a legal estate without knowledge of any secret fraud which might have led to the emanation of the original grant. According to the well known course of equity, their rights could not be affected by such fraud. Their situation was the same, their title was the same, with that of every other member of the community who holds land by regular conveyances from the original patentee.

Is the power of the legislature competent to the annihilation of such title, and to a resumption of the property thus held?

The principle asserted is, that one legislature is competent to repeal any act which a former legislature was competent to pass; and that one legislature cannot abridge the powers of a succeeding legislature.

The correctness of this principle, so far as respects general legislation, can never be controverted. But, if an act be done under a law, a succeeding legislature cannot undo it. The past cannot be recalled by the most absolute power. Conveyances have been made; those conveyances have vested legal estates, and, if those estates may be seized by the sovereign authority, still, that they originally vested is a fact, and cannot cease to be a fact.

When, then, a law is in its nature a contract, when absolute rights have vested under that contract, a repeal of the law cannot devest those rights; and the act of annulling them, if legitimate, is rendered so by a power applicable to the case of every individual in the community.

It may well be doubted whether the nature of society and of government does not prescribe some limits to the legislative power; and, if any be prescribed, where are they to be found, if the property of an individual, fairly and honestly acquired, may be seized without compensation?

To the legislature all legislative power is granted; but the question, whether the act of transferring the property of an individual to the public, be in the nature of the legislative power, is well worthy of serious reflection. . . .

. . . The constitution of the United States declares that no state shall pass any bill of attainder, *ex post facto* law, or law impairing the obligation of contracts.

Does the case now under consideration come within this prohibitory section of the constitution?

In considering this very interesting question, we immediately ask ourselves what is a contract? Is a grant a contract?

A contract is a compact between two or more parties, and is either executory or executed. An executory contract is one in which a party binds himself to do, or not to do, a particular thing; such was the law under which the conveyance was made by the governor. A contract executed is one in which the object of contract is performed; and this, says Blackstone, differs in nothing from a grant. The contract between Georgia and the purchasers was executed by the grant. A contract executed, as well as one which is executory, contains obligations binding on the parties. A grant, in its own nature, amounts to an extinguishment of the right of the grantor, and implies a contract not to re-assert that right. A party is, therefore, always estopped by his own grant.

Since, then, in fact, a grant is a contract executed, the obligation of which still continues, and since the constitution uses the general term contract, without distinguishing between those which are executory and those which are executed, it must be construed to comprehend the latter as well as the former. A law annulling conveyances between individuals, and declaring that the grantors should stand seized of their former estates, notwithstanding those grants, would be as repugnant to the constitution as a law discharging the vendors of property from the obligation of executing their contracts by conveyances. It would be strange if a contract to convey was secured by the constitution, while an absolute conveyance remained unprotected.

If, under a fair construction of the constitution, grants are comprehended under the term contracts, is a grant from the state excluded from the operation of the provision? Is the clause to be considered as inhibiting the state from impairing the obligation of contracts between two individuals, but as excluding from that inhibition contracts made with itself?

The words themselves contain no such distinction. They are general, and are applicable to contracts of every description. If contracts made with the state are to be exempted from their operation, the exception must arise from the character of the contracting party, not from the words which are employed.

Whatever respect might have been felt for the state sovereignties, it is not to be disguised that the framers of the constitution viewed, with some apprehension, the violent acts which might grow out of the feelings of the moment; and that the people of the United States, in adopting that instrument, have manifested a determination to shield themselves and their property from the effects of those sudden and strong passions to which men are exposed. The restrictions on the legislative power of the states are obviously founded in this sentiment; and the constitution of the United States contains what may be deemed a bill of rights for the people of each state. . . .

It is, then, the unanimous opinion of the court, that, in this case, the estate having passed into the hands of a purchaser for a valuable consideration, without notice, the state of Georgia was restrained, either by general principles, which are common to our free institutions, or by the particular provisions of the constitution of the United States, from passing a law whereby the estate of the plaintiff in the premises so purchased could be constitutionally and legally impaired and rendered null and void. . . .

5. JOHN TAYLOR

From INQUIRY INTO THE PRINCIPLES AND POLICY OF THE GOVERNMENT OF THE UNITED STATES (1814)[1]

The same mouth will solemnly assert, that the principles of equity annul every contract, which defrauds an individual; and that justice or policy requires a catalogue of law charters which defraud a nation, to exist and have their effect.

This is owing to the artful conversion of good words, into knavish dogmas. It is not new, to see errour take refuge under the garb of truth. Superstition has in all ages called itself religion. Thus law charters, with the faithless design of enslaving a nation by the introduction of the aristocracy of the present age, crouch behind the good and honest words "publick faith and national credit," to prevent a nation from destroying that, which is destroying it. And they succeed; because we are as unsuspicious that a false and fraudulent dogma, is hidden under fair language, as that a well dressed gentleman indicates a thief.

To come at truth, we ought not to stop at a verbal investigation. We must consider whether the effects of every law and every measure, by whatever names the law or measure are called, are on the side of virtue or vice.

An irrepealable law charter is a standing temptation to governments to do evil, and an invitation to individuals to become their accessaries; by its help, a predominant party may use temporary power, to enact corporate or individual emoluments for itself, at the national expense. Successive parties will repeat the same iniquity; and even the outs or opposition will be corrupted, to do obeisance at the shrine of the dogma, that they also may reap of the fruit it bestows, when a nation shall fall into their hands; which upon every change of administration, will have its hopes of reform gratified, by new pillages under the sanctions of publick faith and national credit.

This modern system of law charters, is founded in the same de-

[1] (Fredericksburg, 1814), pp. 63–64, 274–275, 282.

sign, with the ancient system of a social compact. Under the sanction of social compact, governments have formerly tyrannised over
nations. Under the sanction of law charters, governments now buy
a faction, rob nations of enormous wealth, and soar beyond responsibility. The inviolability of a social compact was the old dogma;
the inviolability of law charters is the new; for effecting the same
end. The last is however an engine in the hands of avarice and ambition, of power far superior to the first. It is able to corrupt and
pillage a nation without limit. The first was an opinion unable to
purchase partisans; the last offers every thing to its disciples, which
can gratify pernicious passions, and meets arguments with bribes.
Thus a nation, which won self-government by exploding the doctrine of the antiquated compact dogma, may lose it again in the
modern law charter dogma; and thus a nation, which thought it
morally wrong to suffer slavery from troops hired by clothes, pay
and rations, may be persuaded that it is morally right to suffer
slavery from troops hired by dividends, interest upon stock, and protecting duty bounties. . . .

Nobility and hierarchy are not the only modes of constituting
orders, proper for fomenting national discontent, and introducing
monarchy, if it is true, as Mr. Adams asserts, and as all mankind
allow, "that wealth, is the great machine for governing the world."
Hence wealth, like suffrage, must be considerably distributed, to
sustain a democratick republick; and hence, whatever draws a considerable proportion of either into a few hands, will destroy it. As
power follows wealth, the majority must have wealth or lose power.
If wealth is accumulated in the hands of a few, either by a feudal
or a stock monopoly, it carries the power also; and a government becomes as certainly aristocratical, by a monopoly of wealth, as by a
monopoly of arms. A minority, obtaining a majority of wealth or
arms in any mode, becomes the government. . . .

Our policy is founded upon the idea, that it is both wise and just,
to leave the distribution of property to industry and talents; that
what they acquire is all their own, except what they owe to society;
that they owe nothing to society except a contribution equivalent
to the necessities of government; that they owe nothing to monopoly or exclusive privilege in any form; and that whether they are
despoiled by the rage of a mob, or the laws of a separate interest,
the genuine sanction of private property is equally violated. Are

these the principles of our policy? Do paper systems correspond with these principles?

If legislative patronage enriches a portion of society, that portion is necessarily converted into an order, possessing the qualities of an aristocracy. It is placed between the government and the nation. It receives wealth from the one, and takes it from the other. This ties it to the government by the passion of avarice, and separates it from the nation by the passion of fear. And these two passions, annexed to any separate interest, have unexceptionably converted it into a political order, and forced it into the ranks of despotism. . . .

From CONSTRUCTION CONSTRUED, AND CONSTITU-TIONS VINDICATED (1820)[1]

The Principles of Our Revolution

These are the keys of construction, and the locks of liberty. The question to be considered is, whether our revolution was designed to establish the freedom both of religion and property, or only of the former.

It is strange that the human mind should have been expanded in relation to religion, and yet should retain narrow notions in relation to property. Objects unseen, and incapable of being explained by the information of the senses, afford less perfect materials for the exercise of reason, than those capable of being investigated by evidence, within the scope of the human understanding. As the difficulties opposed to the correction of religious fanaticism seemed less surmountable, whilst its effects were more pernicious, the zeal of philosophers was condensed in an effort to relieve mankind from an evil the most distressing; and their attention was diverted from another, at this period the most prominent. But having wrested religious liberty from the grasp of fanaticism, it now behooves them to turn their attention towards pecuniary fanaticism, and to wrest civil liberty from its tyranny also. Between an absolute power in governments over the religion and over the property of men, the analogy is exact, and their consequences must therefore be the same. Freedom of religion being the discovery by which religious liberty could only be established; freedom of property must be the only means also, for the establishment of civil liberty. . . .

[1] (Richmond, 1820), pp. 9–13, 67, 78.

No form of government can foster a fanaticism for wealth, without being corrupted. The courtiers of republicks, able to exercise an absolute power over the national property, are more numerous and more vicious than the courtiers of kings, because access to patrons is easier; they have more occasion for partisans, and a multiplication of despots over property multiplies the channels of fraud. New ones also are frequently opened by a revolution of parties, and of patrons, who with their favorites and dependants, are in haste to bolster power or amass wealth, during the continuance of a fleeting authority. Against a propensity so mischievous, and so fatal to republicks, there seems to be no resource, but a constitutional prohibition of the power by which it is nurtured; and a rejection of precedents, by which infringements of so wholesome a prohibition are usually justified. Both reason and morality unite to impress upon nations, a necessity for imposing restraints upon a propensity, which may so easily be concealed under the most glittering robes of patriotism. What real patriot would feel himself molested, by restraints upon avarice and ambition? Are not both unfriendly to human happiness? Some patriots have sacrificed their lives for the happiness of their country. Is the sacrifice of an error, by which fraud and avarice are nurtured, too much to expect of ours?

A love of wealth, fostered by honest industry, is an ally both of moral rectitude, and national happiness, because it can only be gratified by increasing the fund for national subsistence, comfort, strength and prosperity; but a love of wealth, fostered by partial laws for enriching corporations and individuals, is allied to immorality and oppression, because it is gratified at the expense of industry, and diminishes its ability to work out national blessings. . . .

. . . Would liberty be well established in England, if her hierarchy was destroyed, whilst the government retained the absolute power of distributing wealth and poverty? Is not that establishment merely one of the modes for exercising this species of despotism; and what substantial or lasting remedy could arise from abolishing one mode, whilst others remained amply sufficient to establish the same pernicious principle? Is not a power of transferring property by pensions, bounties, corporations and exclusive privileges; and even of bestowing publick money by the unlimited will of legislative bodies, as dangerous to liberty, as a power of doing the same thing by the instrumentality of a privileged church? Is the casuistry consistent, which denies to a government the power of infringing the freedom of religion, and yet invests it with a despotism over the freedom of property? A corporation, combination, or chartered church for one purpose, in its pecuniary effects, is analagous to corporations for effecting the other. It has been said, that government in its best form is an evil. This absurd idea seems to have been suggested, by its being usually invested with an army of supernumerary powers wholly unnecessary for effecting the end of preserving social tranquillity and safety. Against these supernumerary powers, the United States waged a long war, upon the ground, that governments are instituted to secure, and not to bestow the freedom of property; and it would be highly absurd to suppose, that having established their great principle, they directly became contented with an unfruitful theory, and surrendered the idea of its application. It was tyrannical in the English government, said the colonies, to insist upon taking away their property, and giving it to placemen and pensioners; and they very justly considered life and liberty as so intimately connected with property, that the rights of the latter could not be invaded, without invading the other rights also. They fought for a revolution, and established governments to secure all three of these natural rights, because a loss of one was equivalent to a loss of all, in a national view. . . .

Property

Blackstone has treated of "The rights of persons, and the rights of things;" but the rights of man include life, liberty and property, according to the prevalent fashion of thinking in the United States. The last right is the chief hinge upon which social happiness depends. It is therefore extremely important to ascertain, whether it is secured by the same principle with our other rights; and whether the security, if the same, ought to be equivalently efficacious; before we proceed to the contemplated examination of several constructions of our constitutions. The rights to life, liberty and property, are so intimately blended together, that neither can be lost in a state of society without all; or at least, neither can be impaired without wounding the others. Being indissolubly united, a principle which embraces either must embrace all; and by allowing it to constitute the only solid security for one, we admit it to be the only solid security of the rest. A sovereignty in governments,

of every form, has universally claimed and exercised a despotick
power over life, liberty and property. Whether enjoyed by a monarchy, aristocracy, democracy, or by a mixture of the three, it acknowledges no controul, and submits to no limitations. . . .

. . . The freedom of property from the indefinite despotism of
sovereignty, is the best security to be found against those unjust
laws by which social liberty is so often injured; and against that
despotism of majorities, by which it has been so often destroyed.
This wise and just principle even denies to the sovereignty of the
people, a right to the private property of individuals, because the
conventional act by which that species of sovereignty was created,
conceded a right to tax for social purposes only, and withheld a
right to tax for individual aggrandizement. I conclude therefore,
that neither the state governments nor congress have a sovereign
power over property; that neither of them has any right at all to
create modes for transferring it artificially from one man or one
interest to another; that the right of taxation, with which they are
invested, is limited to the attainment of social ends or specified
objects; and that the right of appropriation, being merely an ap-
pendage of the right of taxation, is restrained to the same ends or
objects. . . .

From TYRANNY UNMASKED (1822) [1]

Neither ambition nor avarice could ever succeed in depriving nations of their liberty and property, if they did not by some artifice
enlist the services of a body of men, numerically powerful. The
general promises the plunder of a town to his soldiers; they take
it; and he keeps most of it for himself and his officers. These are
enriched, and the soldiers remain poor. A demagogue promises
liberty to a rabble, and by their help makes himself their tyrant.
And capitalists, by promising wealth to mechanicks, accumulate
it for themselves, and become their masters. The Committee disclaim a predilection for factory capitalists, and an enmity towards
agriculture. I balance this argument by disclaiming also a predilection for agriculturists, and an enmity towards mechanicks; but I
avow an enmity against all modes for transferring property by exclusive privileges. As no man, however, can find the seeds from

[1] (Washington, 1822), pp. 194–201, 345–349.

which his opinions have germinated, such protestations are frivolous, and they are also unworthy of weight; because the consequences, and not the origin of opinions, constitute their material-
ity. . . . At the threshold of this enquiry, I have changed a term,
by substituting mechanicks for manufacturers, to display truth more
clearly. The term agriculture needs no such correction, because
we have not the two conflicting classes of landlords and tenants,
as we have of capitalists and mechanicks. Where the land of a
country is owned by landlords, and worked by tenants, the phrase
"landed interest" refers to the landlords, who may enjoy exclusive
privileges of which the tenants do not partake; and the impoverishment of one interest may contribute to the enrichment of the other.
In like manner, where the factories belong to capitalists, and are
worked by mechanicks, the phrase "manufacturing interest" refers
to the capitalists, who may enjoy exclusive privileges of which the
workmen do not partake; and their impoverishment may contribute
to the enrichment of the capitalists, as the impoverishment of
tenants may enrich landlords. In deciding the questions, therefore, by the test of friendship or enmity, we ought to exhibit persons, and not confound distinct interests, as the objects of these
passions. A cold calculation of the profit to be made by factories,
may be a vice of avarice, but a friendly sympathy for the calamities
of workmen, arising from the policy of making laws to accumulate
this profit, can only flow from good will towards them.

The interest of mechanicks against the factory policy, advocated
by the Committee, is infinitely stronger than that of farmers, because, they may more easily be swept into factories, and the profits
of their labour more completely carried into the pockets of the capitalists, than can be effected in the case of land owners. These are
so powerful as to be able, when they feel a loss, to give themselves
a compensation, as the English landlords have done by the corn
laws; and between the capitalists and landlords in that country, the
mechanicks find poverty. . . . A mechanick employed in a factory rarely acquires a competence; opulence is out of the question;
and he is completely excluded from publick employments, by being
doomed to a situation in which he can never acquire a capacity for
them. He can hardly be considered as a citizen. A code of laws
draws around him a magick circle, by making mechanical combina-

tions punishable, lest they should check capitalist combinations; and he is re-imbursed by penalties for the loss of hope.

The condition of the mechanick in the United States has hitherto been extremely different. It neither excites insurrections, nor inculcates a hatred of the government. It does not require a regular army to cure the agonies of misery. It neither shortens life, nor devotes old age to an hospital. It never fails to acquire a competency by industry and good conduct; sometimes rises to opulence; and receives its due share of publick employments. Instead of being deemed mean and servile, it is capable of respectability, and the whole magistracy is open to it. . . .

To counteract facts established by a double example, the same bribe is offered to land-owners here, which has created in England, a conspiracy between landlords and capitalists against mechanicks, by which they have been reduced to perpetual labour and perpetual poverty.—The land-owners are told, that by coercing mechanicks into factories, the prices of their manufactures will be reduced, and that the land-owners will then be reimbursed for the bounties now paid to capitalists, by a future cheapness to be effected at the expense of mechanicks, thus coerced into factories. I do not deny that such would be the case, if the factory scheme could be carried to the same extent here as in England. This could not be effected, even if our populousness could furnish the materials, except by the English system of legislation to prevent mechanicks from breaking their factory chains, and compelling them to labour hard for low wages to supply the conspirators cheaply. But is not this coerced cheapness evidently imposed upon the mechanical occupation? If it could be effected in the United States, the first class of valuable and respectable citizens which would be ruined by it, would be the great body of mechanicks scattered throughout the country, who would be undersold by the factory capitalists, and compelled to relinquish their free occupations, and become hirelings at the factories. The promised consummation of the factory project, therefore, however tempting to farmers, would be a complete degradation of mechanicks from the equal and comfortable station they hold in society, to one much less desirable. Every present fraud offers a future bribe. The future cheapness offered to land-holders is too distant and uncertain, to induce them to enter into this conspiracy with the capitalists against the mechanicks; and besides, why should they get less than the English landlords for doing so? These have had their rents, and of course the value of their lands doubled or trebled into the bargain, and if without this additional bribe, cheapness would have been insufficient to compensate them for the evils of the capitalist-policy, the land-owners here may safely conclude that they will not be compensated by this promise alone, for co-operating in the conspiracy; and that to make a good bargain, they ought to have the price of their lands doubled or trebled, like the English landlords. . . .

The prices paid by farmers to the great number of free mechanicks, scattered throughout the country, and by these mechanicks to farmers, promote neighbourhood consumptions; create much domestick commerce regulated by free exchanges, and not by a fraudulent monopoly; stimulate mutual industry, and increase the value of property; but the prices paid to factory capitalists, so long as their monopoly operates, will to a great extent be employed in transferring and accumulating capital. A transfer of profit from industry to the accumulation of capital, whether the profit is agricultural or mechanical, is a mutual diminution of the fund, acting and reacting between industrious occupations, and begetting mutual prosperity. The more of his profits the agriculturist can save from the capitalist, the more employment he will give to his friend and neighbour, the mechanick; and the more of his are retained by the mechanick, the more he will consume of agricultural products, or enhance by his savings, the value of land.—In either case would domestick commerce be rendered more beneficial to the society, by diverting these funds from this intercourse, to the accumulation of pecuniary capitals?

. . . The most enormous monopoly is that of monarchs of all the land within their territories, once established in Europe by the feudal system, and still subsisting in Turkey and some Asiatic countries.—This deprives industry of its power to acquire, to a great extent. Of the same nature is the protecting-duty monopoly. A monopoly of land, enables the monopolist to extract wealth from the produce of land; and a monopoly of mechanicks, enables the monopolist to extract wealth from the produce of mechanicks. The monopolist in both cases is able to enhance the price of land or its produce, or the produce of his mechanicks, at the expense of buyers. Land was monopolized by the feudal system, incidentally to monopolize labour; by the factory system, the labour itself is directly monopolized. Next to that of land, a monopoly of manufacturing is the most extensive and oppressive of which we can have a conception. It even appears to operate more widely than a monopoly of land, because all are consumers of manufactures. It does not indeed take away the land itself of agriculturists, but it effects the same end which the feudal monopoly effected; it obtains a portion of its profits. If a law was made to bestow all the lands of the United States upon a few persons, it would be equivalent to a policy for enabling capitalists to build factories, and monopolize mechanicks. . . .

Is it enthusiasm or reason which causes me to behold the finger of God conducting the United States into a situation happily contrived to try and place at rest for ever, the doubt, whether human nature is able to maintain a fair, free, mild, and cheap government? No other people ever were, or ever will be in so good a situation to settle this question affirmatively; and their practical testimony will therefore be considered as conclusive. A great nation was made to nurture them up to independence. A despotick government was made an instrument towards effecting it. Their soils and climates bestow subsistence and energy, without possessing the exuberant fertility or alluring softness, by which conquerors are invited and the mind is enervated. They cover the largest space of the whole world, in which one language is spoken; so that ideas may be exchanged, prejudices encountered, and opinions examined, by one easy, rapid and familiar mode of communication throughout all their territories. A surprising concurrence of circumstances excluded orders and exclusive privileges; and the experience of two centuries taught them that they could do without these remnants of barbarous ages, and instruments of civilized tyranny. Various sects of Christians were wafted into them, without being actuated by the intention of establishing religious freedom, which yet it sprung out of this circumstance without man's agency, except as the humble instrument of an overruling providence. Had all emigrants been of one faith, this half of human liberty would probably have been lost for ever. Apparently, accident also produced a division of States, not less efficacious in favour of civil liberty, than are different sects in favour of religious. The wonderful concurrence of circumstances for effecting both ends, admonishes us to behold the division into States as also the work of providence. We have been taught that religion flourishes best, without oppressing the people by expensive establishments, as if to disclose to man the next great truth, that civil liberty does not require them. Make religion rich, and she becomes the patron of vice. Let a government become expensive, and it becomes the patron of ambition and avarice. In neither case can self-government exist, because both are founded upon a supposed necessity, that men must be robbed of their property to preserve social order; and this policy invariably terminates in despotism. Providence seems to have shielded us against it, by producing the division of religious sects, and of a vast territory into separate States; and as if still more securely to protect us against the endless pretext for exposing nations to enslaving privileges and impoverishing expenses, (drawn from the contiguity of powerful governments,) so often used to destroy both religious and civil liberty; it has blessed us with a geographical position, apparently, that our understandings might have the fairest opportunity to detect impositions framed with national antipathies, but directed against private property; and increased our population, so as to place us beyond the reach of fear. In these circumstances I behold a miracle, worked for the salvation of liberty, and creating an awful responsibility on the people of the United States. They seem to have been selected to evince the capacity of man for sustaining a fair and free government; and if by their failure, with such pre-eminent advantages, they shall renounce the favours of heaven, and consign a whole world of endless generations to the tyranny of expensive governments, they will be reprobated as another infatuated and rebellious people, who have rejected benefactions visibly flowing from an Almighty source.

The commission to overturn political idolatry thus entrusted to the United States, like that to overturn religious idolatry entrusted to the Jews, requires only that portion of sagacity, sufficient to discover a fact, of universal notoriety, incapable of contradiction, and acknowledged by every honest man, learned or unlearned. It is, that no species of property transferring policy, past or existing, foreign or domestick, ever did or ever can enrich the labouring classes of any society whatever; but that it universally impoverishes them. To this fact not a single exception appears in the whole history of mankind. What then can be more absurd, than that the agricultural and mechanical classes, or either of them, should conceive that they will be benefited by such a policy? What except labour, can permanently supply the property transferred? The mercantile class, as merchants only, must be impoverished by this policy; but a few individuals of this class, more frequently evade its oppression, than of other labouring classes, by blending the capitalist with the mercantile character; and becoming bankers, lenders to government, or factory owners. So far also, as the agricultural and mechanical classes are interspersed with individuals endowed with pecuniary privileges, such individuals derive emolument from the property-transferring policy, not as mechanicks or agriculturists, but in their privileged characters.—Those who gain more by banking, by the protecting-duty monopoly, or by loaning to the government, than they lose by these property-transferring machines, constitute no exception to the fact, that the property-transferring policy invariably impoverishes all labouring and productive classes. A few individuals are enriched by every species of tyranny, as its essence in civilized countries consists of transferring property by laws. If the general good is the end of self government, and if the property-transferring policy defeats the general good, it also defeats self-government. Therefore the United States cannot fulfil the great purpose to which they seem almost to have been destined, except by a degree of sagacity sufficient to discern, that the property-transferring policy in all its forms, however disguised, is a tyrannical imposition, only sustainable by the same species of political idolatry, which has blinded mankind to their interest, and is yet enslaving most or all civilized nations. . . .

6. DANIEL WEBSTER [1]

From "FIRST SETTLEMENT OF NEW ENGLAND" (1820) [2]

The nature and constitution of society and government in this country are interesting topics, to which I would devote what remains of the time allowed to this occasion. Of our system of government the first thing to be said is, that it is really and practically a free system. It originates entirely with the people, and rests on no other foundation than their assent. To judge of its actual operation, it is not enough to look merely at the form of its construction. The practical character of government depends often on a variety of considerations, besides the abstract frame of its constitutional organization. Among these are the condition and tenure of property; the laws regulating its alienation and descent; the presence or absence of a military power; an armed or unarmed yeomanry; the spirit of the age, and the degree of general intelligence. In these respects it cannot be denied that the circumstances of this country are most favorable to the hope of maintaining the government of a great nation on principles entirely popular. In the absence of military power, the nature of government must essentially depend on the manner in which property is holden and distributed. There is a natural influence belonging to property, whether it exists in many hands or few; and it is on the rights of property that both despotism and unrestrained popular violence ordinarily commence their attacks. Our ancestors began their system of government here under a condition of comparative equality in regard to wealth, and their early laws were of a nature to favor and continue this equality.

A republican form of government rests not more on political constitutions, than on those laws which regulate the descent and transmission of property. Governments like ours could not have been maintained, where property was holden according to the principles of the feudal system; nor, on the other hand, could the feudal

---

[1] On Webster, see above, pp. 180–182.

[2] Address at the celebration of the two hundredth anniversary of the landing at Plymouth Rock, in The Works of Daniel Webster, Vol. I, pp. 5–50, at 34–40. By the courtesy of Little, Brown & Company.

constitution possibly exist with us. Our New England ancestors brought hither no great capitals from Europe; and if they had, there was nothing productive in which they could have been invested. They left behind them the whole feudal policy of the other continent. They broke away at once from the system of military service established in the Dark Ages, and which continues, down even to the present time, more or less to affect the condition of property all over Europe. They came to a new country. There were, as yet, no lands yielding rent, and no tenants rendering service. The whole soil was unreclaimed from barbarism. They were themselves, either from their original condition, or from the necessity of their common interest, nearly on a general level in respect to property. Their situation demanded a parcelling out and division of the lands, and it may be fairly said, that this necessary act fixed the future frame and form of their government. The character of their political institutions was determined by the fundamental laws respecting property. The laws rendered estates divisible among sons and daughters. The right of primogeniture, at first limited and curtailed, was afterwards abolished. The property was all freehold. The entailment of estates, long trusts, and the other processes for fettering and tying up inheritances, were not applicable to the condition of society, and seldom made use of. On the contrary, alienation of the land was every way facilitated, even to the subjecting of it to every species of debt. The establishment of public registries, and the simplicity of our forms of conveyance have greatly facilitated the change of real estate from one proprietor to another. The consequence of all these causes has been, a great subdivision of the soil, and a great equality of condition; the true basis, most certainly, of a popular government. "If the people," says Harrington, "hold three parts in four of the territory, it is plain there can neither be any single person nor nobility able to dispute the government with them; in this case, therefore, except force be interposed, they govern themselves."

The history of other nations may teach us how favorable to public liberty are the division of the soil into small freeholds, and a system of laws, of which the tendency is, without violence or injustice, to produce and to preserve a degree of equality of property. It has been estimated, if I mistake not, that about the time of Henry the Seventh four fifths of the land in England was holden by the great barons and ecclesiastics. The effects of a growing commerce soon afterwards began to break in on this state of things, and before the Revolution, in 1688, a vast change had been wrought. It may be thought probable, that, for the last half-century, the process of subdivision in England has been retarded, if not reversed; that the great weight of taxation has compelled many of the lesser freeholders to dispose of their estates, and to seek employment in the army and navy, in the professions of civil life, in commerce, or in the colonies. The effect of this on the British constitution cannot but be most unfavorable. A few large estates grow larger; but the number of those who have no estates also increases; and there may be danger, lest the inequality of property become so great, that those who possess it may be dispossessed by force; in other words, that the government may be overturned.

A most interesting experiment of the effect of a subdivision of property on government is now making in France. It is understood, that the law regulating the transmission of property in that country, now divides it, real and personal, among all the children equally, both sons and daughters; and that there is, also, a very great restraint on the power of making dispositions of property by will. It has been supposed, that the effects of this might probably be, in time, to break up the soil into such small subdivisions, that the proprietors would be too poor to resist the encroachments of executive power. I think far otherwise. What is lost in individual wealth will be more than gained in numbers, in intelligence, and in a sympathy of sentiment. If, indeed, only one or a few landholders were to resist the crown, like the barons of England, they must, of course, be great and powerful landholders, with multitudes of retainers, to promise success. But if the proprietors of a given extent of territory are summoned to resistance, there is no reason to believe that such resistance would be less forcible, or less successful, because the number of such proprietors happened to be great. Each would perceive his own importance, and his own interest, and would feel that natural elevation of character which the consciousness of property inspires. A common sentiment would unite all, and numbers would not only add strength, but excite enthusiasm. It is true, that France possesses a vast military force, under the direction of an hereditary executive government; and military power, it is possible, may overthrow any government. It is in vain, however, in this period of the world, to look for security against military power to the arm of the great landholders. That notion is derived from a state of things long since past; a state in which a feudal baron, with his retainers, might stand against the sovereign and his retainers, himself but the greatest baron. But at present, what could the richest landholder do, against one regiment of disciplined troops? Other securities, therefore, against the prevalence of military power must be provided. Happily for us, we are not so situated as that any purpose of national defence requires, ordinarily and constantly, such a military force as might seriously endanger our liberties.

In respect, however, to the recent law of succession in France, to which I have alluded, I would, presumptously perhaps, hazard a conjecture, that, if the government do not change the law, the law in half a century will change the government; and that this change will be, not in favor of the power of the crown, as some European writers have supposed, but against it. Those writers only reason upon what they think correct general principles, in relation to this subject. They acknowledge a want of experience. Here we have had that experience; and we know that a multitude of small proprietors, acting with intelligence, and that enthusiasm which a common cause inspires, constitute not only a formidable, but an invincible power.

The true principle of a free and popular government would seem to be, so to construct it as to give to all, or at least to a very great majority, an interest in its preservation; to found it, as other things are founded, on men's interest. The stability of government demands that those who desire its continuance should be more powerful than those who desire its dissolution. This power, of course, is not always to be measured by mere numbers. Education, wealth, talents, are all parts and elements of the general aggregate of power; but numbers, nevertheless, constitute ordinarily the most important consideration, unless, indeed, there be a *military force* in the hands of the few, by which they can control the many. In this country we have actually existing systems of government, in the maintenance of which, it should seem, a great majority, both in numbers and in other means of power and influence, must see their interest. But this state of things is not brought about solely by written political constitutions, or the mere manner of organizing the govern-

ment; but also by the laws which regulate the descent and transmission of property. The freest government, if it could exist, would
not be long acceptable, if the tendency of the laws were to create
a rapid accumulation of property in few hands, and to render the
great mass of the population dependent and penniless. In such a
case, the popular power would be likely to break in upon the rights
of property, or else the influence of property to limit and control
the exercise of popular power. Universal suffrage, for example,
could not long exist in a community where there was great inequality of property. The holders of estates would be obliged, in
such case, in some way to restrain the right of suffrage, or else such
right of suffrage would, before long, divide the property. In the
nature of things, those who have not property, and see their neighbors possess much more than they think them to need, cannot be
favorable to laws made for the protection of property. When this
class becomes numerous, it grows clamorous. It looks on property
as its prey and plunder, and is naturally ready, at all times, for
violence and revolution.

It would seem, then, to be the part of political wisdom to found
government on property; and to establish such distribution of property, by the laws which regulate its transmission and alienation, as
to interest the great majority of society in the support of the government. This is, I imagine, the true theory and the actual practice of our republican institutions. With property divided as we
have it, no other government than that of a republic could be
maintained, even were we foolish enough to desire it. There is
reason, therefore, to expect a long continuance of our system.
Party and passion, doubtless, may prevail at times, and much temporary mischief be done. Even modes and forms may be changed,
and perhaps for the worse. But a great revolution in regard to
property must take place, before our governments can be moved
from their republican basis, unless they be violently struck off by
military power. The people possess the property, more emphatically than it could ever be said of the people of any other country,
and they can have no interest to overturn a government which protects that property by equal laws.

Let it not be supposed, that this state of things possesses too
strong tendencies towards the production of a dead and uninterest-
ing level in society. Such tendencies are sufficiently counteracted

by the infinite diversities in the characters and fortunes of individuals. Talent, activity, industry, and enterprise tend at all times to produce inequality and distinction; and there is room still for the accumulation of wealth, with its great advantages, to all reasonable and useful extent. It has been often urged against the state of society in America, that it furnishes no class of men of fortune and leisure. This may be partly true, but it is not entirely so, and the evil, if it be one, would affect rather the progress of taste and literature, than the general prosperity of the people. But the promotion of taste and literature cannot be primary objects of political institutions; and if they could, it might be doubted whether, in the long course of things, as much is not gained by a wide diffusion of general knowledge, as is lost by diminishing the number of those who are enabled by fortune and leisure to devote themselves exclusively to scientific and literary pursuits. However this may be, it is to be considered that it is the spirit of our system to be equal and general, and if there be particular disadvantages incident to this, they are far more than counterbalanced by the benefits which weigh against them. The important concerns of society are generally conducted, in all countries, by the men of business and practical ability; and even in matters of taste and literature, the advantages of mere leisure are liable to be overrated. If there exist adequate means of education and a love of letters be excited, that love will find its way to the object of its desire, through the crowd and pressure of the most busy society.

7. JAMES FENIMORE COOPER (1789–1851)

COOPER, famous novelist, was the son of a well-to-do landowner, local officeholder and Federalist politician (who was killed by a political opponent). He was born in Burlington, New Jersey, and reared on his father's extensive estate in a wilderness region near Otsego Lake, New York. He married at twenty-one and lived the life of a country squire on his wife's estate at Scarsdale, New York. After he had made his reputation with his first romantic novels, he lived seven years in Europe, where he met distinguished people and engaged in lively discussions with them on European and American politics. When he returned home, "America no longer seemed American" to him, and he no longer seemed American to home-town commentators. Some of his political judgments, written abroad, had aroused violent criticism in New York newspapers, and he replied savagely. The controversy extended over several years, in the press and in the courts. Cooper, a Democrat, brought a dozen suits for libel against his Whig critics; he won most of the suits, but not much popular favor.

Cooper wrote several works of social and political criticism: *Notions of the Americans* (2 vols., 1828), *A Letter to his Countrymen* (a pamphlet, 1834), and *The American Democrat* (a brief book, 1838). Several of his novels have political themes: notably *The Monikins* (1835), an allegory satirizing contemporary America by relating the experiences of a group of human beings who find themselves in a country run by monkeys. Cooper assailed American democracy in the West and the industrial capitalism of the East: the former for its frontier lawlessness and its leveling politics; the latter for its worship of financial success; both for their social crudities and their tolerance of political demagoguery.

[Political criticism appears also in Cooper's *Homeward Bound* (1838), *Home as Found* (1838), *The Redskins* (1846), and several of his other novels.

See: Henry W. Boynton, *James Fenimore Cooper* (1931); John F. Ross, *The Social Criticism of Fenimore Cooper* (1933); Robert E. Spiller, *Fenimore Cooper, Critic of His Times* (1931); H. L. Mencken, "Introduction" to the 1931 reprint of *The American Democrat*, pp. xi–xx; Vernon L. Parrington, *Main Currents of American Thought*, Vol. II (1927), pp. 222–237.]

"ON PROPERTY" (1838) [1]

As property is the base of all civilization, its existence and security are indispensable to social improvement. Were it possible to have a community of property, it would soon be found that no one would toil, but that men would be disposed to be satisfied with barely enough for the supply of their physical wants, since none would exert themselves to obtain advantages solely for the use of others. The failure of all attempts to form communities, even on a small scale, with a common interest, goes to prove this. Where there is a rigid equality of condition, as well as of rights, that condition must necessarily be one of a low scale of mediocrity, since it is impossible to elevate those who do not possess the requisite qualities any higher. Thus we see that the societies, or religious sects, in which a community of property prevails, are content with merely supplying the wants of life, knowing little or nothing of its elegancies, refinements, or mental pleasures. These communities, moreover, possess an outlet for their idle and dissolute, by resorting to expulsion, a remedy that society itself cannot apply.

The principle of individuality, or to use a less winning term, of selfishness, lies at the root of all voluntary human exertion. We toil for food, for clothes, for houses, lands, and for property, in general. This is done, because we know that the fruits of our labor will belong to ourselves, or to those who are most dear to us. It follows, that all which society enjoys beyond the mere supply of its first necessities, is dependent on the rights of property.

It is not known that man exists anywhere without establishing rules for the protection of property. Even insects, reptiles, beasts and birds, have their several possessions, in their nests, dens and supplies. So completely is animal exertion, in general, whether in man or beast, dependent on the enjoyment of this right, under limitations which mark their several conditions, that we may infer that the rights of property, to a certain extent, are founded in nature. The food obtained by his toil, cannot be taken from the mouth of man, or beast, without doing violence to one of the first of our natural rights. We apply the term of robber, or despoiler, to

[1] In *The American Democrat, or Hints on the Social and Civic Relations of the United States of America* (1838); reprint, with an introduction by H. L. Mencken (1931), at pp. 127–133. By courtesy of Alfred A. Knopf.

the reptile or bird, that preys on the aliment of another animal, as well as to the human thief. So long as natural justice is admitted to exist, the party assailed, in such cases, has a right to defend his own.

The rights of property become artificial and extended, as society becomes civilized. In the savage state the land is without owners, property consisting in the hut, the food, and the arms used in war and in the chase. In pastoral, or semi-barbarous states, use gives claims, not to individuals, but to tribes, and flocks are pastured on grounds that belong to one entire community, but to that one only. Private property is composed of cattle, sheep, tents, horses, camels, with the common claims to share in the common fields.

Civilization has established various, and in some cases, arbitrary and unjust distinctions, as pertaining to the rights of property. These are abuses, the tendency of man being to convert into curses things that Providence designed to prove benefits. Still, most of the ordinances of civilized society, that are connected with this interest, are founded in reason, and ought to be rigidly maintained.

The first great principle connected with the rights of property, is its inviolability in all cases in which the laws leave it in possession of the proprietor. Every child should be taught to respect the sanctity of his neighbour's house, garden, fields and all that is his. On those parts of another's possessions, where it is permitted to go, he should go with care not to abuse the privilege, and from those parts which he is forbidden to use, he should religiously abstain. The child that is properly impressed in infancy, with the rights of property, is in little danger of committing theft in after life, or, in any other manner of invading that which is the just possession of another.

The doctrine that any one "may do what he please with his own," however, is false. One may do with his own, whatever the laws and institutions of his country allow, and no more. One may even respect the letter, and yet violate the spirit of those laws and institutions, committing a moral, if not a legal offence, in so doing. Thus, he, who would bring his money to bear upon the elections of a country like this, abuses his situation, unless his efforts are confined to fair and manly discussions before the body of the people.

In nations where the mass have no political rights, means have been found to accumulate power by the aid of wealth. The pretence has been that none but the rich have a stake in society. Every man who has wants, feelings, affections and character, has a stake in society. Of the two, perhaps, the necessities of men are a greater corrective of political abuses, than their surplus means. Both may lead to evil, beyond a doubt, but, as laws which are framed by all, must be tolerably impartial and general in their operation, less danger arises from the rule of the former, than from the rule of the latter. When property rules, it rules alone; but when the poor are admitted to have a voice in government, the rich are never excluded. Such is the nature of man, that all exclusive power is uniformly directed to exclusive purposes. Property always carries with it a portion of indirect political influence, and it is unwise, and even dangerous, to strengthen this influence by adding to it constitutional privileges; the result always being to make the strong stronger, and the weak weaker.

On the other hand, all who love equal justice, and, indeed, the safety of free institutions, should understand that property has its rights, and the necessity of rigidly respecting them. It is the right of the possessor of property to be placed on an equal footing with all his fellow citizens, in every respect. If he is not to be exalted on account of his wealth, neither is he to be denounced. In this country, it is the intention of the institutions, that money should neither increase nor lessen political influence.

There are habits that belong to every condition of life. The man of hereditary wealth, is usually a man of leisure, and he little understands the true spirit of democracy, who supposes that such a man is not to enjoy the tastes and inclinations, which are the fruits of leisure and cultivation, without let or hindrance. Democracy leaves every man the master of his acts and time, his tastes and habits, so long as he discharges his duty to the publick, and respects the laws. He who declaims against another for holding himself aloof from general association, arrogates to himself a power of censure that he does not rightly possess, and betrays his own consciousness of inferiority. Men of really high social station never make this complaint, for they are above jealousy; and they who do, only discover a feeling that is every way removed from the manliness and spirit of true independence.

One may certainly be purse-proud, and of all the sources of human pride, mere wealth is the basest and most vulgar minded. Real gentlemen are almost invariably above this low feeling, and they who attribute habits, that have their rise in sentiment, tastes, knowledge and refinement, to such a cause, usually make the mistake of letting their own ignorance of the existence of motives so elevated, be known. In a word, if the man of property has no more personal legal immunities, than the man who has none, neither has he fewer. He is privileged to use his own means, under the general regulations of society, in the pursuit of his own happiness, and they who would interfere with him, so far from appreciating liberty, are ignorant of its vital principles.

If left to itself, unsupported by factitious political aid, but sufficiently protected against the designs and rapacity of the dishonest, property is an instrument of working most of the good that society enjoys. It elevates a national character, by affording the means of cultivating knowledge and the tastes; it introduces all above barbarism into society; and it encourages and sustains laudable and useful efforts in individuals. Like every other great good, its abuses are in proportion to its benefits.

The possessor of property is not, half the time, as much the object of envy as the needy imagine, for its corrupting influence endangers eternal peace. Great estates are generally of more benefit to the community than to their owners. They bring with them anxiety, cares, demands, and, usually, exaggerated notions, on the part of the publick, of the duties of the rich. So far from being objects of envy, their possessors are oftener the subjects of commiseration; he who has enough for his rational wants, agreeably to his habits and education, always proving the happier man.

The possessions of new families are commonly exaggerated in the publick mind, while those of long established families are as commonly diminished.

A people that deems the possession of riches its highest source of distinction, admits one of the most degrading of all influences to preside over its opinions. At no time, should money be ever ranked as more than a means, and he who lives as if the acquisition of property were the sole end of his existence, betrays the dominion of the most sordid, base, and grovelling motive, that life offers.

Property is desirable as the ground work of moral independence, as a means of improving the faculties, and of doing good to others, and as the agent in all that distinguishes the civilized man from the savage.

Property has been made the test of political rights, in two distinct forms. It has been *represented*, and it has been established as a *qualification*. The *representation* of property is effected in two modes; first, by giving the proprietor more votes than one, according to the number and situation of his freeholds; and, secondly, by raising the test of qualification so high, as to exclude all but the affluent from the franchise. The first was the English system, previously to the recent changes; the last, is the actual system of France.

A government founded on the representation of property, however direct or indirect, is radically vicious, since it is a union of two of the most corrupting influences to which man is subject. It is the proper business of government to resist the corruptions of money, and not to depend on them.

To a qualification of property, if placed so low as to embrace the great majority of the people, there is no very serious objection, though better tests might, perhaps, be devised. Residence, character, information, and fixed relations with society, ought to be added to this qualification; and it might be better, even, could they be made entirely to supersede it. In local governments, or those of towns and villages, which do little more than control property, a low property qualification is the true test of the franchise, though even in these cases, it might be well to add information and character.

8. HORACE GREELEY (1811–72)

GREELEY, famous newspaper editor and political reformer, was born in Amherst, New Hampshire, son of a farmer and day laborer who was never able to keep his family much above the margin of subsistence. The family shifted to Vermont and then to Pennsylvania; and Greeley, in his fifteenth year, with very little schooling, settled in New York as a journeyman printer. He rose to a partnership in a small printing shop, wrote articles for newspapers, joined a relative in setting up a weekly magazine of social criticism (called the *New Yorker*, 1834–41), edited small Whig dailies, and (at the age of thirty) founded the New York *Tribune*, of which he was the editor until his death thirty years later. He assembled an exceptionally able staff for the *Tribune* and it soon became one of the most influential papers of the country. It was known as a Whig paper during the first decade of its existence, and Greeley gave strong support to Henry Clay's "American System."

Greeley aligned himself with the new Republican party but kept himself free from rigid ties to any political group. He opposed most of the compromises on slavery, yet sought to bring the Civil War to a close by compromise and advocated a conciliatory treatment of the post-war South. He defended tariff protection and attacked the monopolistic beneficiaries of tariffs. He brought new ideas to the attention of the north and west. At a time when *laisser faire* was the policy approved by most of his readers, he insisted that there were serious maladjustments in American society which only organized efforts could correct. He was a persistent and eclectic reformer, setting forth his ideas vigorously in editorials and lectures. He fought for temperance, the abolition of capital punishment, and land and labor reforms. In 1872 he was nominated for President by both the Liberal-Republicans and the Democrats, on platforms substantially the same for the two parties. The platforms did not fit the nominee: they straddled the tariff issue and demanded civil service reform, whereas he was a strong protectionist and had offered excuses for the spoils system. In a campaign of personal vilification, President Grant, the regular Republican candidate, was re-elected by a large majority. Greeley died a few weeks later.

Greeley had been particularly disturbed by the consequences of the rapid industrialization of the east. He attacked monopoly, the unequal distribution of wealth, and the callousness of industrialists in the face of bad living and working conditions among their employees. "Go West"—to the unoccupied lands of the public domain—was one way of escape for the crowded and exploited workingmen. Accordingly the *Tribune* gave powerful aid to the "land reformers'" program (finally made law in the "Homestead Act" of 1862) for alloting family-sized farms, at nominal prices, to actual settlers on the public lands. He approved some forms of labor legislation but held that a general improvement of the laborer's status should be sought chiefly through organized efforts of the workers themselves.

[See: Horace Greeley, *Recollections of a Busy Life* (1868); John R. Commons, "Horace Greeley and the Working Class Origins of the Republican Party," *Political Science Quarterly*, Vol. XXIV (1909), pp. 468–488; Vernon L. Parrington, *Main Currents of American Thought*, Vol. II (1927), pp. 247–258; Don C. Seitz, *Horace Greeley, Founder of the New York Tribune* (1926).]

From "THE EMANCIPATION OF LABOR" (1846) [1]

Work stands in no need of eulogium. From olden times Priests and Poets have vied with Orators and Statesmen in heaping praises and flatteries on the man of honest, independent, useful toil. Not merely have these resonantly proclaimed that he *ought to be*, but that he *is* the most blessed among mortals. Indeed, an unsophisticated listener or reader might well imbibe the notion that all these honeyed eulogists, earth's great and glorious, had been thrust out, by some harsh decree of inexorable Fate, from the plow-field and the work-bench—sent sorrowing exiles into forums or senates—and there compelled to witness afar off the felicities they too might have enjoyed had they been born under kindlier stars, and to be content, in their sublime self-denial, with but depicting the delights of digging and delving, which only the more fortunate millions must enjoy.

Yet, in the midst of all this deluge of flattery and felicitation, the Worker of the Nineteenth Century stands a sad and care-worn man. Once in a while a particularly flowery Fourth-of-July Oration, Political harangue, or Thanksgiving Sermon, catching him well-filled with creature-comforts and a little inclined to soar starward, will take him off his feet, and for an hour or two he will wonder if

[1] In Horace Greeley, *Hints Toward Reform* (New York, 1850), pp. 13–50, at 13–20, 27, 29–34, 36–37, 40, 42–45. By courtesy of Harper & Brothers.

ever human lot was so blest as that of the free-born American laborer. He hurrahs, cavorts, and is ready to knock any man down
who will not readily and heartily agree that this is a great country,
and our industrious classes the happiest people on earth. The hal-
lucination passes off, however, with the silvery tones of the orator,
the exhilarating fumes of the liquor which inspired it. The inhaler
of the bewildering gas bends his slow steps at length to his sorry
domicile, or wakes therein on the morrow, in a sober and practical
mood. His very exaltation, now past, has rendered him more
keenly susceptible to the deficiencies and impediments which hem
him in: his house seems narrow; his food coarse; his furniture scanty;
his prospects gloomy, and those of his children more sombre, if
possible; and as he hurries off to the day's task which he has too
long neglected and for which he has little heart, he too falls into
that train of thought which is beginning to encircle the globe, and
of which the burden may be freely rendered thus—"Why should
those by whose toil ALL comforts and luxuries are produced or made
available enjoy so scanty a share of them? Why should a man able
and eager to work ever stand idle for want of employment in a
world where so much needful work impatiently awaits the doing?
Why should a man be required to surrender something of his independence in accepting the employment which will enable him to
earn by honest effort the bread of his family? Why should the
man who faithfully labors for another and receives therefor less than
the product of his labor be currently held the obliged party, rather
than he who buys the work and makes a good bargain of it? In
short, Why should Speculation and Scheming ride so jauntily in
their carriages, splashing honest Work as it trudges humbly and
wearily by on foot?"—Such, as I interpret it, is the problem which
occupies and puzzles the knotted brain of Toil in our day. Let us
ponder it.

But first, let us look at the whole matter in the light in which it
presents itself to Conservatism, or the champions of the established
order of things. We can lose nothing, we may gain something of
insight, by so regarding it, which will reward a few moments' attention. Inestimable is the value of a Fact, if we do but rightly apprehend it; and very strong is the inherent presumption that the
shape things have actually, and as we say naturally, taken is the
very best they could have taken, all things considered, including

the nature of Man. Let us look, then, at this whole matter of Labor, its Condition and Recompense, as it must appear to the men of substance and of thrift all around us.

All extreme statements begin and end in error, and nothing can be more mistaken than the vulgar presumption that Wealth goes by luck, or in fact that, searchingly regarded, there is any such thing as luck in the Universe. The man of respectability and property, whose blocks of houses adorn the busiest streets of our towns, and whose note goes unquestioned in bank, can you think him distinguished by no substantial qualities from those who were his playmates and schoolmates, and who are now his tenants and hirelings? O rely on it, there is no such instance of results without a cause in Nature! The man may be no better, I readily grant you, than those around him—perhaps in the truest sense no wiser—but very different he must be, and for that one purpose of accumulating property, a vastly superior being. Tried in History or Geography, in Psalmody or the Catechism, he might prove of small account; but in that wisdom which coins dollars from rocks and extracts fertility from marshes and miasms, he must be an adept. Nay, I go farther, and insist that a keen eye would have readily picked him out from among his schoolmates, and said, 'Here is the lad who will die a Bank President, owning factories and blocks of stores!' Now let us see how the questions we meditate must appear to this thrifty, practical man:

Trace his history closely, and you will find that in his boyhood he was provident and frugal—that he shunned expense and dissipation—that he feasted and quaffed seldom, unless at others' cost —that he was rarely seen at balls or frolics—that he was diligent in study and in business—that he did not hesitate to do an uncomfortable job, if it bade fair to be profitable—that he husbanded his hours and made each count one, either in earning or in preparing to work efficiently. He rarely or never stood idle because the business offered him was esteemed ungenteel or disagreeable—he laid up a few dollars during his minority, which proved a sensible help to him on going into business for himself—he married seasonably, prudently, respectably—he lived frugally and delved steadily until it clearly became him to live better, and until he could employ his time to better advantage than at the plow or over the bench. Thus his first thousand dollars came slowly but surely; the next more easily and readily by the help of the former; the next, of course, more easily still; until now he adds thousands to his hoard with little apparent effort or care. But the germ of all this spreading oak was in the tough acorn whence it sprang. Given the original qualities of the lad, all beyond was plainly deducible therefrom, unless prevented by death or some extreme calamity.

Now we shall but waste our breath in attempting to convince this man that the world is not a very good world as it stands, and labor rewarded exactly as it should be. Talk to him of the wants and woes of the Poor, and he will answer you that their sons can afford to smoke and drink freely, which he at their age could not; and that he now meets many of these poor in the market, buying luxuries that he can not afford. Dwell on the miseries occasioned by a dearth of employment, and he will reply that *he* never encountered any such obstacle when poor; for when he could find nothing better, he cleaned streets or stables, and when he could not command twenty dollars a month, he fell to work as heartily and cheerfully for ten or five. In vain will you seek to explain to him that his rare faculty both of doing and of finding to do—his wise adaptation of means to ends in all circumstances, his frugality and others' improvidence—are a part of your case—that it is precisely because all are not created so handy, so thrifty, so worldly-wise, as himself, that you seek so to modify the laws and usages of Society that a man may still labor steadily, efficiently, and live comfortably, although his youth was not improved to the utmost, and though his can never be the hand that transmutes all it touches to gold. Failing here, you urge that at least his children should be guarantied an unfailing opportunity to learn and to earn, and that they, surely, should not suffer nor be stifled in ignorance because of their parent's imperfections. Still you talk in Greek to the man of substance, unless he be one of the few who have, in acquiring wealth, outgrown the idolatry of it, and learned to regard it truly as a means of doing good, and not as an end of earthly effort. If he be a man of wealth merely, still cherishing the spirit which impelled him to his life-long endeavor, the world appears to him a vast battlefield, on which some must win victory and glory while to others are accorded shattered joints and discomfiture, and the former could not be, or would lose their zest, without the latter.

It seems to him quite plain that all might become as rich as he is if they would make the needful sacrifices of ease and mortifications of appetite; and if they won't, what can *he* do for them? To dissipate his fortune in prodigal beneficence would injure thousands and bring lasting good to few; to reduce mankind to some sort of Agrarian level would, if practicable, render life a tame, plodding, humdrum affair, hardly worth taking as a gift. In fine, the world appears to him the best that could be for the men and women who inhabit it,—its usages and laws the plain dictates of Divine benignity contemplating human depravity; and to all your suggestions of radical improvement he simply shakes his head and turns away to inquire the price of Cotton or the chances of an alteration in the Tariff.

Him we will leave for a season to his more congenial pursuits, while we inquire and consider in our own way what changes are necessary to the Emancipation and Social elevation of the laborer. I affirm, then, that there are three important respects in which the condition of the Laboring Mass, even of our own countrymen, may be improved, ought to be improved, and in regard to which it is the duty of the rich and powerful, of the Church and the State, to cowork for the required melioration. Of these I would place first in order, though perhaps not in practical importance,

Their relation to the Soil. I place this first, because I think Society and Government have been guilty of a *positive*, not a negative, wrong in regard to it—a wrong of usurpation and misdoing, and not merely of neglect and short-coming. God created the earth for the use and subsistence of mankind, and not primarily of a part, and of the rest in subordination to these. By Nature's law, use and improvement can alone vest in any individual a right to call some spot of earth his own, and exclude all others from the enjoyment and benefit thereof. Nothing can well be a more palpable subversion of the order of Providence than the assumption by Governments of a right to grant a province or county of virgin soil to some favorite, whether with or without consideration, to be held by him and his heirs for their own use and benefit, and to be cultivated and improved by others on terms which make the landlord class rich without labor or useful doing, and keep the tenant class mainly poor and subservient, though they do their best. If there ever was or can be a monstrous subversion of the order of Providence, it is here. Man has a natural right to such a portion of the earth not already improved by others as he can cultivate and make fruitful; the act of Government is simply officious and impertinent which assumes to give him this, and it is a gross usurpation and moral nullity to undertake to give him more. As well might it attempt to farm out the rain or sunshine, giving to one man all that falls on his own land and several of his neighbors', and directing these to buy so much as they need of him. What Government rightfully may and ought to do in the premises is simply to determine and declare the area of the earth's surface which one man may justly, and therefore legally, appropriate to himself and transmit to his posterity without encroaching on the equal natural rights of others. In a young and thinly-peopled community, this area may be larger; as population increases and arts are perfected, it should be gradually reduced and the freehold left vacant to-day by death be divided among the heirs, so as to leave no one in possession of more than the public good prescribes as the maximum for any one man. At first, a mile square might be allowable, there being so much or more for each family in the community; and we see that this allotment has been decided upon in the settlement of Oregon. I can not doubt that this is far too much, whether we regard individual or general good; that the settlers, thus held apart by their mutual grasping, will lose vastly more in education, social intercourse, neighborly kindnesses, than they can possibly gain in ultimate wealth. If the principle of Limitation had been early adopted and maintained, I presume a much smaller area would have been deemed ample. As it is, the emigrant to Oregon grasps not for himself and his children, his flocks and herds only, but with a view to his future aggrandizement by selling off or renting to others. But let a colony on a territory, say of 50,000 arable square miles, begin by allotting to each pioneer a square mile, if he be unwisely greedy enough to desire so much, with the express understanding, however, that this area is to be diminished to future occupants so soon and so fast as the increase of population shall demand it, and that meantime no person shall be allowed upon any pretext to acquire more than the maximum prescribed by law. . . .

Next in order to Land Reform stands the question of Labor Reform, or the regulation of the hours of daily manual toil. I am not aware that any noted writer on Social Economy, or on the sanitary and moral condition of the Laboring Classes, has failed to condemn the exaction of twelve to thirteen hours' labor per day as excessive and pernicious—an offence against general well-being, and even against the self-interest of the Employers. . . .

I am encouraged to hope for an early and favorable action on this subject by recent action in England. It is sometimes made a reproach to our influential and wealthy class that they pattern closely after England, and copy her fashions, her laws, habits, and thoughts, with servile alacrity. I will not here stop to consider how far this ought to be esteemed a reproach if it were admitted to be a truth. It seems to me that we might learn much from that same England, both by way of example and of warning. Be this as it may, the fact that the British Parliament has passed a law decreeing a reduction of the Hours of Factory Labor to eleven, and after one year to ten per day, will doubtless do much to pave the way for and hasten the adoption of some kindred measure here. Such action on the other side of the Atlantic will be effectual not merely as an example, but by removing the dangers, real or fancied, of unequal Foreign competition, in case of a reduction of hours on this side. And I may fairly presume that the most ferocious hater of British laws and precedents will make little objection to our imitating this.

Yet a Limitation of the Hours of Labor seems to me a secondary though most important Reform. So long as unemployed Labor crowds the market and the street, eagerly chaffering and underbidding for opportunity to earn a bare subsistence, I fear any stringent legislation on this point could not be enforced. Indeed, the difficulties environing the subject are by no means few nor trivial. The evil resembles in character the 'compound fracture' of the physical man. We can all agree at the outset that ten hours' faithful, skillful labor per day *ought* to enable any man to support his family comfortably and respectably. But here are men whose personal burdens are excessive—who owe debts incurred by past sickness or misfortune in business; who have sick or disabled relatives cast upon their hands, and who choose to labor excessively in order to meet manfully the demands made upon them. Can the law wisely interfere to say that such men shall not work twelve or fourteen hours if they choose? Again: a dam gives way, the machinery of a mill breaks, and five hundred workers must stand idle and incur expense until a few can make all right again. Would it be wise and just to prescribe that these few shall be inflexibly restricted to ten hours' labor per day? These instances might be multiplied, but enough. Since it is confessedly impolitic and indeed impossible to fix by law the *price* of any service or commodity, it is not without reason that some have honestly doubted that any law prescribing arbitrarily the boundaries of a day's work would be effective or useful. The end aimed at is at last to be reached, in my judgment, from the other side—by such a change in the Social Condition of the mass of Laborers and in their relation to the Soil, as will leave them *really* free to accept an offer of employment, in view of all its conditions, or decline it. Secure to them this, and they will enforce a suitable limitation of the Hours of Labor without the aid of positive, peremptory statutes; but so long as this is not, I apprehend that no law can surely and uniformly accomplish the desired end.

But, now that we have considered the natural difficulties and limitations to be encountered, I think we are prepared to state clearly what the law can and may do in the premises. All must allow that there should be *some* definite limit to an ordinary day's work, and that that limit should not be fixed and changed as the mere pleasure or interest of the Employing Class shall dictate. I intend by this no reflection on the character of that Class. That would ill become me, since to that Class I at present belong. I do not believe it less wise, humane, or considerate, in the average, than the Employed, nor less likely to do right where the interests of the two may seem to conflict. But the sound general rule that no man is a proper judge in his own case applies here as well as elsewhere. There should always be two parties to a bargain, and to every part of it, otherwise it is apt to prove a hard one. And while I hold that the State can not properly prescribe that no man shall in any case work more for another than ten hours in any one day—still less can it in my view, make one law for Corporations and another for Individuals—it may yet, as the general Protector of the Weak against the Strong, do much, and ought to do much, to mitigate the evils of excessive hours of daily toil. The action I would recommend, and which in one State has already in part received the sanction of the Legislature, is substantially as follows:

1. An act forbidding absolutely the employment of children or minors, whether Apprentices or Hired, for more than ten hours per day. The State has a right to see, and ought to see, that the frames

of the rising generations are not shattered nor their constitutions undermined by excessive labor. She should do this for her own sake as well as Humanity's. She has a vital interest in the strength and vigor of those who are to be her future fathers and mothers, her defenders in war, her cultivators and artisans in peace. She may safely make this limitation imperative, since for whatever service it may be necessary to employ labor for a longer term per day there will always be found an abundance of adults, if proper inducements are offered.

2. A simple declaratory act that in all cases where no other term is specified, the Law shall presume and decide that an agreement to work a week, a month, a year, or any other term, implies ten hours' faithful work on each secular day, and no more. It may be expedient to vary this term in certain out-door employments, especially Farming, making it nine hours between October and March, and eleven between April and September, the four months named standing at ten hours; but this would be in perfect consistency with the general principle that ten hours should constitute a legal day's work, wherever the parties, being responsible and independent adults, do not see fit to vary this by express agreement. The moral effect of such an act, in inducing a very general conformity to its dictates, would be great, and I can not believe that much hired labor would ultimately be performed otherwise than in accordance with the rule it prescribed, save in pressing emergencies.

To the ardent and dogmatic Reformer, who holds the Ten-Hour Rule the chief and sufficient means for the Emancipation of Labor from thraldom and depression, this suggestion will seem tame and halting; but I confidently believe such an act as it contemplates would effect more enduring good than would one that took the more arbitrary and inflexible form. Yet I would see with pleasure the two tried side by side, in sister States, by way of experiment.

—A Limitation of the Hours of Labor, once accomplished, will be valuable mainly for the Opportunity it proffers—the prospect it opens. 'The end is not yet'—very far from it. If the worker, released from excessive drudgery in the mill or the shop, shall mis-improve his new-found leisure in the groggery, the cigar-store, the gambling den, or some other haunt of vileness, it were well for him if he had remained a patient, abject drudge for life. And herein is the discouragement of many from all effort to improve the physical and temporal condition of the less fortunate Laboring Class. They can only see that more wages give more liquor, and more leisure incites to more dissipation. Alas! let us confess in deep humility and sorrow that there is a deplorable truth at the bottom of this. Yet no—I think it is *not* at the bottom, but nearer he surface. Fearfully true it is that many of those whose lives are mechanical merely—whose days are consecrated to drudgery, and the gloom of whose narrow tenements is rarely softened by the sun of Hope—*do* usually spend their hours snatched from toil in degrading, brutalizing sensualities, so as to give plausibility to the conclusion that they would be better if they had no leisure at all and no resources beyond the means of supplying the barest necessaries of life. But the logic which thence infers that the victim of incessant toil and meager recompense ought ever to remain such is that which exalts Slavery into a Divine and beneficent institution, and proves War a general blessing by demonstrating the average worthlessness or worse of those it employs and consumes. We must stop this arguing from existing evils in support of the abuses and wrongs which created them. Let us give Human Nature a fair trial, and see if it utterly lack sense as well as any glimmering of virtue, before we pronounce it a hopeless failure, to be managed only with the strait-jacket and the halter. Let us have a fair and full trial of a Laboring Class thoroughly educated, not overworked, fairly remunerated, with ample leisure, and adequate opportunities for Social, Moral, and Intellectual culture and enjoyment, and then, if the hard-handed multitude shall still persist in squandering their leisure and their means in riot and dissipation, we must sadly, reluctantly, but utterly, abandon all hope of a better day coming for the Toiling Millions, and leave them to the tender mercies of the miser, the forestaller, the pawnbroker, the grog-seller, as fair game. Whether the land-pirate strip the wreck or the sea swallow it, what matter? But I can not doubt that a better Social condition, enlarged opportunities of good, an atmosphere of Humanity and Hope, would insure a nobler and truer Character, and that the dens of dissipation will cease to lure those whom a proper Education has qualified, and whom excessive Toil has not disqualified, for the improvement of Liberty and Leisure. At all events, the momentous consequences depending should impel a speedy trial of the experiment, and insure a fair trial. . . .

Unquestionably the Emancipation of Labor is to be effected through or in conjunction with the mental and moral improvement of the Laboring Class. So far, all are of one mind. But whoever argues thence that nothing is to be done, nor even attempted, in the way of physical or circumstantial melioration, until the Laboring Class shall have wrought out its own thorough spiritual development and moral renovation, might as well declare himself a champion of the Slave-Trade at once. The internal and external renovation are each necessary to the completeness of the other. Merely lightening his tasks and enlarging his comforts will not raise a groveling, sensual, ignorant boor to the dignity of true manhood; but no more can just and luminous ideas of his own nature, relations, duties, and destiny, be expected often to irradiate the mind of one doomed to a life of abject drudgery, penury, and privation. "Tom," said a Colonel on the Rio Grande to one of his command, "how can so brave and good a soldier as you are so demean himself as to get drunk at every opportunity?"—"Colonel!" replied the private, "how can you expect all the virtues that adorn the human character for seven dollars a month?" The answer, however faulty in morals, involves a grave truth. Self-respect is the shield of Virtue; Comfort and Hope are the hostages we proffer the world for our good behavior in it; take these away, and Temptation is left without counteracting force or influence. . . .

Here, then, is the basis of our demand for that integral and all-pervading reform in the circumstances and conditions of human existence which we term ASSOCIATION, and in which rests my hope of a better day at hand for the down-trodden millions. Association affirms that every child born into the world has a rightful claim upon the community around him for Subsistence until able to earn for himself; for an Education which shall enable him to earn efficiently as well as rightly to improve and enjoy; and for Opportunity to earn at all times by honest Industry steadily employed and justly remunerated. . . .

. . . Why may we not give to Labor a republican organization, as we have, in defiance of a croaking world, given one to Government, so that the workers shall freely choose their own chiefs or overlookers, regulate their own hours of daily toil, and divide the general product according to a preconcerted scale whose sole end shall be mutual and universal justice? Is Labor so intractable, so senseless, that it can never run its appointed race without a rider? Let us at least hope not.

Let me rudely sketch you a village, township, school district, or whatever you may term it, organized as we would have it, and as we hope many ultimately will be. The basis is a faith among the associates or members that they can live harmoniously with and deal justly by each other, treating any casual imperfections which may be developed with forbearance and kindness. One hundred families, animated by this spirit, resolve to make an attempt toward a more trustful and genial life, and to that end sell off as they can their immovable possessions and resolve to seek a new home together; we will say in Michigan or Wisconsin. They send out two or three chosen leaders, who, after careful examination, select and purchase a tract of one to five thousand acres, as their means will warrant, embracing the largest circle of advantages—Timber, Prairie, Water-Power, convenience for Transportation, &c., &c. They have carefully foreseen that proper building-materials, including brick or stone, lime and timber, are to be obtained with facility. Mills are erected and various branches of Manufacturing established as fast as they are needed, or as there is any labor which can be spared for and advantageously employed therein. New members who bid fair to be desirable accessions are received, on due probation, as fast as there may be accommodations for them, and so they can be profitably employed. If a blacksmith, a carpenter, a brickmaker, or glazier, is wanted, he is obtained by hiring until, among the wide circle of friends or acquaintances of the members, one is found who would like to unite his fortunes with the Phalanx, and who is deemed a worthy associate. Thus they go on, producing abundant food and other raw staples, steadily extending the bounds of their cultivated area, and increasing its product; enjoying at least the necessaries of life and doing without the superfluities until they are enabled to obtain them without running in debt. Soon an edifice, intended for the permanent home of them all, is commenced and finished piecemeal in the most substantial manner— fireproof so nearly that fire could not spread from one section to another, and so planned that the whole may be warmed, lighted,

supplied with water, and cleared of refuse by arrangements answering as well for a thousand persons as for one. Three or four large
and spacious kitchens, barns, granaries &c., &c., supplied with every
convenience, would answer the purpose of three or four hundred
under our present economy, saving vast amounts now lost by waste,
vermin, the elements, &c. &c. A tenth part of the labor now required for Household service, procuring Fuel, &c., would suffice,
while that now consumed in journeys to the mill, the store, the
blacksmith, the shoemaker, and the like, would be saved entirely.
There would be abundant employment in the various branches of
Industry pursued for all ages, capacities, tastes, and all that would
be saved in the kitchen and the woods could be advantagously and
agreeably employed in the gardens and nurseries, the mills and
factories. The productive force of this population would be vastly
greater than under existing arrangements, while its economies in
other respects would be immense. . . .

. . . Make schools as free and abundant as possible, and there
will still be a class—I fear, increasing in number—who will be
withheld by extreme poverty and consequent shabbiness—by the
stolid ignorance or brutal drunkenness of their parents—by infirmities which forbid their attendance on a school located at some
distance from their homes—by the thousand consequences of
Want, Uncertainty, Disease, and Vice—from the acquirement of
a proper Education. But in an Association such as we contemplate, the thorough Intellectual, Moral, and Physical Education
of each will be the direct and palpable *interest* of all—a matter of
the highest and most intimate concern. The cost of the books
now thinly scattered in five hundred dwellings will procure one
ample and comprehensive Library, with the apparatus and materials required to demonstrate the truths of Chemistry and the whole
range of Natural Science. The best teachers in every branch will
in time be selected—those who unite a natural capacity for teaching with the fullest attainments, and who do not need the stimulus
of high salaries to induce them to devote some hours of each day
to the inculcation of Knowledge, Industry, and Virtue. Frequent
and agreeable alternations from the school-room to the garden, the
factory, the halls and grounds set apart for exercise and recreation,
will benefit alike teachers and scholars, giving a zest to learning as
well as industry unknown to our monotonous drudgery, whether

of work or study. In short, I see no reason why the wildest dreams of the fanatical believer in Human Progress and Perfectibility may not ultimately be realized, and each child so trained as to shun every vice, aspire to every virtue, attain the highest practicable skill in Art and efficiency in Industry, loving and pursuing honest, untasked Labor for the health, vigor, and peace of mind, thence resulting as well as for its more palpable rewards, and joyfully recognising in universal the only assurance of individual good. . . .

9. GEORGE FITZHUGH (1806–81)

W E HAVE seen that a South Carolinian, Calhoun, set forth in broad terms the distinctive virtues of an agrarian aristocracy and proposed constitutional devices for safeguarding southern plantation society from destruction by national policies beneficial to special interests of the industrial north. About the same time George Fitzhugh, a Virginia lawyer and sociological writer, was presenting in more detail a typical southern view of the superior humanitarianism of a slave economy as compared with an economic system based on wage labor. Events soon outmoded Fitzhugh's defense of slavery; but others in his day, even in the north, shared his views that *laisser faire* capitalism was irresponsible and exploitative in its dealings with "free" laborers; and such views have long survived the Civil War.

Fitzhugh wrote two important books and contributed articles to *DeBow's Southern Review* (founded in New Orleans in 1846). This magazine, although persistently defending slavery, devoted its main efforts to informed discussions showing the opportunities and needs of the south for the development of manufacturing, trade and transportation. Fitzhugh himself admitted that some manufactures, properly regulated, might be beneficially introduced into the southern system; but his chief and constant aim was to persuade and prepare southerners to take the offensive in demonstrating the positive practical and moral virtues of a slave economy.

[Fitzhugh's main books are *Sociology for the South* (1854) and *Cannibals All!* or, *Slaves without Masters* (1857). See also his articles in *De Bow's Review*, Vol. XXX (1861).]

From SOCIOLOGY FOR THE SOUTH (1854)[1]

Ch. ii. *Failure of Free Society and Rise of Socialism.*

The phenomena presented by the vassals and villiens of Europe after their liberation, were the opposite of those exhibited by the wealthy and powerful classes. Pauperism and beggary, we are in-

---

[1] George Fitzhugh, *Sociology for the South, or the Failure of Free Society* (Richmond, 1854), at pp. 34–48, 161–163.

formed by English historians, were unknown till the villiens began to escape from their masters, and attempted to practise a predatory and nomadic liberty. A liberty, we should infer from the descriptions we can get of it, very much like that of domestic animals that have gone wild—the difference in favor of the animals being that nature had made provision for them, but had made none for the villiens. The new freemen were bands of thieves and beggars, infesting the country and disturbing its peace. Their physical condition was worse than when under the rule of the Barons, their masters, and their moral condition worse also, for liberty had made them from necessity thieves and murderers. It was necessary to retain them in slavery, not only to support and sustain them and to prevent general mendicity, but equally necessary in order to govern them and prevent crime. The advocates of universal liberty concede that the laboring class enjoy more material comfort, are better fed, clothed and housed, as slaves, than as freemen. The statistics of crime demonstrate that the moral superiority of the slave over the free laborer is still greater than his superiority in animal well-being. There never can be among slaves a class so degraded as is found about the wharves and suburbs of cities. The master requires and enforces ordinary morality and industry. We very much fear, if it were possible to indite a faithful comparison of the conduct and comfort of our free negroes with that of the runaway Anglo-Saxon serfs, that it would be found that the negroes have fared better and committed much less crime than the whites. But those days, the 14th and 15th centuries, were the halcyon days of vagabond liberty. The few that had escaped from bondage found a wide field and plenty of subjects for the practice of theft and mendicity. There was no law and no police adequate to restrain them, for until then their masters had kept them in order better than laws ever can. But those glorious old times have long since passed. A bloody code, a standing army and efficient police keep them quiet enough now. Their numbers have multiplied a hundred fold, but their poverty has increased faster than their numbers. Instead of stealing and begging, and living idly in the open air, they work fourteen hours a day, cooped up in close rooms, with foul air, foul water, and insufficient and filthy food, and often sleep at night crowded in cellars or in garrets, without regard to sex.

In proceeding to prove that this is a correct account of the effects

in England of liberating the laboring class, we are at much difficulty how to select from the mass of testimony that at every turn
presents itself to us. We are not aware that any one disputes the
fact that crime and pauperism throughout Western Europe increased *pari passu* with liberty, equality and free competition. We
know of but a single respectable authority that disputes the fact
that this increase is directly attributable to free competition or liberty. Even the Edinburgh Review, hitherto the great champion of
political economy and free competition, has been silent on the subject for several years. With strange inconsistency, the very men
who assert that universal liberty has, and must ever, from the nature
of things, increase crime, mendicity and pauperism among the laboring class, maintain that slavery degrades this very class whom it
preserves from poverty and crime. The elevation of the scaffold is
the only moral or physical elevation that they can point to which
distinguishes the condition of the free laborer from his servile ancestor. The peasantry of England, in the days of Cressey, Agin-
court and Shrewsbury, when feudalism prevailed, were generally
brave, virtuous, and in the enjoyment of a high degree of physical
comfort—at least, that comfort differed very little from that of
their lords and masters. This same peasantry, when Charles Edward with three thousand Highlanders invaded England, had become freemen and cowards. Starving Frenchmen will at least
fight, but starving Chartists only bluster. How slavery could degrade men lower than universal liberty has done, it is hard to
conceive; how it did and would again preserve them from such
degradation, is well explained by those who are loudest in its abuse.
A consciousness of security, a full comprehension of his position,
and a confidence in that position, and the absence of all corroding
cares and anxieties, makes the slave easy and self-assured in his address, cheerful, happy and contented, free from jealousy, malignity,
and envy, and at peace with all around him. His attachment to his
master begets the sentiment of loyalty, than which none more purifies and elevates human nature. This theory of the moral influences of slavery is suggested and in part borrowed from Alexandre
Dumas' "French Milliner." He, descended from a negro slave,
and we may presume prejudiced against slavery, speaks in glowing
terms of its happy influence on the lives and manners of the Russian serfs. He draws a contrast between their cheerfulness and the

wretchedness of the French laboring class, and attributes solely to the feeling of security which slavery induces, their enviable cheerfulness.

The free laborer rarely has a house and home of his own; he is insecure of employment; sickness may overtake him at any time and deprive him of the means of support; old age is certain to overtake him, if he lives, and generally finds him without the means of subsistence; his family is probably increasing in numbers, and is helpless and burdensome to him. In all this there is little to incite to virtue, much to tempt to crime, nothing to afford happiness, but quite enough to inflict misery. Man must be more than human, to acquire a pure and a high morality under such circumstances.

In free society the sentiments, principles, feelings and affections of high and low, rich and poor, are equally blunted and debased by the continual war of competition. It begets rivalries, jealousies and hatreds on all hands. The poor can neither love nor respect the rich, who, instead of aiding and protecting them, are endeavoring to cheapen their labor and take away their means of subsistence. The rich can hardly respect themselves, when they reflect that wealth is the result of avarice, caution, circumspection and hard dealing. These are the virtues which free society in its regular operation brings forth. Its moral influence is therefore no better on the rich than on the poor. The number of laborers being excessive in all old countries, they are continually struggling with, scandalizing and underbidding each other, to get places and employment. Every circumstance in the poor man's situation in free society is one of harassing care, of grievous temptation, and of excitement to anger, envy, jealousy and malignity. That so many of the poor should nevertheless be good and pure, kind, happy and high-minded, is proof enough that the poor class is not the worst class in society. But the rich have their temptations, too. Capital gives them the power to oppress; selfishness offers the inducement, and political economy, the moral guide of the day, would justify the oppression. Yet there are thousands of noble and generous and disinterested men in free society, who employ their wealth to relieve, and not to oppress the poor. Still these are exceptions to the general rule. The effect of such society is to encourage the oppression of the poor.

The ink was hardly dry with which Adam Smith wrote his

Wealth of Nations, lauding the benign influences of free society, ere the hunger and want and nakedness of that society engendered a revolutionary explosion that shook the world to its centre. The starving artisans and laborers, and fish-women and needle-women of Paris, were the authors of the first French revolution, and that revolution was everywhere welcomed, and spread from nation to nation like fire in the prairies. The French armies met with but a formal opposition, until they reached Russia. There, men had homes and houses and a country to fight for. The serfs of Russia, the undisciplined Cossacks, fought for lares and penates, their homes, their country, and their God, and annihilated an army more numerous than that of Xerxes, and braver and better appointed than the tenth legion of Caesar. What should Western European poor men fight for? All the world was the same to them. They had been set free to starve, without a place to rest their dying heads or to inter their dead bodies. Any change they thought would be for the better, and hailed Buonaparte as a deliverer. But the nature of the evil was not understood; there were some remnants of feudalism, some vigor in the Catholic church; these Buonaparte swept away, and left the poor without a stay or a hope. Buonaparte is conquered and banished, universal peace restored; commerce, mechanic arts, manufactures and agriculture revive and flourish; invention is stimulated, industry urged on to its utmost exertion. Never seemed the world so prosperous, so happy, so progressive. But only seemed! Those awful statistics unfold the sad tale that misery and crime and poverty are on the increase still. The prisons are filled, the poor houses and the penal colonies supplied too fast, and the gallows ever pendant with its subject. In 1830, Paris starves again, builds barricades, continues hungry, and hesitates what next to do. Finally sets up a new king, no better than the one she has expelled. Revolution follows revolution with electric speed throughout great part of Western Europe. Kings are deposed, governments changed; soon new kings put in their places, and things subside—not quietly—into the *status quo ante bellum*. All this, while millions of the poor are fleeing from Europe as men fly from an infected plague spot, to seek their fortunes in other climes and regions. Another eighteen years of hunger, of crime, of riots, strikes, and trades unions, passes over free society. In 1848 the drama of 1830 is almost literally re-enacted. Again

Paris starves, builds barricades, and expels her king. Again Western Europe follows her example. By this time, however, men had
discovered that political changes would not cure the diseases of
society. The poor must have bread; government must furnish it.
Liberty without bread was not worth fighting for. A Republic is
set up in Paris that promises employment and good wages to every
body. The experiment is tried and fails in a week. No employment, except transplanting trees and levelling mounds, could be
found, and the treasury breaks. After struggling and blundering
and staggering on through various changes, Louis Napoleon is made
Emperor. He is a socialist, and socialism is the new fashionable
name of slavery. He understands the disease of society, and has
nerve enough for any surgical operation that may be required to
cure it. His first step in socialism was to take the money of the
rich to buy wheat for all. The measure was well-timed, necessary
and just. He is now building houses on the social plan for working
men, and his Queen is providing nurseries and nurses for the children of the working women, just as we Southerners do for our
negro women and children. It is a great economy. Fourier suggested it long after Southerners had practiced it. During these
times there was a little episode in Ireland—Ireland, the freest country in the world, where law is violated every day, mocked at and
derided, whence the rich and the noble have emigrated, where all
are poor, all equal, and all idle. A few thousands only had usually
starved annually; but the potatoe crop failed; they had no feudal
lords to buy other food for them, and three hundred thousand
starved in a single season. No slave or serf ever did starve, unless
he were a runaway. Irishmen, although they love liberty to distraction, have lost their taste for starving. They are coming en masse
to America, and in a few years, at the present rate of emigration,
will leave the island without inhabitants. The great and increasing
emigration from free society in Europe can only be accounted for
on the ground that they believe their social system so rotten that
no mere political change can help them—for a political revolution
can be had on twenty-four hours' notice.

The Chartists and Radicals of England would in some way subvert and re-construct society. They complain of free competition
as a crying evil, and may be classed with the Socialists. The high
conservative party called Young England vainly endeavors, by

preaching fine sentiments, to produce that good feeling between the rich and the poor, the weak and the powerful, which slavery alone can bring about. Liberty places those classes in positions of antagonism and war. Slavery identifies the interests of rich and poor, master and slave, and begets domestic affection on the one side, and loyalty and respect on the other. Young England sees clearly enough the character of the disease, but is not bold enough to propose an adequate remedy. The poor themselves are all practical Socialists, and in some degree pro-slavery men. They unite in strikes and trades unions, and thus exchange a part of their liberties in order to secure high and uniform wages. The exchange is a prudent and sensible one; but they who have bartered off liberty, are fast verging towards slavery. Slavery to an association is not always better than slavery to a single master. The professed object is to avoid ruinous underbidding and competition with one another; but this competition can never cease whilst liberty lasts. Those who wish to be free must take liberty with this inseparable burden. Odd-Fellows' societies, temperance societies, and all other societies that provide for sick and unfortunate members, are instances of Socialism. The muse in England for many years has been busy in composing dissonant laborer songs, bewailing the hardships, penury and sufferings of the poor, and indignantly rebuking the cruelty and injustice of their hard-hearted and close-fisted. employers.

Dickens and Bulwer denounce the frame-work of society quite as loudly as Carlyle and Newman; the two latter of whom propose slavery as a remedy for existing evils. A large portion of the clergy are professed Socialists, and there is scarcely a literary man in England who is not ready to propose radical and organic changes in her social system. Germany is full of Communists; social discontent is universal, and her people are leaving en masse for America —hopeless of any amelioration at home for the future. Strange to tell, in the free States of Amerca too, Socialism and every other heresy that can be invoked to make war on existing institutions, prevail to an alarming extent. Even according to our own theory of the necessity of slavery, we should not suppose that that necessity would be so soon felt in a new and sparsely-settled country, where the supply of labor does not exceed the demand. But it is probable the constant arrival of emigrants makes the situation of

the laborer at the North as precarious as in Europe, and produces
a desire for some change that shall secure him employment and
support at all times. Slavery alone can effect that change; and
towards slavery the North and all Western Europe are unconsciously marching. The master evil they all complain of is free
competition—which is another name for liberty. Let them remove
that evil, and they will find themselves slaves, with all the advantages and disadvantages of slavery. They will have attained association of labor, for slavery produces association of labor, and is
one of the ends all Communists and Socialists desire. A well-
conducted farm in the South is a model of associated labor that
Fourier might envy. One old woman nurses all the children whilst
the mothers are at work; another waits on the sick, in a house set
aside for them. Another washes and cooks, and a fourth makes
and mends the clothing. It is a great economy of labor, and is a
good idea of the Socialists. Slavery protects the infants, the aged
and the sick; nay, takes far better care of them than of the healthy,
the middle-aged and the strong. They are part of the family, and
self-interest and domestic affection combine to shelter, shield and
foster them. A man loves not only his horses and his cattle, which
are useful to him, but he loves his dog, which is of no use. He
loves them because they are his. What a wise and beneficent provision of Heaven, that makes the selfishness of man's nature a protecting aegis to shield and defend wife and children, slaves and
even dumb animals. The Socialists propose to reach this result
too, but they never can if they refuse to march in the only road
Providence has pointed out. Who will check, govern and control
their superintending authority? Who prevent his abuse of power?
Who can make him kind, tender and affectionate, to the poor,
aged, helpless, sick and unfortunate? *Qui custodiat custodes?* Nature establishes the only safe and reliable checks and balances in
government. Alton Locke describes an English farm, where the
cattle, the horses and the sheep are fat, plentifully fed and warmly
housed; the game in the preserves and the fish in the pond carefully provided for; and two freezing, shivering, starving, half-clad
boys, who have to work on the Sabbath, are the slaves to these animals, and are vainly endeavoring to prepare their food. Now it
must have occurred to the author that if the boys had belonged to

the owner of the farm, they too would have been well-treated, happy and contented. This farm is but a miniature of all England; every animal is well-treated and provided for, except the laboring man. He is the slave of the brutes, the slave of society, produces everything and enjoys nothing. Make him the slave of one man, instead of the slave of society, and he would be far better off. None but lawyers and historians are aware how much of truth, justice and good sense, there is in the notions of the Communists, as to the community of property. Laying no stress on the too abstract proposition that Providence gave the world not to one man, or set of men, but to all mankind, it is a fact that all governments, in civilized countries, recognize the obligation to support the poor, and thus, in some degree, make all property a common possession. The poor laws and poor houses of England are founded on communistic principles. Each parish is compelled to support its own poor. In Ireland, this obligation weighs so heavily as in many instances to make farms valueless; the poor rates exceeding the rents. But it is domestic slavery alone that can establish a safe, efficient and humane community of property. It did so in ancient times, it did so in feudal times, and does so now, in Eastern Europe, Asia and America. Slaves never die of hunger; seldom suffer want. Hence Chinese sell themselves when they can do no better. A Southern farm is a sort of joint stock concern, or social phalastery, in which the master furnishes the capital and skill, and the slaves the labor, and divide the profits, not according to each one's in-put, but according to each one's wants and necessities.

Socialism proposes to do away with free competition; to afford protection and support at all times to the laboring class; to bring about, at least, a qualified community of property, and to associate labor. All these purposes, slavery fully and perfectly attains. . . .

Ch. xv. The Association of Labor.

If the Socialists had done no other good, they would be entitled to the gratitude of mankind for displaying in a strong light the advantages of the association of labor. Adam Smith, in his elaborate treatise on the Division of Labor, nearly stumbled on the same truth. But the division of labor is a curse to the laborer, without the association of labor. Division makes labor ten times more efficient, but by confining each workman to some simple, monotonous employment, it makes him a mere automaton, and an easy prey to the capitalist. The association of labor, like all associations, requires a head or ruler, and that head or ruler will become a cheat and a tyrant, unless his interests are identified with the interests of the laborer. In a large factory, in free society, there is division of labor, and association too, but association and division for the benefit of the employer and to the detriment of the laborer. On a large farm, whatever advances the health, happiness and morals of the negroes, renders them more prolific and valuable to their master. It is his interest to pay them high wages in way of support, and he can afford to do so, because association renders the labor of each slave five times as productive and efficient as it would be, were the slaves working separately. One man could not enclose an acre of land, cultivate it, send his crops to market, do his own cooking, washing and mending. One man may live as a prowling beast of prey, but not as a civilized being. One hundred human beings, men, women and children, associated, will cultivate ten acres of land each, enclose it, and carry on every other operation of civilized life. Labor becomes at least twenty times as productive when a hundred associate, as when one acts alone. The same is as true in other pursuits as in farming. But in free society, the employer robs the laborer, and he is no better off than the prowling savage, although he might live in splendor if he got a fair proportion of the proceeds of his own labor.

We have endeavored to show, heretofore, that the negro slave, considering his indolence and unskilfulness, often gets his fair share, and sometimes more than his share, of the profits of the farm, and is exempted, besides, from the harassing cares and anxieties of the free laborer. Grant, however, that the negro does not receive adequate wages from his master, yet all admit that in the aggregate the negroes get better wages than free laborers; therefore, it follows that, with all its imperfections, slave society is the best form of society yet devised for the masses. When Socialists and Abolitionists, by full and fair experiments, exhibit a better, it will be time to agitate the subject of abolition.

The industrial products of black slave labor have been far greater and more useful to mankind, than those of the same amount of any other labor. In a very short period, the South and South-west have been settled, cleared, fenced in, and put in cultivation, by what were, a century ago, a handful of masters and slaves. This region now feeds and clothes a great part of mankind; but free trade cheats them of the profits of their labor. In the vast amount of our industrial products, we see the advantages of association—in our comparative poverty, the evils of free trade.

10. HENRY C. CAREY (1793–1879)

HENRY CAREY, "first professional economist" of America and a "father" of high tariff protectionism, was the son of Mathew Carey (1760–1839), who was also an economic writer of strong protectionist views. The latter had been a bookseller, printer, and pamphleteer in Ireland and migrated to America (seven years before Henry's birth) after serving a term of imprisonment for his vigorous criticism of the Irish policy of the British government. He settled in Philadelphia, where he founded a newspaper, two influential, although unprofitable, magazines, and a publishing house that soon became the best in the United States. Henry, after little formal schooling and considerable parental instruction, went to work as a young boy in his father's publishing house, joined the firm (Carey, Lea, and Carey) at twenty-four, and later became its head. At the age of forty-five he withdrew from business, with a considerable fortune, and turned his attention to economic writing.

In his earlier writings, Carey was a free trader and an advocate of *laisser faire* in the general terms of traditional classical economics.[1] The financial crisis of 1836–37 left its effects on both his business and his theory; and he soon became a vigorous critic of the classical doctrines and a thoroughgoing protectionist and nationalist. Free trade, he now argued, was a dogma fostered on this country by England, because of her interest in making America the chief producer of raw materials for her factories and the chief purchaser of her commodities. America, he maintained, had almost unlimited possibilities of expansion and improvement, if she made herself self-sufficient; and protective tariffs were necessary to bring out and protect the latent productive capacities of the country. On similar grounds he recommended remonetization of silver, greenback issues, and a monetary system based generally on government credit, in order to secure a non-exportable currency subject to manipulation in accordance with the changing needs of the nation.[2]

Carey set forth a final summation of his views in two extensive works: *The Harmony of Interests: Agricultural, Manufacturing, and Com-*

---

[1] See his *Essay on the Rate of Wages* (1835) and *Principles of Political Economy*, 3 vols. (1837–40).

[2] These views appear in two of Carey's pamphlets (*Commercial Associations in France and England*, 1845, and *The Past, the Present, and the Future*, 1848) and in editorials which he contributed regularly to the New York *Tribune* (while Greeley was editor).

mercial (1851), and *The Principles of Social Science* (1858–59). In these books he stressed the similarities between political economy and the natural sciences and reached optimistic conclusions as to the possibility of economic reform through organized collective efforts directed by government. Under the benevolent design of Nature the varied economic interests of a nation, he held, are normally, or potentially, in harmony. Yet a nation, like an organism, has interdependent parts and functions which require direction from a center or head, to keep them in balance and make them operate in the interests of the whole. Orthodox economists were prevailingly contemptuous of Carey's views; but *The Principles of Social Science* was translated into eight European languages, and into Japanese.

[See: Charles H. Levermore, "Henry C. Carey and His Social System," in *Political Science Quarterly*, Vol. V (1890), pp. 553–582; Vernon L. Parrington, *Main Currents of American Thought*, Vol. III (1930), pp. 105–111; D. H. Kaplan, *Henry Charles Carey: a Study in American Economic Thought* (1931).]

From PRINCIPLES OF SOCIAL SCIENCE (1858–59) [1]

The complex organism of the human body being, by the sympathies and dependencies of its various parts, made an unit in its action and its uses, the entire race, in a sense as real and as true, philosophically and practically, becomes one man, and may so be treated. The species is but so many representatives of the individual—the aggregate differing in degree, but not in kind, from any of the atoms of which it is composed. Politically, we have the idea embraced in our national motto, *e pluribus unum*—the same truth of fact presenting itself in the legal ideas of joint and several obligation, and joint and several right, where each debtor is bound for the whole debt, and each creditor is entitled to look to each and all for payment. The corporation, or artificial man, is another familiar instance of the same idea—the moralist, in his turn, using the word *solidarity*, for indicating the liability of each and all the members of society to suffer for the errors, or profit of the judicious action, of any of its component parts. The recognition of correspondence, analogy, or oneness, here exhibited, runs through all branches of theory and practice having man for their subject—

[1] Text from edition of 1871 (3 vols., Philadelphia), Vol. III, pp. 401, 406, 408–415, 435–436, 455–457. By courtesy of J. B. Lippincott Co.

warranting the study of the many in the one, and promising helpful illustrations of the societary body, to be derived from examination of the individual. . . .

The analogy we have sought to trace, here affords the correspondence. In a state of absolute isolation, or that of feeble and imperfect social relation, man, denied, as he is, the protecting and assisting aid elsewhere resulting from combinations of men with their fellow-men, has but a low grade of individual existence. In the healthy maturity of society, as in that of the man, the independence of the individual, though embracing many of his most important interests, cannot be entire, either in extent, or in degree. The connection of the societary man with his fellows is a double one—its analogue being found in the vegetative organs. The sympathetic system of nerves receives branches directly from the brain and spinal marrow, throughout its entire course in the neck, thorax, and abdomen—the organs which it supplies, as the stomach, liver, and pancreas, having, besides, an immediate connection with the brain and spinal cord by means of nerves sent directly to them. The societary man has his independency rooted in his original relations with his fellow-men—threads of common life holding him in a general dependency upon every neighbor man—organized government, meanwhile, representing his fellows in their aggregate, and stretching its lines of support, protection, and harmonizing restraints, over all the points in which his life has its relative issues. . . .

The theory of political government of these United States is in an obvious general harmony with the vital economy, as it has been here exhibited. The individual, having rights and interests with which no one ventures to interfere—the atom, in its proper isolation—scarcely feels the rein of a nerve of the ruling functionaries, though receiving the vital impulse, and the nourishing circulation, in equal partnership with masses of the highest organization. The family, held together by its proper sympathetic ties, is obedient to an almost unconscious influence on the part of the central life— meeting its restraints and directions only when its offices link it to its daily augmenting relations. The school district has powers which it exercises independently of that larger society from which it derives its powers, and to which it is responsible for the rightful exercise of its functions—the cerebro-spinal nerve touching it only for necessary government. The township enjoys a similar independence—feeling the corresponding control of the county. The county holds its franchises under similar conditions of freedom and limitation. The State is sovereign in all remoter and more general relations, consistent with the supremacy of the Union—that, again, being supreme only in what is essential to the harmony and well-being of the whole of the great confederacy. . . .

Men approach each other, prompted by a desire for association, and by a consciousness that their own strength and power will be increased by combination. Met together, thousands of cases occur, in which unenlightened selfishness is found opposing itself to measures looking to the promotion of the good of all—measures, in the benefits of which, those so acting would participate. Such being the case, it becomes soon obvious that some certain persons must act as umpires, empowered so to co-ordinate and determine the movement of the societary body, as to call into activity all the powers of its members, while requiring each and all to hold in due respect the rights of those around them—the object sought to be obtained being that of removing obstacles which stand in the way of association and combination. The duties to be performed by the persons so empowered, are thus precisely the same with those that, in the physical body, are assigned to the brain, and the health of the social body must as much depend upon their due performance as does that of the physical one upon the performance by the brain of the duties assigned to it—abdication, without injury, being no more possible in the one case than in the other. Order having been well defined, by M. Guizot, as being "only the free and certain exercise of rights," failure in its maintenance among the various members of a society, is as certain to be followed by injurious consequences, as is failure of the intellect to direct the operations of its many subjects. Being Heaven's first and greatest law, the feeling of its necessity exhibits itself, whensoever and wheresoever men come together—the most disorderly of beings, the very pirates of the ocean, always selecting some certain person to be invested with the authority needed for maintaining discipline among themselves, and for securing that there be a fair division of the plunder among both the absent and the present.

The first and greatest obstacle to association being found in the necessity for effecting changes of place, one of the earliest wants of man is found in the need for roads. At first, the footpath supplies the only means of intercourse, but as men increase in number, the pack-horse takes the place of man—the value of the latter rising because of his centering in himself all the power thus obtained. In time, however, other and better roads are needed; but now the difficulty arises, that the owner of the pack-horse, in his ignorant selfishness, opposes their construction, under the belief, that his services and those of his animals, may be thereby lessened in their power to command remuneration. The farmer, too, opposes it, for the reason, that it will divide his farm—wholly overlooking the fact, that the economy of transportation will probably double the money-value of his property. In this state of things, society, by its head, steps in—deciding the terms upon which the land shall be yielded for the general purposes, and upon what terms the owner of the land shall be entitled to use the road.—Later, turnpikes and railroads are needed, but how, in the absence of a co-ordinating head, could such roads be made? Were each and every proprietor along the line, to make his separate piece, each would be owner of his share—determining for himself the charge for its use, and endeavoring to obtain, at the cost of all the others, the largest portion of the tolls. Here, again, society comes in—fixing the terms upon which the land may be taken, and the tolls that may be claimed— at the same time creating an artificial man, and authorizing the head of the body thus created to guide and direct the operations.

Water is needed—each and every person being now obliged to go daily to the distant river for his day's supply, and the whole combined wasting, in each successive year, more labor than would, if at once applied, bring the river to their doors. Who, however, is to do it? Being done by A and B, C and D would profit by it—paying nothing for the service. Society now interferes—deciding that what is for the good of all, must be done by all, and authorizing the authorities of the town to do the work at the public cost. Each then obtains his supplies in return for diminished effort—giving the body corporate only a small per centage of the product of the labor thus economized.

The precious metals pass in lumps, each exchange involving a necessity for weighing of the pieces. Seeing that much labor may be saved, society, by its head, authorizes certain persons to receive such lumps as may be brought to them—to test their quality—to make them up in pieces of a certain weight and shape—and then to stamp them with certain marks, as evidence that they had passed through proper hands.

So, too, with regard to weights and measures—commerce being much facilitated by the determination of the precise idea that is to be conveyed by the expressions—a yard of cloth—a pound of butter—a ton of coal—a bushel of wheat.

Valuable minerals exist, and in abundant quantities, but who shall make the investigations required for bringing such treasures to the light? A and B have tried it, but have failed. All are likely to be largely benefited by such discoveries, but none are willing to risk the large expenditure they may require. Society now steps in—bringing science to their aid, showing where such deposits may be safely looked for, and requiring all to pay their quota towards explorations promotive of the good of all.

The losses by sea are so very great as to add largely to the tax of transportation, to the great detriment of those who own, and those who farm the land. That this evil may be removed, there is needed a knowledge of the laws of the currents and the winds, but who shall study them? Being for the good of all, it should be done at the cost of all, and society, by its head, requires that it be so done.

In default of evidences of marriage and of birth, property is frequently retarded on its way to the proper heirs. Seeing this, society determines that certain persons shall keep records of births, marriages, and deaths—thereby facilitating all future operations in regard to the transfer of lands, houses, stocks, and other property, at the death of their present owners.

Schools are needed, but the rich are indisposed to pay for educating the poor, and the poor are unable to educate themselves. To the former, society now says, that the strength of a community increases in the ratio of the development of the powers of its members; that with every step in that direction, land acquires increase of value; that diffusion of intelligence tends to the promotion of morality, and thereby gives increased security to person and to property; that the rich are, therefore, directly interested in the education of the poor; that it is for the good of all; and that, therefore, all must contribute a small per centage upon the value of their properties, to be so applied.

A city requires to be supplied with gas, and, for that purpose, extensive works are to be erected, and miles of pipes required to be laid. Who shall do it? The city owns the streets, and if it grants permission to use them, without conditions, it thereby creates a monopoly, that may become most oppressive. The city head decides the terms upon which the obstacles to combination among the makers of gas, and those who desire to consume it, may be removed—the head of the State, at the same time, authorizing the former to combine among themselves, for carrying the arrangement into full effect.

Among the community there are some who are blind, while others are deaf, dumb, or otherwise deprived of power to provide for their own support. They cannot be allowed to perish, yet who shall contribute to their relief? In answer to this question, society says, that it is a common burthen, to the carrying of which each shall contribute in the ratio of his means—thus distributing among those who have been favored by Heaven, the care of those who have been less fortunate.

Drainage being needed, the health of the community is affected. Who shall do it? What is the business of all is that of none, and marshes remain undrained. At length, however, society determines that what is for the good of all, must be done at the cost of all—the rich and the poor being required to contribute in the ratio of their respective interests.

Epistolary intercourse must be maintained, but how can it be done? In the absence of combined action, the few who are rich and powerful can afford to send their letters by special messengers —profiting largely by information obtained in advance of their weaker neighbors. To remove this difficulty, and in the interests of all, society takes charge of the correspondence—transmitting letters to a distance of thousands of miles, and receiving in return a smaller amount of money than is usually paid for carrying a single letter to an adjoining street.

A country embraces all the varieties of soil and climate requisite for a very varied agriculture, from the barley of the north to the sugar of the south; and yet, in default of the introduction of many articles, its inhabitants are compelled to go abroad from year to year—paying three, four, or five times, the original cost, and thus losing annually, a greater amount than would, if properly applied, give to its farmers new employment for labor and land, that would add largely to the general wealth. In this state of things, society comes to their aid—asking each and every contributor to the tax of transportation to pay, into a common fund, a small per centage of its amount, to be applied to the introduction of seeds and knowledge, by means of which they may, in a brief period, be relieved from the payment of further contributions.

Schools develop the various faculties of the younger portion of the community, but in default of diversity in the modes of employment, those who would have distinguished themselves in the workshop are compelled to remain idle, if they would not follow the plough, or begin to trade. Iron ore and fuel abound, but, there being no furnaces in which the former can be smelted, both remain idle in the earth, and the farmer can with difficulty obtain a plough. Wool abounds, but there is no woollen mill, and the farmer's daughter is idle, while he, himself, is unable to obtain a coat. Corn abounds, but the cost of transporting it to a distant market, leaves its producer little to pay for either machinery or clothing.—A furnace and a mill are needed, but who shall build them? Building materials, and labor unemployed, abound, but how can they be combined? Those who might undertake the work, would speedily find, that, however much their operations might tend towards increasing the quantity of cloth and iron obtainable in exchange for food and labor, their distant competitors would still so far control the market as to drive them from it, to their own entire ruin— fearing which, the furnace and the mill would remain unbuilt; labor would remain unemployed; fuel, ore, and food, would remain superabundant; the farmer would continue to give the larger part of the clothing-power of his corn for freight on the remainder; and the whole people would continue poor.—In this state of things, society says to the farmers and laborers, that the establishment of mills and furnaces would double the value of both land and labor, and that to enable them to combine their efforts for the erection of such establishments, it will require of the foreign producers of cloth and iron a certain portion of the value of all they may import—applying the proceeds to the making of new and better roads, or to paying the expenses of government; thus, while relieving them, at once and forever, from the oppressive tax of transportation to the distant market, improving the modes of communication among themselves.

In all these cases, the political head does exactly that which, as we have seen, has been provided to be done by the physical one—co-ordinating the movements of the various members of the society in such manner as to remove the obstacles which stand in the way of association, and prevent that diversification of the employments of society which is required for adding value to land and labor, and giving freedom to man. The more perfect that co-ordination, whether in the physical or social body, the more complete must be the development of all the parts, and the more harmonious the action of the whole.

It may, however, be said, that the exercise of these various powers tends towards centralization, yet is the reverse of this the case. Each and every movement above described, tends towards the development of the various powers of the earth and man—towards the creation of local centres—towards increasing the rapidity of the societary circulation—towards creating a counterbalance to the attractions of the political or trading capital—and, therefore, towards concentration. The more perfect the balance of the centripetal and centrifugal forces, the greater must be the steadiness of the societary movement—the larger the proportion borne by fixed to circulating capital—the more perfect the individuality of both people and State—and the greater the tendency towards the perfect establishment of human freedom. Are there, then, no proper limits to the sphere of action of those who guide and direct the commerce of the State? There are—*their whole duty being found in the removal of the obstacles to perfect combination.* Going beyond that point, government leaves its proper sphere—doing then mischief in place of good. . . .

The world is word-governed, unmeaning phrases being made idols of—objects of word-worship—to the great profit of the large class which stand between the producers and consumers of the world—living at the cost of both. Of these phrases, some have reference to the affairs of another world, while others refer to the societary movement of the present one—prominent among the latter being those of *Laisser faire, laisser passer*—the world is governed too much—that country is best governed, which is least governed —&c., &c. . . .

Throughout nature, the rank and perfection of organisms are in direct proportion to the number and dissimilarity of the parts, proof of this being found at every stage of progress from the simplest composition of inorganic matter, up to the structure of MAN, on whom are reproduced all the forms and faculties of being, over which, for the service of his needs, it has been given to him to rule. This law not only marks the relative rank of classes of creatures, but it serves, also, to measure the respective positions of the individuals of whom the several classes are composed—the nearest approach to perfection being found in those men in whom the distinctive human qualities are found most active, and most developed. Following out the rule, those communities of men in which are found the largest variety of differences, and the most effective development of them into action, should present the nearest approach to perfection of societary organization. Seeking such communities, we find them in those in which the demands for human powers are most diversified—those in which men are enabled most fully to combine their efforts—rapid societary motion there stimulating into activity all the power that, thus far, has remained latent, and enabling their members to pass from the brutifying labors of transportation, through those of the workshop, to those of a scientific agriculture.

Subordination of specialties as to a general intention—diversity of functions or uses, so combined as to produce a perfect harmony of related action—is, at once, the mark and test of organization. The individual man is healthy and efficient within himself, in proportion to the vigor and exactness with which the bodily instruments of his will obey the governing brain—those charged with carrying on his automatic life, meanwhile furnishing full support to his voluntary powers. Absolute subordination in the parts of a machine to the moving force, is the constant characteristic of inanimate organizations. In a watch, steam-engine, mill, or ship, all the parts are in prompt and complete obedience—their perfection being measured by the exactness of their subordination.

In societary organizations, we have the same law modified, but not repealed, by the liberty which accompanies human life—bringing with it responsibility to both God and man. The crew of a ship—the hands employed in a factory—the thousands of whom an army is composed—are organized and subordinated, that they may accomplish the work for whose performance they have been brought together. So, too, is it in civil government—subordination of the subjects being essential to the well-being and the progress of the community, and to those very individual liberties which it limits, as well as to the national order for whose security it has been designed—the most remarkable case of societary organization on record, being that under which the Hebrews sojourned in the desert, during the long period that intervened between the passage of the Red Sea, and their entrance into the promised land.

Throughout nature, the more perfect the organization, and the more absolute the subordination, the more harmonious and beautiful is the interdependence of the parts. A rock, or a lump of coal being broken, each and every portion remains as perfect as it had been before. Dividing a polypus into a dozen parts, the vital force is found existing in each and all, and to such extent, that each becomes again a perfect animal. Doing the same by man, he speedily passes into dust.—So, too, is it with societies—the mutuality of interdependence growing with every stage of progress, from that simplest of societary forms presented to view in the history of Crusoe and his Friday, towards that high state of organization in which tens of thousands of persons combine to satisfy the public want for a single newspaper—hundreds of thousands then profiting by its perusal at a cost so small as scarcely to admit of calculation.

Throughout nature, the more complete the subordination, and the more perfect the interdependence of the parts, the greater is the individuality of the whole, and the more absolute the power of self-direction. The rock is chained to earth, obeying but a single force; the bird, at will, rises in the air, or skims across the lake. The dog obeys his master; the master has power to direct himself, and nature too. The man in perfect health, with all the parts moving in perfect subjection to the directing brain, determines for himself if he will go abroad, or stay at home—the invalid, on the contrary, being compelled to keep his chamber.—So, too, must it be with society— its power for self-direction growing with the growth of interdependence among its various parts, and the latter becoming developed as the organization becomes more perfect, and the subordination more complete.

Organization and subordination, association and individuality, responsibility and freedom, travel thus together, throughout the social world. . . .

11. ABRAHAM LINCOLN

FEW of Lincoln's utterances deal with property rights, except in relation to the slavery question. His opposition to slavery was associated with his general faith in *laisser-faire* humanitarianism. He believed that each man will come nearest to attaining that to which he is entitled if rights of competition and association and easy access to unexploited regions are kept open on equal terms to all. At no time in his political experience was he faced with problems connected with demands for the public regulation of either working conditions or business practices.

The selections below contain the brief passages most frequently quoted to indicate Lincoln's views on Capital and Labor.

From *A CAMPAIGN SPEECH IN NEW HAVEN*
(*March 6, 1860*) [1]

Another specimen of this bushwhacking—that "shoe strike." Now be it understood that I do not pretend to know all about the matter. I am merely going to speculate a little about some of its phases, and at the outset I am glad to see that a system of labor prevails in New England under which laborers can strike when they want to, where they are not obliged to work under all circumstances, and are not tied down and obliged to labor whether you pay them or not! I like the system which lets a man quit when he wants to, and wish it might prevail everywhere. One of the reasons why I am opposed to slavery is just here. What is the true condition of the laborer? I take it that it is best for all to leave each man free to acquire property as fast as he can. Some will get wealthy. I don't believe in a law to prevent a man from getting rich; it would do more harm than good. So while we do not propose any war upon capital, we do wish to allow the humblest man an equal chance to get rich with everybody else. When one starts poor, as most do in the race of life, free society is such that he knows he can better his

[1] In *Complete Works of Abraham Lincoln*, ed. by John G. Nicolay and John Hay, Vol. V, pp. 339–371, at 360–361.

condition; he knows that there is no fixed condition of labor for his whole life. I am not ashamed to confess that twenty-five years ago I was a hired laborer, mauling rails, at work on a flatboat—just what might happen to any poor man's son. I want every man to have a chance—and I believe a black man is entitled to it—in which he can better his condition—when he may look forward and hope to be a hired laborer this year and the next, work for himself afterward, and finally to hire men to work for him. This is the true system.

From ANNUAL MESSAGE TO CONGRESS
(December 3, 1861)[1]

It is not needed nor fitting here that a general argument should be made in favor of popular institutions; but there is one point, with its connections, not so hackneyed as most others, to which I ask a brief attention. It is the effort to place *capital* on an equal footing with, if not above, *labor*, in the structure of the government. It is assumed that labor is available only in connection with capital; that nobody labors unless somebody else, owning capital, somehow by the use of it induces him to labor. This assumed, it is next considered whether it is best that capital shall *hire* laborers, and thus induce them to work by their own consent, or *buy* them and drive them to it without their consent. Having proceeded so far, it is naturally concluded that all laborers are either *hired* laborers, or what we call slaves. And further, it is assumed that whoever is once a hired laborer is fixed in that condition for life.

Now there is no such relation between capital and labor as assumed, nor is there any such thing as a free man being fixed for life in the condition of a hired laborer. Both these assumptions are false, and all inferences from them are groundless.

Labor is prior to and independent of capital. Capital is only the

---

[1] In *A Compilation of the Messages and Papers of the Presidents*, ed. by James D. Richardson, Vol. VIII, pp. 3258–3259. Lincoln had expressed similar views, in substantially the same words, in an address before the Wisconsin State Agricultural Society on September 30, 1859 (*Complete Works of Abraham Lincoln*, ed. by John G. Nicolay and John Hay, Vol. V, pp. 236–256, at 247–252). In a letter to "The Workingmen's Association of New York," dated March 21, 1864, he quoted, without change, the passages printed above from the Annual Message of 1861; and he added that "the views then expressed now remain unchanged, nor have I much to add" (*ibid.*, Vol. X, pp. 50–54).

fruit of labor, and could never have existed if labor had not first existed. Labor is the superior of capital, and deserves much the higher consideration. Capital has its rights, which are as worthy of protection as any other rights. Nor is it denied that there is, and probably always will be, a relation between labor and capital producing mutual benefits. The error is in assuming that the whole labor of community exists within that relation. A few men own capital, and that few avoid labor themselves, and with their capital hire or buy another few to labor for them. A large majority belong to neither class—neither work for others nor have others working for them. In most of the Southern States a majority of the whole people of all colors are neither slaves nor masters, while in the Northern a large majority are neither hirers nor hired. Men, with their families—wives, sons, and daughters—work for themselves on their farms, in their houses, and in their shops, taking the whole product to themselves, and asking no favors of capital on the one hand nor of hired laborers or slaves on the other. It is not forgotten that a considerable number of persons mingle their own labor with capital; that is, they labor with their own hands and also buy or hire others to labor for them; but this is only a mixed and not a distinct class. No principle stated is disturbed by the existence of this mixed class.

Again, as has already been said, there is not of necessity any such thing as the free hired laborer being fixed to that condition for life. Many independent men everywhere in these States a few years back in their lives were hired laborers. The prudent, penniless beginner in the world labors for wages awhile, saves a surplus with which to buy tools or land for himself, then labors on his own account another while, and at length hires another new beginner to help him. This is the just and generous and prosperous system which opens the way to all, gives hope to all, and consequent energy and progress and improvement of condition to all. No men living are more worthy to be trusted than those who toil up from poverty; none less inclined to take or touch aught which they have not honestly earned. Let them beware of surrendering a political power which they already possess, and which if surrendered will surely be used to close the door of advancement against such as they and to fix new disabilities and burdens upon them till all of liberty shall be lost. . . .

12. HENRY GEORGE (1839-97)

THE author of *Progress and Poverty* and founder of the "Single-Tax" movement was the son of a devout Episcopalian publisher of religious books in Philadelphia. The father had a large family and a small income, and Henry quit school at thirteen. He worked at various small jobs until, at sixteen, he sailed as foremast boy to Calcutta, where he got a vivid impression of extreme contrasts between wealth and poverty. After a brief sojourn at home again, he made his way to California, a new country where he had been told there were better opportunities for earning a living. Settling in San Francisco, he at first found only small jobs and (after marrying at twenty-two) he lived for several years in great poverty, with a growing family. At twenty-eight, however, he had risen to the managing editorship of a newspaper, the San Francisco *Times*.

Meanwhile, George had begun to reflect both on his own hard times and on the general economic condition of that frontier region of rich resources, rapidly increasing population, large new fortunes made by land speculators, and, with it all, increasing economic insecurity for most of the settlers. The great railway systems played a part in the land speculations, and George wrote an article on "What the Railroad Will Bring Us." (It appeared, in 1868, in a new magazine, the *Overland Monthly*, published in San Francisco and edited by Bret Harte.) The railroads, George argued, were making California both prosperous and poor; if there was less poverty than in the East, that was only because the natural wealth of the West was "not yet monopolized." Next year (George wrote twenty-five years later) a new idea came to him "like a flash." While on a horseback ride in the country he stopped to ask a poor teamster about the price of grazing lands near by; the teamster replied that the lands were held for a thousand dollars per acre. This, said George, made him see clearly that the rapidly growing population of California, although adding nothing to the quality of the land, was enriching a few landowners and at the same time making it more difficult for others to earn a living. Three years later he set forth this idea in a pamphlet entitled *Our Land and Land Policy* (1871). Then he read the works of English classical economists and found in them, particularly in Ricardo's "law of rent," general theoretical confirmation for his new idea. During the depression and labor disturbances of 1877 he began work on a comprehensive statement of his theory of the cause and cure of the ills of society. The result was his *Progress and Poverty*, published in 1879 at his own expense.

George moved to New York City in 1880, and in the following year spent a few months in Ireland as correspondent for the New York *Irish World*. A few years later he made extensive lecture tours of England and Ireland, where he was received with great enthusiasm. Said George Bernard Shaw (in 1905): "When I was swept into the great Socialist revival of 1883, I found that five-sixths of those who were swept in with me had been converted by Henry George." His *Progress and Poverty* had enormous sales in England and America, and George stood high among reformist circles in the eastern States. Labor and socialist groups nominated him for mayor of New York City in 1886; he was only narrowly defeated by the candidate of the strong Democratic organization and received more votes than the Republican nominee, Theodore Roosevelt. Eleven years later, he was again a candidate for the same office; he died during the campaign.

To explain and popularize his central idea and its correlaries, George wrote a half dozen books, edited a single-tax weekly (*The Standard,* 1886–92), and lectured extensively. Since his death small groups of disciples have advocated his views without essential change. He was not the first to hold that there are "unearned" values in landed property; and it is impossible to allocate among George and several other nineteenth-century writers the exact proportions of influence in bringing about the adoption, in various parts of the world, of "increment" taxes on land. There is now, moreover, a wide acceptance of the general idea of community-created values. Progressive taxes on incomes and inheritances, as well as the various forms of social legislation, are often explained as the means for restoring to the mass of people some of the values created by their needs and activities.

[See: Henry George, Jr., *The Life of Henry George* (1900); Broadus Mitchell, "Single Tax," in *Encyclopaedia of the Social Sciences;* Louis F. Post, *The Prophet of San Francisco* (1930); Arthur N. Young, *The Single Tax Movement in the United States* (1916); George R. Geiger, *The Philosophy of Henry George* (1933); F. W. Coker, "The Land Taxers," in *Recent Political Thought* (1934), pp. 88–98.]

From PROGRESS AND POVERTY (1879)[1]

Introductory. The Problem.

The present century has been marked by a prodigious increase in wealth-producing power. The utilization of steam and electricity, the introduction of improved processes and labor-saving machinery, the greater subdivision and grander scale of production, the wonderful facilitation of exchanges, have multiplied enormously the effectiveness of labor.

At the beginning of this marvelous era it was natural to expect, and it was expected, that labor-saving inventions would lighten the toil and improve the condition of the laborer; that the enormous increase in the power of producing wealth would make real poverty a thing of the past. Could a man of the last century—a Franklin or a Priestley—have seen, in a vision of the future, the steamship taking the place of the sailing vessel, the railroad train of the wagon, the reaping machine of the scythe, the threshing machine of the flail; could he have heard the throb of the engines that in obedience to human will, and for the satisfaction of human desire, exert a power greater than that of all the men and all the beasts of burden of the earth combined; could he have seen the forest tree transformed into finished lumber—into doors, sashes, blinds, boxes or barrels, with hardly the touch of a human hand; the great workshops where boots and shoes are turned out by the case with less labor than the old-fashioned cobbler could have put on a sole; the factories where, under the eye of a girl, cotton becomes cloth faster than hundreds of stalwart weavers could have turned it out with their handlooms; could he have seen steam hammers shaping mammoth shafts and mighty anchors, and delicate machinery making tiny watches; the diamond drill cutting through the heart of the rocks, and coal oil sparing the whale; could he have realized the enormous saving of labor resulting from improved facilities of exchange and communication—sheep killed in Australia eaten fresh in England, and the order given by the London banker in the after-

[1] *Progress and Poverty: An Inquiry into the Cause of Industrial Depressions and of Increase of Want with Increase of Wealth. The Remedy* (Garden City, N. Y., 1926); reprint (Fiftieth Anniversary Edition, Robert Schalenbach Foundation, New York, 1940), pp. 3–6, 12, 165–167, 169, 220–221, 326, 331–334, 336–337, 401–405, 431–437. By courtesy of Robert Schalenbach Foundation.

noon executed in San Francisco in the morning of the same day; could he have conceived of the hundred thousand improvements which these only suggest, what would he have inferred as to the social condition of mankind? . . . .

Now, however, we are coming into collision with facts which there can be no mistaking. From all parts of the civilized world come complaints of industrial depression; of labor condemned to involuntary idleness; of capital massed and wasting; of pecuniary distress among business men; of want and suffering and anxiety among the working classes. All the dull, deadening pain, all the keen, maddening anguish, that to great masses of men are involved in the words "hard times," afflict the world to-day. This state of things, common to communities differing so widely in situation, in political institutions, in fiscal and financial systems, in density of population and in social organization, can hardly be accounted for by local causes. There is distress where large standing armies are maintained, but there is also distress where the standing armies are nominal; there is distress where protective tariffs stupidly and wastefully hamper trade, but there is also distress where trade is nearly free; there is distress where autocratic government yet prevails, but there is also distress where political power is wholly in the hands of the people; in countries where paper is money, and in countries where gold and silver are the only currency. Evidently, beneath all such things as these, we must infer a common cause.

That there is a common cause, and that it is either what we call material progress or something closely connected with material progress, becomes more than an inference when it is noted that the phenomena we class together and speak of as industrial depression are but intensifications of phenomena which always accompany material progress, and which show themselves more clearly and strongly as material progress goes on. Where the conditions to which material progress everywhere tends are most fully realized— that is to say, where population is densest, wealth greatest, and the machinery of production and exchange most highly developed— we find the deepest poverty, the sharpest struggle for existence, and the most of enforced idleness. . . . .

I propose in the following pages to attempt to solve by the methods of political economy the great problem I have outlined. I propose to seek the law which associates poverty with progress, and increases want with advancing wealth; and I believe that in the explanation of this paradox we shall find the explanation of those recurring seasons of industrial and commercial paralysis which, viewed independently of their relations to more general phenomena, seem so inexplicable. Properly commenced and carefully pursued, such an investigation must yield a conclusion that will stand every test, and as truth, will correlate with all other truth. For in the sequence of phenomena there is no accident. Every effect has a cause, and every fact implies a preceding fact. . . .

Bk. III, Ch. ii. Rent and the Law of Rent.

The term rent, in its economic sense—that is, when used, as I am using it, to distinguish that part of the produce which accrues to the owners of land or other natural capabilities by virtue of their ownership—differs in meaning from the word rent as commonly used. In some respects this economic meaning is narrower than the common meaning; in other respects it is wider.

It is narrower in this: In common speech, we apply the word rent to payments for the use of buildings, machinery, fixtures, etc.; as well as to payments for the use of land or other natural capabilities; and in speaking of the rent of a house or the rent of a farm, we do not separate the price for the use of the improvements from the price for the use of the bare land. But in the economic meaning of rent, payments for the use of any of the products of human exertion are excluded, and of the lumped payments for the use of houses, farms, etc., only that part is rent which constitutes the consideration for the use of the land—that part paid for the use of buildings or other improvements being properly interest, as it is a consideration for the use of capital.

It is wider in this: In common speech we speak of rent only when owner and user are distinct persons. But in the economic sense there is also rent where the same person is both owner and user. Where owner and user are thus the same person, whatever part of his income he might obtain by letting the land to another is rent, while the return for his labor and capital are that part of his income which they would yield him did he hire instead of owning the land. Rent is also expressed in a selling price. When land is purchased, the payment which is made for the ownership, or right to perpetual use, is rent commuted or capitalized. If I buy land for a small price and hold it until I can sell it for a large price, I have become rich, not by wages for my labor or by interest upon my capital, but by the increase of rent. Rent, in short, is the share in the wealth produced which the exclusive right to the use of natural capabilities gives to the owner. Wherever land has an exchange value there is rent in the economic meaning of the term. Wherever land having a value is used, either by owner or hirer, there is rent actual; wherever it is not used, but still has a value, there is rent potential. It is this capacity of yielding rent which gives value to land. Until its ownership will confer some advantage, land has no value.[1]

Thus rent or land value does not arise from the productiveness or utility of land. It in no wise represents any help or advantage given to production, but simply the power of securing a part of the results of production. No matter what are its capabilities, land can yield no rent and have no value until some one is willing to give labor or the results of labor for the privilege of using it; and what any one will thus give depends not upon the capacity of the land, but upon its capacity as compared with that of land that can be had for nothing. I may have very rich land, but it will yield no rent and have no value so long as there is other land as good to be had without cost. But when this other land is appropriated, and the best land to be had for nothing is inferior, either in fertility, situation, or other quality, my land will begin to have a value and yield rent. And though the productiveness of my land may decrease, yet if the productiveness of the land to be had without charge decreases in greater proportion, the rent I can get, and consequently the value of my land, will steadily increase. Rent, in short, is the price of monopoly, arising from the reduction to individual ownership of natural elements which human exertion can neither produce nor increase. . . .

Perhaps it may conduce to a fuller understanding of the law of rent to put it in this form: The ownership of a natural agent of production will give the power of appropriating so much of the wealth produced by the exertion of labor and capital upon it as exceeds the return which the same application of labor and capital

---

[1] In speaking of the value of land I use and shall use the words as referring to the value of the bare land. When I wish to speak of the value of land and improvements I shall use those words.

could secure in the least productive occupation in which they freely engage. . . .

Bk. III, Ch. viii. The Statics of the Problem . . . Explained.

. . . Nothing can be clearer than the proposition that the failure of wages to increase with increasing productive power is due to the increase of rent.

Three things unite to production—labor, capital, and land.

Three parties divide the produce—the laborer, the capitalist, and the land owner.

If, with an increase of production the laborer gets no more and the capitalist no more it is a necessary inference that the land owner reaps the whole gain.

And the facts agree with the inference. Though neither wages nor interest anywhere increase as material progress goes on, yet the invariable accompaniment and mark of material progress is the increase of rent—the rise of land values.

The increase of rent explains why wages and interest do not increase. The cause which gives to the land holder is the cause which denies to the laborer and capitalist. That wages and interest are higher in new than in old countries is not, as the standard economists say, because nature makes a greater return to the application of labor and capital, but because land is cheaper, and, therefore, as a smaller proportion of the return is taken by rent, labor and capital can keep for their share a larger proportion of what nature does return. It is not the total produce, but the net produce, after rent has been taken from it, that determines what can be divided as wages and interest. Hence, the rate of wages and interest is everywhere fixed, not so much by the productiveness of labor as by the value of land. Wherever the value of land is relatively low, wages and interest are relatively high; wherever land is relatively high, wages and interest are relatively low. . . .

Bk. VI, Ch. ii. The True Remedy.

We have traced the unequal distribution of wealth which is the curse and menace of modern civilization to the institution of private property in land. We have seen that so long as this institution exists no increase in productive power can permanently benefit the masses; but, on the contrary, must tend still further to depress their condition. We have examined all the remedies, short of the abolition of private property in land, which are currently relied on or proposed for the relief of poverty and the better distribution of wealth, and have found them all inefficacious or impracticable.

There is but one way to remove an evil—and that is, to remove its cause. Poverty deepens as wealth increases, and wages are forced down while productive power grows, because land, which is the source of all wealth and the field of all labor, is monopolized. To extirpate poverty, to make wages what justice commands they should be, the full earnings of the laborer, we must therefore substitute for the individual ownership of land a common ownership. Nothing else will go to the cause of the evil—in nothing else is there the slightest hope.

This, then, is the remedy for the unjust and unequal distribution of wealth apparent in modern civilization, and for all the evils which flow from it:

We must make land common property. . . .

Bk. VII, Ch. i. *The Injustice of Private Property in Land.*

When it is proposed to abolish private property in land the first question that will arise is that of justice. Though often warped by habit, superstition, and selfishness into the most distorted forms, the sentiment of justice is yet fundamental to the human mind, and whatever dispute arouses the passions of men, the conflict is sure to rage, not so much as to the question "Is it wise?" as to the question "Is it right?" . . .

What constitutes the rightful basis of property? What is it that enables a man justly to say of a thing, "It is mine?" From what springs the sentiment which acknowledges his exclusive right as against all the world? Is it not, primarily, the right of a man to himself to the use of his own powers, to the enjoyment of the fruits of his own exertions? Is it not this individual right, which springs from and is testified to by the natural facts of individual organization—the fact that each particular pair of hands obey a particular brain and are related to a particular stomach; the fact that each man is a definite, coherent, independent whole—which alone justifies individual ownership? As a man belongs to himself, so his labor when put in concrete form belongs to him.

And for this reason, that which a man makes or produces is his own, as against all the world—to enjoy or to destroy, to use, to exchange, or to give. No one else can rightfully claim it, and his exclusive right to it involves no wrong to any one else. Thus there is to everything produced by human exertion a clear and indisputable title to exclusive possession and enjoyment, which is perfectly consistent with justice, as it descends from the original producer, in whom it vested by natural law. The pen with which I am writing is justly mine. No other human being can rightfully lay claim to it, for in me is the title of the producers who made it. It has become mine, because transferred to me by the stationer, to whom it was transferred by the importer, who obtained the exclusive right to it by transfer from the manufacturer, in whom, by the same process of purchase, vested the rights of those who dug the material from the ground and shaped it into a pen. Thus, my exclusive right of ownership in the pen springs from the natural right of the individual to the use of his own faculties. . . .

. . . With what other power is man by nature clothed, save the power of exerting his own faculties? How can he in any other way act upon or affect material things or other men? Paralyze the motor nerves, and your man has no more external influence or power than a log or stone. From what else, then, can the right of possessing and controlling things be derived? If it spring not from man himself, from what can it spring? Nature acknowledges no ownership or control in man save as the result of exertion. In no other way can her treasures be drawn forth, her powers directed, or her forces utilized or controlled. She makes no discriminations among men, but is to all absolutely impartial. She knows no distinction between master and slave, king and subject, saint and sinner. All men to her stand upon an equal footing and have equal rights. She recognizes no claim but that of labor, and recognizes that without respect to the claimant. . . .

. . . If production give to the producer the right to exclusive possession and enjoyment, there can rightfully be no exclusive possession and enjoyment of anything not the production of labor, and the recognition of private property in land is a wrong. For the right to the produce of labor cannot be enjoyed without the right to the free use of the opportunities offered by nature, and to admit the right of property in these is to deny the right of property in the produce of labor. When non-producers can claim as rent a portion of the wealth created by producers, the right of the producers to the fruits of their labor is to that extent denied. . . .

The moment this distinction is realized, that moment it is seen that the sanction which natural justice gives to one species of property is denied to the other; that the rightfulness which attaches to individual property in the produce of labor implies the wrongfulness of individual property in land; that, whereas the recognition of the one places all men upon equal terms, securing to each the due reward of his labor, the recognition of the other is the denial of the equal rights of men, permitting those who do not labor to take the natural reward of those who do.

Whatever may be said for the institution of private property in land, it is therefore plain that it cannot be defended on the score of justice.

The equal right of all men to the use of land is as clear as their equal right to breathe the air—it is a right proclaimed by the fact of their existence. For we cannot suppose that some men have a right to be in this world and others no right.

If we are all here by the equal permission of the Creator, we are all here with an equal title to the enjoyment of his bounty—with an equal right to the use of all that nature so impartially offers. This is a right which is natural and inalienable; it is a right which vests in every human being as he enters the world, and which during his continuance in the world can be limited only by the equal rights of others. There is in nature no such thing as a fee simple in land. There is on earth no power which can rightfully make a grant of exclusive ownership in land. If all existing men were to unite to grant away their equal rights, they could not grant away the right of those who follow them. For what are we but tenants for a day? Have we made the earth, that we should determine the rights of those who after us shall tenant it in their turn? The Almighty, who created the earth for man and man for the earth, has entailed it upon all the generations of the children of men by a decree written upon the constitution of all things—a decree which no human action can bar and no prescription determine. Let the parchments be ever so many, or possession ever so long, natural justice can recognize no right in one man to the possession and enjoyment of land that is not equally the right of all his fellows. . . .

Bk. VIII, Ch. ii. How Equal Rights to the Land May be Asserted and Secured. . . .

We have weighed every objection, and seen that neither on the ground of equity or expediency is there anything to deter us from making land common property by confiscating rent.

But a question of method remains. How shall we do it?

We should satisfy the law of justice, we should meet all economic requirements, by at one stroke abolishing all private titles, declaring all land public property, and letting it out to the highest bidders in lots to suit, under such conditions as would sacredly guard the private right to improvements.

Thus we should secure, in a more complex state of society, the same equality of rights that in a ruder state were secured by equal partitions of the soil, and by giving the use of the land to whoever could procure the most from it, we should secure the greatest production. . . .

But such a plan, though perfectly feasible, does not seem to me the best. Or rather I propose to accomplish the same thing in a simpler, easier, and quieter way, than that of formally confiscating all the land and formally letting it out to the highest bidders.

To do that would involve a needless shock to present customs and habits of thought—which is to be avoided.

To do that would involve a needless extension of governmental machinery—which is to be avoided. . . .

I do not propose either to purchase or to confiscate private property in land. The first would be unjust; the second, needless. Let the individuals who now hold it still retain, if they want to, possession of what they are pleased to call *their* land. Let them continue to call it *their* land. Let them buy and sell, and bequeath and devise it. We may safely leave them the shell, if we take the kernel. *It is not necessary to confiscate land; it is only necessary to confiscate rent.*

Nor to take rent for public uses is it necessary that the State should bother with the letting of lands, and assume the chances of the favoritism, collusion, and corruption this might involve. It is not necessary that any new machinery should be created. The machinery already exists. Instead of extending it, all we have to do is to simplify and reduce it. By leaving to land owners a percentage of rent which would probably be much less than the cost and loss involved in attempting to rent lands through State agency, and by making use of this existing machinery, we may, without jar or shock, assert the common right to land by taking rent for public uses.

We already take some rent in taxation. We have only to make some changes in our modes of taxation to take it all.

What I, therefore, propose, as the simple yet sovereign remedy, which will raise wages, increase the earnings of capital, extirpate pauperism, abolish poverty, give remunerative employment to whoever wishes it, afford free scope to human powers, lessen crime, elevate morals, and taste, and intelligence, purify government and carry civilization to yet nobler heights, is—*to appropriate rent by taxation.*

In this way the State may become the universal landlord without calling herself so, and without assuming a single new function. In form, the ownership of land would remain just as now. No owner of land need be dispossessed, and no restriction need be placed upon the amount of land any one could hold. For, rent being taken by the State in taxes, land, no matter in whose name it stood, or in what parcels it was held, would be really common property, and every member of the community would participate in the advantages of its ownership.

Now, insomuch as the taxation of rent, or land values, must necessarily be increased just as we abolish other taxes, we may put the proposition into practical form by proposing—

To abolish all taxation save that upon land values.

As we have seen, the value of land is at the beginning of society nothing, but as society develops by the increase of population and the advance of the arts, it becomes greater and greater. In every civilized country, even the newest, the value of the land taken as a whole is sufficient to bear the entire expenses of government. In the better developed countries it is much more than sufficient. Hence it will not be enough merely to place all taxes upon the value of land. It will be necessary, where rent exceeds the present governmental revenues, commensurately to increase the amount demanded in taxation, and to continue this increase as society progresses and rent advances. But this is so natural and easy a matter, that it may be considered as involved, or at least understood, in the proposition to put all taxes on the value of land. That is the first step, upon which the practical struggle must be made. When the hare is once caught and killed, cooking him will follow as a matter of course. When the common right to land is so far appreciated that all taxes are abolished save those which fall upon rent, there is no danger of much more than is necessary to induce them to collect the public revenues being left to individual land holders. . . .

Bk. IX, Ch. i. Of the Effect upon the Production of Wealth. . . .

To abolish the taxation which, acting and reacting, now hampers every wheel of exchange and presses upon every form of industry, would be like removing an immense weight from a powerful spring. Imbued with fresh energy, production would start into new life, and trade would receive a stimulus which would be felt to the remotest arteries. The present method of taxation operates upon exchange like artificial deserts and mountains; it costs more to get goods through a custom house than it does to carry them around the world. It operates upon energy, and industry, and skill, and thrift, like a fine upon those qualities. If I have worked harder and built myself a good house while you have been contented to live in a hovel, the tax-gatherer now comes annually to make me pay a penalty for my energy and industry, by taxing me more than you. If I have saved while you wasted, I am mulct, while you are exempt. If a man build a ship we make him pay for his temerity, as though he had done an injury to the state; if a railroad be opened, down comes the tax-collector upon it, as though it were a public nuisance; if a manufactory be erected we levy upon it an annual sum which would go far toward making a handsome profit. We say we want capital, but if any one accumulate it, or bring it among us, we charge him for it as though we were giving him a privilege. We punish with a tax the man who covers barren fields with ripening grain; we fine him who puts up machinery, and him who drains a swamp. How heavily these taxes burden production only those realize who have attempted to follow our system of taxation through its ramifications, for, as I have before said, the heaviest part of taxation is that which falls in increased prices. But manifestly these taxes are in their nature akin to the Egyptian Pasha's tax upon date-trees. If they do not cause the trees to be cut down, they at least discourage the planting.

To abolish these taxes would be to lift the whole enormous

weight of taxation from productive industry. The needle of the seamstress and the great manufactory; the cart-horse and the locomotive; the fishing boat and the steamship; the farmer's plow and the merchant's stock, would be alike untaxed. All would be free to make or to save, to buy or to sell, unfined by taxes, unannoyed by the tax-gatherer. Instead of saying to the producer, as it does now, "The more you add to the general wealth the more shall you be taxed!" the state would say to the producer, "Be as industrious, as thrifty, as enterprising as you choose, you shall have your full reward! You shall not be fined for making two blades of grass grow where one grew before; you shall not be taxed for adding to the aggregate wealth."

. . . Every productive enterprise, besides its return to those who undertake it, yields collateral advantages to others. If a man plant a fruit-tree, his gain is that he gathers the fruit in its time and season. But in addition to his gain, there is a gain to the whole community. Others than the owner are benefited by the increased supply of fruit; the birds which it shelters fly far and wide; the rain which it helps to attract falls not alone on his field; and, even to the eye which rests upon it from a distance, it brings a sense of beauty. And so with everything else. The building of a house, a factory, a ship, or a railroad, benefits others besides those who get the direct profits. . . .

And to shift the burden of taxation from production and exchange to the value or rent of land would not merely be to give new stimulus to the production of wealth; it would be to open new opportunities. For under this system no one would care to hold land unless to use it, and land now withheld from use would everywhere be thrown open to improvement.

The selling price of land would fall; land speculation would receive its death blow; land monopolization would no longer pay. Millions and millions of acres from which settlers are now shut out by high prices would be abandoned by their present owners or sold to settlers upon nominal terms. And this not merely on the frontiers, but within what are now considered well settled districts. Within a hundred miles of San Francisco would be thus thrown open land enough to support, even with present modes of cultivation, an agricultural population equal to that now scattered from the Oregon boundary to the Mexican line—a distance of 800 miles.

In the same degree would this be true of most of the Western States, and in a great degree of the older Eastern States, for even in New York and Pennsylvania is population yet sparse as compared with the capacity of the land. And even in densely populated England would such a policy throw open to cultivation many hundreds of thousands of acres now held as private parks, deer preserves, and shooting grounds.

For this simple device of placing all taxes on the value of land would be in effect putting up the land at auction to whomsoever would pay the highest rent to the state. The demand for land fixes its value, and hence, if taxes were placed so as very nearly to consume that value, the man who wished to hold land without using it would have to pay very nearly what it would be worth to any one who wanted to use it. . . .

With natural opportunities thus free to labor; with capital and improvements exempt from tax, and exchange released from restrictions, the spectacle of willing men unable to turn their labor into the things they are suffering for would become impossible; the recurring paroxysms which paralyze industry would cease; every wheel of production would be set in motion; demand would keep pace with supply, and supply with demand; trade would increase in every direction, and wealth augment on every hand.

13. GROVER CLEVELAND (1837–1908)

G ROVER CLEVELAND, twice President (1885–89, 1893–97, first Democrat to hold the office since the Civil War) had no sense of critical weaknesses in the prevailing economic system and no general program of reform. He was born (son of a Presbyterian minister) in Caldwell, New Jersey, and reared in upper New York State. Largely self-supporting from his seventeenth year and unable to realize his desire for a college education, he studied law and maintained a successful practice in the intervals between his terms in public office. He was known as a "reformer" in local and State offices (assistant district attorney, later sheriff, of Erie county, mayor of Buffalo, and governor of the State) because he attacked corruption and, although a "straight" party man, maintained his independence of party machines. He made his way up to the presidency largely by a reputation for honesty, courage, and practical wisdom. As President he startled Congress and the country by vetoing over two hundred individual pension bills, an extravagant general pension measure, and a "pork-barrel" rivers-and-harbors bill. He made an unusual number of independent appointments and vigorously supported civil-service reform. He fought stubbornly for lower tariffs, a sound monetary system, and governmental economy. In advocating these aims he expressed generally conservative economic views, yet explicitly recognized the duty of a government to resist overweening claims by property-owners.

Cleveland won and lost elections largely on the tariff issue. The Senate was under Republican control during his first term and he was unable to obtain tariff reductions. Renominated in 1888, he gained a plurality of the popular vote but lost in the electoral vote. Four years later he was nominated for a third time, the tariff was again a major issue, and he won by a decisive margin. Again, however, he suffered a grievous disappointment in his plans for tariff reduction: the rates of a House bill, which had been framed generally in accord with his views, were so extensively raised by the Senate, through a combination of a few Democrats with the Republican minority, that he allowed the bill to become law without his signature.

The third annual message in a President's term comes at a time when thoughts about the next campaign usually preoccupy the minds of party managers. Cleveland ignored such considerations by devoting the third regular message of his first term to a forthright discussion of the existing state of tariff protection and its effects on government revenues and the economic condition of the country. "I would stultify myself," he replied to his alarmed advisers, "if I failed to let the message go forward from any fear that it might offset my election." [1] His general position is revealed in the following passages from the message:

> It is not proposed to entirely relieve the country of this taxation. It must be extensively continued as the source of the Government's income; and in a readjustment of our tariff the interests of American labor engaged in manufacture should be carefully considered, as well as the preservation of our manufactures. It may be called protection or by any other name, but relief from the hardships and dangers of our present tariff laws should be devised with especial precaution against imperiling the existence of our manufacturing interests. But this existence should not mean a condition which, without regard to the public welfare or a national exigency, must always insure the realization of immense profits instead of moderately profitable returns. . . .
>
> It is a *condition* which confronts us, not a theory.

This message evoked extensive and vigorous comment, with extremes of praise and condemnation. The New York *Nation* hailed the message as "the most courageous document that has been sent from the Executive Mansion since the close of the Civil War." The Chicago *Journal* called it "cant and humbug"; the New York *Tribune* said the President had not spoken as "an American"; and the *Commercial Gazette* called him an "ignoramus" and an "idiot."

Cleveland's fourth annual message, reporting generally on the state of the union, again expressed strong views on the tariff.

[See: Robert McElroy, *Grover Cleveland the Man and the Statesman* (2 vols., 1923); Allan Nevins, *Grover Cleveland: a Study in Courage* (1932); Henry Jones Ford, *The Cleveland Era: a Chronicle of the New Order in Politics* (1919).]

From FOURTH ANNUAL MESSAGE
(DECEMBER 3, 1888) [2]

To the Congress of the United States:

As you assemble for the discharge of the duties you have assumed as the representatives of a free and generous people, your meeting is marked by an interesting and impressive incident. With the ex-

[1] Robert McElroy, *Grover Cleveland the Man and the Statesman*, Vol. I, p. 271.
[2] In *A Compilation of the Messages and Papers of the Presidents*, ed. by James D. Richardson, Vol. XII, pp. 5358–5361.

piration of the present session of the Congress the first century of our constitutional existence as a nation will be completed.

Our survival for one hundred years is not sufficient to assure us that we no longer have dangers to fear in the maintenance, with all its promised blessings, of a government founded upon the freedom of the people. The time rather admonishes us to soberly inquire whether in the past we have always closely kept in the course of safety, and whether we have before us a way plain and clear which leads to happiness and perpetuity.

When the experiment of our Government was undertaken, the chart adopted for our guidance was the Constitution. Departure from the lines there laid down is failure. It is only by a strict adherence to the direction they indicate and by restraint within the limitations they fix that we can furnish proof to the world of the fitness of the American people for self-government.

The equal and exact justice of which we boast as the underlying principle of our institutions should not be confined to the relations of our citizens to each other. The Government itself is under bond to the American people that in the exercise of its functions and powers it will deal with the body of our citizens in a manner scrupulously honest and fair and absolutely just. It has agreed that American citizenship shall be the only credential necessary to justify the claim of equality before the law, and that no condition in life shall give rise to discrimination in the treatment of the people by their Government.

The citizen of our Republic in its early days rigidly insisted upon full compliance with the letter of this bond, and saw stretching out before him a clear field for individual endeavor. His tribute to the support of his Government was measured by the cost of its economical maintenance, and he was secure in the enjoyment of the remaining recompense of his steady and contented toil. In those days the frugality of the people was stamped upon their Government, and was enforced by the free, thoughtful, and intelligent suffrage of the citizen. Combinations, monopolies, and aggregations of capital were either avoided or sternly regulated and restrained. The pomp and glitter of governments less free offered no temptation and presented no delusion to the plain people who, side by side, in friendly competition, wrought for the ennoblement and dignity of man, for the solution of the problem of free government, and for the achievement of the grand destiny awaiting the land which God had given them.

A century has passed. Our cities are the abiding places of wealth and luxury; our manufactories yield fortunes never dreamed of by the fathers of the Republic; our business men are madly striving in the race for riches, and immense aggregations of capital outrun the imagination in the magnitude of their undertakings.

We view with pride and satisfaction this bright picture of our country's growth and prosperity, while only a closer scrutiny develops a somber shading. Upon more careful inspection we find the wealth and luxury of our cities mingled with poverty and wretchedness and unremunerative toil. A crowded and constantly increasing urban population suggests the impoverishment of rural sections and discontent with agricultural pursuits. The farmer's son, not satisfied with his father's simple and laborious life, joins the eager chase for easily acquired wealth.

We discover that the fortunes realized by our manufacturers are no longer solely the reward of sturdy industry and enlightened foresight, but that they result from the discriminating favor of the Government and are largely built upon undue exactions from the masses of our people. The gulf between employers and the employed is constantly widening, and classes are rapidly forming, one comprising the very rich and powerful, while in another are found the toiling poor.

As we view the achievements of aggregated capital, we discover the existence of trusts, combinations, and monopolies, while the citizen is struggling far in the rear or is trampled to death beneath an iron heel. Corporations, which should be the carefully restrained creatures of the law and the servants of the people, are fast becoming the people's masters.

Still congratulating ourselves upon the wealth and prosperity of our country and complacently contemplating every incident of change inseparable from these conditions, it is our duty as patriotic citizens to inquire at the present stage of our progress how the bond of the Government made with the people has been kept and performed.

Instead of limiting the tribute drawn from our citizens to the necessities of its economical administration, the Government persists in exacting from the substance of the people millions which, unapplied and useless, lie dormant in its Treasury. This flagrant injustice and this breach of faith and obligation add to extortion the danger attending the diversion of the currency of the country from the legitimate channels of business.

Under the same laws by which these results are produced the Government permits many millions more to be added to the cost of the living of our people and to be taken from our consumers, which unreasonably swell the profits of a small but powerful minority.

The people must still be taxed for the support of the Government under the operation of tariff laws. But to the extent that the mass of our citizens are inordinately burdened beyond any useful public purpose and for the benefit of a favored few, the Government, under pretext of an exercise of its taxing power, enters gratuitously into partnership with these favorites, to their advantage and to the injury of a vast majority of our people.

This is not equality before the law.

The existing situation is injurious to the health of our entire body politic. It stifles in those for whose benefit it is permitted all patriotic love of country, and substitutes in its place selfish greed and grasping avarice. Devotion to American citizenship for its own sake and for what it should accomplish as a motive to our nation's advancement and the happiness of all our people is displaced by the assumption that the Government, instead of being the embodiment of equality, is but an instrumentality through which especial and individual advantages are to be gained.

The arrogance of this assumption is unconcealed. It appears in the sordid disregard of all but personal interests, in the refusal to abate for the benefit of others one iota of selfish advantage, and in combinations to perpetuate such advantages through efforts to control legislation and improperly influence the suffrages of the people.

The grievances of those not included within the circle of these beneficiaries, when fully realized, will surely arouse irritation and discontent. Our farmers, long suffering and patient, struggling in the race of life with the hardest and most unremitting toil, will not fail to see, in spite of misrepresentations and misleading fallacies, that they are obliged to accept such prices for their products as are fixed in foreign markets where they compete with the farmers of the world; that their lands are declining in value while their debts increase, and that without compensating favor they are forced by the action of the Government to pay for the benefit of others such enhanced prices for the things they need that the scanty returns of their labor fail to furnish their support or leave no margin for accumulation.

Our workingmen, enfranchised from all delusions and no longer frightened by the cry that their wages are endangered by a just revision of our tariff laws, will reasonably demand through such revision steadier employment, cheaper means of living in their homes, freedom for themselves and their children from the doom of perpetual servitude, and an open door to their advancement beyond the limits of a laboring class. Others of our citizens, whose comforts and expenditures are measured by moderate salaries and fixed incomes, will insist upon the fairness and justice of cheapening the cost of necessaries for themselves and their families.

When to the selfishness of the beneficiaries of unjust discrimination under our laws there shall be added the discontent of those who suffer from such discrimination, we will realize the fact that the beneficent purposes of our Government, dependent upon the patriotism and contentment of our people, are endangered.

Communism is a hateful thing and a menace to peace and organized government; but the communism of combined wealth and capital, the outgrowth of overweening cupidity and selfishness, which insidiously undermines the justice and integrity of free institutions, is not less dangerous than the communism of oppressed poverty and toil, which, exasperated by injustice and discontent, attacks with wild disorder the citadel of rule.

He mocks the people who proposes that the Government shall protect the rich and that they in turn will care for the laboring poor. Any intermediary between the people and their Government or the least delegation of the care and protection the Government owes to the humblest citizen in the land makes the boast of free institutions a glittering delusion and the pretended boon of American citizenship a shameless imposition.

A just and sensible revision of our tariff laws should be made for the relief of those of our countrymen who suffer under present conditions. Such a revision should receive the support of all who love that justice and equality due to American citizenship; of all who realize that in this justice and equality our Government finds its strength and its power to protect the citizen and his property; of all who believe that the contented competence and comfort of many accord better with the spirit of our institutions than colossal fortunes unfairly gathered in the hands of a few; of all who appreciate that the forbearance and fraternity among our people, which recognize the value of every American interest, are the surest guaranty of our national progress, and of all who desire to see the products of American skill and ingenuity in every market of the world, with a resulting restoration of American commerce.

The necessity of the reduction of our revenues is so apparent as to be generally conceded, but the means by which this end shall be accomplished and the sum of direct benefit which shall result to our citizens present a controversy of the utmost importance. There should be no scheme accepted as satisfactory by which the burdens of the people are only apparently removed. Extravagant appropriations of public money, with all their demoralizing consequences, should not be tolerated, either as a means of relieving the Treasury of its present surplus or as furnishing pretext for resisting a proper reduction in tariff rates. Existing evils and injustice should be honestly recognized, boldly met, and effectively remedied. There should be no cessation of the struggle until a plan is perfected, fair and conservative toward existing industries, but which will reduce the cost to consumers of the necessaries of life, while it provides for our manufacturers the advantage of freer raw materials and permits no injury to the interests of American labor.

The cause for which the battle is waged is comprised within lines clearly and distinctly defined. It should never be compromised. It is the people's cause. . . .

14. WILLIAM GRAHAM SUMNER (1840–1910)

SUMNER'S studies and writings cover a wide range. One of his first publications was an annotated translation of a German commentary on the Book of Kings. He wrote important biographies of American statesmen and authoritative works on American financial history.[1] His *Folkways* (1906) is one of the most original and influential sociological works ever produced in America; and the major conclusions of that work are based on the extensive anthropological data which he had collected and which, enlarged, revised, and classified by Albert G. Keller, his disciple and successor at Yale, now make up the four large volumes of *The Science of Society*, by Sumner and Keller.

Sumner was born in Paterson, New Jersey. His father, an industrious and intelligent mechanic, and his maternal grandparents were immigrants (from Lancashire, England) who had come to America in search of better opportunities for earning a living. They reached New Jersey in the midst of a depression, and in Sumner's infancy the family moved to Hartford, Connecticut, where his father secured employment in a railway repair shop. Sumner was graduated from Yale, spent several years in Europe in the study of metaphysics and biblical criticism, taught freshman subjects at Yale for three years, was ordained as a priest in the Episcopal church and served as an assistant rector in New York City and as a rector in Morristown, New Jersey. In some of his sermons he discussed economic and political subjects, and problems in these fields became of increasing interest to him. When, in 1872, he was offered the appointment to a newly created professorship of political and social science at Yale, he accepted readily; and he held that position, with extraordinary popularity as a teacher, until his retirement a year before his death.

Sumner's selection for the new Yale chair appeared to have been due in part to expectations, on the part of President Noah Porter (a professor of "moral science") and some of the trustees, that Sumner's ecclesiastical background would give assurance that under his tutelage the discussion of problems of social ethics and public policy at Yale

---

[1] *Andrew Jackson as a Public Man* (1882); *Alexander Hamilton* (1890); *Robert Morris* (1892); *A History of American Currency* (1874); *The Financier and the Finances of the American Revolution*, 2 vols. (1891); *A History of Banking in the United States* (1896).

would be safeguarded against current amoral and non-religious tendencies in the teaching of those subjects in America. Sumner, however, helped introduce more of the natural sciences into the Yale curriculum (at the expense of the classics), and he made his own teaching distinctively secular and empirical. In the classroom, and especially in articles and public lectures, he applied his sociological doctrines to current public issues, dealing particularly with questions concerning the proper sphere of governmental action. He vigorously disparaged all attempts to solve such questions by appeals either to so-called "natural rights" or to an assumed natural benevolence and gregariousness in men. He founded his ideas of governmental policy partly on the Darwinian theory of evolution and the Spencerian concept of society as the seat of forces subject to laws; and partly on his own findings concerning the ways of human action, the forms of human beliefs and sentiments, and the social institutions that develop from customary ways of action and thought. He coined the familiar expression, "the forgotten man," to describe (in a somewhat idealizing picture) the ordinary hard-working, self-reliant, patriotic individual who, asking no favors of government, is made to pay the taxes out of which a government gets the means to execute measures which, under pressure from idealizing social reformers, it enacts to protect and assist the inefficient, indolent or vicious members of the community. There is a forgotten idea in Sumner's discussions of governmental functions: for many of his lay admirers ignore his emphatic criticism of tariff protection.

[For Sumner's political ideas see his *The Challenge of Facts and Other Essays, The Forgotten Man and Other Essays, Earth Hunger and Other Essays*, all edited by A. G. Keller, and *What Social Classes Owe to Each Other* (1883).

See also: Albert G. Keller, *Reminiscences (Mainly Personal) of William Graham Sumner* (1933); Charles H. Cooley, "Sumner and Methodology," in Robert C. Angell, ed., *Sociological Theory and Social Research* (1930), ch. 11; Ralph H. Gabriel, *The Course of American Democratic Thought* (1940), ch. 19; Harris E. Starr, *William Graham Sumner* (1925).]

"THE CHALLENGE OF FACTS"[1]

Socialism is no new thing. In one form or another it is to be found throughout all history. It arises from an observation of certain harsh facts in the lot of man on earth, the concrete expression

[1] In *Essays of William Graham Sumner*, ed. by Albert Galloway Keller and Maurice R. Davie, 2 vols. (New Haven, 1934), Vol. II, pp. 87–122. By special arrangement with Yale University Press.

of which is poverty and misery. These facts challenge us. It is folly to try to shut our eyes to them. We have first to notice what they are, and then to face them squarely.

Man is born under the necessity of sustaining the existence he has received by an onerous struggle against nature, both to win what is essential to his life and to ward off what is prejudicial to it. He is born under a burden and a necessity. Nature holds what is essential to him, but she offers nothing gratuitously. He may win for his use what she holds, if he can. Only the most meager and inadequate supply for human needs can be obtained directly from nature. There are trees which may be used for fuel and for dwellings, but labor is required to fit them for this use. There are ores in the ground, but labor is necessary to get out the metals and make tools or weapons. For any real satisfaction, labor is necessary to fit the products of nature for human use. In this struggle every individual is under the pressure of the necessities for food, clothing, shelter, fuel, and every individual brings with him more or less energy for the conflict necessary to supply his needs. The relation, therefore, between each man's needs and each man's energy, or "individualism," is the first fact of human life.

It is not without reason, however, that we speak of a "man" as the individual in question, for women (mothers) and children have special disabilities for the struggle with nature, and these disabilities grow greater and last longer as civilization advances. The perpetuation of the race in health and vigor, and its success as a whole in its struggle to expand and develop human life on earth, therefore, require that the head of the family shall, by his energy, be able to supply not only his own needs, but those of the organisms which are dependent upon him. The history of the human race shows a great variety of experiments in the relation of the sexes and in the organization of the family. These experiments have been controlled by economic circumstances, but, as man has gained more and more control over economic circumstances, monogamy and the family education of children have been more and more sharply developed. If there is one thing in regard to which the student of history and sociology can affirm with confidence that social institutions have made "progress" or grown "better," it is in this arrangement of marriage and the family. All experience proves that monogamy, pure and strict, is the sex relation which conduces most to the vigor and intelligence of the race, and that the family education of children is the institution by which the race as a whole advances most rapidly, from generation to generation, in the struggle with nature. Love of man and wife, as we understand it, is a modern sentiment. The devotion and sacrifice of parents for children is a sentiment which has been developed steadily and is now more intense and far more widely practiced throughout society than in earlier times. The relation is also coming to be regarded in a light quite different from that in which it was formerly viewed. It used to be believed that the parent had unlimited claims on the child and rights over him. In a truer view of the matter, we are coming to see that the rights are on the side of the child and the duties on the side of the parent. Existence is not a boon for which the child owes all subjection to the parent. It is a responsibility assumed by the parent towards the child without the child's consent, and the consequence of it is that the parent owes all possible devotion to the child to enable him to make his existence happy and successful.

The value and importance of the family sentiments, from a social point of view, cannot be exaggerated. They impose self-control and prudence in their most important social bearings, and tend more than any other forces to hold the individual up to the virtues which make the sound man and the valuable member of society. The race is bound, from generation to generation, in an unbroken chain of vice and penalty, virtue and reward. The sins of the fathers are visited upon the children, while, on the other hand, health, vigor, talent, genius, and skill are, so far as we can discover, the results of high physical vigor and wise early training. The popular language bears witness to the universal observation of these facts, although general social and political dogmas have come into fashion which contradict or ignore them. There is no other such punishment for a life of vice and self-indulgence as to see children grow up cursed with the penalties of it, and no such reward for self-denial and virtue as to see children born and grow up vigorous in mind and body. It is time that the true import of these observations for moral and educational purposes was developed, and it may well be questioned whether we do not go too far in our reticence in regard to all these matters when we leave it to romances and poems to do almost all the educational work that is done in the way of spreading ideas about them. The defense of marriage and the family, if their sociological value were better understood, would be not only instinctive but rational. The struggle for existence with which we have to deal must be understood, then, to be that of a man for himself, his wife, and his children.

The next great fact we have to notice in regard to the struggle of human life is that labor which is spent in a direct struggle with nature is severe in the extreme and is but slightly productive. To subjugate nature, man needs weapons and tools. These, however, cannot be won unless the food and clothing and other prime and direct necessities are supplied in such amount that they can be consumed while tools and weapons are being made, for the tools and weapons themselves satisfy no needs directly. A man who tills the ground with his fingers or with a pointed stick picked up without labor will get a small crop. To fashion even the rudest spade or hoe will cost time, during which the laborer must still eat and drink and wear, but the tool, when obtained, will multiply immensely the power to produce. Such products of labor, used to assist production, have a function so peculiar in the nature of things that we need to distinguish them. We call them capital. A lever is capital, and the advantage of lifting a weight with a lever over lifting it by direct exertion is only a feeble illustration of the power of capital in production. The origin of capital lies in the darkness before history, and it is probably impossible for us to imagine the slow and painful steps by which the race began the formation of it. Since then it has gone on rising to higher and higher powers by a ceaseless involution, if I may use a mathematical expression. Capital is labor raised to a higher power by being constantly multiplied into itself. Nature has been more and more subjugated by the human race through the power of capital, and every human being now living shares the improved status of the race to a degree which neither he nor any one else can measure, and for which he pays nothing.

Let us understand this point, because our subject will require future reference to it. It is the most short-sighted ignorance not to see that, in a civilized community, all the advantage of capital except a small fraction is gratuitously enjoyed by the community. For instance, suppose the case of a man utterly destitute of tools, who is trying to till the ground with a pointed stick. He could get something out of it. If now he should obtain a spade with which to till the ground, let us suppose, for illustration, that he could get twenty times as great a product. Could, then, the owner of a spade in a civilized state demand, as its price, from the man who had no spade, nineteen-twentieths of the product which could be produced by the use of it? Certainly not. The price of a spade is fixed by the supply and demand of products in the community. A spade is bought for a dollar and the gain from the use of it is an inheritance of knowledge, experience, and skill which every man who lives in a civilized state gets for nothing. What we pay for steam transportation is no trifle, but imagine, if you can, eastern Massachusetts cut off from steam connection with the rest of the world, turnpikes and sailing vessels remaining. The cost of food would rise so high that a quarter of the population would starve to death and another quarter would have to emigrate. To-day every man here gets an enormous advantage from the status of a society on a level of steam transportation, telegraph, and machinery, for which he pays nothing.

So far as I have yet spoken, we have before us the struggle of man with nature, but the social problems, strictly speaking, arise at the next step. Each man carries on the struggle to win his support for himself, but there are others by his side engaged in the same struggle. If the stores of nature were unlimited, or if the last unit of the supply she offers could be won as easily as the first, there would be no social problem. If a square mile of land could support an indefinite number of human beings, or if it cost only twice as much labor to get forty bushels of wheat from an acre as to get twenty, we should have no social problem. If a square mile of land could support millions, no one would ever emigrate and there would be no trade or commerce. If it cost only twice as much labor to get forty bushels as twenty, there would be no advance in the arts. The fact is far otherwise. So long as the population is low in proportion to the amount of land, on a given stage of the arts, life is easy and the competition of man with man is weak. When more persons are trying to live on a square mile than it can support, on the existing stage of the arts, life is hard and the competition of man with man is intense. In the former case, industry and prudence may be on a low grade; the penalties are not severe, or certain, or speedy. In the latter case, each individual needs to exert on his own behalf every force, original or acquired, which he can command. In the former case, the average condition will be one of comfort and the population will be all nearly on the average. In the latter case, the average condition will not be one of comfort, but the population will cover wide extremes of comfort and misery. Each will find his place according to his ability and his effort. The former society will be democratic; the latter will be aristocratic.

The constant tendency of population to outstrip the means of subsistence is the force which has distributed population over the world, and produced all advance in civilization. To this day the two means of escape for an overpopulated country are emigration and an advance in the arts. The former wins more land for the same people; the latter makes the same land support more persons. If, however, either of these means opens a chance for an increase of population, it is evident that the advantage so won may be speedily exhausted if the increase takes place. The social difficulty has only undergone a temporary amelioration, and when the conditions of pressure and competition are renewed, misery and poverty reappear. The victims of them are those who have inherited disease and depraved appetites, or have been brought up in vice and ignorance, or have themselves yielded to vice, extravagance, idleness, and imprudence. In the last analysis, therefore, we come back to vice, in its original and hereditary forms, as the correlative of misery and poverty.

The condition for the complete and regular action of the force of competition is liberty. Liberty means the security given to each man that, if he employs his energies to sustain the struggle on behalf of himself and those he cares for, he shall dispose of the product exclusively as he chooses. It is impossible to know whence any definition or criterion of justice can be derived, if it is not deduced from this view of things; or if it is not the definition of justice that each shall enjoy the fruit of his own labor and self-denial, and of injustice that the idle and the industrious, the self-indulgent and the self-denying, shall share equally in the product. Aside from the a priori speculations of philosophers who have tried to make equality an essential element in justice, the human race has recognized, from the earliest times, the above conception of justice as the true one, and has founded upon it the right of property. The right of property, with marriage and the family, gives the right of bequest.

Monogamic marriage, however, is the most exclusive of social institutions. It contains, as essential principles, preference, superiority, selection, devotion. It would not be at all what it is if it were not for these characteristic traits, and it always degenerates when these traits are not present. For instance, if a man should not have a distinct preference for the woman he married, and if he did not select her as superior to others, the marriage would be an imperfect one according to the standard of true monogamic marriage. The family under monogamy, also, is a closed group, having special interests and estimating privacy and reserve as valuable advantages for family development. We grant high prerogatives, in our society, to parents, although our observation teaches us that thousands of human beings are unfit to be parents or to be entrusted with the care of children. It follows, therefore, from the organization of marriage and the family, under monogamy, that great inequalities must exist in a society based on those institutions. The son of wise parents cannot start on a level with the son of foolish ones, and the man who has had no home discipline cannot be equal to the man who has had home discipline. If the contrary were true, we could rid ourselves at once of the wearing labor of inculcating sound morals and manners in our children.

Private property, also, which we have seen to be a feature of society organized in accordance with the natural conditions of the struggle for existence produces inequalities between men. The struggle for existence is aimed against nature. It is from her niggardly hand that we have to wrest the satisfactions for our needs, but our fellow-men are our competitors for the meager supply. Competition, therefore, is a law of nature. Nature is entirely neutral; she submits to him who most energetically and resolutely assails her. She grants her rewards to the fittest, therefore, without regard to other considerations of any kind. If, then, there be liberty, men get from her just in proportion to their works, and their having and enjoying are just in proportion to their being and their doing. Such is the system of nature. If we do not like it, and if we try to amend it, there is only one way in which we can do it. We can take from the better and give to the worse. We can deflect the penalties of those who have done ill and throw them on those who have done better. We can take the rewards from those who have done better and give them to those who have done worse. We shall thus lessen the inequalities. We shall favor the survival of the unfittest, and we shall accomplish this by destroying liberty. Let it be understood that we cannot go outside of this alternative: liberty, inequality, survival of the fittest; not-liberty, equality, survival of the unfittest. The former carries society forward and favors all its best members; the latter carries society downwards and favors all its worst members.

For three hundred years now men have been trying to understand and realize liberty. Liberty is not the right or chance to do what we choose; there is no such liberty as that on earth. No man can do as he chooses: the autocrat of Russia or the King of Dahomey has limits to his arbitrary will; the savage in the wilderness, whom some people think free, is the slave of routine, tradition, and superstitious fears; the civilized man must earn his living, or take care of his property, or concede his own will to the rights and claims of his parents, his wife, his children, and all the persons with whom he is connected by the ties and contracts of civilized life.

What we mean by liberty is civil liberty, or liberty under law; and this means the guarantees of law that a man shall not be interfered with while using his own powers for his own welfare. It is, therefore, a civil and political status; and that nation has the freest institutions in which the guarantees of peace for the laborer and security for the capitalist are the highest. Liberty, therefore, does not by any means do away with the struggle for existence. We might as well try to do away with the need of eating, for that would, in effect, be the same thing. What civil liberty does is to turn the competition of man with man from violence and brute force into an industrial competition under which men vie with one another for the acquisition of material goods by industry, energy, skill, frugality, prudence, temperance, and other industrial virtues. Under this changed order of things the inequalities are not done away with. Nature still grants her rewards of having and enjoying, according to our being and doing, but it is now the man of the highest training and not the man of the heaviest fist who gains the highest reward. It is impossible that the man with capital and the man without capital should be equal. To affirm that they are equal would be to say that a man who has no tool can get as much food out of the ground as the man who has a spade or a plough; or that the man who has no weapon can defend himself as well against hostile beasts or hostile men as the man who has a weapon. If that were so, none of us would work any more. We work and deny ourselves to get capital just because, other things being equal, the man who has it is superior, for attaining all the ends of life, to the man who has it not. Considering the eagerness with which we all seek capital and the estimate we put upon it, either in cherishing it if we have it, or envying others who have it while we have it not, it is very strange what platitudes pass current about it in our society so soon as we begin to generalize about it. If our young people really believed some of the teachings they hear, it would not be amiss to preach them a sermon once in a while to reassure them, setting forth that it is not wicked to be rich, nay even, that it is not wicked to be richer than your neighbor.

It follows from what we have observed that it is the utmost folly to denounce capital. To do so is to undermine civilization, for capital is the first requisite of every social gain, educational, ecclesiastical, political, aesthetic, or other.

It must also be noticed that the popular antithesis between persons and capital is very fallacious. Every law or institution which protects persons at the expense of capital makes it easier for persons to live and to increase the number of consumers of capital while lowering all the motives to prudence and frugality by which capital is created. Hence every such law or institution tends to produce a large population, sunk in misery. All poor laws and all eleemosynary institutions and expenditures have this tendency. On the contrary, all laws and institutions which give security to capital against the interests of other persons than its owners, restrict numbers while preserving the means of subsistence. Hence every such law or institution tends to produce a small society on a high stage of comfort and well-being. It follows that the antithesis commonly thought to exist between the protection of persons and the protection of property is in reality only an antithesis between numbers and quality.

I must stop to notice, in passing, one other fallacy which is rather scientific than popular. The notion is attributed to certain economists that economic forces are self-correcting. I do not know of

any economists who hold this view, but what is intended probably
is that many economists, of whom I venture to be one, hold that
economic forces act compensatingly, and that whenever economic
forces have so acted as to produce an unfavorable situation, other
economic forces are brought into action which correct the evil and
restore the equilibrium.   For instance, in Ireland overpopulation
and exclusive devotion to agriculture, both of which are plainly
traceable to unwise statesmanship in the past, have produced a situation of distress.   Steam navigation on the ocean has introduced
the competition of cheaper land with Irish agriculture.   The result
is a social and industrial crisis.   There are, however, millions of
acres of fertile land on earth which are unoccupied and which are
open to the Irish, and the economic forces are compelling the direct
corrective of the old evils, in the way of emigration or recourse to
urban occupations by unskilled labor.   Any number of economic
and legal nostrums have been proposed for this situation, all of
which propose to leave the original causes untouched.   We are told
that economic causes do not correct themselves.   That is true.   We
are told that when an economic situation becomes very grave it
goes on from worse to worse and that there is no cycle through
which it returns.   That is not true, without further limitation.   We
are told that moral forces alone can elevate any such people again.
But it is plain that a people which has sunk below the reach of the
economic forces of self-interest has certainly sunk below the reach
of moral forces, and that this objection is superficial and short-
sighted.   What is true is that economic forces always go before
moral forces.   Men feel self-interest long before they feel prudence,
self-control, and temperance.   They lose the moral forces long
before they lose the economic forces.   If they can be regenerated
at all, it must be first by distress appealing to self-interest and forcing recourse to some expedient for relief.   Emigration is certainly
an economic force for the relief of Irish distress.   It is a palliative
only, when considered in itself, but the virtue of it is that it gives
the non-emigrating population a chance to rise to a level on which
the moral forces can act upon them.   Now it is terribly true that
only the better ones emigrate, and only the better ones among those
who remain are capable of having their ambitions and energy
awakened, but for the rest the solution is famine and death,
with a social regeneration through decay and the elimination of that

part of the society which is not capable of being restored to health and life. As Mr. Huxley once said, the method of nature is not even a word and a blow, with the blow first. No explanation is vouchsafed. We are left to find out for ourselves why our ears are boxed. If we do not find out, and find out correctly, what the error is for which we are being punished, the blow is repeated and poverty, distress, disease, and death finally remove the incorrigible ones. It behooves us men to study these terrible illustrations of the penalties which follow on bad statesmanship, and of the sanctions by which social laws are enforced. The economic cycle does complete itself; it must do so, unless the social group is to sink in permanent barbarism. A law may be passed which shall force somebody to support the hopelessly degenerate members of a society, but such a law can only perpetuate the evil and entail it on future generations with new accumulations of distress.

The economic forces work with moral forces and are their handmaidens, but the economic forces are far more primitive, original, and universal. The glib generalities in which we sometimes hear people talk, as if you could set moral and economic forces separate from and in antithesis to each other, and discard the one to accept and work by the other, gravely misconstrue the realities of the social order.

We have now before us the facts of human life out of which the social problem springs. These facts are in many respects hard and stern. It is by strenuous exertion only that each one of us can sustain himself against the destructive forces and the ever recurring needs of life; and the higher the degree to which we seek to carry our development the greater is the proportionate cost of every step. For help in the struggle we can only look back to those in the previous generation who are responsible for our existence. In the competition of life the son of wise and prudent ancestors has immense advantages over the son of vicious and imprudent ones. The man who has capital possesses immeasurable advantages for the struggle of life over him who has none. The more we break down privileges of class, or industry, and establish liberty, the greater will be the inequalities and the more exclusively will the vicious bear the penalties. Poverty and misery will exist in society just so long as vice exists in human nature.

I now go on to notice some modes of trying to deal with this problem. There is a modern philosophy which has never been taught systematically, but which has won the faith of vast masses of people in the modern civilized world. For want of a better name it may be called the sentimental philosophy. It has colored all modern ideas and institutions in politics, religion, education, charity, and industry, and is widely taught in popular literature, novels, and poetry, and in the pulpit. The first proposition of this sentimental philosophy is that nothing is true which is disagreeable. If, therefore, any facts of observation show that life is grim or hard, the sentimental philosophy steps over such facts with a genial platitude, a consoling commonplace, or a gratifying dogma. The effect is to spread an easy optimism, under the influence of which people spare themselves labor and trouble, reflection and forethought, pains and caution—all of which are hard things, and to admit the necessity for which would be to admit that the world is not all made smooth and easy, for us to pass through it surrounded by love, music, and flowers.

Under this philosophy, "progress" has been represented as a steadily increasing and unmixed good; as if the good steadily encroached on the evil without involving any new and other forms of evil; and as if we could plan great steps in progress in our academies and lyceums, and then realize them by resolution. To minds trained to this way of looking at things, any evil which exists is a reproach. We have only to consider it, hold some discussions about it, pass resolutions, and have done with it. Every moment of delay is, therefore, a social crime. It is monstrous to say that misery and poverty are as constant as vice and evil passions of men! People suffer so under misery and poverty! Assuming, therefore, that we can solve all these problems and eradicate all these evils by expending our ingenuity upon them, of course we cannot hasten too soon to do it.

A social philosophy, consonant with this, has also been taught for a century. It could not fail to be popular, for it teaches that ignorance is as good as knowledge, vulgarity as good as refinement, shiftlessness as good as painstaking, shirking as good as faithful striving, poverty as good as wealth, filth as good as cleanliness—in short, that quality goes for nothing in the measurement of men, but only numbers. Culture, knowledge, refinement, skill, and taste cost labor, but we have been taught that they have only individual, not social value, and that socially they are rather drawbacks than otherwise.   In public life we are taught to admire roughness, illiteracy, and rowdyism.   The ignorant, idle, and shiftless have been taught that they are "the people," that the generalities inculcated at the same time about the dignity, wisdom, and virtue of "the people" are true of them, that they have nothing to learn to be wise, but that, as they stand, they possess a kind of infallibility, and that to their "opinion" the wise must bow.   It is not cause for wonder if whole sections of these classes have begun to use the powers and wisdom attributed to them for their interests, as they construe them, and to trample on all the excellence which marks civilization as on obsolete superstition.

Another development of the same philosophy is the doctrine that men come into the world endowed with "natural rights," or as joint inheritors of the "rights of man," which have been "declared" times without number during the last century.   The divine rights of man have succeeded to the obsolete divine right of kings.   If it is true, then, that a man is born with rights, he comes into the world with claims on somebody besides his parents.   Against whom does he hold such rights?   There can be no rights against nature or against God.   A man may curse his fate becaue he is born of an inferior race, or with an hereditary disease, or blind, or, as some members of the race seem to do, because they are born females; but they get no answer to their imprecations.   But, now, if men have rights by birth, these rights must hold against their fellow-men and must mean that somebody else is to spend his energy to sustain the existence of the persons so born.   What then becomes of the natural rights of the one whose energies are to be diverted from his own interests?   If it be said that we should all help each other, that means simply that the race as a whole should advance and expand as much and as fast as it can in its career on earth; and the experience on which we are now acting has shown that we shall do this best under liberty and under the organization which we are now developing, by leaving each to exert his energies for his own success.   The notion of natural rights is destitute of sense, but it is captivating, and it is the more available on account of its vagueness.   It lends itself to the most vicious kind of social dogmatism, for if a man has natural rights, then the reasoning is clear up to the finished socialistic doctrine that a man has a natural right to whatever he needs, and that the measure of his claims is the wishes which he wants fulfilled. If, then, he has a need, who is bound to satisfy it for him? Who holds the obligation corresponding to his right? It must be the one who possesses what will satisfy that need, or else the state which can take the possession from those who have earned and saved it, and give it to him who needs it and who, by the hypothesis, has not earned and saved it.

It is with the next step, however, that we come to the complete and ruinous absurdity of this view. If a man may demand from those who have a share of what he needs and has not, may he demand the same also for his wife and for his children, and for how many children? The industrious and prudent man who takes the course of labor and self-denial to secure capital, finds that he must defer marriage, both in order to save and to devote his life to the education of fewer children. The man who can claim a share in another's product has no such restraint. The consequence would be that the industrious and prudent would labor and save, without families, to support the idle and improvident who would increase and multiply, until universal destitution forced a return to the principles of liberty and property; and the man who started with the notion that the world owed him a living would once more find, as he does now, that the world pays him its debt in the state prison.

The most specious application of the dogma of rights is to labor. It is said that every man has a right to work. The world is full of work to be done. Those who are willing to work find that they have three days' work to do in every day that comes. Work is the necessity to which we are born. It is not a right, but an irksome necessity, and men escape it whenever they can get the fruits of labor without it. What they want is the fruits, or wages, not work. But wages are capital which some one has earned and saved. If he and the workman can agree on the terms on which he will part with his capital, there is no more to be said. If not, then the right must be set up in a new form. It is now not a right to work, nor even a right to wages, but a right to a certain rate of wages, and we have simply returned to the old doctrine of spoliation again. It is immaterial whether the demand for wages be addressed to an individual capitalist or to a civil body, for the latter can give no wages which it does not collect by taxes out of the capital of those who have labored and saved.

Another application is in the attempt to fix the hours of labor *per diem* by law. If a man is forbidden to labor over eight hours per day (and the law has no sense or utility for the purposes of those who want it until it takes this form), he is forbidden to exercise so much industry as he may be willing to expend in order to accumulate capital for the improvement of his circumstances.

A century ago there were very few wealthy men except owners of land. The extension of commerce, manufactures, and mining, the introduction of the factory system and machinery, the opening of new countries, and the great discoveries and inventions have created a new middle class, based on wealth, and developed out of the peasants, artisans, unskilled laborers, and small shop-keepers of a century ago. The consequence has been that the chance of acquiring capital and all which depends on capital has opened before classes which formerly passed their lives in a dull round of ignorance and drudgery. This chance has brought with it the same alternative which accompanies every other opportunity offered to mortals. Those who were wise and able to profit by the chance succeeded grandly; those who were negligent or unable to profit by it suffered proportionately. The result has been wide inequalities of wealth within the industrial classes. The net result, however, for all, has been the cheapening of luxuries and a vast extension of physical enjoyment. The appetite for enjoyment has been awakened and nourished in classes which formerly never missed what they never thought of, and it has produced eagerness for material good, discontent, and impatient ambition. This is the reverse side of that eager uprising of the industrial classes which is such a great force in modern life. The chance is opened to advance, by industry, prudence, economy, and emigration, to the possession of capital; but the way is long and tedious. The impatience for enjoyment and the thirst for luxury which we have mentioned are the greatest foes to the accumulation of capital; and there is a still darker side to the picture when we come to notice that those who yield to the impatience to enjoy, but who see others outstrip them, are led to malice and envy. Mobs arise which manifest the most savage and senseless disposition to burn and destroy what they cannot enjoy. We have already had evidence, in more than one country, that such a wild disposition exists and needs only opportunity to burst into activity.

The origin of socialism, which is the extreme development of the sentimental philosophy, lies in the undisputed facts which I described at the outset. The socialist regards this misery as the fault of society. He thinks that we can organize society as we like and that an organization can be devised in which poverty and misery shall disappear. He goes further even than this. He assumes that men have artificially organized society as it now exists. Hence if anything is disagreeable or hard in the present state of society it follows, on that view, that the task of organizing society has been imperfectly and badly performed, and that it needs to be done over again. These are the assumptions with which the socialist starts, and many socialists seem also to believe that if they can destroy belief in an Almighty God who is supposed to have made the world such as it is, they will then have overthrown the belief that there is a fixed order in human nature and human life which man can scarcely alter at all, and, if at all, only infinitesimally.

The truth is that the social order is fixed by laws of nature precisely analogous to those of the physical order. The most that man can do is by ignorance and self-conceit to mar the operation of social laws. The evils of society are to a great extent the result of the dogmatism and self-interest of statesmen, philosophers, and ecclesiastics who in past time have done just what the socialists now want to do. Instead of studying the natural laws of the social order, they assumed that they could organize society as they chose, they made up their minds what kind of a society they wanted to make, and they planned their little measures for the ends they had resolved upon. It will take centuries of scientific study of the facts of nature to eliminate from human society the mischievous institutions and traditions which the said statesmen, philosophers, and ecclesiastics have introduced into it. Let us not, however, even then delude ourselves with any impossible hopes. The hardships of life would not be eliminated if the laws of nature acted directly and without interference. The task of right living forever changes its form, but let us not imagine that that task will ever reach a final solution or that any race of men on this earth can ever be emancipated from the necessity of industry, prudence, continence, and temperance if they are to pass their lives prosperously. If you believe the contrary you must suppose that some men can come to exist who shall know nothing of old age, disease, and death.

The socialist enterprise of reorganizing society in order to change what is harsh and sad in it at present is therefore as impossible, from the outset, as a plan for changing the physical order. I read the other day a story in which a man dreamt that somebody had invented an application of electricity for eradicating certain facts from the memory. Just think of it! What an emancipation to the human race, if a man could so emancipate himself from all those incidents in his past life which he regrets! Let there no longer be such a thing as remorse or vain regret! It would be half as good as finding a fountain of eternal youth. Or invent us a world in which two and two could make five. Two two-dollar notes could then pay five dollars of debts. They say that political economy is a dismal science and that its doctrines are dark and cruel. I think the hardest fact in human life is that two and two cannot make five; but in sociology while people will agree that two and two cannot make five, yet they think that it might somehow be possible by adjusting two and two to one another in some way or other to make two and two equal to four and one-tenth.

I have shown how men emerge from barbarism only by the use of capital and why it is that, as soon as they begin to use capital, if there is liberty, there will be inequality. The socialist looking at these facts says that it is capital which produces the inequality. It is the inequality of men in what they get out of life which shocks the socialist. He finds enough to criticize in the products of past dogmatism and bad statesmanship to which I have alluded, and the program of reforms to be accomplished and abuses to be rectified which the socialists have set up have often been admirable. It is their analysis of the situation which is at fault. Their diagnosis of the social disease is founded on sectarian assumptions, not on the scientific study of the structure and functions of the social body. In attacking capital they are simply attacking the foundations of civilization, and every socialistic scheme which has ever been proposed, so far as it has lessened the motives to saving or the security of capital, is anti-social and anti-civilizing.

Rousseau, who is the great father of the modern socialism, laid accusation for the inequalities existing amongst men upon wheat and iron. What he meant was that wheat is a symbol of agriculture, and when men took to agriculture and wheat diet they broke up their old tribal relations, which were partly communistic, and

developed individualism and private property. At the same time
agriculture called for tools and machines, of which iron is a symbol;
but these tools and machines are capital. Agriculture, individualism, tools, capital were, according to Rousseau's ideas, the causes of
inequality. He was, in a certain way, correct, as we have already
seen by our own analysis of the facts of the social order. When
human society reached the agricultural stage machinery became
necessary. Capital was far more important than on the hunting or
pastoral stage, and the inequalities of men were developed with
great rapidity, so that we have a Humboldt, a Newton, or a Shakespeare at one end of the scale and a Digger Indian at the other. The
Humboldt or Newton is one of the highest products produced by
the constant selection and advance of the best part of the human
race, *viz.*, those who have seized every chance of advancing; and the
Digger Indian is a specimen of that part of the race which withdrew from the competition clear back at the beginning and has
consequently never made any advance beyond the first superiority
of man to beasts. Rousseau, following the logic of his own explanation of the facts, offered distinctly as the cure for inequality a
return to the hunting stage of life as practiced by the American Indians. In this he was plainly and distinctly right. If you want
equality you must not look forward for it on the path of advancing
civilization. You may go back to the mode of life of the American
Indian, and, although you will not then reach equality, you will
escape those glaring inequalities of wealth and poverty by coming
down to a comparative equality, that is, to a status in which all are
equally miserable. Even this, however, you cannot do without sub-
mitting to other conditions which are far more appalling than any
sad facts in the existing order of society. The population of Massachusetts is about two hundred to the square mile; on the hunting
stage Massachusetts could not probably support, at the utmost, five
to the square mile; hence to get back to the hunting stage would
cost the reduction of the population to two and a half where there
are now one hundred. In Rousseau's day people did not even
know that this question of the power of land to support population
was to be taken into account.

Socialists find it necessary to alter the definition of capital in
order to maintain their attacks upon it. Karl Marx, for instance,
regards capital as an accumulation of the differences which a mer-

chant makes between his buying price and his selling price. It is, according to him, an accumulation of the differences which the employer gains between what he pays to the employees for making the thing and what he obtains for it from the consumer. In this view of the matter the capitalist employer is a pure parasite, who has fastened on the wage-receiving employee without need or reason and is levying toll on industry. All socialistic writers follow, in different degrees, this conception of capital. If it is true, why do not I levy on some workers somewhere and steal this difference in the product of their labor? Is it because I am more honest or magnanimous than those who are capitalist-employers? I should not trust myself to resist the chance if I had it. Or again, let us ask why, if this conception of the origin of capital is correct, the workmen submit to a pure and unnecessary imposition. If this notion were true, co-operation in production would not need any effort to bring it about; it would take an army to keep it down. The reason why it is not possible for the first comer to start out as an employer of labor is that capital is a prerequisite to all industry. So soon as men pass beyond the stage of life in which they live, like beasts, on the spontaneous fruits of the earth, capital must precede every productive enterprise. It would lead me too far away from my present subject to elaborate this statement as it deserves and perhaps as it needs, but I may say that there is no sound political economy and especially no correct conception of wages which is not based on a complete recognition of the character of capital as necessarily going before every industrial operation. The reason why co-operation in production is exceedingly difficult, and indeed is not possible except in the highest and rarest conditions of education and culture amongst artisans, is that workmen cannot undertake an enterprise without capital, and that capital always means the fruits of prudence and self-denial already accomplished. The capitalist's profits, therefore, are only the reward for the contribution he has made to a joint enterprise which could not go on without him, and his share is as legitimate as that of the hand-worker.

The socialist assails particularly the institution of bequest or hereditary property, by which some men come into life with special protection and advantage. The right of bequest rests on no other grounds than those of expediency. The love of children is the strongest motive to frugality and to the accumulation of capital.

The state guarantees the power of bequest only because it thereby encourages the accumulation of capital on which the welfare of society depends. It is true enough that inherited capital often proves a curse. Wealth is like health, physical strength, education, or anything else which enhances the power of the individual; it is only a chance; its moral character depends entirely upon the use which is made of it. Any force which, when well used, is capable of elevating a man, will, if abused, debase him in the same proportion. This is true of education, which is often and incorrectly vaunted as a positive and purely beneficent instrumentality. An education ill used makes a man only a more mischievous scoundrel, just as an education well used makes him a more efficient, good citizen and producer. So it is with wealth; it is a means to all the higher developments of intellectual and moral culture. A man of inherited wealth can gain in youth all the advantages which are essential to high culture, and which a man who must first earn the capital cannot attain until he is almost past the time of life for profiting by them. If one should believe the newspapers, one would be driven to a philosophy something like this: it is extremely praiseworthy for a man born in poverty to accumulate a fortune; the reason why he wants to secure a fortune is that he wants to secure the position of his children and start them with better advantages than he enjoyed himself; this is a noble desire on his part, but he really ought to doubt and hesitate about so doing because the chances are that he would do far better for his children to leave them poor. The children who inherit his wealth are put under suspicion by it; it creates a presumption against them in all the activities of citizenship.

Now it is no doubt true that the struggle to win a fortune gives strength of character and a practical judgment and efficiency which a man who inherits wealth rarely gets, but hereditary wealth transmitted from generation to generation is the strongest instrument by which we keep up a steadily advancing civilization. In the absence of laws of entail and perpetuity it is inevitable that capital should speedily slip from the hold of the man who is not fit to possess it, back into the great stream of capital, and so find its way into the hands of those who can use it for the benefit of society.

The love of children is an instinct which, as I have said before, grows stronger with advancing civilization. All attacks on capital have, up to this time, been shipwrecked on this instinct. Consequently the most rigorous and logical socialists have always been led sooner or later to attack the family. For, if bequest should be abolished, parents would give their property to their children in their own life-time; and so it becomes a logical necessity to substitute some sort of communistic or socialistic life for family life, and to educate children in masses without the tie of parentage. Every socialistic theory which has been pursued energetically has led out to this consequence. I will not follow up this topic, but it is plain to see that the only equality which could be reached on this course would be that men should be all equal to each other when they were all equal to swine.

Socialists are filled with the enthusiasm of equality. Every scheme of theirs for securing equality has destroyed liberty. The student of political philosophy has the antagonism of equality and liberty constantly forced upon him. Equality of possession or of rights and equality before the law are diametrically opposed to each other. The object of equality before the law is to make the state entirely neutral. The state, under that theory, takes no cognizance of persons. It surrounds all, without distinctions, with the same conditions and guarantees. If it educates one, it educates all— black, white, red, or yellow; Jew or Gentile; native or alien. If it taxes one, it taxes all, by the same system and under the same conditions. If it exempts one from police regulations in home, church, and occupation, it exempts all. From this statement it is at once evident that pure equality before the law is impossible. Some occupations must be subjected to police regulation. Not all can be made subject to militia duty even for the same limited period. The exceptions and special cases furnish the chance for abuse. Equality before the law, however, is one of the cardinal principles of civil liberty, because it leaves each man to run the race of life for himself as best he can. The state stands neutral but benevolent. It does not undertake to aid some and handicap others at the outset in order to offset hereditary advantages and disadvantages, or to make them start equally. Such a notion would belong to the false and spurious theory of equality which is socialistic. If the state should attempt this it would make itself the servant of envy. I am entitled to make the most I can of myself without hindrance from anybody, but I am not entitled to any guarantee that I shall make as much of myself as somebody else makes of himself.

The modern thirst for equality of rights is explained by its historical origin. The mediaeval notion of rights was that rights were special privileges, exemptions, franchises, and powers given to individuals by the king; hence each man had just so many as he and his ancestors had been able to buy or beg by force or favor, and if a man had obtained no grants he had no rights. Hence no two persons were equal in rights and the mass of the population had none. The theory of natural rights and of equal rights was a revolt against the mediaeval theory. It was asserted that men did not have to wait for a king to grant them rights; they have them by nature, or in the nature of things, because they are men and members of civil society. If rights come from nature, it is inferred that they fall like air and light on all equally. It was an immense step in advance for the human race when this new doctrine was promulgated. Its own limitations and errors need not now be pointed out. Its significance is plain, and its limits are to some extent defined when we note its historical origin.

I have already shown that where these guarantees exist and where there is liberty, the results cannot be equal, but with all liberty there must go responsibility. If I take my own way I must take my own consequences; if it proves that I have made a mistake, I cannot be allowed to throw the consequences on my neighbor. If my neighbor is a free man and resents interference from me he must not call on me to bear the consequences of his mistakes. Hence it is plain that liberty, equality before the law, responsibility, individualism, monogamy, and private property all hold together as consistent parts of the same structure of society, and that an assault on one part must sooner or later involve an assault on all the others.

To all this must be added the political element in socialism. The acquisition of some capital—the amount is of very subordinate importance—is the first and simplest proof that an individual possesses the industrial and civil virtues which make a good citizen and a useful member of society. Political power, a century ago, was associated more or less, even in the United States, with the possession of land. It has been gradually extended until the suffrage is to all intents and purposes universal in North and South America, in Australia, and in all Europe except Russia and Turkey. On this system political control belongs to the numerical majority, limited only by institutions. It may be doubted, if the terms are taken strictly and correctly, whether the non-capitalists outnumber the capitalists in any civilized country, but in many cities where capital is most collected they certainly do. The powers of government have been abused for ages by the classes who possessed them to enable kings, courtiers, nobles, politicians, demagogues, and their friends to live in exemption from labor and self-denial, that is, from the universal lot of man. It is only a continuation of the same abuse if the new possessors of power attempt to employ it to secure for themselves the selfish advantages which all possessors of power have taken. Such a course would, however, overthrow all that we think has been won in the way of making government an organ of justice, peace, order, and security, without respect of persons; and if those gains are not to be lost they will have to be defended, before this century closes, against popular majorities, especially in cities, just as they had to be won in a struggle with kings and nobles in the centuries past.

The newest socialism is, in its method, political. The essential feature of its latest phases is the attempt to use the power of the state to realize its plans and to secure its objects. These objects are to do away with poverty and misery, and there are no socialistic schemes yet proposed, of any sort, which do not, upon analysis, turn out to be projects for curing poverty and misery by making those who have share with those who have not. Whether they are paper-money schemes, tariff schemes, subsidy schemes, internal improvement schemes, or usury laws, they all have this in common with the most vulgar of the communistic projects, and the errors of this sort in the past which have been committed in the interest of the capitalist class now furnish precedents, illustration, and encouragement for the new category of demands. The latest socialism divides into two phases: one which aims at centralization and despotism—believing that political form more available for its purposes; the other, the anarchical, which prefers to split up the state into townships, or "communes," to the same end. The latter furnishes the true etymology and meaning of "communism" in its present use, but all socialism, in its second stage, merges into a division of property according to the old sense of communism.

It is impossible to notice socialism as it presents itself at the present moment without pointing out the immense mischief which has been done by sentimental economists and social philosophers who have thought it their professional duty, not to investigate and teach the truth, but to dabble in philanthropy. It is in Germany that this development has been most marked, and as a consequence of it the judgment and sense of the whole people in regard to political and social questions have been corrupted. It is remarkable that the country whose learned men have wrought so much for every other science, especially by virtue of their scientific method and rigorous critical processes, should have furnished a body of social philosophers without method, discipline, or severity of scholarship, who have led the nation in pursuit of whims and dreams and impossible desires. Amongst us there has been less of it, for our people still possess enough sterling sense to reject sentimental rubbish in its grosser forms, but we have had and still have abundance of the more subtle forms of socialistic doctrine, and these open the way to the others. We may already see the two developments forming a congenial alliance. We have also our writers and teachers who seem to think that "the weak" and "the poor" are terms of exact definition; that government exists, in some especial sense, for the sake of the classes so designated; and that the same classes (whoever they are) have some especial claim on the interest and attention of the economist and social philosopher. It may be believed that, in the opinion of these persons, the training of men is the only branch of human effort in which the labor and care should be spent, not on the best specimens but on the poorest.

It is a matter of course that a reactionary party should arise to declare that universal suffrage, popular education, machinery, free trade, and all the other innovations of the last hundred years are all a mistake. If any one ever believed that these innovations were so many clear strides towards the millennium, that they involve no evils or abuses of their own, that they tend to emancipate mankind from the need for prudence, caution, forethought, vigilance—in short, from the eternal struggle against evil—it is not strange that he should be disappointed. If any one ever believed that some "form of government" could be found which would run itself and turn out the pure results of abstract peace, justice, and righteousness without any trouble to anybody, he may well be dissatisfied.

To talk of turning back, however, is only to enhance still further the confusion and danger of our position. The world cannot go back. Its destiny is to go forward and to meet the new problems which are continually arising. Under our so-called progress evil only alters its forms, and we must esteem it a grand advance if we can believe that, on the whole, and over a wide view of human affairs, good has gained a hair's breadth over evil in a century. Popular institutions have their own abuses and dangers just as much as monarchical or aristocratic institutions. We are only just finding out what they are. All the institutions which we have inherited were invented to guard liberty against the encroachments of a powerful monarch or aristocracy, when these classes possessed land and the possession of land was the greatest social power. Institutions must now be devised to guard civil liberty against popular majorities, and this necessity arises first in regard to the protection of property, the first and greatest function of government and element in civil liberty. There is no escape from any dangers involved in this or any other social struggle save in going forward and working out the development. It will cost a struggle and will demand the highest wisdom of this and the next generation. It is very probable that some nations—those, namely, which come up to this problem with the least preparation, with the least intelligent comprehension of the problem, and under the most inefficient leadership—will suffer a severe check in their development and prosperity; it is very probable that in some nations the development may lead through revolution and bloodshed; it is very probable that in some nations the consequence may be a reaction towards arbitrary power. In every view we take of it, it is clear that the general abolition of slavery has only cleared the way for a new social problem of far wider scope and far greater difficulty. It seems to me, in fact, that this must always be the case. The conquest of one difficulty will only open the way to another; the solution of one problem will only bring man face to face with another. Man wins by the fight, not by the victory, and therefore the possibilities of growth are unlimited, for the fight has no end.

The progress which men have made in developing the possibilities of human existence has never been made by jumps and strides. It has never resulted from the schemes of philosophers and reformers. It has never been guided through a set program by the wisdom of any sages, statesmen, or philanthropists. The progress which has been made has been won in minute stages by men who had a definite task before them, and who have dealt with it in detail, as it presented itself, without referring to general principles, or attempting to bring it into logical relations to an *a priori* system. In most cases the agents are unknown and cannot be found. New and better arrangements have grown up imperceptibly by the natural effort of all to make the best of actual circumstances. In this way, no doubt, the new problems arising in our modern society must be solved or must solve themselves. The chief safeguard and hope of such a development is in the sound instincts and strong sense of the people, which, although it may not reason closely, can reject instinctively. If there are laws—and there certainly are such—which permit the acquisition of property without industry, by cunning, force, gambling, swindling, favoritism, or corruption, such laws transfer property from those who have earned it to those who have not. Such laws contain the radical vice of socialism. They demand correction and offer an open field for reform because reform would lie in the direction of greater purity and security of the right of property. Whatever assails that right, or goes in the direction of making it still more uncertain whether the industrious man can dispose of the fruits of his industry for his own interests exclusively, tends directly towards violence, bloodshed, poverty, and misery. If any large section of modern society should rise against the rest for the purpose of attempting any such spoliation, either by violence or through the forms of law, it would destroy civilization as it was destroyed by the irruption of the barbarians into the Roman Empire.

The sound student of sociology can hold out to mankind, as individuals or as a race, only one hope of better and happier living. That hope lies in an enhancement of the industrial virtues and of the moral forces which thence arise. Industry, self-denial, and temperance are the laws of prosperity for men and states; without them advance in the arts and in wealth means only corruption and decay through luxury and vice. With them progress in the arts and increasing wealth are the prime conditions of an advancing civilization which is sound enough to endure. The power of the human race to-day over the conditions of prosperous and happy living are sufficient to banish poverty and misery if it were not for folly and vice. The earth does not begin to be populated up to its power to support population on the present stage of the arts; if the United States were as densely populated as the British Islands, we should have 1,000,000,000 people here. If, therefore, men were willing to set to work with energy and courage to subdue the outlying parts of the earth, all might live in plenty and prosperity. But if they insist on remaining in the slums of great cities or on the borders of an old society, and on a comparatively exhausted soil, there is no device of economist or statesman which can prevent them from falling victims to poverty and misery or from succumbing in the competition of life to those who have greater command of capital. The socialist or philanthropist who nourishes them in their situation and saves them from the distress of it is only cultivating the distress which he pretends to cure.

15. THE RT. REV. WILLIAM LAWRENCE
(1850–1941)

HE father and grandfather of William Lawrence were wealthy and religious merchants, manufacturers, and philanthropists of Lawrence, Massachusetts, a city founded by the family. He was graduated from Harvard in 1871 and received his theological degree from the Episcopal Theological School (Cambridge) where he later became professor and dean. He was Bishop of Massachusetts for thirty-three years (1893–1926). Known as the "banker bishop," he was distinguished both for his tolerance in matters of ritual and theological doctrine and for his administrative ability. He raised large endowments for pensions for the Episcopal clergy and led two successful financial drives for Harvard University. He was the author of several works on ecclesiastical and ethical subjects and of biographies of Amos A. Lawrence (his father), Henry Cabot Lodge (his classmate), Phillips Brooks (his predecessor as bishop), and Roger Wolcott (his friend and a governor of Massachusetts). The article reprinted below was first delivered as an address at an annual dinner of the Chamber of Commerce of New York.

[See: William Lawrence, *Memories of a Happy Life* (1926).]

"THE RELATION OF WEALTH TO MORALS" (1901)[1]

There is a certain distrust on the part of our people as to the effect of material prosperity on their morality. We shrink with some foreboding at the great increase of riches, and question whether in the long run material prosperity does not tend toward the disintegration of character.

History seems to support us in our distrust. Visions arise of their fall from splendor of Tyre and Sidon, Babylon, Rome, and Venice, and of great nations too. The question is started whether England is not to-day, in the pride of her wealth and power, sowing the wind from which in time she will reap the whirlwind.

[1] Rt. Rev. William Lawrence, "The Relation of Wealth to Morals," *The World's Work*, Vol. I (1900–1901), pp. 286–292.

Experience seems to add its support. Is it not from the ranks of the poor that the leaders of the people have always risen? Recall Abraham Lincoln and patriots of every generation.

The Bible has sustained the same note. Were ever stronger words of warning uttered against the deceitfulness of riches than those spoken by the peasant Jesus, who Himself had no place to lay His head? And the Church has through the centuries upheld poverty as one of the surest paths to Heaven: it has been a mark of the saint.

To be sure, in spite of history, experience, and the Bible, men have gone on their way making money and hailing with joy each age of material prosperity. The answer is: "This only proves the case; men are of the world, riches are deceitful, and the Bible is true; the world is given over to Mammon. In the increase of material wealth and the accumulation of riches the man who seeks the higher life has no part."

In the face of this comes the statement of the chief statistician of our census—from one, therefore, who speaks with authority: "The present census, when completed, will unquestionably show that the visible material wealth in this country now has a value of ninety billion dollars. This is an addition since 1890 of twenty-five billion dollars. This is a saving greater than all the people of the Western Continent had been able to make from the discovery of Columbus to the breaking out of the Civil War."

If our reasoning from history, experience, and the Bible is correct, we, a Christian people, have rubbed a sponge over the pages of the Bible and are in for orgies and a downfall to which the fall of Rome is a very tame incident.

May it not be well, however, to revise our inferences from history, experience, and the Bible? History tells us that, while riches have been an item and an indirect cause of national decay, innumerable other conditions entered in. Therefore, while wealth has been a source of danger, it has not necessarily led to demoralization.

That leaders have sprung from the ranks of the poor is true and always will be true, so long as force of character exists in every class. But there are other conditions than a lack of wealth at the source of their uprising.

And as to the Bible:—while every word that can be quoted against the rich is as true as any other word, other words and deeds are as true; and the parables of our Lord on the stewardship of wealth, His association with the wealthy, strike another and complementary note. Both notes are essential to the harmony of His life and teachings. His thought was not of the conditions, rich or poor, but of a higher life, the character rising out of the conditions —fortunately, for we are released from that subtle hypocrisy which has beset the Christian through the ages, bemoaning the deceitfulness of riches and, at the same time, working with all his might to earn a competence, and a fortune if he can.

Man "Born to be Rich." Now we are in a position to affirm that neither history, experience, nor the Bible necessarily sustains the common distrust of the effect of material wealth on morality. Our path of study is made more clear. Two positive principles lead us out on our path.

The first is that man, when he is strong, will conquer Nature, open up her resources, and harness them to his service. This is his play, his exercise, his divine mission.

"Man," says Emerson, "is born to be rich. He is thoroughly related, and is tempted out by his appetite and fancies to the conquest of this and that piece of Nature, until he finds his well-being in the use of the planet, and of more planets than his own. Wealth requires, besides the crust of bread and the roof, the freedom of the city, the freedom of the earth." "The strong race is strong on these terms."

Man draws to himself material wealth as surely, as naturally, and as necessarily as the oak draws the elements into itself from the earth.

The other principle is that, in the long run, it is only to the man of morality that wealth comes. We believe in the harmony of God's Universe. We know that it is only by working along His laws natural and spiritual that we can work with efficiency. Only by working along the lines of right thinking and right living can the secrets and wealth of Nature be revealed. We, like the Psalmist, occasionally see the wicked prosper, but only occasionally.

Put two men in adjoining fields, one man strong and normal, the other weak and listless. One picks up his spade, turns over the earth, and works till sunset. The other turns over a few clods, gets a drink from the spring, takes a nap, and loafs back to his work. In a few years one will be rich for his needs, and the other a pauper dependent on the first, and growling at his prosperity.

Put ten thousand immoral men to live and work in one fertile valley and ten thousand moral men to live and work in the next valley, and the question is soon answered as to who wins the material wealth. Godliness is in league with riches.

Now we return with an easier mind and clearer conscience to the problem of our twenty-five billion dollars in a decade.

My question is: Is the material prosperity of this Nation favorable or unfavorable to the morality of the people?

The first thought is, Who has prospered? Who has got the money?

I take it that the loudest answer would be, "The millionaires, the capitalists, and the incompetent but luxurious rich;" and, as we think of that twenty-five billion, our thoughts run over the yachts, the palaces, and the luxuries that flaunt themselves before the public.

Who the Rich Are. As I was beginning to write this paper an Irishman with his horse and wagon drew up at my back door. Note that I say *his* horse and wagon. Twenty years ago that Irishman, then hardly twenty years old, landed in Boston, illiterate, uncouth, scarcely able to make himself understood in English. There was no symptom of brains, alertness, or ambition. He got a job to tend a few cows. Soon the American atmosphere began to take hold. He discovered that here every man has his chance. With his first earnings he bought a suit of clothes; he gained self-respect. Then he sent money home; then he got a job to drive a horse; he opened an account at the savings bank; then evening school; more money in the bank. He changed to a better job, married a thrifty wife, and to-day he owns his house, stable, horse, wagon, and bicycle; has a good sum at the bank, supports five children, and has half a dozen men working under him. He is a capitalist, and his yearly earnings represent the income on $30,000. He had no "pull"; he has made his own way by grit, physical strength, and increasing intelligence. He had had material prosperity. His older brother, who paid his passage over, has had material prosperity, and his younger brother, whose passage my friend paid, has had material prosperity.

Now we are beginning to get an idea as to where the savings are. They are in the hands of hundreds of thousands of just such men, and of scores of thousands of men whose incomes ten years ago were two and five thousand, and are now five and ten thousand; and of thousands of others whose incomes have risen from ten to thirty thousand. So that, when you get to the multi-millionaires, you have only a fraction to distribute among them. And of them the fact is that only a small fraction of their income can be spent upon their own pleasure and luxury; the bulk of what they get has to be reinvested, and becomes the means whereby thousands earn their wages. They are simply trustees of a fraction of the national property.

When, then, the question is asked, "Is the material prosperity of this nation favorable or unfavorable to the morality of the people?" I say with all emphasis, "In the long run, and by all means, favorable!"

In other words, to seek for and earn wealth is a sign of a natural, vigorous, and strong character. Wherever strong men are, there they will turn into the activities of life. In the ages of chivalry you will find them on the crusades or seeking the Golden Fleece; in college life you will find them high in rank, in the boat, or on the athletic field; in an industrial age you will find them eager, straining every nerve in the development of the great industries. The race is to the strong. The search for material wealth is therefore as natural and necessary to the man as is the pushing out of its roots for more moisture and food to the oak. This is man's play, his exercise, the expression of his powers, his personality. You can no more suppress it than you can suppress the tide of the ocean. For one man who seeks money for its own sake there are ten who seek it for the satisfaction of the seeking, the power there is in it, and the use they can make of it. There is the exhilaration of feeling one's self grow in one's surroundings; the man reaches out, lays hold of this, that, and the other interest, scheme, and problem. He is building up a fortune? Yes, but his joy is also that he is building up a stronger, abler, and more powerful man. There are two men that have none of this ambition: the gilded, listless youth and the ragged, listless pauper to whom he tosses a dime; they are in the same class.

We are now ready to take up the subject in a little more detail.

How is it favorable? The parable of my Irish friend gives the answer.

In the first place, and as I have already suggested, the effort to make his living and add to his comforts and power gives free play to a man's activities and leads to a development of his faculties. In an age and country where the greater openings are in commercial lines, there the stronger men and the mass of them will move. It is not a question of worldliness or of love of money, but of the natural use and legitimate play of men's faculties. An effort to suppress this action is not a religious duty, but a disastrous error, sure to fail.

Self-Respect and Self-Mastery. Besides this natural play of the faculties comes the development of self-respect and ambition. In the uprise from a lower to a higher civilization, these are the basal elements. Watch the cart-loads of Polish or Italian immigrants as they are hauled away from the dock. Study their lifeless expression, their hang-dog look, and their almost cowering posture. Follow them and study them five years later: note the gradual straightening of the body, the kindling of the eye, and the alertness of the whole person as the men, women, and children begin to realize their opportunities, bring in their wages, and move to better quarters. Petty temptations and deep degradations that might have overwhelmed them on their arrival cannot now touch them.

With this comes also the power of self-mastery. The savage eats what he kills and spends what he has. In the movement towards civilization through material wealth, questions come up for decision every hour. Shall I spend? Shall I save? How shall I spend? How can I earn more? Shall I go into partnership with a capital of ten dollars, or shall I wait until I have fifty dollars?

Wage earners are not to-day, as they were in earlier days, hungering for the bare physical necessities of life. They are hungering now, and it marks an upward movement in civilization, for higher things, education, social life, relaxation, and the development of the higher faculties.

To be sure, a certain fraction wilt under the strain, take to drink, to lust, to laziness. There is always the thin line of stragglers behind every army, but the great body of the American people are marching upwards in prosperity through the mastery of their lower tastes and passions to the development of the higher. From rags to clothes, from filth to cleanliness, from disease to health; from bare walls to pictures; from ignorance to education; from narrow and petty talk to books and music and art; from superstition to a more rational religion; from crudity to refinement; from self-centralization to the conception of a social unity.

Here in this last phrase we strike the next step in development. In this increase of wealth, this rapid communication which goes with it, this shrinking of the earth's surface and unifying of peoples through commerce, men and women are realizing their relations to society.

That there are those who in the deepest poverty sustain the spirit of unselfishness and exhibit a self-sacrifice for others which puts their richer neighbors to the blush we know by experience. At the same time, the fact is that for the mass and in the long run grinding poverty does grind down the character: in the struggle for bare existence and for the very life of one's children there is developed an intense self-centralization and a hardness which is destructive of the social instinct and of the finer graces. When, however, through the increase of wealth man has extended his interests, his vision, and his opportunities, "he is thoroughly related." His lines run out in every direction; he lays his finger upon all the broader interests of life, the school, the church, and the college. He reaches through commerce to the ends of the earth. He discovers one bond which is essential to the social unity in this commercial age— the bond of faith in other men; for in credit, on belief in others, our whole social and commercial fabric is built. And when a man has reached this point, he has indeed reached one of the high plateaus of character: from this rise the higher mountain peaks of Christian graces, but here he is on the standing-ground of the higher civilization.

As I write I can almost feel the silent protest of some critics. Are not these qualities, self-respect, self-mastery, a sense of social unity, and mutual confidence, the commonplaces of life? Is this the only response of material wealth in its relation to morality?

These are to us now the commonplaces of life: they are at the same time the fundamentals of character and of morality. If material prosperity has been one of the great instruments (and I believe it has) in bringing the great body of our people even to approach this plateau of character, it has more than justified itself.

One might, however, mention other and finer qualities that follow in these days the train of prosperity. I instance only one. We will strike up one mountain peak: it is that of joyful and grateful service.

The Privilege of Grateful Service. In other days we have heard much of "the sweet uses of adversity": the note still lingers in sermons and will linger as long as Christianity stands. There is, however, the other note that sounds strong in these days,—the privilege of grateful service.

I have in mind now a man of wealth (you can conjure up many like him) who lives handsomely and entertains; he has everything that purveys to his health and comfort. All these things are tributary to what? To the man's efficiency in his complete devotion to the social, educational, and charitable interests to which he gives his life. He is Christ's as much as was St. Paul, he is consecrated as was St. Francis of Assisi; and in recognition of the bounty with which God has blessed him he does not sell all that he has, but he uses all that he has, and, as he believes, in the wisest way, for the relief of the poor, the upbuilding of social standards, and the upholding of righteousness among the people. The Christian centuries, with all their asceticism and monasticism, with their great and noble saints, have, I believe, never witnessed a sweeter, more gracious, and more complete consecration than that which exists in the lives of hundreds of men and women in the cities and towns of this country, who, out of a sense of grateful service to God for His bounty, are giving themselves with all joy to the welfare of the people. And if ever Christ's words have been obeyed to the letter, they are obeyed to-day by those who are living out His precepts of the stewardship of wealth.

As we think of the voluntary and glad service given to society, to the State, the Church, to education, art, and charity, of the army of able men and women who, without thought of pay, are serving upon directories of savings banks and national banks, life insurance companies, railroads, mills, trusts and corporations, public commissions, and offices of all sorts, schools and colleges, churches and charities; as we run our thoughts over the free services of the doctors, of the lawyers, for their poorer clients, we are amazed at the magnitude of unpaid service, which is now taken for granted, and at the cheerful and glad spirit in which it is carried through. Material prosperity is helping to make the national character sweeter, more joyous, more unselfish, more Christlike. That is my answer to the question as to the relation of material prosperity to morality.

Again I feel a silent protest. Is not the writer going rather far? We did not believe that our twenty-five billions would lead to orgies; but is he not getting rather close to the millennium? Are there no shadows and dark spaces in the radiance which he seems to think that wealth is shedding around us?

Yes, my friendly critic, there are, and to a mention of a few of them I give the pages that are left.

The Spirit of Commercialism. First and most pervasive, I name the spirit of commercialism. It crops up in many forms and places, hydra-headed.

Is it any wonder? When one realizes that in the last ten years seventy millions of people have earned their living, paid their bills, and have at the same time increased the property of the Nation by twenty-five billions of dollars, we reach a slight conception of the intensity, the industry, the enterprise, and the ability with which those people have thought, worked, and reaped. One wonders that religion, charity, or culture have survived the strain at all. When the eye and ambition of a strong man are set upon a purpose, he sometimes neglects other considerations; he is not over nice about the rights of others; he occasionally overrides the weak, crushes out the helpless, and forgets to stop and pick up those that have fallen by the way.

We know how that was in England: we remember the report of the Commission by Lord Shaftesbury as to the horrible condition of the miners, men, women, and children. That was simply one phase in the development of the great movement of modern industrialism. It was a neglect and forgetfulness under a new pressure, rather than deliberate cruelty. The facts once known, attention called,—and reforms began; and they have been going on in behalf of the working people ever since. Much, very much, has been done.

As conditions change, much remains to do. The better adjustment of rights, wages, and taxes will call for the highest intelligence and strongest character. Again, the small tradesman has driven away the little counter where a widow earned her living, the larger tradesman has wiped out the small tradesman, and the department store is now finishing off some of the large tradesmen. It is hard, but it is a part of the great economic movement. It endangers some of the fundamentals of morality, and destroys for the time some of the finer graces.

Ephemeral success sometimes follows deceit, and that breeds a body of commercial frauds; but they cannot endure. A fortune is won by an unscrupulous adventurer; and a hundred fortunes are lost and characters spoiled in trying to follow suit. An ignorant man happens upon wealth or by some mysterious commercial ability wins wealth, and he then thinks himself omniscient. He, not God, is his own creator. He goes to church, but he is Godless. When a nation of people have been seeking for clothes, houses, and comforts in the upbuilding of civilization, is it any wonder that they do not realize that a man's life consisteth not in the abundance of things that he possesseth? There are deceit, hardness, materialism, and vulgarity in the commercial world; and to me the vulgarest of all is not the diamond-studded operator, but the horde of mothers crushing each other around the bargain counter in their endeavor to get something, and that so small, for nothing. The worst of commercialism is that it does not stop at the office, but enters the home, taints the marriage vow, and poisons social life at its springs.

Beyond these rudimentary forms of commercialism, there is another, even more dangerous, because it threatens the liberties and rights of the people. The eye of the public is on it now. I refer to the relation of concentrated masses of wealth to the public service.

I have no time to more than suggest a few of the conditions that have led up to this. Industrial enterprise has drawn many of the strongest and ablest men from political to commercial interests; society and legislation now do for the people what in other days the landlord did; they are concerned more and more with industrial, commercial, and financial questions, from the national tariff to the size of a house-drain. Just at this time, and because of our great industrial development and prosperity, a horde of ignorant voters waiting to be moulded by any strong leader have come to this shore. The wide distribution of wealth has driven merchants and mechanics, widows and trustees of orphans, doctors and ministers, to invest their savings in great enterprises, corporations, and trusts, which, to succeed, must be directed by a few men. We have therefore this situation: a few men responsible for the safekeeping and development of enormous properties, dependent upon legislation, and a great mass of voters, many of them ignorant, represented by their own kind in city or state government, strongly organized by a leader who is in it for what he can get out of it, and who is ever alert with his legislative cohorts to "strike" the great corporations. The people believe that the officers of great corporations so manage that they can get what they want, call it by assessment, bribery, ransom, or what you will, and they brand those otherwise respectable men as cowards and traitors to public liberty.

The Rich Man and the Burglar. A burglar breaks into your house, awakes you, and "strikes" you for $500 which is in your safe downstairs. You expostulate: he answers that he will burn your house. But your children, you cry, will they be safe? He does not know: he wants the money. But if you give it to him, he will try the same on other people. It is against all public duty for you to yield. Again, the threat that he will burn your house; and you, miserable, conscience-stricken that you are doing a cowardly thing, and one against the safety of the public, crawl downstairs, open the safe, and hand over the cash. You have saved your house and children, but how about your duty to the public and your neighbors, as well as to yourself?

This is very much the position of the great trustees of capital, the heads of our great corporations, at the hands of the modern bandit. Shall they jeopardize the income of women and children, merchants and mechanics, and perhaps drive them into poverty? Or shall they accept the situation, yield to the threat, and trust to the authorities to seize the robber, or through an aroused public opinion so to vote, act, and legislate as to change the law and stop this modern brigandage? That some of the promoters and managers of great corporations are unscrupulous is undoubtedly true. The jail is none too good for them, if only the law would touch them. Nor have we a word of apology or justification for any man who yields to or encourages blackmail. The difficulty, however, is not a simple one. It concerns more than the directors and the politicians; it relates to the rights and liberties of the people. I do not have so much fear of the rich man in office, as I do of the poor but weak man in office and the rich man outside. Through the interplay of aroused public opinion, better legislation, and intelligent action, the relief will come. A younger generation, with its eye keen upon that danger-point, is coming to the front.

In some cities of China the houses have no windows on the street, only bare walls and the little door. The families are isolated, narrow, and selfish: there is no public spirit. When the Chinese boy returns home from his Christian Mission School, touched with the spirit of Christian civilization, his first work in bringing civilization to his home is to take a crowbar, knock a hole in the front wall, and make a window, that he may see out and the people see in. He unifies society and creates a public opinion. What is needed as our next step in civilization is to break a hole and make a window that the public may see into the great corporations and trusts and, what is just as important, that the managers may see out and recognize the sentiment of the public.

Light and action—heroic action! There are men to-day waiting and wanting to act, to throw off the shackles of the modern bandit; but they dare not alone: their trusts are too great. What is wanted is a group of men, high in position, great in power, who at great cost, if need be, will stand and say, "Thus far, up to the lines of the nicest honor, shalt thou go, and no farther."

The people have their eye upon the public service. An administration may pay political debts by pushing ignorant and unworthy men into the lower offices, but when it comes to filling positions of great responsibility the President could not, and would not if he could, appoint men less worthy than Wood in Cuba, Allen in Porto Rico, and Taft in the Philippines, men of force, intelligence, and character. Collegiate education does not insure character, but it does sift men and insure intelligence; and, as President Pritchett of the Massachusetts Institute of Technology pointed out in his inaugural address, though less than one per cent of our population are college men, yet from this very small fraction a majority of the legislative, executive, and judicial places of the General Government which have to do in any large way with shaping the policy and determining the character of the government, are chosen.

The Danger from Luxury. One other dark shadow, and I am done. The persistent companion of riches,—luxury and an ability to have what you want. That vice and license are rampant in certain quarters is clear; that vulgar wealth flaunts itself in the face of the people is beyond question; and that the people are rather amused at the spectacle must be confessed. The theatre syndicate will turn on to the boards whatever the people want; and the general tone of the plays speaks not well for the taste and morality of the people. The strain of temptation overwhelms a fraction of our youth. But one has no more right to test the result of prosperity by the small class of the lazy and luxurious than he has to test the result of poverty by the lazy tramp.

With all this said, the great mass of the people are self-restrained and simple. Material prosperity has come apace, and on the whole it uplifts. Responsibility sobers men and nations. We have learned how to win wealth: we are learning how to use and spend it. Every year marks a long step in advance in material prosperity, and character must march in step. Without wealth, character is liable to narrow and harden. Without character, wealth will destroy. Wealth is upon us, increasing wealth. The call of to-day is, then, for the uplift of character,—the support of industry, education, art, and every means of culture; the encouragement of the higher life; and, above all, the deepening of the religious faith of the people; the rekindling of the spirit, that, clothed with her material forces, the great personality of this Nation may fulfil her divine destiny.

I have been clear, I trust, in my opinion that material prosperity is in the long run favorable to morality. Let me be as clear in the statement of that eternal truth, that neither a man's nor a nation's life consists in the abundance of things that he possesseth.

In the investment of wealth in honest enterprise and business, lies our path of character. In the investment of wealth in all that goes towards the uplift of the people in education, art, and religion is another path of character. Above all, and first of all, stands the personal life. The immoral rich man is a traitor to himself, to his material as well as spiritual interests. Material prosperity is upon us; it is marching with us. Character must keep step, ay, character must lead. We want great riches; we want also great men.

16. CHARLES HORTON COOLEY (1864–1929)

CHARLES H. COOLEY, son of Thomas M. Cooley (author of famous treatises on the American Constitution and an original member of the Interstate Commerce Commission), was for many years a professor of sociology at the University of Michigan. He wrote several works on the nature and processes of social organization and he was president of the American Sociological Society in 1918. Cooley did not believe that sociology could be made a science that is exact in the sense of the physical sciences. Careful observation of the actual behavior of individuals in relation to one another provides indispensable data for the understanding of man and society; but it does not supply all the necessary data. Mental introspection and the interpretation of other men's minds furnish other data as well as essential cues for the understanding of the "factual" data. Society, Cooley believed, is organic—an integrated, coordinated, whole of fundamentally interdependent units. Man's consciousness is as social as it is individual. "Society is mental" and "mind is social." Thus Cooley found materials for the interpretation of society not only in the records of cultural anthropologists and social statisticians, but also in the literature of philosophy and ethics and in the intellectual history of great men: in the Psalms, Plato, Marcus Aurelius, Dante, Shakespeare, Montaigne, Emerson, etc. All this gave him a solid basis for recognizing functions of political government beyond the mere policing of a perpetual conflict between self-centered, competitive, individuals.

[See: George H. Mead, "Cooley's Contribution to American Social Thought" and Arthur Evans Wood, "Charles Horton Cooley: An Appreciation," *American Journal of Sociology*, Vol. 35 (1930), pp. 693–706 and 707–717.]

From SOCIAL ORGANIZATION (1909) [1]

Chapter XXIII. On the Ascendency of a Capitalist Class.

Since in our age commerce and industry absorb most of the practical energy of the people, the men that are foremost in these activi-

[1] Charles Horton Cooley, *Social Organization: A Study of the Larger Mind* (New York, 1909); from chs. xxiii and xxvi. By special arrangement with Charles Scribner's Sons.

ties have a certain ascendency, similar to that of warriors in a military age.

Although this sort of men is not sharply marked off, it is well enough indicated by the term capitalist or capitalist-manager class; the large owner of capital being usually more or less of a manager also, while the large salaries and other gains of successful managers soon make them capitalists. . . .

Like everything else that has power in human life, the money-strong represent, in some sense, the survival of the fittest—not necessarily of the best. That is, their success, certainly no guaranty of righteousness, does prove a certain adaptation to conditions, those who get rich being in general the ablest, for this purpose, of the many who devote their energies to it with about the same opportunities. They are not necessarily the ablest in other regards, since only certain kinds of ability count in making money; other kinds, and those often the highest, such as devotion to intellectual or moral ideals, being even a hindrance. Men of genius will seldom shine in this way, because, as a rule, only a somewhat commonplace mind will give itself whole-heartedly to the commercial ideal.

There is much likeness in the persons and methods by which, in all ages, the cruder sort of power is acquired. When the military system is ascendent over the industrial it is acquired in one way, when property is secure from force in another, but this makes less difference than might be supposed. In either case it is not mere personal prowess, with the sword or with the tool, that gains large success, but power in organization. Aggressiveness, single-minded devotion to the end and, above all, organizing faculty—these were the methods of Clovis and Pepin and William of Normandy, as they are of our rulers of finance. And now, as formerly, much of the power that is alive in such men falls by inheritance into weaker hands.

As to righteousness, in the sense of good intention, they probably do not, on the whole, differ much from the average. Some may be found of the highest character, some of gross unscrupulousness. The majority are doubtless without moral distinction and take the color of their associates. The view sometimes set forth on behalf of men of wealth that riches go with virtue, and the view, more popular among non-possessors, that it comes by wickedness, are equally untrustworthy. The great mass of wealth is accumulated by solid qualities—energy, tenacity, shrewdness and the like—which may coexist with great moral refinement or with the opposite.

As a group, however, they are liable to moral deficiencies analogous to those of the conquerors and organizers of states just referred to. There is, especially, a certain moral irresponsibility which is natural to those who have broken away from customary limitations and restraints and are coursing almost at will over an unfenced territory. I mean that business enterprise, like military enterprise, deals largely with relations as to which there are no settled rules of morality, no constraining law or public opinion. Such conditions breed in the ordinary actor a Macchiavellian opportunism. Since it is hard to say what is just and honest in the vast and abstract operations of finance, human nature is apt to cease looking for a standard and to seize booty wherever and however it safely can. Hence the truly piratical character of many of our great transactions. And in smaller matters also, as in escaping taxation, it is often fatally easy for the rich to steal.

It must be allowed that such ascendency as the capitalist class has rests, in part at least, upon service. That is to say, its members have had an important function to perform, and in performing that function have found themselves in a position to grasp wealth. The great work of the time has been, or has seemed to be, the extension and reconstruction of industry. In this work leadership and organization have been needed on a great scale, and our captains of industry have nobly met this demand. That their somewhat autocratic control of production was called for by the situation seems to be shown by the rather general failure of coöperative enterprises intended to dispense with it. . . .

At the same time it is plain that a large part of the accumulation of wealth—hard unfortunately to distinguish from other parts—is accomplished not by social service but, as just intimated, by something akin to piracy. This is not so much the peculiar wickedness of a predatory class as a tendency in all of us to abuse power when not under definite legal or moral control. The vast transactions associated with modern industry have come very little under such control, and offer a field for freebooting such as the world has never seen.

Nor need we affirm that even the gains of the great organizers are in the highest sense right, only that they are natural and do not necessarily involve conscious wrong-doing.

The question of the rather arbitrary control of industry by the capitalist-manager, which now prevails, and of the possibility of this control being diminished or modified in the future, calls for some analysis of underlying forces. Evidently there is a conflict of principles here—the democratic or popular and the autocratic. The latter, now ascendant, has the advantages of concentration, secrecy and promptness—the same which give it superiority in war. On the other hand, the democratic principle should have the same merit in industry and commerce that it has in politics; namely that of enlisting the pride and ambition of the individual and so getting him to put himself into his work. Other things being equal, a free system is a more vital and energetic organism than one in which the initiative and choice come from a central authority.

And it is apparent that the working of the autocratic system in our economic life shows just the strength and weakness that would naturally be expected. The prompt undertaking and execution of vast schemes at a favorable moment, and the equally prompt recession when conditions alter; the investment of great resources in enterprises which yield no immediate return; the decision and secrecy important in overcoming competitors; the unhesitating sacrifice of workmen and their families when the market calls for a shut-down of production—such traits as these are of the utmost importance to commercial success, and belong to arbitrary control rather than to anything of a more popular sort. On the other hand, it would be easy to show at any length desired that such control is accompanied by a wide-spread disaffection of spirit on the part of the working classes, which, expressed in unwilling labor, strikes and agitation, is a commercial disadvantage, and a social problem so urgent as to unsettle the whole economic system.

The autocratic system has evidently a special advantage in a time of rapid and confused development, when conditions are little understood or regulated, and the state of things is one of somewhat blind and ruthless warfare; but it is quite possible that as the new industries become established and comparatively stable, there will be a commercial as well as a social demand for a system that shall invite and utilize more of the good-will and self-activity of the workman. . . . Indeed the rise, on purely commercial grounds, of a more humane and individualizing tendency, aiming in one way or another to propitiate the self-feeling of the workman and get him to identify himself with his work, is well ascertained. Among the familiar phases of this are the notable growth of coöperative production and exchange in Belgium, Russia and other European countries, the increasing respect for labor unions and the development by large concerns of devices for insurance, for pensions, for profit-sharing and for the material and social comfort of their employees. "As a better government has come up from the people than came down from the kings, so a better industry appears to be coming up from the people than came down from the capitalists."

In some form or other the democratic principle is sure to make its way into the economic system. Coöperation, labor unions, public regulation, public ownership and the informal control of opinion will no doubt all have a part; the general outcome being that the citizen becomes a more vital agent in the life of the whole. . . .

In discussing the power of the capitalist class there is no question of the finer and higher forms of power. We shall rarely find among the rich any pregnant spiritual leadership, theirs being a pedestrian kind of authority which has a great deal to do with the every-day comfort of their contemporaries but does not attempt to sway the profounder destinies of the race. Nor does the world often accord them enduring fame: lacking spiritual significance their names are writ in water. Even in industry the creative thought, the inventions which are the germs of a new era, seldom come from money-winners, since they require a different kind of insight.

The capitalist represents power over those social values that are tangible and obvious enough to have a definite standing in the market. His money and prestige will command food, houses, clothes, tools and all conventional and standard sorts of personal service, from lawn-mowing to the administration of a railroad, not genius or love or anything of that nature. That wealth means social power of this coarser sort is apparent in a general way, and yet merits a somewhat closer examination.

We have, first, its immediate power over goods and services: the master of riches goes attended by an invisible army of potential servitors, ready to do for him anything that the law allows, and often more. He is in this way, as in so many others, the successor of the nobleman of mediaeval and early modern history, who went about with a band of visible retainers eager to work his will upon all opposers. He is the ruler of a social system wherever he may be.

The political power of wealth is due only in part to direct corruption, vast as that is, but is even more an indirect and perfectly legal pressure in the shape of inducements which its adroit use can always bring to bear—trade to the business man, practice to the lawyer and employment to the handworker: every one when he thinks of his income wishes to conciliate the rich. Influence of this sort makes almost every rich man a political power, even without his especially wishing to be. But when wealth is united to a shrewd and unscrupulous political ambition, when it sets out to control legislation or the administration of the laws, it becomes truly perilous. We cannot fail to see that a large part of our high offices are held by men who have no marked qualification but wealth, and would be insignificant without it; also that our legislation—municipal, state and national—and most of our administrative machinery, feel constantly the grasp of pecuniary power. Probably it is not too much to say that except when public opinion is unusually aroused wealth can generally have its way in our politics if it makes an effort to do so.

As to the influence of the rich over the professional classes—lawyers, doctors, clergymen, teachers, civil and mechanical engineers and the like—we may say in general that it is potent but somewhat indirect, implying not conscious subservience but a moral ascendency through habit and suggestion. The abler men of this sort are generally educated and self-respecting, have a good deal of professional spirit and are not wholly dependent upon any one employer. At the same time, they get their living largely through the rich, from whom the most lucrative employment comes, and who have many indirect ways of making and marring careers. The ablest men in the legal profession are in close relations with the rich and commonly become capitalists themselves; physicians are more independent, because their art is not directly concerned with property, yet look to wealthy patients for their most profitable practice; clergymen are under pressure to satisfy wealthy parishioners, and teachers must win the good will of the opulent citizens who control educational boards.

Now there is nothing in social psychology surer than that if there is a man by whose good will we desire to profit, we are likely to adapt our way of thinking to his. Impelled to imagine frequently his state of mind, and to desire that it should be favorable to our aims, we are unconsciously swayed by his thought, the more so if he treats us with a courtesy which does not alarm our self-respect. It is in this way that wealth imposes upon intellect. Who can deny it?

Newspapers are generally owned by men of wealth, which has no doubt an important influence upon the sentiments expressed in them; but a weightier consideration is the fact that they depend for profit chiefly upon advertisements, the most lucrative of which come from rich merchants who naturally resent doctrines that threaten their interest. Of course the papers must reach the people, in order to have a value for advertising or any other purpose, and this requires adaptation to public opinion; but the public of what are known as the better class of papers are chiefly the comparatively well-to-do. And even that portion of the press which aims to please the hand-working class is usually more willing to carry on a loud but vague agitation, not intended to accomplish anything but increase circulation, than to push real and definite reform.

All phases of opinion, including the most earnest and honest inquiry into social questions, finds some voice in print, but—leaving aside times when public opinion is greatly aroused—those phases that are backed by wealthy interests have a great advantage in the urgency, persistence and cleverness with which they are presented. At least, this has been the case in the past. It is a general feeling of thoughtful men among the hand-working class that it is hard to get a really fair statement of their view of industrial questions from that portion of the newspaper and magazine press that is read by well-to-do people. The reason seems to be mainly that the writers live unconsciously in an atmosphere of upper-class ideas from which they do not free themselves by thorough inquiry. Besides this, there is a sense of what their readers expect, and also, perhaps, a vague feeling that the sentiments of the hand-working class may threaten public order.

Since the public has supplanted the patron, a man of letters has least of all to hope or fear from the rich—if he accepts the opinion of Mr. Howells that the latter can do nothing toward making or marring a new book.

The power of wealth over public sentiment is exercised partly through sway over the educated classes and the press, but also by the more direct channel of prestige. Minds of no great insight, that is to say the majority, mould their ideals from the spectacle of visible and tangible success. In a commercial epoch this pertains to the rich; who consequently add to the other sources of their influence power over the imagination. Millions accept the money-making ideal who are unsuited to attain it, and run themselves out of breath and courage in a race they should never have entered; it is as if the thin-legged and flat-chested people of the land should seek glory in football. The money-game is mere foolishness and mortification for most of us, and there is a madness of the crowd in the way we enter into it. Even those who most abuse the rich commonly show mental subservience in that they assume that the rich have, in fact, gotten what is best worth having. . . .

Chapter XXVI. Poverty.

The most practical definition of poverty is that now widely adopted which relates it to function, and calls those the poor whose income is not sufficient to keep up their health and working efficiency. This may be vague but is not too much so to be useful, and is capable of becoming quite definite through exact inquiry. At least it indicates roughly a considerable portion of the people who are poor in an obvious and momentous sense of the word.

Being undernourished, the poor lack energy, physical, intellectual and moral. Whatever the original cause of their poverty, they cannot, being poor, work so hard, think so clearly, plan so hopefully, or resist temptation with so much steadfastness as those who have the primary means of keeping themselves in sound condition.

Moreover, the lack of adequate food, clothing and housing commonly implies other lacks, among which are poor early training and education, the absence of contact with elevating and inspiring personalities, a narrow outlook upon the world, and, in short, a general lack of social opportunity.

The poor are not a class in the sense of having a distinct psychical organization. Absorbed in a discouraging material struggle, or perhaps in the sensuality and apathy to which a discouraging outlook is apt to lead, they have no spirit or surplus energy adequate to effectual coöperative endeavor on their own initiative, or even to grasping the benefits of existing organization. As a rule they get far less from the law and its administration, from the church, the schools, the public libraries and the like, than the classes more capable of self-assertion, and this is particularly true in a *laissez-faire* democracy, such as ours, which gives rights pretty much in proportion to the vigor with which they are demanded. It is this lack of common consciousness and purpose that explains the ease with which, in all ages, the poor have been governed, not to say exploited, from above. And if they are getting some consciousness and purpose at the present time, it is largely for the very reason that they are less inveterately and hopelessly poor now than in the past.

The familiar question whether poverty is due to personal or social causes is in itself somewhat fallacious, as smacking of a philosophy that does not see that the personal and social are inseparable. Everything in personality has roots in social conditions, past or present. So personal poverty is part of an organic whole, the effect in one way or another, by heredity or influence, of the general life. The question has significance, however, when we understand it as asking whether or not the cause is so fixed in personality that it cannot be counteracted by social influences. We find that in a community generally prosperous a part of the people—say ten per cent.—are poor in the urgent sense indicated above. The practical question is, Are these people poor from causes so established in their characters (however originating) that the rest of the community can do nothing effectual for them, or are they plastic to forces which might raise them to a normal standard of living?

As to this—leaving out the various extreme opinions which attend all such questions—there is a fair measure of agreement among competent observers somewhat to the following effect: There is a considerable number of individuals and families having intrinsic defects of character which must always keep them poor so long as they are left in the ordinary degree of self-dependence. The great majority of the poor, however, have no ineradicable personal weakness but are capable of responding to influences which might raise them to a normal standard of living. In other words, the nine-tenths of the community which is not poor might conceivably bring influences to bear which would—in a healthy manner and without demoralizing alms-giving—remove all but a small part of the poverty of the other tenth. It is only a question of putting into the matter sufficient knowledge and good will. As to the view, still not uncommon, that the laziness, shiftlessness and vice of the poor are the source of their difficulties, it may be said that these traits, so far as they exist, are now generally regarded by competent students as quite as much the effect as the cause of poverty. If a man is under-vitalized he will either appear lazy or will exhaust himself in efforts which are beyond his strength—the latter being common with those of a nervous temperament. Shiftlessness, also, is the natural outcome of a confused and discouraging experience, especially if added to poor nutrition. And as to drink and other sensual vices, it is well understood that they are the logical resource of those whose life does not meet the needs of human nature in the way of variety, pleasantness and hope. There are other causes of vice besides poverty, as appears from its prevalence among the unresource-ful rich, but there can be no doubt that good nurture, moderate work, wholesome amusement and a hopeful outlook would do away with a great, probably the greater, part of it. There are, no doubt, among the poor, as among the well-to-do, many cases of incurable viciousness and incompetence, but it would be no less unjust and foolish to assume that any individual is of this sort than to give up a scarlet fever patient because some will die of that disease in spite of the best treatment.

I find that the ablest and most experienced workers have generally the most confidence as to what may be done even with the apparently lazy, shiftless or vicious by bringing fresh suggestions, encouragements and opportunities to bear upon them. And it is only a small portion of the poor that are even apparently lazy, shiftless or vicious; the majority comparing not unfavorably with the well-to-do classes in these respects.

Leaving aside general conditions which may depress whole nations or races, the main cause of poverty in a prosperous country like the United States is without doubt some sort of maladjustment between the individual, or the family or neighborhood group, and the wider community, by reason of which potential capacity does not yield its proper fruit in efficiency and comfort. This is evidently the case, for example, with the sort of poverty most familiar in our American cities; that due to the transplanting of vast numbers of Europeans to a society, not too good for them as we carelessly assume, but out of connection with their habits and traditions. The Italians, Slavs and Russian Jews who just now throng our cities are by no means deficient, on the whole, either in intelligence, industry or thrift; and those who know them best find them prolific in some qualities, such as artistic sensibility of various kinds, in which America is otherwise rather deficient. But the process of adaptation to our industrial conditions is trying and leaves many in poverty and demoralization.

Among the native population also, poverty and the moral degradation which is often found with it is due largely, perhaps chiefly, to various kinds of maladjustment between the working classes and the industrial system—to loss of employment from periodical depressions or from the introduction of new methods, to the lack of provision for industrial education, to the perils attending migration from country to city, and so on.

What shall we say of the doctrine very widely, though perhaps not very clearly, held that the poor are the "unfit" in course of elimination, and are suffering the painful but necessary consequences of an inferiority that society must get rid of at any cost? A notion of this kind may be discovered in the minds of many men of fair intelligence, and is due to remote, obscure and for the most part mistaken impressions of the teaching of Malthus and Darwin.

The unfit, in the sense of Darwin and of biology in general, are those whose hereditary type is so unsuited to the conditions of life that it tends to die out, or at least suffer relative diminution in numbers, under the action of these conditions—as white families tend to die out in the tropics. In other words, they have an inferiority due to heredity, and this inferiority is of such a character that they do not leave as many children to continue their race as do those of a superior or fitter type.

It is very questionable whether any great part of the poor answer the description in either of these respects. As to the first, it is the prevailing opinion with those most familiar with the matter that their inferiority, except possibly where a distinct race is in question, as with the Negroes, is due chiefly to deficient nurture, training and opportunity, and not to heredity. This view is supported by the fact that under the conditions which a country of opportunity, like the United States, affords, great masses of people rise from poverty to comfort, and many of them to opulence, showing that the stock was as capable as any. Something of this sort has taken place with German and Irish immigrants, and is likely to take place with Jews, Slavs and Italians.

As to elimination, it is well known that only poverty of the most extreme and destructive kinds avails to restrict propagation, and that the moderately poor have a higher rate of increase than the educated and well-to-do classes. It is, in fact, far more the latter that are the "unfit" in a biological sense than the former.

The truth is that poverty is unfitness, but in a social and not a biological sense. That is to say, it means that feeding, housing, family life, education and opportunity are below the standards that the social type calls for, and that their existence endangers the latter in a manner analogous to that in which the presence of inferior cattle in a herd endangers the biological type. They threaten, and to a greater or less degree actually bring about, a general degradation of the community, through ignorance, inefficiency, disease, vice, bad government, class hatred (or, still worse, class servility and arrogance) and so on.

But since the unfitness is social rather than biological, the method of elimination must also be social, namely, the reform of housing and neighborhood conditions, improvement of the schools, public teaching of trades, abolition of child-labor and the humanizing of industry.

That there are strains of biological unfitness among the poor—hereditary idiocy, or nervous instability tending toward vice and crime, for example—is not to be denied, and certainly these should be eliminated, but poverty, far from effecting elimination, is perhaps their main cause. This will, no doubt, be duly considered by students of the new science of eugenics, for which those of us who approach social problems from another point of view may yet have the highest regard and expectation. Only a shallow sort of mind will suppose there is any necessary conflict between biological and psychological sociology.

As to the question, who is to blame for poverty, let us remember that the whole question of praise or blame is one of point of view and expediency. Blame the poor if it will do them any good, and sometimes, perhaps, it will, but not so often probably as the well-to-do are apt to imagine. It used to be thought that people must always be held responsible for their condition, and that the main if not the only source of improvement was to prod their sense of this responsibility; but more thoughtful observation shows that it is not always a good thing to urge the will. . . .

The main blame for poverty must rest upon the prosperous, because they have, on the whole, far more power in the premises. However, poverty being due chiefly to conditions of which society is only just beginning to become conscious, we may say that in the past nobody has been to blame. It is an unintended result of the economic struggle, and is "done with the elbows rather than the fists." But consciousness is arising, and with it comes responsibility. We are becoming aware of what makes poverty and how it can in great part be done away with, and if accomplishment does not keep pace with knowledge we shall be to blame indeed.

All parts of society being interdependent, the evils of poverty are not confined to one class, but spread throughout the whole; and the influence of a low standard of living is felt in the corruption of politics, the prevalence of vice and the inefficiency of labor. The cause of the poor is therefore the cause of all, and from this point of view those of them who in spite of weakness, discouragement and neglect keep up the fight for a decent life and shun dependence and degradation, should be regarded as heroic defenders of the general welfare, deserving praise as much as the soldier at the front. If we do not so regard them, it is because of our lack of intelligence and social consciousness. . . .

17. THOMAS NIXON CARVER (1865–   )

THOMAS N. CARVER was professor of economics at Oberlin College for six years and in 1900 joined the department of economics in Harvard University, becoming professor emeritus in 1935. He is the author of *The Distribution of Wealth* (1904), *Sociology and Social Progress* (1905), *Principles of Political Economy* (1919), *The Essential Factors of Social Evolution* (1935), *What Must We Do to Save Our Economic System* (1938), and works on rural economics, rural sociology, and the ethical aspects of modern economic society.

From "ECONOMIC COMPETITION" (1915)[1]

It is time to stop talking about protecting the weak against the strong. There is not better ground for this than for the Nietzschean proposal to allow the strong to do as they please. What the state must do is to protect production against predation. Whether the predacious individual be weak or strong does not enter into the case, neither does the question as to whether the productive individual be strong or weak. However strong the productive individual may be, it is a waste of energy for him to have to defend himself and his products against the predacious individual. The state can do it more economically. However weak the predacious individual may be, he must be restrained.

Of all forms of human conflict, economic competition is the highest. In no other form of conflict does success depend so much upon production or service and so little upon destruction or deception. There are three forms of economic competition: competitive production, competitive bargaining, and competitive consumption. Competitive production always works well; competitive bargaining sometimes works well and sometimes badly; competitive consumption always works badly. Of these three forms of economic competition, therefore, the highest is competitive production, the lowest

[1] Chapter v of *Essays in Social Justice* (Cambridge, Mass., 1915), pp. 93–129. By courtesy of Harvard University Press.

is competitive consumption, while competitive bargaining occupies a middle position.

Most of the opponents of economic competition propose to substitute for this form of conflict another form, namely, political competition. The more the state absorbs the enterprises now carried on by private initiative, the more will political competition displace economic competition. Political competition is a lower form. Before pursuing this topic further, let us examine the fundamental factors involved in all human conflict.

That the chief purpose of all living beings is to keep on living is too obvious to need discussion. The universal struggle for existence has occupied the attention of all students of the problems of life, both human and sub-human, for many generations. Some of the most revolutionary and far-reaching scientific generalizations of modern times have grown out of this study. It is clearly perceived by every student that economic competition is, in some way, a part of this universal struggle. It is not always understood just how it relates itself to that struggle as it is carried on in the sub-human world. There is abroad a very uncritical and undiscriminating opinion to the effect that there is no essential difference between economic competition and the brutal struggle for existence as studied by the zoölogist.

In assuming the universality of the struggle for existence, however, it is not necessary to exclude such facts as love, friendship, play, and mutual aid, either among men or animals. These are facts which cannot be denied, and they must have a place in any philosophy of life that is worth a moment's consideration. In the effort of living beings to keep on living these benign agencies have a place as well as the sterner facts of war and slaughter. In a preliminary and superficial way it may be suggested that the key to the problem of harmonizing such unlike things as love and war, friendship and strife, mutual aid and mutual slaughter, is found in the observation that human interests are sometimes harmonious and sometimes antagonistic. Where they are harmonious, love, friendship, and mutual aid promote the effort to keep on living. Where they are antagonistic, some form of struggle is inevitable. It may take any one of a multitude of forms. The rivals may, in an unthinking way, absorb the limited supply of nutriment, moisture, or light, leaving the less successful competitors to perish of starvation;

it may take the form of a conscious and deliberate extermination of rivals by the method of slaughter, or it may take on the idyllic, but none the less deadly form of gracious social intercourse which accompanies courtship, and leaves the less fortunate competitors to go unmated and eventually to perish without reproducing themselves. From this point of view, love and friendship are only specialized forms of battle and slaughter. . . .

The very nature of wealth involves a conflict of interests and consequent rivalry. Nothing is ever regarded as wealth, commercially evaluated, or bought and sold, unless it be scarce. A thing is scarce only when there is less of it available, in a given time and place, than is wanted. Where there is less of it than is wanted, if some one gets all he wants, some one else must necessarily get less than he wants. Instantly there is rivalry for the possession of the scarce article.

In an unrestrained and brutal state of existence, there are no limits to the form which this rivalry may take. The rivals may strive with tooth and claw, or with manufactured implements of destruction, or they may strive to win the desired article by useful and meritorious service; but strive they will in one form or another. Not every form of struggle for wealth is economic competition. The only forms to which that name can accurately be applied are those wherein some form of service, real or imagined, is a condition of success. These alone are economical forms of rivalry, all others are uneconomical. They consist in contributing to social production as much as is acquired by the competitor. Rivalry in acquisition becomes rivalry in production; all other forms of rivalry in acquisition being more and more suppressed by enlightened governments.

. . . Wherever there is any kind of social control or legal restraint, an effort is made to distinguish between the economic and the uneconomic, and to suppress the uneconomic methods, particularly the destructive methods, of acquiring wealth. In fact, the enlightenment and efficiency of a system of government or social control may be tested by the accuracy with which it makes that discrimination, and the success of its efforts to suppress the uneconomical methods.

By an economical method of acquiring wealth is meant a method by which an individual succeeds in proportion as he contributes to the wealth of the community. By an uneconomical method is meant a method by which the individual impoverishes others in proportion as he succeeds himself. The more people there are in a community acquiring wealth by uneconomical methods, and the more successful they are, the poorer they tend to make the community; but the more there are acquiring wealth by economical methods, and the more successful they are, the richer they make the rest of the community.

The fact that we can make such a distinction as this between the economical and the uneconomical ways of making a living shows how far we have progressed beyond the brutal struggle for existence. Neither brutes nor unrestrained human beings make any such distinction. All the grosser and less refined of the destructive ways of acquiring the means of subsistence are practiced by brutes. The only reason they do not practice the more refined methods is that they do not know how. But unrestrained and uncontrolled human beings have not even the limitations of ignorance. . . .

Wherever this primordial struggle is carried on, among individuals or groups, among men, animals or plants, the supreme command of nature is, be strong! This is the whole of the law. To disobey this is to disobey every other command. Strength comes with self-discipline. To the sovereign social group this command enjoins the enforcement of discipline within. Murder must be suppressed because the group that permits it weakens itself. Thieving, swindling, monopolizing, and all other destructive activities must be suppressed for the same all-sufficient reason, and for no other reason whatsoever. . . .

But how shall a nation grow strong? One way is to secure the maximum economy of its fund of human energy. When human energy, or labor power, is allowed to go to waste, either in idleness, or in non-productive effort, the nation weakens itself to that extent. One of the most effective ways of preventing idleness is to establish the rule that only he who works shall eat, and, further, that each shall be allowed to possess in proportion as his production exceeds his consumption. . . . When men can acquire wealth in no other way whatsoever except by producing it or its equivalent, or rendering a positive service commensurate with it, then they will strive to acquire it by these productive and useful methods. Instead of enriching himself at the expense of some one else, each individual will then find it impossible to enrich himself except by enriching the nation.

This means in a most distinct and important sense that, in order that the sovereign group may be successful in the unmitigated, primordial struggle which it must of necessity wage, it must discipline its individuals and prevent them from waging such a conflict among themselves. It must repress all destructive methods of acquiring wealth within its own jurisdiction by means of a criminal law. That is what criminal law is for. A crime is that which weakens the group. The more crimes there are committed the weaker the group becomes, other things equal.

When farmers rival one another in growing corn, there is a struggle among them, but it is not the unmitigated brutal struggle. It is the kind of a struggle which increases the corn crop and strengthens, to that extent, the group. There is no reason why the state should repress that kind of a struggle, or even regulate it beyond seeing that each one acts fairly and does not try to win by destroying other men's crops or interfering with their work. But when they quarrel over line fences, one trying to move his fence over on another man's land, there is a struggle which produces nothing. What one wins another loses, and there is no net gain. All the energy expended in this kind of a struggle is, from a social point of view, wasted. It, therefore, tends to weaken rather than strengthen the group. Therefore it is to the interest of the group to suppress, as promptly as possible, this kind of a struggle,—not to regulate it, not merely to see fair play, and let the stronger win; but to settle it. Therefore we have courts of law to take such quarrels out of private hands and settle them. It is even more important that such a quarrel be settled than that it be settled justly, though this is very important. To settle it justly is to give the land in dispute to the man who had earned it, i.e., who had given an equivalent for it. Otherwise the other man would acquire wealth uneconomically, that is, without having contributed anything for it.

From this point of view, it will appear that the purpose of a just government is not, strictly, to protect the weak and restrain the strong, though there is a sense in which that may be true. If by the weak are meant those weak in body, and by the strong those strong in body, it is one purpose of government to prevent the strong from imposing upon the weak by means of his bodily strength alone. If, however, the strong is able to contribute more to the strength of the state through superior production or service, the state must allow him to profit by his success, and if the weak is unable, because of bodily weakness to contribute anything to the strength of the state, he must fail. The state may support him, but it must be called charity and not justice. At any rate, it would be suicidal for any state to make it a practice to restrain the strong in this sense, from performing superior service lest he should succeed better than the weak, with his inferior service.

In this restrained economic struggle or competition, a new definition of strength is virtually adopted, and a new standard of fitness for success in the struggle is put into effect. In the unmitigated brutal struggle, weapons of destruction are quite as important as serviceable qualities. Success comes to whomsoever is able to fight successfully where there are no rules of the game. The state must lay down rules for the struggle among individuals, and, in proportion as it approximates to justice, these rules will make productivity, or usefulness to the state, the condition of success. The struggle thus becomes a struggle to see who can become most useful or productive, and the prizes are awarded accordingly.

In this struggle strength succeeds on condition that it be used in service, and it fails if it is not. Weakness, of the kind which can render little service, is sure to fail and has and deserves no protection against the normal consequences of that kind of weakness. In this kind of a regulated struggle, it becomes literally true that greatness depends upon service. "And whosoever will be chief among you, let him be your servant"—not a servant in the sense of one who is in servitude under your beck and call, but a servant in the sense of one who contributes most largely to the life and strength of "you all," i.e., the whole of society.

Under these conditions, if any state can reach them, economic success would be an accurate measure of economic merit. The more men there were getting rich, and the richer they got, the better it would be for the whole. A large crop of multi-millionaires would then be a favorable sign because it would mean that there were a large number of individuals, each of whom had contributed millions to the wealth of the state. This fact, however, would probably not make them popular, nor protect them from the envy and covetousness of the weak.

There is no denying that, even under these ideal conditions there would be a real and intense struggle among individuals within the state. What we are laboring to show is that it differs in the most fundamental qualities from the unmitigated brutal struggle for existence. The enemies of the competitive system not only fail, but refuse to see this important difference. To fail to see this difference is to fail to see the difference between production and destruction, between service and harm. Brutes and sovereign human groups sometimes succeed by means of implements of destruction, and in proportion to the harm they do. Under economic competition men succeed only by means of instruments of production, and in proportion to the service they do. . . .

Under a state which accurately distinguishes between the economic and uneconomic ways of getting wealth, and effectively suppresses all of the latter, it follows of necessity that every individual will be forced, with respect to wealth, to act in his own self-interest precisely as he would if he were animated by the most completely altruistic motives and patriotic sentiments. If as an altruist he saw that there was a great and intense need for a certain product or service, he would feel impelled to supply it. As a self-interested person he would find it profitable to do the same. If as an altruist he saw that he could use the price for which his product or service would sell in supplying other needs, he would exact the price and use it thus. As a self-interested person he would find it profitable to do the same. If as an altruist he saw that he could, by reducing his consumption, use his surplus income in purchasing tools, rather than consumers' goods, thus turning the productive forces of the community into the tool-making rather than the luxury-producing industries, and thus, in turn, increasing the productive power of the community, he would thus reduce his consumption and increase his investment. As a far-sighted or wisely self-interested person he would find it advantageous to do the same thing. If as an altruist he saw that he could, by exacting a price for the use of his new tools and using this price in purchasing still other tools, he could still further increase the productive power of the community, he would exact the price, that is, interest on his capital, and reinvest it. As a self-interested person he would find it to his advantage to do the same. And so on, throughout the whole list of possibilities, the wisest philanthropy and the wisest self-interest would lead to identical conduct, until we reach the missionary field where the people are to be given services which they do not want and will refuse to pay for. . . .

This appeal to self-interest to do for the community precisely what altruism would do, is in no sense whatever, an attempt to set up self-interest as the sole motive to action, or to refuse to appeal to altruism and patriotism even in matters of wealth. The appeal is to both. Every human being has a certain amount of altruism and patriotism about him, and can always be appealed to, more or less powerfully on this basis. It is quite proper to make this appeal and turn this sentiment to the public good. On the other hand, no human being is free from self-interest or, as it was previously called, self-centered appreciation, and there is no one who cannot be appealed to on this ground. If he can be appealed to on this ground also, as well as on the ground of altruism or patriotism, we have a double appeal moving him in the direction of public service. It is like harnessing two great natural forces and compelling them to work together toward the same end. Where this can be done successfully, it would be silly to attempt to dispense with one and depend upon the other alone.

At this point it is well to be on our guard against a common interpretation of Adam Smith's famous dictum regarding a beneficent order of nature under which the individual is led, "as by an invisible hand, to promote the public interest while trying to promote his own." Adam Smith saw clearly, as has every clear-headed student of the problem since his day, that under the competitive system, properly safeguarded, men are led by their self-interest to do many things which result in good to society. In fact it would not be difficult to show that, in the mass, most of the good and useful things that are done in any progressive community are done through self-interest. The few really good things which are done through pure altruism are so conspicuous because of their unfamiliarity, as to attract notice.

But it is a mistake to assume that this beneficent order of nature exists, or can possibly exist, in the absence of very careful and strict government supervision and interference. Government and government alone prevents competition from lapsing into the brutal struggle for existence, where self-interest leads to uneconomic as well as to economic,—to destructive as well as to productive activity

on the part of the individual. But where governmental interference
is wisely and efficiently directed, so that men are not allowed to
follow their self-interest in the direction of destructive, harmful,
or uneconomic activities, they will still follow their self-interest.
Since the only ways left open to them are the productive, useful,
and economic activities, their self-interest impels them into these
activities. Thus it is that, *under proper government interference
and control*, men are led as by an invisible hand, to promote the
public interest while trying to promote their own. . . .

Let it not be understood, however, that merely because government supervision and control are necessary to the maintenance of
the competitive system as distinguished from the unmitigated
struggle for existence, that all government interference is, therefore,
justifiable. Speaking broadly, it would not be so very unsafe to
say that government interference is almost as frequently harmful
as beneficial. It is only when it is wisely planned that it can be
justified. To be wisely planned is, essentially, to distinguish accurately between economic and uneconomic activities, and to suppress
the latter efficiently.

The reliance upon the motive of self-interest as one means of
harnessing men to useful work does not necessarily mean the reliance upon greed. They who object to this principle of government
sometimes make the mistake of using opprobrious words where
nothing really opprobrious is involved. The desire to possess goods
for oneself, one's family, and others in whom one is specially interested is not an unworthy desire, though it is, by the high-souled
partizans of another system, characterized as greed. In its place
it is sometimes proposed to substitute the desire for social esteem,
or some other agreeable motive. But if the desire to possess goods
is greed, then the desire for social esteem is vanity. As between
greed and vanity there is little to choose. Besides, the appeal to
the desire for goods does not, in the slightest degree, interfere with
the appeal to the desire for social esteem. They are equally self-
interested. If we can appeal to both, we have a more powerful
combination of motives than if we appeal to one alone. There is
thus the same reason for appealing to both forms of self-interest, in
order to induce strenuous production, that we found in favor of
appealing to both self-interest and altruism. . . .

. . . Is it better that the state should take over most of the industrial functions, thus narrowing the field of business competition and enlarging the field of political competition? For if the state runs most of our industries as it now runs the post-offices, then most of our industrial positions will be filled as postal positions are now filled. One's success in getting desirable positions will depend upon the same qualities which now advance him in the civil or governmental service. But if most of our industrial enterprises are left in the hands of individuals, then the rivalry will be business rivalry and one's success in getting desirable positions will depend upon the qualities which bring success in business. The question as to the relative desirability of these two forms of rivalry depends upon which is the more accurate method of selecting men for desirable positions, the political method or the business method. Under the political method, generally speaking, the man's advancement will depend upon his ability to convince voters of his fitness for the place. Under business competition, a man's success will depend primarily upon his ability to convince buyers of the value of his products or services. It would seem, therefore, that this question depends upon whether the voter votes more intelligently than the buyer buys. The question is: Does the average man when he votes spend his vote as intelligently as he does his dollar when he buys products or services? If he is more likely to be prejudiced in his votes than in his purchases, or is more likely to vote ignorantly than he is to purchase ignorantly, one should conclude that buying is a more accurate test of merit than voting, and vice versa. Suppose that a private individual should produce and put on the market a good product which appeals to the buyer, but the producer is a member of an unpopular race or an unpopular religious body, that is, that there is a great deal of prejudice against him and his class; is this prejudice as likely to interfere with the sale of his product or his services as it is to interfere with his getting votes for a desirable position? It would seem not. To that extent, at least, buying is a less inaccurate method of determining merit than voting, that is, the racial and religious prejudices are less likely to be factors in buying than in voting. If that be true, the man who succeeds in getting the money of purchasers is in this respect, at least, more likely to have earned that money than is the man who gets their votes through racial or religious prejudices likely to have deserved their votes. Thus far, at any rate, the argument is in favor of the business rather than the political form of rivalry.

Again, as to the matter of ignorance or intelligence: Does the average purchaser purchase as intelligently or more intelligently than he votes? Does he know as accurately what he is getting for his money as he does what he is getting for his vote? Doubtless many improvements can be made in our balloting system. Any one who will examine himself or his own experience will probably agree that he votes very unintelligently, that is to say, he knows very little about the candidates whose names appear on the ballot, and he has very inadequate methods of finding out about them. Though the writer has tried consistently to do his duty as a voter, he has to confess that in a majority of cases the candidates for whom he votes are absolutely unknown to him and that, therefore, a man who could not read at all could vote quite as intelligently as he can in more than half the cases. In other words, in more than half the cases, voting with him is wholly a matter of guess work, and he has no adequate means of finding out in advance what he is voting for, in the way of men, and seldom in the way of measures. If this be the experience of the average man, it would seem to imply that the average man votes very unintelligently, and that therefore there is little reason to expect that the individuals who get his votes have earned them or deserved them. . . .

There are, however, some services which have to be rendered and which we cannot possibly get by the process of buying and selling, or, through business rivalry. We could not have several governors trying to rule the state and giving the governed the option of paying for the service of the one he liked best. This, however, is the result of what is known as territorial sovereignty in government. The only absolute monopoly in the world is government. The individual has no choice in the matter except by the process of migration, and even that may be forbidden by the government of the territory in which he happens to be born. Where you have an absolute monopoly there can obviously be no such thing as business or economic competition, for the two are contradictory. Then the only method by which the governed can have a voice in the determination of the kind of service which he is to receive is by the ballot. Where there is no territorial sovereignty, or territorial monopoly, but where rivals may really be in the field offering their services, he who would secure a service may take his choice and give his vote, that is, his money, to the one that satisfies him best. Thus business and industry which have not become monopolistic are all extremely democratic, in that sense more democratic in fact than any government can ever possibly hope to be. Balloting is only a clumsy device to try to make government partially democratic. But it is, even at its best, less democratic than industry is already. If industry once became as absolutely monopolistic as government is, then they who are served by the industry would be helpless to control it without the ballot—as helpless as they are to control government without the ballot. Even then they would have less control of that industry than they now have over competitive industry through their ability to purchase or to withhold their purchase, that is, to give or to withhold their industrial, as opposed to their political, votes. . . .

The simple fact is that industry is more democratic without the ballot than government can possibly be made even with the ballot. First as to the open road to talent; that has always existed in industry in a higher degree than in politics. However meritorious a man may be in politics, if his opinions are in advance of those of the majority he gets no advancement. A very small and select minority may approve his work in industry and reward it. He secures his advancement as the result of this without waiting for the crude majority to approve. It is true even here he may fail through being so very far in advance of his times as not to secure the support even of the elect minority, but it is obviously easier for an advanced person to secure the support of a small and highly-intelligent minority than to transform this into a majority, which would require that much less intelligent people should be convinced. Even under the best of democracies the man of genius stands a better chance outside of than in politics, whereas, of course, in an aristocratic or autocratic government he stands no chance at all.

It is of course also true that a trickster who would not succeed at all in politics, may succeed in business by deceiving a small and select body of imbeciles. However, he must, even in business unless he violates the criminal law, succeed in giving even these few people something which they *think* they want. Any field of endeavor in which men succeed in proportion to the number of desires they can satisfy, necessarily involves the opportunity for abuse so long as there are evil desires to be satisfied. Individuals come more nearly getting what they want from business men than they do from politicians and government agents. If they happen to want evil things of course they get them from business caterers, unless the law in some way restrains and forbids them to get what they want, as in a prohibition state. This in itself implies greater democracy in business and industry than in government. . . .

. . . Still industries sometimes develop monopolistic tendencies. They then begin to lose something of their sensitiveness to the desires of the people to whom they cater. This is true where they make such advances toward absolute monopoly as to practically control the field for the sale of a certain product. Though the individuals are still free to reject the product or to buy other partial substitutes for it, still some control must be exercised over such partial monopolies, and this control can only be exercised through politics and the ballot. This control must eventually take the form of price regulation in order to take away their control of markets.

Incidentally, this would destroy most of the trusts. No trust exists by virtue of its superior productive powers. Every one depends for its existence upon its superiority in buying or selling, that is upon its power over prices. Take away this power and enable the outside concerns to match their productivity against that of the trust, and outside competition will increase and force the trust to break up into its most effective *productive* units, as distinguished from the most efficient *bargaining* units.

This means, however, that the necessity for the ballot as a means of directly controlling the policy of an industry arises only when an industry begins to take on some of the qualities and characteristics of government. Enough has doubtless been said to show how purely shallow and senseless it is to repeat such vague generalities as "the democracy of industry" when industry is already more thoroughly democratic than government has ever been or can ever possibly become.

In short, the more nearly an industry approaches that condition of complete monopolization which characterizes all government, the more we shall find it necessary to resort to the ballot to exercise a check upon the power of the monopoly as we now use it to exercise a check upon government. Concretely, this means government control. But government control merely means playing the vote-getting monopolist against the money-getting monopolist. The politician, that is, the vote-getter, cares no more for the people than does the trust magnate. He merely wants their votes as the trust magnate wants their money. He wants their votes in order that he may further his own interests just as the trust magnate wants their money in order that he may further his own interests. If it came to a detailed comparison, it is impossible to predict which would suffer most. But when one is played against the other, one bidding for the people's votes and the other bidding for their money, the people themselves may profit as the result of this new kind of competition. When they can no longer play one against the other, that is, when they are completely in the hands of either the one or the other, they will be helpless indeed. That is to say, when politicians cease baiting trusts and corporations, on the one hand, and when, on the other, there is no field of enterprise outside of publicly owned industry in which the private individual may pursue his interest, but must seek it in the public service, then will the people suffer. In the one case, monopoly will crush all initiative. In the other, the successful vote-getter will place his heel on the neck of the man who opposed his candidacy and who must come to him for a job in the public service after he is elected to a high position.

Again, the dollar is less likely to be influenced by class prejudice or race hatred than the ballot. No one refuses to buy cotton grown by a negro, though many would refuse to vote for him for a public office. No one refuses to buy clothes of a Jew though there are people who would refuse to vote for him. In short the negro, the Jew, or a member of any other unpopular class stands a better chance of getting what he deserves in business than he does in politics. Suppose cotton planting were handled as a government enterprise; negroes might be given positions as field hands, but no one, however capable or meritorious would be likely to get a position which a white man wanted, except where negro votes outnumbered the white. There the conditions would be reversed provided the negroes would vote together. In those communities where there is a prejudice against the Jew, he would seldom secure a desirable position under the political form of competition, except where Jews had large voting strength. But in business he can rise to the highest positions if he possesses the ability to render good service. Gentiles will buy his products or services, thus enabling him to secure their dollars, who would not give him their votes. . . .

We now come to the question of the morality of the competitive spirit. Is it true, as some high idealists would have us believe, that competition is in spirit incompatible with ethics and religion, that we ought neither to run for office, thus engaging in political competition, nor engage in business competition? We have tried to show that, where the principle of self-interest or self-centered appreciation is present, competition in one form or another is inevitable and cannot possibly be avoided,—that as between the two forms, namely, political and economic competition, economic competition is less wasteful and more accurate as a test of fitness, that industrial competition is more in harmony with the spirit of true democracy than is political competition. But is any form of competition compatible with the ideal of Christianity or of Christian ethics?

In the first place, it would seem that those who hold the view that competition is antagonistic to the spirit of Christianity would find it impossible to engage in a game of tennis or croquet, for there is certainly competition here. In fact, if we look at the matter fairly and squarely, we should find that it would be very difficult even to amuse ourselves without some form of competition. But the answer will probably be made that it may be proper to compete in minor matters, but that it is wrong to compete for the necessaries of existence. I do not think that the difference is logically brought out by this contrast. Even in sport competition may take on an extremely unethical and irreligious tone, and in industry it may be as harmless and benign as the competition which takes place in a friendly game of golf. Whenever and wherever sports are engaged in primarily for the sake of a prize, where the contestants regard victory as the one desirable thing in terms of which everything else is evaluated, even sport becomes vicious. Then the rule is, anything to win; everything is evaluated in terms of its relation to the one desideratum, namely, victory. It is this, and this only, which tends to make sport vicious, unethical, or unchristian. This spirit will spoil any form of competition. . . .

Thus it will be seen that the fundamental question which must be settled before anything else can be settled is the question of the philosophy of life which dominates the competitive process. If the world is dominated by the pig-trough philosophy, competition is not only inevitable, but it will invariably take on the morals of the pig-trough and become unethical and unchristian. But it would be futile to attempt to correct this by doing away with industrial competition so long as the same philosophy of life dominated individuals. So long as we had learned books written on the "economy of happiness" and the "efficiency of consumption," in which everything is expressed in terms of consumers' satisfactions, so long as it was conceived to be the chief end of industry and human effort to enable men to fill their bellies with the husks of material wealth, the rivalry would be unethical and unchristian no matter what form it took, whether it were political rivalry, military rivalry, or economic rivalry. Merely changing the machinery of government, or the methods of holding property, or of conducting industry, would in no way alleviate the grim and deadly character of that rivalry.

But let the community become dominated by the work-bench philosophy, under which productive action rather than consumption, either graceful or ungraceful, is the end, then competition in whatever field it may be carried on, or in whatever channel it may be directed, loses its unethical and unchristian character and comes to be the very expression of the highest ideals of Christian ethics. Incidentally it will be found that every single statement or pronouncement by the founder of Christianity on the subject of wealth, industry, and property is in the strictest harmony with this point of view. Not a single word did he ever utter in condemnation of private property or large possessions or large accumulations; but on every occasion he showed his disapproval of selfish consumption.

He who does less well than he can does ill. He who spends a dollar in selfish gratification when he might spend it for tools or productive services, does less well than he can. This is the logic back of every pronouncement of the Nazarene regarding wealth.

18. THORSTEIN VEBLEN (1857–1929)

VEBLEN, leader of an "institutional" school of American economists, was as independent of traditional trends in economic writing
as William Graham Sumner was among the sociologists. He was born
in Wisconsin of Norwegian parentage and reared in Norwegian farm
communities of the northwest. After his graduation from Carleton College he went to Yale, to study philosophy and sociology under Noah
Porter and Sumner. He wrote his doctoral dissertation on "Ethical
Grounds of a Doctrine of Retribution." Somewhat unconventional in
his ways of thought and expression, he found no teaching position. Accordingly, he returned to live and work on farms in the west; yet he continued to devote most of his time to reading widely and to serious reflection on the maladjustments of contemporary economic society.
Then, in his thirty-fourth year, he decided to accept the advice and aid
of his father, a farmer, and again prepare himself for a scholar's life.
He went to Cornell University, where J. Laurence Laughlin, professor of
economics, found a fellowship for him; next year he followed Laughlin
to the University of Chicago, where he was soon appointed to the teaching staff and rose to the rank of an assistant-professorship; for nine years
he was managing editor of the *Journal of Political Economy*, published
at the University. He later taught at Stanford University, the University
of Missouri, and the New School of Social Research in New York City.
For a year he was on the editorial board of *The Dial*, a fortnightly
magazine of literary criticism and liberal political opinion; during that
year the magazine was commonly referred to as "the Veblenian Dial."

Veblen's first book, *The Theory of the Leisure Class* (1899), was immediately popular among historians, literary critics, sociologists, younger
economists, and some of the more distinguished of the older economists.
He gave a more comprehensive statement of his doctrines in his *Theory
of Business Enterprise* (1904); and he developed some of his particular
themes in *The Instinct of Workmanship* (1914), *The Engineers and the
Price System* (1921, a forerunner of the "technocracy" of the nineteen-
thirties), and *Absentee Ownership and Business Enterprise* (1923). His
Higher Learning in America (1918) is a caustic criticism of the management of universities by business men.

Veblen analysed existing economic society from an evolutionary, institutional, point of view: we adapt our economic theories and our moral creeds to established ways of behavior; we reinterpret accepted theories and creeds in order to make them fit our changing practical notions of social necessity. Our economic society, he held, has not been traditionally liberal or individualistic in its motivation and practice; its distinguishing mark has been its "pecuniary" character. Veblen laid stress on the distinction between making goods (industrial employment, the machine process) and making money (pecuniary employment, business enterprise). Making money, the chief mark of "success" in our society, interferes with making goods; business-minded men are not qualified to manage industry most productively; business enterprise is the chief cause of crises and depressions; and our whole pecuniary system tends to thwart a deeply ingrained human instinct of workmanship.

Veblen gave no clear details of the system he expected to succeed the present business or pecuniary economy; he looked forward generally to a system in which engineers and other technicians exercise chief control over production and distribution. He wrote in a somewhat eccentric style. Most contemporary economists opposed or slighted his doctrines. When, in his sixty-eighth year, a nominating committee of the American Economics Association (in which there had been some wrangling over the matter) told him they were prepared to nominate him for the presidency of the Association (if he would join the body), Veblen rejected their proposal and remarked that he had not been offered such a recognition when he had needed it.

[See: Wesley C. Mitchell, ed., *What Veblen Taught: Selected Writings . . . with an Introduction* (1936); Joseph Dorfman, *Thorstein Veblen and His America* (1934).]

From *THE THEORY OF THE LEISURE CLASS* (1899)[1]

Ch. ii. Pecuniary Emulation. . . .

Wherever the institution of private property is found, even in a slightly developed form, the economic process bears the character of a struggle between men for the possession of goods. It has been customary in economic theory, and especially among those economists who adhere with least faltering to the body of modernised classical doctrines, to construe this struggle for wealth as being

[1] Thorstein Veblen, *The Theory of the Leisure Class: An Economic Study in the Evolution of Institutions* (New York, 1899), from chs. ii, iii, iv. By special arrangement with the Viking Press.

substantially a struggle for subsistence. Such is, no doubt, its character in large part during the earlier and less efficient phases of industry. Such is also its character in all cases where the "niggardliness of nature" is so strict as to afford but a scanty livelihood to the community in return for strenuous and unremitting application to the business of getting the means of subsistence. But in all progressing communities an advance is presently made beyond this early stage of technological development. Industrial efficiency is presently carried to such a pitch as to afford something appreciably more than a bare livelihood to those engaged in the industrial process. It has not been unusual for economic theory to speak of the further struggle for wealth on this new industrial basis as a competition for an increase of the comforts of life,—primarily for an increase of the physical comforts which the consumption of goods affords.

The end of acquisition and accumulation is conventionally held to be the consumption of the goods accumulated—whether it is consumption directly by the owner of the goods or by the household attached to him and for this purpose identified with him in theory. This is at least felt to be the economically legitimate end of acquisition, which alone it is incumbent on the theory to take account of. Such consumption may of course be conceived to serve the consumer's physical wants—his physical comfort—or his so-called higher wants—spiritual, aesthetic, intellectual, or what not; the latter class of wants being served indirectly by an expenditure of goods, after the fashion familiar to all economic readers.

But it is only when taken in a sense far removed from its naïve meaning that consumption of goods can be said to afford the incentive from which accumulation invariably proceeds. The motive that lies at the root of ownership is emulation; and the same motive of emulation continues active in the further development of the institution to which it has given rise and in the development of all those features of the social structure which this institution of ownership touches. The possession of wealth confers honour; it is an invidious distinction. Nothing equally cogent can be said for the consumption of goods, nor for any other conceivable incentive to acquisition, and especially not for any incentive to the accumulation of wealth. . . .

Ch. iii.   Conspicuous Leisure.

If its working were not disturbed by other economic forces or other features of the emulative process, the immediate effect of such a pecuniary struggle as has just been described in outline would be to make men industrious and frugal. This result actually follows, in some measure, so far as regards the lower classes, whose ordinary means of acquiring goods is productive labour. This is more especially true of the labouring classes in a sedentary community which is at an agricultural stage of industry, in which there is a considerable subdivision of property, and whose laws and customs secure to these classes a more or less definite share of the product of their industry. These lower classes can in any case not avoid labour, and the imputation of labour is therefore not greatly derogatory to them, at least not within their class. Rather, since labour is their recognised and accepted mode of life, they take some emulative pride in a reputation for efficiency in their work, this being often the only line of emulation that is open to them. For those for whom acquisition and emulation is possible only within the field of productive efficiency and thrift, the struggle for pecuniary reputability will in some measure work out in an increase of diligence and parsimony. But certain secondary features of the emulative process, yet to be spoken of, come in to very materially circumscribe and modify emulation in these directions among the pecuniarily inferior classes as well as among the superior class.

But it is otherwise with the superior pecuniary class, with which we are here immediately concerned. For this class also the incentive to diligence and thrift is not absent; but its action is so greatly qualified by the secondary demands of pecuniary emulation, that any inclination in this direction is practically overborne and any incentive to diligence tends to be of no effect. The most imperative of these secondary demands of emulation, as well as the one of widest scope, is the requirement of abstention from productive work. This is true in an especial degree for the barbarian stage of culture. During the predatory culture labour comes to be associated in men's habits of thought with weakness and subjection to a master. It is therefore a mark of inferiority, and therefore comes to be accounted unworthy of man in his best estate. By virtue of this tradition labour is felt to be debasing, and this tradition has never died out. On the contrary, with the advance of social differ-entiation it has acquired the axiomatic force due to ancient and un-questioned prescription.

In order to gain and to hold the esteem of men it is not sufficient merely to possess wealth or power. The wealth or power must be put in evidence, for esteem is awarded only on evidence. And not only does the evidence of wealth serve to impress one's importance on others and to keep their sense of his importance alive and alert, but it is of scarcely less use in building up and preserving one's self-complacency. In all but the lowest stages of culture the normally constituted man is comforted and upheld in his self-respect by "de-cent surroundings" and by exemption from "menial offices." En-forced departure from his habitual standard of decency, either in the paraphernalia of life or in the kind and amount of his everyday activity, is felt to be a slight upon his human dignity, even apart from all conscious consideration of the approval or disapproval of his fellows.

The archaic theoretical distinction between the base and the honourable in the manner of a man's life retains very much of its ancient force even to-day. So much so that there are few of the better class who are not possessed of an instinctive repugnance for the vulgar forms of labour. We have a realising sense of ceremonial uncleanness attaching in an especial degree to the occupations which are associated in our habits of thought with menial service. It is felt by all persons of refined taste that a spiritual contamination is inseparable from certain offices that are conventionally required of servants. Vulgar surroundings, mean (that is to say, inexpen-sive) habitations, and vulgarly productive occupations are unhesi-tatingly condemned and avoided. They are incompatible with life on a satisfactory spiritual plane—with "high thinking." From the days of the Greek philosophers to the present, a degree of leisure and of exemption from contact with such industrial processes as serve the immediate everyday purposes of human life has ever been recognised by thoughtful men as a prerequisite to a worthy or beau-tiful, or even a blameless, human life. In itself and in its conse-quences the life of leisure is beautiful and ennobling in all civilised men's eyes. . . .

Ch. iv. Conspicuous Consumption. . . .

During the earlier stages of economic development, consumption
of goods without stint, especially consumption of the better grades
of goods,—ideally all consumption in excess of the subsistence minimum,—pertains normally to the leisure class. This restriction
tends to disappear, at least formally, after the later peaceable stage
has been reached, with private ownership of goods and an industrial system based on wage labour or on the petty household economy. But during the earlier quasi-peaceable stage, when so many
of the traditions through which the institution of a leisure class has
affected the economic life of later times were taking form and consistency, this principle has had the force of a conventional law. It
has served as the norm to which consumption has tended to conform, and any appreciable departure from it is to be regarded as
an aberrant form, sure to be eliminated sooner or later in the further course of development.

The quasi-peaceable gentleman of leisure, then, not only consumes of the staff of life beyond the minimum required for subsistence and physical efficiency, but his consumption also under-
goes a specialisation as regards the quality of the goods consumed.
He consumes freely and of the best, in food, drink, narcotics, shelter, services, ornaments, apparel, weapons and accoutrements,
amusements, amulets, and idols or divinities. In the process of
gradual amelioration which takes place in the articles of his consumption, the motive principle and the proximate aim of innovation is no doubt the higher efficiency of the improved and more
elaborate products for personal comfort and well-being. But that
does not remain the sole purpose of their consumption. The canon
of reputability is at hand and seizes upon such innovations as are,
according to its standard, fit to survive. Since the consumption of
these more excellent goods is an evidence of wealth, it becomes
honorific; and conversely, the failure to consume in due quantity
and quality becomes a mark of inferiority and demerit.

This growth of punctilious discrimination as to qualitative excellence in eating, drinking, etc., presently affects not only the manner
of life, but also the training and intellectual activity of the gentleman of leisure. He is no longer simply the successful, aggressive
male,—the man of strength, resource, and intrepidity. In order
to avoid stultification he must also cultivate his tastes, for it now

becomes incumbent on him to discriminate with some nicety between the noble and the ignoble in consumable goods. He becomes a connoisseur in creditable viands of various degrees of merit,
in manly beverages and trinkets, in seemly apparel and architecture,
in weapons, games, dances, and the narcotics. This cultivation of
the aesthetic faculty requires time and application, and the demands made upon the gentleman in this direction therefore tend
to change his life of leisure into a more or less arduous application
to the business of learning how to live a life of ostensible leisure in
a becoming way. Closely related to the requirement that the gentleman must consume freely and of the right kind of goods, there
is the requirement that he must know how to consume them in a
seemly manner. His life of leisure must be conducted in due form.
Hence arise good manners in the way pointed out in an earlier
chapter. High-bred manners and ways of living are items of conformity to the norm of conspicuous leisure and conspicuous consumption.

Conspicuous consumption of valuable goods is a means of reputability to the gentleman of leisure. As wealth accumulates on his
hands, his own unaided effort will not avail to sufficiently put his
opulence in evidence by this method. The aid of friends and competitors is therefore brought in by resorting to the giving of valuable
presents and expensive feasts and entertainments. Presents and
feasts had probably another origin than that of naïve ostentation,
but they acquired their utility for this purpose very early, and they
have retained that character to the present; so that their utility in
this respect has now long been the substantial ground on which
these usages rest. Costly entertainments, such as the potlatch or
the ball, are peculiarly adapted to serve this end. The competitor
with whom the entertainer wishes to institute a comparison is, by
this method, made to serve as a means to the end. He consumes
vicariously for his host at the same time that he is a witness to the
consumption of that excess of good things which his host is unable
to dispose of single-handed, and he is also made to witness his
host's facility in etiquette.

In the giving of costly entertainments other motives, of a more
genial kind, are of course also present. The custom of festive gath-
erings probably originated in motives of conviviality and religion;
these motives are also present in the later development, but they

do not continue to be the sole motives. The latter-day leisure-class festivities and entertainments may continue in some slight degree to serve the religious need and in a higher degree the needs of recreation and conviviality, but they also serve an invidious purpose; and they serve it none the less effectually for having a colourable non-invidious ground in these more avowable motives. But the economic effect of these social amenities is not therefore lessened, either in the vicarious consumption of goods or in the exhibition of difficult and costly achievements in etiquette. . . .

From the foregoing survey of the growth of conspicuous leisure and consumption, it appears that the utility of both alike for the purposes of reputability lies in the element of waste that is common to both. In the one case it is a waste of time and effort, in the other it is a waste of goods. Both are methods of demonstrating the possession of wealth, and the two are conventionally accepted as equivalents. The choice between them is a question of advertising expediency simply, except so far as it may be affected by other standards of propriety, springing from a different source. On grounds of expediency the preference may be given to the one or the other at different stages of the economic development. The question is, which of the two methods will most effectively reach the persons whose convictions it is desired to affect. Usage has answered this question in different ways under different circumstances. . . .

But there are other standards of repute and other, more or less imperative, canons of conduct, besides wealth and its manifestation, and some of these come in to accentuate or to qualify the broad, fundamental canon of conspicuous waste. Under the simple test of effectiveness for advertising, we should expect to find leisure and the conspicuous consumption of goods dividing the field of pecuniary emulation pretty evenly between them at the outset. Leisure might then be expected gradually to yield ground and tend to obsolescence as the economic development goes forward, and the community increases in size; while the conspicuous consumption of goods should gradually gain in importance, both absolutely and relatively, until it had absorbed all the available product, leaving nothing over beyond a bare livelihood. But the actual course of development has been somewhat different from this ideal scheme.

Leisure held the first place at the start, and came to hold a rank very much above wasteful consumption of goods, both as a direct exponent of wealth and as an element in the standard of decency, during the quasi-peaceable culture. From that point onward, consumption has gained ground, until, at present, it unquestionably holds the primacy, though it is still far from absorbing the entire margin of production above the subsistence minimum.

The early ascendency of leisure as a means of reputability is traceable to the archaic distinction between noble and ignoble employments. Leisure is honourable and becomes imperative partly because it shows exemption from ignoble labour. The archaic differentiation into noble and ignoble classes is based on an invidious distinction between employments as honorific or debasing; and this traditional distinction grows into an imperative canon of decency during the early quasi-peaceable stage. Its ascendency is furthered by the fact that leisure is still fully as effective an evidence of wealth as consumption. Indeed, so effective is it in the relatively small and stable human environment to which the individual is exposed at that cultural stage, that, with the aid of the archaic tradition which deprecates all productive labour, it gives rise to a large impecunious leisure class, and it even tends to limit the production of the community's industry to the subsistence minimum. This extreme inhibition of industry is avoided because slave labour, working under a compulsion more rigorous than that of reputability, is forced to turn out a product in excess of the subsistence minimum of the working class. The subsequent relative decline in the use of conspicuous leisure as a basis of repute is due partly to an increasing relative effectiveness of consumption as an evidence of wealth; but in part it is traceable to another force, alien, and in some degree antagonistic, to the usage of conspicuous waste.

This alien factor is the instinct of workmanship. Other circumstances permitting, that instinct disposes men to look with favour upon productive efficiency and on whatever is of human use. It disposes them to deprecate waste of substance or effort. The instinct of workmanship is present in all men, and asserts itself even under very adverse circumstances. So that however wasteful a given expenditure may be in reality, it must at least have some colourable excuse in the way of an ostensible purpose. The manner in which, under special circumstances, the instinct eventuates in a taste for exploit and an invidious discrimination between noble and ignoble classes has been indicated in an earlier chapter. In so far as it comes into conflict with the law of conspicuous waste, the instinct of workmanship expresses itself not so much in insistence on substantial usefulness as in an abiding sense of the odiousness and aesthetic impossibility of what is obviously futile. Being of the nature of an instinctive affection, its guidance touches chiefly and immediately the obvious and apparent violations of its requirements. It is only less promptly and with less constraining force that it reaches such substantial violations of its requirements as are appreciated only upon reflection.

So long as all labour continues to be performed exclusively or usually by slaves, the baseness of all productive effort is too constantly and deterrently present in the mind of men to allow the instinct of workmanship seriously to take effect in the direction of industrial usefulness; but when the quasi-peaceable stage (with slavery and status) passes into the peaceable stage of industry (with wage labour and cash payment) the instinct comes more effectively into play. It then begins aggressively to shape men's views of what is meritorious, and asserts itself at least as an auxiliary canon of self-complacency. All extraneous considerations apart, those persons (adults) are but a vanishing minority to-day who harbour no inclination to the accomplishment of some end, or who are not impelled of their own motion to shape some object or fact or relation for human use. The propensity may in large measure be overborne by the more immediately constraining incentive to a reputable leisure and an avoidance of indecorous usefulness, and it may therefore work itself out in make-believe only; as for instance in "social duties," and in quasi-artistic or quasi-scholarly accomplishments, in the care and decoration of the house, in sewing-circle activity or dress reform, in proficiency at dress, cards, yachting, golf, and various sports. But the fact that it may under stress of circumstances eventuate in inanities no more disproves the presence of the instinct than the reality of the brooding instinct is disproved by inducing a hen to sit on a nestful of china eggs. . . .

From *THE THEORY OF BUSINESS ENTERPRISE (1904)*[1]

Ch. viii. Business Principles in Law and Politics.

Popular welfare is bound up with the conduct of business; because industry is managed for business ends, and also because there prevails throughout modern communities a settled habit of rating the means of livelihood and the amenities of life in pecuniary terms. But apart from their effect in controlling the terms of livelihood from day to day, these principles are also in great measure decisive in the larger affairs of life, both for the individual in his civil relations and for the community at large in its political concerns. Modern (civilized) institutions rest, in great part, on business principles. This is the meaning, as applied to the modern situation, of the current phrases about the Economic Interpretation of History, or the Materialistic Theory of History.

Because of this settled habit of seeing all the conjunctures of life from the business point of view, in terms of profit and loss, the management of the affairs of the community at large falls by common consent into the hands of business men and is guided by business considerations. Hence modern politics is business politics, even apart from the sinister application of the phrase to what is invidiously called corrupt politics. This is true both of foreign and domestic policy. Legislation, police surveillance, the administration of justice, the military and diplomatic service, all are chiefly concerned with business relations, pecuniary interests, and they have little more than an incidental bearing on other human interests. All this apparatus is also charged with the protection of life and personal liberty, but its work in this bearing has much of a pecuniary color.

Legislation and legal decisions are based on the dogma of Natural Liberty. This is peculiarly true as regards the English-speaking peoples, the foundation of whose jurisprudence is the common law, and it holds true in an especial degree of America. In other European communities the sway of natural-rights preconceptions is not so unmitigated, but even with them there is a visibly growing

[1] Thorstein Veblen, *The Theory of Business Enterprise* (New York, 1904), at pp. 268–280, 288–292. By special arrangement with Charles Scribner's Sons.

predilection for the natural-rights standpoint in all matters touching business relations. The dogma of natural liberty is peculiarly conducive to an expeditious business traffic and peculiarly consonant with the habits of thought which necessarily prevail in any business community.

The current body of natural-rights preconceptions antedates the modern business situation. The scheme of natural rights grew up and found secure lodgement in the common sense of the community, as well as with its lawgivers and courts, under the discipline of the small industry and petty trade ("domestic industry") whose development culminated in the eighteenth century. In industrial matters the efficient and autonomous factor in the days of the small industry was the individual workman, his personal force, dexterity, and diligence; similarly in the petty trade of the precapitalistic English situation the decisive factor was the discretion and sagacity of the small merchant and the petty employer, who stood in direct personal relations with their customers and their employees. In so far as trade and industry was not restrained by conventional regulations, statutory or customary, both trade and industry was in effect an open field of free competition, in which man met man on a somewhat equable footing. While the competitors were not on a footing of material equality, the industrial system was sufficiently loose-jointed, of a sufficiently diffuse growth, to make competition effective in the absence of mandatory restrictions. The like will hold of the business organization associated with the small industry. Both trade and industry were matters of personal efficiency rather than comprehensively organized processes of an impersonal character.

Natural rights, as they found their way into the conceptions of law and equity, were in effect the assumed equal rights of men so situated on a plane of at least constructive equality that the individuals concerned would be left in a position of effectively free choice if conventional restrictions were done away. The organization was not, mechanically, a close-knit one, in the sense that the concatenation of industrial processes or of business transactions was not rigorous either in point of time relations or of the quantity and character of the output or the work. Neither were the place, pace, circumstances, means, or hours of work closely determined for the workman or his employer by mechanical circumstances of the industrial process or of the market. The standardization of life under the old régime was of a conventional character, not of a mechanical kind such as is visible in the more recent development. And this conventional standardization was gradually losing force.

The movement of opinion on natural-rights ground converged to an insistence on the system of natural liberty, so called. But this insistence on natural liberty did not contemplate the abrogation of all conventional prescription. "The simple and obvious system of natural liberty" meant freedom from restraint on any other prescriptive ground than that afforded by the rights of ownership. In its economic bearing the system of natural liberty meant a system of free pecuniary contract. "Liberty does not mean license;" which in economic terms would be transcribed, "The natural freedom of the individual must not traverse the prescriptive rights of property." Property rights being included among natural rights, they had the indefeasibility which attaches to natural rights. Natural liberty prescribes freedom to buy and sell, limited only by the equal freedom of others to buy and sell; with the obvious corollary that there must be no interference with others' buying and selling, except by means of buying and selling.

This principle of natural (pecuniary) liberty has found its most unmitigated acceptance in America, and has here taken the firmest hold on the legal mind. Nowhere else has the sacredness of pecuniary obligations so permeated the common sense of the community, and nowhere does pecuniary obligation come so near being the only form of obligation that has the unqualified sanction of current common sense. Here, as nowhere else, do obligations and claims of the most diverse kinds, domestic, social, and civil, tend to take the pecuniary form and admit of being fully discharged on a monetary valuation. To a greater extent than elsewhere public esteem is awarded to artists, actors, preachers, writers, scientists, officials, in some rough proportion to the sums paid for their work.

American civil rights have taken an extreme form, with relatively great stress on the inviolability of pecuniary relations, due to the peculiar circumstances under which the American community has grown up. The pioneers, especially in that North-Atlantic seaboard community that has been chiefly effective in shaping American traditions, brought with them a somewhat high-wrought variant of the English preconception in favor of individual discretion, and this tradition they put in practice under circumstances peculiarly favorable to a bold development. They brought little of the remnants of that prescriptive code that once bound the handicraft system, and the conditions of life in the colonies did not foster a new growth of conventional regulations circumscribing private initiative. America is the native habitat of the self-made man, and the self-made man is a pecuniary organism.

Presently, when occasion arose, the metaphysics of natural liberty, pecuniary and other, was embodied in set form in constitutional enactments. It is therefore involved in a more authentic form and with more incisive force in the legal structure of this community than in that of any other. Freedom of contract is the fundamental tenet of the legal creed, so to speak, inviolable and inalienable; and within the province of law and equity no one has competence to penetrate behind this first premise or to question the merits of the natural-rights metaphysics on which it rests. The only principle (attested habit of thought) which may contest its primacy in civil matters is a vague "general welfare" clause; and even this can effectively contest its claims only under exceptional circumstances. Under the application of any general welfare clause the presumption is and always must be that the principle of free contract be left intact so far as the circumstances of the case permit. The citizen may not be deprived of life, liberty, or property without due process of law, and the due process proceeds on the premise that property rights are inviolable. In its bearing upon the economic relations between individuals this comes to mean, in effect, not only that one individual or group of individuals may not legally bring any other than pecuniary pressure to bear upon another individual or group, but also that pecuniary pressure cannot be barred.

Now, through gradual change of the economic situation, this conventional principle of unmitigated and inalienable freedom of contract began to grow obsolete from about the time when it was fairly installed; obsolescent, of course, not in point of law, but in point of fact. Since about the time when this new conventional standardization of the scheme of economic life in terms of free contract reached its mature development, in the eighteenth century,[1] a new standardizing force, that of the machine process, has

---

[1] This date is true for England. For America the discipline favorable to the growth of the natural-liberty dogma lasted nearly a century longer. In America the new,

invaded the field. The standardization and the constraint of the system of machine industry differs from what went before it in that it has had no conventional recognition, no metaphysical authentication. It has not become a legal fact. Therefore it neither need nor can be taken account of by the legal mind. It is a new fact which fits into the framework neither of the ancient system of prescriptive usage nor of the later system of free personal initiative. It does not exist *de jure*, but only *de facto*. Belonging neither to the defunct system nor to the current legal system, since it neither constitutes nor traverses a "natural right," it is, as within the cognizance of the law, non-existent. It is, perhaps, actual, with a gross, material actuality; but it is not real, with a legal, metaphysically competent reality. Such coercion as it may exert, or as may be exercised through its means, therefore, is, in point of legal reality, no coercion.

Where physical impossibility to fulfil the terms of a contract arises out of the concatenation of industrial processes, this physical impossibility may be pleaded as invalidating the terms of the contract. But the pecuniary pressure of price or subsistence which the sequence and interdependence of industrial processes may bring to bear has no standing as such in law or equity; it can reach the cognizance of the law only indirectly, through gross defection of one of the contracting parties, in those cases where the pressure is severe enough to result in insolvency, sickness, or death. The material necessities of a group of workmen or consumers, enforced by the specialization and concatenation of industrial processes, is, therefore, not competent to set aside, or indeed to qualify, the natural freedom of the owners of these processes to let work go on or not, as the outlook for profits may decide. Profits is a business proposition, livelihood is not.

---

modern, technological and business era can scarcely be said to have set in in good vigor until the period of the Civil War. Hence, with a longer and later training, the preconceptions of natural liberty are fresher and more tenacious in America. For the Continental peoples the case is different again. With them the modern technological and business situation is of approximately the same date as in America, but their training up to the date of the transition to the modern situation was in a much less degree a training in individual initiative, free scattered industry, and petty trade. The Continental peoples for the most part made a somewhat abrupt transition after the middle of the nineteenth century from a stale and dilapidated system of guild and feudalistic prescriptions to the (for them) exotic system of modern technology and business principles. [Author's note.]

Under the current *de facto* standardization of economic life enforced by the machine industry, it may frequently happen that an individual or a group, e.g., of workmen, has not a *de facto* power of free contract. A given workman's livelihood can perhaps, practically, be found only on acceptance of one specific contract offered, perhaps not at all. But the coercion which in this way bears upon his choice through the standardization of industrial procedure is neither assault and battery nor breach of contract, and it is, therefore, not repugnant to the principles of natural liberty. Through controlling the processes of industry in which alone, practically, given workmen can find their livelihood, the owners of these processes may bring pecuniary pressure to bear upon the choice of the workmen; but since the rights of property which enforce such pressure are not repugnant to the principles of natural liberty, neither is such pecuniary pressure repugnant to the law,—the case is therefore outside the scope of the law. The converse case, where the workmen take similar advantage of their employers to bring them to terms, is similarly outside the scope of the common law,—supposing, of course, that there has in neither case been a surrender of individual liberty, a breach of contract, theft, a resort to violence, or threats of violence. So long as there is no overt attempt on life, liberty of the person, or the liberty to buy and sell, the law cannot intervene, unless it be in a precautionary way to prevent prospective violation of personal or property rights.

The "natural," conventional freedom of contract is sacred and inalienable. *De facto* freedom of choice is a matter about which the law and the courts are not competent to inquire. By force of the concatenation of industrial processes and the dependence of men's comfort or subsistence upon the orderly working of these processes, the exercise of the rights of ownership in the interests of business may traverse the *de facto* necessities of a group or class; it may even traverse the needs of the community at large, as, e.g., in the conceivable case of an advisedly instituted coal famine; but since these necessities, of comfort or of livelihood, cannot be formulated in terms of the natural freedom of contract, they can, in the nature of the case, give rise to no cognizable grievance and find no legal remedy.

The discrepancy between law and fact in the matter of industrial freedom has had repeated illustration in the court decisions on disputes between bodies of workmen and their employers or owners. These decisions commonly fall out in favor of the employers or owners; that is to say, they go to uphold property rights and the rights of free contract. The courts have been somewhat broadly taken to task by a certain class of observers for alleged partiality to the owners' side in this class of litigation. It has also been pointed out by faultfinders that the higher courts decide, on the whole, more uniformly in favor of the employer-owner than the lower ones, and especially more so than the juries in those cases where juries have found occasion to pass on the law of the case. The like is true as regards suits for damages arising out of injuries sustained by workmen, and so involving the question of the employer's liability. Even a casual scrutiny of the decisions, however, will show that in most cases the decision of the court, whether on the merits of the case or on the constitutionality of the legal provisions involved,[1] is well grounded on the metaphysical basis of natural liberty. That is to say in other words, the decisions will be found on the side of the maintenance of fundamental law and order, "law and order" having, of course, reference to the inalienable rights of ownership and contract. As should fairly be expected, the higher courts, who are presumably in more intimate touch with the principles of jurisprudence, being more arduously trained and more thoroughly grounded in the law at the same time that they have also presumably a larger endowment of legal acumen,—these higher courts speak more unequivocally for the metaphysical principles and apply them with a surer and firmer touch. In the view of these higher adepts of the law, free contract is so inalienable a natural right of man that not even a statutory enactment will enable a workman to forego its exercise and its responsibility. By metaphysical necessity its exercise attaches to the individual so indefeasibly that it cannot constitutionally be delegated to collective action, whether legislative or corporate.[2] This extreme

[1] E.g., as to employer's liability for accidents or unsanitary premises, the safeguarding of machinery, age limit of laborers or hour limit of working time, etc. [Author's note.]

[2] E.g. where a workman's accepting employment on machinery which is not safeguarded as the law requires is construed as an exercise of the indefeasible right of free contract on his part, which thereby exempts the employer from liability for eventual accidents. [Author's note.]

consequence of the principle of natural liberty has at times aroused indignation in the vulgar; but their grasp of legal principles is at fault. The more closely the logical sequence is followed up, the more convincingly does the legitimacy of such a decision stand out. . . .

The ground of sentiment on which rests the popular approval of a government for business ends may be summed up under two heads: patriotism and property. Both of these terms stand for institutional facts that have come down out of a past which differed substantially from the present situation. The substance of both is of the nature of unreasoning sentiment, in the sense that both are insisted on as a matter of course, as self-legitimating grounds of action which, it is felt, not only give expedient rules of conduct, but admit of no question as to their ulterior consequences or their value for the life-purposes of the community. The former of these fundamental institutional habits of thought (perhaps better, habits of mind) runs back to the discipline of early barbarism, through the feudal days of fealty to the earlier days of clan life and clannish animosity. It has therefore the deep-rooted strength given by an extremely protracted discipline of predation and servitude. Under modern conditions it is to be rated as essentially an institutional survival, so ingrained in the populace as to make any appeal to it secure of a response irrespective of the material merits of the contention in whose behalf the appeal is made.

By force of this happy knack of clannish fancy the common man is enabled to feel that he has some sort of metaphysical share in the gains which accrue to the business men who are citizens of the same "commonwealth"; so that whatever policy furthers the commercial gains of those business men whose domicile is within the national boundaries is felt to be beneficial to all the rest of the population.

The second institutional support of business politics, viz. property, is similarly an outgrowth of the discipline of the past, and similarly, though perhaps in a less degree, out of touch with the discipline of the more recent cultural situation. In the form in which it prevails in the current popular animus, the principle of ownership comes down from the days of handicraft industry and petty trade, as pointed out above. As it is of less ancient and less unbroken descent, so it seems also to be a less secure cultural heritage than the sense of patriotic solidarity. It says that the ownership of property is the material foundation of human well-being, and that this natural right of ownership is sacred, after the manner in which individual life, and more especially national life, is sacred. The habits of life and thought inculcated by joint work under the manorial system and by joint rules under the handicraft system have apparently contributed much to the notion of a solidarity of economic interests, having given the notion such a degree of consistency as has enabled it to persist in the face of a visible discrepancy of interests in later, capitalistic times. Under this current, business régime, business gains are the basis of individual wealth, and the (pseudo) notion of joint acquisition has taken the place of the manorial notion of joint work. The institutional animus of ownership, as it took shape under the discipline of early modern handicraft, awards the ownership of property to the workman who has produced it. By a dialectical conversion of the terms, this metaphysical dictum is made to fit the circumstances of later competitive business by construing acquisition of property to mean production of wealth; so that a business man is looked upon as the putative producer of whatever wealth he acquires. By force of this sophistication the acquisition of property by any person is held to be, not only expedient for the owner, but meritorious as an action serving the common good. Failure to bargain shrewdly or to accumulate more goods than one has produced by the work of one's own hands is looked upon with a feeling of annoyance, as a neglect, not only of opportunity, but of duty. The pecuniary conscience commonly does not, of course, go to quixotic lengths in a public-spirited insistence on everybody's acquiring more than an aliquot part of the aggregate wealth on hand, but it is felt that he best serves the common good who, other things equal, diverts the larger share of the aggregate wealth to his own possession. His acquiring a defensible title to it makes him the putative producer of it.

The natural-rights basis of ownership is by this paralogism preserved intact, and the common man is enabled to feel that the business men in the community add to the aggregate wealth at least as much as they acquire a title to; and the successful business men are at least as well persuaded that such is their relation to the aggregate wealth and to the material well-being of the community at large. So that both the business men whose gains are sought to be enhanced by business politics and the populace by whose means the business gains are secured work together in good faith towards a well-advised business end,—the accumulation of wealth in the hands of those men who are skilled in pecuniary matters. . . .

19. CHARLES A. BEARD (1874–   )

CHARLES A. BEARD, formerly a professor of politics at Columbia University, is the author of numerous works in the fields of European and American history and politics, and has been president of both the American Political Science and the American Historical Associations. He was director of the Training School of Public Service in New York City (1917–22) and adviser to the Institute of Municipal Research in Tokio (1922) and to the Japanese minister of home affairs, after the earthquake of 1923. His books include the *Economic Interpretation of the Constitution* (1913), *The Economic Origins of Jeffersonian Democracy* (1915), *The Supreme Court and the Constitution* (1912), *The Idea of National Interest* (1934); also (with Mary Ritter Beard) *The Rise of American Civilization* (1927) and *America in Midpassage* (1939); and (with George H. E. Smith) *The Open Door at Home* (1934) and *The Old Deal and the New* (1940).

From THE ECONOMIC BASIS OF POLITICS (1922, 1934)[1]

Economic Groups and the Structure of the State. . . .

An examination of the first American state constitutions reveals no abandonment of the Old-World notion that government rests upon property. Take, for instance, the Massachusetts Constitution of 1780 drawn by John Adams and adopted after long and serious deliberation. In this document we discover that no man could vote for members of the legislature or for governor, unless he had a freehold estate of the annual value of three pounds, or some estate of the value of sixty pounds. Here is a distinct recognition of two classes of property interests in the government,— real property and personalty. To add further security to the two orders or "estates" the constitution provided that no one could be elected governor who did not possess a freehold of the value of one thousand pounds, and furthermore, that the senators should

[1] Charles A. Beard, *The Economic Basis of Politics* (New York, 1922, rev. ed., 1934), from chs. ii, iii, iv. By special arrangement with Alfred A. Knopf.

be distributed among the respective districts of the state on the score of the amount of taxes paid in each of them. It was in defence of this last provision that Daniel Webster made his famous speech in the Massachusetts convention of 1820, defending the economic basis of government. If the Massachusetts constitution proved to be rather democratic in its operations, that was, as Webster pointed out, due to the wide distribution of property, not to any desire of the Massachusetts Fathers to sacrifice the security of property to a political shibboleth. . . .

Admitting the plain evidence of the first state constitutions, that the wise founders of this Republic recognized the place of property interests in political processes, it may be said that the Constitution of the United States, drawn in that period, nowhere takes into account the existence of economic divisions. This is true, if we read merely the language of the instrument and not the records of the convention which drafted it. In the document itself there are no provisions similar to those which appear in the first state constitutions, placing landed- and personal-property qualifications on the suffrage and office holding; but the omission was not made because the framers of that immortal instrument were indifferent to the rights of property or unaware of the influence wielded by economic groups upon the course of government. Neither was it because they disapproved of property qualifications, for such existed in nearly every state in the Union. In fact property qualifications for officers and for voters were proposed in the convention, but it was impossible to agree on their precise form. Inasmuch as many of the troubles under the Articles of the Confederation had arisen from attacks on capital by state legislatures elected by freeholders, and inasmuch as the convention was especially eager to safeguard the rights of personal property, a freehold qualification did not seem to offer an adequate remedy. On the other hand, to impose a large personal-property qualification on voters would have meant the defeat of the Constitution by the farmers who were, of necessity, called upon to ratify it. Under the circumstances the framers of the Constitution relied, not upon direct economic qualifications, but upon checks and balances to secure the rights of property—particularly personal property—against the assaults of the farmers and the proletariat. . . .

The Doctrine of Political Equality.

The great political philosophers, with few exceptions, have regarded property as the fundamental element in political power, and have looked upon a constitution as a balance of economic groups. The governments founded and developed before the nineteenth century were in fact complexes of group interests. Nowhere was the representative system, in its origin, designed to reflect the opinions of mere numerical aggregations of human beings considered in the abstract apart from property and employment. On the contrary, it reflected the sentiments and views of different sorts and conditions of men, estates or orders: clergy, nobility, burghers, and peasants.

In the United States where there was no clerical estate or established nobility to be represented in the government, the existence of the two fundamental property groups—the owners of realty and the owners of personalty—was taken into account either in positive constitutional law or in the check and balance system provided by the separation of powers. If the first American constitutions were more democratic than those of Europe, the fact is not to be attributed to radical changes in human nature, induced by a voyage across the Atlantic, but, as the great Webster pointed out, to a very wide distribution of property, due mainly to cheap land.

So things stood in the closing years of the old régime. Then suddenly came two great revolutions, one in economic fact, and the other in political theory. The first was brought about by the invention of the steam engine and machinery, creating an immense amount of property which had hitherto existed only as a minor element in economic life, namely, industrial and mercantile capital. So rapidly did this new form of property accumulate that even in the United States, by the middle of the nineteenth century, it exceeded in value the agricultural land of the country.

Being more mobile and more easily concentrated than land, a vast portion of it quickly fell into the hands of, relatively speaking, a small portion of society. As land was the great stabilizer of the old order, so capital became the great disturber in the new order. Like a mighty giant tossing to and fro in a fever, in its quest for profits, it tore masses of men from the land, from their sleepy villages and hamlets, and hurled them here and there all over the globe. Under its influence the old sharp class differences were disarranged. The peasant might become a successful cotton spinner, a financial magnate, a contributor to party war-chests, a peer of the realm. The Manchester individualists, Cobden and Bright, looking upon the new order which they had helped to create, pronounced it good and declared that because any hustling individual might rise from poverty to wealth, the era of *individual* equality had arrived. Instead of studying the new groups, the new class divisions, more subtle and complex than ever before, they proclaimed the glad day of equality.

While James Watt was experimenting in Glasgow with the steam engine, and thus preparing to blow up the old economic order in the realm of fact, a French philosopher, Jean Jacques Rousseau, was experimenting with ideas scarcely less dangerous to the *ancien régime* than the operations of the Scotch mechanic. Unlike his distinguished predecessor in political science, Montesquieu, Rousseau did not search assiduously among the institutions and habits of mankind to find a basis for his political philosophy. Rousseau was not a man of science or a detached scholar. He was a passionate propagandist. He formulated the sentiments and views of the third estate in France then beginning to thunder against the monarchy, which was buttressed by the special privileges of the clergy and the nobility. In his *Social Contract* he set forth the moral and philosophic justification for the revolt of the third estate. . . .

Having found the origin of society in a general agreement of free and equal men, Rousseau naturally places sovereign power by moral right in "the people"—a collectivity of all the individual members of the state. The law of the state is therefore not the will of some class (like the landed gentry) imposed upon all others, or a compromise rule produced by a balance of conflicting group interests, but is, according to Rousseau, an expression of "the general will." This alone is its justification. . . .

But Rousseau is face to face with the fact that unanimity among citizens is impossible and that the general will cannot be the will of the whole ten thousand or the whole hundred thousand, as the case may be, but must, perforce, be the will of a certain fraction of the citizens. He boldly meets the problem, and following the old philosophers he holds that the exercise of sovereignty is by the majority. The *general will* of which he makes so much, is in practice, the will of a majority. With fine confidence he contends that the will of the majority is right and works for the good of the state. . . .

But it may be asked, how did this levelling doctrine of universal political equality find a foothold in the United States where there were no official clergy and nobility to be overthrown by the third estate? Well, some writers have laboured hard to show that it is a French creation utterly at variance with Anglo-Saxon tradition— whatever that may mean. In the interest of truth, however, it should be said that the free-and-equal doctrine is not French, but English in origin. Its beginnings among English-speaking peoples may be traced to the flood of speculation that broke loose in England during the seventeenth century when the merchants and gentry were engaged in a revolt against the crown and aristocracy— the clergy having been broken a century earlier by the bluff king, Henry VIII, who confiscated much of their property. It was from English defenders of revolution, like John Locke, rather than from French authors, that Jefferson derived the gospel of the Declaration of Independence. Moreover the economic circumstances in the United States were on the whole favorable to the propaganda of that word. There was no established clergy here. There was no titled aristocracy. There was no such proletariat as formed the "mob" of Paris. Land was the chief form of property and its wide distribution among the whites (leaving the slaves out of account) brought about in fact a considerable economic equality to correspond to the theory of political equality.

Moreover, at the time that America was committed to the theory of political equality, the people were engaged in a revolt against the government imposed on them under the authority of Great Britain. Like the third estate in France they needed some effective and compelling justification for their extraordinary conduct. Of course the leaders of the American Revolution could have said coldly: "We are fighting for the plantation owners of the South, the merchants and landed gentry of the North, and the free farmers in both sections, in order that they may govern themselves."

Obviously, such a chilly declaration of fact would not have thrilled the masses, especially the mechanics of the towns who enjoyed no political rights under either system, the old or the new. It was necessary to have something that would ring throughout the country. Hence the grand words of the Declaration of Independence: "All men are created equal" and "governments derive their just powers from the consent of the governed." There were critics ready to point out that these high principles did not square with slavery, indentured servitude, and political disfranchisement, but they did not prevail. In the fervour of the moment, Jefferson, while bent on justifying the revolt against George III, in fact challenged the rule of property which was guaranteed by the state constitutions drafted by his fellow revolutionists in that very epoch. Even Jeffersonians, when confronted, like Rousseau's followers, with the logical consequences of their doctrine shrank from applying it. Nevertheless the grand words stood for all time, and advocates of manhood suffrage and woman suffrage afterward appealed to them with great effect in attacking property and sex qualifications on the right to vote.

When once the free-and-equal doctrine had been let loose in the New World and the Old, it was impossible to check its course. Steadily it made headway against governments founded upon a class basis. Steadily it supplanted the old philosophy of politics which gave to property and to estates a place in the process of government. Within seventy years after the Declaration of Independence the battle for white manhood suffrage was virtually won in the United States. Some remnants of the old system of class privilege in politics remained, but they were regarded as anachronisms. Time was to dispose of them. America was committed to the great doctrine that in politics all heads are equal and all are entitled to the same share of power in the government. . . .

The logical application of Rousseau's doctrine of complete and abstract human equality is clear. It means that the number of members in any legislature shall be apportioned among geographical districts approximately according to the number of inhabitants without reference to their wealth, occupations, or interests. It means that all high public officers shall be elected by majorities or pluralities. Man is to be regarded as a "political" animal. No account is to be taken of those sentiments and views which, as Madison says, arise from the possession of different degrees and kinds of property. All heads are equal and, from the point of view of politics, alike. The statesman is a mathematician concerned with counting heads. The rule of numbers is enthroned. The homage once paid to kings is to be paid to the statistics of election returns.

Surely, in all the history of thought, there is nothing more wonderful than this.

While this political revolution has been going on, have the economic groups once recognized by statesmen and political philosophers disappeared? The answer is emphatic. It is to be found in the census returns, which, as certainly as the doomsday book of William the Conqueror, record the perdurance of group and class interests despite the rhetoric of political equality. It is to be found in practical politics day by day. Does any one think that a thousand farmers or labourers, going on about their tasks, have the same influence in the formation of a protective tariff bill as a thousand manufacturers represented by spokesmen in the lobbies and committee rooms of the Congress of the United States? Does any one suppose that the exemption of trade unions from the provisions of the Sherman Anti-Trust Law was the result of the platonic wishes of "the people," rather than the determined and persistent activity of The American Federation of Labor?

We are therefore confronted by an inherent antagonism between our generally accepted political doctrines, and the actual facts of political life. In the world of natural science men do not tarry long with hypotheses that will not square with observed phenomena. Shall we in the field of political science cling to a delusion that we have to deal only with an abstract man divorced from all economic interests and group sentiments?

The Contradiction and the Outcome. . . .

Nevertheless, the democratic device of universal suffrage does not destroy economic classes or economic inequalities. It ignores them. Herein lies the paradox, the most astounding political contradiction that the world has ever witnessed. Hence the question arises: Has political democracy solved the problem of the ages, wrung the answer from the sphinx? Is it a guarantee against the storms of revolution? Does it make impossible such social conflicts as those which tore ancient societies asunder? Does it afford to mankind a mastery over its social destiny?

To ask these questions is to answer them. Nothing was more obvious in the thinking of western civilization before the outbreak of the World War than dissatisfaction with political democracy. Equally obvious was the discontent with representative government based on the doctrine of abstract numbers and civic equality. Whether one went into the countryside of Oregon or strolled along Quai d'Orsay, one heard lively debates over "the failure of representative government." The initiative and referendum and recall —direct government—more head counting on the theory of numbers and abstract equality, such was the answer of the Far West to the riddle. . . .

The upshot of all this seems to be that in a modern industrial society, the problem of property, so vital in politics, is not as simple as it was in old agricultural societies. It was one thing for peasants to destroy their landlords and go on tilling the soil as they had long been wont to do. It is another thing for workingmen to destroy capitalists as a class and assume all the complex and staggering burdens of management and exchange. It is also clear that, as efficient production depends to a great extent upon skill, skill itself is a form of property even if property in capital is abolished.

In short a great society, whether capitalist or communist, must possess different kinds and grades of skill and talent and carry on widely diversified industries. There must be miners, machinists, electricians, engineers, accountants, transport workers, draftsmen, managers, and a hundred other kinds of specialists. They may be temporarily welded together in a conflict with their capitalist employers, but they will be divided over the distribution of wealth among themselves after the capitalists have been disposed of. Conceivably a highly militarist government might destroy their organizations and level them down, but the result would be ruin of production and of the state itself. Even a communist could hardly defend his system on the theory that all must choose between military despotism and utter ruin.

The grand conclusion, therefore, seems to be exactly that advanced by our own James Madison in the Tenth Number of the Federalist. To express his thought in modern terms: a landed interest, a transport interest, a railway interest, a shipping interest, an engineering interest, a manufacturing interest, a public-official interest, with many lesser interests, grow up of necessity in all great societies and divide them into different classes actuated by different sentiments and views. The regulation of these various and interfering interests, whatever may be the formula for the ownership of property, constitutes the principal task of modern statesmen and involves the spirit of party in the necessary and ordinary operations of government. In other words, there is no rest for mankind, no final solution of eternal contradictions. Such is the design of the universe. The recognition of this fact is the beginning of wisdom —and of statesmanship.

20. THEODORE ROOSEVELT (1858-1919)

THEODORE ROOSEVELT, famed for his colorful verbal assaults on "malefactors of great wealth" and for his vigorous reform activities in local, State, and national politics, was born in New York City of an old and well-to-do New York family. After his graduation from Harvard he studied law, but soon gave that up and chose politics as his career. He was elected to the lower house of the New York legislature at the age of twenty-three and held office for most of the rest of his life. At twenty-five he was a delegate to the Republican National Convention, where he tried unsuccessfully to prevent the presidential nomination of James Blaine, old-guard Republican leader. At twenty-eight he was Republican candidate for mayor of New York City; he was defeated by the Tammany candidate and outrun by the single-taxer, Henry George, a labor-socialist nominee whom some conservative groups in the city feared less than they feared the young Roosevelt. He was aggressively interested in civil service reform and was for six years a member of the United States Civil Service Commission. As president of the board of police commissioners of New York City he worked to clean up slums and drive corruption out of the police department. President McKinley made him an assistant secretary of the navy in 1897; he resigned this office after fourteen months in order to take part in the Spanish-American War. With Leonard Wood (member of the army medical corps and White House physician) he organized the "Rough Riders," a cavalry regiment made up chiefly of men from the cattle ranges and mining camps of the southwest. Part of the regiment reached Cuba and took part (on foot) in the siege of San Juan Hill. He served a term as governor of New York . His vigorous sponsorship of political and economic reform so disturbed the Republican party leaders that they helped secure his nomination for vice-president in 1900. The assassination of President McKinley in September 1901 made him President, and he was elected for a second term.

In foreign policy Theodore Roosevelt was an active "expansionist" and "interventionist." Before becoming President he energetically supported the acquisition of the trans-oceanic colonies of Spain (after the Spanish-American war) and the annexation of Hawaii. As President he brought about (by swift and independent executive action) the acquisition of the Panama canal zone ("I took the Canal Zone and let Congress debate"). He pursued a "big stick" policy toward Latin America and created the "Roosevelt Corollary to the Monroe Doctrine," which established the right of the United States to intervene when Latin-American countries failed to keep domestic order or to pay their foreign debts. He backed the "open door" in China, brought about the Portsmouth conference ending the Russo-Japanese war, and had a hand in the Algeciras conference of 1906. He sent the United States navy on a cruise around the world, which included a "visit" to Japan. After his presidency he advocated an international league to prevent war, by force if necessary; and soon after the outbreak of the World War he demanded active participation by the United States on the side of the Allies.

In domestic policy, Roosevelt, as President, stood somewhere between "regular" Republicans, who urged "hands-off" private business, and "Insurgents" and "Progressives," who demanded a vigorous and varied regulation of business. He did little to upset the conservative leadership of the House and Senate and made a good many concessions in order to avoid a party split. Yet he promoted some successful "anti-trust" prosecutions and secured the enactment of laws for the promotion of public health, the better conservation and utilization of natural resources, and the more effective regulation of inter-state railways. Many congressmen complained that he was usurping legislative powers.

A definite split between conservative and progressive Republicans took place during the administration of President Taft, whose nomination Roosevelt had virtually dictated. Roosevelt, now charging his successor with complete subservience to reactionary leadership, aligned himself wholeheartedly with the insurgents. On a speaking tour through the West in the summer of 1910 he outlined his program for a "square deal" and a "new nationalism." When the progressives failed to wrest control from the old guard in the Republican convention of 1912, he led the secession which resulted in the formation of the National Progressive party. The party, with Roosevelt and Hiram Johnson, reform governor of California, as its standard bearers, adopted a platform calling for political and economic changes then regarded as radical: woman suffrage, direct primaries, the initiative, referendum, and recall, an easier method of amending the Constitution, a popular referendum on State judicial decisions invalidating legislation under the police power, and State and national legislation to prohibit child labor, establish insurance against sickness, unemployment, and old age, and restrain the courts in the issue of injunctions in labor disputes.

Theodore Roosevelt was a prolific, versatile, and spirited writer. Besides his numerous political articles, he wrote a book on the United States navy in the War of 1812, two political biographies, several histories of the American frontier, and descriptions of his hunting and exploring trips. He was "Contributing Editor" of *The Outlook* (a weekly magazine of political opinion) from 1909 to 1914; and he was president of the American Historical Association in 1912.

[Theodore Roosevelt's works fill twenty-four volumes (memorial edition, New York, 1923–26). See also: Henry F. Pringle, *Theodore Roosevelt* (1931); J. B. Bishop, *Theodore Roosevelt and His Time Shown in His Own Letters* (2 vols., 1920).]

From "THE NEW NATIONALISM" (1910) [1]

. . . Our interest is primarily in the application to-day of the lessons taught by the contest of half a century ago. It is of little use for us to pay lip loyalty to the mighty men of the past unless we sincerely endeavor to apply to the problems of the present precisely the qualities which in other crises enabled the men of that day to meet those crises. It is half melancholy and half amusing to see the way in which well-meaning people gather to do honor to the men who, in company with John Brown, and under the lead of Abraham Lincoln, faced and solved the great problems of the nineteenth century, while, at the same time, these same good people nervously shrink from, or frantically denounce, those who are trying to meet the problems of the twentieth century in the spirit which was accountable for the successful solution of the problems of Lincoln's time.

Of that generation of men to whom we owe so much, the man to whom we owe most is, of course, Lincoln. Part of our debt to him is because he forecast our present struggle and saw the way out. He said:—

> I hold that while man exists it is his duty to improve not only his own condition, but to assist in ameliorating mankind.

And again:—

> Labor is prior to, and independent of, capital. Capital is only the fruit of labor, and could never have existed if labor had not first existed. Labor is the superior of capital, and deserves much the higher consideration.

[1] A Speech before the "Grand Army of the Republic" at Osawatomie, Kansas, August 31, 1910; in *The Works of Theodore Roosevelt*, Memorial Edition, 24 vols. (New York, 1923–1926), Vol. XIX, pp. 13–21, 22–28. By courtesy of The Roosevelt Memorial Association.

If that remark was original with me, I should be even more strongly denounced as a communist agitator than I shall be anyhow. It is Lincoln's. I am only quoting it; and that is one side; that is the side the capitalist should hear. Now, let the workingman hear his side.

> Capital has its rights, which are as worthy of protection as any other rights. . . . Nor should this lead to a war upon the owners of property. Property is the fruit of labor; . . . property is desirable; is a positive good in the world.

And then comes a thoroughly Lincolnlike sentence:—

> Let not him who is houseless pull down the house of another, but let him work diligently and build one for himself, thus by example assuring that his own shall be safe from violence when built.

It seems to me that, in these words, Lincoln took substantially the attitude that we ought to take; he showed the proper sense of proportion in his relative estimates of capital and labor, of human rights and property rights. Above all, in this speech, as in many others, he taught a lesson in wise kindliness and charity; an indispensable lesson to us of to-day. But this wise kindliness and charity never weakened his arm or numbed his heart. We cannot afford weakly to blind ourselves to the actual conflict which faces us to-day. The issue is joined, and we must fight or fail.

In every wise struggle for human betterment one of the main objects, and often the only object, has been to achieve in large measure equality of opportunity. In the struggle for this great end, nations rise from barbarism to civilization, and through it people press forward from one stage of enlightenment to the next. One of the chief factors in progress is the destruction of special privilege. The essence of any struggle for healthy liberty has always been, and must always be, to take from some one man or class of men the right to enjoy power, or wealth, or position, or immunity, which has not been earned by service to his or their fellows. That is what you fought for in the Civil War, and that is what we strive for now.

At many stages in the advance of humanity, this conflict between the men who possess more than they have earned and the men who have earned more than they possess is the central condition of progress. In our day it appears as the struggle of free men to gain and hold the right of self-government as against the special interests, who twist the methods of free government into machinery for defeating the popular will. At every stage, and under all circumstances, the essence of the struggle is to equalize opportunity, destroy privilege, and give to the life and citizenship of every individual the highest possible value both to himself and to the commonwealth. That is nothing new. All I ask in civil life is what you fought for in the Civil War. I ask that civil life be carried on according to the spirit in which the army was carried on. You never get perfect justice, but the effort in handling the army was to bring to the front the men who could do the job. Nobody grudged promotion to Grant, or Sherman, or Thomas, or Sheridan, because they earned it. The only complaint was when a man got promotion which he did not earn.

Practical equality of opportunity for all citizens, when we achieve it, will have two great results. First, every man will have a fair chance to make of himself all that in him lies; to reach the highest point to which his capacities, unassisted by special privilege of his own and unhampered by the special privilege of others, can carry him, and to get for himself and his family substantially what he has earned. Second, equality of opportunity means that the commonwealth will get from every citizen the highest service of which he is capable. No man who carries the burden of the special privileges of another can give to the commonwealth that service to which it is fairly entitled.

I stand for the square deal. But when I say that I am for the square deal, I mean not merely that I stand for fair play under the present rules of the game, but that I stand for having those rules changed so as to work for a more substantial equality of opportunity and of reward for equally good service. One word of warning, which, I think, is hardly necessary in Kansas. When I say I want a square deal for the poor man, I do not mean that I want a square deal for the man who remains poor because he has not got the energy to work for himself. If a man who has had a chance will not make good, then he has got to quit. And you men of the Grand Army, you want justice for the brave man who fought, and punishment for the coward who shirked his work. Is not that so?

Now, this means that our government, national and state, must be freed from the sinister influence or control of special interests.

Exactly as the special interests of cotton and slavery threatened our political integrity before the Civil War, so now the great special business interests too often control and corrupt the men and methods of government for their own profit. We must drive the special interests out of politics. That is one of our tasks to-day. Every special interest is entitled to justice—full, fair, and complete,— and, now, mind you, if there were any attempt by mob violence to plunder and work harm to the special interest, whatever it may be, that I most dislike, and the wealthy man, whomsoever he may be, for whom I have the greatest contempt, I would fight for him, and you would if you were worth your salt. He should have justice. For every special interest is entitled to justice, but not one is entitled to a vote in Congress, to a voice on the bench, or to representation in any public office. The Constitution guarantees protection to property, and we must make that promise good. But it does not give the right of suffrage to any corporation.

The true friend of property, the true conservative, is he who insists that property shall be the servant and not the master of the commonwealth; who insists that the creature of man's making shall be the servant and not the master of the man who made it. The citizens of the United States must effectively control the mighty commercial forces which they have themselves called into being.

There can be no effective control of corporations while their political activity remains. To put an end to it will be neither a short nor an easy task, but it can be done.

We must have complete and effective publicity of corporate affairs, so that the people may know beyond peradventure whether the corporations obey the law and whether their management entitles them to the confidence of the public. It is necessary that laws should be passed to prohibit the use of corporate funds directly or indirectly for political purposes; it is still more necessary that such laws should be thoroughly enforced. Corporate expenditures for political purposes, and especially such expenditures by public service corporations, have supplied one of the principal sources of corruption in our political affairs.

It has become entirely clear that we must have government supervision of the capitalization, not only of public service corporations, including, particularly, railways, but of all corporations doing an interstate business. I do not wish to see the nation forced into the ownership of the railways if it can possibly be avoided, and the only alternative is thoroughgoing and effective regulation, which shall be based on a full knowledge of all the facts, including a physical valuation of property. This physical valuation is not needed, or, at least, is very rarely needed, for fixing rates; but it is needed as the basis of honest capitalization.

We have come to recognize that franchises should never be granted except for a limited time, and never without proper provision for compensation to the public. It is my personal belief that the same kind and degree of control and supervision which should be exercised over public service corporations should be extended also to combinations which control necessaries of life, such as meat, oil, and coal, or which deal in them on an important scale. I have no doubt that the ordinary man who has control of them is much like ourselves. I have no doubt he would like to do well, but I want to have enough supervision to help him realize that desire to do well.

I believe that the officers, and, especially, the directors, of corporations should be held personally responsible when any corporation breaks the law.

Combinations in industry are the result of an imperative economic law which cannot be repealed by political legislation. The effort at prohibiting all combination has substantially failed. The way out lies, not in attempting to prevent such combinations, but in completely controlling them in the interest of the public welfare. For that purpose the Federal Bureau of Corporations is an agency of first importance. Its powers, and, therefore, its efficiency, as well as that of the Interstate Commerce Commission, should be largely increased. We have a right to expect from the Bureau of Corporations and from the Interstate Commerce Commission a very high grade of public service. We should be as sure of the proper conduct of the interstate railways and the proper management of interstate business as we are now sure of the conduct and management of the national banks, and we should have as effective supervision in one case as in the other. The Hepburn Act, and the amendment to the Act in the shape in which it finally passed Congress at the last session, represent a long step in advance, and we must go yet further.

There is a widespread belief among our people that, under the methods of making tariffs which have hitherto obtained, the special interests are too influential. Probably this is true of both the big special interests and the little special interests. These methods have put a premium on selfishness, and, naturally, the selfish big interests have gotten more than their smaller, though equally self-ish, brothers. The duty of Congress is to provide a method by which the interest of the whole people shall be all that receives consideration. To this end there must be an expert tariff commission, wholly removed from the possibility of political pressure or of improper business influence. Such a commission can find the real difference between cost of production, which is mainly the difference of labor cost here and abroad. As fast as its recommendations are made, I believe in revising one schedule at a time. A general revision of the tariff almost inevitably leads to log-rolling and the subordination of the general public interest to local and special interests.

The absence of effective state, and, especially, national, restraint upon unfair money getting has tended to create a small class of enormously wealthy and economically powerful men, whose chief object is to hold and increase their power. The prime need is to change the conditions which enable these men to accumulate power which it is not for the general welfare that they should hold or exercise. We grudge no man a fortune which represents his own power and sagacity, when exercised with entire regard to the welfare of his fellows. Again, comrades over there, take the lesson from your own experience. Not only did you not grudge, but you gloried in the promotion of the great generals who gained their promotion by leading the army to victory. So it is with us. We grudge no man a fortune in civil life if it is honorably obtained and well used. It is not even enough that it should have been gained without doing damage to the community. We should permit it to be gained only so long as the gaining represents benefit to the community. This, I know, implies a policy of a far more active governmental interference with social and economic conditions in this country than we have yet had, but I think we have got to face the fact that such an increase in governmental control is now necessary.

No man should receive a dollar unless that dollar has been fairly earned. Every dollar received should represent a dollar's worth of service rendered—not gambling in stocks, but service rendered. The really big fortune, the swollen fortune, by the mere fact of its size acquires qualities which differentiate it in kind as well as in degree from what is possessed by men of relatively small means. Therefore, I believe in a graduated income tax on big fortunes, and in another tax which is far more easily collected and far more effective—a graduated inheritance tax on big fortunes, properly safeguarded against evasion and increasing rapidly in amount with the size of the estate. . . .

Moreover, I believe that the natural resources must be used for the benefit of all our people, and not monopolized for the benefit of the few, and here again is another case in which I am accused of taking a revolutionary attitude. People forget now that one hundred years ago there were public men of good character who advocated the nation selling its public lands in great quantities, so that the nation could get the most money out of it, and giving it to the men who could cultivate it for their own uses. We took the proper democratic ground that the land should be granted in small sections to the men who were actually to till it and live on it. Now, with the water power, with the forests, with the mines, we are brought face to face with the fact that there are many people who will go with us in conserving the resources only if they are to be allowed to exploit them for their benefit. That is one of the fundamental reasons why the special interests should be driven out of politics. Of all the questions which can come before this nation, short of the actual preservation of its existence in a great war, there is none which compares in importance with the great central task of leaving this land even a better land for our descendants than it is for us, and training them into a better race to inhabit the land and pass it on. Conservation is a great moral issue, for it involves the patriotic duty of insuring the safety and continuance of the nation. Let me add that the health and vitality of our people are at least as well worth conserving as their forests, waters, lands, and minerals, and in this great work the national government must bear a most important part.

I have spoken elsewhere also of the great task which lies before the farmers of the country to get for themselves and their wives and children not only the benefits of better farming, but also those of better business methods and better conditions of life on the farm. The burden of this great task will fall, as it should, mainly upon the great organizations of the farmers themselves. I am glad it will, for I believe they are all well able to handle it. In particular, there are strong reasons why the Departments of Agriculture of the various states, the United States Department of Agriculture, and the agricultural colleges and experiment stations should extend their work to cover all phases of farm life, instead of limiting themselves, as they have far too often limited themselves in the past, solely to the question of the production of crops. And now a special word to the farmer. I want to see him make the farm as fine a farm as it can be made; and let him remember to see that the improvement goes on indoors as well as out; let him remember that the farmer's wife should have her share of thought and attention just as much as the farmer himself.

Nothing is more true than that excess of every kind is followed by reaction; a fact which should be pondered by reformer and reactionary alike. We are face to face with new conceptions of the relations of property to human welfare, chiefly because certain advocates of the rights of property as against the rights of men have been pushing their claims too far. The man who wrongly holds that every human right is secondary to his profit must now give way to the advocate of human welfare, who rightly maintains that every man holds his property subject to the general right of the community to regulate its use to whatever degree the public welfare may require it.

But I think we may go still further. The right to regulate the use of wealth in the public interest is universally admitted. Let us admit also the right to regulate the terms and conditions of labor, which is the chief element of wealth, directly in the interest of the common good. The fundamental thing to do for every man is to give him a chance to reach a place in which he will make the greatest possible contribution to the public welfare. Understand what I say there. Give him a chance, not push him up if he will not be pushed. Help any man who stumbles; if he lies down, it is a poor job to try to carry him; but if he is a worthy man, try your best to see that he gets a chance to show the worth that is in him. No man can be a good citizen unless he has a wage more than sufficient to cover the bare cost of living, and hours of labor short enough so that after his day's work is done he will have time and energy to bear his share in the management of the community, to help in carrying the general load. We keep countless men from being good citizens by the conditions of life with which we surround them. We need comprehensive workmen's compensation acts, both state and national laws to regulate child labor and work for women, and, especially, we need in our common schools not merely education in book learning, but also practical training for daily life and work. We need to enforce better sanitary conditions for our workers and to extend the use of safety appliances for our workers in industry and commerce, both within and between the states. Also, friends, in the interest of the workingman himself we need to set our faces like flint against mob violence just as against corporate greed; against violence and injustice and lawlessness by wage workers just as much as against lawless cunning and greed and selfish arrogance of employers. If I could ask but one thing of my fellow countrymen, my request would be that, whenever they go in for reform, they remember the two sides, and that they always exact justice from one side as much as from the other. I have small use for the public servant who can always see and denounce the corruption of the capitalist, but who cannot persuade himself, especially before election, to say a word about lawless mob violence. And I have equally small use for the man, be he a judge on the bench, or editor of a great paper, or wealthy and influential private citizen, who can see clearly enough and denounce the lawlessness of mob violence, but whose eyes are closed so that he is blind when the question is one of corruption in business on a gigantic scale. Also remember what I said about excess in reformer and reactionary alike. If the reactionary man, who thinks of nothing but the rights of property, could have his way, he would bring about a revolution; and one of my chief fears in connection with progress comes because I do not want to see our people, for lack of proper leadership, compelled to follow men whose intentions are excellent, but whose eyes are a little too wild to make it really safe to trust them. Here in Kansas there is one paper which habitually denounces me as the tool of Wall Street, and at the same time frantically repudiates the statement that I am a Socialist on the ground that that is an unwarranted slander of the Socialists.

National efficiency has many factors. It is a necessary result of the principle of conservation widely applied. In the end it will

determine our failure or success as a nation. National efficiency
has to do, not only with natural resources and with men, but it is
equally concerned with institutions. The state must be made efficient for the work which concerns only the people of the state;
and the nation for that which concerns all the people. There
must remain no neutral ground to serve as a refuge for lawbreakers,
and especially for lawbreakers of great wealth, who can hire the
vulpine legal cunning which will teach them how to avoid both
jurisdictions. It is a misfortune when the national legislature fails
to do its duty in providing a national remedy, so that the only national activity is the purely negative activity of the judiciary in forbidding the state to exercise power in the premises.

I do not ask for overcentralization; but I do ask that we work in
a spirit of broad and far-reaching nationalism when we work for
what concerns our people as a whole. We are all Americans. Our
common interests are as broad as the continent. I speak to you
here in Kansas exactly as I would speak in New York or Georgia,
for the most vital problems are those which affect us all alike. The
national government belongs to the whole American people, and
where the whole American people are interested, that interest can
be guarded effectively only by the national government. The betterment which we seek must be accomplished, I believe, mainly
through the national government.

The American people are right in demanding that New Nationalism, without which we cannot hope to deal with new problems.
The New Nationalism puts the national need before sectional or
personal advantage. It is impatient of the utter confusion that
results from local legislatures attempting to treat national issues
as local issues. It is still more impatient of the impotence which
springs from overdivision of governmental powers, the impotence
which makes it possible for local selfishness or for legal cunning,
hired by wealthy special interests, to bring national activities to
a deadlock. This New Nationalism regards the executive power
as the steward of the public welfare. It demands of the judiciary
that it shall be interested primarily in human welfare rather than
in property, just as it demands that the representative body shall
represent all the people rather than any one class or section of the
people.

I believe in shaping the ends of government to protect property as well as human welfare. Normally, and in the long run, the ends are the same; but whenever the alternative must be faced, I am for men and not for property, as you were in the Civil War. I am far from underestimating the importance of dividends; but I rank dividends below human character. Again, I do not have any sympathy with the reformer who says he does not care for dividends. Of course, economic welfare is necessary, for a man must pull his own weight and be able to support his family. I know well that the reformers must not bring upon the people economic ruin, or the reforms themselves will go down in the ruin. But we must be ready to face temporary disaster, whether or not brought on by those who will war against us to the knife. Those who oppose all reform will do well to remember that ruin in its worst form is inevitable if our national life brings us nothing better than swollen fortunes for the few and the triumph in both politics and business of a sordid and selfish materialism. . . .

21. ROBERT M. LA FOLLETTE (1855–1925)

THE progressivism of the early twentieth century is perhaps best typified in the program and political technique of R. M. La Follette, Sr.[1] His main objective was to check the rapidly growing economic and political power of great agglomerations of capital. To this end he sought (1) to secure a more effective enforcement of the laws against monopolies, in businesses where competition would be socially beneficial; (2) to subject natural monopolies—the railroads and public utilities—to strong and expert governmental regulation in order to force them to supply adequate services at reasonable rates; (3) to make corporate wealth bear a heavier share of the burden of taxation; and (4) to strengthen popular control over economic policy by a democratization of the electoral process.

La Follette was of agrarian frontier origin. He was born in a log cabin in Wisconsin, worked his way through the State university (where his course included the study of oratory), read law and began practice in the university town of Madison, took office a few years later (in his twenty-sixth year) as county district attorney, and continued in active political life until his death forty-four years later. He held office as a Republican and in his earlier career showed no sharp deviation from orthodox Republican doctrine. Yet he generally maintained his independence of party leaders and became increasingly suspicious of the connections between big business and the party machines. He was a member of the United States House of Representatives for six years, and, as a member of the ways and means committee, took part in framing the high rates of the McKinley tariff law of 1890. He failed of re-election to Congress in the Democratic sweep of 1890 and was out of office for ten years; but in that interval he campaigned actively for the nomination and election of progressive Republicans and worked out and popularized the main lines of a program of political and economic reform, which thenceforth differentiated him from regular Republicans, although he continued to run for office as a Republican. He was governor of Wisconsin for two terms (1901–05) and secured the enact-

[1] Known as "Fighting Bob"; father of Robert M. La Follette, Jr. (United States Senator, 1925–   ) and of Philip La Follette (governor of Wisconsin, 1931–33 and 1935–39).

ment of laws providing for the direct primary in the nomination of elective officers and for the more effective taxation and regulation of railroads. He was United States senator during the last twenty years of his life. Here he fought against the high rates of the tariff measures of 1908 and 1922, opposed other conservative measures of the Republican administrations of Taft, Harding, and Coolidge, and supported most of the progressive measures of Democratic President Wilson. He was author of the "seaman's law" of 1915, requiring improved working and living conditions for employees on ocean, lake, and river craft; he was one of the first to advocate the creation of a separate cabinet department of labor; and he introduced the Senate resolution leading to the investigation of scandals connected with the naval oil leases of Harding's administration. He helped bring about equal suffrage for women, the direct election of United States senators, and the limitation of campaign expenditures.

La Follette was a prominent candidate for the presidential nomination in the Republican conventions of 1908 and 1912; the failure of Theodore Roosevelt to support his candidacy on either occasion confirmed his suspicions that Roosevelt was not a genuine progressive. In 1924 (in his seventieth year) he received the presidential nomination of the "Conference for Progressive Action," a loose federation of farm, labor, socialist, and progressive groups; Democratic Senator Burton K. Wheeler of Montana was his running mate. The platform adopted by the Conference (generally known as "The La Follette party") attacked political corruption and business monopolies and pledged farm relief (chiefly by reducing tariff rates and freight charges), public ownership of railroads and water power, and the submission of constitutional amendments empowering Congress to override court decisions that invalidated congressional statutes and providing for the popular election of federal judges for limited terms. The nominees, who were endorsed by the Socialist Party and the American Federation of Labor, received one-sixth of the popular vote, carried La Follette's home State, and ran ahead of the Democratic candidates in eleven States.

Distinctive features of La Follette's methods were his frequent appeals to popular opinion, in public addresses and in speeches on the Senate floor, and his extensive use of expert aid in the formulation, explanation, and execution of policy. He fortified his popular appeals with extensive arrays of facts and figures. In his home State he established "the Wisconsin idea": using the staff of the State university as a source of information on problems of government, setting up a bureau in the capitol to supply expert guidance to the law-makers, and appointing technically trained men on the regulatory commissions. His methods were widely copied in other States that were under the leadership of progressive governors.

[See: *La Follette's Autobiography: a Personal Narrative of Political Experiences* (1913); Ellen Torelle, *The Political Philosophy of Robert M. La Follette as Revealed in His Speeches and Writings* (1920); Albert O. Barton, *La Follette's Winning of Wisconsin, 1894–1904* (1922); Allen F. Lovejoy, *La Follette and the Establishment of the Direct Primary in Wisconsin, 1890–1904* (1941); Bruce Bliven, "Robert M. La Follette's Place in Our History," *Current History*, Vol. 22 (1925), pp. 716–722.]

From "ADDRESS . . . DEALING WITH . . . TRUSTS, CONSOLIDATED RAILROADS AND . . . BANKING INTERESTS . . ." (1912)[1]

Mr. Toastmaster, President Curtis, and Gentlemen of the Periodical Publishers' Association:

The great issue before the American people to-day is the control of their own government. In the midst of political struggle, it is not easy to see the historical relations of the present Progressive movement. But it represents a conflict as old as the history of man—the fight to maintain human liberty, the rights of all the people.

A mighty power has been builded up in this country in recent years, so strong, yet so insidious and far-reaching in its influence, that men are gravely inquiring whether its iron grip on government and business can ever be broken. Again and again it has proved strong enough to nominate the candidates of both political parties. It rules in the organization of legislative bodies, state and national, and of the committees which frame legislation. Its influence is felt in cabinets and in the policies of administrations, and is clearly seen in the appointment of prosecuting officers and the selection of judges upon the Bench.

In business it has crippled or destroyed competition. It has

[1] "Address of Robert M. La Follette at the Annual Banquet of the Periodical Publishers' Association, Philadelphia, February 2, 1912, Dealing with the History of the Growth of the Power Represented in Trusts, Consolidated Railroads and Consolidated Banking Interests Controlling Money and Credits, and Suggestions for Meeting Recognized Evils," in *La Follette's Autobiography: A Personal Narrative of Political Experiences* (Madison, c. 1913), pp. 762–797. By courtesy of Fola La Follette.

stifled individual initiative. It has fixed limitations in the field of production. It makes prices and imposes its burdens upon the consuming public at will.

In transportation, after a prolonged struggle for government control, it is, with only slight check upon its great power, still master of the highways of commerce.

In finance its power is unlimited. In large affairs it gives or withholds credit, and from time to time contracts or inflates the volume of the money required for the transaction of the business of the country, regardless of everything excepting its own profits.

It has acquired vast areas of the public domain, and is rapidly monopolizing the natural resources—timber, iron, coal, oil.

And this THING has grown up in a country where, under the Constitution and the law, the citizen is sovereign!

The related events which led to this centralized control are essential to a clear understanding of the real danger—the magnitude of this danger now menacing the very existence of every independent concern remaining in the field of business enterprise.

The First Period—The Individual and the Partnership.—For nearly a century after Jefferson declared for a government of "equal rights for all, and special privileges for none," the business of the country was conducted by individuals and partnerships. During this first period business methods were simple, its proportions modest, and there was little call for larger capital than could be readily furnished by the individual or, in the most extreme cases, a partnership of fair size.

From the beginning, when men bartered their products in exchange, down through all the ages, the business of the world had been conducted under the natural laws of trade—demand, supply, competition. Like all natural laws, they were fair and impartial; they favored neither the producer nor the consumer. They had ruled the market and made the prices when the individual and the partnership conducted substantially all commercial enterprises during the first period of our business life.

But as the country developed, as the population poured over the Alleghenies, occupied the Mississippi Valley, pushed on to the Rocky Mountains and down the western slope to California, discovering the boundless wealth of our natural resources—the fields and forests, the mountains of iron and coal and precious metals, there was a pressing call on every hand for larger capital beyond the power of any individual or any partnership to supply. We had outgrown the simple methods; there was a demand for a new business device strong enough to unlock the treasure house of the new world.

The Second Period—The Private Corporation.—The modern corporation was invented to meet that demand, and general statutes for incorporation were soon upon the statute books of every state. Their adoption marked the beginning of the second period of our business life. It was the best machine ever invented for the purpose; simple in organization, effective in operation.

A hundred, a thousand, any number of men could associate their capital, and employing the representative principle upon which our country was based, vote for and elect a president, a general manager, a board of directors, a body of men, no larger than an ordinary partnership, and clothe them with power to conduct the business to the success of which the aggregate capital was contributed.

Men no longer stood baffled by the magnitude of any undertaking, but promptly enlisted an army of contributors, large or small, massed together the required capital and under the direction of the officers and directors of the corporation, a small executive body, seized upon these waiting opportunities, and this second period marked a material development, surpassing anything in the world's history. It was not the era of greatest individual fortune building, but it was the period of greatest general prosperity. And why?

The natural laws of trade—demand, supply and competition—still ruled the market and made the prices in the second period of our business life. The private corporation, in a large measure, supplanted the individual, and the partnership in mining, manufacturing and large commercial enterprises, but each corporation competed with every other in the same line of business. Production was larger, development more rapid, but, under the free play of competition, the resulting prosperity was fairly distributed between the producer and the consumer, the seller and the buyer, because profits and prices were reasonable.

Big capital behind the private corporations drove business at a pace and upon a scale never before witnessed. Competition was at once the spur to the highest efficiency and the check against waste and abuse of power.

In this period of our industrial and commercial progress, America amazed and alarmed our business rivals of the old world. We were soon foremost among the nations of the earth in agriculture, in mines and mining, in manufactures and in commerce as well.

The American market became the greatest thing in all the material world. Its control became the one thing coveted.

The Third Period—The Combination of Corporations.—The evil hour was come upon us. Daring, unscrupulous men plotted in violation of the common law, the criminal statutes and against public right to become masters of that market and take what toll they pleased. To do this thing it was necessary to set aside, abrogate, nullify the natural laws of trade that had ruled in business for centuries. Production was to be limited, competition stifled and prices arbitrarily fixed by selfish decree. And thus we entered upon the third period of our business and commercial life—the period of a combination of the corporations under a single control in each line of business. It was not an evolution; it was a revolution.

And yet certain economists set it down in the literature of the day that the Supreme Ruler of the universe reserved in His great plan a divinely appointed place and time for a Rockefeller, a Morgan, a Carnegie, a Baer, to evolve this new law, which should enable them to appropriate the wealth of the country and Mexicanize its business and its people.

The combination became supreme in each important line, controlling the markets for the raw material and the finished product, largely dictating the price of everything we sell and the price of everything we buy—beef, sugar, woolens, cottons, coal, oil, copper, zinc, iron, steel, agricultural implements, hardware, gas, electric light, food supplies.

Monopoly acquired dominion everywhere.

It brought with it the inevitable results of monopoly—extortionate prices, inferior products. We soon found shoddy in everything we wear, and adulteration in everything we eat.

Did these masters of business stop there? By no means! "Increase of appetite had grown by what it fed on." The floodgates of fictitious capitalization were thrown wide open. These organizations of combinations overcapitalized for a double purpose. The issue of bonds and stocks in excess of investment covered up the exaction of their immense profits, and likewise offered an unlimited field for promotion and speculation.

The establishment of this third period was the beginning of rapidly advancing prices, increasing the cost of living upon people of average earning power until the burden is greater than they can bear.

The Fourth Period—The Combination of Combinations.—The strife for more money, more power—more power, more money—swept everything before it.

It remained only to bring together into a community of interest or ownership the great combinations which controlled, each in its own field—in short, to combine these combinations.

One needs but to study the directory of directories of the great business concerns of the country to determine the extent to which this combination of combinations has been successfully accomplished, thus carrying us over into the fourth period of our industrial and commercial life—the period of complete industrial and commercial servitude in which we now unhappily find ourselves. And this supreme control of the business of the country is the triumph of men who have at every step defied public opinion, the common law and criminal statutes.

This condition is intolerable. It is hostile to every principle of democracy. If maintained it is the end of democracy. We may preserve the form of our representative government and lose the soul, the spirit of our free institutions. . . .

The Sherman law ["Anti-Trust Act" of 1890] placed in the hands of the executive department of this government the most perfect weapon which the ingenuity of man could forge for the protection of the people against the power of monopoly.

It will be the impartial verdict of history that the executive department of government could have saved the people from the appalling conditions which confront us to-day, if all the power of this great government had been put forth to enforce the anti-trust law. Two or three score of prosecutions dragging along in the courts at a snail's pace, from administration to administration, was little more than notice to these business kings that they might proceed to set up their authority against the government and extend their dominion over trade and transportation; that there was no real danger of the law being so enforced as to do much more than to affect the political situation from time to time.

That this was accepted as the government's position by the interests can now be made very plain.

The organization of combinations began quite actively early in 1898. The high tariff rates of the Dingley law encouraged combination and aided in its ultimate purpose.

Between January 1, 1898, and January 1, 1900, 149 trusts were formed to suppress competition and control prices. These combinations were capitalized for $3,784,000,000. The next four years were years of enormous trust growth.

From January 1, 1900, to January 1, 1904, taking account of only the more important trusts, 8,664 great plants were combined, with a total capitalization of $20,379,162,511.

Prices were mounting higher and higher. The people were crying aloud in protest, but protest and denunciation caused no fear on the part of the trust makers, so long as the government was actually prosecuting less than an average of seven cases a year.

Mark what followed: From January 1, 1904, to January 1, 1908, trust consolidation made mighty strides, and the total capitalization reached the astounding sum of $31,672,160,754. In these four years the capitalization increased more than 55 per cent.

The Centralization of Railroad Control.—In the meantime what were the powers doing in the great field of transportation? A swift backward glance reveals the fact that the same system of consolidation, centralized control and suppressed competition had been forced through in violation of law and public right.

The vital interests of organized society in commerce and the public nature of transportation impose upon government the duty to establish and maintain control over common carriers.

To discharge this obligation the government must exact from the common carrier:

(1) Reasonable rates, (2) impartial rates, (3) adequate and impartial services.

The public is interested in adequate and impartial services. The shipper is especially interested in equal and impartial rates. The consumer is especially interested in reasonable rates.

For forty years after railroads were established there was no attempt to invoke governmental control. The public depended solely upon competition between railroads for the protection of public interests.

Finally it learned the elementary lesson that the railroad is a natural monopoly; that there can be no competition excepting at common points, and that at common points the railroads were destroying all competition by pooling agreements.

Then came the demand in 1870 for governmental control—in order to secure reasonable rates. It originated in the upper Mississippi Valley—in Wisconsin, Iowa, Minnesota, and Illinois, for a control of rates within the state.

It spread east and west and became a national movement for controlling interstate commerce.

The supreme courts of the middle western states sustained the state legislation. The Supreme Court of the United States sustained the state courts, and the power of the state and federal governments to control and fix reasonable transportation rates, each in its own sphere, was adjudicated as a public right thirty-eight years ago.

For a generation of time since those decisions the people have struggled to secure an interstate commerce law which would establish and enforce reasonable rates. That was the relief which the consumer, the great body of the people, demanded—reasonable rates.

The shippers have no interest in reasonable rates. They do not pay the freight. The consumer pays the freight. But the shipper is at a disadvantage in supplying his trade unless he has rates relatively equal to those given to other shippers engaged in the same business.

Shippers could easily present concrete cases of injustice. They could readily organize and appear before committees and make their representatives feel their power.

Not so with the consumer, who, in the end, pays all the freight, as a part of the purchase price of everything he buys. He cannot identify the freight charge, because it is a part of the price he pays when he purchases supplies. However small the item, in the aggregate it is important to him. He cannot maintain a lobby. If his United States Senators and his Congressmen do not represent him, he is helpless.

What is the net result of thirty-eight years' struggle with the railroads? Congress enacted the interstate commerce law of 1887; the Elkins law of 1903; the Hepburn law of 1906; and the recent law of 1910.

Out of all this legislation the shippers have been able to secure a partial enforcement of their contention for an equalization of rates.

The consumers have lost in their long fight for reasonable rates.

After all these years it is not to-day within the power of the interstate commerce commission to take the first step to ascertain a reasonable rate. There is a vast difference between equal rates and reasonable rates.

The consumers are no nearer to securing reasonable rates than they were thirty-eight years ago.

Ninety million people are to-day paying annually to the railroads $2,500,000,000 for transportation—a sum greater than the total cost of maintaining the federal government, the state governments, the county governments, and all the municipal governments of the entire country.

The power of the railroads over Congress has been well-nigh supreme. . . .

The control of transportation was achieved through combination. Less than twenty years ago the railroads, overriding the law, secretly combined to suppress every trace of competition and to advance rates.

By 1897, 922 railroad corporations, with 250 allied railroads, having altogether 178,307 miles of road, constituting 95 per cent. of the vital railway mileage of the country, were organized into six systems, known as the Vanderbilt, Pennsylvania, Morgan-Hill, Gould-Rockefeller, Moore-Leeds and Harriman-Kuhn-Loeb groups and their allies.

Since that time further concentration and control has increased the mileage of these groups to more than 200,000 miles of road. These groups are controlled by eight men, and, as stated by John Moody, in 1904, "the superior dominating influence of Mr. Rockefeller and Mr. Morgan is felt in a greater or less degree in all of the groups."

But an even greater danger was in waiting,—the control of capital and credit, the very life of all business.

The Centralized Control of Banking, Capital, and Credits.—
The country is only just beginning to understand how completely
great banking institutions in the principal money centres have become bound up with the control of industrial institutions, the railroads and franchise combinations.

That there was a tendency on the part of great banking associations to merge and combine could not be overlooked. But while
financial and economic writers had directed public attention to the
fact, and had even pointed out the opportunity and temptation
for the use of this augmented power, in connection with the promotion of the speculative side of business organization, they were
slow to believe that banking institutions could be so prostituted.
Certain critical observers had, however, as long as five or six years
ago, suggested the dangerous tendencies in this direction. . . .

The plain truth is that legitimate commercial banking is being
eaten up by speculative banking. The greatest banks of the financial centre of the country have ceased to be agents of commerce
and have become primarily agencies of promotion and speculation.
By merging the largest banks, trust companies, and insurance companies masses of capital have been brought under one management, to be employed not as the servant of commerce, but as its
master; not to supply legitimate business and to facilitate exchange,
but to subordinate the commercial demands of the country upon
the banks to call loans in Wall Street and to finance industrial organizations, always speculative, and often unlawful in character.
Trained men, who a dozen years ago stood first among the bankers
of the world as heads of the greatest banks of New York City, are,
in the main, either displaced or do the bidding of men who are not
bankers, but masters of organization.

The banks which were then managed by bankers as independent
commercial institutions are now owned in groups by a few men,
whose principal interests are in railroads, traction, telegraph, cable,
shipping, iron and steel, copper, coal, oil, gas, insurance, etc.

This subversion of banking by alliance with promotion and stock
speculation is easily traced.

There was every inducement for those who controlled transportation and a few great basic industries to achieve control of money
in the financial centre of the country.

The centralization of the banking power in New York City

would not only open the way for financing the reorganization and consolidation of industrial enterprises and of public utilities throughout the country, but would place those in authority where they could control the markets on stocks and bonds almost at will.

With this enormous concentration of business it is possible to create, artificially, periods of prosperity and periods of panic. Prices can be lowered or advanced at the will of the "System." When the farmer must move his crops a scarcity of money may be created and prices lowered. When the crop passes into the control of the speculator the artificial stringency may be relieved and prices advanced, and the illegitimate profit raked off the agricultural industry may be pocketed in Wall Street.

If an effort is made to compel any one of these great "Interests" to obey the law, it is easy for them to enter into a conspiracy to destroy whoever may be responsible for the undertaking.

The bare names of the directors of two great bank groups—the Standard Oil group and the Morgan group—given in connection with their other business associations is all the evidence that need be offered of the absolute community of interest between banks, railroads, and all the great industries. . . .

I would not unjustly decry Wall Street or ignore the necessity of a great central market to provide capital for the large business undertakings of this country. I recognize the rights of capital and the service which capital can render to a great producing nation such as ours. But this government guarantees equality of opportunity for all men, and it likewise guarantees equality of opportunity for all capital. And corporations and combinations of corporations, with their centralized banking and extending branch connections from state to state, are not entitled to special favors in legislation.

The whole course of banking and currency legislation has steadily favored the great banking institutions, especially those having community of interest with the industrial and transportation companies of the country. . . .

This is but the barest outline of the upbuilding of the power which now controls.

Is there a way out? Let us consider.

By its decisions in the Standard Oil and Tobacco cases the Supreme Court has all at once created itself into a legislature, an interstate commerce commission and a supreme court, combined in one.

The "rule of reason" gives it legislative power, the power to determine according to its own opinion that some restraints of trade are lawful and other restraints unlawful. The power to carry out the dissolution and reorganization of the trusts and to work out the details is exactly the power that a legislature turns over to a commission. Punishment for contempt is the court's substitute for the criminal penalty that the legislature attaches to the violation of its statutes.

The supreme court has amended the anti-trust act in exactly the way that Congress repeatedly refused to amend it, and has usurped both legislative and executive power in doing it. Whether we wish it or not, Congress is now compelled to create an interstate trade commission to control the trusts, or else leave the control to the federal courts, acting as a commission.

Such a commission should not fix prices. Price regulation assumes that we are dealing with a necessary monopoly, as in the case of railroads and public utilities. But the commercial monopolies are based on unfair and discriminatory practices and special privileges. These can be abolished in several ways.

Amend the Sherman law by enacting specific prohibitions against well-known practices that constitute unreasonable restraints of trade. One of these is the brutal method of the Standard Oil Company of cutting prices in any place where there is a competitor in order to kill him off, while keeping up prices in other places. Another is the club wielded by the tobacco trust, which put the jobbers in a position where, unless they refrained from buying of a competitor, they could not get from the trust the brands which were indispensable to the successful conduct of their business. These and several other obviously unreasonable restraints of trade are definitely prohibited in the bill which I have introduced in the Senate. . . .

It is claimed on all sides that competition has failed. I deny it. Fair competition has not failed. It has been suppressed. When competitors are shut out from markets by discrimination, and denied either transportation, raw material or credit on equal terms, we do not have competition. We have the modern form of highway robbery. The great problem of legislation before us is first for the people to resume control of their government, and then to protect themselves against those who are throttling competition by the aid of government.

I do not say that competition does not have its evils. Labor organizations are the struggling protest against cut-throat competition. The anti-trust law was not intended or understood to apply to them. They should be exempt from its operation.

The tariff should be brought down to the difference in labor cost of the more efficient plants and the foreign competitor, and where there is no difference the tariff should be removed. Where the protective tariff is retained its advantages must be passed along to labor, for whose benefit the manufacturer contends it is necessary.

The patent laws should be so amended that the owners of patents will be compelled to develop them fully or permit their use on equal terms by others.

More vital and menacing than any other power that supports trusts is the control of credit through the control of the people's savings and deposits. . . .

Our National Banking Law is a patchwork of legislation. It should be thoroughly revised. And all authorities agree that a comprehensive plan for an emergency currency is vitally important. When the basic principle of such a plan is once determined, when it is settled that government controlled banks are to be, *in fact,* controlled by the government *in the public interest,* the details can easily be worked out.

An emergency currency circulation should be backed by proper reserves, issued only against commercial paper that represents actual and legitimate business transactions. No plan should be adopted which admits of control by banking interests which, under existing conditions, means, in the end, control by the great speculative banking groups.

In all our plans for progressive legislation, it must not be forgotten that we are only just beginning to get control of the railroads. The present law is an improvement, but the Interstate Commerce Commission requires to be greatly strengthened. It should have a much larger appropriation, enabling it to prosecute investigations in all parts of the country. It should make physical valuations of the railroads, eliminating watered stock, monopoly values and the unwarranted inflation of railway terminals to conceal monopoly values. And the Commerce Court should be abolished as a mere subterfuge interposed to handicap the commission.

As a first necessary step for the regulation of interstate commerce, we *must* ascertain the reasonable value of the physical property of railroads, justly inventoried, upon a sound economic basis, distinguishing *actual* values from *monopoly* values derived from violations of law, and must make such discriminating values the *base line* for determining rates. The country should know how much of the eighteen billions of capitalization was contributed by those who own the railroads, and how much by the people themselves. We should also provide for the extension of the powers and the administrative control of the Interstate Commerce Commission. . . .

One would think that in a democracy like ours, people seeking the truth, able to read and understand, would find the press their eager and willing instructors. Such was the press of Horace Greeley, Henry Raymond, Charles A. Dana, Joseph Medill, and Horace Rublee.

But what do we find has occurred in the past few years since the money power has gained control of our industry and government? It controls the newspaper press. The people know this. Their confidence is weakened and destroyed. No longer are the editorial columns of newspapers a potent force in educating public opinion. The newspapers, of course, are still patronized for news. But even as to news, the public is fast coming to understand that wherever news items bear in any way upon the control of government by business, the news is colored; so confidence in the newspaper as a newspaper is being undermined.

Cultured and able men are still to be found upon the editorial staffs of all great dailies, but the public understands them to be hired men who no longer express honest judgments and sincere conviction, who write what they are told to write, and whose judgments are salaried.

To the subserviency of the press to special interests in no small degree is due the power and influence and prosperity of the weekly and monthly magazines. A decade ago young men trained in journalism came to see this control of the newspapers of the country. They saw also an unoccupied field. And they went out and built up great periodicals and magazines. They were free.

Their pages were open to publicists and scholars and liberty, and justice and equal rights found a free press beyond the reach of the corrupt influence of consolidated business and machine politics. We entered upon a new era.

The periodical, reduced in price, attractive and artistic in dress, strode like a young giant into the arena of public service. Filled with this spirit, quickened with human interest, it assailed social and political evils in high places and low. It found the power of the public service corporation and the evil influences of money in the municipal government of every large city. It found franchises worth millions of dollars secured by bribery; police in partnership with thieves and crooks and prostitutes. It found juries "fixed" and an established business plying its trade between litigants and the back door of blinking justice. . . .

The free and independent periodical turned her searchlight on state legislatures, and made plain as the sun at noonday the absolute control of the corrupt lobby. She opened the closed doors of the secret caucus, the secret committee, the secret conference, behind which United States Senators and Members of Congress betrayed the public interest into the hands of railroads, the trusts, the tariff mongers, and the centralized banking power of the country. She revealed the same influences back of judicial and other appointments. She took the public through the great steel plants and into the homes of the men who toil twelve hours a day and seven days in the week. And the public heard their cry of despair. She turned her camera into the mills and shops where little children are robbed of every chance of life that nourishes vigorous bodies and sound minds, and the pinched faces and dwarfed figures told their pathetic story on her clean white pages.

The control of the newspaper press is not the simple and expensive one of ownership and investment. There is here and there a "kept sheet" owned by a man of great wealth to further his own interests. But the papers of this class are few. The control comes through that community of interests, that interdependence of investments and credits which ties the publisher up to the banks, the advertisers and the special interests.

We may expect this same kind of control, sooner or later, to reach out for the magazines. But more than this: I warn you of a subtle new peril, the centralization of advertising, that will in time seek to gag you. What has occurred on the small scale in almost every city in the country will extend to the national scale, and will ere long close in on the magazines. No men ever faced graver responsibilities. None have ever been called to a more unselfish, patriotic service. I believe that when the final test comes, you will not be found wanting; you will not desert and leave the people to depend upon the public platform alone, but you will hold aloft the lamp of Truth, lighting the way for the preservation of representative government and the liberty of the American people.

22. WOODROW WILSON (1856–1924)

IN THE spring of 1907, Woodrow Wilson, addressing an academic audience and speaking as a scholarly interpreter of the American governmental system, said that the office of President of the United States "does not demand active experience in affairs so much as particular qualities of mind and character which we are at least as likely to find outside the ranks of our public men as within them." Six years later he was elected President after an experience of less than two years in public office. He was born in Staunton, Virginia, son of a Presbyterian minister. After graduation from Princeton, he spent one year in the law school of the University of Virginia, practised for a year in Atlanta, and then entered Johns Hopkins University for advanced study of history and political science. He wrote a notable book on *Congressional Government* (1885) as his doctoral dissertation. He taught at Bryn Mawr College and Wesleyan University, became professor of jurisprudence and political economy at Princeton University in 1890, and twelve years later was made president of Princeton. He was a popular teacher; as university president he introduced important and influential educational reforms, some of which aroused bitter controversies within the Princeton faculty.

Meanwhile Wilson had established a reputation as a penetrating writer and an eloquent and forceful public speaker. Since he took a moderate stand in his discussion of current proposals for reform, conservative Democrats in the east talked of him as a desirable presidential candidate; he might at least block the nomination (for a fourth time) of William J. Bryan, radical monetary reformer. In 1910 the Democratic machine of New Jersey (a normally Republican State) decided that the Democrats might carry the State if they adopted a progressive platform and nominated a good speaker, recommended by conservatives, as candidate for governor. Wilson accepted the nomination and the Democrats carried the State by a surprising majority. A split between the governor and the machine developed almost immediately: the Democratic legislature ignored the governor's demands that the platform be carried out and the governor ignored the party's demands for patronage. Whereupon Governor Wilson (who was without "active experience in affairs") stumped the State so effectively that the legislature enacted most of the platform pledges. This achievement alienated most of

Wilson's original sponsors but put him at the forefront of progressive leaders of the nation. In the Democratic national convention of 1912, after a bitter struggle between conservatives and progressives and a week of balloting, Wilson, supported by Bryan, received the presidential nomination. In a three-cornered race, he was elected by the largest electoral majority since Monroe.[1]

As President, Wilson assumed a vigorous personal direction of governmental policy in both domestic and foreign affairs, thereby putting into effective practice some academic opinions he had expressed a few years earlier. He had said (in 1906):

> The Presidents who have not made themselves leaders have lived no more truly on that account in the spirit of the Constitution than those whose force has told in the determination of law and policy. . . . The President is at liberty, both in law and conscience, to be as big a man as he can. His capacity will set the limit; and if Congress be overborne by him, it will be no fault of the makers of the Constitution,—it will be from no lack of constitutional powers on his part, but only because the President has the nation behind him, and Congress has not.

Wilson maintained his party leadership and persuaded Congress to follow his policies, chiefly by means of his appeals to popular opinion. In his domestic program, he was helped by having behind him several decades of able agitation and action in furtherance of social reform, under such "progressive" and "insurgent" leaders as Senators R. M. LaFollette and G. W. Norris, Governor Hiram Johnson of California and President Theodore Roosevelt. During his first administration Congress enacted a notable program of reform, providing for reduced tariffs, a more flexible monetary system (the federal reserve act), a more effective prevention of unfair methods of competition (the federal trade commission and "Clayton anti-trust" acts), better credit facilities for farmers, improved living and working conditions for seamen, an eight-hour day for employees on interstate railways, and two measures (both invalidated by the Supreme Court) for a national regulation of child labor.

Wilson's general program, as outlined in his messages and campaign speeches, was directed chiefly towards a restoration of individual initiative and free competition rather than towards a positive promotion of the general welfare through elaborate governmental regulations and aids. He called his system "the new freedom."

---

[1] Electoral vote: Wilson 435, Theodore Roosevelt (Progressive) 88, Taft (Republican) 8. Wilson received 42 percent of the popular vote.

[Wilson's most illuminating and scholarly studies of American government are *Congressional Government* (1885) and *Constitutional Government in the United States* (1908).

See: Ray Stannard Baker, *Woodrow Wilson: Life and Letters*, (8 vols., 1927–39); William Allen White, *Woodrow Wilson, the Man, His Times and His Task* (1924); William E. Dodd, *Woodrow Wilson and His Work* (4th ed., 1921); Charles Seymour, *Woodrow Wilson and the World War* (1921).]

From THE NEW FREEDOM (1913)[1]

THE OLD ORDER CHANGETH

There is one great basic fact which underlies all the questions that are discussed on the political platform at the present moment. That singular fact is that nothing is done in this country as it was done twenty years ago.

We are in the presence of a new organization of society. Our life has broken away from the past. The life of America is not the life that it was twenty years ago; it is not the life that it was ten years ago. We have changed our economic conditions, absolutely, from top to bottom; and, with our economic society, the organization of our life. The old political formulas do not fit the present problems; they read now like documents taken out of a forgotten age. The older cries sound as if they belonged to a past age which men have almost forgotten. Things which used to be put into the party platforms of ten years ago would sound antiquated if put into a platform now. We are facing the necessity of fitting a new social organization, as we did once fit the old organization to the happiness and prosperity of the great body of citizens; for we are conscious that the new order of society has not been made to fit and provide the convenience or prosperity of the average man. The life of the nation has grown infinitely varied. It does not centre now upon questions of governmental structure or of the distribution of governmental powers. It centres upon questions of the very structure and operation of society itself, of which government is only the instrument. Our development has run so fast and

[1] Woodrow Wilson, *The New Freedom* (New York and Garden City, 1913), from ch. i. By special arrangement with Doubleday, Doran & Company, Inc.

so far along the lines sketched in the earlier day of constitutional
definition, has so crossed and interlaced those lines, has piled upon
them such novel structures of trust and combination, has elaborated
within them a life so manifold, so full of forces which transcend the
boundaries of the country itself and fill the eyes of the world, that
a new nation seems to have been created which the old formulas
do not fit or afford a vital interpretation of.

We have come upon a very different age from any that preceded
us. We have come upon an age when we do not do business in
the way in which we used to do business,—when we do not carry
on any of the operations of manufacture, sale, transportation, or
communication as men used to carry them on. There is a sense in
which in our day the individual has been submerged. In most
parts of our country men work, not for themselves, not as partners
in the old way in which they used to work, but generally as employees,—in a higher or lower grade,—of great corporations. There
was a time when corporations played a very minor part in our business affairs, but now they play the chief part, and most men are
the servants of corporations.

You know what happens when you are the servant of a corporation. You have in no instance access to the men who are really
determining the policy of the corporation. If the corporation is
doing the things that it ought not to do, you really have no voice
in the matter and must obey the orders, and you have oftentimes
with deep mortification to co-operate in the doing of things which
you know are against the public interest. Your individuality is
swallowed up in the individuality and purpose of a great organization.

It is true that, while most men are thus submerged in the corporation, a few, a very few, are exalted to a power which as individuals they could never have wielded. Through the great organizations of which they are the heads, a few are enabled to play a
part unprecedented by anything in history in the control of the
business operations of the country and in the determination of the
happiness of great numbers of people.

Yesterday, and ever since history began, men were related to one
another as individuals. To be sure there were the family, the
Church, and the State, institutions which associated men in certain

wide circles of relationship. But in the ordinary concerns of life, in the ordinary work, in the daily round, men dealt freely and directly with one another. To-day, the everyday relationships of men are largely with great impersonal concerns, with organizations, not with other individual men.

Now this is nothing short of a new social age, a new era of human relationships, a new stage-setting for the drama of life.

In this new age we find, for instance, that our laws with regard to the relations of employer and employee are in many respects wholly antiquated and impossible. They were framed for another age, which nobody now living remembers, which is, indeed, so remote from our life that it would be difficult for many of us to understand it if it were described to us. The employer is now generally a corporation or a huge company of some kind; the employee is one of hundreds or of thousands brought together, not by individual masters whom they know and with whom they have personal relations, but by agents of one sort or another. Workingmen are marshaled in great numbers for the performance of a multitude of particular tasks under a common discipline. They generally use dangerous and powerful machinery, over whose repair and renewal they have no control. New rules must be devised with regard to their obligations and their rights, their obligations to their employers and their responsibilities to one another. Rules must be devised for their protection, for their compensation when injured, for their support when disabled.

There is something very new and very big and very complex about these new relations of capital and labor. A new economic society has sprung up, and we must effect a new set of adjustments. We must not pit power against weakness. The employer is generally, in our day, as I have said, not an individual, but a powerful group; and yet the workingman when dealing with his employer is still, under our existing law, an individual.

Why is it that we have a labor question at all? It is for the simple and very sufficient reason that the laboring man and the employer are not intimate associates now as they used to be in time past. Most of our laws were formed in the age when employer and employees knew each other, knew each other's characters, were

associates with each other, dealt with each other as man with man.
That is no longer the case. You not only do not come into personal
contact with the men who have the supreme command in those
corporations, but it would be out of the question for you to do it.
Our modern corporations employ thousands, and in some instances
hundreds of thousands, of men. The only persons whom you see
or deal with are local superintendents or local representatives of a
vast organization, which is not like anything that the workingmen
of the time in which our laws were framed knew anything about.
A little group of workingmen, seeing their employer every day, dealing with him in a personal way, is one thing, and the modern body
of labor engaged as employees of the huge enterprises that spread
all over the country, dealing with men of whom they can form no
personal conception, is another thing. A very different thing. You
never saw a corporation, any more than you ever saw a government.
Many a workingman to-day never saw the body of men who are
conducting the industry in which he is employed. And they never
saw him. What they know about him is written in ledgers and
books and letters, in the correspondence of the office, in the reports
of the superintendents. He is a long way off from them.

So what we have to discuss is, not wrongs which individuals intentionally do,—I do not believe there are a great many of those,—
but the wrongs of a system. I want to record my protest against
any discussion of this matter which would seem to indicate that
there are bodies of our fellow-citizens who are trying to grind us
down and do us injustice. There are some men of that sort. I
don't know how they sleep o' nights, but there are men of that
kind. Thank God, they are not numerous. The truth is, we are
all caught in a great economic system which is heartless. The modern corporation is not engaged in business as an individual. When
we deal with it, we deal with an impersonal element, an immaterial
piece of society. A modern corporation is a means of co-operation
in the conduct of an enterprise which is so big that no one man can
conduct it, and which the resources of no one man are sufficient to
finance. A company is formed; that company puts out a prospectus;
the promoters expect to raise a certain fund as capital stock. Well,
how are they going to raise it? They are going to raise it from the
public in general, some of whom will buy their stock. The moment
that begins, there is formed—what? A joint stock corporation.

Men begin to pool their earnings, little piles, big piles. A certain number of men are elected by the stockholders to be directors, and these directors elect a president. This president is the head of the undertaking, and the directors are its managers.

Now, do the workingmen employed by that stock corporation deal with that president and those directors? Not at all. Does the public deal with that president and that board of directors? It does not. Can anybody bring them to account? It is next to impossible to. do so. If you undertake it you will find it a game of hide and seek, with the objects of your search taking refuge now behind the tree of their individual personality, now behind that of their corporate irresponsibility.

And do our laws take note of this curious state of things? Do they even attempt to distinguish between a man's act as a corporation director and as an individual? They do not. Our laws still deal with us on the basis of the old system. The law is still living in the dead past which we have left behind. This is evident, for instance, with regard to the matter of employers' liability for workingmen's injuries. Suppose that a superintendent wants a workman to use a certain piece of machinery which it is not safe for him to use, and that the workman is injured by that piece of machinery. Some of our courts have held that the superintendent is a fellow-servant, or, as the law states it, a fellow-employee, and that, therefore, the man cannot recover damages for his injury. The superintendent who probably engaged the man is not his employer. Who is his employer? And whose negligence could conceivably come in there? The board of directors did not tell the employee to use that piece of machinery; and the president of the corporation did not tell him to use that piece of machinery. And so forth. Don't you see by that theory that a man never can get redress for negligence on the part of the employer? When I hear judges reason upon the analogy of the relationships that used to exist between workmen and their employers a generation ago, I wonder if they have not opened their eyes to the modern world. You know, we have a right to expect that judges will have their eyes open, even though the law which they administer hasn't awakened.

Yet that is but a single small detail illustrative of the difficulties we are in because we have not adjusted the law to the facts of the new order.

Since I entered politics, I have chiefly had men's views confided to me privately. Some of the biggest men in the United States, in the field of commerce and manufacture, are afraid of somebody, are afraid of something. They know that there is a power somewhere so organized, so subtle, so watchful, so interlocked, so complete, so pervasive, that they had better not speak above their breath when they speak in condemnation of it.

They know that America is not a place of which it can be said, as it used to be, that a man may choose his own calling and pursue it just as far as his abilities enable him to pursue it; because to-day, if he enters certain fields, there are organizations which will use means against him that will prevent his building up a business which they do not want to have built up; organizations that will see to it that the ground is cut from under him and the markets shut against him. For if he begins to sell to certain retail dealers, to any retail dealers, the monopoly will refuse to sell to those dealers, and those dealers, afraid, will not buy the new man's wares.

And this is the country which has lifted to the admiration of the world its ideals of absolutely free opportunity, where no man is supposed to be under any limitation except the limitations of his character and of his mind; where there is supposed to be no distinction of class, no distinction of blood, no distinction of social status, but where men win or lose on their merits.

I lay it very close to my own conscience as a public man whether we can any longer stand at our doors and welcome all newcomers upon those terms. American industry is not free, as once it was free; American enterprise is not free; the man with only a little capital is finding it harder to get into the field, more and more impossible to compete with the big fellow. Why? Because the laws of this country do not prevent the strong from crushing the weak. That is the reason, and because the strong have crushed the weak the strong dominate the industry and the economic life of this country. No man can deny that the lines of endeavor have more and more narrowed and stiffened; no man who knows anything about the development of industry in this country can have failed to observe that the larger kinds of credit are more and more difficult to obtain, unless you obtain them upon the terms of uniting your efforts with those who already control the industries of the country; and nobody can fail to observe that any man who tries to set himself up in competition with any process of manufacture which has been taken under the control of large combinations of capital will presently find himself either squeezed out or obliged to sell and allow himself to be absorbed.

There is a great deal that needs reconstruction in the United States. I should like to take a census of the business men,—I mean the rank and file of the business men,—as to whether they think that business conditions in this country, or rather whether the organization of business in this country, is satisfactory or not. I know what they would say if they dared. If they could vote secretly they would vote overwhelmingly that the present organization of business was meant for the big fellows and was not meant for the little fellows; that it was meant for those who are at the top and was meant to exclude those who are at the bottom; that it was meant to shut out beginners, to prevent new entries in the race, to prevent the building up of competitive enterprises that would interfere with the monopolies which the great trusts have built up.

What this country needs above everything else is a body of laws which will look after the men who are on the make rather than the men who are already made. Because the men who are already made are not going to live indefinitely, and they are not always kind enough to leave sons as able and as honest as they are.

The originative part of America, the part of America that makes new enterprises, the part into which the ambitious and gifted workingman makes his way up, the class that saves, that plans, that organizes, that presently spreads its enterprises until they have a national scope and character,—that middle class is being more and more squeezed out by the processes which we have been taught to call processes of prosperity. Its members are sharing prosperity, no doubt; but what alarms me is that they are not *originating* prosperity. No country can afford to have its prosperity originated by a small controlling class. The treasury of America does not lie in the brains of the small body of men now in control of the great enterprises that have been concentrated under the direction of a very small number of persons. The treasury of America lies in those ambitions, those energies, that cannot be restricted to a special favored class. It depends upon the inventions of unknown men, upon the originations of unknown men, upon the ambitions of unknown men. Every country is renewed out of the ranks of the

unknown, not out of the ranks of those already famous and powerful and in control.

There has come over the land that un-American set of conditions
which enables a small number of men who control the government
to get favors from the government; by those favors to exclude their
fellows from equal business opportunity; by those favors to extend
a network of control that will presently dominate every industry in
the country, and so make men forget the ancient time when America lay in every hamlet, when America was to be seen in every fair
valley, when America displayed her great forces on the broad
prairies, ran her fine fires of enterprise up over the mountainsides
and down into the bowels of the earth, and eager men were everywhere captains of industry, not employees; not looking to a distant
city to find out what they might do, but looking about among their
neighbors, finding credit according to their character, not according
to their connections, finding credit in proportion to what was
known to be in them and behind them, not in proportion to the
securities they held that were approved where they were not known.
In order to start an enterprise now, you have to be authenticated, in
a perfectly impersonal way, not according to yourself, but according to what you own that somebody else approves of your owning.
You cannot begin such an enterprise as those that have made America until you are so authenticated, until you have succeeded in obtaining the good-will of large allied capitalists.   Is that freedom?
That is dependence, not freedom.

We used to think in the old-fashioned days when life was very
simple that all that government had to do was to put on a policeman's uniform, and say, "Now don't anybody hurt anybody else."
We used to say that the ideal of government was for every man to
be left alone and not interfered with, except when he interfered
with somebody else; and that the best government was the government that did as little governing as possible.   That was the idea
that obtained in Jefferson's time.   But we are coming now to realize
that life is so complicated that we are not dealing with the old
conditions, and that the law has to step in and create new conditions under which we may live, the conditions which will make it
tolerable for us to live.

Let me illustrate what I mean: It used to be true in our cities
that every family occupied a separate house of its own, that every

family had its own little premises, that every family was separated in its life from every other family. That is no longer the case in our great cities. Families live in tenements, they live in flats, they live on floors; they are piled layer upon layer in the great tenement houses of our crowded districts, and not only are they piled layer upon layer, but they are associated room by room, so that there is in every room, sometimes, in our congested districts, a separate family. In some foreign countries they have made much more progress than we in handling these things. In the city of Glasgow, for example (Glasgow is one of the model cities of the world), they have made up their minds that the entries and the hallways of great tenements are public streets. Therefore, the policeman goes up the stairway, and patrols the corridors; the lighting department of the city sees to it that the halls are abundantly lighted. The city does not deceive itself into supposing that that great building is a unit from which the police are to keep out and the civic authority to be excluded, but it says: "These are public highways, and light is needed in them, and control by the authority of the city."

I liken that to our great modern industrial enterprises. A corporation is very like a large tenement house; it isn't the premises of a single commercial family; it is just as much a public affair as a tenement house is a network of public highways.

When you offer the securities of a great corporation to anybody who wishes to purchase them, you must open that corporation to the inspection of everybody who wants to purchase. There must, to follow out the figure of the tenement house, be lights along the corridors, there must be police patrolling the openings, there must be inspection wherever it is known that men may be deceived with regard to the contents of the premises. If we believe that fraud lies in wait for us, we must have the means of determining whether our suspicions are well founded or not. Similarly, the treatment of labor by the great corporations is not what it was in Jefferson's time. Whenever bodies of men employ bodies of men, it ceases to be a private relationship. So that when courts hold that workingmen cannot peaceably dissuade other workingmen from taking employment, as was held in a notable case in New Jersey, they simply show that their minds and understandings are lingering in an age which has passed away. This dealing of great bodies of men with other bodies of men is a matter of public scrutiny, and should be a matter of public regulation.

Similarly, it was no business of the law in the time of Jefferson to come into my house and see how I kept house. But when my house, when my so-called private property, became a great mine, and men went along dark corridors amidst every kind of danger in order to dig out of the bowels of the earth things necessary for the industries of a whole nation, and when it came about that no individual owned these mines, that they were owned by great stock companies, then all the old analogies absolutely collapsed and it became the right of the government to go down into these mines to see whether human beings were properly treated in them or not; to see whether accidents were properly safeguarded against; to see whether modern economical methods of using these inestimable riches of the earth were followed or were not followed. If somebody puts a derrick improperly secured on top of a building or overtopping the street, then the government of the city has the right to see that that derrick is so secured that you and I can walk under it and not be afraid that the heavens are going to fall on us. Likewise, in these great beehives where in every corridor swarm men of flesh and blood, it is the privilege of the government, whether of the State or of the United States, as the case may be, to see that human life is protected, that human lungs have something to breathe.

These, again, are merely illustrations of conditions. We are in a new world, struggling under old laws. As we go inspecting our lives to-day, surveying this new scene of centralized and complex society, we shall find many more things out of joint. . . .

The transition we are witnessing is no equable transition of growth and normal alteration; no silent, unconscious unfolding of one age into another, its natural heir and successor. Society is looking itself over, in our day, from top to bottom; is making fresh and critical analysis of its very elements; is questioning its oldest practices as freely as its newest, scrutinizing every arrangement and motive of its life; and it stands ready to attempt nothing less than a radical reconstruction, which only frank and honest counsels and the forces of generous co-operation can hold back from becoming a revolution. We are in a temper to reconstruct economic society, as we were once in a temper to reconstruct political society, and political society may itself undergo a radical modification in the process. I doubt if any age was ever more conscious of its task or more unanimously desirous of radical and extended changes in its economic and political practice.

We stand in the presence of a revolution,—not a bloody revolution; America is not given to the spilling of blood,—but a silent revolution, whereby America will insist upon recovering in practice those ideals which she has always professed, upon securing a government devoted to the general interest and not to special interests.

We are upon the eve of a great reconstruction. It calls for creative statesmanship as no age has done since that great age in which we set up the government under which we live, that government which was the admiration of the world until it suffered wrongs to grow up under it which have made many of our own compatriots question the freedom of our institutions and preach revolution against them. I do not fear revolution. I have unshaken faith in the power of America to keep its self-possession. Revolution will come in peaceful guise, as it came when we put aside the crude government of the Confederation and created the great Federal Union which governs individuals, not States, and which has been these hundred and thirty years our vehicle of progress. Some radical changes we must make in our law and practice. Some reconstructions we must push forward, which a new age and new circumstances impose upon us. But we can do it all in calm and sober fashion, like statesmen and patriots.

I do not speak of these things in apprehension, because all is open and above-board. This is not a day in which great forces rally in secret. The whole stupendous program must be publicly planned and canvassed. Good temper, the wisdom that comes of sober counsel, the energy of thoughtful and unselfish men, the habit of co-operation and of compromise which has been bred in us by long years of free government, in which reason rather than passion has been made to prevail by the sheer virtue of candid and universal debate, will enable us to win through to still another great age without violence.

23. FRANKLIN D. ROOSEVELT (1882–   )

FRANKLIN DELANO ROOSEVELT was born at Hyde Park, New York, fifth cousin of former President Theodore Roosevelt. He was educated at Groton, Harvard, and the law school of Columbia University, and was a member of law firms in New York City (1907–10, 1924–33). He held office as New York State senator (1910–13), assistant secretary of the navy (1913–20), and governor of New York (1929–33). He was Democratic candidate for the vice-presidency in 1920. Chosen President in 1933 and twice reelected, he became (in 1941) the first to enter that office for a third term. His political ideas are found in some of his messages and addresses, and in several brief books, including *Whither Bound* (1926), *Looking Forward* (1933), and *On Our Way* (1934).

From LOOKING FORWARD (1933) [1]

Ch. i. Reappraisal of Values.

The issue of government has always been whether individual men and women will have to serve some system of government or economics or whether a system of government and economics exists to serve individual men and women. . . .

There were those who, because they had seen the confusion which attended the years of war for American independence, surrendered to the belief that popular government was essentially dangerous and essentially unworkable. These thinkers were, generally, honest and we cannot deny that their experience had warranted some measure of fear.

The most brilliant, honest and able exponent of this point of view was Hamilton. He was too impatient of slow-moving methods. Fundamentally, he believed that the safety of the Republic lay in the autocratic strength of its government, that the destiny of individuals was to serve that government and that a great and

[1] Franklin Delano Roosevelt, *Looking Forward* (New York, 1933), from chs. i and ii, at pp. 17, 19–27, 31–34, 39, 43–51. By courtesy of The John Day Company.

strong group of central institutions, guided by a small group of able and public-spirited citizens, could best direct all government.

But Jefferson, in the summer of 1776, after drafting the Declaration of Independence, turned his mind to the same problem and took a different view. He did not deceive himself with outward forms. Government with him was a means to an end, not an end in itself; it might be either a refuge and a help or a threat and a danger, depending on the circumstances. We find him carefully analyzing the society for which he was to organize a government:

"We have no paupers—the great mass of our population is of laborers, our rich who cannot live without labor, either manual or professional, being few and of moderate wealth. Most of the laboring class possess property, cultivate their own lands, have families and from the demands for their labor are enabled to extract from the rich and the competent such prices as enable them to feed abundantly, clothe above mere decency, to labor moderately and raise their families."

These people, he considered, had two sets of rights, those of "personal competency" and those involved in acquiring and possessing property. By "personal competency" he meant the right of free thinking, freedom of forming and expressing opinions and freedom of personal living, each man according to his own lights.

To insure the first set of rights a government must so order its functions as not to interfere with the individual. But even Jefferson realized that the exercise of the property rights must so interfere with the rights of the individual that the government, without whose assistance the property rights could not exist, must intervene, not to destroy individualism but to protect it.

We are familiar with the great political duel which followed; and how Hamilton and his friends, building toward a dominant, centralized power, were at length defeated in the great election of 1800 by Jefferson's party. Out of that duel came the two parties, Republican and Democratic, as we know them today.

So began, in American political life, the new day, the day of the individual against the system, the day in which individualism was made the great watchword in American life. The happiest of economic conditions made that day long and splendid. On the Western frontier land was substantially free. No one who did not shirk the task of earning a living was entirely without opportunity to do so. Depressions could, and did, come and go; but they could not alter the fundamental fact that most of the people lived partly by selling their labor and partly by extracting their livelihood from the soil, so that starvation and dislocation were practically impossible. At the very worst there was always the possibility of climbing into a covered wagon and moving West, where the untilled prairies afforded a haven for men to whom the East did not provide a place.

So great were our natural resources that we could offer this relief not only to our own people but to the distressed of all the world. We could invite immigration from Europe and welcome it with open arms.

When a depression came a new section of land was opened in the West. This became our tradition. So even our temporary misfortune served our manifest destiny.

But a new force was released and a new dream created in the middle of the nineteenth century. The force was what is called the industrial revolution, the advance of steam and machinery and the rise of the forerunners of the modern industrial plant. The dream was that of an economic machine, able to raise the standard of living for everyone; to bring luxury within the reach of the humblest; to annihilate distance by steam power and later by electricity, and to release everyone from the drudgery of the heaviest manual toil.

It was to be expected that the force and the dream would necessarily affect government. Heretofore, government had merely been called upon to produce conditions within which people could live happily, labor peacefully and rest secure. Now it was called upon to aid in the consummation of this new dream. There was, however, a shadow over it. To make the dream real required use of the talents of men of tremendous will and tremendous ambition, since in no other way could the problems of financing and engineering and new development be met.

So manifest were the advantages of the machine age, however, that the United States fearlessly, cheerfully and, I think, rightly accepted the bitter with the sweet. It was thought that no price was too high for the advantages which we could draw from a finished industrial system.

The history of the last half century is accordingly in large measure a history of financial titans, whose methods were not scrutinized with too much care and who were honored in proportion as they produced the results, irrespective of the means they used. The financiers who pushed the railroads to the Pacific, for example, were always ruthless, often wasteful and frequently corrupt, but they did build railroads and we have them today. It has been estimated that the American investor paid for the American railway system more than three times over in the process, but despite this fact the net advantage was to the United States.

As long as we had free land, as long as population was growing by leaps and bounds, as long as our industrial plants were insufficient to supply our own needs, society chose to give the ambitious man free play and unlimited reward, provided only that he produced the economic plant so much desired.

During the period of expansion there was equal economic opportunity for all, and the business of government was not to interfere but to assist in the development of industry. This was done at the request of the business men themselves. The tariff was originally imposed for the purpose of "fostering our infant industry," a phrase which the older among my readers will remember as a political issue not so long ago.

The railroads were subsidized, sometimes by grants of money, oftener by grants of land. Some of the most valuable oil lands in the United States were granted to assist the financing of the railroad which pushed through the Southwest. A nascent merchant marine was assisted by grants of money or by mail subsidies, so that our steam shipping might ply the seven seas. . . .

In retrospect we can see now that the turn of the tide came with the turn of the century. We were reaching our last frontier then; there was no more free land and our industrial combinations had become great uncontrolled and irresponsible units of power within the State.

Clear-sighted men saw with fear the danger that opportunity would no longer be equal; that the growing corporation, like the feudal baron of old, might threaten the economic freedom of individuals to earn a living. In that hour our anti-trust laws were born.

The cry was raised against the great corporations. Theodore Roosevelt, the first great Republican Progressive, fought a Presidential campaign on the issues of "trust busting" and talked freely about malefactors of great wealth. If the government had a policy it was rather to turn the clock back, to destroy the large combinations and to return to the time when every man owned his individual small business. This was impossible. Theodore Roosevelt, abandoning his idea of "trust busting," was forced to work out a difference between "good" trusts and "bad" trusts. The Supreme Court set forth the famous "rule of reason" by which it seems to have meant that a concentration of industrial power was permissible if the method by which it got its power and the use it made of that power was reasonable.

The situation was seen more clearly by Woodrow Wilson, elected in 1912. Where Jefferson had feared the encroachment of political power on the lives of individuals, Wilson knew that the new power was financial. He saw, in the highly centralized economic system, the despot of the twentieth century, on whom great masses of individuals relied for their safety and their livelihood, and whose irresponsibility and greed (if it were not controlled) would reduce them to starvation and penury. . . .

Opportunity in business has further narrowed since Wilson's time, just as freedom to farm has ceased. It is still true that men can start small enterprises, trusting to their native shrewdness and ability to keep abreast of competitors; but area after area has been pre-empted altogether by the great corporations, and even in the fields which still have no great concerns the small man starts under a handicap. The unfeeling statistics of the past three decades show that the independent business man is running a losing race. Perhaps he is forced to the wall; perhaps he cannot command credit; perhaps he is "squeezed out," in Wilson's words, by highly organized corporate competitors, as your corner grocery man can tell you.

Recently a careful study was made of the concentration of business in the United States. It showed that our economic life was dominated by some six hundred odd corporations who controlled two-thirds of American industry. Ten million small business men divided the other third.

More striking still, it appeared that, if the process of concentration goes on at the same rate, at the end of another century we shall have all American industry controlled by a dozen corporations and run by perhaps a hundred men. Put plainly, we are steering a steady course toward economic oligarchy, if we are not there already.

Clearly all this calls for a reappraisal of values. A mere builder of more industrial plants, a creator of more railroad systems, an organizer of more corporations, is as likely to be a danger as a help. The day of the great promoter or the financial titan, to whom we granted everything if only he would build or develop, is over.

Our task now is not discovery or exploitation of natural resources or necessarily of producing more goods. It is the soberer, less dramatic business of administering resources and plants already in hand, of seeking to reestablish foreign markets for our surplus production, of meeting the problem of under-consumption, or adjusting production to consumption, of distributing wealth and products more equitably, of adapting existing economic organization to the service of the people.

Just as in older times the central government was first a haven of refuge and then a threat, so now, in a closer economic system the central and ambitious financial unit is no longer a servant of national desire but a danger. I would draw the parallel one step further. We do not think, because national government became a threat in the eighteenth century, that therefore we should abandon the principle of national government.

Nor today should we abandon the principle of strong economic units called corporations merely because their power is susceptible to easy abuse. In other times we dealt with the problem of an unduly ambitious central government by modifying it gradually into a constitutional democratic government. So today we are modifying and controlling our economic units.

As I see it, the task of government in its relation to business is to assist the development of an economic declaration of rights, an economic constitutional order. This is the common task of statesmen and business men. It is the minimum requirement of a more permanently safe order of society. Happily, the times indicate that to create such an order is not only the proper policy of government but is the only line of safety for our economic structure as well.

We know now that these economic units cannot exist unless prosperity is uniform—that is, unless purchasing power is well distributed throughout every group in the nation. That is why even the most selfish of corporations, for its own interest, would be glad to see wages restored and unemployment aided, and to bring the farmer back to his accustomed level of prosperity, and to assure a permanent safety for both groups. That is why some enlightened industries endeavor to limit the freedom of action of each man and business group within the industry in the common interest of all. That is why business men everywhere are asking for a form of organization which will bring the scheme of things into balance, even though it may in some measure qualify the freedom of action of individual units within the business. . . .

Ch. ii. Need for Economic Planning.

The evidences of change in our social order are so numerous, so tragic in some of their consequences, and so surely indicative of the necessity of sanity in all our planning for the future that there can be no argument with regard to the patriotic and self-sacrificing attitude all men should take who have been given the duty of governing, of legislating and of administering the business of the people. . . .

In the same way we cannot review carefully the history of our industrial advance without being struck by its haphazardness, with the gigantic waste with which it has been accomplished—with the superfluous duplication of productive facilities, the continual scrapping of still useful equipment, the tremendous mortality in industrial and commercial undertakings, the thousands of dead-end trails in which enterprise has been lured, the profligate waste of natural resources.

Much of this waste is the inevitable by-product of progress in a society which values individual endeavor and which is susceptible to the changing tastes and customs of the people of which it is composed. But much of it, I believe, could have been prevented by greater foresight and by a larger measure of social planning.

Such controlling and directive forces as have been developed in recent years reside to a dangerous degree in groups having special interests in our economic order, interests which do not coincide with the interests of the nation as a whole. I believe that the recent course of our history has demonstrated that, while we may utilize their expert knowledge of certain problems and the special facilities with which they are familiar, we cannot allow our economic life to be controlled by that small group of men whose chief outlook upon the social welfare is tinctured by the fact that they can make huge profits from the lending of money and the marketing of securities—an outlook which deserves the adjectives "selfish" and "opportunist."

There is a tragic irony in our economic situation today. We have not been brought to our present state by any natural calamity —by drouth or floods or earthquakes, or by the destruction of our productive machine or our man power. We have a superabundance of raw materials, of equipment for manufacturing these materials into the goods which we need, and transportation and commercial facilities for making them available to all who need them. A great portion of our machinery and our facilities stand idle, while millions of able-bodied and intelligent men and women, in dire need, are clamoring for the opportunity to work. Our power to operate the economic machine which we have created is challenged.

We are presented with a multitude of views as to how we may again set into motion that economic machine. Some hold to the theory that the periodic slowing down of the machine is one of its inherent peculiarities, a peculiarity which we must grin about and bear, because if we attempt to tamper with it we shall cause even worse trouble. According to this theory, as I see it, if we grin and bear long enough, the economic machine will eventually begin to pick up speed and in the course of an indefinite number of years will again attain the maximum number of revolutions signifying what we have been wont to miscall prosperity—but which, alas, is but a last ostentatious twirl of the economic machine before it again succumbs to that mysterious impulse to slow down again.

This attitude toward our economic machine requires not only greater stoicism but greater faith in immutable economic law and less faith in the ability of man to control what he has created than I, for one, have. Whatever elements of truth lie in it, it is an invitation to sit back and do nothing; and all of us are suffering today, I believe, because this comfortable theory was too thoroughly implanted in the minds of some of our leaders, both in finance and in public affairs.

Other students of economics trace our present difficulties to the ravages of the World War and its bequest of unsolved political and economic and financial problems. Still others trace our difficulties to defects in the world's monetary systems.

Whether it be an original cause, an accentuating cause, or an effect, the drastic change in the value of our monetary unit in terms of the commodities it will buy is a problem which we must meet straightforwardly. It is self-evident that we must either restore commodities to a level approximating their dollar value of several years ago or else that we must continue the destructive process of reducing, through defaults or through deliberate writing down, obligations assumed at a higher price level.

Possibly because of the urgency and complexity of this problem some of our economic thinkers have been occupied with it to the exclusion of other phases of as great importance.

Of these other phases, that one which seems most important to me in the long run is the problem of controlling, by adequate planning, the creation and the distribution of those products which our vast economic machine is capable of yielding.

I do not mean to curtail the use of capital. I do not mean to curtail new enterprise. But think carefully of the vast sums of capital or credit which in the past decade have been devoted to unjust enterprises—to the development of unessentials and to the multiplication of many products far beyond the capacity of the nation to absorb. It has been the same story as the thoughtless turning out of too many school teachers and too many lawyers.

In the field of industry and business many of those whose primary solicitude is confined to the welfare of what they call capital have failed to read the lessons of the past few years and have been moved less by calm analysis of the needs of the nation as a whole than by a blind determination to preserve their own special stakes in the economic order.

I do not mean to intimate that we have come to the end of the period of expansion. We shall continue to need capital for the production of newly invented devices, for the replacement of equipment worn out or rendered obsolete by our technical progress. A great deal will have to be done to make us decent, healthy, and as happy as our several natures will permit. We need better housing in most of our cities. Many parts of our country still need more and better roads. There is urgent necessity for canals, parks and other physical improvements.

But it seems to me that our physical economic plant will not expand in the future at the same rate at which it has been expanded in the past. We may build more factories, but the fact remains that we have enough to supply all of our domestic needs, and more, if they are used. With these factories we can now make more shoes, more textiles, more steel, more radios, more automobiles, more of almost everything than we can use.

Our basic trouble was not an insufficiency of capital. It was an insufficient distribution of buying power, coupled with an over-sufficient speculation in production. While wages rose in many of our industries, they did not as a whole rise proportionately to the reward to capital, and at the same time the purchasing power of other great groups of our population was permitted to shrink. We accumulated such a superabundance of capital that our great bankers were vying with each other, some of them employing questionable methods, in their efforts to lend this capital at home and abroad.

I believe that we are at the threshold of a fundamental change in our economic thought. I believe that in the future we are going to think less about the producer and more about the consumer. Do what we may to inject health into our ailing economic order, we cannot make it endure for long unless we can bring about a wiser, more equitable distribution of the national income.

It is well within the inventive capacity of man, who has built up this great social and economic machine capable of satisfying the wants of all, to insure that all who are willing and able to work receive from it at least the necessities of life. In such a system, the reward for a day's work will have to be greater, on the average, than it has been, and the reward to capital, especially capital which is speculative, will have to be less.

But I believe that after the experience of the last three years, the average citizen would rather receive a smaller return upon his savings in return for greater security for the principal, than to experience for a moment the thrill or the prospect of being a millionaire only to find the next moment that his fortune, actual or expected, has withered in his hand because the economic machine has again broken down.

It is toward stability that we must move if we are to profit by our recent experience. Few will disagree that the goal is desirable.

Yet many of faint heart, fearful of change, sitting tightly to the roof-tops in the flood, will sternly resist striking out for this objective lest they fail to attain it. Even among those who are willing to attempt the journey there will be violent differences of opinion as to how it should be made. So complex, so widely distributed over our whole country are the problems which confront us that men and women of common aim do not agree upon the method of attacking them. Such disagreement leads to doing nothing, to drifting. Agreement may come too late.

Let us not confuse objectives with methods. Too many so-called leaders of the nation fail to see the forest because of the trees. Too many of them fail to recognize the necessity of planning for definite objectives. True leadership calls for the setting forth of the objectives and the rallying of public opinion in support of these objectives.

When the nation becomes substantially united in favor of planning the broad objectives of civilization, then true leadership must unite thought behind definite methods.

The country needs and, unless I mistake its temper, the country demands bold, persistent experimentation. It is common sense to take a method and try it; if it fails, admit it frankly and try another. But above all, try something. The millions who are in want will not stand by silently forever while the things to satisfy their needs are within easy reach.

We need enthusiasm, imagination and ability to face facts, even unpleasant ones, bravely. We need to correct by drastic means if necessary the faults in our economic system from which we now suffer. We need the courage of the young.

24. HENRY A. WALLACE (1888–   )

HENRY A. WALLACE was assistant editor and editor (1924–29) of *Wallace's Farmer* (a leading farm magazine established by his father, Henry Cantwell Wallace, secretary of agriculture, 1921–24), and editor of *Iowa Homestead and Wallace's Farmer* (1929–33). He was United States secretary of agriculture during the first two terms of President F. D. Roosevelt and took office as vice-president on January 20, 1941. He is the author of several books on agricultural subjects. After joining the Roosevelt administration he wrote several works on ethical aspects of present-day economic society and was accepted as a leading theoretical interpreter of the "New Deal"; these works include *America Must Choose* (1934), *New Frontiers* (1934), *Technology, Corporations and the General Welfare* (1937), and *Paths to Plenty* (1938).

From NEW FRONTIERS (1934) [1]

Explorers and Pioneers.

The United States is like a boy eighteen years old, possessed of excellent health and a strong body, but so unsettled in his mind and feelings that he doesn't know what to do next.

In the old days before the World War our fathers and grandfathers had their troubles and disagreements, but they agreed for the most part that this was a land of unlimited opportunity; that we would have continually more machinery and more inventions; that our cities would be getting bigger, our land values higher, and our opportunities for personal profit greater all the time.

For ten generations white people on this continent moved forward in this faith. There were times of serious setback, for example, the thirties, seventies, and nineties of the last century, but in those days depression could be cured by the pioneer virtue of optimistic grab and toil. Continual immigration from abroad, ex-

[1] Henry A. Wallace, *New Frontiers* (New York, 1934), from chs. i, ii, iii. By special arrangement with Reynal & Hitchcock, Inc.

731

pansion into the new lands of the West and the building of railroads and highways acted as feeders to growing cities. These developments confirmed in our fathers those energetic individualistic
traits which are peculiarly American. . . .

The tragic joke on the United States is that we went to bed as a
pioneer debtor nation in 1914 and woke up after a nightmare of
world madness as a presumably mature creditor nation in 1920.
We were full grown in the same sense that a boy of eighteen is
full grown. But ever since 1920 that boy of eighteen has been playing in the sand pile.

We educated our children—among them, millions of unemployed young—in the belief that the United States was still a pioneer country where the rugged, individualistic virtues of hard work
and saving would inevitably bring success. We did not tell our
sons and daughters that they were caught between two worlds, and
that in the new world it will take more than hard work and saving
to insure salvation.

I look at the unemployed, especially the younger ones among
them, and am reminded of the verse from the Psalms: "The stone
which the builders rejected has become the head of the corner."
In all truth, one of the most significant facts of this age is the continuous unemployment of millions of good people. Out of this is
bound to come pressure which will either destroy the old world, or
create a new world, or do both. . . .

My generation must face both ways.

It is our privilege and disadvantage to look at the Bourbons, the
wealthy troglodytes of the preceding generation, repeating in their
ignorance outworn phrases, seeking to patch their outworn economic structure and defend it from the poverty-stricken radicals,
many of whom are just as ignorant as the troglodytes.

My generation wishes the new generation would spend more
time trying to build seaworthy vessels in which to reach a new
world and less time bothering with the troglodytes, who are rapidly
dying off, anyway. . . .

Our young people may wait until we are ready for them to begin,
or they may not; but they will not wait forever. During the past
four jobless years they have become terribly disillusioned. They
are poor in experience, influence, learning, and money. Doubtless

they need to know much more than they do about the facts of to-day. Most of all, they need to have their imaginations aroused to the possibilities of the future.

The younger people of the United States have more marvelous things to work with during the next generation than any people ever had. We have in the United States, extraordinary resources of rich soil and abundant coal, with petroleum and minerals conveniently located. Our proportion of resources to population is very great. With ordinary common sense a high standard of living in terms of material things is almost inevitable. Our climate is invigorating to human beings. The human beings now here have been drawn from among the most intelligent and vigorous racial stocks of the old world. Railways, highways, factories, and all the varied equipment necessary for abundant production and rapid distribution have been built. Able research men are at work in the endowed institutions, the State experiment stations, in the Federal Government and in the commercial laboratories, finding new and better ways of getting things done.

Able men, unequalled resources, inventive genius—here are the materials which the older generation, partly as a result of inept leadership, partly as a result of war, have so terribly foozled. Here is the challenge to all younger adaptable spirits possessing sufficient courage and insight to enter upon a plan of national coordination, realistic, yet idealistic. . . .

What we approach is not a new continent but a new state of heart and mind resulting in new standards of accomplishment. We must invent, build and put to work new social machinery. This machinery will carry out the Sermon on the Mount as well as the present social machinery carries out and intensifies the law of the jungle.

Thus we who live in the land of yesterday exhort each other with high sounding phrases to go pioneering anew. That is all right, but it should also be stated that the hard, daily work in this land of tomorrow will be appalling, and it will not lighten until vast but possible changes have been brought about in human hearts and minds.

The greatest hope is that hearts and minds will be changed in a considerable measure by the changed nature of the work. The work will be literally of a million different kinds; and it will move increasingly to an enforced realization that unrestrained selfishness is ruinous to everyone.

The plan cannot be sketched out definitely in advance any more than William Penn could sketch out for the next 100 years the destiny of Pennsylvania. This does not mean that the central core of a plan will not begin to emerge, or that the smaller segments should not be definitely blueprinted. But it does suggest that there must be a combination of flexibility and determination in definite execution. . . .

New Rules.

Two aspects of the problem stand out clearly. One has to do with planning in the physical sense of the term. The other has to do with changing the rules of the game—with laws governing tariffs, money, the regulation of corporations, taxation, and railroad and public utility rates.

We must control that part of our individualism which produces anarchy and widespread misery. If the majority of us are to have automobiles, we must obey the traffic lights and observe certain rules of common decency in order to get speedily and safely from one place to another. In the process our individuality has been curbed, but once certain habits of mutual consideration are established, we discover that the advantages outweigh the handicaps. The range of individual expression has really been widened.

Insofar as the process of production and distribution operates on a large scale over wide territories, it will be absolutely necessary for the state to assume its true functions of "directing, watching, stimulating and restraining as circumstances suggest or necessity demands." The words quoted are from no less a radical than Pope Pius XI, who has also stated that there should be "a reasonable relationship between the prices obtained for the products of the various economic groups, agrarian, industrial, etc." Most broadminded people will further agree that it is a function of the state to promulgate such a spirit of justice as will bring about that harmonious proportion in which "men's various economic activities combine and unite into one single organism and become members of a common body, lending each other mutual help and services."

Obviously, certain limits must be placed on competition and individualism. These limits should be placed by a state in the justice of whose acts there is absolute confidence. The limits should not deal with irritating particulars but with broad outlines. On these broad outlines, there should be substantial unanimity of opinion among thinking people in both the Republican and Democratic parties, and among leaders of labor, industry and agriculture. If such agreement can be reached there will be infinite opportunities for the 125 million individuals of the United States to develop their ruggedness to mutual advantage instead of to their competitive disadvantage.

It is important for all, and for younger people especially, to realize that the New Deal spirit ebbs and flows. Ordinarily, the progressive liberals get a real opportunity to change the rules only about once in a generation. Human nature is such that complacency prevails and conservatives stay in the saddle until things get pretty bad. From a logical point of view the leadership of the United States from 1920 to 1930 was bad. But the conservatives stayed in power. Most people resolutely refuse to think politically if they have jobs, a place to sleep and something to eat and wear. The economic well-being of the moment was pumped up by a false statesmanship. It took ten years and an economic smash before the people would heed the warnings of those who said, "This thing is built on sand."

Most of the so-called young liberals of today received their first political inspiration between 1906 and 1915 from Woodrow Wilson and Theodore Roosevelt. They saw liberalism go out of date in the '20's and wondered if the American people had permanently accepted a Belly-God. The young men who today are between eighteen and thirty years of age and who are anxious to see America built over fundamentally and completely in line with their dreams, will perhaps also have an opportunity to watch the conservatives get back into power. This may not come for eight, twelve or sixteen years, but it will come almost as surely as prosperity returns. People like to be comfortable and "let alone." The conservative is bound to triumph fully half the time.

But it must also be remembered that there is something inherently inadequate and often rotting about comfort. The conservative type of mind is constitutionally incapable of understanding the inevitability of certain changes. . . .

As a rule the conservative type of mind is so instinctively and continuously self-centered that it is always being surprised by changing forces. The liberals need the conservatives and the conservatives need the liberals. Only by forthright attack and counter-attack can the people be stimulated really to think.

I am not suggesting that all our younger people be liberals. There are many who should be conservatives. I am deeply concerned, however, that the leadership of the future, whether liberal or conservative, should grapple more definitely and clearly with the facts and forces involved. It seems a pity that the liberals and conservatives, the Democrats and the Republicans, as we call them now, should spend so much time calling each other names. There are tremendously important problems to be put before the people. It may not be good politics to conduct this education, but it is absolutely vital if our democracy is to survive.

Middle Courses.

I am hoping we can advance by means of an aroused, educated Democracy. Socialism, Communism, and Fascism, it is true, have the advantage of certain precise rules not available to Democracy. They make the path to the land of tomorrow seem straight and short. The only rules a democracy can rely upon make the path seem by comparison long and tortuous. But the point is that most Americans think less rigid rules and the clash of free opinion allowed by Democracy will in the long run take us farther than will the precise, decisive dogma of Communism or Fascism. So do I.

There is nothing novel or sensational about the rules of the game I have in mind. Until recently, however, the full significance of such rules has been obscured, and the rules have been manipulated more or less secretly for the benefit of the few at the expense of the many. Now the time seems ripe for a change in behalf of the many.

The first step is to understand these rules in all their significance. They have to do with such devices as the tariff, the balance of international payments, monetary policy, subsidies, taxation, price and production policies, and railroad rate regulations. Their significance lies in the fact that by their manipulation it is possible to direct, stimulate, restrain, and balance those forces which have to do with proportioning the national income. All governments that

have advanced beyond the pioneer stage find it necessary to use
such controls, in lieu of free competition. In using them, a democracy worthy of the name must be guided by concern for social
justice and social charity—in other words, the greatest good for
the greatest number.

Reliance upon such devices to redistribute income and opportunity, is not the way of Socialism, of Communism or of Fascism.
Neither is it the way of the free-booter capitalists of the neo-
Manchester school of economics. With their devotion to unlimited competition, these people seem to think the traffic lights
should be removed so motorists and pedestrians might illustrate
the doctrine of the survival of the fittest at every street corner. It
is necessary in a democracy to furnish the red and green lights to
guide the traffic, but not to supply drivers for every car on the
road.

Long before the World War, competition was limited by rules,
both public and private. Since then, it has been limited increasingly. The vital question is: In whose behalf is competition limited? Is the limitation making the rich richer and the poor poorer?
If so, there is danger that a day may come when the extreme left
will join hands with the extreme right to bring about that most
dangerous of all forms of government, a corrupt oligarchy, maintaining itself in power by pandering to the vices and prejudices of
a bitter, materialistic, perennially unemployed multitude.

An enduring democracy can be had only by promoting a balance
among all our major producing groups, and in such a way as does
not build up a small, inordinately wealthy class. The danger in
democracies, as we have known them in the past, is this: All too
easily, under pressure of changing conditions, they play into the
hands of either the extreme left or the extreme right. The same
legislators will allow themselves to be stampeded by scared capitalists toward the extreme right, and by the unemployed toward
the extreme left. The complexities and the confusion of modern
civilization are such that legislators quickly forget objectives of social and economic balance, and give way to the special pressures of
the moment.

There is no likelihood of a dictatorship in this country, whether
of the proletariat, of the technicians, or of the financiers, unless our
middle class is wiped out. If we get into a really big war, the after-

effect might include something of this sort; but without such a catastrophe it would seem that we have much better than an even chance to use our democratic powers and escape such regimentation by government as has been invoked in the totalitarian or autarchic states of Europe.

There is something wooden and inhuman about the government interfering in a definite, precise way with the details of our private and business lives. It suggests a time of war with generals and captains telling every individual exactly what he must do each day and hour. The Great War gave blueprint planning and regimented adherence to a plan a tremendous impetus. For several years hundreds of millions of people had definite objectives held before them in a tone of command. Their psychology was to some extent definitely altered. With their middle classes pauperized, and with the war methods of planning as an inspiration, it is small wonder that Italy, Germany, and Russia have since continued blueprint planning.

I see no reason as yet why we in the United States should go into precise detailed planning except, perhaps, with respect to natural resources and to certain rather small segments of our national life on an emergency basis. With the situation that exists and is likely to exist in the United States for the next ten years, the chief objective of our democracy should be so to manage the tariff, and the money system, to control railroad interest rates; and to encourage price and production policies that will maintain a continually balanced relationship between the income of agriculture, labor, and industry. . . .

25. HERBERT HOOVER (1874–   )

HERBERT CLARK HOOVER, born in West Branch, Iowa, is a graduate in engineering from Stanford University, and for two decades was engaged in professional work in mining, railway, and metal firms in various parts of the world. He served on several commissions during the period of the World War, notably as chairman of the commission for relief in Belgium (1915–19) and as United States food administrator (1917–19). He was secretary of commerce in the administrations of Harding and Coolidge and he was President for one term (1929–33). His political views are set forth in *American Individualism* (1922), *The Challenge to Liberty* (1934), and *American Road* (1938); and in numerous public addresses criticizing the policies of President F. D. Roosevelt.

"WE MAY SUM UP" (1934) [1]

The issue of civilization today is whether Liberty can survive the wounds it has received in these recent years.

After the war Liberalism came into a vast ascendency. The arms of democracy had been victorious over the legions of despotism. Those dismembered nations hastened with high hopes to adopt the forms and endeavored to develop the spirit of individual Liberty. Then came the dreadful aftermaths—the vengeful peace, the continuation of hate, the realization of losses from the gigantic destruction, the rise of bitter nationalism with all its barriers and snatching for advantage, the attempts by inflations to shift and postpone the debt burdens of the day, the vicious speculation and exploitation to which inflation gives opportunity, the dislocations from rapid advances of scientific discovery and labor-saving devices, and the final plunge into the liquidation by the great depression. The human misery that has flowed from it all has discredited the social systems of all nations, no matter how great their concept of liberty, justice, and peace.

Liberalism fell first in its new-born regions, and today it is under

[1] In Herbert Hoover, *The Challenge to Liberty* (New York, 1934), ch. xi. By special arrangement with Charles Scribner's Sons.

739

attack in the great areas of its origins and development. Indeed, the fate of Liberalism rests today mainly upon three great nations, America, the British Commonwealth, and France. It is within these areas where the fortresses of freedom though much weakened can be held. If they fail the lesser outworks will fall. In America, where Liberty blazed brightest and by its glow shed light to all others, it is today impaired and endangered.

In anxiety and hope, in the yearnings of humanity for betterment, alternative philosophies of society have sprung into life, offering "solutions" for all difficulties. Whatever their names be—Fascism, Socialism, or Communism—they have this common result: wherever these systems have been imposed tyranny has been erected, government by the people abolished. The protection of law has vanished before dictation; no person is secure in justice; even the old right of *habeas corpus* is forgotten; the right of property is wholly removed or its use permitted only upon sufferance by the state; free speech, free press, the right of assembly have been banished; whispers and terror replace security and freedom of spirit. From these repressive measures comes the banishment of freedom itself.

Be it noted that even "temporary" dictatorships are achieved by the direct and emphatic promise to the people that their liberties eventually will be restored. In Russia, the theory runs that some liberty will be restored when the revolution of the proletariat is "consummated." In Italy, liberties will be restored as the people earn them by faithful obeisance before the throne of Fascism. Under Naziism, liberties will be restored when the "National Consolidation" is secured.

A sobering commentary upon the processes of mass psychology is the idea in all of these countries that Liberty may be achieved and secured only by sacrifice of liberties to the efficiency of tyranny. Certainly it is not illogical to suggest that if the ultimate purpose of dictatorships is the restoration of Liberty, the first aim of existing liberal governments should be the defense and maintenance of Liberty.

The proponents of these rival programs are often men of burning zeal. In their zeal they are willing to wipe out centuries of achievement, to ignore the bloody road over which the human race has travelled, evolving as it went the very ideals of justice and liberty. They envisage these ideals as their own and sole discovery, they adopt actions and measures which this long road of trial has proved disastrous, and they abandon the gains of freedom so painfully acquired.

From the examples of National Regimentation that we have examined it is obvious that many of its measures represent not reform or relief within the boundaries of Liberty, but that they are emulating parts of some of these other systems with the hope of speeding recovery from the depression.

One may disagree and keep silent as to the justification of some of these measures if they are to be limited to "emergency," for in the march of a great people that is relatively unimportant if that is all of it. Then these dangers and stresses will disappear as an eddy in the stream of national life. The important thing is whether this drift from essential liberties is to be permanent. If not permanent, these emergency measures will have served the purpose of having exhausted the pent-up panaceas of a generation and broken them on the wheel of resistant human behavior and the spirit of a people with a heritage of liberty.

The threat of the continuance of these "emergency" acts is a threat to join the Continental retreat of human progress backward through the long corridor of time. In the demands for continuance there lies a mixture of desperate seeking for justification of their adoption and subtle ambitions of those advocating other philosophies. Whatever the motive, the promise of permanence now stares the American people starkly in the face. It is not the mere evolution of an economic procedure that this Regimentation implies—it steps off the solid highways of true American Liberty into the dangerous quicksands of governmental dictation.

Thus what I am interested in in this inquiry is something that transcends the transitory actions, as important as they are, something far more pregnant with disaster to all that America has been to its people and to the world. No nation can introduce a new social philosophy or a new culture alien to its growth without moral and spiritual chaos. I am anxious for the future of freedom and liberty of men. That America has stood for; that has created her greatness; that is all the future holds that is worth while.

The unit of American life is the family and the home. Through it vibrates every hope of the future. It is the economic unit as well as the moral and spiritual unit. But it is more than this. It is the beginning of self-government. It is the throne of our highest ideals. It is the center of the spiritual energy of our people.

The purpose of American life is the constant betterment of all these homes. If we sustain that purpose every individual may have the vision of decent and improving life. That vision is the urge of America. It creates the buoyant spirit of our country. The inspiring hope of every real American is for an enlarged opportunity for his children. The obligation of our generation to them is to pass on the heritage of Liberty which was entrusted to us. To secure the blessings of Liberty to ourselves and to our posterity was the purpose in sacrifice of our fathers. We have no right to load upon our children unnecessary debts from our follies or to force them to meet life in regimented forms which limit their self-expression, their opportunities, their achievements. St. Paul said nearly two thousand years ago, "Ye have been called unto liberty."

Our American System and its great purpose are builded upon the positive conception that "men are endowed by their Creator with certain unalienable Rights, that among these are Life, Liberty, and the pursuit of Happiness"; that the purpose and structure of government is to protect these rights; that upon them the government itself shall not encroach. From these liberties has come that unloosing of creative instincts and aspirations which have builded this, the greatest nation of all time.

The Bill of Rights—our forefathers' listing of unalienable liberties and personal securities—was written a century and a half ago. We have had need to work out both practical application of these liberties and the machinery for maintaining them in the changing scene of the years. We have seen some of them fade from memory, such as the protection from quartering of troops. We have had to add some new rights to assure freedom from slavery and to give universal franchise. We have had to keep the balance as between some of them and to see that some—chiefly property rights —are not used to override other rights. We have steadily developed from the spirit of freedom high standards and ideals of human relationship, a great system of advancement of mankind.

We have at times failed to live up to our ideals, but that they shall continue to shine brightly is the important thing.

Those are today denounced who, on one hand, dare assert that these liberties and personal securities still live, and, on the other, they are equally denounced who assert that they have been transgressed. It will be denied that any one of them has ever been mentioned in our country for repeal or modification. Nor has it been proposed today that any new rights and securities should be added to those guaranteed by the Constitution. Therein lies the intellectual dishonesty of the attack upon them. If we have discovered that any one of these liberties is not our individual endowment by the Creator, the right thing is to propose a change in the Constitution and allow us to examine it, not to extinguish it by indirection. Such an alteration would not get far, for whether people know them by name or not, the principles of liberty and security are embedded in their daily thought and action. Perhaps not one in a hundred thousand of our people knows the detailed list of liberties our forefathers insisted upon, or the development of them since, but never a day goes by that every man and woman does not instinctively rely upon these liberties.

Yet today forces have come into action from ignorance, panic, or design which, either by subtle encroachment or by the breaking down of their safeguards, do endanger their primary purpose. These liberties are of urgent practical importance. The very employment upon which millions depend for their bread is today delayed because of the disturbance of confidence in their security.

There are those who assert that revolution has swept the United States. That is not true. But there are some who are trying to bring it about. At least they are following the vocal technique which has led elsewhere to the tragedy of Liberty. Their slogans; their promise of Utopia; their denunciation of individual wickednesses as if these were the wards of Liberty; their misrepresentation of deep-seated causes; their will to destruction of confidence and consequent disorganization in order to justify action; their stirring of class feeling and hatred; their will to clip and atrophy the legislative arm; their resentment of criticism; their chatter of boycott, of threat and of force—all are typical enough of the methods of more violent action.

In our blind groping we have stumbled into philosophies which lead to the surrender of freedom. The proposals before our country do not necessarily lead to the European forms of Fascism, of Socialism, or of Communism, but they certainly lead definitely from the path of liberty. The danger lies in the tested human experience, that a step away from liberty itself impels a second step, a second compels a third. The appetite for power grows with every opportunity to assume it, and power over the rights of men leads not to humility but to arrogance, and arrogance incessantly demands more power. A few steps so dislocate social forces that some form of despotism becomes inevitable and Liberty dies.

No country or no society can be conducted by partly acknowledging the securities of Liberty and partly denying them, not by recognizing some of them and denying others. That is part democracy and part tyranny. At once there are conflicts and interferences which not only damage the whole economic mechanism but drive unceasingly for more and more dictation.

Even partial regimentation cannot be made to work and still maintain live democratic institutions. Representative government will sooner or later be at conflict with it along the whole front, both in the incidentals of daily working and in the whole field of free choice by the people. If it be continued the Congress must further surrender its checks and balances on administration and its free criticism since these, with intensified duties to its constituents, create interferences that will make efficient administration of this regimented machine impossible.

For any plan of Regimentation to succeed it must have not only powers of rigid discipline but adamant continuity. Does anyone believe that with the interferences of the Congress and the storms of a free press any government can impose discipline and follow a consistent and undeviating course in directing the activities of 125,000,000 highly diversified people? Because such a course is impossible Fascism and Sovietism have suppressed both free speech and representative government.

We are confronted with a maze of problems. The boom and depression brought discouraging increases and disclosures of the abuses of Liberty and the growth of economic oppressions. I have discussed these abuses at length in previous chapters because these betrayals of trust, exploitation, monopoly, and all the rest of them are the battle-grounds of Liberty.

The American System has steadily evolved the protections of Liberty. In the early days of road traffic we secured a respect for liberties of others by standards of decency and courtesy in conduct between neighbors. But with the crowding of highways and streets we have invented Stop and Go signals which apply to everybody alike, in order to maintain the same ordered Liberty. But traffic signals are not a sacrifice of Liberty, they are the preservation of it. Under them each citizen moves more swiftly to his own individual purpose and attainment. That is a far different thing from the corner policeman being given the right to determine whether the citizen's mission warrants his passing and whether he is competent to execute it, and then telling him which way he should go, whether he likes it or not. That is the whole distance between ordered Liberty and Regimentation.

The achievements of our own economic system have brought us new problems in stability in business, in agriculture, and in employment, and greater security of living. But the first constructive step in solution is the preservation of Liberty, for in that sphere alone are the dynamic forces with which to solve our problems successfully.

The whole history of humanity has been a struggle against famine and want. Within less than half a century the American System has achieved a triumph in this age-long struggle by producing a plenty.

The other systems now urged for permanent adoption propose to solve the remaining problem of distribution of a hard-won plenty by restrictions which will abolish the plenty. To adopt this course would be an abject surrender. Worse, it would be a surrender to the complexities of distribution after the major battle, which is production, has been won. It may be repeated that if we undermine the stimulants to individual effort which come alone from the spirit of Liberty, we may well cease to discuss the greater "diffusion of income," "of wealth," "minimum standards," and "economic security," the "abolition of poverty," and its fears. Those are possibilities only in an economy of plenty.

It is not that the proposals or philosophies or tendencies of National Regimentation are new discoveries to humanity, which offer the bright hope of new invention or new genius in human leadership. They have the common characteristic of these other philosophies of society and of those of the Middle Ages—that the liberties of men flow only from the state; that men are subjective to the state; that men shall be regimented, not free men. Herein is the flat conflict with true Liberalism. It is all old, very, very old, the idea that the good of men arises from the direction of centralized executive power, whether it be exercised through bureaucracies, mild dictatorships or despotisms, monarchies or autocracies. For Liberty is the emancipation of men from power and servitude and the substitution of freedom for force of government.

Liberty comes alone and lives alone where the hard-won rights of men are held unalienable, where governments themselves may not infringe, where governments are indeed but the mechanisms to protect and sustain these liberties from encroachment. It was this for which our fathers died, it was this heritage they gave to us. It was not the provisions with regard to interstate commerce or the determination of weights and measures or coinage, for which the Constitution was devised—it was the guaranties that men possessed fundamental liberties apart from the state, that they were not the pawns but the masters of the state. It has not been for the aid and comfort of any form of economic domination that our liberties have been hallowed by sacrifice. It has not been for the comfort of machinery that we have builded and extended these liberties, but for the independence and comfort of homes.

Those who proclaim that in a Machine Age there is created an irreconcilable conflict in which liberty cannot survive should not forget the battles of liberty over the centuries, for let it be remembered that in the end both big business and machinery will vanish before freedom if that be necessary. But it is not necessary. It is not because Liberty is unworkable, but because we have not worked it conscientiously or have forgotten its true meaning that we often get the notion of the irreconcilable conflict with the Machine Age.

We cannot extend the mastery of government over the daily life of a people without somewhere making it master of people's souls and thoughts. That is going on today. It is part of all regimentation.

Even if the government conduct of business could give us the maximum of efficiency instead of least efficiency, it would be purchased at the cost of freedom. It would increase rather than decrease abuse and corruption, stifle initiative and invention, undermine the development of leadership, cripple the mental and spiritual energies of our people, extinguish equality of opportunity, and dry up the spirit of liberty and the forces which make progress.

It is a false Liberalism that interprets itself into government dictation, or operation of commerce, industry and agriculture. Every move in that direction poisons the very springs of true Liberalism. It poisons political equality, free thought, free press, and equality of opportunity. It is the road not to liberty but to less liberty. True Liberalism is found not in striving to spread bureaucracy, but in striving to set bounds to it. Liberalism is a force proceeding from the deep realization that economic freedom cannot be sacrificed if political freedom is to be preserved. True Liberalism seeks all legitimate freedom first in the confident belief that without such freedom the pursuit of other blessings is in vain.

The nation seeks for solution of its many difficulties. These solutions can come alone through the constructive forces from the system built upon Liberty. They cannot be achieved by the destructive forces of Regimentation. The purification of Liberty from abuses, the restoration of confidence in the rights of men, the release of the dynamic forces of initiative and enterprise are alone the methods by which these solutions can be found and the purpose of American life assured.

The structure of human betterment cannot be built upon foundations of materialism or business, but upon the bedrock of individual character in free men and women. It must be builded by those who, holding to ideals of its high purpose, using the molds of justice, lay brick upon brick from the materials of scientific research, the painstaking sifting of truth from collections of facts and experience, the advancing ideas, morals and spiritual inspirations. Any other foundations are sand, any other mold is distorted; and any other bricks are without straw.

I have no fear that the inherent and unconquerable forces of freedom will not triumph. But it is as true today as when first uttered that "the condition upon which God hath given liberty to man is eternal vigilance." We have in our lifetime seen the subjection of Liberty in one nation after another. It has been defeated by the untruth that some form of dictation by government alone can overcome immediate difficulties and can assure entry into economic perfection. America must not and it will not succumb to that lure. That is the issue of our generation, not a partisan issue but the issue of human liberty.

The spark of liberty in the mind and spirit of man cannot be long extinguished; it will break into flames that will destroy every coercion which seeks to limit it.

26. RT. REV. JOHN A. RYAN (1869–   )

FATHER RYAN, a native of Minnesota, has been a member of the faculties of several Catholic institutions of higher learning, professor of social ethics at the National Catholic School of Social Service since 1921, and director of the social action department of the National Catholic Social Welfare Conference. He has written numerous works on contemporary political applications of Christianity, including *A Living Wage* (1906), *Distributive Justice* (1916), *The Church and Socialism* (1919), *The Church and Labor* (1920), *A Better Economic Order* (1935), and *Seven Troubled Years* (1937).

From "A NEW ECONOMIC ORDER" (1935) [1]

Not Collectivism. Apparently the majority of those who demand a reorganization of the industrial system assume that the new economic order must exemplify some form of collectivistic organization.

It is clear that if we are neither to go back nor to buttress the existing system, the only other choice is an advance toward collectivism.[2]

Cumulative evidence supports the conclusion that, in the United States as in other countries, the age of individualism and laissez-faire in economy and government is closing and that a new age of collectivism is emerging.

As to the specific form which this "collectivism," this integration and interdependence, is taking and will take in the future, the evidence at hand is by no means clear or unequivocal. It may involve the limiting or supplanting of private property by public property or it may entail the preservation of private property, extended and distributed among the masses.[3]

The organization which the writer of the first of these three paragraphs had in mind is undoubtedly genuine collectivism; that

---

[1] Rt. Rev. Msgr. John A. Ryan, *A Better Economic Order* (New York, 1935), from ch. viii.   By courtesy of Harper & Brothers, publishers.

[2] Editorial in the *New Republic*, January 23, 1935.

[3] *Conclusions and Recommendations of the Social Studies Commission of the American Historical Association.*   New York, 1934.

is, public ownership and operation of at least all the great industrial concerns, in addition to mines, oil deposits and public utilities; possibly also public ownership of land and public operation of the large farms. The composer of the second paragraph seems to mean the same, until we come to the third paragraph, where we find that for him collectivism "may entail the preservation of private property, extended and distributed among the masses." If the term is to be used with a reasonable degree of definiteness, "collectivism" should not be taken as a synonym of "distributism." The sentence quoted just now from the third paragraph describes the latter, not the former. The two systems differ fundamentally. The spirit, as well as the proposals, of the one are diametrically opposed to the spirit and proposals of the other.

America does need a new economic order. Nevertheless all Americans who believe in natural rights, democracy and a rational measure of individual liberty, do not want that order to be any form of genuine collectivism. The apparently mild variety desired by Stuart Chase, Norman Thomas, the *New Republic* and a growing number of our university professors and publicists, would gravely diminish all three of these fundamental goods. Even a moderate collectivist regime would inevitably degenerate into intolerable and inefficient bureaucracy and despotism.

Industrial Self-Government: Organization by Occupational Groups. Happily a constitution for a better economic order can be found outside of collectivism. Indeed, it would be the antithesis of collectivism, no less than of capitalism. Such a constitution has been outlined and recommended by Pope Pius XI, in his encyclical, "On Reconstructing the Social Order." [1] . . .

What is the nature of the social order which the Pope wishes to see established? In more than one place he declares that the root cause of all our economic evils is individualism. There is too much individual freedom for the strong, the cunning, and the unscrupulous. There is too much freedom for powerful individuals to combine and dominate the whole of society. There is too much antagonism between economic classes. The remedy can not be more freedom for individuals, or more power for combinations. The

[1] Three ways of identifying this document are in vogue: The designation, *Quadragesimo Anno* simply quotes the opening words of the Latin text. When the same method of reference is used in English, the title becomes "Forty Years After"; i.e. after the appearance of Pope Leo XIII's *Rerum Novarum*. [Author's note.]

excesses of individualism, the tyranny of combinations, and the conflict between classes, can be adequately controlled only by the State. "When we speak of the reform of the social order," says Pope Pius, "it is principally the State we have in mind."

Many social reformers who applaud the Pope's analysis of evils and his proposal to seek a remedy in the State, will assume that he means, or ought to mean, some form of collectivism, some kind of Socialism. These persons are completely mistaken. The Holy Father does not want state ownership and operation of the means of production. He wants more, not less, rational freedom for all individuals. Class conflict he would eliminate not by a futile effort to abolish classes, but by bringing them into a practical scheme of cooperation. On the whole, he would decentralize the economic activities of the State. He would interpose a graded hierarchical order, a system of subsidiary organizations between the individual and the State.

"The aim of social legislation, therefore, must be," says the Pope, "the reestablishment of occupational groups." His choice of the word "reestablishment," instead of "establishment," shows that he is not proposing something entirely new. He is taking as a model that organization of industry known as the Guild System. In that system, masters, journeymen and apprentices, were all united in one association. Of course, that arrangement could not be set up without change in our machine system, where the place of the associated master workman is occupied by the employing capitalist and the place of the associated journeyman by the propertyless employee.

Nevertheless, the main principle and the spirit of the guilds could be adopted and adapted. Occupational groups could be organized, which, in the words of Pope Pius, "would bind men together, not according to the position which they occupy in the labor market but according to the diverse functions which they exercise in society." In the railroad industry, for example, the owners, managers and employees, would be united with reference to the common social function which all these classes perform, namely, that of carrying goods and passengers in cars over steel rails.

In other words, these organizations would comprise both employers and employees, both capitalists and laborers. The occupational group would be empowered by law to fix wages, interest, dividends, and prices, to determine working conditions, to adjust industrial disputes, and to carry on whatever economic planning was thought feasible. All the groups in the several concerns of an industry could be federated into a national council for the whole industry. There might also be a federation of all the industries of the nation. The occupational groups, whether local or national, would enjoy power and authority over industrial matters coming within their competence. This would be genuine self-government in industry.

Of course, the occupational groups would not be entirely independent of the government. No economic group, whether of capitalists or laborers, or of both in combination, can be trusted with unlimited power to fix their own profits and remuneration. While allowing to the occupational groups the largest measure of reasonable freedom in the management of their own affairs, the State, says Pius XI, should perform the tasks which belong to it and which it alone can effectively accomplish, namely, those of "directing, watching, stimulating and restraining, as circumstances suggest or necessity demands."

The occupational group system would not only mean industrial self-government, but it could easily bring about a full measure of industrial democracy. In another part of the Encyclical, the Pope recommends, as we have seen above, that the wage earners be enabled to have some share in the ownership or the management or the profits of industry. Sooner or later, this change must come and the sooner the better. At present, industrial society is made up of two classes, a very small minority that does all the managing, reaps all the profits and exercises all the ownership, and the vast majority that manages nothing, owns nothing, and gets no profits. Such a society always is and always will be in a state of unstable equilibrium.

Considerable discussion has taken place concerning the resemblance, or the difference, between the occupational group system proposed by the Holy Father and the trade associations set up by our National Recovery Administration. Insofar as all the participants in each industry are brought under a code of fair practice and insofar as each association exercises a considerable measure of industrial self-government, there is much resemblance. The most striking difference, and it is a vital difference, between the occupational group arrangement and the NRA organizations is that the latter do not include adequate participation by labor. It is to be hoped that this fundamental defect will soon be removed. Labor should share with capital in all those activities which affect labor. The employees should participate in the drawing up, the administration, and the enforcement of the codes. Until this fundamental change is made, the Pope's proposals will continue to be more radical than the provisions of the New Deal.

It has been asserted that the occupational group system would involve the abolition of capitalism. Whether this is true depends upon our definition. If we take capitalism to mean merely the private ownership of capital, the system of occupational groups might still be called a capitalist system. If, however, we use the word capitalism in its historical sense, with its traditional philosophy, then it is automatically excluded by every important principle and proposal in *Quadragesimo Anno.*

For the underlying principles of capitalism are those of individualism and economic liberalism. In a dozen places, the Holy Father condemns individualism because it calls for unlimited competition and rejects state regulation. In a dozen places, he condemns liberalism because it authorizes men to seek unlimited profits and unlimited interest, and to pay the lowest wages which men can be coerced to accept under the guise of a "free" contract. To repeat the words already quoted of J. L. and Barbara Hammond, liberalism asserted the "right to acquire and use property, subject to no qualifications . . . the right to take what interest and profit you could get; to buy and sell as you pleased . . . for the Divine Right of Kings it substituted the Divine Right of Capitalists." Capitalism in this sense would obviously be impossible under the Pope's system of occupational groups.

It should be noted that the association of employers and employees in the occupational group organizations does not exclude distinct organizations of either or both classes. The Holy Father points out that "those who are engaged in the same trade or profession will form free associations among themselves, for purposes connected with their occupations. . . . Not only is man free to institute those unions which are of a private character, but he has the right further to adopt such organization and such rules as may best conduce to the attainment of their respective objects."

The new social order recommended by the Holy Father would exemplify neither individualism nor socialism. Neither the individual nor the corporation would be permitted to make extortionate and anti-social "free" contracts. The profit motive would continue to function, but not to enjoy unlimited scope. It would be subjected to the restraints of reason and justice. On the other hand, the new social order would not be Socialism. It would not place the entire control and operation of industry in the hands of a supreme general staff. It would not abolish private property. It would not regiment labor or substantially restrict freedom of choice by the consumer.

In a word, the industrial system proposed by the Pope would occupy a middle ground between capitalism and Communism, between individualism and Socialism. It would provide all the freedom and opportunity which every individual needs to develop his personality; and it would avoid that concentration of power which would defeat itself and which free men would not long tolerate. . . .

Economic Planning. Many of the present day intellectuals who are enamored of collectivism seem to be moved largely if not mainly by its capacity to substitute a planned productive system for the unbalanced production, the over-production, the under-consumption and the alternating booms and depressions which characterize the capitalist regime. Undoubtedly the vision of a system of planned production and control, which would put an end to this industrial anarchy, is very alluring. It makes an almost irresistible appeal to experts, engineers and all possessors of the tory mind and outlook. Nevertheless its successful operation would involve a degree of centralized control over all economic actions and processes under which effective democracy could not long survive. This planned production and control would involve genuine "regimentation." In all probability, however, the attempt would fail, owing to the magnitude of the enterprise and the limitations of human powers.

Of course, every realistic student of our industrial system desires some degree of economic planning. He desires that comprehensive and systematic knowledge of our productive resources and capacities and of the economic conditions and needs of all classes of our people be made available to capitalists, workers and legislators. But most of us are not willing that any group of officials should have the power to impose their deductions from this knowledge upon all our people in the form of compulsory regulations. Let us have the knowledge and let us have councils of experts to advise, but let us not permit the experts to translate their advice into legal enactments.

The occupational groups prescribed by the Pope might well provide the best machinery for adequate economic planning. All the groups, for example, in all the great steel concerns, would be united into a national federation. Among the objects which the federation of groups might seek to attain would be the adjustment of output to probable and reasonable demand the allotment of proper proportions of the output to the different steel companies.

Owing to the constitution of the occupational groups, the workers as well as the managers and owners would participate in the activities of economic planning. The interests of the consumers could be protected by admitting them to representation in the federation of economic groups. Indeed, it would seem appropriate and necessary to admit consumer representation to the local as well as the national economic groups whenever the purchasers of goods would be affected by group determinations or policies. As the Pope specifically points out, the occupational groups might take any form of organization which its members prefer, "provided that both justice and the common good be taken into account." The latter consideration would frequently demand representation by the consumers. Finally, the planning agreed upon by the occupational groups as well as the other determinations affecting the public should be supervised and sanctioned by the state. Thus political compulsion would be reduced to a minimum and at the same time placed upon the basis of adequate knowledge.

The capacity of the occupational group organization to effectuate the measure of industrial democracy described in the immediately preceding chapter is obvious. Labor sharing in management, profits, and ownership could be developed to an unlimited extent through the cooperative action of employers and employees which would be easily attained and, indeed, inevitable. In this, as in all other departments of industrial life and government, the occupational group system would promote individual freedom, individual self development and democracy, instead of the bureaucratic regulation, the determination from above of what things are good for the individual and the despotism which is inseparable from a regime of collectivism. . . .

Immediate Duties of the State. In the meantime, there are certain definite, important industrial actions and functions which should be performed by the State.

1. The reduction of the working week and a program of public works, sufficient together to provide employment for all who want to work.

2. Adequate enforcement of all the provisions of the NRA codes.

3. Public ownership of public utilities, mines and petroleum deposits, as rapidly and as soon as it can be wisely accomplished. Public operation would not always be necessary. Operation by capitalists, workers and consumers jointly, would sometimes be preferable. This statement is particularly applicable to mines and petroleum resources.

4. Government competition with great corporations in any industry when this is the only effective means of preventing monopoly.

5. The use of every effective and legitimate means to bring down the rate of interest.

6. Increased taxes on medium and large incomes, inheritances and excess business profits, to the extent required and justified by the canon of ability to pay.

Reforms in Economic Morals. More fundamental to and more necessary for a better economic order than any of the political and industrial arrangements advocated in this volume is an increase of ethical instruction and a lifting of ethical standards throughout the entire field of industrial relations and transactions. There is needed a great quickening of the public and private conscience. Great as is the faith of the Pope in the social order which he recommends, he declares it will not be effective without a reform of ethical conduct and ethical standards. "If we examine matters diligently and thoroughly," he says, "we shall perceive clearly that this longed for social reconstruction must be preceded by a profound renewal of the Christian spirit, from which multitudes engaged in industry in every country have unhappily departed. Otherwise, all our endeavors will be futile and our social edifice will be built not upon a rock but upon shifting sand."

The truth of these weighty words is becoming more and more evident every day in these United States. "Practical Christianity," said President Roosevelt recently, "would go far in helping us to solve the great economic problems confronting us, brought about in large part by greed and selfishness." The extent to which the New Deal has been and still is impeded by exhibitions of cunning, extortion, and downright dishonesty, is causing a rapidly increasing number of observers to doubt whether as a people we have the moral qualities necessary to carry out successfully any plan of social reform or to achieve any considerable measure of social justice.

Consider the numerous efforts of strong business concerns to injure and destroy the weak. Consider the enormous frauds perpetrated upon the consumer through unjustly high prices and upon the laborer through unjustly low wages. Consider the many and varied forms of dishonesty which compelled the invention of a new descriptive term, "chiseling." Consider the trickery and tyranny of powerful corporations that force their employes into company unions and deny the right of free organization. Consider the efforts of certain craft unions to promote their minority interests at the expense of the majority of their fellow workers. Consider the willingness of certain cooperatives of dairymen to join with certain milk distributors in gouging the consumer.

When we contemplate these and many other indications of the same sort, we realize the pertinence of the Holy Father's words about the necessity of a reform in morals. We perceive that if the New Deal fails or if the efforts to establish a better economic order are unsuccessful, the main cause of the failure will be a very ugly and very ancient vice. It is the vice that we call avarice or greed.

27. NORMAN THOMAS (1884–   )

NORMAN THOMAS, born in Marion, Ohio, is a graduate of Princeton University and the Union Theological Seminary, and he is an ordained minister of the Presbyterian church. A leading member of the Socialist Party of the United States, he has been a candidate for governor of New York, twice a candidate for mayor of New York City, and four times a candidate for President of the United States. His views on public questions are set forth in numerous books and pamphlets. His books include *The Conscientious Objector in America* (1923, revised in 1927, under the title *Is Conscience a Crime?*), *America's Way Out* (1930), *Human Exploitation* (1934), *After the New Deal, What?* (1936), *Socialism on the Defensive* (1938), and *We Have a Future* (1941).

From AFTER THE NEW DEAL, WHAT? (1936) [1]

Ch. vii. The Future: Socialism?

To this bleak future of the suicide of western civilization in a new cycle of wars, general chaos, or the organized tyranny of fascism, the Socialist has an answer. He does not trust to kind fortune, vague optimism, or any inevitable victory of good over evil without effort and purpose of man. Of the disintegration of the capitalist system he is sure; it is already far advanced. The victory of socialism is not equally sure. But it must be burned into the conscience of this generation and the next not only that we *can* have new dark ages, but that we *will* have new dark ages unless there is a conscious and creative purpose of building a federation of cooperative commonwealths in an interdependent world. Socialism, we believe, is the reasonable and the only reasonable way of life and social organization in an age of interdependence and collectivism such as power-driven machinery has imposed. Socialism in this day and generation is the condition of true democracy.

[1] Norman Thomas, *After the New Deal, What?* (New York, 1936), from ch. vii. The Macmillan Company.

It is the fulfillment of the prophet's dream of brotherhood. But although socialism is the reasonable form of organization in a machine age and the desirable fulfillment of the dream of prophets, patriots, and sages, it does not follow that it is inevitable. To establish socialism requires struggle and intelligent struggle. It requires the development of new and nobler loyalties. The socialist society is not for fools or cowards. There is no foreordained assurance that man will have the wisdom to use for the social good the machinery which he had the intelligence to invent.

But half the battle for socialism will be won when men understand two things: First, that there is not room for plenty, peace or freedom in the present disintegrating social order; and second, that socialism in itself is a thing infinitely desirable. So far we have been concerned primarily to develop the first argument; now we must turn to the second. Socialism is first of all a reasoned conviction that plenty and peace, freedom and fellowship, lie within the grasp of men. It is the assertion that our failure to conquer poverty in the midst of potential abundance is due to an acceptance of a system which is based on relative scarcity, and upon the exploitation of the masses by an owning class. Socialism believes that men may be free by making power-driven machinery the slave of mankind. It believes in planned production for the use of all rather than an unplanned production for the profit of an owning class. It asserts that this type of production for use requires social ownership of land, natural resources and the principal means of production and distribution, including, of course, the entire system of money, banking and credit. In the name of social ownership of land and tools it does not propose to house men in public barracks or to take from a worker his favorite hammer, violin or typewriter, or anything else which he uses without exploiting others. Socialism does intend to end absentee landlordism, but it intends to make men more, not less, secure in the occupancy and use of homes in which they live.

Because men will be more secure against the loss of their homes and their jobs there will be more real liberty. The statement that socialism will take from men civil and religious liberty is born either of malice or complete misunderstanding of the subject of socialism.

American Socialism has expressly recognized a man's right to the religion of his choice. Many socialists would go farther and quote approvingly the statement I heard a young socialist make to a woman perturbed that if she accepted socialism she would lose her religion. "Madam," said he, "one does not have to be a Christian to be a socialist, but I cannot understand how you can be a true Christian in these times and not be a socialist."

Social ownership of the great means of production and distribution is necessary for planning. It is the only basis on which we can end the dominion of profit. Even under capitalism social ownership has had an encouraging degree of success. Witness for instance such a list of publicly owned enterprises as schools, roads, parks, the post office, the Panama Canal, city water and sewer systems, power plants, and the like. They are supplemented, too, by the success of consumers' cooperatives carried on for the benefit of the consumers who are members of them and not for the private profit of any group of individuals.

It takes custom derived from a long historic development to explain how anything as utterly absurd as the legal control of private enterprises by absentee stockholders could come into existence. These stockholders know nothing about the conduct of the steel mills, electric power systems, railroads or banks which legally they own. They are concerned only with the profit they get. Their enterprises would fail disastrously except for the hired brains and hands employed by boards of directors to run them, not for the use of all, but for the profit of these same absentee stockholders. There was some rhyme and reason to the old individualistic capitalism where the capitalist assumed definite responsibility. In this age when the engineer, the technician, the manager, are the key to productive enterprise there is no reason under the sun why they should not work for society rather than for absentee owners. Logically they could do a much better job because the fact is that the interest of the absentee owners is by no means identical with the interest of the consumers, still less with the interest of the workers. So far is it from being true that the profit system puts the most advanced science and the more advanced inventions automatically to work, that, on the contrary, a great many inventions are kept off the market by the monopolists or semi-monopolists who can control them in order to protect profit. There is no reason to doubt that the engineers who have given us the modern automobile could also have added to the skill of their performance engines which would use less gasoline, but that would not suit powerful financial interests. Progress in railroad travel was held back for years by the belief, probably the mistaken belief, of directors that profits would not be increased by further improvements.

We have already accepted the estimate of experts that it would be possible to provide every American family on the average with an income equivalent to that now enjoyed by those with between $4,000 and $5,000 a year. Or, from a different angle, we have accepted the estimate of those experts who say that we could establish a minimum income for each American worker of between $2,000 and $2,500 a year without notably reducing higher incomes, except the swollen fortunes of the very rich. Economic machinery ought to be operated to make this great possibility a reality. It is hard to imagine any single thing which would do so much to end physical misery, mental anguish, frustration, yes, crime, as the certainty that every family worth holding together at all, every family where breadwinners are willing to work, would be guaranteed a minimum of $2,500 a year.

Above that level, at least during the transition period and the earlier stages of socialism, it would be well to reward men according to deed. . . . One of the ways to attract men is to remunerate them according to deed. There is no such thing as perfect justice in rewarding them according to deed. Differentials in reward, particularly in the earlier stages of socialist transition, will have something to do with traditional holdovers and with the kind of pressure which different groups can exert. Nevertheless, socialism can rapidly apply three principles to the incalculable benefit of mankind: (1) No income for any able-bodied adult without work; no long search for work in vain; (2) a minimum standard of decent living for all; (3) above the minimum an approximation to reward according to deed, far more just than that which prevails in our gamblers' world.

It will be almost the first business of a socialist society to get rid of the ugliness as well as the discomfort of the slums and shacks which now disgrace America. Even more surely, it will be the first business of socialism to see that every boy and girl born into the world shall receive food necessary for physical health, training to enable him to do the work for which he is best fitted, a chance when he comes to working age to do that work, and to do it under conditions which give him both security and leisure.

It is logically possible today to house all our people in comfort and beauty; to feed them amply; to help them through a socialized medical service to get well and stay well; to provide them economic security against the vicissitudes of life; and to substitute for the present alternation between long hours of monotonous, ill-rewarded toil and bitter unemployment a shorter working week and enriched leisure.

To establish and maintain all this Socialists do not depend upon an omnipotent and omniscient state. They regard the state as the principal instrument that must be used for the establishment of a new social order. It is the business of workers with hand and brain to gain control of government in order to accomplish this great change. Between the fascist conception of the totalitarian state as an end in itself, and the socialist conception of the state as something to be used to establish the cooperative commonwealth, there is the difference between darkness and light. A socialist does not believe that the state is the only form of social organization which should be allowed to exist. It has no divine right. Its powers will have to be vigorously asserted and effectively used in a transition period, but as the habit of cooperation and functional self-government grows the coercive state should wither away. It should become a true commonwealth. . . . The power of the state will be necessary to effect the transfer from private to public ownership, but it should not supersede or crush consumers' cooperatives. They would admirably supplement it.

A society which is in a way to achieve a socialist revolution with a minimum of disorder and strife could well afford, as part of the price of achieving it, to offer some compensation to expropriated owners. There would be a certain equity in this as between certain classes of owners because probably certain key industries would be taken first. Such key industries as the public utilities are precisely those in which the savings of the little men are invested. For these reasons, as I have elsewhere explained at more length, socialists generally would offer compensation plus taxation, taxation that would amount to expropriation in the higher brackets. Besides income and inheritance taxes a socialist government should use what has been called a capital levy; that is a tax upon wealth in private hands. It could be paid in money, in bonds, which would be retired, thus lessening the burden of debt, or in stocks of those enterprises which the government is ready to socialize anyway. Even under capitalism such a levy is the best way to deal with the crushing burden of debt. It would be less destructive than wholesale inflation or deflation. It is a way, however, that a capitalist society finds it psychologically impossible to take.

Of course an owning class which stubbornly and blindly resists socialism and which resorts to violence against it, cannot expect compensation. On the other hand, if the day ever comes when, as it were, over night, a smooth-running socialist society should be put into operation it would be better to cut the Gordian knot of vested right and property privilege than to try any kind of compensation. Under such a society, all except the very wealthy would be materially better off than they can ever be under any form of private ownership of the great machinery of production. And even the very wealthy might find new health to their souls!

To carry out a socialist program it is necessary that at least the key industries be taken over under a concerted plan. For example, good as publicly owned electric plants may be, it will be found unsatisfactory to try to carry on a socialized or partially socialized power industry under the capitalist economy. T.V.A. is now doing a remarkably good job. Its success is an encouragement for the future. It is worth while as a yardstick and much more than a yardstick. But the yardstick theory, or any other theory of piecemeal socialization within the confines of capitalism, has its disadvantages in waste and confusion. Socialism is much more than the sum total of certain socialized industries. It involves a general plan impossible on the yardstick theory. It involves also a way of life to which strife between government-owned industry and its privately owned rivals offers more of disadvantage than advantage. There may be a kind of socialist emulation between publicly or cooperatively owned enterprises, but scarcely satisfactory competition between enterprises operating on a different basis and with an appeal to different ideals.

Let us assume, then, that the state has taken over the key industries; that it itself is under the control of workers with hand and brain, well organized on both the industrial and economic fronts; that its activities are supplemented by the activities of consumers cooperatives—under what plan will it control industry? It will put each socialized industry under the administrative direction of a governing authority representing the two permanent interests which always must exist in our economic life. They are the interests of man as consumer and as producer. They are not necessarily in opposition, but they are not identical. A coal miner or a textile worker has a peculiar set of interests in regard to the industry in which he invests his life. He has another set of the interests as a consumer. The interest of the workers as consumers should be dominant. Men work to live, not live to work. It is essential for managing a world where technological advance is rapid that the primary emphasis should not be on the vested rights of workers in one particular trade, but rather on the vested rights of men to enjoy what well-managed work can create. Sidney and Beatrice Webb assert that part of the success of the Russian planned economy is due to "placing the control in the hands of representatives, not of any organizations of producers, but organizations representing the consumers." That general principle should be followed with consumers' interest dominant in the new set-up. Nevertheless the unique interest of the worker in his own industry should be recognized under administration by a board on which there is representation of the general consuming interest and the particular interests of the various categories of workers employed in it. The precise form may vary in different industries. Labor unions will have a function even in a socialist society as an expression and protection of the interests of different groups of producers. They should no longer be organized consciously or subconsciously in terms of the class conflict since society or the mass of workers themselves will be the owners.

Socialized industries, each a law unto itself, cannot plan for work, leisure, security, and abundance for all unless there is over them a general economic planning council to prepare the master plan. This council is the general staff in the war against poverty. It is the expert arm of government, subject to general decisions of Congress or the electorate as to policy, but free from interference in detail. It should be composed of men and women chosen from panels suggested by engineering societies and various industrial and agricultural groups. It must make the most efficient possible use of expert skills in engineering and accounting.

It will be seen that the plan which I have outlined offers as a safeguard against bureaucratic centralization functional self-administration. It may also offer some degree of decentralization through regional machinery of government and of economic planning. That regional machinery cannot conform to present state lines or accept the dogma of states' rights because state lines have no intelligent relation to economic geography. The plan which I have suggested conserves democracy in its truest sense. It permits choices of policy and leadership to be made by those concerned in them. It recognizes that no one organization can express or carry out all a man's interests. It realizes to the full the usefulness of the expert, the engineer, and the technician, and the principle that those engaged in special tasks should have special voice in the way those tasks are carried out.

Agriculture offers somewhat greater difficulties in the earlier stages of socialization than such industries as steel, textiles, coal, or the railroads. That is partly because agriculture is in process of a delayed mechanization. The coming of the mechanical cotton picker will revolutionize hundreds of thousands of lives for better or for worse. The farmer under any kind of social order must reckon not only with new machinery and new methods but also the possibility that for his products there may be substituted the synthetic products of the chemical industry. . . .

Socialist plans in America most assuredly do not call for the forcible elimination of a man who farms his own land. Rather he would be protected against the vicissitudes which have brought it to pass that in the fertile central valleys of California something like 35 per cent of the land, I was recently told, is corporation farmed. One practical method of protection is to be found in crop insurance. A socialist government would socialize the machinery of marketing both what the farmer buys and what he sells. By taxation and otherwise it would abolish absentee landlordism. It would substitute collectives for great privately owned plantations, and train the workers in the democratic management of those collectives or cooperatives. It would enlist the farmers themselves in planning for the conservation and best use of soil. It would guide excess farm workers from the fields into other occupations. There is no inexorable limitation to employment if we set out to meet human needs rather than to preserve private profits. We can then control the rate of introduction of machinery or new technological processes according to our ability to increase production and shorten working hours.

I am still convinced, as I have often said, that the outstanding difficulty for socialism on the theoretical side is not to draw up plans for the operation of socialism within a great country like the United States, but to draw up plans for the operation of socialism throughout the world. Every year gives new proof that the great problem for socialism is nationalism. We have to begin where we are. That means that we must begin in a world divided into national states, each claiming absolute sovereignty. There are certain variations of national culture and traditions which make it both impossible and undesirable to impose so rigid a mould on all nations as the Communists once thought to impose. On the other hand, no nation is economically or culturally self-sufficient. Prosperity as well as peace depends upon international cooperation. Rather, both depend on a world-wide cooperation which does not emphasize the nation as the ultimate unit, fixed and unchangeable. There must be machinery for such cooperation. How shall we set up that machinery and develop the ideals which will make it function effectively? The League of Nations has not even tried to do this fundamental task. It is something yet to be done. How to do it is the most difficult single question which Socialists and all lovers of peace have to face. It is a task which will be easier as Socialists come to power within each nation. But socialism achieved on a national scale will not automatically answer the question. One answer might well be a league of Socialist states, a federation of cooperative commonwealths, not primarily for military defense but rather for economic cooperation. Another answer, not necessarily inconsistent with the first, is an effort after organized world-wide controls of such fundamentals as the allocation of raw materials, a uniform fiscal system or the relation of fiscal systems to one another, universal minimum standards for workers, and the effective limitation of armaments. This . . . is part of the price of peace. Every effort toward it will be worth while, but its satisfactory attainment is incompatible with capitalist nationalism. . . .

Our solution of the problem of world organization cannot proceed as if nationalism did not exist. It exists, and exists with power. It represents at its best a certain cultural variety which enriches the world. For colonial peoples nationalism is an expression, however inadequate, of a determination to break an economic yoke imposed by imperialism. The process of education in world loyalty which is essential under socialism is consistent with the patriotism which would put each country first in the service that it renders its own citizens and the contribution that it makes to mankind. But there is no education in this sort of patriotism except as it deliberately cultivates the loyalties, and builds the organizations, which cross national and racial lines. There never will be the right sort of League of Nations until workers, farmers, and professional men build real international organizations with strength and wisdom and an understanding of national differences consistent with world interdependence. . . .

The argument that we cannot plan successfully is based in its superficial form on a simple denial of the ability of men to manage for their own good the complicated machinery which they have invented. It is rarely accompanied by an attempt to prove that we can use modern power-driven machinery and the collectivism which it entails without plan. It is simply an assertion that the job is too difficult. It ignores, or passes over far too lightly, such partial examples of successful planning as the economic planning of the World War afforded, to say nothing of the success of the Five Year Plan in Soviet Russia.

In particular the critics of planning are fond of proclaiming the impossibility of planning for agriculture because of the uncertainty of the weather and other conditions which make farming, they say, the world's greatest gamble. Here the critics are on fairly sound ground if they confine their remarks to a planning in terms of profit dependent on relative scarcity. Such planning will always cut its margin too fine. It will always think in terms of the profit of a great many individual farmers rather than in terms of the best use of land for the common good. Agricultural planning under socialism must put to the forefront the accumulation of reserves in order to maintain an economy of abundance against drouth and disaster. If this is done it is absurd to say that all agricultural planning must fail. A great deal is known about the proper use of soil, how much land should be restored to buffalo grass and how much to forests here in America. A great deal is known about the average amount of foodstuff necessary for a well-fed population. Under these conditions agricultural planning becomes necessary, desirable, and by no means impossible in a true commonwealth in which the predominant idea is the production and sharing of abundance.

One superficial argument against planning asserts that without the stimulus of future profit there would be no savings, no investment for new enterprises, and hence no "progress." Such a contention overlooks the fact that already we are dependent upon the initiative of the engineer, not the entrepreneur. Great corporations maintain laboratories for invention. They set aside reserves and do not trust much to private savings to provide for their future. The Steel Trust is not dependent for capital for expansion on speculation in the stock market with its stocks. Society can provide its own experimental laboratories and its own working capital at least as well as the Steel Trust or the A. T. and T.

There is a statement of the argument against the possibility of planning which goes deeper and raises some real problems. Certain orthodox economists, of whom Hayek is perhaps the ablest, assert that planned economy not only tends to produce a sort of paralysis by removng any effective consumers' choice, but also that it makes any real cost accounting impossible. In other words, that it strips us of any mechanism by which to judge the way in which the productive resources of the community may most efficiently be used. . . .

Some things are clear. There is nothing scientifically infallible about the determination of costs in our capitalist economy. The cost of producing cotton cloth as compared to the cost of producing automobiles is based on no natural laws. It is based on the historic tradition which has brought it to pass that cotton is grown by half-starved serf labor and made into cloth by underpaid textile workers. The cost accounting of the orthodox economist takes no account of the social cost of this kind of a system. Under our present capitalist economy, the increase of monopoly control, and the steady march of mass advertising certainly interfere with any scientific cost accounting resting on consumers' choice and the free working of the market. Difficulties of cost accounting under a planned economy may be great but they can scarcely be as great as the difficulties which exist today, and make cost accounting in any true sense so weak a defense against recurring crises and continuous waste.

As a general answer to those who assert, rather than prove, that planned economy requires complete loss of consumers' choice, the rationing of goods, and the conscription of workers, it may be pointed out that this would be true only if one were to conceive of the world as a beleaguered garrison with limited supplies. On the contrary, ours is a world with ever-expanding ablity to produce not only necessities but luxuries. It can produce them so generously that what might be regarded as waste in a beleaguered garrison would be justified in order to make possible consumers' choice. A study of the incomes now possible in America shows that there would be a wide margin of what might be called free income over and above what is necessary for subsistence. Experts can calculate on the basis of known facts and observed tendencies the probable direction of consumers' choice. That calculation is no more likely to be equivalent to the rationing which exists among a beleaguered garrison than is the calculation of the average expectancy of life equivalent to a sentence of death to the individual at the expiration of that period. The probable trends of human demands and industrial improvements, the kinds of jobs therefore likely to be open, are matters known to other experts who can then help young men and women to find the type of work for which they are most fit. That is not conscription but guidance, far more compatible with real freedom than the haphazard whims of chance and the need to live which now confine thousands of workers to blind-alley occupations regardless of their temperaments and abilities. . . .

The second argument, that socialism is incompatible with civil and religious liberty, is more popular and in some statements of it weightier. The Liberty League or *Saturday Evening Post* version of it need not greatly concern us. It comes close to pure hypocrisy in the mouths of men who are not really concerned about liberty, but only about profit. Their liberty means not justice for Mooney and Billings, the share-croppers of Alabama and Arkansas, or the workers whose employers arm themselves with machine guns and poison gas. It means the right to get all you can and keep all you get. It is true in practical experience that liberty rests upon tolerance. Tolerance is not and cannot be the chief of virtues to men engaged in the tremendous enterprise of setting up a new social order. But even the tolerance of skepticism or indifference is a virtue against brutality and oppression. Historically, intolerance has often killed or wounded the thing it sought to protect. Even in a transition society the Jeffersonian principle that the state should act only to punish overt acts may be found to minister to social well-being no less than to individual liberty.

But the chief argument of those who say that socialism and liberty are incompatible is not a theory which is confined to the exigencies of the transition period. That argument has been well stated in the April [1936] issue of the *International Journal of Ethics* by H. Gomperz of Vienna: "*I think it was the tragic error of democratic socialism to think that men could be deprived of their economic independence and yet maintain independence of thought.* Loyalty to one's convictions requires an economic prop; where this is lacking the former has no permanence . . . the pillars of spiritual—more especially of religious, but also of political, liberty have everywhere been, first of all the higher and the lower aristocracy; further the burgesses, who if not actually wealthy were at least not without property; occasionally, too, here and there, the yeomen."

Before we come to the heart of this contention certain preliminary things must be said. Liberty, in the sense in which Mr. Gomperz is considering it, has always been the possession of the comparatively few. It is, I forget who first said it, an aristocratic virtue. This will always be true unless and until it can be planted and made to flourish in the soil of economic justice and equality. For years I have been insisting to deaf ears that if and when the time comes when the masses feel that they must choose between liberty and economic security they will take economic security. Fascism in Europe expressed open scorn of liberty and fascism won. A great many men like to be told what to do. It saves them the trouble of thinking, and when the dictator's commands can be sweetened by an emotional appeal to nationalism or by a promise of bread they are doubly acceptable.

Liberty in the sense of assured justice for the individual or of Milton's "right to know, to utter, and to argue freely according to conscience" exists most imperfectly even in the bourgeois democ-

racies of our day, as Mr. Gomperz admits. Very few there are even
in America who have the economic independence which he considers necessary to independence of thought. He overlooks the
fact that many workers have won through their unions a degree of
security which gives them an independence of thought greater
than members of the middle class display. The upper middle
class despite its economic independence is not free. Its members
are bound by prejudice, fear, and desire for social prestige into a
herd of their own. Historically, it is some sense of security rather
than private ownership of property which has furthered freedom
of thought. Indeed there has been an interaction between liberty
and economic security or well-being. Sometimes men have come
to understand that independence of thought is necessary to the
successful working of a society which may provide material security.

This we may affirm with confidence: Socialism, by providing a
wider security to men, provides a better basis for liberty. It is not
animated by the ideals of the totalitarian or servile state. In a
genuine socialist society industries will not be administered by
political appointees of a dominant party. They will be functionally
self-governed. Workers will be protected by an improved civil
service and by their own industrial organizations. If, temporarily,
they should lose their jobs they will not starve but will be automatically eligible to whatever provisions may be made for temporary unemployment. They will have the protection against old
age. They will have an income over and above what it costs them
to exist which they can use in association with their fellows to
support the kind of papers they like and societies in which they
have confidence. There has never been a distribution of property
which gave to the masses the economic security necessary to independence of thought on the same scale on which socialism can
provide it. It would be a sorry outlook if liberty, civil or religious,
were dependent on the right and power of the "free" man to exploit his fellows by private ownership of production goods. The
contrary is true.

What is necessary for the increase of freedom in the socialist
society is that it put in the forefront a conscious recognition of the
value of liberty to the individual and to society. It is possible for
a man to believe something intensely and yet to believe that he
must justify his faith by winning conviction, not by repression.

There may be a stage in social revolution when it will be necessary to deprive recalcitrant enemies of the new order of the right to sabotage it under pretext of democracy. There certainly will be a stage of the social revolution which will call for a firm hand against counter revolution. But even in the transition years, in America with our traditions, the ideal to be held up is not the ideal of dictatorship but of workers' democracy. Such workers' democracy is not psychologically or practically equivalent to the dictatorship of the proletariat. Recent events have made the word "dictatorship" obnoxious to lovers, I shall not say of freedom, but of human decency. To accept the idea of dictatorship means to accept tyranny and oppression. The dictatorship of the proletariat in Russia was not as Communists have sometimes claimed, equivalent to workers' democracy. It was the dictatorship of a particular party. The two are not the same.

We cannot settle all the problems of freedom and cooperation for the future. We can rejoice that some of them, once socialism has triumphed, will automatically grow less difficult. No William Randolph Hearst of the future will be allowed to have a fortune of $220,000,000 which he can use to corrupt public opinion and public taste in the name of freedom of the press.

A new society may also find a way short of censorship to enforce certain standards of factual truth and to prevent the libelling not only of individuals but of races and nations. Liberty should not mean the right to foment wars by lies and slander. On this difficult question I do not dogmatize. Problems of liberty cannot be solved offhand by a formula.

They can be solved if we remember that liberty is a necessity of the good life, that without it society will stagnate and men will be less than men. To hold high the torch of freedom is essential to defense against the brutality and the obscurantism of a Mussolini or a Hitler. Socialism will be untrue to itself if ever it forgets that its purpose is not merely to bring prosperity and peace, but freedom to mankind.

28. RESTORING PRIVATE PROPERTY

M ANY of the familiar arguments for maintaining a social system
based on private property have little validity except in reference
to a society in which ordinary individuals own the properties on which
they labor for their livelihood. Most Americans now own no property
of that sort. Familiar technological, social, and political changes have
made it increasingly difficult for individual enterprisers to survive in
most fields of productive activity. Most of us today work, not on our
own land or with our own tools and materials, but with goods and instruments owned by others. Many recent writers contend that we can
escape the major evils of our present society only through measures to
protect or restore private enterprise in some of its forms, even sacrificing
some productive efficiency for the sake of the individual virtues and social benefits we have traditionally associated with individual ownership
of productive establishments. The selections below are illustrative of
this doctrine.

Allen Tate (1899–   ), poet and literary critic, is a native of Kentucky and a graduate of Vanderbilt University. A free lance writer most
of the time, he served briefly on the faculties of southern institutions and
was appointed Resident Fellow in Creative Writing at Princeton University in 1939. Besides numerous books of poems and critical essays
he has written biographies of Stonewall Jackson and Jefferson Davis.
His views on the restoration of private property are set forth in magazine
articles and in essays in several symposia.

Herbert Agar (1897–   ), born in New Rochelle, New York, is a
graduate of Columbia University and did post-graduate work at Princeton, where he received the degrees of master of arts and doctor of philosophy. He has been London correspondent of Louisville papers, author of
a syndicated news column, and (since 1940) editor of the Louisville
Courier-Journal. He is the author of books of poems and fiction and won
a Pulitzer prize for his The People's Choice (1933), a study of American
Presidents from Washington to Harding. His advocacy of reforms to
preserve and restore the small property-owner in America is set forth at
length in his Land of the Free (1935); and his more general political
ideas appear in his Pursuit of Happiness (1938).

From HERBERT AGAR AND ALLEN TATE, WHO OWNS AMERICA? [1] (1936)

Ch. 6. Notes on Liberty and Property (by Allen Tate).

II. The history of property in the United States is a struggle, from 1787 on, of one kind of property against another. Small ownership, typified by agriculture, has been worsted by big, dispersed ownership—the giant corporation. This must be kept steadily in mind. Without this fact it is easy to fall into the trap of the Big Business interests today, who are tryng to convince the people that there is one kind of property—just property, whether it be a thirty-acre farm in Kentucky or a stock certificate in the United States Steel Corporation. For if there is a contest merely between property and non-property—between real private property, as the average American understands it, and collectivism, the small owner will come to the support of the big corporation. And this is what the big corporation is using every means to make the small owner do.

The owner of the small farm, of the small factory, of the village store, owns a distinct kind of property. It is the familiar, historical kind. The reason why the 'little man' confidently identifies his interests with the big interests is that he cannot imagine another kind of property than his own. He thinks that there is just 'property,' and that he has been less successful in accumulating it than Mr. Mellon. Of course the corporations know better. And they take advantage of the innocent rectitude of the owner of genuine property. . . .

A movement to restore property to the citizens of this country must be based upon a broad distinction. The people must be shown the fundamental difference between tangible property, which means effective control by the owner, and giant corporate property, which usually means control by a clique. The people must learn that giant corporate property is no less hostile to their interests than State, or collectivist, ownership—that the big cor-

---

[1] Herbert Agar and Allen Tate, eds., *Who Owns America? A New Declaration of Independence* (Boston and New York, 1936), from chs. 6 and 7. By special arrangement with Houghton Mifflin Company.

poration is socially less responsible and eventually less efficient than collectivism.

The joint-stock corporation, when overgrown, is the enemy of private property in the same sense as communism is. The collectivist State is the logical development of giant corporate ownership, and, if it comes, it will signalize the final triumph of Big Business. 'All the arts,' said Walter Pater, 'strive toward the condition of music.' Corporate structure strives toward the condition of Moscow.

It will have reached that condition when the integration of the big monopolies requires still further concentration of control in the hands of the State, and when ownership is so dispersed that it will be coextensive with society as a whole.

III. What is effective ownership? It is not a metaphysical essence. Unlike liberty it is not a thing of the spirit. Common sense can recognize it. The effective ownership of property entails personal responsibility for the use which is made of a given portion of the means of production. A true property system will be composed of a large proportion of owners whose property is not to be expressed solely in terms of exchange-value, but retains, for the owner, the possibility of use-value. Pure liberty would be the power of the owner to choose between selling and using. Actual liberty is the power of choice relative to 'conditions.' But as the freedom to 'use' disappears, liberty begins to disappear. There has never been a society in which use-value has been the exclusive kind of value; no such society is being recommended now. But the degree of use-value that any society retains is the degree of its approach to liberty.

A farmer owns a hog. It has two values—use-value and exchange- or market-value. The farmer's ownership is effective because he has the relatively free choice between killing the hog for his smokehouse and selling it on the market.

No such choice is open to the stockholder in the giant corporation. He holds a certificate of rights and expectations. In order to make good the rights and to fulfill the expectations of the 'owners,' the corporation has got to sell its commodity. Its concern is wholly with exchange-value. The 'liberty' available to the stockholder consists in the degree of power the corporation has from time to time over the market. If it lacks this power the stockholder has no liberty whatever. The farmer, if he is protected by a system of prices and distribution favorable to agriculture, enjoys a kind of liberty, the real kind, that can function apart from power over others. Compare his position with that of a corporation which makes tires. The market for tires in a given year is bad. It cannot eat the tires, nor can it operate enough cars of its own to consume them. Neither can the stockholder consume tires to the amount of 'expectations' (dividends) due him. He may look at the pretty pictures on his stock certificate and starve—or he may sell the stock at a price that he cannot dictate.

It is not suggested that everybody make his own tires in a system that requires by law universal production for use. It is rather that finance-capitalism has become so top-heavy with a crazy jigsaw network of exchange-value that the individual citizen is wholly at the mercy of the shifting pieces of the puzzle at remote points where he cannot possibly assert his own needs and rights. This was not originally the American system. We began with the belief that society should be supported by agriculture, the most stable basis of society because it is relatively less dependent upon the market than any other kind of production.

Now this is elementary, and that is why Big Business does not include it in its propaganda today. Nor is Big Business interested in the responsibility of property, an attribute of ownership no less important than legal title itself. Responsibility is a function of control, and is necessary to effective ownership. A stock certificate is a symbol of a certain amount of capital working somewhere to produce a certain amount of exchange-value from which the 'owner' hopes to derive a certain amount of profit. But dispersed ownership guided by concentrated control deprives the owner of the exacting privileges of responsibility. For control alone makes responsibility possible. It doesn't make it inevitable. The history of the big corporation shows that the men in control, having a remote, symbolic, paper connection with the owners, can violate their responsibility in two ways—by milking the stockholders and by stealing from new capital issues.

And the social aspect of responsibility cannot exist. The corporation must produce for the market; labor is necessarily an inhuman item of costs. If the stockholder has no chance to be responsible, neither has the chairman of the board. Both are involved in a system of property rights in which responsibility to labor is on principle irrelevant. The corporation has only the freedom of power, not responsible freedom of choice. It must be un-responsible in the sense that a man may supposedly be un-moral. The corporation may choose to give its labor numerous 'social services' in sheer humanitarian ebullience. Labor gets as philanthropy what is due to the free citizen as a fruit of his labor.

Changes in the character of property since the rise of the big corporation are ably summarized by Berle and Means under seven heads:

(1) Ownership under real private property was active. It is now passive, under the corporation.

(2) Ownership formerly meant an extension of the owner's personality—a connection between personal and physical property that gave to property a moral significance that it now lacks. 'With the corporate revolution, this quality has been lost to the property owner much as it has been lost to the worker through the industrial revolution.'

(3) The individual's wealth is no longer an expression of his own efforts. The moral significance of this is obvious. Wealth is now conditioned by (a) those in actual control of a business and (b) the general confidence of society in its future prosperity—usually herd feeling.

(4) A man's wealth is capital—ownership of a portion of the means of production. It fluctuates under constant appraisal; that is, its exchange-value is subject to constant revision.

(5) Individual wealth has become extremely liquid; it is quickly convertible from one form to another. The facility of the 'market' is a factor to be considered in the decline of the responsibility of ownership, which has become fluid and anonymous.

(6) Wealth exists decreasingly in a form which can be employed directly by the owner. When wealth was in the form of land, it could be used by the owner even if its market-value was negligible. 'The physical quality of such wealth makes possible a subjective value to the owner quite apart from any market value it may have. The newer form of wealth is quite incapable of this direct use. Only through sale in the market can the owner obtain its direct

use. He is thus tied to the market as never before.' (A man can love the land, and I suppose men loved the small, vineclad factories of early New England. The man who loves the United States Steel Corporation could make a good living in a side-show.)

(7) 'Finally, in the corporate system, the "owner" of industrial wealth is left with a mere symbol of ownership, while the power, responsibility, and the substance of ownership which have been an integral part of ownership in the past are being transferred to a separate group in whose hands lies control.'

To summarize, historically, this summary: since about 1760 in Great Britain and since the Civil War in America, *one attribute of property as it existed for five hundred years has been steadily lost.* That attribute is the responsibility of personal control. The other attribute remains: legal ownership. But without control its future security must necessarily be tenuous. If the legal remnant of ownership should disappear, as it must if finance-capitalism cannot get on its feet again, the last vestige of the institution of private property will be gone. It will be replaced by collectivist ownership. Possibly the change will be ushered in by another depression, followed by great industrial liquidations. The big productive plants will remain, with ownership even more dispersed than before: through society as a whole; and with control even more concentrated under a fiction called the State.

IV. Figures obligingly prove anything. But there are no figures to prove that the concentrated control of property is not enormous.

Of the total business property of the country 78 per cent is corporate. There are over five hundred corporations each with assets of over $100,000,000. The two hundred largest control 49 per cent of *all* corporate wealth, which includes the thousands of small corporations. Nearly 40 per cent, then, of all business wealth, both corporate and private, is controlled by the two hundred corporations.

In 1929, the national wealth was about $367,000,000,000. The total assets of the two hundred big corporations was about $81,-000,000,000, or 22 per cent of the national wealth. (These corporations are non-banking.) The figures are taken from Berle and Means, who comment:

[The big corporation's] political influence may be tremendous. Therefore, if roughly half of corporate wealth is controlled by two hundred big corporations and half by smaller companies, it is fair to assume that very much more than half of industry is dominated by these units. This concentration is made even more significant when it is remembered that as a result of it, approximately two thousand individuals out of a population of one hundred and twenty-five million are in a position to control and direct half of industry.

These two thousand men control the wealth of a little under six million investors—a ratio of one to three thousand.

In 1819, Chief Justice Marshall, in the famous Dartmouth College Case, described the corporation as 'an artificial being, invisible, intangible, and existing only in contemplation of law. Being the mere creature of law, it possesses only those properties which the charter of its creation confers upon it, either expressly, or as incidental to its very existence. Among the most important are immortality, and, if the expression may be allowed, individuality; properties by which a perpetual succession of many persons are considered as the same, and may act as a single individual.' . . .

Now, it is said that this state of affairs existing between the immortal corporation and the mortal owner—to say nothing of the present non-owner who is as good as dead—has been brought about by 'economic determinism.' Nature decided in favor of Big Business from the beginning. Nature did nothing of the sort, and there is no determinism about it. There is only the determination of those in power to perpetuate and to continue to control the giant corporate system. What exists in contemplation of law can cease to exist in contemplation of law. Corporate property has reached gigantic dimensions under protection of certain legal fictions: when the law made the abstract corporation a person, gifted with the privileges of real persons but with few of the responsibilities, it established a fiction that has gradually undermined the traditional safeguards, the truly functional property rights, embodied in the older common law.

Shall we make a law to undo bad laws and to set up a better older law? It sounds comfortingly too simple. Yet if the people were convinced that the collectivists wished to eliminate the two thousand men only to dispossess the rest of us more thoroughly, they might decide to eliminate the two thousand themselves—to get control of their property again.

V. The struggle is not new. It is the meaning of American history. Hamilton and Jefferson are the symbols of the struggle. . . . The next phase of the contest is doubtless near, but how the lines will be drawn it is impossible to predict. There are two general possibilities: We shall drift with the corporate structure of emasculated ownership until all trace of widespread control vanishes: that would be the tyrant State where corporations would be bigger than now and the two thousand men reduced, say, to twenty. Or we shall return to real politics, resume our political character, and reassert the rights of effective ownership.

I am not suggesting that the American Telephone and Telegraph Company break up into jealous units, one for each county. But I do suggest, if the institution of property, corporate or private, is to survive at all, that we keep only enough centralization—of production as well as control—to prevent gross economic losses and the sudden demoralization of large classes of workers. Our objective has been the big corporation. We must change it. Our objective should be the private business. Corporations are not yet big enough to satisfy the corporations. Nor doubtless will property ever be widely enough distributed to please the absolute distributist. Distributed property should nevertheless be the aim.

Or put it this way: We have been mere economists, and now we have got to be political economists as well. Economics is the study of wealth. But political economy is the study of human welfare.

We have tried to produce as much wealth as possible. It cannot be denied that technology and corporate ownership have combined to increase staggeringly the aggregate wealth of modern States. But it is an equivocal wealth. The aggregate wealth of a nation may be stupendous, and the people remain impoverished. Let us assume, what need not be true, that the total wealth of the property State would not be so great as the total wealth of the tyrant State. Yet the well-being of the people would be greater all-round. If we are to achieve so desirable an end, we have got to add politics to economics in order to get a sum that we may, perhaps, call citizens. For politics is—or should be—concerned with the welfare of persons, which is not always the same as their capacity to produce the maximum of goods.

VI. The skeptics about the property State, and even some of its friends who misunderstand it, assume that we are advocating something like this: Every man must live on a farm, hew his own logs for his cabin, make his own clothing—after tending the sheep and growing the cotton—raise all his food, and refuse to have electric lights. I should like to use this derisive idyl as a boomerang. Even though personal production for use throughout society is now neither possible nor desirable, it should not be forgotten that the nearer a society is to personal production for use the freer it is. We are not, therefore, crying for absolute liberty; we do want a little of it—as much as can be got when the majority of men own small units of production, whether factories or farms.

We do not ask everybody to live on a farm, nor—since we are allowing ourselves a little exchange-value in the property State—do we ask everybody to rush out as soon as he has read this book and buy a small store, a small factory, a small automobile, or a small football team.

At present the buyer of a farm would probably, in a year, be glad to run from his debts, and give it to the insurance company; or should he not be glad to run, he had better try to be. A farm now is not necessarily property. We want to make it property again. A small grocery store may represent certain paper property rights, but in view of the six chain stores surrounding it, it does not represent the same property rights as it did a hundred years ago. We want the store to be property again. Altogether it does seem to be a modest wish. For it is not only necessary to buy the farm or the factory, it is necessary to keep it. It can be kept if we can restore property rights that unite again ownership and control. . . .

Ch. 7. 'But Can it be Done?' (by Herbert Agar). . . .

III. The first step in making clear our program is to get rid of certain misunderstandings. First, we are not proposing a mere back-to-the-land movement—we believe that our program provides for a good life in urban as well as in rural communities. Second, we are not pretending that the present state of the farmer in America is everywhere an example of the good features of agrarian life. Third, we are not proposing a return to technologically inferior modes of manufacture. If these statements are kept in mind, it will be possible for even the most hostile critics to understand what it is we are advocating. The advantage of such understanding will be that our critics can then attack our actual program (which might be valuable to us), instead of merely attacking some queer mis-shapen notions of their own.

Believing as we do that there are moral and economic virtues in the institution of widespread property, and that monopoly-capitalism is morally ugly as well as economically unsound, our practical proposals look toward the establishment of a genuine property State—that is, a State in which a considerable majority of the families participate in real ownership.

The problem of property can be divided, for convenience, into the problem of property in land and the problem of property in industry and the distributive trades.

Other chapters in this book explain why we believe that real property in land can be saved throughout America, and how we believe it can be saved. I shall not recapitulate; but for the sake of clarity I shall state once again that our aim is to make free men of our present farmers, tenants and croppers, rather than to send a swarm of city-dwellers into the country. We may believe that if farming were given a fair chance more people would choose that way of life. But we do not wish to press it upon anybody.

When it comes to the problem of responsible ownership in industry, it must be admitted that there are certain industries and businesses in which such ownership is not feasible. Obvious examples would be railroads, electric power, and other utilities. Here monopoly is necessary for full efficiency. But, as Mr. Coyle writes, 'Monopoly is not business at all, but public service, to be operated with a single eye to the public benefit.' This is to say that such monopolies as are permitted must be regulated in the interests of the people. Either direct social control, as in Sweden, or indirect control, as in the British Gas Regulation Act, would seem to be indicated. Anyone who says 'impossible,' who says Americans can never do what the Swedes have done, or what the British, is a man who prefers pessimism to truth.

Over a large section of modern industry, however, it is not true that monopoly is efficient. As the Swedes have shown us, the optimum size for many plants is the smallest size which can use the most modern, labor-saving machinery. Decentralized factories producing for local use, on a scale where not more than a hundred people are involved in both management and labor, can be owned by the people directly concerned with them. The ownership would be real in the sense that the owners would have responsibility and control, so that the moral arguments in favor of property would at once become applicable. Such decentralization of ownership as well as of plant would take time. A lot could be done in five years; some of the changes would take a generation; but it is worth spending a little time to save America.

Assuming that the American people want the sort of decentralization I have described, the change can be hastened by two forms of State intervention: differential taxation, and control of new capital issues. Few people realize the short life-history of most big businesses. Textiles, railways, coal—the blue chips of yesterday are often the white elephants of today.

If the amalgamation of existing businesses for purely financial purposes (as opposed to purposes of productive efficiency) were made impossible, the falsity of the so-called economic law of monopoly would quickly be proved. Such amalgamations, so far as the future is concerned, can be prevented by control over new capital issues. So far as the past is concerned, it is possible that retroactive trust-busting acts will be hard to enforce. But the Swedes have shown us a better way to bust trusts—by establishing (with the help and support of local communities and of a public opinion that will not be cowed) small efficient productive units which can break the artificial prices made by the trusts and thus expose their profiteering and their inefficiency. In this way, in a system of genuine competition and small ownership, the plain man can get his share of the dividend created by the machine.

The Swedish example gives us ground for hoping that the change from monopoly-capitalism to real private property can be made with a minimum of State interference. But some interference there must be—more in America than in Sweden because of our vast size. Even people like myself, who believe that the best government is that which governs least, must admit that to resolve the chaos of modern America, State action will have to be employed. The question is whether that State action will be directed to the restoration of real property or to the abolition of all property. In the long run there is no third choice.

Monopoly-capitalism is a half-planned economy with all the vices of communism but none of its virtues. If the American people cannot have genuine property, genuine competition, they will prefer a State planned by communists for the good of the whole rather than a State planned by robber barons for the good of one another.

There remains the question of small property in the distributive trades—the question of the small shopkeeper vis-à-vis the chain store. Wherever an industry has been decentralized, wherever the rule is local production for local use, the merchant who retails the product of that industry has been put in a position to compete with the chain store. In a mass-production consumption-goods industry —for example, the food industry—from half to two thirds of the price paid by the consumer is normally chargeable to advertising, high-pressure salesmanship, and physical distribution. The efficiency of the chain store comes from mass buying, which makes it possible to undercut a percentage of the advertising and distribution costs. The chain store would have no such advantage when buying from the local producer. In a system of local production of consumption-goods the merchant becomes the expert buyer for the community—which is the economic purpose of the middleman and his final justification. . . .

29. PROPERTY RIGHTS AND DUE PROCESS OF LAW

THE fifth and fourteenth amendments in the Federal Constitution prohibit Congress and the State legislatures, respectively, from passing laws depriving any person of life, liberty, or property without due process of law. All the State constitutions impose the same or equivalent limitations on State legislatures. Decisions in thousands of cases during the last half century, in both the federal and State courts, have hinged on interpretations of the due process clause. Yet both lawyers and laymen are uncertain as to just what the clause means. The judges themselves, from the Justices of the United States Supreme Court down to local trial judges, have been in sharp disagreement with one another in the matter; and dominant trends in the court interpretations have changed from time to time. This is somewhat strange; for the phrase is at least six centuries old. It appeared in English statutes as early as the fourteenth century, and even then was almost certainly used as an equivalent of older phrases, such as "the law of the land" or "the course of the law"; and the due process clause, or an equivalent, was repeated in later English statutes as well as in charters and other seventeenth- and eighteenth-century documents of the American colonies.

Until about sixty years ago "due process of law" was almost invariably interpreted by our courts as a procedural rather than as a substantive limitation. In other words, the requirement of due process supplied the courts with a basis for determining, not whether a given limitation might be imposed, but how it might be enforced. Thus the clause applied to the methods by which persons were to be tried for crime, by which civil suits were to be conducted, and by which private property could be taken in the exercise of governmental powers of taxation or eminent domain. In the 1880's both federal and State courts began to interpret the clause as applying to the substance of legislation. This radical change in judicial attitude was due to a variety of familiar influences and pressures. Increased complexities in industrial and social relationships had led to a rapid expansion of governmental regulation of economic affairs; this brought on increasing demands, from the propertied interests affected, for judicial protection against the regulations; many judges, genuinely alarmed by what seemed to them to be unwise and arbitrary regulations,

785

found a way of nullifying many of the regulations through this new interpretation of the due process clause; and the clause thereby soon came to be the chief constitutional restriction on State legislation.   Thus in cases in which statutes limiting property rights were assailed as violative of due process, the question at issue came to be, not whether a statute established some unlawful, novel, or unfair procedure for enforcing a limitation, but whether the limitation in itself, by whatever methods it was to be enforced, was arbitrary or capricious.   The exercise of this new judicial function gave rise to sharp controversies, both within and without the courts: one side maintaining that since popularly elected bodies tend to deal selfishly or ignorantly with economic questions, the legitimate interests of property owners cannot be made properly secure unless judges, who are further removed from the influence of uninformed and emotional popular opinions, are accorded wide discretion in nullifying enactments which they regard as violative of substantive property rights; the other side contending that such a discretion gives the judges themselves the power to act arbitrarily and capriciously by enabling them, under cover of rendering politically impartial opinions, to nullify limitations they consider economically or socially undesirable.

Some of the past differences of opinion among the justices of the Supreme Court are reviewed in the majority and minority opinions in the recent case recorded below, which involved a minimum-wage statute of the State of Washington.   In 1923 the Court had (in a six-to-three decision, Chief Justice Taft delivering the dissenting opinion) invalidated a minimum-wage law enacted by Congress for the protection of women and children in the District of Columbia.   In June, 1936, the Court (Chief Justice Hughes and Justices Brandeis, Stone, and Cardozo dissenting) had followed that decision by invalidating a minimum-wage law of the State of New York.   Only ten months after this the Court reversed its position by sustaining the Washington statute; the shift was brought about by a change in attitude by Justice Roberts.

WEST COAST HOTEL CO. v. PARRISH (1937)[1]

MR. CHIEF JUSTICE HUGHES delivered the opinion of the Court.

This case presents the question of the constitutional validity of the minimum wage law of the State of Washington.

The Act, entitled "Minimum Wages for Women," authorizes the fixing of minimum wages for women and minors. . . . It pro vides:

[1] 300 United States Reports 379.

"SECTION 1. The welfare of the State of Washington demands that women and minors be protected from conditions of labor which have a pernicious effect on their health and morals. The State of Washington, therefore, exercising herein its police and sovereign power declares that inadequate wages and unsanitary conditions of labor exert such pernicious effect.

"SEC. 2. It shall be unlawful to employ women or minors in any industry or occupation within the State of Washington under conditions of labor detrimental to their health or morals; and it shall be unlawful to employ women workers in any industry within the State of Washington at wages which are not adequate for their maintenance.

"SEC. 3. There is hereby created a commission to be known as the 'Industrial Welfare Commission' for the State of Washington, to establish such standards of wages and conditions of labor for women and minors employed within the State of Washington, as shall be held hereunder to be reasonable and not detrimental to health and morals, and which shall be sufficient for the decent maintenance of women."

Further provisions required the Commission to ascertain the wages and conditions of labor of women and minors within the State. Public hearings were to be held. If after investigation the Commission found that in any occupation, trade or industry the wages paid to women were "inadequate to supply them necessary cost of living and to maintain the workers in health," the Commission was empowered to call a conference of representatives of employers and employees together with disinterested persons representing the public. The conference was to recommend to the Commission, on its request, an estimate of a minimum wage adequate for the purpose above stated, and on the approval of such a recommendation it became the duty of the Commission to issue an obligatory order fixing minimum wages. Any such order might be reopened and the question reconsidered with the aid of the former conference or a new one. Special licenses were authorized for the employment of women who were "physically defective or crippled by age or otherwise," and also for apprentices, at less than the prescribed minimum wage. . . .

The appellant conducts a hotel. The appellee Elsie Parrish was employed as a chambermaid and (with her husband) brought this suit to recover the difference between the wages paid her and the minimum wage fixed pursuant to the state law. The minimum wage was $14.50 per week of 48 hours. The appellant challenged the act as repugnant to the due process clause of the Fourteenth Amendment of the Constitution of the United States. The Supreme Court of the State, reversing the trial court, sustained the statute and directed judgment for the plaintiffs. *Parrish* v. *West Coast Hotel Co.*, 185 Wash. 581; 55 P. (2d) 1083. The case is here on appeal.

The appellant relies upon the decision of this Court in *Adkins* v. *Children's Hospital*, 261 U. S. 525, which held invalid the District of Columbia Minimum Wage Act, which was attacked under the due process clause of the Fifth Amendment. On the argument at bar, counsel for the appellees attempted to distinguish the *Adkins* case upon the ground that the appellee was employed in a hotel and that the business of an innkeeper was affected with a public interest. That effort at distinction is obviously futile, as it appears that in one of the cases ruled by the *Adkins* opinion the employee was a woman employed as an elevator operator in a hotel. . . .

The recent case of *Morehead* v. *New York ex rel. Tipaldo*, 298 U. S. 587, came here on certiorari to the New York court, which had held the New York minimum wage act for women to be invalid. A minority of this Court thought that the New York statute was distinguishable in a material feature from that involved in the *Adkins* case, and that for that and other reasons the New York statute should be sustained. But the Court of Appeals of New York had said that it found no material difference between the two statutes, and this Court held that the "meaning of the statute" as fixed by the decision of the state court "must be accepted here as if the meaning had been specifically expressed in the enactment." *Id.*, p. 609. That view led to the affirmance by this Court of the judgment in the *Morehead* case, as the Court considered that the only question before it was whether the *Adkins* case was distinguishable and that reconsideration of that decision had not been sought. Upon that point the Court said: "The petition for the writ sought review upon the ground that this case [Morehead] is distinguishable from that one [Adkins]. No application has been made for reconsideration of the constitutional question there decided. The validity of the principles upon which that decision rests is not challenged. This court confines itself to the ground upon which the writ was asked or granted . . . Here the review granted was no broader than that sought by the petitioner . . . He is not entitled and does not ask to be heard upon the question whether the *Adkins* case should be overruled. He maintains that it may be distinguished on the ground that the statutes are vitally dissimilar." *Id.,* pp. 604, 605.

We think that the question which was not deemed to be opened in the *Morehead* case is open and is necessarily presented here. The Supreme Court of Washington has upheld the minimum wage statute of that State. It has decided that the statute is a reasonable exercise of the police power of the State. In reaching that conclusion the state court has invoked principles long established by this Court in the application of the Fourteenth Amendment. The state court has refused to regard the decision in the *Adkins* case as determinative and has pointed to our decisions both before and since that case as justifying its position. We are of the opinion that this ruling of the state court demands on our part a reëxamination of the *Adkins* case. The importance of the question, in which many States having similar laws are concerned, the close division by which the decision in the *Adkins* case was reached, and the economic conditions which have supervened, and in the light of which the reasonableness of the exercise of the protective power of the State must be considered, make it not only appropriate, but we think imperative, that in deciding the present case the subject should receive fresh consideration. . . .

The principle which must control our decision is not in doubt. The constitutional provision invoked is the due process clause of the Fourteenth Amendment governing the States, as the due process clause invoked in the *Adkins* case governed Congress. In each case the violation alleged by those attacking minimum wage regulation for women is deprivation of freedom of contract. What is this freedom? The Constitution does not speak of freedom of contract. It speaks of liberty and prohibits the deprivation of liberty without due process of law. In prohibiting that deprivation the Constitution does not recognize an absolute and uncontrollable liberty. Liberty in each of its phases has its history and connotation. But the liberty safeguarded is liberty in a social organization which requires the protection of law against the evils which menace the health, safety, morals and welfare of the people. Liberty under the Constitution is thus necessarily subject to the restraints of due process, and regulation which is reasonable in relation to its subject and is adopted in the interests of the community is due process.

This essential limitation of liberty in general governs freedom of contract in particular. More than twenty-five years ago we set forth the applicable principle in these words, after referring to the cases where the liberty guaranteed by the Fourteenth Amendment had been broadly described:

"But it was recognized in the cases cited, as in many others, that freedom of contract is a qualified and not an absolute right. There is no absolute freedom to do as one wills or to contract as one chooses. The guaranty of liberty does not withdraw from legislative supervision that wide department of activity which consists of the making of contracts, or deny to government the power to provide restrictive safeguards. Liberty implies the absence of arbitrary restraint, not immunity from reasonable regulations and prohibitions imposed in the interests of the community." *Chicago, B. & Q. R. Co. v. McGuire*, 219 U. S. 549, 567.

This power under the Constitution to restrict freedom of contract has had many illustrations. That it may be exercised in the public interest with respect to contracts between employer and employee is undeniable. Thus statutes have been sustained limiting employment in underground mines and smelters to eight hours a day (*Holden v. Hardy*, 169 U. S. 366); in requiring redemption in cash of store orders or other evidences of indebtedness issued in the payment of wages (*Knoxville Iron Co. v. Harbison*, 183 U. S. 13); in forbidding the payment of seamen's wages in advance (*Patterson v. Bark Eudora*, 190 U. S. 169); in making it unlawful to contract to pay miners employed at quantity rates upon the basis of screened coal instead of the weight of the coal as originally produced in the mine (*McLean v. Arkansas*, 211 U. S. 539); in prohibiting contracts limiting liability for injuries to employees (*Chicago, B. & Q. R. Co. v. McGuire*, supra); in limiting hours of work of employees in manufacturing establishments (*Bunting v. Oregon*, 243 U. S. 426); and in maintaining workmen's compensation laws (*New York Central R. Co. v. White*, 243 U. S. 188; *Mountain Timber Co. v. Washington*, 243 U. S. 219). In dealing with the relation of employer and employed, the legislature has necessarily a wide field of discretion in order that there may be suitable protection of health and safety, and that peace and good order may be promoted through regulations designed to insure wholesome conditions of work and freedom from oppression. *Chicago, B. & Q. R. Co. v. McGuire, supra,* p. 570.

The point that has been strongly stressed that adult employees should be deemed competent to make their own contracts was decisively met nearly forty years ago in *Holden v. Hardy, supra,* where we pointed out the inequality in the footing of the parties. We said (*Id.,* 397):

"The legislature has also recognized the fact which the experience of legislators in many States has corroborated, that the proprietors of these establishments and their operatives do not stand upon an equality, and that their interests are, to a certain extent, conflicting. The former naturally desire to obtain as much labor as possible from their employes, while the latter are often induced by the fear of discharge to conform to regulations which their judgment, fairly exercised, would pronounce to be detrimental to their health or strength. In other words, the proprietors lay down the rules and the laborers are practically constrained to obey them. In such cases self-interest is often an unsafe guide, and the legislature may properly interpose its authority."

And we added that the fact "that both parties are of full age and competent to contract does not necessarily deprive the State of the power to interfere where the parties do not stand upon an equality, or where the public health demands that one party to the contract shall be protected against himself." "The State still retains an interest in his welfare, however reckless he may be. The whole is no greater than the sum of all the parts, and when the individual health, safety and welfare are sacrificed or neglected, the State must suffer."

It is manifest that this established principle is peculiarly applicable in relation to the employment of women in whose protection the State has a special interest. That phase of the subject received elaborate consideration in *Muller v. Oregon* (1908), 208 U. S. 412, where the constitutional authority of the State to limit the working hours of women was sustained. We emphasized the consideration that "woman's physical structure and the performance of maternal functions place her at a disadvantage in the struggle for subsist ence" and that her physical well being "becomes an object of public interest and care in order to preserve the strength and vigor of the race." We emphasized the need of protecting women against oppression despite her possession of contractual rights. We said that "though limitations upon personal and contractual rights may be removed by legislation, there is that in her disposition and habits of life which will operate against a full assertion of those rights. She will still be where some legislation to protect her seems necessary to secure a real equality of right." Hence she was "properly placed in a class by herself, and legislation designed for her protection may be sustained even when like legislation is not necessary for men and could not be sustained." We concluded that the limitations which the statute there in question "placed upon her contractual powers, upon her right to agree with her employer as to the time she shall labor" were "not imposed solely for her benefit, but also largely for the benefit of all." Again, in *Quong Wing v. Kirkendall*, 223 U. S. 59, 63, in referring to a differentiation with respect to the employment of women, we said that the Fourteenth Amendment did not interfere with state power by creating a "fictitious equality." We referred to recognized classifications on the basis of sex with regard to hours of work and in other matters, and we observed that the particular points at which that difference shall be enforced by legislation were largely in the power of the State. In later rulings this Court sustained the regulation of hours of work of women employees in *Riley* v. *Massachusetts*, 232 U. S. 671 (factories), *Miller* v. *Wilson*, 236 U. S. 373 (hotels), and *Bosley* v. *McLaughlin*, 236 U. S. 385 (hospitals).

This array of precedents and the principles they applied were thought by the dissenting Justices in the *Adkins* case to demand that the minimum wage statute be sustained. The validity of the distinction made by the Court between a minimum wage and a maximum of hours in limiting liberty of contract was especially challenged. 261 U. S., p. 564. That challenge persists and is without any satisfactory answer. As Chief Justice Taft observed: "In absolute freedom of contract the one term is as important as the other, for both enter equally into the consideration given and received, a restriction as to the one is not greater in essence than the other and is of the same kind. One is the multiplier and the other the multiplicand." And Mr. Justice Holmes, while recognizing that "the distinctions of the law are distinctions of degree," could "perceive no difference in the kind of degree of interference with liberty, the only matter with which we have any concern, between the one case and the other. The bargain is equally affected which-ever half you regulate." *Id.*, p. 569. . . .

The minimum wage to be paid under the Washington statute is fixed after full consideration by representatives of employers, em-ployees and the public. It may be assumed that the minimum wage is fixed in consideration of the services that are performed in the particular occupations under normal conditions. Provision is made for special licenses at less wages in the case of women who are incapable of full service. The statement of Mr. Justice Holmes in the *Adkins* case is pertinent: "This statute does not compel any-body to pay anything. It simply forbids employment at rates be-low those fixed as the minimum requirement of health and right living. It is safe to assume that women will not be employed at even the lowest wages allowed unless they earn them, or unless the employer's business can sustain the burden. In short the law in its character and operation is like hundreds of so-called police laws that have been upheld." 261 U. S., p. 570. And Chief Justice Taft forcibly pointed out the consideration which is basic in a statute of this character: "Legislatures which adopt a requirement of maximum hours or minimum wages may be presumed to believe that when sweating employers are prevented from paying unduly low wages by positive law they will continue their business, abating that part of their profits, which were wrung from the necessities of their employees, and will concede the better terms required by the law; and that while in individual cases hardship may result, the restriction will enure to the benefit of the general class of em-ployees in whose interest the law is passed and so to that of the community at large." *Id.*, p. 563.

We think that the views thus expressed are sound and that the decision in the *Adkins* case was a departure from the true applica-tion of the principles governing the regulation by the State of the relation of employer and employed. Those principles have been reënforced by our subsequent decisions. Thus in *Radice v. New York*, 264 U. S. 292, we sustained the New York statute which re-stricted the employment of women in restaurants at night. In *O'Gorman & Young v. Hartford Fire Insurance Co.*, 282 U. S. 251, which upheld an act regulating the commissions of insurance agents, we pointed to the presumption of the constitutionality of a statute dealing with a subject within the scope of the police power and to the absence of any factual foundation of record for deciding that the limits of power had been transcended. In *Nebbia* v. *New York*, 291 U. S. 502, dealing with the New York statute providing for minimum prices for milk, the general subject of the regulation of the use of private property and of the making of private contracts received an exhaustive examination and we again declared that if such laws "have a reasonable relation to a proper legislative purpose, and are neither arbitrary nor discriminatory, the requirements of due process are satisfied"; that "with the wisdom of the policy adopted, with the adequacy or practicability of the law enacted to forward it, the courts are both incompetent and unauthorized to deal"; that "times without number we have said that the legislature is primarily the judge of the necessity of such an enactment, that every possible presumption is in favor of its validity, and that though the court may hold views inconsistent with the wisdom of the law, it may not be annulled unless palpably in excess of legislative power." *Id.*, pp. 537, 538.

With full recognition of the earnestness and vigor which characterize the prevailing opinion in the *Adkins* case, we find it impossible to reconcile that ruling with these well-considered declarations. What can be closer to the public interest than the health of women and their protection from unscrupulous and overreaching employers? And if the protection of women is a legitimate end of the exercise of state power, how can it be said that the requirement of the payment of a minimum wage fairly fixed in order to meet the very necessities of existence is not an admissible means to that end? The legislature of the State was clearly entitled to consider the situation of women in employment, the fact that they are in the class receiving the least pay, that their bargaining power is relatively weak, and that they are the ready victims of those who would take advantage of their necessitous circumstances. The legislature was entitled to adopt measures to reduce the evils of the "sweating system," the exploiting of workers at wages so low as to be insufficient to meet the bare cost of living, thus making their very helplessness the occasion of a most injurious competition. The legislature had the right to consider that its minimum wage requirements would be an important aid in carrying out its policy of protection. The adoption of similar requirements by many States evidences a deepseated conviction both as to the presence of the evil and as to the means adapted to check it. Legislative response to that conviction cannot be regarded as arbitrary or capricious, and that is all we have to decide. Even if the wisdom of the policy be regarded as debatable and its effects uncertain, still the legislature is entitled to its judgment.

There is an additional and compelling consideration which recent economic experience has brought into a strong light. The exploitation of a class of workers who are in an unequal position with respect to bargaining power and are thus relatively defenceless against the denial of a living wage is not only detrimental to their health and well being but casts a direct burden for their support upon the community. What these workers lose in wages the taxpayers are called upon to pay. The bare cost of living must be met. We may take judicial notice of the unparalleled demands for relief which arose during the recent period of depression and still continue to an alarming extent despite the degree of economic recovery which has been achieved. It is unnecessary to cite official statistics to establish what is of common knowledge through the length and breadth of the land. While in the instant case no factual brief has been presented, there is no reason to doubt that the State of Washington has encountered the same social problem that is present elsewhere. The community is not bound to provide what is in effect a subsidy for unconscionable employers. The community may direct its law-making power to correct the abuse which springs from their selfish disregard of the public interest. The argument that the legislation in question constitutes an arbitrary discrimination, because it does not extend to men, is unavailing. This Court has frequently held that the legislative authority, acting within its proper field, is not bound to extend its regulation to all cases which it might possibly reach. The legislature "is free to recognize degrees of harm and it may confine its restrictions to those classes of cases where the need is deemed to be clearest." If "the law presumably hits the evil where it is most felt, it is not to be overthrown because there are other instances to which it might have been applied." . . .

Our conclusion is that the case of Adkins v. Children's Hospital, *supra,* should be, and it is, overruled. The judgment of the Supreme Court of the State of Washington is

Affirmed.

Mr. Justice Sutherland, dissenting:

Mr. Justice Van Devanter, Mr. Justice McReynolds, Mr. Justice Butler and I think the judgment of the court below should be reversed.

The principles and authorities relied upon to sustain the judgment, were considered in *Adkins v. Children's Hospital,* 261 U. S. 525, and *Morehead v. New York ex rel. Tipaldo,* 298 U. S. 587; and their lack of application to cases like the one in hand was pointed out. A sufficient answer to all that is now said will be found in the opinions of the court in those cases. Nevertheless, in the circumstances, it seems well to restate our reasons and conclusions.

Under our form of government, where the written Constitution, by its own terms, is the supreme law, some agency, of necessity, must have the power to say the final word as to the validity of a statute assailed as unconstitutional. The Constitution makes it clear that the power has been intrusted to this court when the question arises in a controversy within its jurisdiction; and so long as the power remains there, its exercise cannot be avoided without betrayal of the trust.

It has been pointed out many times, as in the *Adkins* case, that this judicial duty is one of gravity and delicacy; and that rational doubts must be resolved in favor of the constitutionality of the statute. But whose doubts, and by whom resolved? Undoubtedly it is the duty of a member of the court, in the process of reaching a right conclusion, to give due weight to the opposing views of his associates; but in the end, the question which he must answer is not whether such views seem sound to those who entertain them, but whether they convince him that the statute is constitutional or engender in his mind a rational doubt upon that issue. The oath which he takes as a judge is not a composite oath, but an individual one. And in passing upon the validity of a statute, he discharges a duty imposed upon *him,* which cannot be consummated justly by an automatic acceptance of the views of others which have neither convinced, nor created a reasonable doubt in, his mind. If upon a question so important he thus surrender his deliberate judgment, he stands forsworn. He cannot subordinate his convictions to that extent and keep faith with his oath or retain his judicial and moral independence. . . .

It is urged that the question involved should now receive fresh consideration, among other reasons, because of "the economic conditions which have supervened"; but the meaning of the Constitution does not change with the ebb and flow of economic events. We frequently are told in more general words that the Constitution must be construed in the light of the present. If by that it is meant that the Constitution is made up of living words that apply to every new condition which they include, the statement is quite true. But to say, if that be intended, that the words of the Constitution mean today what they did not mean when written—that is, that they do not apply to a situation now to which they would have applied then—is to rob that instrument of the essential element which continues it in force as the people have made it until they, and not their official agents, have made it otherwise. . . .

If the Constitution, intelligently and reasonably construed in the light of these principles, stands in the way of desirable legislation, the blame must rest upon that instrument, and not upon the court for enforcing it according to its terms. The remedy in that situation—and the only true remedy—is to amend the Constitution. Judge Cooley, in the first volume of his Constitutional Limitations (8th ed.), p. 124, very clearly pointed out that much of the benefit expected from written constitutions would be lost if their provisions were to be bent to circumstances or modified by public opinion. He pointed out that the common law, unlike a constitution, was subject to modification by public sentiment and action which the courts might recognize; but that "a court or legislature which should allow a change in public sentiment to influence it in giving to a written constitution a construction not warranted by the intention of its founders, would be justly chargeable with reckless disregard of official oath and public duty; and if its course could become a precedent, these instruments would be of little avail. . . . What a court is to do, therefore, is *to declare the law as written*, leaving it to the people themselves to make such changes as new circumstances may require. The meaning of the constitution is fixed when it is adopted, and it is not different at any subsequent time when a court has occasion to pass upon it." . . .

Coming, then, to a consideration of the Washington statute, it first is to be observed that it is in every substantial respect identical with the statute involved in the *Adkins* case. Such vices as existed in the latter are present in the former. And if the *Adkins* case was properly decided, as we who join in this opinion think it was, it necessarily follows that the Washington statute is invalid.

In support of minimum-wage legislation it has been urged, on the one hand, that great benefits will result in favor of underpaid labor, and, on the other hand, that the danger of such legislation is that the minimum will tend to become the maximum and thus bring down the earnings of the more efficient toward the level of the less-efficient employees. But with these speculations we have nothing to do. We are concerned only with the question of constitutionality.

That the clause of the Fourteenth Amendment which forbids a state to deprive any person of life, liberty or property without due process of law includes freedom of contract is so well settled as to be no longer open to question. Nor reasonably can it be disputed that contracts of employment of labor are included in the rule *Adair* v. *United States*, 208 U. S. 161, 174–175; *Coppage* v. *Kansas*, 236 U. S. 1, 10, 14. In the first of these cases, Mr. Justice Harlan, speaking for the court, said, "The right of a person to sell his labor upon such terms as he deems proper is, in its essence, the same as the right of the purchaser of labor to prescribe the conditions upon which he will accept such labor from the person offering to sell. . . . In all such particulars the employer and employé have equality of right, and any legislation that disturbs that equality is an arbitrary interference with the liberty of contract which no government can legally justify in a free land."

In the *Adkins* case we referred to this language, and said that while there was no such thing as absolute freedom of contract, but that it was subject to a great variety of restraints, nevertheless, freedom of contract was the general rule and restraint the exception; and that the power to abridge that freedom could only be justified by the existence of exceptional circumstances. This statement of the rule has been many times affirmed; and we do not understand that it is questioned by the present decision.

We further pointed out four distinct classes of cases in which this court from time to time had upheld statutory interferences with the liberty of contract. They were, in brief, (1) statutes fixing rates and charges to be exacted by businesses impressed with a public interest; (2) statutes relating to contracts for the performance of public work; (3) statutes prescribing the character, methods and time for payment of wages; and (4) statutes fixing hours of labor. It is the last class that has been most relied upon as affording support for minimum-wage legislation; and much of the opinion in the *Adkins* case (261 U. S. 547–553) is devoted to pointing out the essential distinction between fixing hours of labor and fixing wages. What is there said need not be repeated. It is enough for present purposes to say that statutes of the former class deal with an incident of the employment, having no necessary effect upon wages. The parties are left free to contract about wages, and thereby equalize such additional burdens as may be imposed upon the employer as a result of the restrictions as to hours by an adjustment in respect of the amount of wages. This court, wherever the question is adverted to, has been careful to disclaim any purpose to uphold such legislation as fixing wages, and has recognized an essential difference between the two. *E. g.*, *Bunting v. Oregon*, 243 U. S. 426; *Wilson v. New*, 243 U. S. 332, 345–346, 353–354; and see Freund, Police Power, § 318. . . .

Neither the statute involved in the *Adkins* case nor the Washington statute, so far as it is involved here, has the slightest relation to the capacity or earning power of the employee, to the number of hours which constitute the day's work, the character of the place where the work is to be done, or the circumstances or surroundings of the employment. The sole basis upon which the question of validity rests is the assumption that the employee is entitled to receive a sum of money sufficient to provide a living for her, keep her in health and preserve her morals. And, as we pointed out at some length in that case (pp. 555–557), the question thus presented for the determination of the board can not be solved by any general formula prescribed by a statutory bureau, since it is not a composite but an individual question to be answered for each individual, considered by herself. . . .

The Washington statute, like the one for the District of Columbia, fixes minimum wages for adult women. Adult men and their employers are left free to bargain as they please; and it is a significant and an important fact that all state statutes to which our attention has been called are of like character. The common-law rules restricting the power of women to make contracts have, under our system, long since practically disappeared. Women to-day stand upon a legal and political equality with men. There is no longer any reason why they should be put in different classes in respect of their legal right to make contracts; nor should they be denied, in effect, the right to compete with men for work paying lower wages which men may be willing to accept. And it is an arbitrary exercise of the legislative power to do so. . . .

An appeal to the principle that the legislature is free to recognize degrees of harm and confine its restrictions accordingly, is but to beg the question, which is—since the contractual rights of men and women are the same, does the legislation here involved, by restricting only the rights of women to make contracts as to wages, create an arbitrary discrimination? We think it does. Difference of sex affords no reasonable ground for making a restriction applicable to the wage contracts of all working women from which like contracts of all working men are left free. Certainly a suggestion that the bargaining ability of the average woman is not equal to that of the average man would lack substance. The ability to make a fair bargain, as everyone knows, does not depend upon sex. . . .

Finally, it may be said that a statute absolutely fixing wages in the various industries at definite sums and forbidding employers and employees from contracting for any other than those designated, would probably not be thought to be constitutional. It is hard to see why the power to fix minimum wages does not connote a like power in respect of maximum wages. And yet, if both powers be exercised in such a way that the minimum and the maximum so nearly approach each other as to become substantially the same, the right to make any contract in respect of wages will have been completely abrogated. . . .

IV. THE PROBLEM OF CHANGE

1. From THE DISCUSSION ON THE LAST DAY OF THE CONVENTION OF 1787 [1]

Monday Sepr. 17. 1787. In Convention

The engrossed Constitution being read,

Docr. Franklin rose with a speech in his hand, which he had reduced to writing for his own conveniency, and which Mr. Wilson read in the words following.

Mr. President

I confess that there are several parts of this constitution which I do not at present approve, but I am not sure I shall never approve them: For having lived long, I have experienced many instances of being obliged by better information or fuller consideration, to change opinions even on important subjects, which I once thought right, but found to be otherwise. It is therefore that the older I grow, the more apt I am to doubt my own judgment, and to pay more respect to the judgment of others. Most men indeed as well as most sects in Religion, think themselves in possession of all truth, and that where ever others differ from them it is so far error. Steele, a Protestant in a Dedication tells the Pope, that the only difference between our Churches in their opinions of the certainty of their doctrines is, the Church of Rome is infallible and the Church of England is never in the wrong. But though many private persons think almost as highly of their own infallibility as of that of their sect, few express it so naturally as a certain french lady, who in a dispute with her sister, said "I don't know how it happens, Sister but I meet with no body but myself, that's always in the right"—*Il n'y a que moi qui a toujours raison.*

In these sentiments, Sir, I agree to this Constitution with all its faults, if they are such; because I think a general Government necessary for us, and there is no form of Government but what may be a blessing to the people if well administered, and believe farther that this is likely to be well administered for a course of years, and

---

[1] In *Records of the Federal Convention*, ed. by Max Farrand, Vol. II, pp. 641–649. By courtesy of Yale University Press.

can only end in Despotism, as other forms have done before it, when the people shall become so corrupted as to need despotic Government, being incapable of any other. I doubt too whether any other Convention we can obtain may be able to make a better Constitution. For when you assemble a number of men to have the advantage of their joint wisdom, you inevitably assemble with those men, all their prejudices, their passions, their errors of opinion, their local interests, and their selfish views. From such an Assembly can a perfect production be expected? It therefore astonishes me, Sir, to find this system approaching so near to perfection as it does; and I think it will astonish our enemies, who are waiting with confidence to hear that our councils are confounded like those of the Builders of Babel; and that our States are on the point of separation, only to meet hereafter for the purpose of cutting one another's throats. Thus I consent, Sir, to this Constitution because I expect no better, and because I am not sure, that it is not the best. The opinions I have had of its errors, I sacrifice to the public good—I have never whispered a syllable of them abroad—Within these walls they were born, and here they shall die—If every one of us in returning to our Constituents were to report the objections he has had to it, and endeavor to gain partizans in support of them, we might prevent its being generally received, and thereby lose all the salutary effects & great advantages resulting naturally in our favor among foreign Nations as well as among ourselves, from our real or apparent unanimity. Much of the strength & efficiency of any Government in procuring and securing happiness to the people, depends on opinion, on the general opinion of the goodness of the Government, as well as well as of the wisdom and integrity of its Governors. I hope therefore that for our own sakes as a part of the people, and for the sake of posterity, we shall act heartily and unanimously in recommending this Constitution (if approved by Congress & confirmed by the Conventions) wherever our influence may extend, and turn our future thoughts & endeavors to the means of having it well administered.

On the whole, Sir, I cannot help expressing a wish that every member of the Convention who may still have objections to it, would with me, on this occasion doubt a little of his own infallibility—and to make manifest our unanimity, put his name to this instrument."—He then moved that the Constitution be signed by the members and offered the following as a convenient form viz. "Done in Convention, by the unanimous consent of *the States* present the 17th. of Sepr. &c—In Witness whereof we have hereunto subscribed our names."

This ambiguous form had been drawn up by Mr. G. M. in order to gain the dissenting members, and put into the hands of Docr. Franklin that it might have the better chance of success.

Mr. Gorham said if it was not too late he could wish, for the purpose of lessening objections to the Constitution, that the clause declaring "the number of Representatives shall not exceed one for every forty thousand—" which had produced so much discussion, might be yet reconsidered, in order to strike out 40,000 & insert "thirty thousand." This would not he remarked establish that as an absolute rule, but only give Congress a greater latitude which could not be thought unreasonable.

Mr. King & Mr. Carrol seconded & supported the ideas of Mr. Gorham.

When the President rose [the only occasion on which George Washington entered into the discussions of the Convention], for the purpose of putting the question, he said that although his situation had hitherto restrained him from offering his sentiments on questions depending in the House, and it might be thought, ought now to impose silence on him, yet he could not forbear expressing his wish that the alteration proposed might take place. It was much to be desired that the objections to the plan recommended might be made as few as possible—The smallness of the proportion of Representatives had been considered by many members of the Convention, an insufficient security for the rights & interests of the people. He acknowledged that it had always appeared to himself among the exceptionable parts of the plan; and late as the present moment was for admitting amendments, he thought this of so much consequence that it would give much satisfaction to see it adopted.

No opposition was made to the proposition of Mr. Gorham and it was agreed to unanimously

On the question to agree to the Constitution enrolled in order to be signed. It was agreed to all the States answering ay.

Mr. Randolph then rose and with an allusion to the observations of Docr Franklin, apologized for his refusing to sign the Constitution, notwithstanding the vast majority & venerable names that would give sanction to its wisdom and its worth. He said however that he did not mean by this refusal to decide that he should oppose the Constitution without doors. He meant only to keep himself free to be governed by his duty as it should be prescribed by his future judgment—He refused to sign, because he thought the object of the convention would be frustrated by the alternative which it presented to the people. Nine States will fail to ratify the plan and confusion must ensue. With such a view of the subject he ought not, he could not, by pledging himself to support the plan, restrain himself from taking such steps as might appear to him most consistent with the public good.

Mr. Govr. Morris said that he too had objections, but considering the present plan as the best that was to be attained, he should take it with all its faults. The majority had determined in its favor and by that determination he should abide. The moment this plan goes forth all other considerations will be laid aside—and the great question will be, shall there be a national Government or not? and this must take place or a general anarchy will be the alternative— . . .

Mr. Hamilton expressed his anxiety that every member should sign. A few characters of consequence, by opposing or even refusing to sign the Constitution, might do infinite mischief by kindling the latent sparks which lurk under an enthusiasm in favor of the Convention which may soon subside. No man's ideas were more remote from the plan than his own were known to be; but is it possible to deliberate between anarchy and Convulsion on one side, and the chance of good to be expected from the plan on the other. . . .

Mr. Gerry described the painful feelings of his situation, and the embarrassment under which he rose to offer any further observations on the subject wch. had been finally decided. Whilst the plan was depending, he had treated it with all the freedom he thought it deserved—He now felt himself bound as he was disposed to treat it with the respect due to the Act of the Convention —He hoped he should not violate that respect in declaring on this occasion his fears that a Civil war may result from the present crisis of the U. S.—In Massachusetts, particularly he saw the danger of this calamitous event—In that State there are two parties, one devoted to Democracy, the worst he thought of all political evils, the other as violent in the opposite extreme. From the collision of these in opposing and resisting the Constitution, confusion was greatly to be feared. He had thought it necessary for this & other reasons that the plan should have been proposed in a more mediating shape, in order to abate the heat and opposition of parties— As it had been passed by the Convention, he was persuaded it would have a contrary effect—He could not therefore by signing the Constitution pledge himself to abide by it at all events. . . .

The members then proceeded to sign the instrument.

Whilst the last members were signing it Doctr. Franklin looking towards the Presidents Chair, at the back of which a rising sun happened to be painted, observed to a few members near him, that Painters had found it difficult to distinguish in their art a rising from a setting sun. I have, said he, often and often in the course of the Session, and the vicissitudes of my hopes and fears as to its issue, looked at that behind the President without being able to tell whether it was rising or setting: But now at length I have the happiness to know that it is a rising and not a setting Sun.

The Constitution being signed by all the Members except Mr. Randolph, Mr. Mason, and Mr. Gerry who declined giving it the sanction of their names, the Convention dissolved itself by an Adjournment sine die——

2. A LETTER OF THOMAS JEFFERSON
TO JAMES MADISON (Paris, September 6, 1789) [1]

DEAR SIR,—I sit down to write to you without knowing by what
occasion I shall send my letter. I do it because a subject comes
into my head which I would wish to develope a little more than is
practicable in the hurry of the moment of making up general des-
patches.

The question Whether one generation of men has a right to
bind another, seems never to have been started either on this or
our side of the water. Yet it is a question of such consequences
as not only to merit decision, but place also, among the fundamental principles of every government. The course of reflection
in which we are immersed here on the elementary principles of
society has presented this question to my mind; and that no such
obligation can be transmitted I think very capable of proof. I set
out on this ground which I suppose to be self evident, *"that the
earth belongs in usufruct to the living;"* that the dead have neither
powers nor rights over it. The portion occupied by any individual
ceases to be his when himself ceases to be, and reverts to the society. If the society has formed no rules for the appropriation of
its lands in severalty, it will be taken by the first occupants. These
will generally be the wife and children of the decedent. If they
have formed rules of appropriation, those rules may give it to the
wife and children, or to some one of them, or to the legatee of the
deceased. So they may give it to his creditor. But the child, the
legatee or creditor takes it, not by any natural right, but by a law
of the society of which they are members, and to which they are
subject. Then no man can by *natural right* oblige the lands he
occupied, or the persons who succeed him in that occupation, to
the paiment of debts contracted by him. For if he could, he might
during his own life, eat up the usufruct of the lands for several
generations to come, and then the lands would belong to the dead,

---

[1] In *The Writings of Thomas Jefferson*, ed. by Paul Leicester Ford, Vol. V, pp.
115–124.

and not to the living, which would be reverse of our principle. What is true of every member of the society individually, is true of them all collectively, since the rights of the whole can be no more than the sum of the rights of individuals. To keep our ideas clear when applying them to a multitude, let us suppose a whole generation of men to be born on the same day, to attain mature age on the same day, and to die the same day, leaving a succeeding generation in the moment of attaining their mature age all together. Let the ripe age be supposed of 21. years, and their period of life 34. years more, that being the average term given by the bills of mortality to persons who have already attained 21. years of age. Each successive generation would, in this way, come on and go off the stage at a fixed moment, as individuals do now. Then I say the earth belongs to each of these generations during it's course, fully, and in their own right. The 2d. generation receives it clear of the debts and incumbrances of the 1st., the 3d. of the 2d. and so on. For if the 1st. could charge it with a debt, then the earth would belong to the dead and not the living generation. Then no generation can contract debts greater than may be paid during the course of it's own existence. At 21. years of age they may bind themselves and their lands for 34. years to come: at 22. for 33: at 23 for 32. and at 54 for one year only; because these are the terms of life which remain to them at those respective epochs. But a material difference must be noted between the succession of an individual and that of a whole generation. Individuals are parts only of a society, subject to the laws of a whole. These laws may appropriate the portion of land occupied by a decedent to his creditor rather than to any other, or to his child, on condition he satisfies his creditor. But when a whole generation, that is, the whole society dies, as in the case we have supposed, and another generation or society succeeds, this forms a whole, and there is no superior who can give their territory to a third society, who may have lent money to their predecessors beyond their faculty of paying.

What is true of a generation all arriving to self-government on the same day, and dying all on the same day, is true of those on a constant course of decay and renewal, with this only difference. A generation coming in and going out entire, as in the first case, would have a right in the 1st year of their self dominion to contract a debt for 33. years, in the 10th. for 24. in the 20th. for 14. in the

30th. for 4. whereas generations changing daily, by daily deaths and births, have one constant term beginning at the date of their contract, and ending when a majority of those of full age at that date shall be dead. The length of that term may be estimated from the tables of mortality, corrected by the circumstances of climate, occupation &c. peculiar to the country of the contractors. Take, for instance, the table of M. de Buffon wherein he states that 23,994 deaths, and the ages at which they happened. Suppose a society in which 23,994 persons are born every year and live to the ages stated in this table. The conditions of that society will be as follows. 1st. it will consist constantly of 617,703 persons of all ages. 2dly. of those living at any one instant of time, one half will be dead in 24. years 8. months. 3dly. 10,675 will arrive every year at the age of 21. years complete. 4thly. it will constantly have 348,417 persons of all ages above 21. years. 5ly. and the half of those of 21. years and upwards living at any one instant of time will be dead in 18. years 8. months, or say 19. years as the nearest integral number. Then 19. years is the term beyond which neither the representatives of a nation, nor even the whole nation itself assembled, can validly extend a debt.

To render this conclusion palpable by example, suppose that Louis XIV. and XV. had contracted debts in the name of the French nation to the amount of 10.000 milliards of livres and that the whole had been contracted in Genoa. The interest of this sum would be 500 milliards, which is said to be the whole rent-roll, or nett proceeds of the territory of France. Must the present generation of men have retired from the territory in which nature produced them, and ceded it to the Genoese creditors? No. They have the same rights over the soil on which they were produced, as the preceding generations had. They derive these rights not from their predecessors, but from nature. They then and their soil are by nature clear of the debts of their predecessors. Again suppose Louis XV. and his contemporary generation had said to the money lenders of Genoa, give us money that we may eat, drink, and be merry in our day; and on condition you will demand no interest till the end of 19. years, you shall then forever after receive an annual interest of 12 $\frac{5}{}$ per cent. The money is lent on these conditions, is divided among the living, eaten, drank, and squandered. Would the present generation be obliged to apply the produce of the earth and of their labour to replace their dissipations? Not at all.

I suppose that the received opinion, that the public debts of one generation devolve on the next, has been suggested by our seeing habitually in private life that he who succeeds to lands is required to pay the debts of his ancestor or testator, without considering that this requisition is municipal only, not moral, flowing from the will of the society which has found it convenient to appropriate the lands become vacant by the death of their occupant on the condition of a paiment of his debts; but that between society and society, or generation and generation there is no municipal obligation, no umpire but the law of nature. We seem not to have perceived that, by the law of nature, one generation is to another as one independant nation to another.

The interest of the national debt of France being in fact but a two thousandth part of it's rent-roll, the paiment of it is practicable enough; and so becomes a question merely of honor or expediency. But with respect to future debts; would it not be wise and just for that nation to declare in the constitution they are forming that neither the legislature, nor the nation itself can validly contract more debt, than they may pay within their own age, or within the term of 19. years? And that all future contracts shall be deemed void as to what shall remain unpaid at the end of 19. years from their date? This would put the lenders, and the borrowers also, on their guard. By reducing too the faculty of borrowing within its natural limits, it would bridle the spirit of war, to which too free a course has been procured by the inattention of money lenders to this law of nature, that succeeding generations are not responsible for the preceding.

On similar ground it may be proved that no society can make a perpetual constitution, or even a perpetual law. The earth belongs always to the living generation. They may manage it then, and what proceeds from it, as they please, during their usufruct. They are masters too of their own persons, and consequently may govern them as they please. But persons and property make the sum of the objects of government. The constitution and the laws of their predecessors extinguished them, in their natural course, with those whose will gave them being. This could preserve that being till it ceased to be itself, and no longer. Every constitution, then, and every law, naturally expires at the end of 19. years. If it be enforced longer, it is an act of force and not of right.

It may be said that the succeeding generation exercising in fact the power of repeal, this leaves them as free as if the constitution or law had been expressly limited to 19. years only. In the first place, this objection admits the right, in proposing an equivalent. But the power of repeal is not an equivalent. It might be indeed if every form of government were so perfectly contrived that the will of the majority could always be obtained fairly and without impediment. But this is true of no form. The people cannot assemble themselves; their representation is unequal and vicious. Various checks are opposed to every legislative proposition. Factions get possession of the public councils. Bribery corrupts them. Personal interests lead them astray from the general interests of their constituents; and other impediments arise so as to prove to every practical man that a law of limited duration is much more manageable than one which needs a repeal.

This principle that the earth belongs to the living and not to the dead is of very extensive application and consequences in every country, and most especially in France. It enters into the resolution of the questions Whether the nation may change the descent of lands holden in tail? Whether they may change the appropriation of lands given antiently to the church, to hospitals, colleges, orders of chivalry, and otherwise in perpetuity? whether they may abolish the charges and privileges attached on lands, including the whole catalogue ecclesiastical and feudal? it goes to hereditary offices, authorities and jurisdictions; to hereditary orders, distinctions and appellations; to perpetual monopolies in commerce, the arts or sciences; with a long train of et ceteras: and it renders the question of reimbursement a question of generosity and not of right. In all these cases the legislature of the day could authorize such appropriations and establishments for their own time, but no longer; and the present holders, even where they or their ancestors have purchased, are in the case of bona fide purchasers of what the seller had no right convey.

Turn this subject in your mind, my Dear Sir, and particularly as to the power of contracting debts, and develope it with that perspicuity and cogent logic which is so peculiarly yours. Your station in the councils of our country gives you an opportunity of producing it to public consideration, of forcing it into discussion. At first blush it may be rallied as a theoretical speculation; but examination will prove it to be solid and salutary. It would furnish matter for a fine preamble to our first law for appropriating the public revenue; and it will exclude, at the threshold of our new government the contagious and ruinous errors of this quarter of the globe, which have armed despots with means not sanctioned by nature for binding in chains their fellow-men. We have already given, in example one effectual check to the Dog of war, by transferring the power of letting him loose from the executive to the Legislative body, from those who are to spend to those who are to pay. I should be pleased to see this second obstacle held out by us also in the first instance. No nation can make a declaration against the validity of long-contracted debts so disinterestedly as we, since we do not owe a shilling which may not be paid with ease principal and interest, within the time of our own lives. Establish the principle also in the new law to be passed for protecting copy rights and new inventions, by securing the exclusive right for 19. instead of 14. years [*a line entirely faded*] an instance the more of our taking reason for our guide instead of English precedents, the habit of which fetters us, with all the political herecies of a nation, equally remarkable for it's encitement from some errors, as long slumbering under others. I write you no news, because when an occasion occurs I shall write a separate letter for that.

3. From ALEXANDER HAMILTON, THE FEDERALIST, NO. 85 (1788) [1]

Thus have I, fellow-citizens, executed the task I had assigned myself; with what success, your conduct must determine. I trust at least you will admit that I have not failed in the assurance I gave you respecting the spirit with which my endeavors should be conducted. I have addressed myself purely to your judgments, and have studiously avoided those asperities which are too apt to disgrace political disputants of all parties, and which have been not a little provoked by the language and conduct of the opponents of the Constitution. The charge of a conspiracy against the liberties of the people, which has been indiscriminately brought against the advocates of the plan, has something in it too wanton and too malignant not to excite the indignation of every man who feels in his own bosom a refutation of the calumny. The perpetual changes which have been rung upon the wealthy, the well-born, and the great, have been such as to inspire the disgust of all sensible men. And the unwarrantable concealments and misrepresentations which have been in various ways practiced to keep the truth from the public eye have been of a nature to demand the reprobation of all honest men. It is not impossible that these circumstances may have occasionally betrayed me into intemperances of expression which I did not intend; it is certain that I have frequently felt a struggle between sensibility and moderation; and if the former has in some instances prevailed, it must be my excuse that it has been neither often nor much.

Let us now pause and ask ourselves whether, in the course of these papers, the proposed Constitution has not been satisfactorily vindicated from the aspersions thrown upon it; and whether it has not been shown to be worthy of the public approbation and necessary to the public safety and prosperity. Every man is bound to answer these questions to himself, according to the best of his conscience and understanding, and to act agreeably to the genuine

[1] In *The Federalist*, ed. by Paul Leicester Ford, pp. 581–588.

and sober dictates of his judgment. This is a duty from which nothing can give him a dispensation. 'Tis one that he is called upon, nay, constrained by all the obligations that form the bands of society, to discharge sincerely and honestly. No partial motive, no particular interest, no pride of opinion, no temporary passion or prejudice, will justify to himself, to his country, or to his posterity, an improper election of the part he is to act. Let him beware of an obstinate adherence to party; let him reflect that the object upon which he is to decide is not a particular interest of the community, but the very existence of the nation; and let him remember that a majority of America has already given its sanction to the plan which he is to approve or reject.

I shall not dissemble that I feel an entire confidence in the arguments which recommend the proposed system to your adoption, and that I am unable to discern any real force in those by which it has been opposed. I am persuaded that this is the best which our political situation, habits, and opinions will admit, and superior to any the revolution has produced.

Concessions on the part of the friends of the plan, that it has not a claim to absolute perfection, have afforded matter of no small triumph to its enemies. "Why," say they, "should we adopt an imperfect thing? Why not amend it and make it perfect before it is irrevocably established?" This may be plausible enough, but it is only plausible. In the first place, I remark that the extent of these concessions has been greatly exaggerated. They have been stated as amounting to an admission that the plan is radically defective, and that without material alterations the rights and the interests of the community cannot be safely confided to it. This, as far as I have understood the meaning of those who make the concessions, is an entire perversion of their sense. No advocate of the measure can be found who will not declare as his sentiment that the system, though it may not be perfect in every part, is, upon the whole, a good one; is the best that the present views and circumstances of the country will permit; and is such an one as promises every species of security which a reasonable people can desire.

I answer, in the next place, that I should esteem it the extreme of imprudence to prolong the precarious state of our national affairs, and to expose the Union to the jeopardy of successive experiments, in the chimerical pursuit of a perfect plan. I never expect to see a perfect work from imperfect man. The result of the deliberations of all collective bodies must necessarily be a compound, as well of the errors and prejudices, as of the good sense and wisdom of the individuals of whom they are composed. The compacts which are to embrace thirteen distinct States in a common bond of amity and union must as necessarily be a compromise of as many dissimilar interests and inclinations. How can perfection spring from such materials?

The reasons assigned in an excellent little pamphlet lately published in this city, are unanswerable to show the utter improbability of assembling a new convention under circumstances in any degree so favorable to a happy issue as those in which the late convention met, deliberated, and concluded. I will not repeat the arguments there used, as I presume the production itself has had an extensive circulation. It is certainly well worthy the perusal of every friend to his country. There is, however, one point of light in which the subject of amendments still remains to be considered, and in which it has not yet been exhibited to public view. I cannot resolve to conclude without first taking a survey of it in this aspect.

It appears to me susceptible of absolute demonstration that it will be far more easy to obtain subsequent than previous amendments to the Constitution. The moment an alteration is made in the present plan, it becomes, to the purpose of adoption, a new one, and must undergo a new decision of each State. To its complete establishment throughout the Union, it will therefore require the concurrence of thirteen States. If, on the contrary, the Constitution proposed should once be ratified by all the States as it stands, alterations in it may at any time be effected by nine States. Here, then, the chances are as thirteen to nine in favor of subsequent amendment, rather than of the original adoption of an entire system.

This is not all. Every Constitution for the United States must inevitably consist of a great variety of particulars, in which thirteen independent States are to be accommodated in their interests or opinions of interest. We may of course expect to see, in any body of men charged with its original formation, very different combinations of the parts upon different points. Many of those who form a majority on one question may become the minority on a second, and an association dissimilar to either may constitute the majority on a third. Hence the necessity of molding and arranging all the particulars which are to compose the whole in such a manner as to satisfy all the parties to the compact; and hence, also, an immense multiplication of difficulties and casualties in obtaining the collective assent to a final act. The degree of that multiplication must evidently be in a ratio to the number of particulars and the number of parties.

But every amendment to the Constitution, if once established, would be a single proposition, and might be brought forward singly. There would then be no necessity for management or compromise, in relation to any other point—no giving nor taking. The will of the requisite number would at once bring the matter to a decisive issue. And consequently, whenever nine, or rather ten States, were united in the desire of a particular amendment, that amendment must infallibly take place. There can, therefore, be no comparison between the facility of effecting an amendment, and that of establishing in the first instance a complete Constitution.

In opposition to the probability of subsequent amendments, it has been urged that the persons delegated to the administration of the national government will always be disinclined to yield up any portion of the authority of which they were once possessed. For my own part, I acknowledge a thorough conviction that any amendments which may, upon mature consideration, be thought useful, will be applicable to the organization of the government, not to the mass of its powers; and on this account alone, I think there is no weight in the observation just stated. I also think there is little weight in it on another account. The intrinsic difficulty of governing thirteen States at any rate, independent of calculations upon an ordinary degree of public spirit and integrity, will, in my opinion, constantly impose on the national rulers the necessity of a spirit of accommodation to the reasonable expectations of their constituents. But there is yet a further consideration, which proves beyond the possibility of a doubt that the observation is futile. It is this, that the national rulers, whenever nine States concur, will have no option upon the subject. By the fifth article of the plan, the Congress will be obliged "on the application of the legislatures of two-thirds of the States (which at present amount to nine), to call a convention for proposing amendments, which shall be valid, to all intents and purposes, as part of the Constitution, when ratified by the legislatures of three-fourths of the States, or by conventions in three-fourths thereof." The words of this article are peremptory. The Congress "shall call a convention." Nothing in this particular is left to the discretion of that body. And of consequence all the declamation about the disinclination to a change vanishes in air. Nor, however difficult it may be supposed to unite two-thirds or three-fourths of the State legislatures, in amendments which may affect local interests, can there be any room to apprehend any such difficulty in a union on points which are merely relative to the general liberty or security of the people. We may safely rely on the disposition of the State legislatures to erect barriers against the encroachments of the national authority.

If the foregoing argument is a fallacy, certain it is that I am myself deceived by it, for it is, in my conception, one of those rare instances in which a political truth can be brought to the test of a mathematical demonstration. Those who see the matter in the same light with me, however zealous they may be for amendments, must agree in the propriety of a previous adoption as the most direct road to their own object.

The zeal for attempts to amend, prior to the establishment of the Constitution, must abate in every man who is ready to accede to the truth of the following observations of a writer equally solid and ingenious: "To balance a large state or society (says he), whether monarchical or republican, on general laws, is a work of so great difficulty that no human genius, however comprehensive, is able, by the mere dint of reason and reflection, to effect it. The judgments of many must unite in the work; experience must guide their labor; time must bring it to perfection, and the feeling of inconveniences must correct the mistakes which they *inevitably* fall into in their first trials and experiments." These judicious reflections contain a lesson of moderation to all the sincere lovers of the Union, and ought to put them upon their guard against hazarding anarchy, civil war, a perpetual alienation of the States from each other, and perhaps the military despotism of a victorious demagogue, in the pursuit of what they are not likely to obtain but from time and experience. It may be in me a defect of political fortitude, but I acknowledge that I cannot entertain an equal tranquillity with those who affect to treat the dangers of a longer continuance in our present situation as imaginary. A nation without a national government is in my view an awful spectacle. The establishment of a Constitution, in time of profound peace, by the voluntary consent of a whole people, is a prodigy, to the completion of which I look forward with trembling anxiety. I can reconcile it to no rules of prudence to let go the hold we now have, in so arduous an enterprise, upon seven out of the thirteen States, and, after having passed over so considerable a part of the ground, to recommence the course. I dread the more the consequences of new attempts because I know that powerful individuals, in this and in other States, are enemies to a general national government in every possible shape.   **PUBLIUS**

4. MERCY OTIS WARREN (1728–1814)

MRS. WARREN, poet, political playwright, sister of James Otis, was the first historian of the American Revolution. She was the wife of a Revolutionary leader, James Warren, a gentleman-farmer of nearby Plymouth, of "Mayflower blood," who was an intimate associate and adviser of Samuel and John Adams, held several local offices, and was president of the Massachusetts provincial congress, pay-master and major-general in the provincial militia, and speaker of the first house of representatives under the State constitution of 1780. By their Plymouth fireside, said Mrs. Warren, "were many political plans originated, discussed and digested." To help foster patriotism, she wrote several dramatic sketches; containing scathing satires on Hutchinson, Leonard, and other prominent Tories, they received high praise from John Adams and enjoyed general popularity. She wrote her history of the Revolution, she said, in order to give her children a record "of their mother's mental life." The work (written during the 1790's and published, in three volumes, in 1805) was "Interspersed with Biographical, Political and Moral Observations"; some of the biographical sketches are again malevolent characterizations of Tory leaders. The *History* gives a fresh and valuable picture of the political background of the Revolution. The author was intimately acquainted with many of the leading characters of the movement she was describing. Moreover she had access to public documents, and she used her own diary and notes.

Mrs. Warren showed considerable independence in her political observations. She and her husband were Jeffersonian agrarians in New England and had strong democratic convictions; but they were alarmed by the reckless financiering of the early State governments; and she believed there was no guaranteed permanency for democracy in its then existing forms. America, she said in 1789, is "too poor for Monarchy —too wise for Despotism, and too dissipated selfish and extravagant for Republicanism." Yet she had no doubt that the American people would have enough political intelligence and courage to be able constantly to readapt their institutions to changing needs, thereby preserving the essentially democratic achievement of their revolution.

[See: Alice Brown, *Mercy Warren* (1896); Annie Russell Marble, "Mistress Mercy Warren: Real Daughter of the American Revolution," *New England Magazine*, New Series, Vol. 28 (1903), pp. 163–180.]

From HISTORY OF . . . THE AMERICAN REVOLUTION (1805)[1]

Ch. XXXI.   Supplementary Observations on succeeding Events . . .

There is a propensity in mankind, to enlist themselves under the authority of names, and to adopt the opinions of men of celebrity, more from the fashion of the times, than from the convictions of reason. Thus with the borrowed language of their chieftain, they impose upon themselves, until they think his opinions are their own, and are often wrought up to such a fierce spirit of contention, that they appear ready to defend them in all the cruel modes of the savage, who is seldom actuated by motives of candor and forgiveness of injuries.

Both history and experience have proved, that when party feuds have thus divided a nation, urbanity and benevolence are laid aside; and, influenced by the most malignant and corrupt passions, they lose sight of the sacred obligations of virtue, until there appears little difference in the ferocious spirits of men in the most refined and civilized society, or among the rude and barbarous hordes of the wilderness. Though some symptoms of this degradation of the human character have appeared in America, we hope the cloud is fast dissipating, and that no vicissitudes in human affairs, no intrigues of the interested, nor any mistakes of upright men will ever damp the prospect of the establishment and continuance of a republican system, which appears to be best adapted to the genius of Americans. This form of government has the voice of the majority; the energies and sacrifices of the sons of Columbia, have been exerted to leave a republic form, defined, modified, and digested, as a model to promote the happiness of posterity.

Yet there is still a division of parties, and a variety of sentiment, relative to a subject that has heated the imaginations, and divided the opinions of mankind, from the rise of the Roman republic to the destruction of her splendid empire; and from that day to the

[1] Mrs. Mercy Warren, *History of the Rise, Progress and Termination of the American Revolution. Interspersed with Biographical, Political and Moral Observations,* 3 vols. (Boston, 1805), from Vol. III, ch. xxxi (pp. 228–436) at 396–404, 423–424.

present, when the divisions of the literati of every age, have called the attention of genius and ability to speculate and to dissent in their ideas of the best modes and forms of government.

It may be a subject of wonder and inquiry, that though so many ages have elapsed, and so great a part of the world been civilized and improved, that the science of politics is still darkened by the variety of opinions that prevail among mankind. It may be beyond the reach of human genius, to construct a fabric so free as to release from subordination, nor in the present condition of mankind ought it ever to be wished. Authority and obedience are necessary to preserve social order, and to continue the prosperity or even the existence of nations. But it may be observed, that despotism is not always the certain consequence of monarchy, nor freedom the sure result of republican theories.

It would be presumption in the writer, to entangle herself on a subject of such magnitude and importance, as to decide peremptorily, whether aristocratic, monarchic, or democratic government, is best adapted to the general happiness of the people. This shall be left to bolder pens; she will indulge little farther aberration of her's, after the expression of her wishes, that amidst the heterogeneous opinions of a theoretic age, America may not trifle away her advantages by her own folly and levity, nor be robbed of any of the essential rights which have cost her so dear, by the intrigues or ambition of any class of men.

The speculative of every age have theorized on a system of perfect republicanism, but the experiment has much oftener failed in practice, among all mankind, than been crowned with success. Those that have come nearest thereto, the free states of Greece, the Achean league, the Amphyctions, and other confederacies, fell under the power of Philip, Alexander, and their successors. The republic of Athens, the most conspicuous among the ancients, corrupted by riches and luxury, was wasted and lost by the intrigues of its own ambitious citizens.

The Roman commonwealth, the proud boast, the pattern, and exemplar of all republics, fell under the despotism of a long line of Caesars, generally the most debauched and brutal race of emperors that ever disgraced human nature. More modern experiments, Venice, and indeed all the Italian states, who boasted their freedom, were subjected to the tyranny of an oligarchy or aristocracy, frequently more severe and cruel than that of monarchy. In England, the struggles of Hampden and his virtuous associates were lost, and the strong reasonings of the patriots of that day in favor of freedom were obliterated, after the death of Charles, by the artful, the hypocritical, and the arbitrary Cromwell; and the most voluptuous of kings was restored, and re-seated on the throne of Britain.

Thus, from the first of the Stuarts to the last of the line of Brunswick who have yet reigned, their republican opinions and the freedom of the nation have been in the wane, and have finally sunk into an empty name under the tyranny of George the third. Indeed the most enlightened, rational, and independent characters in Great Britain continue still to defend the principles of liberty with their pens, while they have had reason to apprehend its total extinction through the realm.

Innumerable other instances might be adduced of the defeat of republicanism, in spite of the efforts of its most zealous friends: yet this is no proof that this system of government may not be more productive of happiness to mankind than that of monarchy or aristocracy. The United States of America have now a fair experiment of a republican system to make for themselves; they may perhaps be possessed of more materials that promise success than have ever fallen to the lot of any other nation. From the peculiar circumstances of the emigration of their ancestors, there is little reason to fear that a veil of darkness, tyranny, and barbarity will soon overspread the land to which they fled. These were a set of men very different in principles and manners from any that are to be found in the histories of colonization, where it may be observed, the first planters have been generally either men of enterprise for the acquisition of riches or fame, or convicted villains transported from more civilized societies.

In the outset of the American Revolution, the arm of foreign power was opposed by a people uncontaminated by foreign luxury, the intricacies of foreign politics, or the theological jargon of metaphysical sceptics of foreign extract. Philosophy then conveyed honorable ideas of science, of religion, and morals: the character is since degraded by the unprincipled sarcasms of men of letters, who assume the dignity of philosophic thought. Instead of unfolding the sources of knowledge, and inculcating truth, they often confound without convincing, and by their sophistical reasonings leave the superficial reader, their newly initiated disciple, on the comfortless shores of annihilation.

These observations are not confined to any particular nation or character; the historians of Britain, and the philosophers and poets of France, Germany, and England, are perhaps equally culpable; and it is to be regretted that America has not preserved a national character of her own, free from any symptoms of pernicious deviation from the purest principles on morals, religion, and civil liberty. She has been conducted through a revolution that will be ever memorable, both for its origin, its success, and the new prospects it has opened both at home and abroad. The consequences of this revolution have not been confined to one quarter of the globe, but the dissemination of more liberal principles in government, and more honorable opinions of the rights of man, and the melioration of his condition, have been spread over a considerable part of the world.

But men, prone to abuse the best advantages, lent by the beneficent hand of providence, sometimes sport them away, or confound causes with effects, which lead to the most erroneous conclusions. Thus it has been the recent fashion of courtiers, and of a great part of the clergy, under monarchic governments, to impute the demoralization and scepticism that prevails, to the spirit of free inquiry, as it regards the rights of civil society. This fashion has been adopted by all anti-republicans in America; but it may be asked, whether the declamation and clamor against the dissemination of republican opinions on civil government, as originating the prevalence of atheistical folly, is founded on the basis of truth?

Examine the history of the ancient republics of Greece, and the splendid commonwealth of Rome; was not the strictest regard paid to the worship of their gods, and a sacred observance of their religious rites enjoined, until the Grecian republics were overthrown by ambitious individuals? It was then that sceptical disputes more generally employed the philosophers; in consequence of which the rulers and the people sunk into an indifference to all religion. The rich city of Athens particularly, was early corrupted by the influx of wealth, the influence of aristocratic nobles, and the annihilation of every principle connected with religion.

Survey the Roman commonwealth before its decline, when it

was most worthy of the imitation of republicans. Was not a general regard paid to the worship of their deities, among this celebrated people, and a superstitious attention observed, relative to omens, prodigies and judgments, as denounced and executed by their gods, until republicanism was extinguished, the commonwealth subverted, and the sceptre of a single sovereign was stretched over that vast empire? It was then that Caligula set up his horse to be worshipped, as a burlesque on religion, and the sycophants of the court encouraged every caprice of their emperor. The people did not become so universally corrupt as to throw off all regard for religion, and all homage to the deities of their ancestors, until the libidinous conduct of their august sovereigns, and the nobles of the court, set the example.

Nor do we read in more sacred history, through all the story of the Israelites, that the fool ever said in his heart, there is no God, until under the dominion of kings.

It may be observed in the character of more modern republics, that religion has been the grand palladium of their institutions. Through all the free states of Italy, democracy and religion have been considered in union; some of them have indeed been darkened by superstition and bigotry, yet not equally hoodwinked under republican governments, as are the neighbouring kingdoms of Spain and Portugal, subjected to monarchic despotism.

By no fair deduction can it be asserted, that the scepticism and the late appearance of a total disregard to religious observances in France, are in consequence of the democratic struggles of the nation. The dereliction of all religious principles among the *literati* of France, and the abominable opinions of some of their philosophers, cannot be too much detested; but they have sprung from various causes, remote from political freedom, and too complicated to trace their origin, in a page of cursory observations. . . .

Perfection in government is not to be expected from so imperfect a creature as man; experience has taught, that he falls infinitely short of this point; that however industrious in pursuit of improvements in human wisdom, or however bold the inquiry that employs the human intellect, either on government, ethics, or any other science, man yet discovers a deficiency of capacity to satisfy his researches, or to announce that he has already found an unerring standard on which he may rest.

Perhaps genius has never devised a system more congenial to their wishes, or better adapted to the condition of man, than the American constitution. At the same time, it is left open to amendments whenever its imperfections are discovered by the wisdom of future generations, or when new contingencies may arise either at home or abroad, to make alterations necessary. On the principles of republicanism was this constitution founded; on these it must stand. Many corrections and amendments have already taken place, and it is at the present period as wise, as efficient, as respectable, as free, and we hope as permanent, as any constitution existing on earth. It is a system admired by statesmen abroad, envied by distant nations, and revered by Americans. They pride themselves on this palladium of safety, fabricated at a dangerous crisis, and established on the broad basis of the elective voice of the people. It now depends on their own virtue, to continue the United States of America an example of the respectability and dignity of this mode of government.

5. RALPH WALDO EMERSON (1803–82)

E MERSON, famous as a philosophical essayist and poet, had serious interests in social and political questions. From his basic philosophical beliefs he drew general conclusions as to the nature of human society and applied them to issues of the day. He approved utopian social experiments (e.g., Brook Farm and Bronson Alcott's Fruitlands), although he took no active part in them. He was an ardent abolitionist; he called the fugitive-slave act a "filthy enactment," avowing he would "not obey it, by God"; and he joined the bitter attack on Daniel Webster for recommending (in his "Seventh-of-March" speech) compromises on the slavery question.

Emerson stood generally for democracy and individual liberty: since all existence is unified by the "over-soul" and "every man hath in him the divine Reason," then all men are "created capable" of contributing to reasonable judgments by the community, and each man should be left free in forming and expressing his opinions and, under normal conditions, in deciding on his personal behavior. Yet there is a duality in human as in all nature. Men have gross animal instincts that lead them into selfish rivalries. In actual society there is conflict as well as cooperation, and "a government of force" is necessary. Emerson deplored the materialism and acquisitiveness of contemporary society. Like Jefferson, he believed that there were fewer obstacles to reasonable and refined living in an agricultural society, where every man stands in natural, "primary," relations "with the work of the world." It is "the invasion of Nature by Trade" that upsets the "balance of man." Thus governmental intervention and political reform are not barred by Emerson's philosophy. He believed that there were no dogmas fixing permanently the right lines between state and individual action, and that any community is benefited by the presence of both conservative and progressive views on the pace and direction of political change.

[See: Emerson's *Essay on Politics* (1849), in his *Complete Works*, ed. by E. W. Emerson (Centenary edition, 1903–04), Vol. III, pp. 197–221; *Man the Reformer* (1841), *ibid.*, Vol. I, pp. 225–256; *Journals*, ed. by E. W. Emerson and W. E. Forbes (1909–14), Vol. III, pp. 369–390, Vol. V, pp. 285–286, Vol. VIII, pp. 236, 259.

Vernon L. Parrington, *Main Currents of American Thought*, Vol. II
(1927), pp. 386–399; Van Wyck Brooks, *The Flowering of New England*
(1936), ch. x; Raymer McQuiston, *The Relation of Ralph Waldo Emerson
to Public Affairs* (1923); F. O. Matthiessen, *American Renaissance* (1941),
pp. 100–115, 180–186.]

From "THE CONSERVATIVE" (1841) [1]

The two parties which divide the state, the party of Conservatism and that of Innovation, are very old, and have disputed the
possession of the world ever since it was made. This quarrel is
the subject of civil history. The conservative party established the
reverend hierarchies and monarchies of the most ancient world.
The battle of patrician and plebeian, of parent state and colony, of
old usage and accommodation to new facts, of the rich and the
poor, reappears in all countries and times. The war rages not only
in battle-fields, in national councils and ecclesiastical synods, but
agitates every man's bosom with opposing advantages every hour.
On rolls the old world meantime, and now one, now the other gets
the day, and still the fight renews itself as if for the first time, under
new names and hot personalities.

Such an irreconcilable antagonism of course must have a correspondent depth of seat in the human constitution. It is the opposition of Past and Future, of Memory and Hope, of the Understanding and the Reason. It is the primal antagonism, the appearance in trifles of the two poles of nature.

There is a fragment of old fable which seems somehow to have
been dropped from the current mythologies, which may deserve
attention, as it appears to relate to this subject.

Saturn grew weary of sitting alone, or with none but the great
Uranus or Heaven beholding him, and he created an oyster. Then
he would act again, but he made nothing more, but went on
creating the race of oysters. Then Uranus cried, 'A new work, O
Saturn! the old is not good again.'

Saturn replied 'I fear. There is not only the alternative of making and not making, but also of unmaking. Seest thou the great

---

[1] "The Conservative: A Lecture Delivered at the Masonic Temple, Boston, December 9, 1841," in *Nature, Addresses, and Lectures*, Vol. I of *Emerson's Complete
Works*, Riverside Edition, 12 vols. (Cambridge, Mass., 1883), pp. 277–307, at 279
(beginning of text)–284, 284–297, 298–307. By courtesy of Houghton Mifflin
Company.

sea, how it ebbs and flows? so is it with me; my power ebbs; and if I put forth my hands, I shall not do, but undo. Therefore I do what I have done; I hold what I have got; and so I resist Night and Chaos.'

'O Saturn,' replied Uranus, 'thou canst not hold thine own but by making more. Thy oysters are barnacles and cockles, and with the next flowing of the tide they will be pebbles and sea-foam.'

'I see' rejoins Saturn, "thou art in league with Night, thou art become an evil eye; thou spakest from love; now thy words smite me with hatred. I appeal to Fate, must there not be rest?'—'I appeal to Fate also,' said Uranus, 'must there not be motion?'— But Saturn was silent, and went on making oysters for a thousand years.

After that, the word of Uranus came into his mind like a ray of the sun, and he made Jupiter; and then he feared again; and nature froze, the things that were made went backward, and to save the world, Jupiter slew his father Saturn.

This may stand for the earliest account of a conversation on politics between a Conservative and a Radical which has come down to us. It is ever thus. It is the counteraction of the centripetal and the centrifugal forces. Innovation is the salient energy; Conservatism the pause on the last movement. 'That which is was made by God,' saith Conservatism. 'He is leaving that, he is entering this other,' rejoins Innovation.

There is always a certain meanness in the argument of conservatism, joined with a certain superiority in its fact. It affirms because it holds. Its fingers clutch the fact, and it will not open its eyes to see a better fact. The castle which conservatism is set to defend/ is the actual state of things, good and bad. The project of innovation is the best possible state of things. Of course conservatism always has the worst of the argument, is always apologizing, pleading a necessity, pleading that to change would be to deteriorate: it must saddle itself with the mountainous load of the violence and vice of society, must deny the possibility of good, deny ideas, and suspect and stone the prophet; whilst innovation is always in the right, triumphant, attacking, and sure of final success. Conservatism stands on man's confessed limitations, reform on his indisputable infinitude; conservatism on circumstance, liberalism on power; one goes to make an adroit member of the social frame, the other to postpone all things to the man himself; conservatism is debonair and social, reform is individual and imperious. We are reformers in spring and summer, in autumn and winter we stand by the old; reformers in the morning, conservers at night. Reform is affirmative, conservatism negative; conservatism goes for comfort, reform for truth. Conservatism is more candid to behold another's worth; reform more disposed to maintain and increase its own. Conservatism makes no poetry, breathes no prayer, has no invention; it is all memory. Reform has no gratitude, no prudence, no husbandry. It makes a great difference to your figure and to your thought whether your foot is advancing or receding. Conservatism never puts the foot forward; in the hour when it does that, it is not establishment, but reform. Conservatism tends to universal seeming and treachery, believes in a negative fate; believes that men's temper governs them; that for me it avails not to trust in principles, they will fail me, I must bend a little; it distrusts nature; it thinks there is a general law without a particular application,— law for all that does not include any one. Reform in its antagonism inclines to asinine resistance, to kick with hoofs; it runs to egotism and bloated self-conceit; it runs to a bodiless pretension, to unnatural refining and elevation which ends in hypocrisy and sensual reaction.

And so, whilst we do not go beyond general statements, it may be safely affirmed of these two metaphysical antagonists, that each is a good half, but an impossible whole. Each exposes the abuses of the other, but in a true society, in a true man, both must combine. Nature does not give the crown of its approbation, namely beauty, to any action or emblem or actor but to one which combines both these elements; not to the rock which resists the waves from age to age, nor to the wave which lashes incessantly the rock, but the superior beauty is with the oak which stands with its hundred arms against the storms of a century, and grows every year like a sapling; or the river which ever flowing, yet is found in the same bed from age to age; or, greatest of all, the man who has subsisted for years amid the changes of nature, yet has distanced himself, so that when you remember what he was, and see what he is, you say, What strides! what a disparity is here! . . .

In nature, each of these elements being always present, each theory has a natural support. As we take our stand on Necessity, or on Ethics, shall we go for the conservative, or for the reformer. If we read the world historically, we shall say, Of all the ages, the present hour and circumstance is the cumulative result; this is the best throw of the dice of nature that has yet been, or that is yet possible. If we see it from the side of Will, or the Moral Sentiment, we shall accuse the Past and the Present, and require the impossible of the Future.

But although this bifold fact lies thus united in real nature, and so united that no man can continue to exist in whom both these elements do not work, yet men are not philosophers, but are rather very foolish children, who, by reason of their partiality, see everything in the most absurd manner, and are the victims at all times of the nearest object. There is even no philosopher who is a philosopher at all times. Our experience, our perception is conditioned by the need to acquire in parts and in succession, that is, with every truth a certain falsehood. As this is the invariable method of our training, we must give it allowance, and suffer men to learn as they have done for six millenniums, a word at a time; to pair off into insane parties, and learn the amount of truth each knows by the denial of an equal amount of truth. For the present, then, to come at what sum is attainable to us, we must even hear the parties plead as parties.

That which is best about conservatism, that which, though it cannot be expressed in detail, inspires reverence in all, is the Inevitable. There is the question not only what the conservative says for himself, but, why must he say it? What insurmountable fact binds him to that side? Here is the fact which men call Fate, and fate in dread degrees, fate behind fate, not to be disposed of by the consideration that the Conscience commands this or that, but necessitating the question whether the faculties of man will play him true in resisting the facts of universal experience? For although the commands of the Conscience are *essentially* absolute, they are *historically* limitary. Wisdom does not seek a literal rectitude, but an useful, that is a conditioned one, such a one as the faculties of man and the constitution of things will warrant. The reformer, the partisan, loses himself in driving to the utmost some specialty of right conduct, until his own nature and all nature resist him; but Wisdom attempts nothing enormous and disproportioned to its powers, nothing which it cannot perform or nearly perform. We have all a certain intellection or presentiment of reform existing in the mind, which does not yet descend into the character, and those who throw themselves blindly on this lose themselves. Whatever they attempt in that direction, fails, and reacts suicidally on the actor himself. This is the penalty of having transcended nature. For the existing world is not a dream, and cannot with impunity be treated as a dream; neither is it a disease; but it is the ground on which you stand, it is the mother of whom you were born. Reform converses with possibilities, perchance with impossibilities; but here is sacred fact. This also was true, or it could not be: it had life in it, or it could not have existed; it has life in it, or it could not continue. Your schemes may be feasible, or may not be, but this has the endorsement of nature and a long friendship and cohabitation with the powers of nature. This will stand until a better cast of the dice is made. The contest between the Future and the Past is one between Divinity entering and Divinity departing. You are welcome to try your experiments, and, if you can, to displace the actual order by that ideal republic you announce, for nothing but God will expel God. But plainly the burden of proof must lie with the projector. We hold to this, until you can demonstrate something better.

The system of property and law goes back for its origin to barbarous and sacred times; it is the fruit of the same mysterious cause as the mineral or animal world. There is a natural sentiment and prepossession in favor of age, of ancestors, of barbarous and aboriginal usages, which is a homage to the element of necessity and divinity which is in them. The respect for the old names of places, of mountains and streams, is universal. The Indian and barbarous name can never be supplanted without loss. The ancients tell us that the gods loved the Ethiopians for their stable customs; and the Egyptians and Chaldeans, whose origin could not be explored, passed among the junior tribes of Greece and Italy for sacred nations.

Moreover, so deep is the foundation of the existing social system, that it leaves no one out of it. We may be partial, but Fate is not. All men have their root in it. You who quarrel with the arrangements of society, and are willing to embroil all, and risk the indisputable good that exists, for the chance of better, live, move, and have your being in this, and your deeds contradict your words every day. For as you cannot jump from the ground without using the resistance of the ground, nor put out the boat to sea without shoving from the shore, nor attain liberty without rejecting obligation, so you are under the necessity of using the Actual order of things, in order to disuse it; to live by it, whilst you wish to take away its life. The past has baked your loaf, and in the strength of its bread you would break up the oven. But you are betrayed by your own nature. You also are conservatives. However men please to style themselves, I see no other than a conservative party. You are not only identical with us in your needs, but also in your methods and aims. You quarrel with my conservatism, but it is to build up one of your own; it will have a new beginning, but the same course and end, the same trials, the same passions; among the lovers of the new I observe that there is a jealousy of the newest, and that the seceder from the seceder is as damnable as the pope himself.

On these and the like grounds of general statement, conservatism plants itself without danger of being displaced. Especially before this *personal* appeal, the innovator must confess his weakness, must confess that no man is to be found good enough to be entitled to stand champion for the principle. But when this great tendency comes to practical encounters, and is challenged by young men, to whom it is no abstraction, but a fact of hunger, distress, and exclusion from opportunities, it must needs seem injurious. The youth, of course, is an innovator by the fact of his birth. There he stands, newly born on the planet, a universal beggar, with all the reason of things, one would say, on his side. In his first consideration how to feed, clothe, and warm himself, he is met by warnings on every hand that this thing and that thing have owners, and he must go elsewhere. Then he says, 'If I am born in the. earth, where is my part? have the goodness, gentlemen of this world, to show me my wood-lot, where I may fell my wood, my field where to plant my corn, my pleasant ground where to build my cabin.'

'Touch any wood, or field, or house-lot, on your peril,' cry all the gentlemen of this world; 'but you may come and work in ours, for us, and we will give you a piece of bread.'

'And what is that peril?'

'Knives and muskets, if we meet you in the act; imprisonment, if we find you afterward.'

'And by what authority, kind gentlemen?'

'By our law.'

'And your law,—is it just?'

'As just for you as it was for us. We wrought for others under this law, and got our lands so.'

'I repeat the question, Is your law just?'

'Not quite just, but necessary. Moreover, it is juster now than it was when we were born; we have made it milder and more equal.'

'I will none of your law,' returns the youth; 'it encumbers me. I cannot understand, or so much as spare time to read that needless library of your laws. Nature has sufficiently provided me with rewards and sharp penalties, to bind me not to transgress. Like the Persian noble of old, I ask "that I may neither command nor obey." I do not wish to enter into your complex social system. I shall serve those whom I can, and they who can will serve me. I shall seek those whom I love, and shun those whom I love not, and what more can all your laws render me?'

With equal earnestness and good faith, replies to this plaintiff an upholder of the establishment, a man of many virtues:

'Your opposition is feather-brained and over-fine. Young man, I have no skill to talk with you, but look at me; I have risen early and sat late, and toiled honestly and painfully for very many years. I never dreamed about methods; I laid my bones to, and drudged for the good I possess; it was not got by fraud, nor by luck, but by work, and you must show me a warrant like these stubborn facts in your own fidelity and labor, before I suffer you, on the faith of a few fine words, to ride into my estate, and claim to scatter it as your own.'

'Now you touch the heart of the matter,' replies the reformer. 'To that fidelity and labor I pay homage. I am unworthy to arraign your manner of living, until I too have been tried. But I should be more unworthy if I did not tell you why I cannot walk in your steps. I find this vast network, which you call property, extended over the whole planet. I cannot occupy the bleakest crag of the White Hills or the Alleghany Range, but some man or corporation steps up to me to show me that it is his. Now, though I am very peaceable, and on my private account could well enough die, since it appears there was some mistake in my creation, and that I have been missent to this earth, where all the seats were already taken,—yet I feel called upon in behalf of rational nature, which I represent, to declare to you my opinion that if the Earth is yours so also is it mine. All your aggregate existences are less to me a fact than is my own; as I am born to the Earth, so the Earth is given to me, what I want of it to till and to plant; nor could I, without pusillanimity, omit to claim so much. I must not only have a name to live, I must live. My genius leads me to build a different manner of life from any of yours. I cannot then spare you the whole world. I love you better. I must tell you the truth practically; and take that which you call yours. It is God's world and mine; yours as much as you want, mine as much as I want. Besides, I know your ways; I know the symptoms of the disease. To the end of your power you will serve this lie which cheats you. Your want is a gulf which the possession of the broad earth would not fill. Yonder sun in heaven you would pluck down from shining on the universe, and make him a property and privacy, if you could; and the moon and the north star you would quickly have occasion for in your closet and bed-chamber. What you do not want for use, you crave for ornament, and what your convenience could spare, your pride cannot.'

On the other hand, precisely the defence which was set up for the British Constitution, namely that with all its admitted defects, rotten boroughs and monopolies, it worked well, and substantial justice was somehow done; the wisdom and the worth did get into parliament, and every interest did by right, or might, or sleight, get represented;—the same defence is set up for the existing institutions. They are not the best; they are not just; and in respect to you, personally, O brave young man! they cannot be justified. They have, it is most true, left you no acre for your own, and no law but our law, to the ordaining of which you were no party. But they do answer the end, they are really friendly to the good, unfriendly to the bad; they second the industrious and the kind; they foster genius. They really have so much flexibility as to afford your talent and character, on the whole, the same chance of demonstration and success which they might have if there was no law and no property.

It is trivial and merely superstitious to say that nothing is given you, no outfit, no exhibition; for in this institution of *credit*, which is as universal as honesty and promise in the human countenance, always some neighbor stands ready to be bread and land and tools and stock to the young adventurer. And if in any one respect they have come short, see what ample retribution of good they have made. They have lost no time and spared no expense to collect libraries, museums, galleries, colleges, palaces, hospitals, observatories, cities. The ages have not been idle, nor kings slack, nor the rich niggardly. Have we not atoned for this small offence (which we could not help) of leaving you no right in the soil, by this splendid indemnity of ancestral and national wealth? Would you have been born like a gipsy in a hedge, and preferred your freedom on a heath, and the range of a planet which had no shed or boscage to cover you from sun and wind,—to this towered and citied world? to this world of Rome, and Memphis, and Constantinople, and Vienna, and Paris, and London, and New York? For thee Naples, Florence, and Venice; for thee the fair Mediterranean, the sunny Adriatic; for thee both Indies smile; for thee the hospitable North opens its heated palaces under the polar circle; for thee roads have been cut in every direction across the land, and fleets of floating palaces with every security for strength and provision for luxury, swim by sail and by steam through all the waters of this world. Every island for thee has a town; every town a hotel. Though thou wast born landless, yet to thy industry and thrift and small condescension to the established usage,—scores of servants are swarming in every strange place with cap and knee to thy command; scores, nay hundreds and thousands, for thy wardrobe, thy table, thy chamber, thy library, thy leisure; and every whim is anticipated and served by the best ability of the whole population of each country. The king on the throne governs for thee, and the judge judges; the barrister pleads, the farmer tills, the joiner hammers, the postman rides. Is it not exaggerating a trifle to insist on a formal acknowledgment of your claims, when these substantial advantages have been secured to you? Now can your children be educated, your labor turned to their advantage, and its fruits secured to them after your death. It is frivolous to say you have no acre, because you have not a mathematically measured piece of land. Providence takes care that you shall have a place, that you are waited for, and come accredited; and as soon as you put your gift to use, you shall have acre or acre's worth according to your exhibition of desert,—acre, if you need land;—acre's worth, if you prefer to draw, or carve, or make shoes or wheels, to the tilling of the soil.

Besides, it might temper your indignation at the supposed wrong which society has done you, to keep the question before you, how society got into this predicament? Who put things on this false basis? No single man, but all men. No man voluntarily and knowingly; but it is the result of that degree of culture there is in the planet. The order of things is as good as the character of the population permits. Consider it as the work of a great and beneficent and progressive necessity, which, from the first pulsation in the first animal life, up to the present high culture of the best nations, has advanced thus far. Thank the rude foster-mother though she has taught you a better wisdom than her own, and has set hopes in your heart which shall be history in the next ages. You are yourself the result of this manner of living, this foul compromise, this vituperated Sodom. It nourished you with care and love on its breast, as it had nourished many a lover of the right and many a poet, and prophet, and teacher of men. Is it so irremediably bad? Then again, if the mitigations are considered, do not all the mischiefs virtually vanish? The form is bad, but see you not how every personal character reacts on the form, and makes it new? A strong person makes the law and custom null before his own will. Then the principle of love and truth reappears in the strictest courts of fashion and property. Under the richest robes, in the darlings of the selectest circles of European or American aristocracy, the strong heart will beat with love of mankind, with impatience of accidental distinctions, with the desire to achieve its own fate and make every ornament it wears authentic and real.

Moreover, as we have already shown that there is no pure reformer, so it is to be considered that there is no pure conservative, no man who from the beginning to the end of his life maintains the defective institutions; but he who sets his face like a flint against every novelty, when approached in the confidence of conversation, in the presence of friendly and generous persons, has also his gracious and relenting moments, and espouses for the time the cause of man; and even if this be a shortlived emotion, yet the remembrance of it in private hours mitigates his selfishness and compliance with custom. . . .

The reformer concedes that these mitigations exist, and that if he proposed comfort, he should take sides with the establishment. Your words are excellent, but they do not tell the whole. Conservatism is affluent and openhanded, but there is a cunning juggle in riches. I observe that they take somewhat for everything they give. I look bigger, but am less; I have more clothes, but am not so warm; more armor, but less courage; more books, but less wit. What you say of your planted, builded and decorated world is true enough, and I gladly avail myself of its convenience; yet I have remarked that what holds in particular, holds in general, that the plant Man does not require for his most glorious flowering this pomp of preparation and convenience, but the thoughts of some beggarly Homer who strolled, God knows when, in the infancy and barbarism of the old world; the gravity and sense of some slave Moses who leads away his fellow slaves from their masters; the contemplation of some Scythian Anacharsis; the erect, formidable valor of some Dorian townsmen in the town of Sparta; the vigor of Clovis the Frank, and Alfred the Saxon, and Alaric the Goth, and Mahomet, Ali and Omar the Arabians, Saladin the Curd, and Othman the Turk, sufficed to build what you call society on the spot and in the instant when the sound mind in a sound body appeared. Rich and fine is your dress, O conservatism! your horses are of the best blood; your roads are well cut and well paved; your pantry is full of meats and your cellar of wines, and a very good state and condition are you for gentlemen and ladies to live under; but every one of these goods steals away a drop of my blood. I want the necessity of supplying my own wants. All this costly culture of yours is not necessary. Greatness does not need it. Yonder peasant, who sits neglected there in a corner, carries a whole revolution of man and nature in his head, which shall be a sacred history to some future ages. For man is the end of nature; nothing so easily organizes itself in every part of the universe as he; no moss, no lichen is so easily born; and he takes along with him and puts out from himself the whole apparatus of society and condition extempore, as an army encamps in a desert, and where all was just now blowing sand, creates a white city in an hour, a government, a market, a place for feasting, for conversation, and for love.

These considerations, urged by those whose characters and whose fortunes are yet to be formed, must needs command the sympathy of all reasonable persons. But beside that charity which should make all adult persons interested for the youth, and engage them to see that he has a free field and fair play on his entrance into life, we are bound to see that the society of which we compose a part, does not permit the formation or continuance of views and practices injurious to the honor and welfare of mankind. The objection to conservatism, when embodied in a party, is that in its love of acts it hates principles; it lives in the senses, not in truth; it sacrifices to despair; it goes for availableness in its candidate, not for worth; and for expediency in its measures, and not for the right. Under pretence of allowing for friction, it makes so many additions and supplements to the machine of society that it will play smoothly and softly, but will no longer grind any grist.

The conservative party in the universe concedes that the radical would talk sufficiently to the purpose, if we were still in the garden of Eden; he legislates for man as he ought to be; his theory is right, but he makes no allowance for friction; and this omission makes his whole doctrine false. The idealist retorts that the conservative falls into a far more noxious error in the other extreme. The conservative assumes sickness as a necessity, and his social frame is a hospital, his total legislation is for the present distress, a universe in slippers and flannels, with bib and papspoon, swallowing pills and herb-tea. Sickness gets organized as well as health, the vice as well as the virtue. Now that a vicious system of trade has existed so long, it has stereotyped itself in the human generation, and misers are born. And now that sickness has got such a foothold, leprosy has grown cunning, has got into the ballot-box; the lepers outvote the clean; society has resolved itself into a Hospital Committee, and all its laws are quarantine. If any man resist and set up a foolish hope he has entertained as good against the general despair, Society frowns on him, shuts him out of her opportunities, her granaries, her refectories, her water and bread, and will serve him a sexton's turn. Conservatism takes as low a view of every part of human action and passion. Its religion is just as bad; a lozenge for the sick; a dolorous tune to beguile the distemper; mitigations of pain by pillows and anodynes; always mitigations, never remedies; pardons for sin, funeral honors,—never self-help, renovation, and virtue. Its social and political action has no better aim; to keep out wind and weather, to bring the week and year about, and make the world last our day; not to sit on the world and steer it; not to sink the memory of the past in the glory of a new and more excellent creation; a timid cobbler and patcher, it degrades whatever it touches. The cause of education is urged in this country with the utmost earnestness,—on what ground? Why on this, that the people have the power, and if they are not instructed to sympathize with the intelligent, reading, trading, and governing class; inspired with a taste for the same competitions and prizes, they will upset the fair pageant of Judicature, and perhaps lay a hand on the sacred muniments of wealth itself, and new distribute the land. Religion is taught in the same spirit. The contractors who were building a road out of Baltimore, some years ago, found the Irish laborers quarrelsome and refractory to a degree that embarrassed the agents and seriously interrupted the progress of the work. The corporation were advised to call off the police and build a Catholic chapel, which they did; the priest presently restored order, and the work went on prosperously. Such hints, be sure, are too valuable to be lost. If you do not value the Sabbath, or other religious institutions, give yourself no concern about maintaining them. They have already acquired a market value as conservators of property; and if priest and church-member should fail, the chambers of commerce and the presidents of the banks, the very innholders and landlords of the county, would muster with fury to their support. . . .

But not to balance reasons for and against the establishment any longer, and if it still be asked in this necessity of partial organization, which party on the whole has the highest claims on our sympathy,—I bring it home to the private heart, where all such questions must have their final arbitrement. How will every strong and generous mind choose its ground,—with the defenders of the old? or with the seekers of the new? Which is that state which promises to edify a great, brave, and beneficent man; to throw him on his resources, and tax the strength of his character? On which part will each of us find himself in the hour of health and of aspiration?

I understand well the respect of mankind for war, because that breaks up the Chinese stagnation of society, and demonstrates the personal merits of all men. A state of war or anarchy, in which law has little force, is so far valuable that it puts every man on trial. The man of principle is known as such, and even in the fury of faction is respected. In the civil wars of France, Montaigne alone, among all the French gentry, kept his castle gates unbarred, and made his personal integrity as good at least as a regiment. The man of courage and resources is shown, and the effeminate and base person. Those who rise above war, and those who fall below it, it easily discriminates, as well as those who, accepting its rude conditions, keep their own head by their own sword.

But in peace and a commercial state we depend, not as we ought, on our knowledge and all men's knowledge that we are honest men, but we cowardly lean on the virtue of others. For it is always at last the virtue of some men in the society, which keeps the law in any reverence and power. Is there not something shameful that I should owe my peaceful occupancy of my house and field, not to the knowledge of my countrymen that I am useful, but to their respect for sundry other reputable persons, I know not whom, whose joint virtue still keeps the law in good odor?

It will never make any difference to a hero what the laws are. His greatness will shine and accomplish itself unto the end, whether they second him or not. If he have earned his bread by drudgery, and in the narrow and crooked ways which were all an evil law had left him, he will make it at least honorable by his expenditure. Of the past he will take no heed; for its wrongs he will not hold himself responsible: he will say, All the meanness of my progenitors shall not bereave me of the power to make this hour and company fair and fortunate. Whatsoever streams of power and commodity flow to me, shall of me acquire healing virtue, and become fountains of safety. Cannot I too descend a Redeemer into nature? Whosoever hereafter shall name my name, shall not record a malefactor but a benefactor in the earth. If there be power in good intention, in fidelity, and in toil, the north wind shall be purer, the stars in heaven shall glow with a kindlier beam, that I have lived. I am primarily engaged to myself to be a public servant of all the gods, to demonstrate to all men that there is intelligence and good will at the heart of things, and ever higher and yet higher leadings. These are my engagements; how can your law further or hinder me in what I shall do to men? On the other hand, these dispositions establish their relations to me. Wherever there is worth, I shall be greeted. Wherever there are men, are the objects of my study and love. Sooner or later all men will be my friends, and will testify in all methods the energy of their regard. I cannot thank your law for my protection. I protect it. It is not in its power to protect me. It is my business to make myself revered. I depend on my honor, my labor, and my dispositions for my place in the affections of mankind, and not on any conventions or parchments of yours.

But if I allow myself in derelictions and become idle and dissolute, I quickly come to love the protection of a strong law, because I feel no title in myself to my advantages. To the intemperate and covetous person no love flows; to him mankind would pay no rent, no dividend, if force were once relaxed; nay, if they could give their verdict, they would say that his self-indulgence and his oppression deserved punishment from society, and not that rich board and lodging he now enjoys. The law acts then as a screen of his unworthiness, and makes him worse the longer it protects him.

In conclusion, to return from this alternation of partial views to the high platform of universal and necessary history, it is a happiness for mankind that innovation has got on so far and has so free a field before it. The boldness of the hope men entertain transcends all former experience. It calms and cheers them with the picture of a simple and equal life of truth and piety. And this hope flowered on what tree? It was not imported from the stock of some celestial plant, but grew here on the wild crab of conservatism. It is much that this old and vituperated system of things has borne so fair a child. It predicts that amidst a planet peopled with conservatives, one Reformer may yet be born.

6. CARL L. BECKER (1873–   )

A NATIVE of Iowa, Professor Becker has been a member of the
faculties of history in Pennsylvania State College, Dartmouth College, University of Kansas, University of Minnesota, and (since 1917)
Cornell University. He was president of the American Historical Association in 1931. He is the author of numerous books and essays on
American history, the nature of history, and the interpretation of the
ideologies of particular periods of history. His books include *The Declaration of Independence: a Study in the History of Political Ideas*
(1922), *The Heavenly City of the Eighteenth Century Philosophers*
(1932), *Every Man His Own Historian* (1935), and *Progress and Power*
(1936).

From MODERN DEMOCRACY (1941) [1]

Chapter III. The Dilemma

I

The problem of modern democracies as I have just defined it
may be . . . stated: Can the flagrant inequality of possessions and
of opportunity now existing in democratic societies be corrected by
the democratic method? If it cannot be so corrected the resulting
discontent and confusion will be certain, sooner or later, to issue
in some form of revolutionary or military dictatorship. This then
is the dilemma which confronts democratic societies: to solve the
economic problem by the democratic method, or to cease to be
democratic societies.

It is obvious that the problem, intrinsically, is an economic one.
At the present moment it takes the spectacular form of unemployment. For the past ten years, in the most prosperous democratic
societies, from 10 to 20 per cent of the working population, for the
most part willing but unable to find work, has been kept alive by

[1] Carl L. Becker, *Modern Democracy* (New Haven, 1941: "The volume is based
upon three lectures delivered at the University of Virginia on the Page-Barbour
Foundation"), from ch. iii. By special arrangement with the Yale University Press.

public or private charity or by jobs created for that purpose by the
government.   Unemployment is no new thing, but never before in
democratic societies has it reached the proportions of a major social catastrophe.

The catastrophe cannot be explained as an act of God, cannot be
attributed to destructive natural forces beyond human control.
The people are famished, but there is no famine.   On the contrary, there is wealth in abundance, or should be.   Given our natural resources, man power, and technical equipment, there could
be produced, in this country at least, sufficient wealth to provide
all the people with the necessities of life and many of the desired
comforts and luxuries besides.   Yet in spite of widespread and insistent human need, the technical equipment is used only in part,
the man power is not full employed.   In a land of plenty millions
are destitute.   Obviously the situation is one which arises not from
lack of potential wealth, but from some defect in the method of
producing and distributing wealth.   That the defect is a serious one
is indicated by a simple, ironic fact—the fact that in a world in
which millions are destitute it is thought necessary, and under the
prevailing system of production and distribution of wealth apparently is so, to limit the production of the necessities of life in
order to keep people from starving.

The prevailing system for the production and distribution of
wealth is variously denoted by the phrases capitalist system, competitive system, price system, system of free enterprise, system of
laissez-faire.   Its theoretical justification derives from the general
assumption of the liberal-democratic ideology—the assumption
that social welfare can best be achieved by reducing governmental
interference with the freedom of the individual to a minimum.
The assumption was never better stated than by John Stuart Mill
in his famous essay *On Liberty*.   Governmental interference with
the activities of the individual, he maintained, is never justified except when manifestly necessary to prevent the activities of some individuals from injuring others.   The principle is similarly, but more
succinctly, formulated in the French Declaration of the Rights of
Man: "Liberty is the right of everyone to do whatever does not injure others."

Applied to the economic realm, this principle was interpreted to
mean the maximum freedom of the individual to choose his oc-

cupation or business, and to enter freely into contracts for the acquisition or disposal of private property and for the purchase or sale of personal services. It was assumed that the free play of individual initiative, stimulated by the acquisitive instinct, would result in the maximum production of wealth, and that the competitive instinct, operating through the law of supply and demand and the resulting price system, would result in as equitable a distribution of wealth as the natural qualities and defects of men would permit. In this system the function of the government was reduced to defining and guaranteeing the rights of private property, enforcing the rules of contract, and preserving social order. Having defined the rules of the game, the government would see that they were enforced, but would not otherwise interfere with the players. Let the game go on and the best man win. *Laissez-faire, laissez-passer!*

Contrary to a wide-spread belief, *laissez-faire* was never more than a theory imperfectly applied. The happy, imagined time when government did not interfere in the freedom of the individual by meddling in business never in fact existed. The institution of private property is itself a most drastic regulation of business enterprise, the law of contract a fundamental interference with the liberty of the individual. But assuming private property and the law of contract as part of the system, there never was a time when government did not find it necessary, according to Mill's famous definition, to interfere with the activities of some individuals in order to prevent those activities from injuring others.

In England the trend toward *laissez-faire* was reversed before it was completed. A decade before 1846, when the doctrine was officially adopted by the repeal of the corn laws, the government had found it necessary to restrict free enterprise by passing the first Factory Acts for the protection of women and children. And from that day to this, in England and in every industrialized country, including the United States, the governmental regulation of private property, of free competition and free contract, of the price of commodities and of labor, of the inheritance of property and of the disposal of income from it, has steadily increased. This extension of governmental regulation, this trend toward what is called social legislation, was brought about by the pressure of labor unions supported by the humane sentiment of the community, and underlying it is the assumption, avowed or unavowed, that the system of *laissez-faire*, so eminently successful in stimulating the production of wealth, is incapable, without governmental regulation, of bringing about an equitable or even a tolerable distribution of it. It is far too late to ask whether government should interfere in business enterprise. It always has interfered in business enterprise. The only relevant question is in what ways and to what extent it should so interfere.

Nevertheless, in spite of increasing governmental regulation, the theory of *laissez-faire* was never abandoned. The prevailing assumption was, and still is in democratic societies, that governmental regulation should be kept to a minimum, however high the minimum might in the event prove to be. It was taken for granted that the basic right and the assured foundation of the economic structure of society was private property in the means of production, free enterprise, and the competitive system. Social legislation was regarded as no more than a limited, if necessary, concession to adverse circumstances, a series of minor adjustments that would leave the system intact while enhancing its efficiency. In the optimistic decade before the Great War, social legislation came to be widely regarded, indeed, as in some sense an integral part of the system of free enterprise, a kind of insurance against the subversive doctrine of Socialism, a preordained and peaceful means of transforming that anomaly of progress and poverty which Henry George had so graphically described into that progress and prosperity which the prophets of democracy had so confidently predicted.

Since the Great War faith in social legislation as a means of validating the system of free enterprise has been much impaired. Surveying the history of a century of governmental regulation of business enterprise, it is obvious that while regulation has done much to correct minor evils it has as yet failed to solve the fundamental problem of an equitable distribution of wealth. On the contrary, the problem of the distribution of wealth is more serious and more insistent now than it was in the time of Henry George, so much so, indeed, that if the anomaly of progress and poverty is less glaring than it was, the only reason is that while the poverty is more patent the progress is less assured.

Inevitably, therefore, the question, long since raised, becomes every day more insistent: Can the problem of the production and distribution of wealth be solved, within the framework of the exist-ing system of private property and free enterprise, by any amount of governmental regulation? In short, are the defects of the system of private property in the means of production incidental or in-herent?

II

That the defects of the capitalist system are inherent is the con-tention of those ideologies known as Socialism and Communism. Socialism and Communism, taken in the generic sense of the words, are at least as old as Plato; but in their modern forms they derive from the doctrines formulated by Karl Marx in the middle of the last century.

Marxian Socialism, inspired by the failure of democratic institu-tions to effect an equitable distribution of wealth, was essentially a reinterpretation of the modern doctrine of progress, and as such it comprised a social theory and a philosophy of history. As a so-cial theory it maintained that the social structure at any time is fundamentally determined by the methods of production and dis-tribution of wealth, and that the prevailing institutions and ideas are those best adapted to maintain the interests of the class which, by ownership and control of the chief forms of wealth, dominates the social structure in its own interest. As a philosophy of history it maintained that social change, or progress, is the result, not of a conflict of ideas, but of economic forces, a conflict between the economic interests of the ruling and the dispossessed classes. Not by the persuasive force of ideas, but only by the impersonal pres-sure of economic conditions, could the ruling class ever be dis-possessed, or the institutions and ideas through which its power operates ever be transformed.

Applying this theory to European history, Marx found that the liberal-democratic revolution was the result of the conflict between the economic interests of the landed aristocracy and the rising capitalist class. So far from reflecting the triumph of true over false ideas, it reflected the triumph of capital over land as the pre-dominant factor in production; and the superstructure of liberal-democratic ideas and institutions, so far from having a universal validity, had merely the relative and temporary value of being suited to the functioning of the capitalist system and the interests of the ruling bourgeois class. The liberal-democratic revolution could not, therefore, be regarded as the final term in the historic process. On the contrary, the capitalist system once established, there necessarily developed within it a new conflict between the interests of the ruling bourgeois class and the dispossessed proletariat which would inevitably issue in another social revolution.

The coming social revolution was inevitable, according to Marx, because the capitalist system, like the landed aristocratic system before it, contained within it the defects that would transform it— defects inherent in the institution of private property and the competitive system. The ruthless competition for profits would necessarily result in an increasing concentration of wealth in the hands of those who proved most able in the ruthless competition for profits, thereby reducing the laborers and the defeated capitalists to the level of a bare subsistence; and when this process reached a certain stage the system would collapse for the simple reason that there would be no profit in producing commodities when the underlying proletarian population was no longer able to purchase them at a price that would yield a profit. When this stage was reached, the proletariat, made class conscious by their misery, instructed in the dialectic of social change by their leaders, and united for the defense of their class interests, would by revolutionary action abolish private property in land and capital, and through a democratic government based upon a classless society, organize the production and distribution of wealth for the common good.

The Marxian doctrine provided a new and persuasive ideology for the oppressed working classes whose hopes were persistently defeated by liberal-democracy as a going concern. Its analysis of the capitalist system justified their grievances against their employers, while its philosophy of history promised them that all would be made right in the future, and assured them that in defending their class interests they could not fail since they were supported by the indefeasible forces that shaped the destiny of mankind.

Inspired by the Marxian faith, the industrial workers formed new political parties, for the most part called Socialist, and for the most part accepting the Marxian doctrine of the social revolution. But meantime, while waiting for the coming revolution, and as a preparation for it, the Socialist parties adopted a program of social legislation designed to benefit the masses at the expense of the classes. Attracted by this practical program, lower middle-class people, mostly timid folk who abhorred the idea of violence, voted in increasing numbers for Socialist candidates in the hope of benefiting from the legislation which the Socialist parties promised to support. One result of this trend in practical politics was that the Socialist parties derived their chief support from voters who were not Marxian socialists; another was that the leaders of the Socialist parties, in order to win and hold non-Marxian voters, found it necessary to soft-pedal the doctrine of imminent, catastrophic revolution. In the decade before the Great War the dominant Socialist parties had therefore virtually abandoned the Marxian conception of the revolution as a violent upheaval, and conceived of it as a slow and peaceful process in which the masses, by established political methods, would gain control of the government, and by normal legislative procedure within the existing democratic regime would abolish private property in land and capital and socialize the production and distribution of wealth.

During the Great War the influence of Socialism naturally declined, but the orthodox Marxian tradition, barely kept alive by minority groups within and without the dominant Socialist parties, was given a dramatic and world-wide significance by the Russian Revolution. As reinterpreted by Lenin and realized in the Soviet regime, neo-Marxianism took the name of Communism, and must be clearly distinguished from Socialism as understood by such pre-war Socialists as Bernheim and Kautsky, and such present-day Socialists as Norman Thomas. Present-day Socialism and neo-Marxian Communism agree in one thing only—the necessity of abolishing private property in the means of production. In respect to the means for accomplishing this desired end they disagree radically. Socialism maintains that it can be accomplished by peaceful political methods within the framework of the existing democratic regime; Communism maintains that it can be accomplished only by violent revolutionary expropriation of the capitalist class, carried through for the masses by the dictatorship of a disciplined Communist party.

It was also an essential part of Communist theory that the establishment of Communism in one country would be the prelude to an international Communist revolution. So far, the prediction has not been realized. Revolutions there have been, in Italy, in Germany, in many European countries. But these revolutions, stimulated in part by the fear of Communism rather than by devotion to it, have taken the name of Fascist; and until recently at all events Communism and Fascism have been commonly regarded, especially by the Communists and Fascists themselves, as being fundamentally opposed to each other.

In respect to political theory there are certain differences between Communism and Fascism. In theory Communism maintains that the dictatorship, a drastic technique essential to the revolution but ending with it, will be replaced by a democratic government of free and equal individuals, while Fascism rejects the democratic ideal altogether in favor of the permanent dictatorship. In theory Communism professes to be international, while Fascism frankly accepts the doctrine of racial superiority and national egoism. In theory Communism recognizes the value of reason and science, while Fascism is essentially anti-intellectual in its subordination of reason to will.

In theory, yes; but the Soviet regime in Russia has failed, even more conspicuously than existing democratic societies, to harmonize theory and practice. Although the revolution has long since ended, the classless society has not emerged. The dictatorship is now more firmly established, the prospect for a democratic government is now more remote, than in the time of Lenin. The Stalin regime is no less nationalist and no more international than the regime of Hitler, and its regimentation of opinion and scholarship no less effectively subordinates reason to the will of the dictator. The revolution in Russia, as Trotsky said, has been betrayed; but it has been betrayed less by men and circumstances than by a radical contradiction in Communist theory. The rational and humane values proclaimed in Communist theory are frankly divorced from the means by which they can be realized; they are regarded as ideal ends projected into the future, but incapable of being attained except by the temporary resort to antirational and inhumane means. So far at least the result of this radical contradiction between ends and means has been, and as I think must under any circumstances have been, that the ideal ends were defeated by the very means employed to attain them.

It is in this fundamental discord between ends and means that

Communism and Fascism, as they actually function, are alike—alike in the methods they employ and in the assumptions by which the methods are justified. The Communist and the Fascist revolutions were carried through by the same political technique and the same resort to naked force. The personal power of Mussolini and Hitler is no more arbitrary, more complete, or more ruthlessly employed than that of Stalin. Both Communism and Fascism assume that the welfare of the community and the progress of mankind are in some mystical fashion identified with an abstract entity, called in the one case the dialectic of history and in the other the totalitarian state. Both assume that this abstract entity is realized in the person of an inspired leader to whom the truth has been revealed and the direction of affairs committed. Both assume that the individual, in comparison with the state or the dialectic process, has no significance except as an instrument to be used, with whatever degree of brutality may be necessary, for realizing ends which the leader judges to be good. Both do in effect, whatever they may proclaim in theory, subordinate reason to will, identify right with naked force as an instrument of will, and accord value to the disinterested search for truth only in so far as the leader judges it to be temporarily useful for the attainment of immediate political ends.

Communism and Fascism claim to be theoretical formulations of a "new order" in the world. But as revealed in their works they are no more than the recurrence of old political forms, that is to say, the recurrence in practice of what is variously known as tyranny, dictatorship, absolute monarchy; the recurrence in theory of what is known as divine right. As such they are alike, and alike at war with the fundamental values and assumptions which liberal-democracy, if it is to retain any significance, must preserve.

III

The infinitely complicated process which we call history continuously gives rise to what are called social problems, and at the same time generates those political and intellectual trends which indicate the direction which the solution of those problems is likely to take. The term "solution," used in this connection, is misleading. It connotes a certain perfection or finality, comparable to the solution of a mathematical or a chemical problem, which is never possible in social relations. "The function of history," as J. B. Bury

once remarked, "is not to solve problems but to transform them." In our time the historical process has given rise to the problem of the distribution of wealth, a problem which assumes the double form of social conflict within the nations and of diplomatic and military conflict between them. It would be naïve indeed to suppose that this problem, in either of its forms, will be "solved" with any notable degree of perfection or finality. It will be solved only in the sense of being transformed; and in looking for the direction which this transformation will take, we must consult, not merely our hopes or our preferences, but also the dominant political and intellectual trends which the history of our time discloses.

Those political and intellectual trends I have discussed and discriminated under the terms Liberal-Democracy, Socialism, Communism, and Fascism. The differences between them, both as ideological systems and as going concerns, are obvious and important; but underneath their differences we can note, in respect to what they propose to do and are doing to solve the problem of the distribution of wealth, an interesting and significant similarity. It is a similarity of direction: all these systems are carrying us, with or without our consent, toward an extension of governmental regulation of economic enterprise.

That this is the direction is evident. In all liberal-democratic countries, for the last hundred years, there has been a steadily increasing amount of such regulation of economic enterprise. Both Communism and Socialism propose to make the regulation complete by abolishing private property in the means of production, and the Communist regime in Russia has already accomplished this object. Fascism, no less than Communism, proposes to subordinate the individual to the state; and in the principal Fascist countries, although private property in land and capital has not been formally abolished, the national economy has been so far subjected to governmental direction that free economic enterprise has virtually disappeared. Like it or not, the complexities of a highly integrated technological civilization are carrying us in a certain direction, that is to say, away from freedom of the individual in economic enterprise and toward an extension of social control. This is therefore the direction which, in democratic as well as in other countries, the transformation of the problem of the distribution of wealth will surely take.

The question that chiefly concerns us is whether the necessary social regulation of economic enterprise can be effected by the democratic method, that is to say, without a corresponding social regimentation of opinion and political freedom. Can the possessors be sufficiently dispossessed and the dispossessed be sufficiently reinstated without resort to violence—to revolution and the temporary or the permanent dictatorship. The Communists say no—sooner or later the revolution. The Fascists say no—the totalitarian state is the only solution. They may of course be right. It is futile to suppose that democracy must survive because it accords with the law of nature or some transcendent increasing purpose. Nor can we dismiss the rise of dictatorship in half the world as a temporary aberration brought to birth by the ingenuity of sinister or psychopathic individuals. Common men, when sufficiently distressed, instinctively turn to the inspired leader; and dictatorship in our time, as in past times, is the normal price exacted for the failure of democracy to bind common men by their hopes and fears. The survival of democratic institutions thus depends, not upon the attractiveness or logical consistency of theories of government, but upon the possibility of effecting, by the pragmatic democratic method, a sufficient equalization of possessions and of opportunity to provide common men with what they will consent to regard as tolerable. . . .

Considered as a problem in scientific engineering, providing for the material needs of common men presents no insuperable difficulties: the necessary resources, equipment, man power, and knowledge are available. Given Plato's ruling class of philosopher kings, and a docile population responding to suggestion as smoothly as molten iron yields to physical pressure, adequate wealth could be produced and equitably distributed. Unfortunately perhaps, there are no such philosopher kings; fortunately, there are no such docile people. Government is much less a matter of knowing what is good to be done than of persuading average human beings, stubbornly rooted in conventional habits of thought and action, to do what fallible intelligence judges on incomplete data to be for the moment necessary or desirable. Democratic government is a matter of persuading them to do it voluntarily by registering their wishes in the form of ballots freely given. In democratic countries, therefore, the measures taken for effecting a more equitable distribution of wealth can never be based solely upon the best scientific knowledge available; they can be such only as the majority of citizens will voluntarily sanction and the minority voluntarily submit to.

It is as essential that the minority should voluntarily submit to the measures taken as it is that the majority should voluntarily approve them. Democratic government rests upon the principle that it is better to count heads than it is to break them. The principle is a good one, but unfortunately men will not, under certain conditions, so regard it. By and large the principle works well enough so long as the issues to be decided do not involve those interests which men will always fight for rather than surrender. By and large, democratic government, being government by discussion and majority vote, works best when there is nothing of profound importance to discuss, when the rival party programs involve the superficial aspects rather than the fundamental structure of the social system, and when for that reason the minority can meet defeat at the polls in good temper since it need not regard the decision as either a fatal or a permanent surrender of its vital interests. When these happy conditions disappear democratic government is always in danger.

The danger has already proved fatal in many countries. It exists, although it may not prove fatal, even in those countries where the democratic tradition is most strongly intrenched. For in these countries too the insistent problem of the distribution of wealth is beginning to involve those fundamental class interests which do not readily lend themselves to friendly discussion and mutual concession. The flagrant inequality of possessions and of opportunity is creating an ever sharper differentiation between the beneficiaries of private property in the means of production and the masses whose present circumstances and future prospects depend less upon individual character and talent than upon the hazards of the business cycle. Accompanying this differentiation there has been and is going on a confused but persistent realignment of political parties: on the Right, conservative parties representing the beneficiaries of the system of free enterprise; on the Left, radical parties representing the poor and the dispossessed. As the divergence between Right and Left becomes sharper and more irreconcilable, moderate and conciliatory parties tend to disappear, and the rival party programs of the extreme groups, no longer confined to the superficial aspects of policy within the framework of the traditional system, are increasingly concerned with the validity of the assumptions on which the system rests. Underlying the question of the equitable distribution of wealth is the more fundamental question of the validity of the institution of private property as a means of effecting it. The present power of the possessing classes rests upon the institution of private property; the present distress of the masses is somehow involved in it. If the present discords should be prolonged and intensified, the danger is that the masses will turn to revolution rather than submit to a system which fails to relieve them, that the classes will welcome forcible repression rather than surrender a system which guarantees their power.

The danger is not one to be lightly dismissed. It is certainly greater than many profess to think. But for all that we need not be browbeaten, by dogmatic assumptions, into believing that the discords in the capitalist system cannot under any circumstances be corrected by the democratic procedure. It is an article of Communist faith, which many advanced liberals seem to accept as a matter of course, that history offers no instance of a ruling aristocracy which has surrendered its power voluntarily, and that accordingly nothing short of violent revolutionary expropriation will induce the capitalist class to surrender the power which the institution of private property now confers upon it.

The premise is correct enough, but the conclusion is a *non sequitur*. True enough, no ruling class has ever surrendered its power voluntarily, but it does not follow that no ruling class has ever surrendered its power except under compulsion of naked force. The Roman Patricians did not surrender their power voluntarily, on demand; but they nevertheless surrendered it, gradually, under pressure, without incurring the destruction of republican institutions. The English aristocracy did not surrender its power voluntarily; but since the eighteenth century it has, under pressure exerted through the democratic political procedure, conceded one strategic position after another. And indeed in all those countries where democratic institutions still persist, the capitalist classes have, during the last fifty years or more, conceded bit by bit much of the control over private property which they formerly possessed and once thought indispensable. There is no compelling reason to suppose that, in those countries where the democratic tradition is strongly intrenched, this process of increasing governmental regulation of economic enterprise should not continue, even to the point, if that should prove necessary, of a virtual if not a formal socialization of certain basic industries, without incurring the destruction of democratic institutions.

It is not a question of keeping what we have or scrapping it for some untried ideal social system. At best it is a question of sufficiently improving what we have to avoid the intolerable distress which if unrelieved ends in despair and the resort to violence. No infallible panacea for accomplishing this end is available. The desired end can be accomplished, if at all, only by the method of trial and error, by employing the best knowledge available, so far as it can be employed by the democratic political method, to effect those adjustments which will put idle money to work in productive enterprises and idle men to work at a living wage. What particular measures are best adapted to do this I am incompetent to say. It is for the experts to suggest the particular measures. Since the experts disagree, the measures adopted, however carefully considered, will in the event no doubt be attended with unforeseen consequences calling for still further measures. That attempts to remedy the evil are not wholly successful is no reason for abandoning the task. Something must be done, and much must be attempted that a little may be gained. What is chiefly needed is time—time for experiment, for making mistakes and correcting them, time for the necessary adjustment in vested interests and the necessary psychological adaptation to new ideas, time for the slow crystallization of public opinion and for registering public opinion in legislative enactments by the cumbersome democratic technique.

It is true, of course, that there may not be time enough. There may not be time enough in any case. Technological advance has so accelerated the tempo and complicated the character of social change that present social ills can scarcely be properly diagnosed before they have been so far transformed that the proposed remedies are no longer adequate. But if time fails us, it will be less because of inherent defects in the capitalist system or the democratic procedure than because of the disastrous results of modern war in dislocating the national economy and in impairing the democratic morale. . . .

When we consider the problem of preserving democratic institutions broadly, from both the national and the international point of view, we seem to be helplessly caught in a vicious circle. We know that democratic institutions are threatened by social discords within the nations, and still more by war between them. We know that if we could avoid war it would be much easier to resolve our social discords, and that if we could resolve our social discords it would be much easier to avoid war. If we could do either of these things without the other, the future of democracy would be fairly secure; if we could do both of them it would be altogether so. Yet we know that social discords are a major cause of war, and that war is the one thing that will make it impossible, if anything does, to resolve our social discords. It is in such situations that reason succumbs to force, in such situations that dictators flourish and democracy declines.

It is possible that the crisis which confronts the modern world involves something more serious even than the collapse of democratic institutions. The contradictions in the capitalist system may be no more than symbols of a discord more profound—the discord between the physical power at our disposal and our capacity to make a good use of it. It is obvious at all events that the history of the last two centuries presents us with a disturbing paradox: whereas the application of reason to the mastery of the physical world has proceeded with unanticipated success and mounting optimism, the persistent effort to shape the world of human relations to humane and rational ends has been so far unavailing that we are oppressed with a sense of frustration and defeat.

Long ago it was said that man can more easily take a city than govern himself. Never was the saying more true than now. Never before has the intelligence of man placed so much material power at his disposal: never before has he employed the power at his disposal for the realization of purposes more diverse or more irreconcilable. The hand of man is subdued to what it works in, and the mind admires what the hand can accomplish. Modern man is therefore enamored of mechanical force. Fascinated by the esthetic precision and sheer power of the instruments he has devised, he will use them for doing whatever by their aid can be done, in the confident expectation that what can be done with such clean efficiency must be worth doing. Thus the machines we have invented tend to enslave us. Compelling us to use them on their own terms, and to adjust our conduct to their virtues and limitations, they somehow generate social forces which, being too complex and too intangible to be easily understood, shape our lives to ends we do not will but cannot avoid.

In times past certain civilizations, long established, brilliant and prosperous and seemingly secure against mischance, slowly decayed and either disappeared altogether or were transformed past recognition and forgotten. What has happened many times in the history of mankind may happen again. There are no barbarian hosts without the gates, but there are plenty of potential barbarians within them. It is then within the range of possibility that the flagrant discord between the mechanical power at man's disposal and his capacity to make good use of it is carrying the world into another period of widespread and chronic confusion in which democracy will everywhere succumb to dictatorship, reason to naked force, and naked force prove to be the prelude to another dark age of barbarism.

I do not say that this will happen. I do not think it will. But it is futile to suppose that it cannot happen, futile to rely upon the saving grace of some transcendent increasing purpose (a law of nature, or dialectic of history, or totalitarian state) to bring us in spite of ourselves to a predestined good end. For the solution of our difficulties the only available purposes are our own, the only available intelligence such as we can command. If then democracy survives, if civilization in any tolerable form survives, it will be because, in some favored parts of the world the human mind remains unshackled and, aided by time and fortunate circumstances, proves capable of subordinating the unprecedented material power at its command to the achievement of rational and humane ends. More obvious now even than in the seventeenth century is the truth of Pascal's famous dictum: "Thought makes the whole dignity of man; therefore endeavor to think well, that is the only morality." The chief virtue of democracy, and in the long run the sole reason for cherishing it, is that with all its defects it still provides the most favorable conditions for the maintenance of that dignity and the practice of that morality.

APPENDIX

CONSTITUTION OF THE UNITED STATES

WE the people of the United States, in order to form a more perfect union, establish justice, insure domestic tranquillity, provide for the common defense, promote the general welfare, and secure the blessings of liberty to ourselves and our posterity, do ordain and establish this Constitution for the United States of America.

ARTICLE I

SECTION 1. All legislative powers herein granted shall be vested in a Congress of the United States, which shall consist of a Senate and House of Representatives.

SECTION 2. 1. The House of Representatives shall be composed of members chosen every second year by the people of the several States, and the electors in each State shall have the qualifications requisite for electors of the most numerous branch of the State legislature.

2. No person shall be a representative who shall not have attained to the age of twenty-five years, and been seven years a citizen of the United States, and who shall not, when elected, be an inhabitant of that State in which he shall be chosen.

3. Representatives and direct taxes [1] shall be apportioned among the several States which may be included within this Union, according to their respective numbers, which shall be determined by adding to the whole number of free persons, including those bound to service for a term of years, and excluding Indians not taxed, three fifths of all other persons.[2] The actual enumeration shall be made within three years after the first meeting of the Congress of the United States, and within every subsequent term of ten years, in such manner as they shall by law direct. The number of representatives shall not exceed one for every thirty thousand, but each State shall have at least one representative; and until such enumeration shall be made, the State of New Hampshire shall be entitled to choose three, Massachusetts eight, Rhode Island and Providence Plantations one, Connecticut five, New York six, New Jersey four, Pennsylvania eight, Delaware one, Maryland six, Virginia ten, North Carolina five, South Carolina five, and Georgia three.

4. When vacancies happen in the representation from any State, the executive authority thereof shall issue writs of election to fill such vacancies.

5. The House of Representatives shall choose their speaker and other officers; and shall have the sole power of impeachment.

[1] See the 16th Amendment, below, p. 871.
[2] Partly superseded by the 14th Amendment. (See below, pp. 870–871.)

SECTION 3. 1. The Senate of the United States shall be composed of two senators from each State, chosen by the legislature thereof,[1] for six years; and each senator shall have one vote.

2. Immediately after they shall be assembled in consequence of the first election, they shall be divided as equally as may be into three classes. The seats of the senators of the first class shall be vacated at the expiration of the second year, of the second class at the expiration of the fourth year, and of the third class at the expiration of the sixth year, so that one third may be chosen every second year; and if vacancies happen by resignation, or otherwise, during the recess of the legislature of any State, the executive thereof may make temporary appointments until the next meeting of the legislature, which shall then fill such vacancies.[1]

3. No person shall be a senator who shall not have attained to the age of thirty years, and been nine years a citizen of the United States, and who shall not, when elected, be an inhabitant of that State for which he shall be chosen.

4. The Vice President of the United States shall be President of the Senate, but shall have no vote, unless they be equally divided.

5. The Senate shall choose their other officers, and also a president pro tempore, in the absence of the Vice President, or when he shall exercise the office of President of the United States.

6. The Senate shall have the sole power to try all impeachments. When sitting for that purpose, they shall be on oath or affirmation. When the President of the United States is tried, the chief justice shall preside: and no person shall be convicted without the concurrence of two thirds of the members present.

7. Judgment in cases of impeachment shall not extend further than to removal from office, and disqualifications to hold and enjoy any office of honor, trust or profit under the United States: but the party convicted shall nevertheless be liable and subject to indictment, trial, judgment and punishment, according to law.

SECTION 4. 1. The times, places, and manner of holding elections for senators and representatives, shall be prescribed in each State by the legislature thereof; but the Congress may at any time by law make or alter such regulations, except as to the places of choosing senators.

2. The Congress shall assemble at least once in every year, and such meeting shall be on the first Monday in December, unless they shall by law appoint a different day.

SECTION 5. 1. Each House shall be the judge of the elections, returns and qualifications of its own members, and a majority of each shall constitute a quorum to do business; but a smaller number may adjourn from day to day, and may be authorized to compel the attendance of absent members, in such manner, and under such penalties as each House may provide.

2. Each House may determine the rules of its proceedings, punish its members for disorderly behavior, and, with the concurrence of two thirds, expel a member.

[1] See the 17th Amendment, below, p. 871.

3. Each House shall keep a journal of its proceedings, and from time to time publish the same, excepting such parts as may in their judgment require secrecy ; and the yeas and nays of the members of either House on any question shall, at the desire of one fifth of those present, be entered on the journal.

4. Neither House, during the session of Congress, shall, without the consent of the other, adjourn for more than three days, nor to any other place than that in which the two Houses shall be sitting.

Section 6. 1. The senators and representatives shall receive a compensation for their services, to be ascertained by law, and paid out of the Treasury of the United States. They shall in all cases, except treason, felony and breach of the peace, be privileged from arrest during their attendance at the session of their respective Houses, and in going to and returning from the same; and for any speech or debate in either House, they shall not be questioned in any other place.

2. No senator or representative shall, during the time for which he was elected, be appointed to any civil office under the authority of the United States, which shall have been created, or the emoluments whereof shall have been increased during such time, and no person holding any office under the United States shall be a member of either House during his continuance in office.

Section 7. 1. All bills for raising revenue shall originate in the House of Representatives; but the Senate may propose or concur with amendments as on other bills.

2. Every bill which shall have passed the House of Representatives and the Senate, shall, before it become a law, be presented to the President of the United States; if he approve he shall sign it, but if not he shall return it, with his objections to that House in which it shall have originated, who shall enter the objections at large on their journal, and proceed to reconsider it. If after such reconsideration two thirds of that House shall agree to pass the bill, it shall be sent, together with the objections, to the other House, by which it shall likewise be reconsidered, and if approved by two thirds of that House, it shall become a law. But in all such cases the votes of both Houses shall be determined by yeas and nays, and the names of the persons voting for and against the bill shall be entered on the journal of each House respectively. If any bill shall not be returned by the President within ten days (Sundays excepted) after it shall have been presented to him, the same shall be a law, in like manner as if he had signed it, unless the Congress by their adjournment prevent its return, in which case it shall not be a law.

3. Every order, resolution, or vote to which the concurrence of the Senate and House of Representatives may be necessary (except on a question of adjournment) shall be presented to the President of the United States; and before the same shall take effect, shall be approved by him, or being disapproved by him, shall be repassed by two thirds of the Senate and House of Representatives, according to the rules and limitations prescribed in the case of a bill.

Section 8. 1. The Congress shall have the power to lay and collect taxes, duties, imposts, and excises, to pay the debts and provide for the common defense and general welfare of the United States; but all duties, imposts, and excises shall be uniform throughout the United States;

2. To borrow money on the credit of the United States;

3. To regulate commerce with foreign nations, and among the several States, and with the Indian tribes;

4. To establish an uniform rule of naturalization, and uniform laws on the subject of bankruptcies throughout the United States;

5. To coin money, regulate the value thereof, and of foreign coin, and fix the standard of weights and measures;

6. To provide for the punishment of counterfeiting the securities and current coin of the United States;

7. To establish post offices and post roads;

8. To promote the progress of science and useful arts, by securing for limited times to authors and inventors the exclusive right to their respective writings and discoveries;

9. To constitute tribunals inferior to the Supreme Court;

10. To define and punish piracies and felonies committed on the high seas, and offenses against the law of nations;

11. To declare war, grant letters of marque and reprisal, and make rules concerning captures on land and water;

12. To raise and support armies, but no appropriation of money to that use shall be for a longer term than two years;

13. To provide and maintain a navy;

14. To make rules for the government and regulation of the land and naval forces;

15. To provide for calling forth the militia to execute the laws of the Union, suppress insurrections and repel invasions;

16. To provide for organizing, arming, and disciplining the militia, and for governing such part of them as may be employed in the service of the United States, reserving to the States respectively the appointment of the officers, and the authority of training the militia according to the discipline prescribed by Congress;

17. To exercise exclusive legislation in all cases whatsoever, over such district (not exceeding ten miles square) as may, by cession of particular States, and the acceptance of Congress, become the seat of the government of the United States, and to exercise like authority over all places purchased by the consent of the legislature of the State in which the same shall be, for the erection of forts, magazines, arsenals, dockyards, and other needful buildings; and

18. To make all laws which shall be necessary and proper for carrying into execution the foregoing powers, and all other powers vested by this Constitution in the government of the United States, or in any department or officer thereof.

SECTION 9. 1. The migration or importation of such persons as any of the States now existing shall think proper to admit, shall not be prohibited by the Congress prior to the year one thousand eight hundred and eight, but a tax or duty may be imposed on such importation, not exceeding ten dollars for each person.

2. The privilege of the writ of *habeas corpus* shall not be suspended, unless when in cases of rebellion or invasion the public safety may require it.

3. No bill of attainder or *ex post facto* law shall be passed.

4. No capitation, or other direct, tax shall be laid, unless in proportion to the census or enumeration hereinbefore directed to be taken.[1]

5. No tax or duty shall be laid on articles exported from any State.

6. No preference shall be given by any regulation of commerce or revenue to the ports of one State over those of another: nor shall vessels bound to, or from, one State be obliged to enter, clear, or pay duties in another.

7. No money shall be drawn from the treasury, but in consequence of appropriations made by law; and a regular statement and account of the receipts and expenditures of all public money shall be published from time to time.

8. No title of nobility shall be granted by the United States: and no person holding any office or profit or trust under them, shall, without the consent of the Congress, accept of any present, emolument, office, or title, of any kind whatever, from any king, prince, or foreign State.

SECTION 10. 1. No State shall enter into any treaty, alliance, or confederation; grant letters of marque and reprisal; coin money; emit bills of credit; make anything but gold and silver coin a tender in payment of debts; pass any bill of attainder, *ex post facto* or law impairing the obligation of contracts, or grant any title of nobility.

2. No State shall, without the consent of the Congress, lay any imposts or duties on imports or exports, except what may be absolutely necessary for executing its inspection laws: and the net produce of all duties and imposts laid by any State on imports or exports, shall be for the use of the treasury of the United States; and all such laws shall be subject to the revision and control of the Congress.

3. No State shall, without the consent of Congress, lay any duty of tonnage, keep troops, or ships of war in time of peace, enter into any agreement or compact with another State, or with a foreign power, or engage in war, unless actually invaded, or in such imminent danger as will not admit of delay.

ARTICLE II

SECTION 1. 1. The executive power shall be vested in a President of the United States of America. He shall hold his office during the term of four years, and, together with the Vice President, chosen for the same term, be elected, as follows:

2. Each State shall appoint, in such manner as the legislature thereof may direct, a number of electors, equal to the whole number of senators and representatives to which the State may be entitled in the Congress: but no senator or representative, or person holding an office of trust or profit under the United States, shall be appointed an elector.

[1] See the 16th Amendment, below, p. 871.

The electors shall meet in their respective States, and vote by ballot for two persons, of whom one at least shall not be an inhabitant of the same State with themselves. And they shall make a list of all the persons voted for, and of the number of votes for each; which list they shall sign and certify, and transmit sealed to the seat of the government of the United States, directed to the president of the Senate. The president of the Senate shall, in the presence of the Senate and House of Representatives, open all certificates, and the votes shall then be counted. The person having the greatest number of votes shall be the President, if such number be a majority of the whole number of electors appointed; and if there be more than one who have such majority, and have an equal number of votes, then the House of Representatives shall immediately choose by ballot one of them for President; and if no person have a majority, then from the five highest on the list the said House shall in like manner choose the President. But in choosing the President, the votes shall be taken by States, the representation from each State having one vote; a quorum for this purpose shall consist of a member or members from two thirds of the States, and a majority of all the States shall be necessary to a choice. In every case, after the choice of the President, the person having the greatest number of votes of the electors shall be the Vice President. But if there should remain two or more who have equal votes, the Senate shall choose from them by ballot the Vice President.[1]

3. The Congress may determine the time of choosing the electors, and the day on which they shall give their votes; which day shall be the same throughout the United States.

4. No person except a natural born citizen, or a citizen of the United States, at the time of the adoption of this Constitution, shall be eligible to the office of President; neither shall any person be eligible to that office who shall not have attained to the age of thirty-five years, and been fourteen years a resident within the United States.

5. In case of the removal of the President from office, or of his death, resignation, or inability to discharge the powers and duties of the said office, the same shall devolve on the Vice President, and the Congress may by law provide for the case of removal, death, resignation, or inability, both of the President and Vice President, declaring what officer shall then act as President, and such officer shall act accordingly, until the disability be removed, or a President shall be elected.[2]

6. The President shall, at stated times, receive for his services a compensation, which shall neither be increased nor diminished during the period for which he shall have been elected, and he shall not receive within that period any other emolument from the United States, or any of them.

7. Before he enter on the execution of his office, he shall take the following oath or affirmation:—"I do solemnly swear (or affirm) that I will faithfully execute the office of President of the United States, and will to the best

[1] The preceding paragraph was superseded in 1804 by the 12th Amendment; see below, pp. 869–870.

[2] See the 20th Amendment, below, p. 872.

of my ability, preserve, protect and defend the Constitution of the United States."

SECTION 2. 1. The President shall be commander in chief of the army and navy of the United States, and of the militia of the several States, when called into the actual service of the United States; he may require the opinion, in writing, of the principal officer in each of the executive departments, upon any subject relating to the duties of their respective offices, and he shall have power to grant reprieves and pardons for offenses against the United States, except in cases of impeachment.

2. He shall have power, by and with the advice and consent of the Senate, to make treaties, provided two thirds of the senators present concur; and he shall nominate, and by and with the advice and consent of the Senate, shall appoint ambassadors, other public ministers and consuls, judges of the Supreme Court, and all other officers of the United States, whose appointments are not herein otherwise provided for, and which shall be established by law: but the Congress may by law vest the appointments of such inferior officers, as they think proper, in the President alone, in the courts of law, or in the heads of departments.

3. The President shall have power to fill up all vacancies that may happen during the recess of the Senate, by granting commissions which shall expire at the end of their next session.

SECTION 3. 1. He shall from time to time give to the Congress information of the state of the Union, and recommend to their consideration such measures as he shall judge necessary and expedient; he may, on extraordinary occasions, convene both Houses, or either of them, and in case of disagreement between them with respect to the time of adjournment, he may adjourn them to such time as he shall think proper; he shall receive ambassadors and other public ministers; he shall take care that the laws be faithfully executed, and shall commission all the officers of the United States.

SECTION 4. The President, Vice President, and all civil officers of the United States, shall be removed from office on impeachment for, and conviction of, treason, bribery, or other high crimes and misdemeanors.

ARTICLE III

SECTION 1. The judicial power of the United States shall be vested in one Supreme Court, and in such inferior courts as the Congress may from time to time ordain and establish. The judges, both of the Supreme and inferior courts, shall hold their offices during good behavior, and shall, at stated times, receive for their services, a compensation, which shall not be diminished during their continuance in office.

SECTION 2. 1. The judicial power shall extend to all cases, in law and equity, arising under this Constitution, the laws of the United States, and treaties made, or which shall be made, under their authority;—to all cases affecting ambassadors, other public ministers and consuls;—to all cases of admiralty and maritime jurisdiction;—to controversies to which the United States shall be a party;—to controversies between two or more States;—between a State and citizens of another State; [1]—between citizens of different States,—between citizens of the same State claiming lands under grants of different States, and between a State, or the citizens thereof, and foreign States, citizens or subjects.

2. In all cases affecting ambassadors, other public ministers and consuls, and those in which a State shall be party, the Supreme Court shall have original jurisdiction. In all the other cases before mentioned, the Supreme Court shall have appellate jurisdiction, both as to law and to fact, with such exceptions, and under such regulations as the Congress shall make.

3. The trial of all crimes, except in cases of impeachment, shall be by jury; and such trial shall be held in the State where the said crimes shall have been committed; but when not committed within any State, the trial shall be at such place or places as the Congress may by law have directed.

SECTION 3. 1. Treason against the United States, shall consist only in levying war against them, or in adhering to their enemies, giving them aid and comfort. No person shall be convicted of treason unless on the testimony of two witnesses to the same overt act, or on confession in open court.

2. The Congress shall have power to declare the punishment of treason, but no attainder of treason shall work corruption of blood, or forfeiture except during the life of the person attained.

ARTICLE IV

SECTION 1. Full faith and credit shall be given in each State to the public acts, records, and judicial proceedings of every other State. And the Congress may by general laws prescribe the manner in which such acts, records and proceedings shall be proved, and the effect thereof.

SECTION 2. 1. The citizens of each State shall be entitled to all privileges and immunities of citizens in the several States.

2. A person charged in any State with treason, felony, or other crime, who shall flee from justice, and be found in another State, shall on demand of the executive authority of the State from which he fled, be delivered up to be removed to the State having jurisdiction of the crime.

3. No person held to service or labor in one State under the laws thereof, escaping into another, shall, in consequence of any law or regulation therein, be discharged from such service or labor, but shall be delivered up on claim of the party to whom such service or labor may be due.

SECTION 3. 1. New States may be admitted by the Congress into this Union; but no new State shall be formed or erected within the jurisdiction of any other State; nor any State be formed by the junction of two or more States, or parts of States, without the consent of the legislatures of the States concerned as well as of the Congress.

2. The Congress shall have power to dispose of and make all needful rules and regulations respecting the territory or other property belonging to the United States; and nothing in this Constitution shall be so construed as to prejudice any claims of the United States, or of any particular State.

[1] See the 11th Amendment, below, p. 869.

SECTION 4. The United States shall guarantee to every State in this Union a republican form of government, and shall protect each of them against invasion; and on application of the legislature, or of the executive (when the legislature cannot be convened) against domestic violence.

ARTICLE V

The Congress, whenever two thirds of both Houses shall deem it necessary, shall propose amendments to this Constitution, or, on the application of the legislatures of two thirds of the several States, shall call a convention for proposing amendments, which, in either case, shall be valid to all intents and purposes, as part of this Constitution when ratified by the legislatures of three fourths of the several States, or by conventions in three fourths thereof, as the one or the other mode of ratification may be proposed by the Congress; Provided that no amendment which may be made prior to the year one thousand eight hundred and eight shall in any manner affect the first and fourth clauses in the ninth section of the first article; and that no State, without its consent, shall be deprived of its equal suffrage in the Senate.

ARTICLE VI

1. All debts contracted and engagements entered into, before the adoption of this Constitution, shall be as valid against the United States under this Constitution, as under the Confederation.

2. This Constitution, and the laws of the United States which shall be made in pursuance thereof; and all treaties made, or which shall be made, under the authority of the United States, shall be the supreme law of the land; and the Judges in every State shall be bound thereby, anything in the Constitution or laws of any State to the contrary notwithstanding.

3. The senators and representatives before mentioned, and the members of the several State legislatures, and all executive and judicial officers, both of the United States and of the several States, shall be bound by oath or affirmation to support this Constitution; but no religious test shall ever be required as a qualification to any office or public trust under the United States.

ARTICLE VII

The ratification of the conventions of nine States shall be sufficient for the establishment of this Constitution between the States so ratifying the same.

Done in Convention by the unanimous consent of the States present the seventeenth day of September in the year of our Lord one thousand seven hundred and eighty-seven, and of the independence of the United States of America the twelfth. In witness whereof we have hereunto subscribed our names. [Names omitted]

Articles in addition to, and amendment of, the Constitution of the United States of America, proposed by Congress, and ratified by the legislatures [1] of the several States pursuant to the fifth article of the original Constitution.

[1] The twenty-first amendment (1933) was ratified by conventions in the several States.

ARTICLE I [1]

Congress shall make no law respecting an establishment of religion, or prohibiting the free exercise thereof; or abridging the freedom of speech, or of the press; or the right of the people peaceably to assemble, and to petition the government for a redress of grievances.

ARTICLE II

A well regulated militia, being necessary to the security of a free State, the right of the people to keep and bear arms shall not be infringed.

ARTICLE III

No soldier shall, in time of peace, be quartered in any house, without the consent of the owner, nor in time of war, but in a manner to be prescribed by law.

ARTICLE IV

The right of the people to be secure in their persons, houses, papers, and effects, against unreasonable searches and seizures, shall not be violated, and no warrants shall issue, but upon probable cause, supported by oath or affirmation, and particularly describing the place to be searched, and the persons or things to be seized.

ARTICLE V

No person shall be held to answer for a capital, or otherwise infamous crime, unless on a presentment or indictment of a grand jury, except in cases arising in the land or naval forces, or in the militia, when in actual service in time of war or public danger; nor shall any person be subject for the same offense to be twice put in jeopardy of life or limb; nor shall be compelled in any criminal case to be a witness against himself, nor be deprived of life, liberty, or property, without due process of law; nor shall private property be taken for public use without just compensation.

ARTICLE VI

In all criminal prosecutions, the accused shall enjoy the right to a speedy and public trial, by an impartial jury of the State and district wherein the crime shall have been committed, which district shall have been previously ascertained by law, and to be informed of the nature and cause of the accusation; to be confronted with the witnesses against him; to have compulsory process for obtaining witnesses in his favor, and to have the assistance of counsel for his defense.

ARTICLE VII

In suits at common law, where the value in controversy shall exceed twenty dollars, the right of trial by jury shall be preserved, and no fact tried by a

[1] The first ten Amendments were adopted in 1791.

jury shall be otherwise reëxamined in any court of the United States, than according to the rules of the common law.

ARTICLE VIII

Excessive bail shall not be required, nor excessive fines imposed, nor cruel and unusual punishments inflicted.

ARTICLE IX

The enumeration in the Constitution of certain rights shall not be construed to deny or disparage others retained by the people.

ARTICLE X

The powers not delegated to the United States by the Constitution, nor prohibited by it to the States, are reserved to the States respectively, or to the people.

ARTICLE XI [1]

The judicial power of the United States shall not be construed to extend to any suit in law or equity, commenced or prosecuted against one of the United States by citizens of another State, or by citizens or subjects of any foreign State.

ARTICLE XII [2]

The electors shall meet in their respective States, and vote by ballot for President and Vice President, one of whom, at least, shall not be an inhabitant of the same State with themselves; they shall name in their ballots the person voted for as President, and in distinct ballots, the person voted for as Vice President, and they shall make distinct lists of all persons voted for as President and of all persons voted for as Vice President, and of the number of votes for each, which lists they shall sign and certify, and transmit sealed to the seat of the government of the United States, directed to the President of the Senate;—The President of the Senate shall, in the presence of the Senate and House of Representatives, open all the certificates and the votes shall then be counted;—The person having the greatest number of votes for President, shall be the President, if such number be a majority of the whole number of electors appointed; and if no person have such majority, then from the persons having the highest numbers not exceeding three on the list of those voted for as President, the House of Representatives shall choose immediately, by ballot, the President. But in choosing the President, the votes shall be taken by States, the representation from each State having one vote; a quorum for this purpose shall consist of a member or members from two thirds of the States, and a majority of all the States shall be necessary to a choice. And if the House of Representatives shall not choose a President whenever the right of choice shall devolve upon them, be-

[1] Adopted in 1798.
[2] Adopted in 1804.

fore the fourth day of March next following, then the Vice President shall act as President, as in the case of the death or other constitutional disability of the President. The person having the greatest number of votes as Vice President shall be the Vice President, if such number be a majority of the whole number of electors appointed, and if no person have a majority, then from the two highest numbers on the list, the Senate shall choose the Vice President; a quorum for the purpose shall consist of two thirds of the whole number of Senators, and a majority of the whole number shall be necessary to a choice. But no person constitutionally ineligible to the office of President shall be eligible to that of Vice President of the United States.

ARTICLE XIII [1]

SECTION 1. Neither slavery nor involuntary servitude, except as punishment for crime whereof the party shall have been duly convicted, shall exist within the United States, or any place subject to their jurisdiction.

2. Congress shall have power to enforce this article by appropriate legislation.

ARTICLE XIV [2]

1. All persons born or naturalized in the United States, and subject to the jurisdiction thereof, are citizens of the United States and of the State wherein they reside. No State shall make or enforce any law which shall abridge the privileges or immunities of citizens of the United States; nor shall any State deprive any persons of life, liberty, or property, without due process of law; nor deny to any person within its jurisdiction the equal protection of the laws.

2. Representatives shall be apportioned among the several States according to their respective numbers, counting the whole number of persons in each State, excluding Indians not taxed. But when the right to vote at any election for the choice of electors for President and Vice President of the United States, representatives in Congress, the executive and judicial officers of a State, or the members of the legislature thereof, is denied to any of the male inhabitants of such State, being twenty-one years of age, and citizens of the United States, or in any way abridged, except for participation in rebellion, or other crime, the basis of representation therein shall be reduced in the proportion which the number of such male citizens shall bear to the whole number of male citizens twenty-one years of age in such State.

3. No person shall be a senator or representative in Congress, or elector of President and Vice President, or hold any office, civil or military, under the United States, or under any State, who, having previously taken an oath, as a member of Congress, or as an officer of the United States, or as a member of any State legislature, or as an executive or judicial officer of any State, to support the Constitution of the United States, shall have engaged in insurrection or rebellion against the same, or given aid or comfort to the enemies

[1] Adopted in 1865.
[2] Adopted in 1868.

thereof. But Congress may by a vote of two thirds of each House, remove such disability.

4. The validity of the public debt of the United States, authorized by law, including debts incurred for payment of pensions and bounties for services in suppressing insurrection or rebellion, shall not be questioned. But neither the United States nor any State shall assume or pay any debt or obligation incurred in aid of insurrection or rebellion against the United States, or any claim for the loss or emancipation of any slave; but all such debts, obligations and claims shall be held illegal and void.

5. The Congress shall have power to enforce, by appropriate legislation, the provisions of this article.

ARTICLE XV [1]

SECTION 1. The right of citizens of the United States to vote shall not be denied or abridged by the United States or by any State on account of race, color, or previous condition of servitude.

SECTION 2. The Congress shall have power to enforce this article by appropriate legislation.

ARTICLE XVI [2]

The Congress shall have power to lay and collect taxes on incomes, from whatever source derived, without apportionment among the several States, and without regard to any census or enumeration.

ARTICLE XVII [3]

The Senate of the United States shall be composed of two senators from each state, elected by the people thereof, for six years; and each senator shall have one vote. The electors in each State shall have the qualifications requisite for electors of the most numerous branch of the State legislature.

When vacancies happen in the representation of any State in the Senate, the executive authority of such State shall issue writs of election to fill such vacancies: *Provided,* That the legislature of any State may empower the executive thereof to make temporary appointments until the people fill the vacancies by election as the legislature may direct.

This amendment shall not be so construed as to affect the election or term of any senator chosen before it becomes valid as part of the Constitution.

ARTICLE XVIII [Repealed by 21st Amendment] [4]

After one year from the ratification of this article, the manufacture, sale, or transportation of intoxicating liquors within, the importation thereof into, or the exportation thereof from the United States and all territory subject to the jurisdiction thereof for beverage purposes is hereby prohibited.

[1] Adopted in 1870.
[2] Adopted in 1913.
[3] Adopted in 1913.
[4] Adopted in 1919.

The Congress and the several States shall have concurrent power to enforce this article by appropriate legislation.

This article shall be inoperative unless it shall have been ratified as an amendment to the Constitution by the legislatures of the several States, as provided in the Constitution, within seven years from the date of the submission hereof to the states by Congress.

ARTICLE XIX [1]

The right of citizens of the United States to vote shall not be denied or abridged by the United States or by any State on account of sex.

The Congress shall have power by appropriate legislation to enforce the provisions of this article.

ARTICLE XX [2]

Section 1. The terms of the President and Vice President shall end at noon on the 20th day of January, and the terms of Senators and Representatives at noon on the 3d day of January, of the years in which such terms would have ended if this article had not been ratified; and the terms of their successors shall then begin.

Section 2. The Congress shall assemble at least once in every year, and such meeting shall begin at noon on the 3d of January, unless they shall by law appoint a different day.

Section 3. If, at the time fixed for the beginning of the term of the President, the President elect shall have died, the Vice President elect shall become President. If a President shall not have been chosen before the time fixed for the beginning of his term, or if the President elect shall have failed to qualify, then the Vice President elect shall act as President until a President shall have qualified; and the Congress may by law provide for the case wherein neither a President elect nor a Vice President elect shall have qualified, declaring who shall then act as President, or the manner in which one who is to act shall be selected, and such person shall act accordingly until a President or Vice President shall have qualified.

Section 4. The Congress may by law provide for the case of the death of any of the persons from whom the House of Representatives may choose a President whenever the right of choice shall have devolved upon them, and for the case of the death of any of the persons from whom the Senate may choose a Vice President whenever the right of choice shall have devolved upon them.

Section 5. Sections 1 and 2 shall take effect on the 15th day of October following the ratification of this article.

Section 6. This article shall be inoperative unless it shall have been ratified as an amendment to the Constitution by the legislatures of three-fourths of the several States within seven years from the date of its submission.

[1] Adopted in 1920.
[2] Adopted in 1933.

ARTICLE XXI [1]

SECTION 1. The eighteenth article of amendment to the Constitution of the United States is hereby repealed.

SECTION 2. The transportation or importation into any state, territory, or possession of the United States for delivery or use therein of intoxicating liquors, in violation of the laws thereof, is hereby prohibited.

SECTION 3. This article shall be inoperative unless it shall have been ratified as an amendment to the Constitution by convention in the several States, as provided in the Constitution, within seven years from the date of the submission hereof to the States by the Congress.

[1] Adopted in 1933.

ARTICLE XXI

Section 1. The eighteenth article of amendment to the Constitution of the United States is hereby repealed.

Section 2. The transportation or importation into any state, territory, or possession of the United States for delivery or use therein of intoxicating liquors, in violation of the laws thereof, is hereby prohibited.

Section 3. This article shall be inoperative unless it shall have been ratified as an amendment to the Constitution by convention in the several States, as provided in the Constitution, within seven years from the date of the submission hereof to the States by the Congress.

Adopted in 1933.

INDEX